ON EQUALITY OF EDUCATIONAL OPPORTUNITY

On Equality of Educational Opportunity

PAPERS DERIVING FROM THE HARVARD UNIVERSITY
FACULTY SEMINAR ON THE COLEMAN REPORT

EDITED BY

Frederick Mosteller
&
Daniel P. Moynihan

VINTAGE BOOKS
A Division of Random House
New York

For distinguished and sustained services to education, this work is respectfully dedicated to The Carnegie Corporation of New York

Preface

The report on Equality of Educational Opportunity appeared in the summer of 1966. From the first it was clear that this was a study of the greatest consequence, but also that the educational community and the public at large would have great difficulty assessing its implications. The methodological sophistication of the analysis, and the inherent difficulty of the material itself, made much of the report all but inaccessible to nonspecialists. Moreover, the analysis of the data had been carried out in a matter of months, there being a legislative deadline for the report. While this was a feat of seldom equaled physical and intellectual exertion, it nonetheless suggested that further work could and should be done. As a most original step, the Office of Education initiated this idea by suggesting in the Report that scholars carry out further analyses. Finally, the Federal government, or at least the higher reaches of the Department of Health, Education, and Welfare, had shown serious concern over what seemed to be the "anti-education" findings of the study.

All this suggested to a number of members of the Harvard University faculty that an independent study ought to be made, both to further the analysis and to make its findings available to educators and others concerned with the achievement of equality of educational opportunity. The Carnegie Corporation generously provided funds to support a faculty seminar for the academic year 1966–1967. What had been expected to be rather a specialized undertaking soon attracted widespread interest in the Cambridge community. Here was a subject of such inherent intellectual and social interest as to challenge the best of minds. Before long the evening seminar assumed near conference proportions, with fifty to sixty faculty members, and other interested persons, swarming about among panels, committees, groups, and subgroups. It was a spirited and rewarding experience.

In the aftermath it was the judgment of a number of persons that a collection of papers bearing on the main themes of the seminar should be prepared and published. Mr. Jason Epstein of Random House was immediately encouraging, and remained unreasonably patient as this process slowly wound to a conclusion. Yet another grant from The Carnegie Corporation has supported the reanalyses, especially of Chapters 2, 5, 6, 7, and 11.

The consequences of the seminar were not limited to Harvard Yard, nor to the pages of this book. Participants have published and discussed the Report in many journals and at many meetings. Researchers at other universities have been given considerable aid through the work done by seminar participants on the computer tapes. And both undergraduates and graduate students have written theses based on work first developed through the seminar.

Professors Thomas F. Pettigrew and Daniel P. Moynihan were co-chairmen of the seminar. Mr. Gordon Ambach and Mr. Robert Schwartz served successively as staff secretary to the group, a task to which they brought a rarely encountered but much needed combination of social tact and intellectual rigor.

Dean Theodore R. Sizer of the Harvard Graduate School of Education was both a participant in the seminar, and an unfailing source of support throughout an enterprise that stretched several years longer than anyone had anticipated. Alexander M. Mood of the U.S. Office of Education was also a member of the seminar, and an indispensable source of encouragement and assistance. The seminar was deeply in their debt and the authors of this volume were especially so.

Marshall Smith has aided not only the editors but also several authors in both administrative and substantive ways in the preparation of the manuscripts; it is a pleasure to record that his contribution to this volume completed his last requirement for the doctorate.

Dr. Nancy Dorfman helped the editors organize the ideas in the volume in preparation for writing the opening article.

In preparing the manuscript and computations, the seminar had the aid of Marian Boyd, Elizabeth Chamberlain, Muriel Ferguson, Holly Grano, Elizabeth Harshbarger, Nancy Larson, Ruth McCawley, and Cleo Youtz.

Beyond the assistance of the U.S. Office of Education in obtaining the basic materials for this work, we appreciate the cooperation of George W. Mayeske for repeated discussions and tabulations and of Tetsuo Okada for special tabulation work. Harry Piccariello kindly supplied special data.

During much of the editing process, Frederick Mosteller held a Guggenheim Fellowship.

The following list of people, which is not complete, attended at least one session of the seminar.

F. M.
D. P. M.

Cambridge, February 12, 1971

Gordon M. Ambach
David J. Armor
Albert Beaton

James M. Beshers
William G. Buss
Clark Byse

Robert Campbell
Jeanne Chall
Abram J. Chayes

Antonia Chayes
William G. Cochran
James S. Coleman
Vincent F. Conroy
Andre Daniere
Henry S. Dyer
Jason Epstein
Mario Fantini
Judith Fellows
John P. Gilbert
Fred L. Glimp

Cliff Goldman
Edmund W. Gordon
William Gorham
Neal Gross
Charles C. Halbower
Eric A. Hanushek
Elizabeth Harshbarger
John D. Herzog
Eugene Hixson
Harold Howe

Herold C. Hunt
Christopher S. Jencks
John F. Kain
Sydney J. Key
Frederick R. Kling
Richard Leone
J. Leeson
Gerald S. Lesser
Seymour M. Lipset
Gordon MacInness

Roland McKean
James McPartland

Frank I. Michelman
John U. Monro
Alexander M. Mood
Donald R. Moore
Anton S. Morton
Frederic A. Mosher
Frederick Mosteller
Daniel P. Moynihan

Charles R. Nesson
Thomas F. Pettigrew
H. Douglas Price
Howard Raiffa
Robert T. Riley
Kristine M. Rosenthal
Robert A. Rosenthal
Paul F. Ross
Richard Rowe
Albert M. Sacks

Nancy H. St. John
Robert B. Schwartz
David S. Seeley
Florence Shelton
Charles E. Silberman
Nancy Sizer
Theodore R. Sizer
Gene M. Smith
Marshall S. Smith
Robert J. Solomon

Frank Stefanich
Susan S. Stodolsky
Nathan B. Talbot
Marc S. Tucker
John W. Tukey
Ralph W. Tyler
Frederic D. Weinfeld
Sheldon H. White
Dean K. Whitla

Contents

PREFACE   ix

THE COLEMAN REPORT

1. A Pathbreaking Report Further Studies of the Coleman Report   3   FREDERICK MOSTELLER AND DANIEL P. MOYNIHAN

2. The Coleman Report and the Conventional Wisdom   69   CHRISTOPHER S. JENCKS

3. On the Value of *Equality of Educational Opportunity* as a Guide to Public Policy   116   ERIC A. HANUSHEK AND JOHN F. KAIN

4. The Evaluation of *Equality of Educational Opportunity*   146   JAMES S. COLEMAN

5. School and Family Effects on Black and White Achievement: A Reexamination of the USOE Data   168   DAVID J. ARMOR

6. *Equality of Educational Opportunity:* The Basic Findings Reconsidered   230   MARSHALL S. SMITH

7. Race and the Outcomes of Schooling   343   DAVID K. COHEN THOMAS F. PETTIGREW AND ROBERT T. RILEY

xiii

IMPLICATIONS FOR THE FUTURE

8. The Urgent Need for Experimentation   JOHN P. GILBERT AND FREDERICK MOSTELLER   371

9. Some Thoughts About Future Studies   HENRY S. DYER   384

10. Toward Defining Equality of Educational Opportunity   EDMUND W. GORDON   423

APPENDICES: THE PROBLEM OF MEASUREMENT: Survey & Model

11. The Quality of the Data Collected by *The Equality of Educational Opportunity* Survey   CHRISTOPHER S. JENCKS   437

12. The Measurement of Educational Opportunity   HENRY S. DYER   513

13. Models of the Educational Process: A Sociologist's Perspective   JAMES M. BESHERS   528

14. The Two-Year Compensatory Program of the College of Basic Studies: Implications of a Successful Model   GENE M. SMITH   541

INDEX   547

THE COLEMAN REPORT

1

A Pathbreaking Report

FREDERICK MOSTELLER & DANIEL P. MOYNIHAN

PART I: Background, Importance, and Findings
of the Report on Equality of Educational Opportunity

Science is the criticism of Myths
— W. B. YEATS[1]

In the course of the 1960's the critique of social myths and beliefs acquired a significant role in American national life. Economists had for some time secured themselves a position in national councils, but now a wide range of other disciplines was brought in and social science information became increasingly central to the formulation and evaluation of social policies.

The reasons for this had to do with specific problems afflicting the American government during the 1960's. These problems had proved notably intractable in the face of "common sense" solutions. More complex forms of diagnosis were obviously needed, and increasingly it became possible to provide them. But a general transformation in human society was also shaping that social development. Kenneth Boulding described it as mankind becoming widely conscious not only of its own societies but also of the larger "sociosphere" of which they are a part.

This movement of the social system into self-consciousness is perhaps one of the most significant phenomena of our time, and it represents a very fundamental break with the past, as did the development of personal self-consciousness many millennia earlier.[2]

The process was especially evident in the United States in the 1950's and 1960's as a result of the conjunction of two large forces. A combination of political, economic, and social events led to unprecedented national commitments to restructure the society so as to overcome the injustices and instabilities associated with the historic problems of poverty and race. Simultaneously the methodology of the social sciences made rapid advances, primarily those associated with the development of the high-speed computer, so that large-scale, complex investigations became possible to a degree that had never previously existed. In the words of Karl Deutsch, a "revolution of competence" occurred.

The report on *Equality of Educational Opportunity*[3] is one product of these developments but it is more than just that. It is almost certainly the most important effort of its kind ever undertaken by the United States government. (That it was not done perfectly; that it has raised more problems than it has solved; that it doesn't tell us what to do next—all these shortcomings merely reflect the current state of the large-scale one-shot social survey as an instrument of national policy-making.) The present volume presents further analyses of these survey data. Explicitly and by implication it comments on where this new investigation leaves—or leads—our society. In our description of EEOR,* we shall report its findings without ordinarily stopping to agree or disagree. A description by us in Part I of this chapter of an EEOR finding does not necessarily mean that we support it, for it would make the flow of information very jerky if we were to haggle over the precise degree of our agreement as each point is presented. By and large we do agree, but with reservations that we explain in later parts of this article, and that the other authors of this volume spell out in careful detail in their own chapters.

ORIGINS OF THE REPORT ON THE EQUALITY OF EDUCATIONAL OPPORTUNITY

The origins of the *Equality of Educational Opportunity* report are at once explicit and somewhat obscure. Explicitly, Section 402 of the Civil Rights Act of 1964 provided that the U.S. Office of Education should undertake the survey in question.

Sec. 402.   The Commissioner shall conduct a survey and make a report to the President and the Congress, within two years of the enactment of this title, concerning the lack of availability of equal educational opportunities for individuals

---

* The *report* on *Equality of Educational Opportunity*, as transmitted to the President and Congress, will henceforth be designated EEOR. The *survey* on which the report was based, and which has been the subject of further analysis, will henceforth be designated EEOS.

by reason of race, color, religion, or national origin in public educational institutions at all levels in the United States, its territories and possessions, and
the District of Columbia.

If any clearly conceived objective for the survey did exist, the sequence of
events obscured and muddled it. Initially Congress seems to have intended
the study to become a tool for legal actions opposing formal discrimination
against minority groups. As it became evident that the statute would forbid
outright any such discriminatory acts, the final intent may have been to
establish once and for all that gross differences in school facilities did exist,
especially as between black and white children in the United States. At all
events, the statute implied that there was "lack of availability of equal educational opportunities" and the Office of Education set out to document it.

What followed was the second largest social science research project
in history.[4] Some 570,000 school pupils in the nation were tested, together
with some 60,000 teachers, while information on the facilities available in
some 4,000 schools was gathered in elaborate detail. United States Commissioner of Education Francis Keppel entrusted the operation to a team
headed by James S. Coleman of Johns Hopkins University. Other members
were Ernest Q. Campbell of Vanderbilt University, and five officials of the
Office of Education: Carol J. Hobson, James McPartland, Alexander M.
Mood, Frederic D. Weinfeld, and Robert L. York. Two years later, the
report was released on the Fourth of July weekend, 1966.

The findings constitute the most powerful empirical critique of the
myths (the unquestioned basic assumptions, the socially received beliefs)
of American education ever produced. It is the most important source of
data on the sociology of American education yet to appear. It was the most
complex analysis ever made of educational data in such quantity. And,
again, it is more than that. Flowing from the very provisions of the Civil
Rights Act of 1964, it is a document of profound significance for the future
of racial and ethnic relations in America. Robert A. Dentler has judged it to
make "a contribution to the study of American intergroup relations second
only to Myrdal's *American Dilemma*."[5,6] And yet how much more ambiguous, how much less reassuring, than the earlier document. And how representative of the period in which it appeared!

WHAT IS EQUALITY OF EDUCATIONAL OPPORTUNITY?

The ambiguity of the report begins with the statute that commissioned it. What *is* "equality of educational opportunity"? Congress gave no explanation of the term, nor did the executive branch provide any. This left the matter up to the authors of the EEOR. They in turn adopted not one but, in succession, two definitions.* These alternative meanings had large consequences for their report and are likely now to have profound effects on American education and, indeed, American society.

It is neither necessary nor valuable to demonstrate that the authors of the EEOR went through any formal transition from one concept of equality to another. There are indications that they did, not least the personal testimony of those concerned. But these might be isolated, even idiosyncratic events. Of far greater importance is the increasingly evident fact that, before the EEOR, equality of educational opportunity was measured one way, and thereafter another. This was a change that was coming, part of a general transition, but the EEOR gave it concrete form long before it might otherwise have entered general usage. Stated briefly, before EEOR "equality of educational opportunity" was measured in terms of school inputs, including racial mixture. By inputs, we mean physical facilities of schools and training of teachers; by racial mixture, the Supreme Court's emphasis on integration. With the publication of the EEOR it became increasingly the practice, even the demand, that equality be measured by school outputs; that is to say, by the results of tests of academic achievement.†

(At the same time that we emphasize the importance of outputs, the reader must note that academic achievement is but one output, and that schooling is expected to produce many others. Retention rates, proportion going to college, income and occupation of graduates, even happiness, are a few of many outputs that might be measured. Although the EEOR studied academic achievement with some attention to self-image and self-esteem, the long-run implication of the EEOR is that outputs should be measured much more generally. Because the EEOR devotes so much space to academic achievement, the reader is likely to lose sight of that more general picture,

---

* Coleman's chapter in this book discusses several other definitions, but the major pair for long-run policy are the ones we discuss.
† Gordon's chapter in this book discusses the historical evolution of the meanings of "equality of educational opportunity" in the United States.

since inevitably this book must often describe these variables both for EEOR and for the reanalysis. Lest it seem that academic achievement must be the only job of the schools, let us remember that studies do *not* find adult social achievement well predicted by academic achievement.)

To repeat, this was part of a changing climate of opinion, but part also of a very old story. It may perhaps best be thought of in terms of the long struggle between liberty and equality in the American culture. One tradition in the culture—the more central one—has defined equality essentially in terms of liberty. William Faulkner put it so: "there is no such thing as equality *per se*, but only equality *to:* equal right and opportunity to make the best one can of one's life within one's capacity and capability, without fear of injustice or oppression or violence." [7] The emphasis is entirely on individuals. Another tradition has defined equality in terms of outcomes, but not for individuals, rather for groups; what Warren Weaver calls, in the medical context, statistical morality.

Herein lies the fundamental conflict. The Civil Rights Act of 1964 was on the surface the very embodiment of the former tradition. In effect it *outlawed* group identification. No individual was to be labeled: not by race, religion, national origin, not even, for certain purposes, by sex. Yet the act arose largely out of concern for the status of a specific group: the Negro.* Inevitably its enactment and administrative interpretation led to the formal assertion of *group* rights and interests by the national government.[8] That precisely is the sequence followed by the authors of the EEOR.

SEPARATION AND
SEGREGATION

The EEOR did definitely demonstrate that American school children were to a pronounced degree separated by race. Eighty percent of all white pupils in the 1st grade and the 12th grade were found to attend schools that were from 90 to 100 percent white. Sixty-five percent of all Negro students in the 1st grade attended schools that were between 90 and 100 percent Negro, while at the 12th grade 48 percent attended schools in which half or more of the students were Negro.

* We shall use the terms Negro and Negroes in referring to data from the EEOS. Beyond that we shall sometimes use language more current in 1971, such as "blacks" where it seems appropriate.

SCHOOL FACILITIES *

The presumption, implicit in the statute, and explicit within the EEOS re-search team, was that the schools for minority students were grossly infe-rior. The survey was expected to establish this once and for all. Interviewed in the *Southern Education Report* of November-December, 1965, Coleman put it:

. . . the study will show the difference in the quality of schools that the aver-age Negro child and the average white child are exposed to. You know yourself that the difference is going to be striking. And even though everybody knows there is a lot of difference between suburban and inner city schools, once the statistics are there in black and white, they will have a lot more impact.

Similarly, the investigators were as much appalled by the presumed exist-ence of those differences as were the authors of the Civil Rights Act.

The EEOS began with a concentration on school facilities. At that time, many people believed that educational "inputs" determined educational "outputs," which is to say that the "quality of the schools" measured in the conventional terms of the EEOS rigorously determined the level of academic achievement in them.

It is tempting to state that the conventional wisdom proved wrong on both scores, but this would not be quite fair. *Had* there been the *large* differences in the school facilities of the races that had been assumed, such differences *might* have proved of great consequence. But there did not turn out to be differences of such magnitude between the schools of Negroes and whites, within regions. Differences within races, while substantial, did not relate closely to achievement.

Given these facts, and the further one of unquestioned differences be-tween the races in achievement, perhaps all that could have been established by the EEOS was that "good" schools by themselves are not enough to assure good education. In any event, the findings were quite unexpected.

For those school facilities measured by EEOS, while there are reported differences in those available to the majority as against the minority groups, they are surprisingly small differences. And while on balance the differences favor the majority, it is by no means the case that they consistently do so. Obviously this was disconcerting. No one then thought the result would be even close, not the investigators for the Office of Education, nor the authors of this chapter. The *Summary Report*,[9] issued slightly in advance of the

* David J. Armor's chapter in this book reevaluates school facilities, supporting some findings reported here and weakening others.

EEOR itself, seems to be at heart a political document designed to ease the blow of the findings, even perhaps to deflect them somewhat. It is preoccupied with questions concerning Negroes. Therein it reflects the preoccupations of the Civil Rights Act of 1964. It acknowledges that there was "not a wholly consistent pattern" in the findings and that "minorities are not at a disadvantage in every item." (EEOR, p. 9)

Nationally, Negro pupils have fewer of *some* of the facilities that *seem* most related to academic achievement: They have less access to physics, chemistry, and language laboratories; there are fewer books per pupil in their libraries; their textbooks are less often in sufficient supply. *To the extent that physical facilities are important* to learning, such items *appear* to be more relevant than some others, such as cafeterias, in which minority groups are at an advantage. [(Our italics) EEOR pp. 9 and 12]

Clearly this is a delicately worded statement some distance removed from the certainties of 1964. Even so, from another point of view a somewhat different statement could have been made based on the same reported data. Perhaps the most noteworthy thing about chemistry laboratories, for example, is that the great majority of secondary schools have them available: 94 percent of Negroes and 98 of whites attend such a school. ("Available" here means that there is something the principal calls a chemistry laboratory in the school.) In the Midwest and the West, the reported sample proportion is 100 percent for both groups. There is a greater discrepancy in physics laboratories: 80 percent of Negroes and 94 percent of whites in the nation attend schools that claim to have such a laboratory.* This differential is most extreme not in the South but in the West, where, contrary to that region's general pattern of near parity between the races in other variables, 100 percent of white students have such a laboratory in their schools and only 76 percent of Negroes. But next one learns that in the West 95 percent of Negroes but only 80 percent of whites have language laboratories. And so it goes.

It might as readily have been pointed out that in the whole nation 30 percent of Negroes in elementary schools have a full-time librarian, but only 22 percent of whites. Or that Negro students have a considerably higher proportion of elementary school teachers with tenure than do whites;† that Negro students have secondary school teachers with more teaching experience;† or that their teachers earn equal salaries in elementary schools in the nation as a whole, though about $200 a year less in secondary schools. (See EEOR, Tables 1, 2, 3, 4, 5, 6a, 6b, and Armor's reanalysis.)

More systematic differences between Negro and white groups were that

---

* Jencks's appendix in this book gives consideration to errors of reporting in data of this kind. The possible inequality of use and of excellence of such facilities is discussed in several places in this book.
† Not necessarily an advantage (see Jencks, Chapter 2).

Negro schools were less frequently accredited, Negro students were less likely to repeat when they failed, they had less testing, less academic curriculum, and less accelerated curriculum. Furthermore the teachers of Negroes had lower verbal test scores than those of whites. (See Armor's chapter.)

Let us not lose sight of the effect of regional differences. The South as a whole does not have as strong school facilities as the North. Since about half of the Negroes live in the South, a national index of their school facilities would put them at a disadvantage compared with whites even if Negroes and whites had identical facilities in each region, just because the South has poorer facilities. (See Armor, Chapter 5, Table 2.)

The most striking finding dealt with Southern school facilities. The Civil Rights Act of 1964 was enacted by Northerners in an atmosphere which attributed a generalized social backwardness to the South.

Everyone in the North expected the EEOS to establish that Southern states systematically discriminated against Negroes in the provision of school facilities. While neither the EEOR nor the Summary *Report* comments on these particular findings at any length, the tabulated data do not support the presumption of gross discrimination in the provision of school facilities in the South.

Later, Ernest Q. Campbell,[10] drawing on his experience as a coauthor of the EEOR, explained the point further:

The *Equality of Educational Opportunity* survey secured information about schools on a large set of items relating to the physical plant, teachers, curriculums, extracurricular activities, facilities, fellow classmates, and related matters. I have found and used 238 such items on which I am able to say, at times arbitrarily, that having it is better (or worse) for the student than not having it. Here I use results for the nation and the South in nonmetropolitan areas and for the Northeast and the South in metropolitan areas. Whites have the advantage over Negroes on 129 of these items in the rural South and there are 16 ties; considering non-ties only, the advantage is to the whites on 62 percent of the items. And in the metropolitan South, 60 percent of the non-tied items go in favor of whites. Since absolute justice would produce either all ties or a 50–50 split across items, it is obvious that inequality exists in the South to the disadvantage of Negroes. But if we ask a different question—Is the Negro *relative to whites in the same region* more often at a disadvantage in the South or in the non-South?—we observe somewhat different answers. In the rural areas, Negroes are less disadvantaged (or more advantaged) in the non-South on 114 items and in the South on 101. This is not a large difference. Furthermore, it is the case in metropolitan areas that Negroes fare relatively better in the non-South on 112 items but relatively better in the South on 116. This is not a large difference either, and it runs in a surprising direction. [Campbell's italics]

Campbell went on to select 41 items from the 238 which "either are, or are analogous to, items that in a regression analysis contribute with relatively great power to the explained variance in standardized test score." Again the

results were not those implied by Section 402 of the Civil Rights Act. Negroes by no means had uniformly poorer school facilities than whites, nor in
particular was this pattern most evident in, much less confined to, the
South.* "In other words," Campbell sums up, "though the Negro suffers
disadvantage on educational items that count educationally, his disadvantage is a national and not a regional phenomenon, so much so that for most
items the disadvantage is less in the South than elsewhere."

Many people reviewing these results on school facilities are reluctant
to accept them at face value. As these data stand they suggest that by the
time of the EEOS, the nation had, within geographical regions, come
close to supplying equal, though largely separate, facilities to Negroes and
whites according to the classical notion of traditional physical inputs. Insofar as that is true, the country, having chosen a goal in a social problem,
had come close to reaching it.

The objections are, of course, that there may be biases owing to nonresponse, to errors in response, and to facilities not being of equal quality,
that may make the survey results look fairer than the conditions actually
are. Beyond this, it has turned out that, however nearly equal these variables, they have not produced equality of achievement, as we shall shortly
see. When the second definition of "equality" implying equality of output is
the one in a person's mind, it will be hard for him to give any credit of
accomplishment for steps toward the achievement of a goal that he no
longer regards as pertinent. A typical comment is "optimism arising from
past accomplishments is no cure for present failures." Whether this is a
wise comment or not depends upon an appraisal of the direction in which
the society is moving. Have we continued to solve welfare problems? Have
we invested heavily in education? Are we continuing to do so? If society is
moving to redress inequities, past accomplishments are an indication of future ones and moreover may be their indispensable foundations.

The authors of this chapter believe that in 1966 the nation had come

---

* A recent study by Robert J. Havighurst and others found that in certain facilities
presumed to be crucial the children of the poor in large-city high schools were likely
to be considerably better off than those of the well-to-do.

One change which is favorable to the low-economic-status schools is a result of the
use of federal funds in the War on Poverty through the Elementary and Secondary
Education Act and the Office of Economic Opportunity. The student-teacher ratio
is now substantially lower in low-status schools than in high-status schools—the
percentage of high-status schools with student-teacher ratios of 25 : 1 or less is
about 42, compared with 70 percent of working-class schools. Also, the lower-status
schools are generally employing more paraprofessionals than the higher-status
schools—approximately 50 percent of the working-class schools employed 11 or more
adult paraprofessionals, against 33 percent of the middle-class schools.

(From *A Profile of the Large-City High School,* by Robert J. Havighurst, University
of Chicago, Frank L. Smith, Teachers College, Columbia University, and David E.
Wilder, Teachers College, Columbia University, Published by National Association
of Secondary School Principals, November, 1970, p. 10 : 6)

much closer to achieving this classical notion of equality of educational opportunity than most of us realized then or realize now. And because social goals are so terribly hard to achieve, we think it would be unfortunate if the nation were not informed about the achievements that have been made, for we all get downhearted waiting. When a society makes clear to itself that it has in fact achieved a goal it has set—even though, in retrospect, it may turn out that achieving the particular goal did not do the job that was expected of it—it is better prepared to set out to reach a yet more difficult goal that it hopes will do the job. (That is to say, the achievement of a set of social arrangements that corresponds to normative desires.) An issue of morale is involved here. If the progressive mode of American social behavior is to be maintained, as by and large it has been maintained throughout our history, it is necessary to be clear that by and large we do achieve what we set out to achieve. A certain atmosphere of "cultural despair" was gathering in the nation at the time of the EEOS, and has since become more in evidence. Some would say more in order. We simply disagree with such despair. We do, however, feel this to be a serious matter indeed, and on that ground feel it especially important that inquiries such as the present one, which in a superficial way appear to depict failure, be at some pains also to point out success.

It would be easy to misunderstand our remarks. We share the views of many that the accomplishments of 1966 and 1971 do not nearly reach the levels that the nation needs. The difference between the kind of equality we have and the kind that we want should shape our goals, programs, and policy, but we do want to take stock of advances when they have occurred.

SOME REMARKS ABOUT CRUDE STATISTICS

At the risk of seeming to defend the measurements of EEOS too strongly, we introduce a few remarks about crude measurements for those who may be especially concerned about crude versus refined measurements.

In trying to appraise large organizational matters, it is frequently necessary to count and measure things as a first step in an evaluation. The complaint is then often made, and correctly too, that the things counted are not all equally good, of equal age, or equally serviceable. Surveys are often attacked for overlooking these difficulties, and the EEOS can be subjected to much such criticism. It would be nice to be able to say that such difficulties do not matter, but they can and sometimes do. Two teachers who both earn $11,000 are not necessarily equally good teachers or even good teachers at all. Nor does it necessarily help to know how each was trained, etc. The differences among teachers, as among mathematicians and violinists, are personal. Two textbooks at $5 apiece may both be bad, both good, or one each way. Price does not settle quality.

Nevertheless, when we think of the process of evaluation as proceeding by steps, rather than as a one-time thing, the matter is not quite so unnerving. One must remember that it is easy for the size of a survey to get out of hand and make it unmanageable. One may have to settle for something crude to get started, and this is a fair remark about the educational appraisal we discuss. The nation had to get started. If one stops thinking of EEOS as the once and only survey of education, and instead thinks of it as part of a larger process of appraisal (reconsider policy, get new information, then repeat), he can appreciate why we are going to pass over some things on a first round and hope to do them better another time.

Take the question of science laboratories. If EEOS had found that few schools with predominantly Negro students had science laboratories but most predominantly white schools had them, scarcely anyone would have raised a question about the possibility that the few laboratories were of much higher quality than the many, or vice versa. The information would have been in and the policy rather clear. The reason the quality issue comes up so forcefully is that the count was *not what was expected*. Thus a simple count can do a lot if we do not expect too much of it.

Now in addition to the fact that these counts and measures may actually be biased because of inequities of various kinds, it is well not to take too much refuge in that escape from the facts found. First, merely pointing to a possible weakness does not discredit a study. One has to show that the bias exists and that it matters.

Second, it is the experience of statisticians that when fairly "crude" measurements are refined, the change more often than not turns out to be small. Merely counting the number of laboratories in a school system is, in this sense, a "crude" measurement. It is possible to learn a good deal more about the quality of those laboratories. It could be that on further assessment the judgment to be had from the original crude measurement would be changed. But to repeat, statisticians would not leap too readily to that expectation. Mencken is said to have remarked that romance is the illusion that one woman is different from another. Sadly, perhaps, in real life the similarities of basic categories are often far more powerful and important than the nice differences which can come to absorb individuals so disposed, but which really don't make a great difference in the aggregate.

The statistician would wholeheartedly say go ahead and make the better measurements, but he would often give a low probability to the prospect that the finer measures would produce information that would lead to different policy.

The reasons are several. One is that policy decisions are often rather insensitive to the measures—the same policy is often a good one across a great variety of measures. Secondly, the finer measures, as in the case of laboratories, can be thought of as something like weights. For example, perhaps one science laboratory is only half as good as another—well and good, let us count it ½. It turns out as an empirical fact that in a great variety of occasions, we get much the same policy decisions in spite of the weights. So there are some technical reasons for thinking that the finer measurement may not change the main thrust of one's policy. None of this is an argument against getting better information if it is needed, or against having reservations. More data cost money, and one has to decide where the good places are to put the next money acquired for investigations. If we think it matters a lot, by all means let us measure it better.

Still another point about aggregative statistics is worth emphasizing for large social studies. Although the data may sometimes not be adequate for decisions about individual persons, they may well be adequate for deciding policy for groups. Thus we may not be able to predict which of two ways of teaching spelling will be preferable for a given child, but we may well be able to say that, on the average, a particular method does better. And then the policy is clear, at least until someone learns how to tell which children would do better under the differing methods.

ACADEMIC ACHIEVEMENT
BY ETHNIC, RACIAL,
AND REGIONAL GROUPS

One solid finding of the EEOR had to do with the levels of educational achievement of the six ethnic/racial groups that were studied: Indian Americans, Mexican Americans, Oriental Americans, Puerto Ricans, Negroes, and a final group, the presumedly white "Majority." The range of achievement among these groups is wide. In the words of the EEOR, "With some exceptions—notably Oriental Americans—the average minority pupil scores distinctly lower on these tests at every level than the average white pupil." [EEOR, p. 21] This gap is there in the 1st grade, and it persists. "For example, Negroes in the metropolitan Northeast are about 1.1 standard deviations* below whites in the same region at grades 6, 9, and 12. But

---

* "Standard deviation" is the technical name of a widely used measure of variability which we shall describe but not define. For the type of data described here it is the number of points that must be added to the middle score, that is the score that is higher than just 50 percent of the scores, to make a score just higher than 84 percent of the scores. In a class of 100, the difference between the test scores of the man ranked 50th and the man ranked 84th is about a standard deviation if the test is like those used in EEOS. Slightly over two thirds of the scores are found within one standard

at grade 6 this represents 1.6 years behind; at grade 9, 2.4 years; and at grade 12, 3.3 years." [EEOR, p. 21]

There are also, especially with respect to the South, regional inequalities of achievement. Thus in a standard achievement test in mathematics, 12th-grade whites in the metropolitan South are 1.2 grade levels behind whites in the metropolitan Northeast. And, finally, there are large inequalities of educational achievement between different social classes in all ethnic/racial groups, although these are most often only inferred in the EEOR, and must be derived from the data of the EEOS.

This range of achievement between ethnic, racial, and, by implication, class groups in the United States was a matter generally understood. The EEOR strengthened the knowledge explicitly and quantitatively and demonstrated the important fact that the differences were to be found at all grade levels, and in approximately the same degree.

EFFECT OF VARIATION
OF RESOURCES ON
ACADEMIC ACHIEVEMENT

The pathbreaking quality of the EEOR had to do with its analysis of the relation of variation in school facilities to variation in levels of academic achievement. It reported so little relation as to make it almost possible to say there was none.

School facilities have traditionally been defined and measured in gross terms. We speak of the facilities in a school that might be available to all the students in that school who took the relevant courses. The variation in these facilities seemed to have astonishingly—remember the time—little effect on educational achievement. One example is the importance to educational achievement of the pupil-teacher ratio. The EEOR presented tables on the "effects" of an extraordinary range of school "facilities," but none whatever on this one.

Some facilities measures, such as the pupil/teacher ratio in instruction, are not included because they showed a consistent lack of relation to achievement among all groups under all conditions. [EEOR, p. 312]

This, to be sure, was not exactly new knowledge. Peter Rossi[11] and others have pointed out that this was one of the earliest subjects in education to come under careful, controlled scrutiny. At the time of the EEOR there ex-

deviation each way from the average score in the type of data under study. About 95 percent of the scores fall within two standard deviations each way from the average.

isted nearly half a century of small-scale observations which the EEOR find-ing precisely confirmed. But they had not been commissioned by an Act of Congress, nor were they accompanied by such a mass of comparable find-ings.

It *was* new, moreover, to learn that, after controlling six student-background variables, district per pupil instructional expenditure for grades 6, 9, and 12 accounted for 0.09 percent of the "variance" in educational achievement of Negro students in the North, and 0.29 percent for white Northerners. [EEOR, Table 3.24.1] Fractions of one percent! Nothing re-motely approaching the assumed relationship.

MEANING OF VARIANCE
—AN EXAMPLE

The word "variance" and the idea of partitioning variance are so much used in EEOR that we must stop and describe them. "Variance" is the technical name for the square of the standard deviation. If the standard deviation is 8, the variance is 8×8, or 64. The variance is much used as a measure of variation when it is desired to break the variability into portions and assign them to various sources. The analogy is with the Pythagorean property of right triangles, where the square on the hypotenuse is the sum of the squares on the other two sides. The lengths of the sides correspond to stand-ard deviations from different sources, the squares of lengths to variances. Just as for the sides of a triangle in geometry, in statistics it is the squares or variances that have the nice additive property: the variance of a sum is the sum of the variances.

An idealized illustration may help explain the idea of variation and the reason for breaking it into components. For convenience, we consider eight hypothetical schools, each of which has provided scores for ten children, say, in the 6th grade. To make the example doubly informative, the school averages are actual averages taken from the EEOR for eight groups in the nation based on three variables (using two categories each): Negroes and whites, urban and rural, North and South. (Note, however, that the varia-bilities within the groups are more similar in our example than in the actual EEOR.) Figure 1 shows how the scores vary within these schools. In this idealized example, each school has the same pattern of variation. The whole set of ten scores is just moved up or down according to the group mean. At the right, we also show how the scores of the whole eighty pupils vary. Notice that the whole eighty seem to vary more than do the scores in any one school. This happens because there are differences between (or, for grammar's sake, among) the schools—they have different averages. If they had all had the same average, in our example the eighty scores would have had the same variation as each of the schools do separately.

When we speak of the total variation or total variance, we refer to the variability of all the scores taken together, as in the right-hand distribution. This total variation has as one component the variation within schools; the rest is said to be between schools, and arises essentially because the schools have different averages. In the present hypothetical example 32 percent of the total variation is accounted for by schools, and 68 percent by the variation of students within schools.

Our example has played two roles. First, it explains the idea of variance and of allocating total variance to "between" and "within" hypothetical schools. The more the school averages vary, the more variation there is between schools. At one extreme, if all the students in each school got the same score, but different schools got different scores, then 100 percent of the variance would be "between schools." At the other extreme, if the school averages were all equal and students differed in their scores, none of the variation would be "between schools."

Second, the example illustrates the large fraction of variation in scores on verbal ability that can actually be attributed to ethnicity, region, and degree of urbanization. It also shows clearly that the Negro-white difference makes the largest contribution, and that while regions definitely differ, the range of averages is about 4 points compared to the 10 points for race. Educators from a region should not minimize the importance of the regional difference. Four points is 8 percent of the average score for the white, urban, South's sixth grader.

The policy implications of the example are also clear. One wants to reduce the big differences, and so among those represented here the ethnic and regional differences are the ones to work at. (Socioeconomic status, while important, is only indirectly represented in the example.)

Elsewhere we discuss much smaller proportions of variance being attributed to differences between schools. One reason is that most authors have controlled for region, urbanization, and/or ethnic groups before computing the variance attributed to differences between schools.

Why would most of the variation lie within schools? The reader's own school experience tells him that there is considerable variation in ability in the same schoolroom, and additional variation from room to room. Much of this variation comes from differences in intelligence within the same family. In a review of genetic studies of intelligence Eckland[12] reports that 50 percent or more of the variation may be *within* families. We need not fuss over the possibility that some of this variation may be from congenital or environmental sources, rather than hereditary; the point is that individuals in families exhibit large variation. Sir Cyril Burt[13] notes that many people have the misconception that "Heredity means the tendency of like to beget like," a definition from the *Oxford English Dictionary*, but he says, "What

Figure 1.

Verbal ability score	1	2	3	4	5	6	7	8	Distribution of total group
65					65				65
64							64		64
62								62	62
61					61	61			61 61
60							60		60
58					58	58			58 58
57							57	57	57 57
56					56				56
55	55				55	55			55 55 55
54		54	54				54	54	54 54 54 54
53						53		53	53 53
52				52		52	52		52 52 52
51	51				51			51	51 51 51
50		50	50		50	50			50 50 50 50
49						49	49		49 49
48	48			48	48			48	48 48 48 48
47		47	47			47	47		47 47 47 47
46	46							46	46 46
45		45	45	45	45		45		45 45 45 45 45
44	44					44		44	44 44 44
43		43	43	43					43 43 43
42	42							42	42 42
41		41	41	41	41	41			41 41 41 41 41
40	40						40		40 40
39		39	39	39					39 39 39
38	38							38	38 38
37		37	37	37			37		37 37 37 37
35	35			35					35 35
34		34	34						34 34
32				32					32
31	31								31
30		30	30						30 30
28				28					28

Hypothetical school number

Figure 1. Each number in a column represents a hypothetical score for a hypothetical pupil from a school with the characteristics of one of eight national groups. The frequency distribution at the right shows the general shape that the counts of scores for all schools might take. The averages for the illustrative hypothetical "schools" equal the actual averages in verbal facility for grade 6 found in EEOR for the following subgroups:

1. Negro, urban, Northeast
2. Negro, rural, North and West
3. Negro, urban, South
4. Negro, rural, South

5. White, urban, Northeast
6. White, rural, North and West
7. White, urban, South
8. White, rural, South

they fail to realize is that heredity is responsible not only for resemblances between members of the same family, but also for much of the differences."

One way to think of neighborhood schools is that they are a way of grouping families. If the variation in verbal scores behaves within families like that of intelligence—and it seems reasonable that it should—then the most variation we could get between schools from grouping families would be the amount for between families. And insofar as the sorting is not perfect, it would be less, perhaps considerably less. All we are trying to do in this discussion is to see whether it is reasonable that the proportion of variation in achievement attributable to schools might not turn out to be large. Of course, when we add the special effects due to facilities and teachers we can get increased variation to be attributed to schools. At any rate, the idea that school-to-school variation might be well under 50 percent, even as small as 5 or 10 percent, is not outrageous in the light of these studies. Part of the point of these remarks is to note that much of the variation within schools is probably not the sort of thing a school can do much about as long as it tries to improve all equally.

FURTHER DISCUSSION
OF SCHOOL EFFECTS

Let us return now to the tiny fractions of one percent of variance in educational achievement accounted for by pupil expenditure. These fractions were a part of the already small *between-school variance*. For some parts of the school population, about 90 percent of the variance in student achievement was found to lie *within*—not between—schools. This was as true in the later grades as in the early ones. Therefore the attributes of schools, *described in aggregative terms*, that is, a whole school at a time, could not possibly account for much variation in individual achievement.

Writing shortly after the publication of EEOR, Coleman summarized the overall findings in explicit terms.

Thus, by the criterion stated earlier—that the effectiveness of schools in creating equality of educational opportunity lies in making the conditional probabilities of success less conditional—the schools appear to fail. At the end of school, the conditional probabilities of high achievement are even *more* conditional upon racial or ethnic background than they are at the beginning of school.

There are a number of results from the survey which give further evidence on this matter. First, within each racial group, the strong relation of family economic and educational background to achievement does not diminish over the period of school, and may even increase over the elementary years. Second, most of the variation in student achievement lies within the same school, very little of it is between schools. The implication of these last two results is clear: family background differences account for much more variation in achievement than do school differences.*

Even the school-to-school variation in achievement, though relatively small, is itself almost wholly due to the *social* environment provided by the school: the educational backgrounds and aspirations of other students in the school, and the educational backgrounds and attainments of the teachers in the school. *Per pupil expenditure, books in the library, and a host of other facilities and curricular measures show virtually no relation to achievement if the "social" environment of the school—the educational backgrounds of other students and teachers—is held constant.* [Coleman's italics.]

The importance of this last result lies, of course, in the fact that schools, as currently organized, are quite culturally homogeneous as well as quite racially segregated; teachers tend to come from the same cultural groups (and especially from the same race) as their students, and the student bodies are themselves relatively homogeneous. Given this homogeneity, the principal agents of effectiveness in the schools—teachers and other students—act to maintain or reinforce the initial differences imposed by social origins.

One element illustrates well the way in which the current organization of schools maintains the differences over generations: a Negro prospective teacher leaves a Negro teacher's college with a much lower level of academic competence (as measured by the National Teacher's Examination) than does his white counterpart leaving his largely white college; then he teaches Negro children (in school with other Negro children, ordinarily from educationally deficient backgrounds), who learn at a lower level, in part because of his lesser competence; some of these students, in turn, go into teacher training institutions to become poorly-trained teachers of the next generation.

Altogether, *the sources of inequality of educational opportunity appear to lie first in the home itself and the cultural influences immediately surrounding the home; then they lie in the schools' ineffectiveness to free achievement from the impact of the home, and in the schools' cultural homogeneity which perpetuates the social influences of the home and its environs.* [Coleman's italics.] [14]

To be sure, the EEOR found that some school characteristics mattered. Students mattered. The higher the social class of the other students the higher any given student's achievement. "*Attributes of other students account for far more variation in the achievement of minority group children than do any attributes of school facilities and slightly more than do attributes of staff.*" [(Their italics.) EEOR, p. 302] Teachers appeared to matter, at least for Negroes. A list of variables concerning such matters as teachers' scores on a vocabulary test, their own level of education, their years of experience, showed little relation to achievement of white students, but some for Negroes, and increasingly with higher grade levels. Even so, none of these effects was large: the between-school variance was so little to begin with, dividing it up, parceling it out between this factor and that, produced results unimpressive at best, and demoralizing at worst.

* This implication is not clear to us.

The opening paragraph of the long Coleman quotation above can be viewed, in part, as a statement that after receiving students who are unequally prepared, and unequally supported at home, the schools do not bring those students to educational equality. One way of looking at it is that the school does not slow down those who are ahead and speed up those who are behind. Put this latter way, the policy question arises whether this should be a goal that the regular school system wants to achieve. Marshall Smith's chapter in this book discusses this point and its implications.

In sum, the EEOR found that schools receive children who already differ widely in their levels of educational achievement. The schools thereafter do not close the gaps between students aggregated into ethnic/racial groups. Things end much as they begin. To the simple of mind or heart, such findings might be interpreted to mean that "schools don't make any difference." This is absurd. Schools make a very great difference to children. Children don't think up algebra on their own. It took a whole sequence of civilizations even to invent it. But given that schools have reached their present levels of quality, the observed variation in schools was reported by EEOR to have little effect upon school achievement. This actually means a large joint effect owing to both schools and home background (including region, degree of urbanization, socioeconomic status, and ethnic group), little that is unique to schools or homes. They vary together.

(One may of course ask whether algebra makes an important difference to the lives of children, especially since a high-school or college graduate may well not be able to recall the binomial theorem at all. This is a fair question and it deserves an answer. Training in mathematics through arithmetic is useful for everyday life, but training beyond that has other purposes. For those who are interested in certain occupations, what early and continued training in mathematics does is to keep a variety of occupational options open. When one drops mathematics from his training, he cuts the number of careers he can readily choose. Very little mathematics is "picked up" in everyday life. It is learned in schools. Moreover, careers which once were regarded as having little use for mathematics beyond common arithmetic, such as biology and business and political science, to mention a few, are today requiring more and more training in mathematics. Mathematics comes hard to one who has interrupted his training. And since it is strongly cumulative and slow to gather, remedial work can take so long as to make the desired program of education impossible. Mathematicians, like musicians and artists, want mathematics appreciated for its own sake, but this reason can be put forward for most school subjects. There is, though, an additional reason, and that is the need for us to be able to communicate with one another. When a man says he found something out by solving an equation, an educated man has an idea of what happened, and some grip on how much and how little that might mean. The poet Yeats[15] moans that while he knew Bertrand Russell to be wrong about everything, he is helpless to do anything about it because he himself knows no mathematics. Having some mathematics in one's education does provide some defense against innocent acceptance of inflated claims.)

EFFECTS OF
SOCIAL CLASS

Without too much anticipating the papers of this volume, it would be well early on to emphasize that one important difference between the EEOS groups is that of social class. Most ethnic/racial groups in the United States go through a period when the group label attached to them is a kind of surrogate designation of their social-economic status. For a long period, to refer to "the Irish," "the Italians," "the Central Europeans" (latterly "the ethnics") was to speak generally of day laborers or factory employees, and so on.

The EEOR, conceived in the concern for racial equality of blacks, and expanded, partly as a measure to obtain wider political support, to include all persons, regardless of "race, color, religion, or national origin," did not include any analysis of educational achievement by social class.* But presence of social class was implicit in the stated finding that family background, measured in social class terms—primarily education of parents, but including many other considerations such as the presence of an encyclopedia in the home—is apparently a major determinant of educational achievement.

In a further analysis of the EEOS, Tetsuo Okada, Wallace M. Cohen, and George W. Mayeske of the U.S. Office of Education were able to show this. The authors constructed two indices, first that of Socio-Economic Status (SES), giving the heaviest weights to Father's and Mother's Educational Level and to Father's Occupational Level, and, second, a Grade Level Equivalent (GLE) relating test scores obtained from the EEOS to the corresponding school grade. Using the Verbal Ability tests (which generally provide a good predictor of scores on other tests), they found the Grade Level Equivalents, based on national averages, for the six groups identified by the EEOR as shown in Table 1.

Before discussing these data, we should emphasize that the results for Puerto Rican, Mexican, Indians, and Oriental students are not as solidly based as those for Negroes and whites.

---

* Nor, it may be noted, was there any discussion of differences as between *religious* groups, albeit, the statute clearly authorized and may have dictated such an inquiry. There are some subjects no American government will investigate. It may be just as well.

TABLE 1

Grade Level Equivalents for Various Groups

	Grade 6	Grade 9	Grade 12
Negro	4.4	7.0	8.8
White	6.5	9.8	12.9
Puerto Rican	3.4	7.0	9.3
Mexican	4.5	7.5	9.4
Indian	4.8	7.7	10.5
Oriental	5.9	9.0	11.8

SOURCE: Tetsuo Okada, Wallace M. Cohen, and George W. Mayeske, "Growth in Achievement for Different Racial, Regional, and Socio-economic Groupings of Students," U.S. Office of Education. Mimeographed, May 16, 1969.

Table 1 shows for each group that the grade level of academic achievement increases with actual grade, as one would hope. And it shows considerable variation in level of achievement between the groups at each grade. This is, of course, the standard finding of the EEOR. Okada, Cohen, and Mayeske proceeded to break down these scores by socioeconomic status, as shown in Table 2, whereupon the social class component of group differentials appeared with great emphasis and clarity.

TABLE 2

Grade Level Equivalents for Social Class Groups

Ethnic Group	Grades: SES:	Six			Nine			Twelve		
		Low	Med.	High	Low	Med.	High	Low	Med.	High
Negro		4.1	4.7	5.3	6.5	7.3	8.4	8.1	9.3	10.7
White		5.6	6.5	7.3	8.1	9.5	11.4	10.6	12.6	*
Puerto Rican		3.1	3.6	4.6	6.6	7.2	8.4	8.8	9.8	10.6
Mexican		4.1	4.8	5.7	6.9	7.8	9.0	8.9	9.8	11.6
Indian		4.4	5.1	6.0	7.1	8.2	9.7	9.0	11.2	13.7
Oriental		4.7	6.1	7.0	8.0	9.3	10.3	10.7	11.8	*

Asterisk (*) denotes GLE equal to or greater than 14.0.
SOURCE: Tetsuo Okada, Wallace M. Cohen, and George W. Mayeske, "Growth in Achievement for Different Racial, Regional, and Socio-economic Groupings of Students," U.S. Office of Education. Mimeographed, May 16, 1969.

We note that the difference in achievement between low and high social class is considerable, averaging 1.7 grade levels in the 6th grade, giving equal weight to the six groups. But we also note that the difference between the lowest-scoring and highest-scoring ethnic/racial group in each socioeconomic column continues to be large, averaging 2.7 grade levels in the 6th grade. The data need not have come out this way. It was conceivable that the values in a given socioeconomic column would be approximately equal in spite of the original differences between ethnic groups. Had that occurred, we could have attributed the differences in the performances of ethnic groups to their unequal representation in the social classes. What social class did in the 6th grade was to reduce a difference of 3.1 grade levels in Table 1 (white grade level minus Puerto Rican grade level), to an average difference of 2.7. This is a big reduction, but it still leaves ethnic group accounting for most of the variation. Had we attended to Negroes alone versus whites in the 6th grade, the reduction in variation owing to social class would be from 2.1 to 1.8, a noticeable effect. (We focused on the 6th grade because of a variety of technical problems of making comparisons for the other grades.)

Children whose parents had less than eight grades of education scored lower on these tests than those whose parents had a college education. Joseph Froomkin[16] has calculated that for the children of the poorly educated this represents from 0.8 to 1.0 standard deviations below the average of children of the well educated. Another way of looking at this is that the average scores of poor Negro children in urban slums cluster around the 25th percentile of the whole nation. In terms of grade levels, by grade 3 the middle black child is half a year behind, a year and a half by grade 6, and three years by grade 12. In other words, half these children finish the 12th grade with less than the equivalent of a 9th grade education. For 12th-grade Negro students throughout the nation, only 16 percent were at or above grade level. Similar results hold for Puerto Ricans, Mexican Americans, and American Indians. And this, of course, is the compelling, undisputed finding of the EEOR. This is a central social fact of American society. It having been established, it would seem impossible for that society to ignore it.

FINDINGS ON
INTEGRATION

The EEOR might have been greeted with greater enthusiasm had it offered any substitutes for the beliefs it presumably discredited. But it did not. Given the great pressure of time upon them, and the unexpected nature of their central findings, the authors could not be expected to produce a whole new theory. Racial integration where minority group students were not a majority seemingly improved the level of achievement for them, without lowering it for others. But the improvement was not great. (See Armor's chapter, Figure 2, and also the chapter by Cohen, Pettigrew, and Riley.) In any event, by this time there was a growing movement in the North away from integration and toward concepts of "quality" neighborhood schools, which for the most part was a way of describing slum schools with large per pupil expenditures. Even so, the EEOR made the best of it.

The general picture that all these results give of schools that come closest to taking full advantage of their student input is one with generally greater resources. The relations are not large, but they are all in the direction of somewhat higher achievement: higher per pupil instructional expenditure, a curriculum that offers greater challenges, more laboratories and more activities. However, probably the most important result is the one stated in the preceding section: that characteristics of facilities and curriculum are much less highly related to achievement than are the attributes of a child's fellow students in school. [EEOR, p. 316]

FINDINGS ON CONTROL
OF ENVIRONMENT

As much as could be was also made of the finding that a child's sense of "control of his environment" correlated strongly with his educational achievement. "Of all the variables measured in the survey," the EEOR reported, "including all measures of family background and all school variables, these attitudes showed the strongest relation to achievement. . . ." [EEOR, p. 319] Negro students who had a strong sense of control of environment did better than white students with a weak sense. But could not such feeling of control be essentially a feedback reaction from reality? Bright students who got good marks might well feel good about themselves. And, after all, there was a large number of intelligent black children doing very well in school, and an even greater number of rather unintelligent white children doing poorly. Similarly there were any number of well-to-do black children and any number of poor white children attending schools, some in prosperous parts of the nation, others in urban or rural slums. Even so, much was made of the matter in the EEOR and by other commentators, as for example Marilyn Gittell,[17] who pressed the finding to support a particular position in New York City.

There is every reason to believe that community control of city schools will enhance educational quality. *Equality of Educational Opportunity*, the most extensive educational study ever conducted . . . emphasized the need for an educational system capable of stimulating a strong sense of self among students. . . . Coleman discovered that the secret to learning lay with student attitudes. Attitudes toward self, of power to determine one's future, influence academic achievement far more than factors of class size, teacher qualifications, or condition of school plant.

But the more impressive finding of the EEOR is that such a large number of students, black and white, report that they *do* have a sense of control of their destiny, *do* have a healthy, even exaggerated, sense of their ability. They are ambitious. In the 12th grade, 69 percent of Negroes in the nonmetropolitan South said they wished to be one of the best students in the class; 46 percent of whites in the area said they felt the same way. Forty-six percent of 12th-grade whites and 31 percent of Negroes in the metropolitan Northeast "definitely" planned to go to college. Although only 13 percent of the work force is in professional occupations, 37 percent of 12th-grade whites and 27 percent of Negroes reported they expected to have a professional career. Here, as elsewhere, Negroes expressed greater confidence than any minority save Orientals, of whom 43 percent expected professional careers. [EEOR, Table 10]

The high-school seniors were not especially depressed about life. Thirty-nine percent of whites in the metropolitan Northeast and 29 percent of Negroes agreed with the statement "I sometimes feel that I just can't learn." But only 4 percent of 12th-grade whites in that area and 9 percent of Negroes felt that good luck is more important for success than hard work. Thirteen percent of the whites and 21 percent of the Negroes agreed to the statement "Every time I try to get ahead, something or somebody stops me." Only 5 percent of such whites and 12 percent of Negroes agreed that "People like me don't have much of a chance to be successful in life." Given that a sixth of the population has an I.Q. under 85, and that success typically is judged to be occupational success, this is hardly the portrait of a depressed generation for whom different forms of school management might bring about dramatic changes in attitude.

What then was to be made of it all? At best it was cold comfort, at worst a refutation of fundamental beliefs that bore not just on education, but on some of the central issues of American politics in the 1960's. The result was perhaps inevitable: the EEOR was either ignored or disputed. The former course was facilitated, to say the least, by the response of the U.S. Office of Education and the Federal government generally. There was no immediate response. A small force within the Office of Education undertook a continuing analysis of the EEOS, but for practical purposes until 1970 the EEOR had not the least effect on Federal education policy, which went forward with programs of general financial support and compensatory assistance for poverty areas.

Let us note that insofar as programs provided some entirely new educational ventures, such as preschool training, there is no conflict with the findings of the EEOR even if they are totally accepted. (Section 8.1 of EEOR discusses Project Headstart.) The small variation in effects of facilities was observed for active full-fledged schools. The EEOR did not deal with the effects of "no program" as compared with having a program. What the report did suggest was that existing variations in a full-blown school program would produce comparatively little change in academic achievement.

As an example of the effects of "no schooling," the City of New York reported a loss of two months in reading level for the year 1968–69 owing to the two months' teachers' strike. The Acting Superintendent of Schools, Dr. Nathan Brown, said, "Since the decline cut across every section of the city, I must conclude that schooling does mean something. Some people have said that children learn regardless of school, but here we have a situation where there was not a full school year and children did suffer." [18]

GENERAL APPRAISAL

All in all, the EEOR is a formidable achievement. The outstanding feature of the EEOS is that it was proposed and executed. In normal times, everything would have been against it, especially school and regional politics. It may be useful to note that these were not normal times. The survey was taken and the report written during the years when the forces of political liberalism, and especially the pro-civil rights forces, were dominant as at almost no other time. Certainly there have been not more than three or four—widely separated—such moments in the nation's history. (And even so the EEOS encountered its share of political problems, especially with school districts. We note that the earlier Project Talent, although supported by government funds, was not directed by a special Act of Congress, and it got considerably more cooperation than did EEOS, indeed 93 percent, see Flanagan et al.,[19] as compared with about 72 percent of schools in the sample returning questionnaires for EEOS (Tables 9.6.3, 9.6.4, EEOR, p. 567).

The EEOR is pathbreaking, a watershed. Henceforth no study of the quality of education or the equality of educational opportunity can hope to be taken seriously unless it deals with educational achievement or other accomplishment as the principal measure of educational quality. To be sure, new and more subtle and varied measures of achievement may be expected and should be encouraged. The 3 R's do not end the list of things we want schools to give our children. (Surely, for example, we want children to emerge from their school years with a sense of social dignity and place, and with a commitment to their community. And we want them to learn how to work and live with others.) But educational output, not input alone, must henceforth be the central issue. This is not to say that inputs are of no interest. We want safe buildings for our schools, and we all like a pleasant environment for our work. Similarly there is a general public interest in having a well-paid teaching profession. But henceforth the measure of quality in education is output.

The EEOR wrought this transformation, and great credit is owing to all concerned: to the Congress for asking its question in so sophisticated a form that it required more than perfunctory counting; to the civil-rights coalition that helped enact the bill; to the Department of Health, Education, and Welfare, and its Office of Education, for appreciating the depth of the question and for assembling such singularly gifted persons to design the survey and carry forward the analysis; and to those school systems, school boards, superintendents, principals, teachers, parents, and pupils that participated.

A survey of this scope and depth—once it is done—raises the sights of the nation with respect to educational research. The EEOR was based on advanced ideas of education, sociology, social psychology, survey techniques, and computing.

Further, in a development that we believe could profitably be emulated by others, the Office of Education (OE) encouraged scholars to make more use of the EEOS data, to reanalyze the survey, and reassess the conclusions of the EEOR. The OE has made great efforts to assist scholars on this road to reanalysis, whether the persons concerned were friendly or hostile to the findings of the original report. Those familiar with the difficulties found in moving data from one high-speed computer to another will appreciate the magnitude of the assistance required. The main body of the papers in this book are, of course, based upon such reanalyses.

RESPONSE TO THE
REPORT

In view of these singular merits, it might be asked why the EEOR has not been received with more enthusiasm, more notice. A variety of answers may be proffered.

To begin with, it is a difficult document. It is 737 pages in length, accompanied by a second volume consisting wholly of means, standard deviations, and correlation coefficients (548 pages). It was assembled under intense pressure of time. (Recall the two-year Congressional deadline. It may be noted that five years elapsed from the beginning of the Harvard Seminar to the appearance of the present volume.) But the central fact is that its findings were seen as threatening to the political coalition that sponsored it. This need not have been the case. (*We* would argue that the EEOR is, if anything, a radical document. But it was greeted as a conservative one.)

The *Summary Report* went to great effort to avoid raising the implications of some of the EEOR findings. The question of the "relation of achievement to school characteristics" is not raised until more than halfway through the summary, and then in terms that scarcely seize the attention or rouse the imagination of the unsuspecting reader.

The first finding is that the schools are remarkably similar in the way they relate to the achievement of their pupils when the socioeconomic background of the students is taken into account. [EEOR, p. 21]

Writing in *Science*, Robert C. Nichols[20] described the EEOR findings as "literally of revolutionary significance. . . . [U]ntil these findings are clarified by further research they stand like a spear pointed at the heart of the cherished American belief that equality of educational opportunity will increase the equality of educational achievement." Robert A. Dentler expressed a similar view on a wider canvas.

More crucially, many of the findings run contrary to the favorite assumptions of three of the most concerned audiences: militant school integrationists, militant school segregationists . . . and the many professional educators who focus their effort too exclusively upon school facilities, curriculum reform, and teacher training.[21]

All this suggests a document destined to be greeted with disfavor. In the event, attitudes varied, and were muted. The educational establishment, on the whole, chose to overlook the matter, rather as a person of generous mind and sufficient status might choose to let pass an impropriety on the part of another person ordinarily well enough behaved and reasonably discreet. The educational establishment is not insensitive to criticism, nor impervious to new information, but the EEOR findings were, in a sense, easy to ignore. The report named no names, proposed no remedies. An editorial in *Science*[22] accused the educators of the nation of having no scientific basis for their activities. It had as well have accused a cornfield of ignoring photosynthesis.

The "civil-rights community," the widely based coalition of Negro leaders and organizations, trade unions, and middle-class white liberals, did not take the appearance of EEOR with equal serenity. It is fair enough to compare the EEOR with Myrdal's *American Dilemma* (interestingly, both collective efforts) but the reception of the two two-volume works was altogether different. Myrdal's was an instant classic. It confirmed all the views, documented all the arguments, of those who wished to bring about basic changes in the relationship of the black minority in America to the white majority. But it also proclaimed that these changes were taking place, and would continue to do so. The American Creed would win out—certainly not least through the mediation of universal, equal public education.

Equal educational opportunity, defined as desegregated education, had become a central—perhaps *the* central—demand of the civil-rights movement by 1950. This strategy in turn led to one of the central Supreme Court decisions of American history, *Brown v. Board of Education of Topeka*, which declared, in 1954, that "separate but equal" school facilities were inherently *un*equal and ultimately ordered the South to desegregate "with all deliberate speed." [23] At the risk of oversimplifying, it may be stated that the central purpose of the EEOS was to support that strategy and hasten that process.

How then could the civil-rights community greet such findings as those of the EEOR? The South came off as something less than a horror, while the schools were hardly depicted as the potent agents of social change which so many had assumed them to be, not least the schoolmen themselves. In a *Fortune* article entitled "A Devastating Report on U.S. Education" which appeared a year after the publication of the EEOR, Charles E. Silberman summed up the view of informed liberal opinion.

. . . the Coleman Report suggests forcibly that the public schools do not—and as now constituted cannot—fulfill what has always been considered to be one of their main purposes and justifications: to ensure equality of opportunity . . . or, in Horace Mann's phrase, to be "the balance wheel of the social machinery." [24]

These findings had great relevance to the North as well as to the South. Until the passage of the Civil Rights Act of 1964, civil rights had been a Southern issue. Violence in the South had been white violence. Threats, rhetorical denunciations, and general misbehavior had been almost wholly confined to those whites who resisted the clear implications of the American Creed. However, just after the signing of the Civil Rights Act on July 2, 1964, black violence began in the North. Harlem rioted in 1964, and there was trouble in other cities. With 1965 came Watts, and much more widespread disorder; 1967 saw general near-conflagration. In the meantime, the civil-rights movement in the South had flagged. For both reasons, the nation's attention turned to the problem of the northern "ghettos." These now became the subject of intense scrutiny, analysis, concern. The Northeast in particular, the intellectual center of the country, and the stronghold of liberalism, became ever more aware that conditions for its most deprived minorities ranged from bad to intolerable, at least among the poor thereof. Inevitably and properly concern mounted for the condition of the "ghetto" schools.

This latter is a point requiring comment. Quite insistently the condition of the Negro in the Northern city was likened to that of earlier Jewish immigrants. He was seen as stigmatized, discriminated against, and confined to certain quarters of the city, namely the "ghetto." This was in many ways a badly misleading analogy, and nowhere more so than with respect to education. The "ghetto" schools of Europe no doubt had many problems, but educational achievement was not one of them. To the contrary, if one will extend the medieval term to the nineteenth- and twentieth-century neighborhoods of European Jews, the ghetto schools by and large produced the formative intellects of the modern age.[25]

The "discovery" that Northern Negro students attended schools that were strongly segregated, and that the levels of educational achievement were only slightly higher than those of the South, inevitably led to a torrent of schemes for improvement, for the most part buttressed with evidence of some kind that "ghetto" schools were shortchanged on school facilities defined in the traditional terms of the EEOS. What then was to be made of a massive government report, bearing the impeccable pedigree of the Civil Rights Act itself, which reported that such variation in facilities had hardly any effect on school achievement? A myth—given that myths are not of necessity untrue—of the utmost social and political importance was being challenged in a most dangerous manner.

In this respect the EEOR was part of a generally new phenomenon which was unsettling both to the advocates of social change and to the analysts of social conditions. Especially with respect to matters of race, the period of the EEOR, which is to say the mid-1960's, had been preceded by a half century, at very least, in which social science had been the unfailing ally of social change in this field. Not infrequently social scientists had been advocates as well as analysts, and there had been little if any tension between their dual roles. Social science had come to the aid of the widest range of causes, and not least that of educational equality. A distinctive feature of *Brown v. Board of Education of Topeka* had been the introduction by the plaintiffs of social science information purporting to prove that segregated schools were inherently unequal, and that the disadvantage was sustained by the Negro children. What then was to be made of social scientists apparently turning on their old allies with a report that implied that this was all greatly exaggerated, and that the low levels of educational achievement came from generalized social conditions against which schools could hardly expect to prevail, save in the most marginal ways? This latter was perhaps the unkindest cut of all.

Social scientists were not alone in their "defection." Before long the upper reaches of the business community became involved—genuinely—with the social issues of the slums. But businesslike analysis produced findings surprisingly similar to those of the EEOR. In 1969 the First National City Bank published a study *Public Education in New York*, prepared by its Regional Economics Section. Two paragraphs are of interest in relation to the EEOR findings.

Expenditures for each school include the amount of City and State money allocated to the school (exclusive of funds for capital improvements) and money from Federal aid, primarily funds under Title I and other provisions of the Elementary and Secondary Education Act. Per capita costs in . . . schools with enrollments 90 percent or more black and Puerto Rican averaged $839 in 1967–68, ranging from a low of $529 per pupil to a high of $1,560.

Regardless of the variations in socioeconomic characteristics of the students in these 150 schools, there is no statistical correlation between the aggregate amounts of money spent per pupil and the improvement in reading scores from one year to the next. In other words, in these 150 schools, preliminary evidence does not appear to indicate that an expenditure of one amount is any more effective in changing a pupil's level of achievement than an expenditure of another.

The per capita expenditure of $839 was well above the national average for 1968, which was $623. Even so, the study reported, "Slightly over one of every three fifth graders was reading one or more years below grade level; one in seven was reading two or more years below grade. The race/poverty nexus appears to correlate highest with low reading levels. . . ." These, of course, are the essential findings of the EEOR.

CHALLENGES TO EEOR

Inevitably, the report was challenged as to its accuracy. We have noted that the material is difficult to master, even for those who had the time, facilities, and technical equipment to try. As a result, in these technical areas society must depend upon the judgment of experts. (Thus does science re-create an age of faith!) Increasingly the most relevant findings concerning the state of society are the work of elites, and must simply be taken—or rejected—by the public at large, at times even by the professional public involved, on such faith. Since the specialists often disagree, however, the public is frequently at liberty to choose which side it will, or, for that matter, to choose neither and continue comfortable in the old myths.

Both the EEOS and the EEOR are particularly vulnerable to such disagreement. The study was done under great pressure of time. (It was not, for example, until January, 1966, that the survey was finally completed, leaving a bare five months to complete the report: an absolutely heroic effort.)

Professional judgments were made in the survey design and analysis that are open to dispute. This is not always a matter of being right or wrong, but simply of the absence of professional consensus on the points involved. Inevitably a fair amount of technical controversy arose over the study. Not a great deal was published, but enough to serve as ground for suspicion for any so disposed. A range of criticisms was made. The sample was not properly done. The nonresponses were too many. The number of school systems refusing to cooperate invalidated any results. The reliance on school administrators to report accurately the facilities in their schools was naive. Etc., etc. The subsequent analysis also came under scrutiny, perhaps most notably by Samuel Bowles and Henry M. Levin in *The Journal of Human Resources.* Bowles and Levin reached conclusions somewhat like that of the Scottish verdict "Not Proven." (Not all of Bowles and Levin's conclusions are "optimistic" from the point of view of the sponsors of the Civil Rights Act. They argued, for example, that the EEOR finding that Negro achievement is positively associated with the proportion of fellow students who are white cannot be supported by the evidence of the EEOR.) In the end Bowles and Levin came near to suggesting that the whole thing needed doing over again.

. . . some of the Report's most widely publicized findings concerning the determinants of scholastic achievement, namely, those relating to the ineffectiveness of school resources, the influence of student peers, and the effects of integration, are not substantiated by the evidence. We have attempted to show that both the measurement of the school resources and the control of social background of the student were inadequate, and that the statistical techniques used were inappropriate. By no means do we wish to suggest that the actual relations are the opposite of what the Report concludes or that further research will not substantiate some of the Report's findings; but until better evidence is found, we will have to remain agnostic about which relationships prevail.

   Equality of Educational Opportunity addressed itself to some of the most difficult questions that our society faces: what are the determinants of different educational outcomes, and what is the relative importance of each of the relevant influences? Unfortunately, the survey that led to the Report was handicapped by a severe time constraint. It was also hampered by a more serious impediment, for the learning processes by which different influences alter achievement are largely unknown, and no set of data and statistical analyses can easily compensate for a missing theoretical framework.

   The Report has a distinct contribution to make, but not directly in the arena of educational or social policy. Rather, its strength lies in the fact that it has stimulated a great deal of thought and new research efforts to uncover the largely unknown and complex relationships among family, school, and community influences on one hand, and educational outcomes on the other. Further, it has provided some of the necessary data to test the new hypotheses that it has stimulated. In short, while the Report did not provide the answers, it has brought us closer to being able to use large scale research efforts as a basis for making intelligent policy decisions for our schools.[26]

   We would go further than this. We feel that EEOR has changed our understanding of education in many ways. (And it may, for the time being at least, have created some new myths.) Even more to the point, the availability of the EEOS makes it possible to reanalyze some issues that the EEOR dealt with, and to investigate other matters left relatively untouched. The primary purpose of the present volume is to present the result of three years of reanalysis and new inquiry. Much of what we have found is not at all to our liking—but then neither was much of the EEOR. We had best, however, get used to living with it, and even begin responding, for it is the best purchase anyone now has on an extraordinarily complex and elusive reality.

PART II: Highlights of the Reanalyses

What were the results of the Seminar and the reanalyses that grew out of it?

In the analyses presented here, the variation in achievement among schools was found to be small compared to that among individual students within the same school. This agrees generally with the findings of EEOR. The disagreements concern the components and their sizes. But beyond that the methods are different, the conclusions are sometimes opposed to those of EEOR, and a number of new conclusions have emerged.

THE REANALYSES AND REGRESSION METHODS

The reanalysts of the present volume did not care for the particular methods of analysis used in the EEOR to attribute school-to-school variation in achievement to variables such as teachers, facilities, community, and so on. And therefore they, including Coleman (who explains in his chapter the technical difficulty that originally led him to the EEOR method), use other techniques here. The original method had as one drawback that the answers depended upon the order in which the variables were considered. And so different orders gave somewhat different answers, as some authors in this book demonstrate, for example, Hanushek and Kain, and M. Smith.

Earlier we described the method of attributing the percentage of variance to various sources. Many authors have noted that this technique does not face the policy questions directly either. The key questions they feel are these: When a school changes its facilities in various ways, how much improvement in achievement scores (or other desired good) will be obtained and for how much money? Stripped of the economic aspects, the methods ordinarily used to find the effects of variables are called regression analyses.

The word "regression" in this context comes from a historical accident. Francis Galton happened to use the methods in treating data on inheritance, where "regressing" is a standard term used by biologists. He asked, "Why don't great fathers have great sons?" and to the joy of every boy he also asked, "Why don't great sons have great fathers?" And so he found the world going to the dogs whether he looked forward or backward in time.

And it is this "regression toward average" that the term regression refers to, although it is by no means the main point of most regression analyses.

When regression analyses are completed one has an equation or a set of equations from which one can forecast outputs like academic achievement from various inputs like teachers' salaries, teachers' experience, books in the library, and so on. Some of our authors use such methods.

These methods have weaknesses, especially when derived from a one-shot survey. First, we can estimate the difference in achievement between schools not having and those having a language laboratory, say. But we cannot tell whether actually adding or removing a language laboratory would produce nearly the same differences. Through the years, regression forecasts made in this manner in other fields have often failed in their predictions.

Second, when the effects, as measured here, turn out to be small and their magnitudes uncertain one cannot hope for very pointed policy directions.

Third, where the work involves what J. W. Tukey calls "exploratory data analysis," the usual tests of significance and other safeguards break down. In exploring these data our authors are doing their best, as they should, to find effects and suggestions for improving the schools. In the course of their work they naturally analyze, reanalyze—indeed, ransack—some portion of the EEOS data. Since they are rummaging through many small imperfectly estimated effects, the largest of these may only be one that was especially affected by sampling error. And so one cannot be as comfortable with the apparent effects reported as in the case of "confirmatory data analysis." An idealized version of the latter is that just one analysis required by a theory is evaluated, and its uncertainty assessed. We then say how nearly right the theory is. This is not the way of many large analyses of social-survey data. Big effects are less affected by these problems of multiplicity and selection. For example, the findings on ethnic/racial achievement are quite solid. But it is exactly in the details of the "production function"—the search for the variables that "produce" high test scores—that these problems impede us most.

In laying out these warnings, we must emphasize that the analyses in EEOR suffer from these same difficulties—it is still the same one-shot survey, EEOS, that is being analyzed. And so we are not raising new criticisms against our own reanalyses, merely making clear a few general difficulties applicable to all such studies, but often not mentioned.

FINDINGS OF
REANALYSES

———————

If the present volume poses a major disagreement with the findings of EEOR, it is with how firmly and directly the major analytical questions have been addressed. The details of the difficulties appear in several of the chapters where authors* take up specific issues, but we might mention a few to give the flavor. Considerable nonresponse occurred, some from whole school districts and some from pupils, teachers, principals, and superintendents. Some kinds of questions, such as father's occupation and education, may not be well answered by young children and are often omitted. The teacher's own verbal tests are self-administered. For the most part there is no way to relate the teacher to the pupils he or she taught. The facilities that were studied are unlikely to effect a direct improvement in a pupil's achievement in the area tested. (A science laboratory does not directly strengthen verbal achievement, but it might directly strengthen laboratory work in a science or scores on a science information test.) The quality and actual use of the facilities were not measured. Without meaning to carp, we note that these are by no means all the criticisms about the data, their gathering, and their interpretation.

As a result of such criticisms, the support for several of the conclusions of the EEOR seems much weaker than before. For some issues, the problem now arises whether the data were actually capable of testing the question. A good illustration of this sort of trouble appears in the Cohen, Pettigrew, and Riley chapter of this book. They try to check whether integration of schools directly benefits the academic achievement of the Negro child. (It is fair to say on the basis of their past work that they formerly believed it does.) They now find that EEOR and other studies may not have been successful in disentangling the effects of race and social class, and that selection effects are probably interfering with the analysis, and so it is possible that the "racial" effects observed in the EEOR are due to social-class composition. They have, however, a further finding on integration that we save until later.

This sort of "infirming" conclusion arises on issues several times in several of the papers. Why is it important? Because whenever a large study is available, and little else is known for policy purposes, the temptation is strong to say, as we have said at the close of Part I, that, however feeble this study may be, it is the best we have and that we must base policy on this. Where the study does bear directly upon the question at issue, this is a

* See especially Jencks's appendix for problems of nonresponse.

rather compelling position. But where the study turns out not to have dealt with a question, but only seems to have, then we need not pay it much attention on that point. Why any? Because if an effect is of great magnitude it often will stick out boldly in the analysis, and if it does not the failure to find it suggests that the effect may be small or difficult to appraise.

In Chapter 2 of this book, Christopher Jencks concentrates his effort on Northern urban elementary schools. He reanalyzes the EEOS data with a view to checking several of the original EEOR conclusions. The findings that he feels many people distrusted were (1) that Negro and white children had nearly comparable school resources within regions, and (2) that once one takes account of race and family background, academic achievement is weakly related to school policies and resources. His general finding is that the EEOR was right, and that the "common sense" that led to disbelief was mistaken.

In agreement with the first point above, he finds little racial bias in the allocation of resources among schools of the type he studied. Going beyond this to an area not discussed by EEOR, he also finds little social-class bias in the allocation of resources in these schools.

In agreement with the second point above, he finds that the relations of the school's physical facilities and programs to academic achievement are slight after taking account of student background, with similar findings for weak relations with teacher characteristics.

He disagrees with EEOR findings on the matter of Negro student achievement, for in his sample of schools he finds it less rather than more strongly related to school policies and resources than that of whites.

In trying to assess the effect of socioeconomic level of classmates on a student's own achievement—the social composition effect—he finds a strong relation even after taking account of the student's own race and family background, but regards the inference to be drawn from this as ambiguous. Is it the schoolmates of the lower-class student who attends a middle-class school who help him, or is the family that sends him there more supportive than one which doesn't? For a given socioeconomic composition in the school, he finds that the relation between school racial composition and achievement is small.

To those concerned about the development of educational policy, the dialogue offered in the chapters by Hanushek and Kain, and by Coleman, should be especially enlightening. The former argue that by not concentrating its efforts on inputs or on both inputs and outputs, and instead going on much further to try to find the elements of the educational process whose change would improve education, the EEOR went beyond what it could do and so fell short of its purpose. Coleman argues that without a knowledge of what inputs are important, one cannot know whether opportunities are equal. The value of this debate comes not from its hashing over of the past, but from its implications for the future, not only for studies of education *but also for other studies of programs intended to relieve social problems.* We emphasize again that the existence of the study itself has raised the sights of research workers in the field of education, as this dialogue shows. Hanushek and Kain, like Bowles and Levin mentioned above, especially emphasize the need for a model that will show the process by which inputs affect educational achievement, if they do, and we can confidently look forward to the development and appraisal of such models in the future.

The Armor chapter reanalyzes the USOE data for elementary schools. Instead of looking at the characteristics of individual students, as EEOR did, Armor chooses schools as the units of analysis. By considering such measures as average student achievement or average teacher preparation within each school, he analyzes the between-school variation. This appears to be about one third of the total variation due to schools and individuals combined. This is larger than that considered in earlier discussions because the races and the regions are combined rather than stratified.

In answering questions about school inputs, Armor's findings are similar to those of EEOR. On many input measures, schools with almost all Negro students seem no worse off than schools with almost all whites, although there are some important regional variations. On his summary measures of school facilities and expenditures, no consistent within-region differences are found between schools with almost all Negro students and those with almost all whites. He stresses that schools in the South were significantly more disadvantaged than schools elsewhere. Even though Negro schools are little or no worse off than white schools there, the fact that so many Negroes live in the South means that as a group they are more disadvantaged than whites. This disadvantage appears even greater when, as during the period studied, so many Negroes migrated to the North, where they then had to compete with the products of the better Northern schools.

Two of Armor's input measures showed differences between Negro schools and white schools. Negro schools were far behind white schools in teacher verbal achievement, and quite far ahead of them in teacher professional training (degrees, courses) and commitment (years of experience and professional reading). These somewhat paradoxical findings can both be explained, he argues, by the fact that in most Negro schools the majority of the faculty is Negro (at least in those regions where the two input measures have the largest differences), while white schools have predominantly white faculties. In other words, Negro teachers are ahead in extent of teacher professional training (experience, commitment, etc.), but they show far less verbal achievement than white teachers. In fact, the achievement gap between Negro and white teachers is just about as wide as the gap for students. This finding, which is *not* stressed by EEOR, though it was by Coleman, gives another reason for integration. To the extent that teacher verbal skills are important for student achievement, Negro students will be handicapped if they remain in schools whose faculties are just as deficient as they are.

Evaluating student outputs, as measured by verbal achievement, Armor also documents that Negro students start 1st grade far behind whites, and that they appear to be further behind whites by the time they reach 6th grade. In certain samples, Negro 1st grades were about 1.5 standard deviations behind whites, and this difference reached 2 standard deviations for 6th grades. The large Negro-white differences in verbal skills before formal schooling even begins is one of the strongest pieces of evidence for the importance of family and community background characteristics, and the failure of six years of schooling to narrow the gap raises hard questions about the ability of schools alone ever doing so.

Armor also provides regression analyses using all of his school and family input measures, and he analyzes Negro and white student achievement separately within several regions of the country. He verified that, contrary to the opinions of some of the critics of the methods used in EEOR, no matter how one looks at the associations—controlled or uncontrolled, schools controlled before family, or family controlled before schools—family inputs are far more powerful predictors of achievement than school inputs, and this is true for both races. He stresses that the strongest associations between achievement and school inputs occurred for Negroes in the South (as did EEOR in discussing expenditure per pupil). This has important policy implications, in that Southern Negroes are the most disadvantaged with respect to achievement of any group. It may be that the achievement of Negroes in the South is at such a low level that schools can begin to make an important contribution over and above the family.

On the issue of integration, Armor finds that the lowest-achieving students were white students attending mostly Negro schools. Although Negroes in integrated schools have higher scores than Negroes in mostly Negro schools, they are still achieving about 1.5 standard deviations behind whites in integrated schools. Most of these differences can be explained by family input characteristics; that is, individuals reporting themselves as whites in mostly Negro schools show the lowest family socioeconomic status, and Negroes in integrated schools have higher SES than Negroes in Negro schools but lower socioeconomic status than whites in integrated schools.

Marshall Smith (Chapter 6) reappraises several of the more controversial findings of the EEOR. In calculating the amounts of among-school variation in achievement attributable to family background as compared with other sources of variation, Smith found an error in the EEOR calculations, produced because the wrong variables had been put into the calculations. The effect of the mistake was to produce an *underestimate* in the importance of family factors. Of the original 10 percent variance in achievement between schools (10 percent of total), in the population Smith studied, the maximum proportion to be "explained" by home background ranged from 50 to 70 percent for whites and was about 30 percent for Negroes. These results are about 3 or 4 times as large as those reported by EEOR, and they give no comfort to those who objected that too much credit was being given in EEOR to home background and not enough to school factors. (Note the considerable difference in the amount explained for whites and for Negroes. These numbers imply a considerable difference in sensitivity—or possibly restricted range or poor measurements—to family background for the two groups, as far as academic achievement goes.)

Partly because of the original EEOR error, Smith's analysis of objective family variables (household items, parents' education, number of siblings) does not confirm the EEOR's conclusion of decreasing importance of family background from grades 6 to 12. The author does not necessarily believe that the EEOR conclusion is wrong as a fact, but only that the data do not now seem to support the conclusion. Smith finds an increasing relation through the years between subjective family background variables (child's perception of parents' educational expectations for him) and verbal achievement. Smith's interpretation is that parents perceive the child's achievement in school and that their expectations change as they see how the child shapes up. This interpretation differs from that of EEOR, which suggested that the parents' expectations affected the child's achievement.

Although EEOR concluded that the characteristics of the other members of the student body influenced the verbal achievement of individual students, Smith, like Cohen, Pettigrew, and Riley, while not denying the possibility, also finds no evidence in EEOR to support the position. The complications of the problem are such that nothing short of a longitudinal study, if indeed that would be adequate, would be required to get the truth. In this same vein, although EEOR found differential sensitivity for Negroes and whites to characteristics of the student body, of the school facilities and curriculum, and of teachers, Smith's reanalysis gives no support to this position. Note that it did support differential sensitivity to home background, Negroes being less influenced.

In his regression analyses for predicting verbal achievement, Smith found the coefficients of the facilities and of the teacher variables to be small and therefore his findings lend support to the interpretation reached in EEOR and in the chapters by Jencks and by Armor.

Smith raises a serious point concerning the analysis of the data used in EEOR. He points out that these analyses overlooked the effects that school placement and student self-selection practices might have on inferences about the relationships between school resources and student achievement. This effect is particularly important at the secondary level. The authors of EEOR neglected to distinguish between trade, academic, and comprehensive high schools in their analyses. Furthermore, at the 9th grade they did not distinguish between junior high and senior high schools. The result of this is to put into question any specific findings at the secondary level about relationships between school resources and student achievement. Future studies of secondary school effects should note this problem.

One of the principal sources of conflict over schooling during the past decade has been school desegregation. In their chapter, Cohen, Pettigrew, and Riley pursue some of the issues involved in these disputes. One of these was the degree of relationship between racial composition and achievement. Their analysis yielded two conclusions.

First, the racial composition of schools has only a minimal relationship to the verbal achievement of Negro students, once other factors (school quality, individual student background, and the school's social class composition), were taken into account. This reinforces the conclusion of the original report.

Second, the racial composition of classrooms *within* schools relates to Negro students' verbal ability, even after many relevant influences have been accounted for. This second result suggests that if desegregated schools are internally integrated, Negro students' achievement may benefit. Although the effect is not huge, neither is it negligible.

Cohen, Pettigrew, and Riley also tried to explore other problems related to school integration. They focused a good deal of attention on the relation between schools' interracial climates and student achievement. They sought to determine the degree of relation between the level of interracial hostility of biracial schools and the achievement of Negro or white students. They found, however, that the range of variation in interracial friendship in the EEOS sample of schools was so slight—once variation in schools' racial composition was taken into account—that the problem could not be pursued further with these data.

In general, their results do little to disturb the EEOR conclusions.

CONCLUSIONS OF THE
REANALYSTS

Without going into full detail, the general policy implications of some of these studies should be mentioned. Coleman (Chapter 4) believes that in addition to the use of the method of scientific experimentation we need to develop new methods of discovering variables of importance to policy. He suggests a few techniques that might be tried out. He agrees with Hanushek and Kain on the need for more thoroughly developed models that have both costs and effects in them, at the same time that he feels that we are not so clear about just what the variables are that should be included. (One might at first feel that the nation can afford "whatever" it costs to provide "quality" education for "all" our children. But this simply is not so. Resources for education, as for all other purposes, public or private, are limited. There is a shortage of everything, including knowledge as to what combinations of educational inputs maximize educational outputs. It has been the repeated experience of benefit-cost analysis that things turn up that surprise everyone, such being the counterintuitive nature of solutions to so many problems of complex systems. The sociologist Coleman, and the economists Hanushek and Kain, simply argue for knowledge in an area where the quest for knowledge has been too frequently thwarted or obstructed.)

Coleman notes that as policy research is only beginning in the social area, the social scientist has much to learn about how to answer policy-related questions. By implication then, training programs in this direction are needed, as well as research on policy for social science. These needs have recently been noted in several reports at a national level.

(The report of the Advisory Committee on Government Programs in the Behavioral Sciences of the National Research Council [27] recommended the creation of a National Institute for Advanced Research on Public Policy. The Special Commission on the Social Sciences of the National Sciences Board [28] recommended the creation of research institutes for social problems. The Behavioral and Social Science Survey of the National Academy of Sciences and the Social Science Research Council [29] recommended new graduate schools of applied behavioral science to work on policy problems. As these recommendations are implemented we can expect progress on this problem of training for work on social policy.)

Jencks and Armor regard the low fraction of variance attributable to school variables and teacher variables as discouraging for bringing about improvement and change within the present framework.

Jencks concludes further that (1) the least promising approach to raising achievements is to raise expenditures, since the data give little evidence that any widely used school policy or resource has an appreciable effect on achievement scores. (This does not mean one can get behind in the teacher-salary market or let the buildings fall apart.) He feels that (2) the evidence does not rule out the possibility that radically different policies and approaches might have an impact on achievement. These might or might not cost more than present approaches. He feels that we have no direct evidence to indicate that they *will* work either. Although Jencks does not specify, presumably such devices as giving parents funds that can be spent on the private education of their children, or the removal to boarding schools of children from family situations that are unsatisfactory for the purpose of academic and citizenship improvement, or the development of new kinds of schools, would fall within the framework of such radical developments.

(3) A more promising alternative, based on present evidence, is

socioeconomic integration. This step is more difficult politically, at least at the moment. We don't *know* that integration will boost the achievement of disadvantaged children, but all the EEOS evidence and the bulk of other evidence suggest that it will help *somewhat*.

(4) The most promising alternative would be to alter the way in which parents deal with their children at home. Unfortunately, it is not obvious how this could be done. Income maintenance, family allowances, etc., seem a logical beginning.

(5) The *social* benefits of increasing school resources and altering school policies may be significant even though the *cognitive* benefits are not. This possibility has scarcely been looked at.

The above conclusions by Jencks do not appear in his Chapter 2.

Armor concludes that while integration of schools could help, that *alone* could not close the black-white achievement gap. He believes that closing it requires that major attention be given to the socioeconomic condition of the individual black family. In other words, neither school upgrading nor school integration will close the black-white achievement gap if the black-white gap in socioeconomic status is ignored.

Marshall Smith concludes that insofar as the schools are merely selecting and assigning students to various sorts of educational tracks, they can be regarded as doing a competent job. The complaint arises because they are not performing well as an equalizing agent. Dramatic changes are needed if we want an equalizing agency.

Cohen, Pettigrew, and Riley conclude that any further research on the relation between racial composition and student achievement needs to improve on the EEOR design. The most useful work is likely to arise from longitudinal studies of school districts where desegregation is being undertaken.

Finally, we have mentioned several times the need to consider the schools as having many responses they are trying to train for. We cannot therefore settle for measures of achievement which are restricted to academic accomplishments.

PART III: Looking Forward

What now? There are two ways at very least of looking at the EEOR and its aftermath. It can, in effect, be judged a worthy enterprise but so flawed in its execution as to be of no real use beyond the indisputable fact that it has raised some interesting questions and suggested a new way of looking at programs in education. This is the view of Henry M. Levin, who was quoted directly to this effect: "For a piece of large-scale research, there are big portions of data that are worthwhile and salvageable. But there is absolutely nothing in the report to support policy decisions. Its social value is zero." [30] An alternative view would hold that some findings of EEOR already offer policy-makers important information in some areas and point to new questions requiring investigation in others. From this it would follow that policy should be informed by the report, if not exactly based on it.

We hold this latter view. On reexamination we find the EEOS data do not confirm all of the purported findings of the EEOR. But they confirm many of them, and just as importantly they established new parameters of what is *likely* to be true about education. Henceforth, for example, it is likely we shall find that American school systems are more like one another than otherwise. Henceforth, it is likely we shall find that increasing the "supply" of education for schools that are going concerns by merely increasing gross "inputs" will not have any great effect on gross "outputs." This seems clear.

These remarks do not, however, speak against the value of pointed programs designed for specific payoffs with careful plans for their assessment and improvement. Clearly EEOR does not inform us about such programs, and it scarcely could be expected to have done so.

Public policy is almost invariably based on inadequate information, if for no other reason than that institutions informing day-to-day policy decisions scarcely exist, and certainly not for school systems. But we can afford to distinguish day-to-day decisions, middle-term policy, and long-run policy. For immediate decisions EEOR, plus other research studies and knowledge of the current states of the educational institutions, represent all the policy-maker can hope to have, and he is used to such a state of affairs. More, he is better off than usual. For the middle run he can be organizing planning groups for studies whose results could become available within three to five years. For the long run we all have to take a different attitude toward educational research from that of the hysteria produced by those who want all answers immediately. In the field of pollution, where weather represents an annual cycle, and where a generation of flora and fauna might represent a five-year cycle, we already realize that ten-year plans are required. Our current school system is based on a twelve-year cycle for most pupils and a sixteen- or twenty-year cycle for our professional cadre. Though change is probably desirable, this structure will not change very rapidly. Consequently some wise administrators need to lay plans for investigations that are both long-range and flexible, but much longer-range than anything we are used to.

To return to the present, a document produced in the U.S. Office of Education says:

Most programs to be effective must be based either on proven results or failing that on a consistent body of theory. As of 1968, we have few unequivocal proofs, and only a glimmering of a theory to support these proofs. We do have considerable evidence that pragmatism has not worked.

The statement is a little gloomier than necessary—after all many people have learned to read, write, and add. But even such a negative statement can be the basis of an explicit and positive policy. From assuming, as was done until just a short while ago, that the essential processes of education were well understood, and that the only serious issue of public policy in this field was to provide sufficient resources to bring all sectors up to the level of best practice, we now learn that the processes are *not* well understood. Not understood at all! Well and good. It is entirely feasible to live with this "knowledge," even to make it the central tenet of a coherent and effective educational policy. It is after all clear that a very great deal of education gets done, regardless of how well we "understand" the process. It may just be that even more will get done as there emerges a higher order of understanding.

There is, moreover, good reason to think that the nation is reasonably disposed to proceeding boldly in spite of our weak foundations. The educational world has been shaken. Not so much by the EEOR, or its counterparts in small-scale research projects, as by the relatively indifferent performance turned in by the great compensatory programs of the 1960's. The nation has acquired a goal, or, if it has not, we think it should accept it—equal educational opportunity defined as approximately equal distributions of achievement (but not just for cognitive skills) for the different ethnic/racial groups. This is a goal it does not know how to attain. Given a vital, prosperous, and still largely optimistic society, it follows that a period of fairly intensive educational experimentation and research is in order—and is likely to occur.

WHAT CAN BE ACCOMPLISHED

Other reasons for optimism may be adduced. Not least is that the subject turns out to be interesting. Which is to say it turns out to be difficult, demanding of considerable skill and patience: a worthy challenge to persons seeking to do something of excellence for the nation. But clearly the most important reason is that racial peace in the United States will depend in part on how well the American educational system succeeds in turning out students of approximately equal competence.

In the field of public elementary and secondary education this can mean only one thing. It is no doubt "the plain fact," as the New York City Master Plan declared in 1969, "that no one yet knows how to make a ghetto school work." This is not quite the same as saying that no ghetto schools work, because some do. (Perhaps it should have said no one knows how to make a public ghetto school work.) Very well, someone must learn. Or alternate social arrangements must be devised that will offset the disadvantage which accrues to the slum resident in consequence of his level of development in the fairly narrow range of qualities measured by tests of verbal and mathematical ability. This is true for blacks; it is equally true for Puerto Ricans, Mexican Americans, Indian Americans, and in general that whole range of population groups whose socioeconomic status is sharply below that of the American mean.

There is, moreover, considerable reason to think that an era of experiment and discovery is feasible in the 1970's. The overall number of children in school will decline during the early 1970's, owing to the declining birthrates of the preceding decade. A reasonable estimate is that during the period 1970–74 elementary enrollments will decline by 3 million students and secondary enrollments will grow by only 1.3 to 2.2, even with a zero dropout rate. Post-secondary enrollments will continue to grow, but at a considerably lower rate than that of the late 1960's. Thus there could be a considerable increase in resources per pupil in the school system without a great overall increase in resources applied to education. The latter is possible, but the former is in any event easier and will be more or less automatic. It would be easy to underestimate the quantities involved here. In 1974 the potential supply of elementary and secondary teachers will be close to 2.75 million. If student-teacher ratios remain at the levels of the late 1960's, it will be possible to deploy three quarters of a million teachers to new tasks. What resources can do is likely to be done in the 1970's. And, as we have argued, the actual impact of resources on educational achievement in the individual child remains to be assessed. We know little about the effect of existing arrangements, nothing about the effect of arrangements yet to be invented.

A PILOT MODEL FOR EDUCATION, OCCUPATION, AND INCOME

In thinking about how much can be accomplished by improvements in education we should probably go outside the internal system of school achievement, and especially cognitive achievement, to consider the possible size of long-run effects of improvements in education for occupation and income for

those who have been deprived. This sort of consideration is especially necessary as an antidote to the general test-score mania that we fear extending by
our preoccupation with cognitive achievement as a measure of accomplishment. It will serve to warn us that equality of educational achievement, in
the sense of school years completed, is unlikely to accomplish as much toward equality in income and occupation as those pressing for equality of
educational opportunity probably hope for it. It thereby emphasizes the
need in striving for equalization to move on more than one front.

At the same time that we introduce this study to get some general
notions of what might be accomplished by equalizing years of education, we
also illustrate the kinds of models that are often used in economic studies
and in operational research.

Otis Dudley Duncan[31] has constructed a model intended to show how
several variables combine to forecast a person's occupational and income
levels. In one version of this model he considers how the family head's education and occupation and the family size influence his child's amount of
education, and how they all influence his child's occupation, and finally how
all these influence the child's adult income.

The model uses a type of regression analysis usually called "causal."
This means that the author of the model supplies the hierarchy in which
variables influence one another. His key judgment is "X causes Y but is not
caused by it." For example, family head's education and occupation help
decide (cause) the number of siblings a child will have, but Duncan assumes that their number does not influence father's education or occupation.
That is the sort of "causal" assumption that is made.

What Duncan develops is a model intended to tell us something about
the effects of various disparities between the Negro and white groups in the
country, and the extent to which they could be expected to be redressed if
certain steps could magically be taken. He tries to "explain" the $3,790
difference in family income level for the two races found in a survey as of
about 1962. His data suggest that if the difference in years of schooling for
comparable family backgrounds could be wiped out, it would account for
$520 of this differential. Although this is a good-sized amount, it is very far
from wiping out most of the differential. He finds that adjusting family
background differentials would account for $940, and occupational differ-
ences for people with equal preparation $830. That is, this analysis sug-
gests that from where things stand now, fair employment practices could be
more remunerative than equal schooling. These findings give the flavor of
the main results. The proportions here are more important than the absolute
figures. For our present purposes the suggestion is that about 14 percent of
the difference in income levels might be wiped out if equal years of equal
quality education were suddenly available to Negroes. Since family background and occupational differentials each account for a considerably larger

proportion of the income differential, those interested in money will see the model as suggesting a better payoff from emphasizing family and occupation.

We must caution—and we are sure Duncan would agree—that such an analysis is subject to the weaknesses we have already mentioned for regression analyses based on survey data, rather than experimental data. We do not know what would actually happen if these adjustments could be made. Nevertheless, such an analysis does give us more perspective on what changing amounts of education might or might not be able to accomplish. Some will complain that "years in school" is not identical with "cognitive achievement"; for the illustrative purpose at hand, there is probably less to this criticism than meets the eye.

SOME MYTHS ABOUT THE PRESENT AND NEAR FUTURE

Still, there are probabilities here, or intuitions, as you will. Our intuition is that the EEOR finding on the effect of school characteristics is more likely to prove true than otherwise. It is simply not very likely that equalized or compensated school environment can erase the effects of widely varying levels of educational stimulus which different social groups acquire from the home or neighborhood environment. Dennis J. Dugan, of the U.S. Office of Education, has, for example, estimated the dollar value of the educational services a child received from his mother according to different levels of mother's education. By the 12th grade the accumulated value of such services received from a mother with eight years of education was about $6,200; for a mother who was a college graduate it was about $17,100. Clearly, if this is true, the schools have an extraordinary obstacle to overcome, and it is little wonder that they do not often do so.[32] Similarly, Donald P. Hayes and Judith Grether have developed evidence suggesting—but only suggesting—that middle-class and lower-class children progress at about the same rate during the school year, but that learning during the summer, as measured by achievement tests, almost ceases for the lower-class child while it continues apace for his middle-class schoolmates.[33] If this finding holds up, the gap would continue to widen despite the most impeccably even-handed treatment of children by the school system. It may be that schools can significantly change these outcomes, and it is worth trying. But it should not be supposed that it will be easy.

Other strategies are also worth trying, primarily those dealing with early childhood development and those dealing with the general question of social class. The *fact* of early learning was, in a sense, rediscovered in the middle third of the twentieth century, and toward the end of that period its processes were beginning to be understood. This knowledge was at hand to explain the otherwise baffling finding of the EEOR that the educational disadvantage of minority groups was already there in the 1st grade, and in just about the proportions in which it persisted through the succeeding years. "The differences in language and number competence between lower and middle class children," Jerome Kagan writes, "are significant by the time the child is four years old, and are awesome by the time he enters the first grade." How could marginal differences in school facilities be expected to overcome "awesome" differences in verbal and mathematical competence? How could even large differences do so? The logical course is to turn attention and resources to the period before the lowered level of competence sets in. As Kagan has it, the task is to change "the ecology of the lower class child in order to increase the probability that he will be more successful in attaining normative skills." [34] The variety of ways this might be done are considerable and it requires no very great imagination to think of some, but finding and verifying those that work will take both imagination and extensive sophisticated research. What is now reasonably clear is that a "good" school is a necessary but not a sufficient condition for a child or young person receiving a "good" education. Other conditions are also necessary, and of these knowledge is only beginning to emerge.

One basic caveat is in order. One of the patterns of the 1960's was that of middle-class persons, in largest measure professionals, conceiving a great range of social programs, supported by tax monies, which undertook to assist the poor through a process of employing middle-class persons. Professionally trained persons would provide services of various sorts. Reform was becoming professionalized. The founding of Headstart was a typical instance, which Sheldon H. White has described.

There was social action dictated not by grass roots demands but by the social diagnostician; there was the urge to establish a solution outside the system which had "failed"; there was scientific backing offered by the expert-turned-advocate.[35]

These programs are costly—full-year Headstart costs about $1,600 per child per year, roughly a third more than the per capita expenditure in regular elementary and secondary grades in 1969–70. And, most importantly, the *money* typically ends up in the hands of middle-class professional persons, although there will usually be a penumbra of "paraprofessional" employment associated with such activities. Let us not overlook the point that medical costs form an important part of the budget of the program and that community start-up costs do also. Nevertheless, the total costs make it worth asking whether the thousand dollars plus per year spent on Headstart might not have as great or greater total social advantage if it were simply turned over to parents of the poor child. We don't know.

This raises the question whether a social strategy designed to increase the incomes of lower-class families by raising occupational levels or wage rates, by tax exemptions or income supplementation, might not in the end do more to raise levels of educational achievement than direct spending on schools. This indirect approach has other social justifications: improved nutrition, clothing, and living conditions. (One would not expect very rapid educational improvement from it, but rather an effect that would be felt through successive generations.)

An alternative possibility is that without necessarily strengthening educational achievement, increased parental income might improve occupational and income prospects for the child's future. These effects may be of more immediate concern than direct improvement of education. Further, a bare possibility exists that experiments on the negative income tax going on in 1971 will teach us something about these matters.

Whatever the truths here, the essential fact is that we have only the weakest grasp on any of them. There is no reason whatever to expect a laboratory type of breakthrough in which an explicitly stated problem will be precisely and finally solved.

SOME DIFFERENT
INFORMATION

As always, some information runs counter to that we have described. First, we have repeatedly discussed the proposition that variation in schools doesn't make much difference. Here is a puzzle for those who believe this. The Northeast's white children in 1st grade according to EEOR rank sixth in verbal achievement among the eight national regions. Just how is it that such poor starters wind up in top position after only a few grades? Better TV? The weather? Different tests? Is it that parents who couldn't get them up to average before they went to school suddenly take an interest when they do go? Or may it not be possible that the schools just do have a substantial effect on verbal achievement in the Northeast?

Second, the investigations of St. John and Smith reported by Cohen, Pettigrew, and Riley suggest that schools and integration may matter. They found Negroes who moved from an all-Negro school to an integrated school, although reducing their self-esteem, and leaving their reading achievement unchanged, improved their mathematics achievement.

Third, preliminary reports, by Dyer in his chapter on Future Studies, of the Hartford busing experiment suggest noticeable improvements in scores. Substantial effects may really be available from integration and other changes in the school system. Careful studies like this genuine controlled field investigation are so rare and so easily spoiled that we are not used to thinking about them. If society wants to get its money's worth out of education and other social programs, then it will need to encourage such studies rather than hinder them. Otherwise our power to analyze will have outrun our power to investigate.

Fourth, insofar as gains were registered by Title I programs,* the majority were obtained in the higher grades, Piccariello[36] found. This finding is contrary to the myth that all the remedial work must be packed into the very young, and it opens the possibility of some flexibility that did not seem to be available.

On the other hand, the Title I program as a whole has not produced the gains hoped from it. Indeed, for what are believed to be programs selected in a manner likely to be biased toward higher scores, the record of 189 programs is that 58 showed positive gains in reading scores, 50 showed losses, and 81 showed no significant change. The tragedy here is that little will be learned from the early Title I efforts because there is no social plan for evaluation and evolution. In their chapter in this book Gilbert and Mosteller emphasize the need for the evolutionary development of these large social programs through genuine controlled field investigations. Donald T. Campbell also discusses this need in his notable article "Reforms as experiments." [37]

Some will wish to press the point that improvement in reading is not the primary goal or the primary gain arising from these programs. Although it is true that whenever programs get low marks their proponents tend to find that the wrong features have been evaluated, let us accept this criticism. Suppose that the programs are primarily intended to strengthen children in other ways, ways such as we have mentioned before: improved socialization, improved self-image, improved facility with the spoken language, improved nutrition and medical care, or improved parental care for the child. Then these variables should be assessed both to find out what progress is being made and what methods seem to produce the best yield. The principles we discuss are not limited to programs of cognitive improvement. We must also make clear that, in many problems, before one can decide how to make things "better" he needs first to be able to answer the question "What goes on?", "How does the process work?"

The nation can ill afford full-scale social programs of unknown value that cost large amounts but have no automatic self-improvement features—no way of genuinely assessing their contribution so that policy can be im-

---

* Title I of the Elementary and Secondary Education Act of 1965 provides Federal funds for schools in low income areas. (The association between low family incomes and low educational achievement is, of course, quite strong, as EEOR showed.) Appropriations for this program for 1969 were $1.12 billion, for 1970, $1.34 billion, for 1971, $1.5 billion, and for 1972, $1.5 billion requested.

proved. An atmosphere needs to be created in which this process can become routine.

This, surely, is an essential implication of the EEOR. Henceforth to ignore it will be a mark of irresponsibility or worse. *And it will be so for educational lobbyists demanding "more" no less than for school boards and legislatures resisting such demands.* It is necessary, moreover, not only to assert this requirement, but also to understand and to accept it as a formidably demanding one. The early experience of Title I, the central feature of the first great program of Federal aid to elementary and secondary education, is a prime example of what happens when we do not plan for improvement.

RECOMMENDATIONS

No single program can be expected to close the gap in educational achievement between the disadvantaged minorities and the white group. Furthermore, we do not know what school programs might offer the largest improvements for the cost involved. We must also recognize that strengthened educational achievement may not be the most important social reform needed. Indeed, higher income and better occupational chances probably are more immediate targets of reform groups, with educational achievement regarded as part of the means toward such change, as well as having value in itself. Consequently, we mention here a few key recommendations; others are to be found in the final section of Part II of this chapter, and, of course, each chapter has its own recommendations.

1. *Educational goals. Both nationally and locally, we should reappraise the aims, goals, and measures of success in education. We should adopt equality of educational opportunity, defined for the moment as equality of educational achievement for the several ethnic/racial groups, as a national goal.*

Equality of educational opportunity has had a changing meaning over the years, and it will continue to change. It is essential both to understand *and to accept* this fact. We must also accept a future where people hold sharply divergent views as to just what the term implies. The tensions, touched upon earlier, between the ideals of liberty and equality in American life will almost certainly persist, so that we must not expect that any final understanding of the term will ever be achieved. Nor need it be. But clearly a good deal more systematic thought could be addressed to this subject. In addition, it is possible to hope that at least some persons who now employ the same term to refer to widely differing conceptions of social equity will learn to perceive, and to accept, these differences.

We recommend further that thought be given to the goals and needs of education in the nation. This thought needs to challenge platitudes (and avoidances) about making the most of oneself in every possible way. It must recognize the limitations imposed by the twenty-four-hour day, as well as by the personal weaknesses and strengths each of us has. Perhaps most especially in the period immediately ahead, it will be necessary for all involved in education—researchers not least—to bear ever in mind the dictum that tastes differ. Both Gordon's chapter dealing with the historical evolution of the conception of equality of educational opportunity, and Dyer's, on measuring the extent to which educational goals have been met, relate to this recommendation.

2. *Long-range research programs. We recommend that the nation launch a vigorous program in educational research for the purpose of improving national, state, and local educational policy.*

The economist Boulding says "I am struck . . . with the relatively meager resource which is devoted to the problem of human learning, in spite of the fact that this is the core of virtually all developmental processes." [38] The nation needs to mount a substantial program of educational research which has the definite intent of informing policy. The program should be long-range, but flexible. It needs to be evolutionary rather than revolutionary. (But see recommendation 5.) It needs to take account of the very long cycle time of education. It should prepare the nation to accept the idea of controlled field investigations on a large scale that actually involve randomization at some level—the school or the school district. As Campbell [39] says, "We need to develop the political postures and ideologies that make randomization at these levels possible." Some of the ideas required here are discussed further in the Gilbert and Mosteller chapter.

What sorts of future studies are needed? Dyer mentions several in his chapter. We have recommended long-range planning, but let us add some obvious needs.

Planned-in-advance appraisals of year-long preschool programs are conspicuously missing. Such appraisals cannot be carried out properly unless well planned. The programs and the appraisal should be designed to concentrate upon some *few* specific school gains—whether cognitive gains, social gains, or athletic gains—rather than the whole child. It is not that the whole child isn't important, it is just that we would prefer to find out how to teach *something* to poor children rather than continue to learn that we fail at teaching *everything*. It should be anticipated that the first attempts at appraisal may not be well done. We mustn't be too upset when first-time programs appraised for the first time don't give satisfactory results. We have to learn to teach and to appraise. Feedback should help.

The summer-loss effect for lower-class students should certainly be followed up and either verified or put to bed. If it holds then active steps should be taken to compensate for it.

The problems of tracking and ability grouping have not been much discussed in this chapter. Furthermore, years of research on these problems have not reached stable conclusions. If a student gets into a slow track, he will not be able to catch up with people in faster groups because the pace of the track is slower. On the other hand, maybe he couldn't have kept up anyway. Since the evidence on tracking goes both ways, and since the intellectual and ideological arguments do the same, society may not wish to pay for more evidence on this point, but may prefer to decide on the basis of its own value system to what extent it regards tracking as acceptable. Although both teachers and educational administrators have discussed the arguments for and against tracking and ability grouping until they are weary, parents need to be made aware of these arguments and of the available choices.

One rather basic study should try to find out how teachers and students actually use their time and the effect of this time on various sorts of achievement. To what extent is the teacher actually teaching a group or an individual? To what extent is he keeping order, filling out forms, or working on supplementary school activities? Philip W. Jackson's opening chapter in *Life in Classrooms*[40] illuminates the problem of what is required of a teacher just to keep the class going without teaching them anything. We realize that time budgets have been researched in the past, but we need them studied from the point of view of differential achievement.

To what extent are students working on cognitive material inside and outside the class? We speak here of actual attention, not physical presence in a room or being near a book.

We have discussed the whole problem of education largely from the rather simple point of view of gross results of cognitive tests given to masses of students. We must not forget that in the end learning is an individual accomplishment. No matter how many teachers, friends, computing machines, and relatives surround a student, he himself finally has to learn to spell and memorize the multiplication tables. And as for the famous institution of higher learning composed of Mark Hopkins on one end of a log and a student on the other, Socrates himself could do no good if the student paid no attention to him or the subject. And so we must find out about attention and motivation, much more difficult problems than those of time budgets or achievement. For example, it is said that few Americans read books compared with Europeans. If this is true, have they been turned off by reading in school? Not turned on by it? Or have they better things to do?

The compensatory programs, begun on a massive national scale during the 1960's, pose a set of problems worth noting. A sequence was followed that seems guaranteed to produce confusion, if not bitterness. First, the programs were launched on a crash basis across a continent. Inevitably, the activities that followed varied enormously from one place to another. They were subsumed under a standard heading, however, and it was promptly reported that they were succeeding beautifully. This, as we have argued, is something no one can know so soon. Thereupon, more sophisticated evaluations began, and alas, it typically turned out that there had been no success at all, or at best, little. Again, as we have argued, this is almost the preordained conclusion to be had from the kind of survey made. This is followed by allegations of methodological inadequacy in the surveys, also by assertions that the real aims of the program were not those purportedly tested. Before long a bright and promising enterprise has been reduced to a dismal squabble.

There *is* an alternative. It is absurd to reject the possibility of compensatory educational programs' doing what they set out to do. However, it is equally absurd to suppose that this achievement can be established in the time perspectives that have so far been imposed upon them. It takes a long time for a child to grow up, and perhaps an even longer time to learn what has strengthened or weakened his education. We simply must submit to the discipline of the growth process. Simultaneously, it is surely just as important to be clear at the outset that a variety of goals—not just cognitive achievement—are appropriate to all forms of education, compensatory education included, and that just as we ought to seek to achieve such goals, we ought also to try to assess that achievement.

3. *Periodic assessment. At regular intervals, the nation should measure the state of the schools, its students and teachers, with a view to appraising progress toward its goals.*

Drawing upon the experiences of the EEOR, there should be a regular assessment of schools on a national level, designed to monitor the progress toward equality of educational achievement and other goals, and to help guide us in our further work. This overall monitoring would be carried out independently of the experimental and developmental programs. The survey should be taken at regular time intervals, about every five years.

For the moment it is enough to be clear that the social science critique of widely held social beliefs is not something that is wisely left to random and intermittent initiatives, whether by government, foundations, or individual researchers. Once begun, a kind of collective commitment to keep at the task is necessary if the new truths are not to cause more mischief than the old myths. Ultimately one might expect such periodic assessments of schools to be part of a general system of social indicators, but there is no need to wait and we should not wait for that development.

The National Assessment of Educational Progress of the Education Commission of the States gives us the first appraisal of what this country's schoolchildren and young adults know and can do. The assessment includes ten subjects: citizenship, science, writing, literature, mathematics, reading, music, art, social studies, and career and occupational development. The Commission plans to appraise and reappraise each subject, some every three and some every six years. Since the subjects, such as writing, are so broad, they are broken into ten to fourteen parts, and individuals respond to one or a few parts. The assessment does not report at the level of individuals, schools, school districts, or states, but at the level of four regions of the country and the country as a whole.

Insofar as possible, the reports of the assessments offer factual results and avoid discussing policy implications. Naturally, others should and will use the results for policy.

As first results appear, policy-makers have age, region of country, community size, sex, and race as background variables, together with the absolute and comparative performance for the questions and tasks studied. When the resurveys begin to appear, assessments of change in amounts and kinds of knowledge and skill will become possible for the first time.

Once the goals discussed in recommendation 1 have been established, individual school districts may well wish to monitor the extent to which their individually chosen goals have been achieved.

4. *Employment and income programs. We recommend increased family-income and employment-training programs, together with plans for the evaluation of their long-run effects on education.*

Recognizing that what can be done at school is conditioned by the situation in the home, we believe that employment and income strategies designed to strengthen the home environment of the child and his family have over the long run a chance to produce a great additional component to educational achievement of a child. This belief is not a proven fact, and it would be valuable to try to determine the contributions these social developments make. This will be difficult because we have no more apparatus for appraising the contributions of various social reforms and choosing among or strengthening them than we have for school improvements.

5. *New kinds of schools. We recommend that new kinds of schools be developed and evaluated, and that in existing schools new sorts of educational policies substantially different from those of the past be tried in a research and development manner.*

Returning to schools as a source to consider changing, we recommend that there be explorations of new methods of handling schools and that new types of schools be developed and evaluated. Here, as opposed to the situation in recommendation 2, revolutionary ideas can be most valuable. The caveat as always is not to get locked into an idea. We are not searching for *the* one good way to educate people, only for better ways and for a variety of ways that will serve the individual and the nation well.

Let us mention a couple of possible developments in addition to those in the Conclusions section of Part II. For a small fraction of the costs of national compensatory educational programs, it is probably possible for the nation to purchase the entire daytime program time of the equivalent of a national commercial television network (say from dawn to 7 P.M. weekdays and until noon on Saturday). Included in the price would be funds to create programs all through the week. We could have a national school of the air, indeed several of them, if this idea proved to have merit. Naturally there are political problems, but these could probably be solved. (There is political danger in just one large school.) The real question is, would such a school of the air do much for education in this country? We know that when such courses have been tied in with credit courses in secondary schools and in colleges and in industry, many students have learned enough to pass national examinations in the subject. The preschool program *Sesame Street* is being well received. Would we want such a national school to be primarily preschool, elementary school, secondary school, junior college, four-year college, or adult education? Or should there be a mix? Surely such a possibility should be considered with great care. Young people already spend as much of their time watching TV as on anything else, perhaps 1000 hours a year. Presumably what could be done with lectures and color tape could be done with such a school of the air. Naturally, problem sections and laboratory work would have to supplement such a school program. We are not proposing this as a labor-saving device but as a procedure for offering a high-quality supplement to present educational procedures.

Urie Bronfenbrenner[41] has just completed a comparative study of elementary education in Russia and in the United States. He finds that the Soviet children understand better than ours how to share and cooperate to reach a common goal. He finds that our children have more individual initiative and resourcefulness, theirs more conformity. He finds too that adults there spend more time with children than we do in this country now, although he points out that in earlier periods we did the same. Now our leisure as well as our working hours are stratified by age group. May it not be to our advantage to explore further this work of Bronfenbrenner's with a view to finding out whether some features of Soviet education could profitably be adapted to our system, just as they are finding it worthwhile to adapt some of our capitalistic production methods to their economic system?

6. *Optimism. We recommend that the electorate maintain persistent pressure on its government agencies, school boards, legislatures, and executives to set specific targets, develop and revise programs, and report on progress toward local, state, and national goals in education with an attitude that optimistically expects gains, but, knowing their rarity, appreciates them when they occur.*

Much of our discussion has focused on the touchy problem of the effect of modest changes in facilities, teachers, or curricula on academic achievement. Let us look at the matter differently. The third-best American dream, third after "Anyone Can Be President" and "Anyone Can Make a Million Dollars," is "Anyone Can Go To College." Through the years we have grown to think that more and more members of our population should go. Taubman and Wales[42] find that the average ability level of high-school graduates who enter college was as high in the '60's as at any time since the

'30's. By 1970, we have managed to put about 80 percent of seventeen-year-olds through the 12th grade. We send about 50 percent of the eighteen- to twenty-one-year-olds to college, and nearly half of those attending four-year colleges complete the degree.[43]

How does this compare with the rest of the world? It is hard to get comparable figures, but the data in Table 3 bear on the point.

Table 3 shows that we are sending 1.5 to 3 times as many to colleges and universities as other industrialized countries. (The figure 23.9 percent here differs from the 50 percent mentioned earlier because of the different age group used as a base.) Thus for substantial parts of our population we have learned how to provide access to the educational process reasonably well.

TABLE 3

Percentage of Age Group 20–24 Years Enrolled in Higher Education in Twelve Countries

Country	1965 (percent)	Country	1965 (percent)
Austria	7.5	Netherlands	14.3
Canada	8.6[c]	Norway	7.8
France	14.1[a]	Sweden	11.1[d]
Germany	8.9	United Kingdom	8.5
Italy	7.7	USSR	11.8[b]
Japan	14.6[c]	USA	23.9[c]

[a] Universities only.
[b] Includes evening and correspondence students.
[c] Age group 18–24 years (Canada, USA, Japan).
[d] Universities and degree-granting institutions only.
SOURCES: "Access to higher education in Europe," UNESCO Conference Report, Vienna, November 20–25, 1967, published by UNESCO, Paris, 1968.
  Development of Secondary Education, Organization for Economic Cooperation and Development, Paris, 1969.

It is easy to ask the inevitable question whether sending so many young people to college, and especially colleges as now taught, is a wise social goal. It is a question well worth discussing at some other place and time, one worthy of many a book. But answering it would deflect us from our main point. Society still sets these goals for itself. It has been willing to pay the bills to achieve this dream and in spite of violent debate there is little sign of interest slackening. Thus in the midst of all our discussion of how little we know about the educational process, we should reflect that we have through a great variety of types of colleges and universities been able to come close to satisfying the third dream.

The middle third of the twentieth century in the United States was, for all its ambiguities, a period of extraordinary social idealism and not less extraordinary social progress. There were no two areas of social policy in which progress toward a social ideal largely conceived and widely propounded was more conspicuous than those of equality of educational opportunity and equality of the races. The nation entered this period bound to the mores of caste and class. The white race was dominant. Negro Americans, Mexican Americans, Indian Americans, Oriental Americans, were all somehow subordinate, somehow something less than fully American. (Puerto Ricans had barely touched the national consciousness.) Education beyond a fairly rudimentary point was largely determined by social status. In a bare third of a century these circumstances have been extensively changed. *Changed!* Not merely a sequence of events drifting in one direction or another. To the contrary, events have been bent to the national will. Things declared to be desirable have been attained through sustained and systematic effort.

It is a paradoxical quality of such achievements that they are typically accompanied by intense feelings of dissatisfaction and disappointment on the part of those principally involved. It would have to be said that the nation ended this period (for there was a kind of ending in the late 1960's) with racial tensions higher than at any time in our history, and with dissatisfaction with the educational system approaching the point of crisis. These developments are not to be undone, and their aftermath will be with us for years to come. We see no way to avoid this, but, that being the case, we do recommend that some attention be paid to our national achievements, even as dissatisfaction mounts with respect to newer goals as yet unachieved. For this is the point. To a striking degree, things thought to be desirable in the area of racial equality, and even more so in the area of educational opportunity, have been achieved.

Especially in the period after World War II, Negroes made pronounced gains on whites in the areas of income, occupation, and education. During this period the income gap between young blacks and young whites narrowed. The education gap closed sharply. In 1940, only 12 percent of nonwhites twenty-five to twenty-nine years old had graduated from high school. By 1965 half had done so. High-school graduations became normal for all groups, while in the years immediately following, the number of black students in colleges doubled. Clearly some gaps are narrowing.

The statistics are familiar; the lesson to be drawn from them is not. The United States made extraordinary efforts to achieve certain social goals during this period, and given the way the goals were at first defined, they were substantially achieved. Especially with regard to educational goals, this involved large public expenditures, and these expenditures were forthcoming. Thus between 1955 and 1968 educational expenditures for operating purposes in higher education increased *five times*, from $4 billion per year to $20 billion. The proportion of the gross national product devoted to higher education more than doubled during this same period. As the nation entered the 1970's, it was commonly forecast that upwards of two thirds of young persons would be attending college by the 1980's.

As the 1970's began, the issues of education and race in the United States commenced to enter a new phase, involving new and yet more difficult issues. For most purposes it is accurate to state that these issues first appeared in connection with the continued existence in the eleven states of the South (Alabama, Arkansas, Florida, Georgia, Louisiana, Mississippi, North Carolina, South Carolina, Tennessee, Texas, Virginia) of a legally established dual school system which separated students on the basis of "race." In 1954 the Supreme Court declared that separate education was "inherently unequal," and in 1955 the Court issued its mandate for "all deliberate speed" in according all children equal protection of the laws. Litigation had only begun. Some black children were placed in previously all-white schools, and later the courts insisted that all students be given "freedom of choice," that is to say be allowed to attend any school of their choosing within their school system. The rules were changed, but the results were not. For practical purposes a dual school system persisted in the South. In the 1960's a combination of civil-rights statutes and the beginning of large-scale federal aid to elementary and secondary education gave the executive branch of the national government its first real leverage with respect to the dual school system in the South. Steadily pressure mounted.

The courts continued to play an active role. In 1968 the Supreme Court held, in *Green v. New Kent County Board of Education*, that freedom of choice is an acceptable desegregation device only if it is effective in accomplishing desegregation. By this point the courts were, in effect, insisting on a mixture of races as a measure of compliance with earlier rulings. In 1969, in *Alexander v. Holmes County Board of Education*, the Court further determined that the time for "all deliberate speed has passed" and positive desegregation must take place immediately.

Under explicit holding of this Court the obligation of every school system is to terminate dual school systems at once and to operate now and hereafter only unitary school systems.

A combination of court rulings, program leverage, and executive initiative led to rapid changes thereafter. In the spring of 1970 the dual school system of the South was still essentially intact. In the fall of 1970 it was almost entirely disestablished. A statement issued October 22, 1970, by the Secretary of Health, Education, and Welfare recounts this transformation.

Of the approximately 2,700 school districts in the 11 Southern States more than 97 percent—or all but 76 districts—have desegregated pursuant to voluntary plans and court orders.

Of the 3.1 million black children in these States, 27.4 percent—or 825,024 —live in districts that desegregated prior to this year; an additional 63.0

percent (or more than 1.89 million) live in the more than 600 districts desegregating by voluntary plan and court order this fall. 9.6 percent—or 288,485—live in the 76 districts still not listed in compliance.

Of the 7.4 million white students in these States, 48.3 percent—or 3,570,163—live in districts that desegregated prior to this fall; 42.2 percent—or 3,134,358—live in the more than 600 districts desegregating this fall. 9.5 percent—or 705,576—live in the 76 districts not yet in compliance.

Of the 76 districts not yet in compliance, 59 are currently in litigation, and the remaining 17 are either involved in negotiations or subject to administrative proceedings by HEW or litigation.

In the fall of 1967, 4.3 percent of the South's black children were in *school systems* that had desegregated under [then] current law. In the fall of 1968, this percentage rose to 6.1 percent; in 1969, it reached 27.2 percent; and in 1970, the percentage reached 90.5 as noted above.

With regard to the number of minority children presently attending desegregated *schools*, the figures are presently being ascertained. During the last three years, HEW has arbitrarily defined "desegregated schools" as those schools which are 50 percent or more white. Under this standard, in the fall of 1967, 13.9 percent of the black children in the South attended such schools. In 1968, this percentage rose to 18.4; and in the fall of 1969 it rose to an estimated 28.9 percent. The National Schools Survey, the government's method for determining school enrollment by race and ethnic group, was conducted throughout the Nation this fall, and virtually every school district in the country was required to complete survey forms by October 15. These survey forms are now arriving at HEW, and the results will be compiled by this winter.

The percentage of black children attending majority white schools is not, of course, the only measure of successful desegregation. About 35 percent of the black children in the South live in school districts where minority children constitute 50 percent or more of the school enrollment. In such districts, most of which have desegregated for the first time this fall, defining "desegregation" only by the fact that black children attend majority white schools misses the point.

Indeed, the desegregation of schools in such districts eliminates majority white schools.

Now the new phase was to begin. Stated simply, the end of the dual school system did not necessarily mean the end of all-white or all-black schools. Patterns of residential separation of blacks and whites led to schools of corresponding composition. The issue was the persistence or elimination of racial identity of schools, quite apart from the existence of a dual school system.

The final results of the 1970 National Schools Survey carried out by the Department of HEW suggested both the extent and the limits of the effects to be had from the desegregation efforts of the 1950's and 1960's. The Department was justified in claiming that "unprecedented progress has been made in school desegregation since 1968." During that short time the number of black children in all-black schools in the South dropped from 68 percent to 14 percent! The proportion of black students attending majority white schools in the South rose from 18.4 percent in 1968 to 39.0 percent in 1970. In the thirty-two Northern and Western states (excluding, that is, the South and the six Border States and the District of Columbia), there was virtually no change during this period. In 1968, 27.6 percent of Negro pupils were in majority white schools; in 1970, the proportion was 27.7 percent. Thus, at the outset of the new decade, the schools of the Old South were, at least statistically, more racially integrated than those of the North and West.

In the fall of 1970 the Supreme Court heard arguments in which the school boards of Charlotte, North Carolina, and Mobile, Alabama, contended that they were obligated under the Constitution merely to draw non-racially motivated attendance areas, just as school districts outside the South are generally permitted to do. Attorneys for the plaintiffs, as well as the United States as *amicus curiae*, asserted that a school district which, over the years, has taken steps to segregate children, has a legal obligation to take affirmative steps to undo the results of that segregation. In a word, busing.

In one form or another, this new set of issues is bound to trouble the 1970's. Will the courts require that the schools of the South integrate in the future because they have segregated in the past, while allowing Northern and Western schools to segregate on grounds that they had been integrated in the past—or at least that they had never tried to prevent integration? The point here is that residential patterns resulting from a cumulation of individual acts are nonetheless held to reflect a certain kind of social will, which may or may not be in accordance with fundamental law. Certainly the experience of urban areas outside the South has not been one of rapid or easy racial mixture. The contrary appears to be the case. But is this unconstitutional? At the outset of the 1970's no one knew. Was it desirable? Here again views, on the part both of blacks and whites, differed. In a city such as New York, for example, the demand was increasingly heard from black parents that the teachers and administrators dealing with their children also be black. This was a demand, in effect, for the creation of situations which in the South civil-rights attorneys were asserting to be unconstitutional. In the elections of 1970 in California, a black school administrator was elected Superintendent of Public Instruction, but a white judge who had ordered large-scale busing in Los Angeles County was defeated. Nothing any longer was simple.

Large efforts at social change are rarely carried out with ease and precision. As the 1970 school year proceeded, charges of fraud and bureaucratic bungling were heard from civil-rights groups. (See Jack Rosenthal, "Rights Groups Call School Plan a Fraud." *The New York Times*, November 28, 1970.) It is important to note that a considerable shift had occurred. Where previously these groups had charged that little or no school desegregation was taking place, they now tended to argue that the new unitary school systems continued to discriminate against blacks in various ways, that blacks still did not receive "quality" education, and that special federal funds were not being used for educational purposes. Clearly, a major social change had in fact occurred by the fall of 1970. That other problems remained, or that new ones had been created, is normal enough. We have a long way to go, but we are advancing.

It is simply extraordinary that so much has been done, and—again—scarcely to be remarked that it has not been done flawlessly. The difficulties of the EEOR can be better appreciated in this time-expenditure perspective. Education research scarcely existed as a Federal activity prior to the 1960's. Then in the span of a year—1964 to 1965—the Office of Education funds for this purpose doubled from $19 million to $37 million. The next year they tripled, to $100 million. Indeed, over 80 percent of Federal monies appropriated by 1969 for educational research and development were forthcoming in the years 1965–69. It is hardly to be wondered that the EEOS raised more questions than it answered. The Federal government had only that moment begun seriously attending to such questions. But—again—*it had begun.* Further, for all the disappointments and miscalculations of the period, public support for educational expenditure remained high. During the 1960's, for example, public willingness to see more funds expended in such areas as defense and space exploration dropped off considerably, even sharply. But at the end of the decade, as at the outset, opinion surveys recorded nearly two thirds of the public willing to spend *more* money on education.

No small achievement! In truth, a splendid one. More the reason, as even more difficult goals are set for the future, to pause and take note of what has been accomplished. It truly is not sinful to take modest satisfaction in our progress.

NEEDS AND HOPES

What is needed is innovation, experiment, effort, measurement, analysis. What may be hoped for is a process by which the great gaps separating the educational achievement of different ethnic/racial groups begin to narrow. It may be hoped that before the century is out the great gaps will have disappeared. It may also happen that in the process a general theory of education will have evolved, been tested, replicated, and accepted. Just possibly. The creation of this new myth would be a great intellectual achievement, its critique the challenge of the twenty-first century. For the moment, we should strive for equalization. That would be a great social achievement, one the society needs, and one it will probably support with funds, patience, and good sense.

References and Notes

1. Letter to Sturge Moore, reported by Richard Ellmann in *The Identity of Yeats*, New York: Oxford University Press, 1964, p. 234.

2. Kenneth Boulding. *The Impact of the Social Sciences*. New Brunswick, N.J.: Rutgers University Press, 1966, p. 4.

3. James S. Coleman, Ernest Q. Campbell, Carol J. Hobson, James McPartland, Alexander M. Mood, Frederic D. Weinfeld, Robert L. York. *Equality of Educational Opportunity*. 2 volumes. Washington, D.C.: Office of Education, U.S. Department of Health, Education, and Welfare, U.S. Government Printing Office, 1966. OE–38001; Superintendent of Documents Catalog No. FS 5.238:-38001.

4. Project Talent was apparently the largest. It also concerned education. But as a product of the 1950's, its main concern was with high achieving students. Relatively little attention was paid to race.

5. Robert A. Dentler. "Equality of educational opportunity." *The Urban Review*, December, 1966, p. 27.

6. Gunnar Myrdal, with the assistance of Richard Sterner and Arnold Rose. *An American Dilemma, The Negro Problem and Modern Democracy*, Volumes I and II. New York: Harper & Brothers, 1944.

7. William Faulkner. "On Fear: Deep South in Labor: Mississippi" in *Essays, Speeches & Public Letters by William Faulkner*, edited by James B. Meriwether. New York: Random House, 1965, p. 105.

8. Within months of the enactment of the Civil Rights Act of 1964 forbidding the identification of employees, students, *et al.*, in terms of race or ethnicity, the Federal government was requiring recipients of grants or other forms of assistance to specify the proportion of minority employees, students, or whatever, labeled by race or ethnicity, as a condition of government assistance. *Results* were the measure of compliance. This was foreseen. For example, Moynihan, in a government report *The Negro Family, The Case for National Action* (U.S. Department of Labor, 1965), written in the winter of 1964–65, about the time the EEOs began, asserted it to be inevitable.

9. *Equality of Educational Opportunity* [Summary Report]. Washington, D.C.: Office of Education, U.S. Department of Health, Education, and Welfare, U.S. Government Printing Office, 1966. OE–38000; Superintendent of Documents Catalog No. FS 5.238:38000. [Essentially Chapter 1 of reference 3.]

10. Ernest Q. Campbell. "Negroes, Education, and the Southern States." *Social Forces*, Vol. 47, No. 3, March, 1969, pp. 255–56.

11. Peter H. Rossi. "Social Factors in Academic Achievement: A Brief Review," in A. H. Halsey, Jean Floud, and C. Arnold Anderson, editors, *Education, Economy, and Society*. New York: The Free Press of Glencoe, Inc., 1961, pp. 269–72.

12. Bruce K. Eckland. "Genetics and Sociology: A reconsideration." *American Sociological Review*, Vol. 32, No. 2, April, 1967, pp. 173–94.

13. Sir Cyril Burt. "Intelligence and heredity: Some common misconceptions." *The Irish Journal of Education*, Vol. 3, No. 2, 1969, p. 80.

14. James S. Coleman. "Equal schools or equal students?" *The Public Interest*, No. 4, Summer 1966, pp. 73–74. Copyright © 1966 by National Affairs, Inc.

15. Joseph Hone. *W. B. Yeats 1865–1939*. New York: Macmillan Company, 1943, p. 450.

16. Joseph Froomkin. "Major Policy Issues and Implementation Problems in the Office of Education." October, 1969, mimeographed.

17. Marilyn Gittell and Maurice R. Berube. *Educational Achievement and Community Control*. Institute for Community Studies, Queens College, New York, undated.

18. An article by Nancy Hicks in *The New York Times*, Sunday, February 15, 1970, p. 1.

19. John C. Flanagan, John T. Dailey, Marion F. Shaycoft, William A. Gorham, David B. Orr, and Isadore Goldberg. *Design for a Study of American Youth.* Boston: Houghton Mifflin, 1962, p. 51.

20. Robert C. Nichols. "Schools and the Disadvantaged." *Science*, Vol. 154, No. 3754, December 9, 1966, p. 1314.

21. Dentler, *ibid.*

22. Lloyd N. Morrisett. "Preschool Education," editorial in *Science*, Vol. 153, No. 3741, September 9, 1966.

23. It should be noted that by the end of the 1960's the central tenets of *Brown v. Board of Education* were coming under intense revisionist scrutiny. Alexander M. Bickel in the 1969 Holmes Lectures at the Harvard Law School took strong issue with the implied position of the Warren Court that the public schools are charged with an "equalizing, socializing, nationalizing—assimilationist and secular—mission," which dictates integration. The nation, he suggested, was heading for a future quite different from that envisioned by the justices. For one thing "the assimilationist objective is far from universally shared—in the middle class, or in the principal group, the Negroes, that remains to be assimilated." For another, "it appears that segregation by socio-economic class much more than by race may affect the quality of education for the individual child." It would be reasonable to see in the latter statement a diffusion of the EEOR findings (see EEOR, p. 330). The point is elaborated by Cohen, Riley, and Pettigrew in the present volume. Alexander M. Bickel. *The Supreme Court and the Idea of Progress.* New York: Harper & Row, 1970, pp. 121, 137–38.

24. Charles E. Silberman. "A Devastating Report on U.S. Education." *Fortune*, August, 1967, p. 181.

25. A further point of interest: About 6 percent of Negro children come from white-collar families, as compared with 34 percent for white children. Approximately 40 percent of Negro middle-class high-school-age children attend private schools as compared with 13 percent for whites. This almost certainly has a variety of consequences. The public schools are deprived of an important cadre of Negroes. Also, possibly, there are fewer middle-class Negro parents directly involved with the public schools than might otherwise be the case. See Charles B. Nam, A. Lewis Rhodes, and Robert E. Herriott: "Inequalities in Educational Opportunities, A Demographic Analysis of Educational Differences in the Population," Florida State University, May, 1966, Table 15.

26. Samuel Bowles and Henry M. Levin. "The Determinants of Scholastic Achievement—An Appraisal of Some Recent Evidence." *The Journal of Human Resources*, Vol. III, No. 1, Winter 1968, pp. 3–24.

27. *The Behavioral Sciences and the Federal Government*. Advisory Committee on Government Programs in the Behavioral Sciences, National Research Council. Publication 1680, National Academy of Sciences. Washington, D.C., 1968, pp. 15–16, pp. 91–107.

28. *Knowledge into Action: Improving the Nation's Use of the Social Sciences*. Report of the Special Commission on the Social Sciences of the National Science Board. National Science Foundation. Washington, D.C.: U.S. Government Printing Office, 1969, pp. xvii–xx, pp. 87–95.

29. *The Behavioral and Social Sciences; Outlook and Needs*, National Academy of Sciences, Social Science Research Council. Washington, D.C.: National Academy of Sciences, 1969. Commercially available from Prentice-Hall, Inc., Englewood Cliffs, N.J., pp. 193–210.

30. Quoted in James F. Welsh, "The Coleman Report." In D.C. Perspectives in *Edu-*

cational Researcher, Official Newsletter of the American Educational Research Association. July, 1967, pp. 8–9.

31. Otis Dudley Duncan. "Inheritance of Poverty or Inheritance of Race?" Chapter 4 in Daniel P. Moynihan, editor, *On Understanding Poverty: Perspectives from the Social Sciences*. New York: Basic Books, Inc., 1969, pp. 85–110.

32. Dennis J. Dugan. *The Impact of Parental and Educational Investments upon Student Achievement*. U.S. Office of Education, June, 1969, Table 1, mimeographed. In *Inequality: Studies in Elementary and Secondary Education*, edited by Joseph Froomkin and Dennis J. Dugan.

33. Donald P. Hayes and Judith Grether. "The School Year and Vacations: When Do Students Learn?" Presented to the Eastern Sociological Association Convention, April 19, 1969. Mimeographed.

34. Jerome Kagan. "Social Class and Academic Progress: An Analysis and Suggested Solution Strategies," 1969, mimeographed, p. 4.

35. Sheldon H. White. "The National Impact Study of Head Start." In J. Helmuth (ed.), *Disadvantaged Child. Compensatory Education: A National Debate* (Vol. 3). New York: Brunner/Mazel Inc., 1970.

36. Harry Piccariello. "Evaluation of Title I." In Joseph Froomkin and Dennis J. Dugan, editors, *Inequality: Studies in Elementary and Secondary Education*. U.S. Office of Education, Department of Health, Education, and Welfare, June, 1969. Office of Program Planning and Evaluation, Planning Paper 69–2.

37. Donald T. Campbell. "Reforms as experiments." *American Psychologist*, Vol. 24, No. 4, April, 1969, pp. 409–29.

38. Boulding, *ibid.*, pp. 106–07.

39. Donald T. Campbell, *ibid.*, p. 425.

40. Philip W. Jackson. *Life in Classrooms*. New York: Holt, Rinehart, and Winston, Inc., 1968.

41. Urie Bronfenbrenner. *Two Worlds of Childhood, U.S. and U.S.S.R.* New York: Russell Sage Foundation, 1970.

42. Paul Taubman and Terence J. Wales. "Mental Ability and Higher Educational Attainment Since 1910." National Bureau of Economic Research, Discussion Paper No. 139, October, 1969.

43. Abbott L. Ferriss. *Indicators of Trends in American Education*. New York: Russell Sage Foundation, 1969, pp. 52, 105, 115.

FURTHER STUDIES OF THE COLEMAN REPORT

2

The Coleman Report
and the
Conventional Wisdom*

CHRISTOPHER S. JENCKS

1 ♦ Introduction

Equality of Educational Opportunity (EEOR) made four major points about American education in 1965.

(1) Most black and white Americans attended different schools.

(2) Despite popular impressions to the contrary, the physical facilities, the formal curriculums, and most of the measurable characteristics of teachers in black and white schools were quite similar.

(3) Despite popular impressions to the contrary, measured differences in schools' physical facilities, formal curriculums, and teacher characteristics had very little effect on either black or white students' performance on standardized tests.

(4) The one school characteristic that showed a consistent relationship to test performance was the one school characteristic to which most poor black children had been denied access: classmates from affluent homes.

These findings suggested that America had almost reached the goal of "separate but equal" services established by the Supreme Court (*Plessy v. Ferguson*) in 1896. They also suggested that the Supreme Court had been

* The research reported in this chapter was supported by the Carnegie Corporation of New York and the U.S. Office of Economic Opportunity (Contract # CG 8708 8/0). I was also supported by a Guggenheim Fellowship for part of the period during which the research was conducted.

I am especially indebted to Marshall S. Smith of the Harvard Center for Educational Policy Research for his generous contributions of time and imagination to the work reported here. I have also profited from discussions with David Cohen and Stephan Michelson of the Center for Educational Policy Research, with Samuel Bowles of the Harvard Department of Economics, and with Frederick Mosteller of the Harvard Department of Statistics. Steve Chilton, Christine Schmahl Cowan, Martha Kay, Carol Ann Moore, Paul Smith, and Randall Weiss assisted at various stages in the data processing.

right in 1954 when it reversed itself and declared that "separate but equal" education had been the wrong goal. The EEOR supported the plaintiffs' arguments in *Brown* and innumerable other cases that separate education, at least in the public sector, was inherently unequal. The Report did not, of course, suggest that integration would solve all the problems of black children. But it put the weight of social science behind what was then a national priority, endorsed by the President, the Congress, the Federal courts, and the "liberal establishment," namely integration.

At about the time of the EEOR's appearance, however, national priorities began to change. More and more people began to doubt the political feasibility of either racial or socioeconomic integration in the schools. Having convinced themselves that integration was unattainable, many of the doubters also tried to convince themselves that it was unnecessary. This wishful thinking led to a gradual shift in national priorities, away from integration and back to "separate but equal."

The purpose of the present chapter is simply to demonstrate that despite all the changes in national priorities, the original message of the EEOR was correct. Many reasonable (and some unreasonable) criticisms have been made of the sampling procedures, information-gathering techniques, and analytic methods used in producing the Report.[1] But when these criticisms are taken into account, its conclusions hold up surprisingly well.

Before I report the details of the analysis, the reader may find it useful to contrast my nine major conclusions with those of the original report.

(1) There was racial bias in the allocation of resources among Northern urban elementary schools in 1965, but it was very slight relative to the variation caused by other factors. This finding is consistent with Chapter 2 of EEOR.

(2) There was also social-class bias in the allocation of resources among Northern urban elementary schools, but again it was slight relative to the variation caused by other factors. This issue was not discussed in the EEOR.

(3) When schools with economically and racially similar students were compared, differences in school policies and resources were rarely associated with pedagogically significant or statistically reliable differences in verbal achievement. This finding is consistent with Chapter 3 of the EEOR.

(4) Reading and math scores showed slightly less relationship than verbal scores to schools' social composition. When schools of similar social composition were compared, reading and math scores showed even less relationship to school characteristics than verbal scores. This issue was not fully explored in the EEOR, but my findings are consistent with those reported there.

(5) Even when a school characteristic was associated with high or low achievement (relative to racial or socioeconomic norms), the evidence

seldom suggests that the school characteristic actually affected achievement. This issue was not fully explored in the EEOR.

(6) The achievement of lower-class students, both black and white, was fairly strongly related to the socioeconomic level of their classmates. This usually meant that a student's achievement was also related to the race of his classmates, since black classmates tended to be poor classmates and vice versa. If the socioeconomic level of a lower-class child's classmates was held constant, however, their race had no relationship to his achievement. This is consistent with Chapter 3 of the EEOR.

(7) Black children's achievement was even less related to their schools' policies and resources (other than socioeconomic mix) than white children's achievement. This finding is *not* consistent with Chapter 3 of the EEOR.

(8) The relationship between school characteristics, student background, and student achievement varied slightly from one kind of Northern urban elementary school to another. The relationship in the Northeast was not quite like that in the Midwest, the relationship in Philadelphia was not quite like that in New York, the relationship for lower-class schools was not quite like that for middle-class schools, and so on. This issue was not examined in the EEOR.

(9) The effect of any given increase in school resources did not seem to depend on the amount of resources already available to a school, at least so long as the level remained within the range found in the urban North. This issue was not investigated in the EEOR.

2 ♦ *The Data*

This chapter is exclusively concerned with the 684 Northern urban elementary schools that returned principal, teacher, and 6th-grade student data to the EEOS. The chapter looks briefly at the relationship between the achievement of particular kinds of students (e.g., black students, lower-class white students, etc.) and the overall social composition of the schools in which they were enrolled. It then examines the relationships between schools' mean achievement, their socioeconomic composition, their racial composition, and 119 measures of their "resources" and "policies." [2] I will group these 119 school characteristics under 13 headings.[3]

(1) Regional and Community Characteristics (9 measures)
(2) Expenditures (5 measures)
(3) Preschooling (5 measures)
(4) Exposure to School (4 measures)
(5) Physical Facilities (18 measures)
(6) Access to Books (7 measures)

(7) Curriculum (22 measures)
(8) Numbers and Kinds of Personnel (12 measures)
(9) Characteristics of Principals (7 measures)
(10) Teacher Selection Devices (3 measures)
(11) Teachers' Background and Training (14 measures)
(12) Teachers' Professional Standing (7 measures)
(13) Teacher Morale (6 measures)

The chapter does *not* look at the relationship of student achievement to principals' or teachers' attitudes and opinions.[4]

The reader may wonder whether my 684 sample schools are representative of the urban North as a whole, whether the urban North is similar to the rural North, whether the North is similar to the South, and whether elementary schools are similar to secondary schools. None of these questions is easy to answer.

The EEOS's original Northern urban sample included approximately 1030 elementary schools, 346 of which did not return complete data.[5] The causes and consequences of losing these 346 schools are discussed in detail in Chapter 11. That chapter concludes that the 684 schools examined here are probably sufficiently representative of the urban North as a whole to sustain the generalizations made in this chapter.[6]

I have conducted no analyses of either the rural North or the South. The original EEOR suggested that the North and South were similar but not identical. A replication of the present analyses would probably yield the same conclusion, not only for the North and South, but for urban and rural schools as well.[7]

I have begun an analysis of the EEOS high-school sample. Thus far, the results are very similar to those reported in this chapter for elementary schools. In particular, mean 9th-grade scores appear to explain almost all the variation in mean 12th-grade scores.[8] I have not analyzed the relationship between lower-class achievement and peer-group characteristics at the secondary level.

The reader may also wonder whether it is legitimate to generalize about an entity as heterogeneous as the "urban North." As indicated in the summary, there are differences between schools in the Northeast, Midwest, and Far West, between inner-city and suburban schools, between schools in Detroit, Milwaukee, New York, Philadelphia, and San Francisco, between predominantly lower-class schools and predominantly middle-class schools, and so forth. Nonetheless, all these schools appear to be sufficiently similar so that more is gained by averaging them together than by reporting a multitude of separate analyses which show only minor differences.[9]

All in all, the sample used in this analysis is reasonably satisfactory. The quality of the data collected from the sample schools was less satisfactory. Chapter 11 describes some of the internal inconsistencies in the data. Four general conclusions are relevant to the present chapter:

(1) The estimates of schools' mean 6th-grade verbal, reading, and math scores were probably quite reliable.

(2) The estimates of schools' mean socioeconomic and racial composition were also quite reliable.

(3) The estimates of schools' policies and resources were not very reliable, though the measures based on several teachers' replies were probably better than the measures based on the reply of a single principal.[10]

(4) Errors in measuring school policies and resources may bias estimates of the relationship between these school characteristics and student achievement. The bias is generally such as to reduce the estimated relationship.[11]

Nonetheless, it would be surprising if *more accurate* data were to yield results appreciably different from those reported in this chapter. Data on *different* school or student characteristics might well yield different results.

TABLE 1

Means, Standard Deviations, and Derivations of School Variables
Used in Analysis of 684 Northern Urban Elementary Schools

	Grand Mean	Standard Devia- tion	Mean for Black Pupils	Mean for White Pupils	Mean for Lower- Class Pupils	Mean for Middle- Class Pupils
Regional and Community Characteristics						
26 No elementary accred- itation system in state* (Pr. Q. 5 & 6)	0.42	0.49	0.41	0.41	0.39	0.43
130 School in New Eng- land* (OE Code, 1st digit)	0.08	0.27	0.01	0.10	0.06	0.09
131 School in Mid- Atlantic* (OE Code, 1st digit)	0.30	0.45	0.35	0.27	0.32	0.29
132 School in Great Lakes* (OE Code, 1st digit)	0.23	0.42	0.19	0.25	0.24	0.23
133 School in Plains* (OE Code, 1st digit)	0.06	0.24	0.06	0.07	0.07	0.06
134 School in Far West* (OE Code, 1st digit)	0.33	0.47	0.39	0.31	0.32	0.33
135 School in residential suburb* (Pr. Q. 72)	0.36	0.48	0.11	0.43	0.18	0.40
136 School in industrial suburb* (Pr. Q. 72)	0.03	0.16	0.01	0.03	0.02	0.03
137 School in town of 5–50,000* (Pr. Q. 72)	0.15	0.36	0.08	0.16	0.14	0.16

* Variables marked with an asterisk are dichotomous. Their means indicate the proportion of schools having the attribute.

TABLE 1 (*Continued*)

	Grand Mean	Standard Deviation	Mean for Black Pupils	Mean for White Pupils	Mean for Lower-Class Pupils	Mean for Middle-Class Pupils
138 School in big-city residential area* (Pr. Q. 72)	0.23	0.42	0.30	0.22	0.24	0.23
139 School in inner city* (Pr. Q. 72)	0.17	0.38	0.49	0.10	0.36	0.14
140 School in town of less than 5000* (Pr. Q. 72)	0.05	0.23	0.01	0.06	0.06	0.05
142 Neighborhood school* (Pr. Q. 39)	0.64	0.48	0.57	0.65	0.60	0.65
143 PTA attendance (Pr. Q. 74)	30.70	18.77	24.74	32.12	24.99	31.84
144 Average daily attendance for pupils (Pr. Q. 42)	94.72	2.85	93.45	95.16	93.75	94.91
145 Pct. sixth graders who have attended only present school (6th Gr. Pup. Q. 30)	35.35	19.60	34.79	36.13	34.71	35.48
146 Pct. sixth graders who walk to school (6th Gr. Pup. Q. 49)	68.99	24.81	75.24	67.77	71.07	68.57
148 Pct. white in high school to which sixth graders will go (OE Code, 9th digit)	85.54	21.29	61.23	91.48	77.17	87.20
Student Body Characteristics						
147 School size in 100's (Pr. Q. 40)	6.50	2.86	8.27	6.01	7.20	6.37
149 Pct. white in sixth grade (6th Gr. Pup. Q. 4 + 5)	75.83	29.73	27.31	87.89	58.37	79.29
150 Mean 6th-grade socio-economic status—1st Principal Component (See Chapter 11)	3.11	7.37	−4.61	5.31	−2.44	4.21
Expenditures						
24 State accreditation not complete* (Pr. Q. 5)	0.08	0.27	0.12	0.08	0.07	0.08
25 Regional accreditation not complete* (Pr. Q. 6)	0.31	0.46	0.24	0.34	0.28	0.33
27 Staff salaries per pupil in 100's (Mean T. Q. 32/ Pr. Q. 40)	2.54	0.48	2.58	2.53	2.53	2.54

* Variables marked with an asterisk are dichotomous. Their means indicate the proportion of schools having the attribute.

		Grand Mean	Standard Deviation	Mean for Black Pupils	Mean for White Pupils	Mean for Lower-Class Pupils	Mean for Middle-Class Pupils
94	Principal Salary in 100's (Pr. Q. 71)	123.87	22.26	133.39	121.58	126.72	123.30
95	Mean teacher salary in 100's (T. Q. 32)	70.44	7.62	73.43	69.89	70.66	70.52

Preschooling

		Grand Mean	Standard Deviation	Mean for Black Pupils	Mean for White Pupils	Mean for Lower-Class Pupils	Mean for Middle-Class Pupils
15	Number of preprimary grades (Pr. Q. 1, 3, 4)	0.95	0.43	1.12	0.89	1.02	0.93
16	Free kindergarten* (Pr. Q. 3)	0.88	0.32	0.98	0.85	0.91	0.88
17	Pct. sixth graders who attended kindergarten (6th Gr. Pup. Q. 45)	80.12	16.36				
18	Pct. black sixth graders who attended kindergarten (6th Gr. Pup. Q. 45 + 4A)			77.85			
19	Pct. white sixth graders who attended kindergarten (6th Gr. Pup. Q. 45 + 4B)				82.38		
20	Free nursery school* (Pr. Q. 4)	0.03	0.18	0.08	0.02	0.07	0.03
21	Pct. sixth graders who attended nursery school (6th Gr. Pup. Q. 46)	17.41	11.23				
22	Pct. white sixth graders who attended nursery school (6th Gr. Pup. Q 46 + 4B)				18.11		
23	Pct. black sixth graders who attended nursery school (6th Gr. Pup. Q 46 + 4A)			15.57			

Exposure to School

		Grand Mean	Standard Deviation	Mean for Black Pupils	Mean for White Pupils	Mean for Lower-Class Pupils	Mean for Middle-Class Pupils
8	Automatic promotion* (Pr. Q. 89)	0.58	0.49	0.62	0.57	0.58	0.59
9	Hold back slow learners* (Pr. Q. 89)	0.38	0.49	0.36	0.40	0.39	0.38

* Variables marked with an asterisk are dichotomous. Their means indicate the proportion of schools having the attribute.

TABLE 1 (*Continued*)

		Grand Mean	Standard Deviation	Mean for Black Pupils	Mean for White Pupils	Mean for Lower-Class Pupils	Mean for Middle-Class Pupils
10	Transfer slow learners*						
	(Pr. Q. 89)	0.02	0.14	0.01	0.03	0.02	0.02
12	Percent students on split session						
	(Pr. Q. 21)	2.68	14.15	3.61	1.91	2.84	2.65
13	Days in school year						
	(Pr. Q. 8)	180.64	3.48	181.21	180.48	181.12	180.55
14	Length of school day						
	(Pr. Q. 76)	5.49	0.54	5.39	5.54	5.44	5.50

Physical Facilities

		Grand Mean	Standard Deviation	Mean for Black Pupils	Mean for White Pupils	Mean for Lower-Class Pupils	Mean for Middle-Class Pupils
28	Pupils/room (Pr. Q. 40/ (Pr. Q. 11 + 12))	28.21	4.27	29.63	27.91	28.56	28.15
29	Pct. makeshift rooms (Pr. Q. 12/ (Pr. Q. 11 + 12))	1.40	3.78	2.01	1.31	1.63	1.36
30	Teachers/room (Pr. Q. 26/Pr. Q. 11)	1.00	0.12	1.02	0.99	1.00	1.00
31	Site acres (Pr. Q. 9)	5.39	3.28	3.74	5.77	4.25	5.61
32	Building age (Pr. Q. 10)	22.88	17.35	28.27	21.15	28.04	21.87
33	Auditorium* (Pr. Q. 13c)	0.26	0.44	0.49	0.21	0.35	0.25
34	Cafeteria* (Pr. Q. 13d)	0.25	0.43	0.34	0.23	0.29	0.24
35	Gym (Pr. Q. 13e)	0.23	0.43	0.25	0.21	0.26	0.23
36	Athletic field* (Pr. Q. 13p)	0.67	0.47	0.58	0.69	0.58	0.69
37	Biology lab* (Pr. Q. 13k)	0.05	0.23	0.02	0.06	0.05	0.06
38	Chemistry lab* (Pr. Q. 13l)	0.04	0.19	0.02	0.05	0.03	0.04
39	Physics lab* (Pr. Q. 13m)	0.02	0.13	0.01	0.02	0.01	0.02
40	Language facilities* (Pr. Q. 13n)	0.11	0.32	0.12	0.09	0.13	0.11
41	Typing lab* (Pr. Q. 30)	0.001	0.04	0.001	0.001	0.001	0.001
42	Number of movie projectors (Pr. Q. 13g)	2.03	1.07	2.28	1.97	2.13	2.01
43	Infirmary* (Pr. Q. 25)	0.88	0.32	0.81	0.90	0.82	0.89
44	Kitchen* (Pr. Q. 13r)	0.59	0.49	0.58	0.60	0.56	0.60

* Variables marked with an asterisk are dichotomous. Their means indicate the proportion of schools having the attribute.

		Grand Mean	Standard Deviation	Mean for Black Pupils	Mean for White Pupils	Mean for Lower-Class Pupils	Mean for Middle-Class Pupils
45	Pct. pupils receiving free lunch (Pr. Q. 14)	4.59	10.90	7.00	3.67	6.95	4.12

Access to Books

		Grand Mean	Standard Deviation	Mean for Black Pupils	Mean for White Pupils	Mean for Lower-Class Pupils	Mean for Middle-Class Pupils
46	Age of average textbook (Pr. Q. 17)	3.49	2.09	3.35	3.46	3.48	3.49
47	Years since reading text copyrighted (Pr. Q. 18)	3.95	3.16	3.93	3.94	3.95	3.96
48	Enough texts* (Pr. Q. 20)	0.95	0.23	0.94	0.94	0.94	0.95
49	Library volumes in 100's (Pr. Q. 13b)	39.19	27.48	42.69	38.17	38.05	39.41
50	Library volumes/ 100 students (Pr. Q. 13b/ Pr. Q. 40)	6.43	4.82	5.59	6.63	5.66	6.57
51	Library* (Pr. Q. 13a)	0.84	0.36	0.76	0.86	0.79	0.86
52	Free texts* (Pr. Q. 16)	0.88	0.33	0.94	0.86	0.88	0.88
84	Librarians/1000 pupils (Pr. Q. 36/Pr. Q. 40)	0.60	0.60	0.51	0.61	0.55	0.61

Curriculum

		Grand Mean	Standard Deviation	Mean for Black Pupils	Mean for White Pupils	Mean for Lower-Class Pupils	Mean for Middle-Class Pupils
53	Teacher specialization* (Pr. Q. 77)	0.33	0.47	0.20	0.34	0.32	0.33
54	Biology courses* (Pr. Q. 13k)	0.14	0.34	0.11	0.14	0.12	0.14
55	Chemistry courses* (Pr. Q. 13l)	0.09	0.28	0.10	0.09	0.10	0.09
56	Physics courses* (Pr. Q. 13m)	0.06	0.24	0.02	0.07	0.04	0.06
57	Typing courses* (Pr. Q. 13o)	0.15	0.36	0.20	0.15	0.16	0.15
58	Language courses* (Pr. Q. 13n)	0.39	0.49	0.55	0.36	0.42	0.39
59	Number prior I.Q. tests (Pr. Q. 22 × 5/ grades in school)	2.03	0.84	2.10	2.04	1.98	2.05
60	Number prior achievement tests (Pr. Q. 23 × 5/ grades in school)	3.78	1.22	3.60	3.81	3.75	3.78

* Variables marked with an asterisk are dichotomous. Their means indicate the proportion of schools having the attribute.

TABLE 1 (Continued)

	Grand Mean	Standard Deviation	Mean for Black Pupils	Mean for White Pupils	Mean for Lower-Class Pupils	Mean for Middle-Class Pupils
61 Accelerated courses* (Pr. Q. 86)	0.49	0.50	0.31	0.53	0.41	0.51
62 Hours homework (Pr. Q. 91)	0.55	0.39	0.62	0.53	0.60	0.55
63 Pct. in special English classes (Pr. Q. 93)	4.42	5.73	5.23	3.70	5.54	4.20
64 Pct. in special math classes (Pr. Q. 92)	2.35	4.37	2.31	2.06	2.91	2.27
65 Special low I.Q. classes* (Pr. Q. 94a)	0.58	0.49	0.69	0.58	0.63	0.57
66 Special classes for problem children* (Pr. Q. 94a)	0.21	0.41	0.21	0.21	0.19	0.21
67 Verbal extracurricular activities (Pr. Q. 90d, e, f, g, h, p)	1.10	1.00	1.18	1.10	1.04	1.11
68 Nonverbal extra-curricular activities (Pr. Q. 90d, e, f, g, h, p)	2.42	1.48	2.58	2.35	2.45	2.41
69 Principal says no tracking* (Pr. Q. 80)	0.52	0.50	0.51	0.54	0.49	0.53
70 Principal says all tracked* (Pr. Q. 80)	0.40	0.49	0.43	0.38	0.44	0.39
74 Pct. teachers who say no tracking in school (T. Q. 57)	21.17	18.90	17.22	22.51	20.55	21.29
Number and Kinds of Personnel						
75 Pupils/staff (Pr. Q. 40/ Pr. Q. 26)	28.35	3.97	29.04	28.21	28.42	28.31
76 Mean teacher estimate of class size (Pr. Q. 53)	29.26	2.92	29.85	29.01	29.53	29.21
77 Pupils/room (Pr. Q. 40/ Pr. Q. 11 + 12)	28.22	4.27	29.63	27.91	28.56	28.15
78 Art teachers/1000 pupils (1000 × Pr. Q. 30/ Pr. Q. 40)	0.48	0.58	0.33	0.50	0.44	0.49

* Variables marked with an asterisk are dichotomous. Their means indicate the proportion of schools having the attribute.

	Grand Mean	Standard Deviation	Mean for Black Pupils	Mean for White Pupils	Mean for Lower-Class Pupils	Mean for Middle-Class Pupils
79 Music teachers/1000 pupils (1000 × Pr. Q. 31/ Pr. Q. 40)	0.72	0.62	0.57	0.75	0.68	0.72
80 Speech therapists/ 1000 pupils (Pr. Q. 32/Pr. Q. 40)	0.47	0.34	0.44	0.49	0.47	0.47
81 Psychologists/1000 pupils (Pr. Q. 33/Pr. Q. 40)	0.64	0.49	0.54	0.67	0.56	0.66
82 Remedial reading teachers (Pr. Q. 34/Pr. Q. 40)	0.68	0.92	0.98	0.60	0.75	0.67
83 Guidance counselors/ 1000 pupils (Pr. Q. 35/Pr. Q. 40)	0.32	0.65	0.61	0.26	0.42	0.30
85 Nurses/1000 pupils (Pr. Q. 37/Pr. Q. 40)	0.89	0.58	0.74	0.73	0.84	0.90
86 Attendance officers/ 1000 pupils (Pr. Q. 38/Pr. Q. 40)	0.91	0.92	0.82	0.94	0.93	0.91
Characteristics of Principals						
88 Principal experience (Pr. Q. 56)	11.42	7.83	12.20	11.44	11.40	11.42
89 Principal age (Pr. Q. 58)	46.23	9.21	48.45	45.97	47.16	46.04
90 Male principal* (Pr. Q. 59)	0.76	0.43	0.75	0.75	0.75	0.76
91 Principal years of school (Pr. Q. 60)	17.11	0.59	17.19	17.10	17.11	17.11
92 Black principal* (Pr. Q. 67 & 68)	0.02	0.14	0.11	0.00	0.06	0.01
93 Full-time principal* (Pr. Q. 70)	0.77	0.42	0.76	0.77	0.77	0.77
Teacher Selection Devices						
105 No teacher tenure* (Pr. Q. 28)	0.08	0.27	0.02	0.10	0.07	0.08
106 Automatic tenure* (Pr. Q. 28)	0.74	0.43	0.82	0.73	0.79	0.75
107 Tenure if recommended* (Pr. Q. 28)	0.16	0.37	0.15	0.17	0.14	0.17
119 National teacher exam for teachers* (Pr. Q. 29)	0.14	0.34	0.30	0.10	0.24	0.12

* Variables marked with an asterisk are dichotomons. Their means indicate the proportion of schools having the attribute.

TABLE 1 (Continued)

		Grand Mean	Standard Deviation	Mean for Black Pupils	Mean for White Pupils	Mean for Lower-Class Pupils	Mean for Middle-Class Pupils
Teacher Background and Training							
96	Pct. teachers who attended liberal arts college or university (T. Q. 13)	55.29	20.06	57.88	54.66	55.77	55.19
97	Mean college quality of teachers (T. Q. 23)	27.17	6.98	26.90	27.31	26.65	27.28
98	Pct. teachers from high quality college (T. Q. 19)	71.04	13.49	74.80	70.32	72.30	70.78
99	Teacher pct. white in college (T. Q. 16)	84.78	11.92	71.45	88.81	81.74	86.58
100	Pct. teachers who had an academic major (T. Q. 12)	26.53	13.83	29.64	25.28	28.11	26.22
101	Pct. teachers who were in college honor society (T. Q. 36)	13.83	10.11	13.39	14.13	12.59	14.07
102	Pct. teachers with degrees above B.A. (T. Q. 11)	19.17	14.01	21.37	18.97	19.31	19.14
104	Mean years of school of teachers' parents (T. Q. 9 & 10)	10.50	1.24	10.40	10.53	10.29	10.54
114	Professional experience of teachers (curvilinear) (T. Q. 25)	2.26	0.58	2.28	2.26	2.18	2.27
115	Staff verbal (T. Q. 73–102)	24.82	1.28	23.91	25.04	24.43	24.90
116	Pct. male teachers (T. Q. 1)	16.46	9.86	15.65	16.05	16.54	16.45
117	Pct. black male teachers (T. Q. 1 + 5 + 6)	1.39	3.85	4.59	0.52	2.65	1.14
118	Pct. black teachers (T. Q. 5 & 6)	7.60	16.81	30.83	2.54	14.99	6.14
124	Teacher hours beyond degree (T. Q. 24)	13.11	5.92	15.26	12.43	13.59	13.01
125	Pct. teachers who have attended summer institutes (T. Q. 30)	4.07	5.43	5.55	3.80	4.53	3.98

	Grand Mean	Standard Devia-tion	Mean for Black Pupils	Mean for White Pupils	Mean for Lower-Class Pupils	Mean for Middle-Class Pupils
Teacher Professional Standing						
108 Pct. tenured teachers (T. Q. 35)	52.99	20.74	55.97	52.51	53.69	52.85
109 Pct. temporary or noncertified teachers (T. Q. 28)	13.92	14.38	15.16	13.80	14.89	13.73
110 Pct. substitute teachers (T. Q. 35)	2.58	6.07	4.75	1.94	4.19	2.26
113 Professional experience of teachers (T. Q. 25)	10.94	4.31	11.33	10.97	11.32	10.86
120 Teacher association membership (T. Q. 48)	1.23	0.24	1.14	1.24	1.18	1.23
121 Teacher journals read (T. Q. 49)	1.27	0.45	1.28	1.28	1.22	1.28
127 Teachers' plans stay in teaching (T. Q. 50)	2.29	0.43	2.40	2.27	2.34	2.28
Teacher Morale						
111 Teachers' years experience in present school (T. Q. 26)	5.42	3.03	5.52	5.46	5.80	5.34
112 Pct. teacher turnover (Pr. Q. 27)	10.21	11.39	10.20	9.85	10.86	10.09
122 Mean hours of teacher preparation (T. Q. 51)	2.42	0.53	2.35	2.44	2.32	2.44
123 Mean days missed last year by teachers (T. Q. 27)	4.26	1.63	4.92	4.11	4.49	4.22
126 Pct. teachers who asked this school (T. Q. 29)	36.24	22.14	32.03	36.82	35.97	36.29
128 Pct. possible gripes among teachers (T. Q. 47a, c, j, l, n, o, r & t)	18.76	12.39	31.52	15.08	25.86	17.36

3 ♦ *The Analysis*

I will often compare the policies or resources of schools teaching black children to those of schools teaching white children. I will also compare schools teaching poor children to schools teaching middle-class children. Table 1 shows the weighted mean and standard deviation for each characteristic of the Northern urban elementary schools in this sample. It also shows weighted means for schools attended by different kinds of pupils.[12] The reader can appraise the importance of group differences by comparing such differences with the standard deviation for the whole Northern urban sample. Thus 2.68 percent of all students in this sample were on split sessions (Variable 12), compared to 3.61 percent of all pupils in the schools attended by the typical black. The difference was about $\frac{1}{15}$ of a standard deviation, which is trivial. Note, however, that the comparisons in Table 1 are between schools, not individuals. If there was systematic discrimination *within* schools in making a policy or allocating a resource, Table 1 could be misleading. If, for example, most schools put black children on split sessions before putting white children in the same school on split sessions, the percentage difference would be greater than that shown in Table 1.[13]

Having reported differences in a school policy or resource for students of different background, I will turn to differences in achievement between schools which have similar students but different policies or resources. This will lead to such statements as: "In Northern urban elementary schools with the same socioeconomic and racial composition, an extra year of teacher experience was associated with an extra two days of sixth grade verbal achievement." [14] Sometimes this statement will be shortened to read, "An extra year of teacher experience was associated with two days of student overachievement." "Overachievement" will be defined as the difference between a school's mean test score and the score that would be anticipated on the basis of the students' backgrounds.[15]

A difference in achievement between schools with a certain characteristic and schools without this characteristic does not usually mean that the characteristic *causes* the difference. Such differences generally arise for one of two other reasons.

(1) In many cases achievement differences cause variations in school characteristics, not the other way around. Schools with remedial-reading teachers, for example, had lower verbal scores than schools without remedial-reading teachers, and this held true even after students' family backgrounds had been controlled. Some might use this as evidence that remedial-reading teachers reduce children's verbal scores. A more plausible explanation is that schools with underachievers got proportionately more remedial-reading teachers, while schools with overachievers got proportionately less.

Similarly, there was a small but statistically significant difference in mean achievement between schools with experienced and inexperienced teachers. Some have argued that this testifies to the superior competence of experienced teachers. But in fact the causal relationship seems to work the other way around, at least in Northern urban elementary schools. This can be seen by breaking experience into two categories: experience the teachers had accumulated before they came to their 1965 school, and experience accumulated after coming to it. Schools that had *hired* experienced teachers had overachieving students. Schools that had *retained* their present teachers for a long time did not have overachieving students. This suggests that experience per se was not associated with effective teaching. Instead, teachers with experience appear to have had more bargaining power than teachers who lacked experience, and experienced teachers appear to have used their bargaining power to transfer to schools with overachieving students.

These two examples are by no means atypical. It is almost never clear whether a school characteristic affects student achievement or vice versa. If schools with accelerated curriculums and language laboratories enroll overachievers, are we to assume that the curriculum and the laboratory boosted their achievement? Or are we to assume that the school developed the curriculum and got the laboratory because it already enrolled overachievers (perhaps because it had an unusually effective principal who got the most out of both his teachers and the board of education)? Similar ambiguities recur everywhere.

(2) Even if we rule out the possibility that achievement affects the school characteristic under study, achievement differences are often caused by unmeasured school or pupil characteristics that happen to be correlated with the school characteristic under study. Schools with small classes, for example, enrolled students with unusually high verbal scores for their socioeconomic and racial background. Some might conclude that small classes had a direct effect on student achievement. On closer scrutiny, however, it looks as though districts which spent money on small classes had some other (unmeasured) attribute (education-conscious parents?) that caused the children to overachieve. When I compared districts with similar students but different class sizes, the districts with small classes outscored those with large classes. But when I compared otherwise similar schools in the same district, those with small classes did *not* outscore those with large ones. This pattern was extremely common. Only a handful of school characteristics were associated with high achievement *both* at the district level *and* at the school level within districts.[16]

The foregoing examples could be expanded *ad nauseam*, but the message should already be clear. Despite a lot of claims to the contrary, social scientists simply do not know enough to interpret differences in schools' mean achievement with any confidence. Differences are almost always consistent with a variety of alternative theories. Still, the differences are almost never consistent with *all* the alternative theories. On the contrary, many of the explanations for variation in student achievement offered by laymen, educators, and social scientists can be rejected with considerable confidence on the basis of EEOS data.

Let us take the case of teacher training. If the EEOS had shown higher mean achievement in schools staffed by teacher-training-college alumni than in schools staffed by liberal-arts-college alumni, this would hardly have sufficed to prove that liberal-arts alumni were less effective in the classroom than teachers-college alumni. But in point of fact the EEOS shows *no* difference between the two types of schools. Assuming the survey measured what it seemed to measure, this finding suggests that so far as teaching the three R's is concerned, teachers-college alumni and liberal-arts alumni average about the same.

At first glance, this argument may seem illogical. If correlation cannot prove causation, then the absence of correlation cannot prove the absence of causation. Suppose, for example, that teachers-college alumni made better elementary school teachers than liberal-arts alumni. But suppose that school administrators *believed* that liberal-arts alumni are better. If this were the case, teachers with liberal-arts degrees would have a better chance of getting jobs in schools with unusually high student motivation and potential achievement.[17] If teachers-college alumni got pupils with less academic potential but taught them more effectively, there might be no difference in 6th-grade performance.

The foregoing example of a concealed causal relationship differs from my earlier examples of spurious apparent relationships in only one important respect: it is imaginary. This is no accident. Real instances of noncorrelation concealing causation are extremely rare, whereas real instances of correlation without causation abound in every field. After several years of manipulating the EEOS data, I have found only one or two school characteristics that seemed initially to have no relationship to achievement but were more strongly related to achievement once other factors had been taken into account. I have found dozens of characteristics that had an initial relationship to achievement, but whose relationship disappeared once other factors were taken into account.

The reason for this is that education follows the general rule of human affairs: "whosoever hath, to him shall be given." Schools which have highly motivated students are also likely to get more than their share of most important resources. Schools that have more than their share of one resource usually have more than their share of other resources as well.[18] This means that advantages (or disadvantages) tend to compound one another, and that when we look at any one advantage in isolation, we usually overestimate its effect. One of the EEOS's major findings was that this process was less pervasive and less influential than most people had thought. Nonetheless, it was still far more common than its opposite, in which schools with any given advantage had some offsetting disadvantage.

This suggests an interpretive strategy which I will pursue throughout this chapter. I will first report the relationship of a school characteristic to student background characteristics. I will then report the relationship of the school characteristic to achievement, with background characteristics controlled. If there is no difference in achievement between schools which have a given characteristic and those which do not (after background characteristics have been controlled), I will conclude that the characteristic does not affect achievement in Northern urban elementary schools.[19] If, on the other hand, schools with a given characteristic have different levels of mean achievement from schools that lack the characteristic, I will investigate whether these differences can be explained by other differences between these same sets of schools. Overall, I will make a number of negative inferences about the effect of school characteristics on achievement, but no firm positive inferences.

Because the EEOS collected very little data on the allocation of resources or the application of policies within schools, I will concentrate on the relationship between school characteristics and the average verbal achievement of *all* students in the school.[20] I will not report the precise difference in achievement between sample schools with different characteristics, since this is subject to an unknown amount of sampling error. Instead, I will estimate the range within which the "true" difference for all Northern urban elementary schools probably lay.[21] I will report these relationships in terms of days, weeks, or months of verbal growth.[22] The result will be a series of statements of the following kind: "Students in schools where the teachers had an extra year of experience were between half a day and four days ahead of similar students whose teachers had a year less experience." This may simply be abbreviated to read, "An extra year of teacher experience was associated with between 0.5 and 4.0 days of overachievement." In most cases even the direction of the difference will be unclear, and I will have to say things like, "this school characteristic was associated with between two days of underachievement and four days of overachievement." When the true relationship was almost as likely to be positive as negative, and the range of the likely relationship was less than a month, I will simply say there was "no relationship." [23] Whatever the form of the statement, the reader should assume that the comparison is between mean scores for students from comparable regional, neighborhood, and family backgrounds. Unless I indicate otherwise, the comparisons are for verbal scores.

In general, I will describe the relationship between any given school resource and achievement in terms of the *average* relationship for schools with varying amounts of the resource. The achievement increment associated with an extra year of teacher experience, for example, will be the average difference between schools with mean experience levels of 1 versus 2 years, schools with means of 2 versus 3 years, schools with means of 20 versus 21 years, and so forth. Such descriptions occasionally conceal more than they reveal. Suppose, for example, that teachers improve rapidly in their first five years, but gradually become less effective after ten years. Averaging all sorts of schools could easily lead to the conclusion that additional teacher experience had no effect, when in fact it simply had different effects under different circumstances. When this is the case, I will report it. In general, however, the average relationship turns out to be a satisfactory measure.[24]

4 ♦ Family Background, School Social Composition, and Achievement

The EEOS data are by no means ideal for studying the relationship between a student's family background, his school's social composition, and his achievement. Nonetheless, a brief description of these relationships helps put the findings about school characteristics and student achievement in a realistic perspective.

The EEOS tests showed enormous variation in the performance of students entering 6th grade. Children entering 6th grade in the 5th percentile of their age group had about the same verbal fluency as the average child just entering 3rd grade. Their reading competence was comparable to that of the average child halfway through the 1st grade. Their mathematical ability was comparable to the average child halfway through 2nd grade. Sixth graders at the 95th percentile had verbal scores equal to those of the typical student halfway through 9th grade. Their reading and math scores were equal to those of the typical twelfth grader.[25]

Contrary to popular belief, the students who performed best on these tests were often enrolled in the same schools as the students who performed worst. Marshall Smith found that the range of variation within the typical Northern urban elementary school was about 90 percent of the range for the urban North as a whole.[26] The range of variation for school means was less than half the range for individuals. In some ways this is the most important and most neglected single finding of the EEOS. It means that if our objective is to equalize the outcomes of schooling, efforts to reduce differences *between* schools cannot possibly take us very far. If by some magic we were able to make the mean achievement of every Northern urban elementary school the same, we would only have reduced the variance in test scores by 16–22 percent. If, on the other hand, we left the disparities between schools untouched but were somehow able to eliminate all disparities within schools, we would eliminate 78–84 percent of the variation in 6th-grade competence.

The implications of this are in many ways more revolutionary than anything else in the EEOS. In the short run it remains true that our most pressing political problem is the achievement gap between Harlem and Scarsdale. But in the long run it seems that our primary problem is not the disparity between Harlem and Scarsdale but the disparity between the top and the bottom of the class in both Harlem and Scarsdale. Anyone who doubts this ought to spend some time talking to children in the bottom half of a "good" middle-class suburban school.

The importance of this point is underlined by the EEOS findings about variation in children's performance on different kinds of tests. Most people assume that schools teach reading and mathematics directly, while verbal ability is more susceptible to the influence of home environment, television, and neighborhood chums. The finding that reading and math scores are more variable than verbal score therefore seems to imply that the effects of schooling are more variable than the effects of the home, the TV, the neighborhood, and so forth.[27] This may be true. But when we look more closely at the variation in each test, we find that the greater variability of reading and math scores is not explained primarily by greater differences between schools, but by greater differences between children in the same school. This makes it hard to argue that differences between one school and another play a major role in exacerbating inequality among children. Instead, it appears that differences in the way the same school treats different children must be largely responsible for exacerbating inequalities. By making learning highly competitive and therefore defining some children as "successes" while others are "failures," schools may make it more difficult for the slower children to learn anything and more attractive for the quickest to learn a lot than is the case at home or on the street corner.

There are, of course, several possible alternative reasons for the greater variability of reading and math scores. First, children's genetic potential for comprehending what they read and for doing arithmetic may vary more than their genetic potential for manipulating words. Second, the appearance of variability may be a function of the chronological metric used for comparing tests. "Eighteen months" of verbal growth may not really be less than "twenty-seven months" of reading growth for eleven-year-olds. The "differences," in other words, may be a function of the test, not the developmental process.

The foregoing estimates of overall variation in achievement provide a context for describing racial and socioeconomic differences. In the urban North, the average black sixth grader was about 18 months behind the average white. The gap was about 20 months on reading and math tests. The average "poor" child was about 14 months behind his "middle-class" classmates in the urban North on the verbal test.[28] Again, these differences were almost as great when I compared children in the same school as when I compared children in different schools.

Now let us look at students of the same race and class in schools of differing socioeconomic composition. Poor black sixth graders in overwhelmingly middle-class schools were about 20 months ahead of poor black sixth graders in overwhelmingly lower-class schools. Poor students in schools of intermediate socioeconomic composition fell neatly in between. The differences for poor white sixth graders were similar.

One explanation for these differences, at least among whites, was that the average "poor" white in a middle-class school actually came from a more affluent and better-educated home than the average "poor" white in a lower-class school. This explanation did not apply to poor blacks. When background differences among poor students were taken into account, the difference in achievement between the poorest and richest schools was only 10 months for poor whites, though it was still almost 20 months for poor blacks.

Regardless of their socioeconomic background, poor families who send their children to middle-class schools may also be more achievement-oriented and more competent than poor families who send their children to lower-class schools. The EEOS does not provide adequate data for testing this theory.

A third possible explanation is that middle-class schools have more resources, more sensible policies, better teacher attitudes, and so forth. This might explain the high achievement of poor students in these schools. The EEOS data do not provide a completely adequate test of this hypothesis, since the EEOS did not measure all the policies, resources, and attitudes that could theoretically affect poor children's achievement. Nonetheless, it did measure quite a lot of policies, resources, and attitudes, and none explained an appreciable fraction of the observed differences in achievement.[29]

Finally, let us look at schools in the same region, the same type of neighborhood, and with the same socioeconomic and racial composition. If we compare schools that are similar in these respects, 95 percent score within 6 months of their predicted mean on the verbal test, within 8 months on the math test, and within 10 months on the reading test. Sixty-eight percent are within 3 months of their predicted verbal mean, within 4 months of their predicted math mean, and 5 months of the reading mean. While this similarity could in theory reflect uniformity in the policies or resources of schools with similar students, the policies and resources measured in the EEOS show no such uniformity.[30]

5 ♦ Regional and Community Characteristics

I have already indicated that for many purposes the urban North is not a single homogeneous region but several regions. Even after socioeconomic and racial factors have been taken into account, the difference between the most and least verbal region of the North was from three to five months. The ranking was New England, the Great Lakes, the Plains, the Mid-Atlantic, and finally the Far West. This held for reading and math as well. This ranking would have been slightly different if socioeconomic differences between regions had been ignored, but New England would still have been at the top and the Far West would have remained at the bottom. Regional differences in test scores presumably reflect differing attitudes toward school achievement and differing traditions in the use of language and numbers.

There were also variations among states in the same region. The mean achievement of EEOS sample schools in a given state often averaged several months above or below the level predicted on the basis of their region, race, and class. Since the EEOS samples for specific states were not representative of those states, detailed comparisons would prove little. (The three "underachieving" states in this sample were New York, Michigan, and California, none of which is generally reputed to have particularly bad schools.) A theoretically and empirically unsatisfactory measure of state interest in "school quality," namely whether the principal said there was elementary accreditation in the state, had no relationship to mean achievement.

I also compared large and small school districts. The differences were trivial. First, I compared sample schools in the 8 largest cooperative EEOS districts (Baltimore, Detroit, Milwaukee, New York, Philadelphia, St. Louis, San Francisco, and Washington, D.C.) with schools in the 116 smaller cooperative districts. After racial and socioeconomic factors had been taken into account, the "true" difference was somewhere between a three-month advantage for the big districts and a one-month advantage for the small districts. I also compared the 30 major cooperative cities in the EEOS Northern urban sample with the 96 suburbs and satellite towns. There was even less difference than when only the biggest cities were compared to the rest. These results provide cold comfort to reformers who claim that student achievement in the great cities could be improved by Balkanizing the cities into smaller districts, such as those in the surrounding suburbs. *No* district, large or small, seems to have been very successful in boosting achievement in predominantly black or lower-class schools. This suggests that decentralization and community control have primarily political rather than pedagogic effects.

Within school districts, two neighborhood characteristics were significantly related to 6th-grade achievement. The most powerful and puzzling of these characteristics was the racial composition of the high school into which an elementary school fed its alumni. This relationship persisted even after the elementary school's own racial and socioeconomic composition had been taken into account, and it held for reading and math as well as verbal scores. Those elementary schools which fed predominantly but not entirely black high schools scored from four to six months below the level predicted on the basis of their own racial and socioeconomic mix.[31] The most plausible explanation of this, so far as I can see, is that education-conscious white parents remove their children from the public schools prior to 6th grade if the high school to which the child would go is predominantly black. Children who remain in the public elementary schools therefore have lower scores than we would expect on the basis of their socioeconomic and racial backgrounds. This explanation is speculative, however, and the whole subject deserves further study.

PTA attendance was also significantly related to achievement. Race and class explained about 15 percent of the variance in schools' PTA attendance. But even after this was taken into account, schools whose principals reported that almost all parents attended PTA meetings scored between two and four months above schools whose principals reported not having a PTA. Schools with more moderate PTA attendance were strung out between. PTA attendance seems to be a proxy for districtwide parental interest in education. Variations in PTA attendance *within* a given district were not associated with variations in achievement *within* that district. Differences *between* districts accounted for the overall relationship. The relationship of PTA attendance to student achievement did not change much when other school characteristics were controlled. Thus if the PTA was having an effect on achievement, it was an indirect effect on the attitudes of the district staff, or other unmeasured factors, not a direct effect on measurable characteristics of the district. The relationship did hold for reading or math scores.

Other measures of neighborhood character showed no consistent relationship to student achievement. Principals were asked, for example, to categorize the community in which their school was located as "inner city," "residential suburban," a "small town," and so forth. Once socioeconomic and racial background had been taken into account, schools in these various types of communities all scored within a month of one another.

Nor was student achievement related to whether students had been assigned to their school on the basis of residence, to the percentage of students who walked to school, to the percentage who had been in the same school since first grade, or to the average daily attendance rate. When every sixth grader said he walked to school, for example, verbal achievement was between 1.4 months better and 0.6 months worse than in schools to which no child walked. Contrary to a good deal of folklore, the percentage of sixth graders who reported having been in the same school since first grade had almost no relationship to a school's being located in the inner city, being predominantly black, or being poor. Rich white suburbanites evidently move a lot too. Nor did pupil turnover have any appreciable relationship to achievement. Principals' reports of average daily attendance showed almost no relationship to achievement.[32]

6 ♦ *Expenditures*

Coleman *et al.* estimated school expenditures from district-wide data, ignoring variations between schools in the same district. They found almost no relationship between district expenditures and district achievement once they had controlled socioeconomic differences.

I tried to estimate expenditures at the *school* level. First, I estimated each school's per pupil expenditures for teacher salaries. Such expenditures account for more than half of all school spending, and they probably correlate 0.7 or 0.8 with overall per pupil expenditure in any given school. Sample schools spent from $175 to $625 per pupil per year on teacher salaries, with the mean being $253. The difference in expenditures on blacks and whites was less than $5 per pupil, and the difference between lower- and middle-class children was only $1. A $100 increase in salaries per pupil was associated with between one month of verbal overachievement and three days of underachievement.

The apparent positive relationship between achievement and this measure of per pupil expenditure reflected the relationship between achievement and the teacher-pupil ratio, not the relationship between achievement and teacher salaries. An increase in the salary of the average teacher was as likely to be associated with underachievement as with overachievement. Thus while teachers of blacks averaged $350 per year more salary than teachers of whites, this evidently did black pupils little good. Districts with high ratios of teachers to pupils, on the other hand, outscored districts with low ratios fairly consistently on the verbal test, though not on the reading or math test. I will return to this later.

The principal's salary provides another general indication of the level of affluence that a board of education judges appropriate in its schools. The association between the principal's salary and student achievement is hard to interpret, however. The average black pupil's principal is paid nearly $1200 more than the average white pupil's principal. Very poorly paid and very well paid principals have students who overachieve by an average of about a month. The great majority of principals fall in the middle-income range, and they have students who underachieve by a week or two. This relationship may simply be attributable to sampling error, though more complex theories could also be invented to explain it.[33]

Accreditation should provide another crude index of expenditures. State and regional accreditation agencies often apply their standards unevenly, but at least in theory accreditation is an indication that a school has adequate overall physical and human resources. Black children had about one chance in eight of attending a school whose principal reported being in trouble with his state accreditation agency, while white children had one chance in twelve. Lower-class pupils suffered no similar disadvantage. Unfortunately, the data collected in the EEOS on elementary-school accreditation seem to have been extremely unreliable (see Chapter 11). Perhaps this accounts for the fact that once other relevant factors had been taken into account, schools which reported being in difficulty with their state accreditation agency had higher verbal achievement scores than schools which said they had received a clean bill of health. The difference was less than two days, however, and could easily be explained by chance.

Neither raising salaries nor buying the other things that impress accreditation agencies seems to boost student achievement. Increasing the ratio of adults to children looks slightly more promising, and I will return to this possibility later.

7 ♦ *Preschooling*

The sixth graders covered by the EEOS had mostly entered school in 1960. The revival of national interest in early childhood education that culminated in OEO's Project Headstart did not begin until several years later. It had had little impact even in 1965, when the EEOS was conducted. While 88 percent of the Northern urban EEOS schools reported free kindergartens, only 3 percent reported free nursery schools. Schools with black and/or poor pupils were slightly more likely to have free kindergartens and nurseries than schools with white and/or middle-class pupils. Nonetheless, 82 percent of the whites reported having attended kindergarten, compared to 78 percent of the blacks. And 18 percent of the whites versus 16 percent of the blacks reported having attended a nursery school.[34] The differences between poor and middle-class pupils were larger.

These discrepancies between reported opportunity and reported utilization reinforce the suspicion that children who are sent to nursery school probably come from more education-conscious families than children who are not sent, even when their socioeconomic status is the same. This makes it difficult to interpret the relationship between nursery-school attendance and 6th-grade achievement. An increase from zero to a third, or from a third to two thirds, in the proportion of self-proclaimed nursery-school alumni was associated with between two months of verbal overachievement and a week of underachievement.[35] The results for reading and math were equally unimpressive. This is not very strong evidence for the theory that nursery-school attendance boosts achievement. Doubts on this score are reinforced by the even weaker relationship between kindergarten attendance and achievement. An increase from zero to 33 percent in kindergarten alumni, or from 33 to 67 percent, or from 67 to 100 percent, was associated with between two weeks of overachievement and a week of underachievement. The presence of a free nursery or kindergarten in a school had even less relationship to achievement. Separate analyses for blacks and for poor whites indicated even weaker relationships for these groups than for the general population.

It seems safe to conclude that if the nursery and kindergarten programs prevalent around 1960 had an effect on achievement, it was extremely small. This does not, however, mean that highly structured preschool programs aimed specifically at the development of cognitive skills could not have larger effects. This question cannot be answered with the EEOS data, because no effort was made to identify children who had been in such programs. Indeed, hardly any programs of this type existed at the time the EEOS sixth graders would have been in nursery school.

8 ◆ Exposure to School

Of the many things that ought logically to affect student achievement, dramatic variations in the amount of time a child spends in school seem especially likely to make a difference. If a child quits school after six years, he is unlikely to learn algebra. If school is in session only two months each year, as was common in the nineteenth century, the American history course is unlikely to get past the War of 1812. If school operates only three hours each day, there may be enough time to teach reading, but nature study and music are likely to get short shrift.

The EEOS suggests, however, that Northern urban elementary schools have reached or exceeded the point of diminishing returns with respect to exposure. Almost all the sample schools operated at least 5 hours per day, 175 days per year. Virtually none operated more than 6.5 hours per day, 190 days per year. Only a few of the sample schools had children on split sessions, though this was slightly more common in schools with large black enrollments. Exposure to schooling showed no appreciable relationship to achievement. A one-day increase in the school year, for example, was associated with between five days of underachievement and one day of over-achievement.[36] The length of the school day was not associated with achievement. Neither was the percentage of children on half-day sessions. These findings do not suggest that efforts to develop "year round schooling" or "after-school" programs are likely to boost achievement on tests of the type used in the EEOS[37]

9 ◆ Facilities

Those who urge better physical facilities for schooling usually do so for nonacademic reasons. They want a gym so the students can play basket-ball; they want a new building because the old one is ugly, depressing, or a firetrap; etc. Still, there is also a variety of theories which imply some indi-rect relationship between facilities and academic achievement. School super-intendents campaigning for new buildings sometimes argue, for example, that new buildings will relieve crowding, reduce class size, and thus help boost achievement. Or they argue that new buildings improve morale and help attract good teachers, who in turn boost achievement.

I examined the relationship between achievement and a rather exten-sive list of physical facilities, including the number of pupils per room, the number of rooms per teacher, the percentage of makeshift rooms, the acre-age of the school site, the age of the building, and whether the school had an auditorium, a cafeteria, a gym, an athletic field, a biology laboratory, a chemistry laboratory, a physics laboratory, special facilities for teaching languages, a typing room, an infirmary, a kitchen, and movie projectors.

Black children attended schools with about 1.7 more pupils per room than white children. A reduction of 1.7 children per room was associated with between a five-day gain in verbal achievement and a one-day loss for the average student. Reducing the number of pupils per room from 38 to 15 (the range within which 98 percent of this sample fell) was associated with between 2.8 months' gain in verbal achievement and 0.4 month's loss. The relationships for blacks were weaker. The overall trend is consistent with the slight improvement in achievement found in schools with favorable teacher-pupil ratios, but the differences are depressingly small relative to the magnitude of the problem.

The number of rooms per teacher showed no relationship to student achievement. Neither did most of the other physical facilities. One exception was physics laboratories, which were found in only 10 of the 684 sample elementary schools. Such labs, or at least principals who claimed to have them, were associated with between a week and four months' *under*achievement. Other science laboratories had smaller but nonetheless uniformly negative relationships to achievement. I can think of no obvious reason for this. The differences in achievement associated with the presence or absence of the other facilities were all well within the range to be expected from sampling error.[38] These results held for reading and math as well as verbal scores.

I also examined the relationship between the percentage of children receiving free lunches and student achievement. The EEOS measures of socioeconomic level explained only 11 percent of the variation in free lunch distribution. Free lunches had virtually no relationship to verbal achievement once their relationship to school social class had been taken into account. They had a slight relationship to reading scores, but not to math scores.[39]

The likelihood of a black or a poor child attending a school with each facility can be compared with the likelihood for a white or middle-class child by looking at Table 1. The differences were seldom large and showed no consistent direction.

10 ◆ *Access to Books*

While many educators acknowledge that physical facilities have little relationship to student achievement, many would probably expect a relationship between achievement and students' access to books. Table 1 indicates that a child's access to books is only slightly influenced by his race and class. Both black and poor children were somewhat more likely to be in an elementary school without a library or librarian. But even when this was taken into account, the average black child had access to slightly more library books than the average white child. The age and number of textbooks available to Northern urban elementary school children were unrelated to their race or class.

Schools with a library were likely to score between two weeks behind and five days ahead of schools without a library on the verbal test. Schools with an extra 100 library volumes had pupils who scored from three days above the expected level to one day below it. A school with an extra librarian per 1000 pupils had scores between 12 days below the norm and 4 days above it.

Textbooks were no more efficacious. A school which reported "enough" textbooks achieved from three weeks below par to one week above. A school which gave out free texts fell anywhere from a month below the norm for its race and class to exactly at the norm on the verbal test. There was even less relationship between free texts and reading or math scores. A school which kept its textbooks a year longer than another school with similar pupils achieved from four days to half a day higher on the verbal test than its more up-to-date competitor. Even this tiny unexpected difference did not hold for reading or math scores. A school which had bought reading texts of recent copyright was more likely to underachieve than overachieve, but each additional year since the text had been copyrighted was accompanied by no more than two days' loss or one day's gain in mean verbal score.[40]

These differences are so uniformly trivial that one is tempted to dismiss them entirely. They do, however, suggest an interesting point. Students with greater access to books, and especially new books, do fairly consistently worse on the verbal test than similar students with less access. This pattern is unlikely to be explained by chance alone.[41] Yet it also seems unlikely that access to books depresses students' verbal scores, especially since the pattern does not hold for reading. Perhaps the explanation is that when schools have unusually nonverbal students, they are more likely to hire extra librarians, buy new textbooks, develop a more adequate library, and so forth. Access to books, in other words, may be a response to nonachievement rather than a cause of it.

This conclusion will not please the publishing industry, but perhaps publishers will find some comfort in the fact that when books are found in children's *homes* the children do far better in school than if they have no books at home. One need not labor the implications of this fact for the relative importance of home and school.

Publishers may also take comfort from another point. As I note in chapter 11, the EEOS measures of achievement, like all nationally standardized tests of verbal, reading, and mathematical competence, were designed to test general skills, not familiarity with the contents of any specific text. Thus, while we can say that the typical new reading text did not result in higher reading comprehension than its predecessors, we cannot say that access to books about flatworms had no effect on children's knowledge of flatworms. On the contrary, it would be remarkable if such a relationship did not exist.

11 ♦ *Curriculum*

Many of the curriculum measures used in the EEOS were designed for high schools rather than elementary schools, and many appear to be unreliable. Even when the reported data appear plausible and consistent, moreover, they seldom tell us much about what actually happens in different classrooms.

One "curriculum" measure that showed a fairly consistent relationship to verbal achievement was the frequency of I.Q. testing in the school. The frequency of I.Q. tests was not appreciably related to the social or racial composition of a school. Nonetheless, when I estimated the number of I.Q. tests the average sixth grader had probably taken prior to the EEOS, I found that each additional test was associated with between a week and a month of overachievement on the EEOS verbal test. This relationship did not hold for reading or math tests. Some might argue that this proves the value of practice in taking I.Q.-type tests. But this argument is hard to square with the fact that the number of *achievement* tests sixth graders had taken showed almost no relationship to their scores on any of the EEOS tests.[42]

The diversity of a school's curriculum was somewhat related to its social composition (see Table 1). Once this was taken into account, however, diversity was not related to 6th-grade achievement on verbal, reading, or math tests. The relationship of test scores to the presence of biology courses, chemistry courses, physics courses, and typing courses (all rare), as well as to teacher specialization by subject, accelerated courses for fast learners, and language courses (all common), was always weak and more often negative than positive.

Schools that assigned an extra hour of homework each night scored between five weeks above the norm for their race and class and one week below the norm on the verbal test. The relationship was even weaker for reading and math.

Ability grouping showed an interesting but inconsistent relation to achievement. This is hardly surprising in light of the equally inconsistent results of experimental studies.[43] Poor and/or black pupils were slightly more likely to be in schools where the principal said all students were grouped by ability. These schools outscored other schools with similar students by from three days to five weeks on the verbal test, but they did not overachieve on the reading or math test. Schools where the principal said students were grouped separately by ability in different subjects outscored both schools where there was no ability grouping and schools where all students were grouped the same way for all subjects by between a month and two months on the verbal test, and by one week to two months on the reading test. Such schools did not overachieve on the math test.

These results seem to vindicate educators, almost all of whom favor some kind of ability grouping, as against parents, many of whom oppose it. Yet before reaching any firm conclusions on the subject it is worth noting that principals' reports on this issue appear to be quite unreliable.[44] Furthermore, the percentage of teachers who report ability grouping in their school has no relationship to achievement. The relationship between principals' reports and achievement may therefore tell us more about the kinds of schools that report ability grouping than about the effect of different kinds of grouping on achievement.

Schools that had what I called "verbal" extracurricular activities (newspapers, student government, drama, etc.) tended to underachieve while schools with "nonverbal" extra-curricular activities (athletics, bands, etc.) tended to overachieve. In both cases, however, the differences were a matter of weeks rather than months, and the relationship did not hold for reading and math scores.

The percentage of children in both Special English and Special Math classes had an appreciable negative relationship to verbal achievement. It is conceivable that putting children in these classes depresses their verbal achievement, but it seems more likely that schools with nonverbal students set up more such classes than schools with unusually verbal students.

12 ✦ Numbers and Kinds of Personnel

If there is one thing on which almost all educators seem to agree, it is that high ratios of adults to children are better than low ratios. The most popular version of this theory is that small classes are more effective than large ones. I looked at three measures of class size: the ratio of total enrollment to the number of full-time equivalent teachers reported by the principal, the ratio of total enrollment to the number of classrooms reported by the principal, and the average class size reported by the teachers. The teachers' reports showed a more consistent relationship to achievement than the measures derived from principals' reports.[45] The average size of classes as reported by teachers ranged from 15 to 40, with 98 percent of the schools averaging between 20 and 36. In general, black children were in schools with slightly larger classes than whites, but the mean difference was only one or two pupils. The gap between poor and middle-class pupils was even less.

Eliminating one child from the average class was associated with between one and six days of verbal overachievement. Thus schools with classes of 20 scored from two weeks to three months above schools with classes of 36. The differences for reading and math scores were much smaller and were not consistently positive.

We can ask at least three different questions about this kind of relationship. First, is it attributable to unmeasured differences between children in districts with small as against large classes? This interpretation is supported by the fact that when we compare schools with the same 1st-grade nonverbal mean as well as the same socioeconomic level, the relationship of class size to achievement is cut in half.[46] It is also supported by the fact that when we compare similar schools in the same district we find almost no difference in achievement between those with large and those with small classes. The relationship between class size and achievement arises only when we compare one district to another. Indeed, it arises only when we weight the districts by enrollment, indicating that it is a function of differences among a few big cities.

Second, we can ask whether class size is affecting student achievement or vice versa. We know, for example, that districts with unusually high achievement often try to establish special classes for advanced students, and that those classes are often small. We also know that experimental research on class size has yielded consistently ambiguous results, and it is hard to believe that this would happen if smaller classes had a consistently beneficial effect on test scores.[47]

Third, we can assume that the observed differences indicate an underlying cause-effect relationship. We can then ask whether the resulting changes in achievement are big enough to justify the cost of cutting class size. There is no way to answer this question definitively. Halving class size means almost doubling per pupil expenditure. As far as verbal development is concerned, the result *might* be that eleven-year-olds would reach their present level of achievement a month or two sooner. There is no evidence that cutting class size would narrow the gap between disadvantaged and advantaged pupils. On the contrary, the shaky evidence of the EEOS suggests that a general reduction in class size might even *widen* the gap.[48] I conclude that while reductions in class size can often be justified in terms of teachers' sanity, pleasant classroom atmosphere, and other advantages, they are hard to justify in terms of test scores.

Nonteaching personnel were more numerous in schools attended by white and/or middle-class pupils than in schools attended by black and/or lower-class pupils. The differences are shown in Table 1. They are mostly small and by no means consistent. Once these relationships had been taken into account, there was no evidence that most ancillary personnel had any appreciable effect on student achievement scores. I examined the number of art teachers, music teachers, speech therapists, psychologists, remedial-reading teachers, counselors, librarians, nurses, and truant officers per 1000 pupils. The difference between well-staffed and poorly staffed schools was less than a month in eight of the nine categories, and in three cases the schools with more resources appeared to underachieve. Such results are best explained in terms of random sampling variation. In the ninth category, speech therapists per 1000 pupils, each extra therapist was associated with from two days to seven weeks of verbal overachievement. Considering that speech therapists see only a minority of a school's pupils, this could indicate large individual effects. The relationship was weaker but in the same direction for reading and math achievement.

13 ♦ Characteristics of Principals

"Great man" theories always have strong intuitive appeal, especially when all other theories have proven inadequate to the problem at hand. If we find a school in which disadvantaged children do unusually well, we almost automatically assume that the principal must be in some way extraordinary.[49] Unfortunately, a survey like the EEOS cannot really test this thesis. Principals were asked their race, age, sex, educational attainment, how long they had been principals, how much they made, and whether they were full-time administrators or also had to teach. None of these variables had a significant relationship to achievement for either blacks or whites.[50]

14 ♦ Teacher Selection Devices

Probably the most common proposal for solving school problems is to "get better teachers." The most obvious device for doing this is to raise salaries, but we have seen that changes in salaries within the range found in the urban North had little relationship to achievement. A second device for improving the quality of teachers is to administer exams which supposedly identify incompetents. The National Teacher Examination is often used for this purpose, but there are also many local variants. Exams of this type are especially common in big cities. Teachers of poor and/or black children are therefore especially likely to have been selected on the basis of exam performance. Districts which use such exams to select teachers have pupil verbal scores from two weeks to two months lower than similar districts which do not use the exam. There is a smaller difference in the opposite direction on the reading test, and no difference on the math test.

Teacher selection also takes place *after* hiring. Some districts retain almost everyone who wants to stay, making tenure automatic after a certain number of years. Other districts provide tenure only on the recommendation of the principal or other supervisors. Still other districts have no tenure system. Blacks were a little more likely to be in districts with automatic tenure while whites tend to be in districts with no tenure. Verbal achievement differences among such districts were small but statistically significant. Schools in which the principal said that tenure was conditional on some supervisor's recommendation underachieved by from one to six weeks on both the verbal and reading tests. The differences on the math test were trivial. Schools which reported either no tenure or automatic tenure were slightly above the norm.[51]

The overall implication of the foregoing findings is very discouraging. The most commonly used devices for selecting effective teachers appear at best inefficient and at worst counterproductive.

15 ◆ Teacher Background and Training

The EEOS asked teachers a variety of questions about their family background and about the colleges they had attended. I extracted fourteen schoolwide measures from these questions: the percentage of male teachers, the percentage of black teachers, the percentage of black male teachers, the mean number of years of school completed by the teachers' parents, the teachers' verbal scores, the percentage of teachers who had attended a liberal arts college or university, the mean percentage of black students in the colleges attended by the teachers, two subjective estimates of the mean quality of the colleges attended by the teachers, the percentage of teachers who had majored in an academic subject in college, the percentage who had been in a college honor society, the percentage of teachers with degrees higher than a B.A., the amount of study teachers had done beyond their highest degree, and the percentage who had attended a summer institute.

One common complaint about elementary schools, especially elementary schools serving lower-class children, is that they are dominated by overprotective women. This allegedly makes the boys feel that learning is "sissy." The solution to this problem is supposed to be hiring male teachers to serve as role models for the boys. Students in Northern urban elementary schools with unusually high percentages of male teachers seem, however, to *under*achieve on verbal and reading tests, though not on math tests. The one exception was the verbal achievement of lower-class blacks. For them, high percentages of male teachers were associated with verbal overachievement.[52] Since 94 percent of the sample schools had at least two thirds women teachers, it is hard to say much about increasing the percentage of males beyond a third. An increase from zero to 33 percent was associated with verbal and reading scores between one day and three weeks below the norm. This relationship held up when other teacher characteristics were controlled.

Schools with large numbers of black pupils were more likely to have black teachers than schools with mostly white pupils. Neither black nor white students' achievement on any test was related to the color of the teachers in their schools. Many black teachers had, however, attended black colleges in the South.[53] The percentage of teachers from such colleges was negatively related to white students' verbal achievement, although not to reading or math scores. Schools where all teachers came from black colleges scored 0.5 to 3.5 months behind schools where no teacher had attended a black college. This may simply be a regional artifact. Schools with teachers from black colleges are likely to be in border states with low verbal scores. Black students' achievement was unrelated to the percentage of teachers from black colleges.

Section 1 discussed the trivial relationship of student achievement to the percentage of teachers who had attended liberal arts colleges. Teachers were also asked to make subjective judgments about the quality of their alma mater. One of these questions yielded an index which showed a very weak positive relationship to achievement. The other showed an even weaker negative relationship. Both could easily be attributed to chance. Teachers who majored in academic subjects were somewhat more likely to be in schools where the students underachieved than in schools where students overachieved, but this somewhat startling result could also be explained by chance. The percentage of teachers who were in a college honors society showed no relationship to achievement. The same held true for the percentage of teachers holding more than a bachelor's degree. Schools where every teacher had a master's degree were from six weeks ahead to two weeks behind schools which had no teacher with more than a B.A. Teachers who had taken additional courses beyond their highest degree were generally found in schools where the students underachieved, but the difference was well within the range expected on the basis of sampling error. Teachers who had attended summer institutes were found in schools which scored almost exactly as one would expect, given their student bodies.

When we turn from the racial and academic origins of teachers to their socioeconomic background, we find that an extra year of parental education for every teacher was associated with between ten days of verbal overachievement and one day of underachievement on the part of students.

Teacher verbal scores, on the other hand, showed a weak but consistently positive relationship to achievement. A one-standard-deviation increase in teacher verbal score was associated with from zero to two weeks' increase in student verbal achievement. It is not clear whether this reflects the selective recruitment or the superior effectiveness of verbally adept teachers. Unlike most relationships, this one was stronger within districts than between. It also held for math scores, though not for reading scores.

None of the foregoing data lends much support to those who claim that better teacher recruitment and training will appreciably boost student achievement. Effective teachers are about equally likely to be born rich or poor, black or white, male or female. They appear no more likely to graduate from liberal arts colleges than from teachers colleges, to major in academic subjects rather than education, to attend what they view as "good" rather than "bad" colleges, or to hold higher degrees. Verbally fluent teachers may be slightly more effective than verbally inept teachers, but it is not clear whether they are better at teaching their pupils or only at negotiating their way into schools where pupils overachieve for other reasons.

16 ♦ Teacher Professional Standing

Over the years the teaching profession has developed a variety of formal and informal criteria for ranking its members and the schools in which they are employed. This section examines seven such criteria: the professional experience of the teachers, the percentage of teachers who had achieved tenure, the percentage who were temporarily certified, the percentage of substitute teachers in the school on the day of the EEOS, the percentage who were members of a teachers' association or union, the number of professional journals read by the average teacher, and whether the teacher planned to continue in education until retirement.

The teachers' average prior professional experience had almost no relationship to either the social or racial composition of a school. The relationship between teacher experience and student achievement has already been discussed. It was small but statistically significant. It seemed to reflect the selective recruitment of teachers to overachieving schools rather than the superior effectiveness of experienced teachers. Unlike most of the other relationships discussed in this chapter, it held up when schools in the same district were compared as well as when different districts were compared. It did not hold up for reading or math.

The relationship between the percentage of tenured teachers and student achievement was negative. The percentage of tenured teachers was correlated with the average level of teacher experience, so I expected schools with large percentages of tenured teachers to have overachieving students.[54] They did not. A 10 percent increase in tenured teachers (i.e., an increase from 0–10, 10–20, 20–30, etc.) was associated with between three days of verbal underachievement and one day of overachievement. This suggested that schools with experienced but nontenured teachers were overachieving, while those with equally experienced tenured teachers were underachieving. This turned out to be the case. When I compared schools with students from similar backgrounds and equally experienced teachers, a 10 percent increase in the percentage of tenured teachers was associated with from two days to two weeks of underachievement. This relationship also held for reading and math scores.

The percentage of temporarily certified teachers in a school had little relationship to the school's social composition and no relationship whatever to its mean achievement. The percentage of substitute teachers, on the other hand, had a relationship to both. Three quarters of the sample schools had no substitute teachers on the day of the survey. No school had more than 46 percent substitutes. There were more substitutes in both poor and black schools, but even after this had been taken into account, the percentage of substitutes had a negative relationship to achievement. A 10 percent increase in substitutes was associated with between two and five weeks of underachievement. At first glance this seemed to imply that children learn less from substitutes—a theory strongly supported by casual observation. But the relationship did not hold up when I compared schools with high and low percentages of substitutes in the same district. Nor did the relationship hold up when I looked at reading and math scores. Causal inferences therefore seem risky. Districts with underachieving students may simply have trouble getting enough regular teachers.[55]

The percentage of teachers in some kind of professional association showed a small positive relationship to verbal achievement, with the best-organized schools outscoring the worst-organized by anywhere from one day to one month. There was no relationship for reading or math achievement. The degree of involvement, at least in 1965, was somewhat greater in white and/or middle-class schools than elsewhere. The average number of journals read by the teaching staff showed no relationship to achievement when other teacher characteristics were ignored. Once other teacher characteristics were taken into account, the reading of journals was associated with from zero to four weeks of verbal *under*achievement. The relationship for reading and math scores was weaker but still negative.

The commitment of teachers to their profession, as indicated by their assertions that they planned to remain teachers for the rest of their lives, showed no relationship either to students' family backgrounds or to their achievement.

17 ♦ Teacher Morale

The relationship between various measures of teacher morale and student achievement is even harder to interpret than most, since student achievement is likely to affect morale as well as vice versa. Six measures will be discussed: the length of time the average teacher had been in his or her present school, the annual turnover rate among teachers, the number of days the average teacher had missed in 1964, the number of hours the average teacher reported spending in preparing for the next day's classes, the percentage of teachers who had asked for assignment to their present school, and the percentage of teachers listing various kinds of complaints about the school.

There was no relationship between the number of years teachers had spent in their present school and either the students' family backgrounds or their achievement scores. The same generalization held for the teacher turnover rate as well. Teachers were slightly more likely to have asked for white and/or middle-class schools, but once this was taken into account there was no appreciable relationship between the proportion of teachers who had asked for their present school and the achievement of students in that school.

There was a slight difference between the preparation time of teachers with black and white students, and there was also a modest relationship between preparation time and verbal achievement for both groups. Overall, an extra hour of preparation was associated with from zero to four weeks of verbal overachievement. This was true both when I compared districts and when I compared schools in the same district. It was not true for reading or math scores. Whether teacher preparation causes high student verbal scores or vice versa remains unclear.

Teacher absenteeism was slightly higher in black and in lower-class schools. It was probably also associated with slight underachievement. The schools with the highest rates of absenteeism were from two months below to two days above those with the lowest rates of absenteeism. Since the number of days missed never averaged more than 12, it seems more likely that underachievement causes absenteeism than vice versa. The relationship of absenteeism to reading and math achievement was nil.

Finally, the percentage of possible complaints about a school reported by teachers showed a strong relationship to both the racial and the socioeconomic composition of the school. Even when this was taken into account, however, schools where the teachers had large numbers of gripes tended to enroll verbal underachievers. The direction of causality here is clearly ambiguous. The difference between the schools where teachers complained the most and those where they complained the least was between a week and three months on the verbal test.

18 ♦ *Summary*

(1) Eliminating all school-to-school differences in mean achievement would only reduce the overall inequality of 6th-grade academic outcomes by 16–22 percent in the urban North.

(2) Only a handful of the school policies and resources measured in the EEOS were appreciably related to the racial and socioeconomic backgrounds of Northern urban sixth graders.

(3) Differences in achievement among students from the same socioeconomic and racial background were not related to most of the school characteristics measured in the EEOS. This was especially true of reading and math achievement. Where achievement was associated with a school characteristic, the nature and direction of causality were almost always in doubt.

(4) Ninety percent of the variation in Northern urban elementary schools' mean verbal achievement, 85 percent of the variation in their mean math achievement, and 80 percent of the variation in their mean reading

achievement were accounted for by region, racial composition, and socioeconomic composition. An additional two or three percent could probably be accounted for by variations in initial ability.[56]

19 ♦ *Predictions*

On the basis of the foregoing findings and a variety of other evidence, I would offer six predictions.

(1) If controlled experiments were conducted in a substantial number of schools, no school characteristic measured in the EEOS except the socioeconomic level of the school would have a consistent effect of more than a month on 6th-grade reading, math, or verbal achievement.

(2) The effect of schools' socioeconomic composition on reading, math, and verbal achievement under experimental conditions would also turn out to be modest, but it might be large enough to influence decisions about the allocation of pupils to different schools.

(3) Controlled experiments would show that children in some classrooms gain significantly more on reading, math, and verbal tests in a given year than similar children in other classrooms. Over a period of time, such studies would also show that some teachers were more effective than others. But the differences among teachers per se would not explain more than a fraction of the overall difference in impact of different classrooms. The remaining variation would be a function of the unique interaction of particular students with one another and with their teacher in that year.

(4) While experimental studies would show that teachers differ in effectiveness, they would show that not only the variables measured in the EEOS but other more complex variables (such as teachers' scores on attitude and personality scales) are only slightly correlated with teaching effectiveness.

(5) If and when we begin to unravel the determinants of children's eventual life chances, we will find that attending a school which boosts achievement scores is of very limited value. Attending a school which develops the "right" habits and attitudes will prove to be of somewhat greater value, but we will find it extraordinarily difficult to define what the "right" habits and attitudes are. Schools which develop the habits and values that facilitate adult success will often not be especially effective at boosting children's test scores.

(6) If and when we develop a comprehensive picture of inequality in American life, we will find that educational inequality is of marginal importance for either good or ill. Such things as control over capital, occupational specialization, and the traditions of American politics will turn out to be far more important than the schools.

Notes

1. Many of the attacks on Coleman and his colleagues must be understood as part of the continuing warfare between economists and sociologists. Coleman was a sociologist, and he reached a conclusion which was neither surprising nor unsettling to other sociologists, namely that family background and peers have a large effect on children, whereas teachers and physical surroundings have small effects. Had he *not* found that peers were important, other sociologists would doubtless have subjected his work to severe methodological criticism. Sewell and Armer (1966), for example, examined a body of Wisconsin data rather like the EEOS and concluded that once individual background had been taken into account, "neighborhood context" had a negligible effect on high-school students' college plans. Their work was immediately subjected to vigorous methodological criticism by sociologists (Turner *et al.*, 1966). Economists have different preconceptions. They are trained to believe that resources make a difference, i.e., that costs are associated in some way with benefits. Since the EEOR did not support this conclusion, many economists were very critical (Bowles and Levin, 1968; Hanushek and Kain, Chapter 3). Had Coleman *et al.* emulated educational economists by searching out those school resources which showed a statistically significant relationship to achievement and then estimating "production functions" which purported to show the effect of the resources on achievement, the economists' complaints would almost certainly have been less vehement.

2. I will use the term "resource" to describe the things money can buy: a new building, a free lunch, small classes, experienced teachers, principals with Ed.D.'s and so forth. I will use the term "policy" to describe the way resources are utilized. Whether the school teaches Spanish or French, whether teacher tenure depends on a principal's recommendation, and whether students are grouped by ability are matters of "policy" in this sense. The socioeconomic and racial composition of a school is clearly a result of "policy" in this sense, and it clearly provides a "resource" to any given student. Nonetheless, I will *not* use these terms to cover the mix of students. At times, I will lump "policies" and "resources" together, and speak of "school characteristics." Most specific "school characteristics" result from a combination of "policies" and "resources." A school may have a high percentage of male teachers, for example, either because it pays usually high salaries which allow men to remain in the classroom rather than becoming administrators, because it discriminates against female applicants, or both. It may also have a lot of male teachers for reasons that reflect *neither* its resources *nor* its policies, e.g., a surplus of male B.A.'s in the local job market.

3. Because some of the measures (e.g., region) are not ordinal, they have been broken into several dummy variables for analytic purposes. The number of school "variables" used in the analysis is therefore considerably greater than the number of independent "measures" mentioned in the text. A list of school variables and the EEOS questionnaire items from which they were derived is given in Table 1. A description of the coding procedures is available on request from the author.

4. I omitted "attitude" variables because: (a) it is even less clear what they measure than what the "resource" and "policy" variables measure; (b) it is even harder to argue that "attitudes" are causally prior to achievement than to argue this for "resources" and "policies," and (c) a preliminary examination showed generally small differences in achievement between schools with similar student background, but different teacher and principal attitudes.

5. Detailed definitions of the terms "Northern," "urban," and "elementary school" are found in Chapter 11. The reader should bear in mind that the term "urban" includes suburbs as well as cities.

6. The EEOS sample was stratified so as to ensure an adequate number of integrated and all-black schools. In order to make the sample "representative," each school must be assigned a weight which is inversely proportional to the probability

of the school's having been included in the sample. When a school was lost, Coleman *et al.* gave nearby participating schools of similar racial composition larger weights (EEOR, p. 588). Some of the preliminary analyses reported in this chapter and in Chapter 11 were conducted with an unweighted sample. The final analyses were conducted with a weighted sample. All analyses are based on a weighted sample unless otherwise indicated. Comparisons of weighted and unweighted results suggest that the differences are seldom very important. The coefficients of school characteristics are so weak and unstable, however, that even minor changes in the sample sometimes substantially alter the apparent statistical significance of a variable.

7. See Armor, Chapter 5, and Smith, Chapter 6, for further evidence on similarities and differences between regions. Since completing this chapter I have also conducted research on the EEOS high schools in all regions. The main difference seems to be that initial achievement does not predict final achievement as well in rural as in urban areas.

8. See Chapter 11 for additional comparisons between elementary and secondary schools.

9. Unweighted regression equations were estimated separately for schools in the Northeast, Midwest, and Far West; for the five Standard Metropolitan Statistical Areas with the largest number of cooperative schools (New York, Philadelphia, Detroit, Milwaukee, and San Francisco); for the five districts with the most cooperative schools (the same districts as SMSA's); for "inner-city" and "residential/suburban" schools; for schools with above and below average socioeconomic levels, and for schools with above and below average 1st-grade scores. The school-wide 6th-grade verbal mean was the dependent variable in all analyses. In the first set of comparisons, the independent variables were those family background and school characteristics that had proven statistically significant in equations for the full sample. This procedure contained a built-in bias against finding statistically significant differences between subsamples, since variables with similar coefficients in several subsamples are more likely to be statistically significant in a pooled sample than variables with radically different coefficients in different subsamples. A second set of comparisons was therefore made, in which the independent variables were the background characteristics of the pupils and a dozen randomly selected school characteristics. *Every* comparison showed a statistically significant difference between equations from different subsamples. On the other hand, *no* comparison suggested that pooling subsamples was seriously misleading. The coefficients in the pooled sample usually approximated the weighted mean of the coefficients in the subsamples. There were no instances in which the coefficients for the subsamples had statistically significant coefficients with opposite signs.

The standard errors of equations that controlled only student background were never more than four months in any subsample, and the importance of background was never appreciably altered by introducing school characteristics. Coefficients for the pooled sample therefore describe the "average relationship" for the entire urban North fairly well, even though variations around this average are not random.

Ideally, it would be desirable to identify school and background characteristics that had different relationships to achievement in different subsamples, and then to recognize these differences in equations for the full sample. Efforts to do this turned out to take more time and money than they were worth, however.

I approached the problem as follows. When a variable had a noticeably different coefficient in, say, the East and the West, this variable was replaced with two new ones. The first new variable had a value of zero in all Eastern schools and a value equal to the original variable in all Western schools. The second variable had a value of zero in all Western schools, and a value equal to the original variable in all Eastern schools. This allowed the variable to have one coefficient for predicting achievement in the East, and another for the West. When the variable was not applicable, its zero value made it drop out.

Substitutions of this kind almost never yielded statistically significant improvements in the predictive accuracy of the overall equations. This is simply another way of saying that while the overall differences between subsamples were usually significant, the differences between the coefficients of specific variables usually were not. Furthermore, the number of new variables required to take full account of all the potential differences between subsamples was unmanageable. If, for example, I had begun with an equation that included four background measures and a dozen school measures, and if I had allowed these sixteen variables to have different coefficients in each of five regions, each of six types of community within each region, and each of two socioeconomic levels in each type of community, I would have had 960 independent variables in my full equation. Estimating such an equation was impossible both in theory and in practice. One could, it is true, estimate each variable's coefficient for each subsample and then collapse variables which took on the same coefficient under several conditions. However, this would result in some variables' appearing only once, while others would appear under many different conditions with different coefficients. Given a sample of "only" 684 schools, this procedure seems as likely to pick up random relationships as genuine interactions.

My decision to treat Northern urban schools as a single sample rested on another consideration as well. The EEOS sample was drawn in such a way that it can, with appropriate weights, be made relatively representative of the entire urban North. It can *not* easily be made representative of any subdivision of the urban North. The "inner-city" schools in the EEOS sample, for example, differ to an unknown extent from the norm for all Northern urban inner-city schools. Similarly, the "Philadelphia" schools in the EEOS sample differ in unknown ways from the overall Philadelphia norm. It is therefore even more dangerous to generalize from subsamples than from the full Northern urban sample.

10. Perhaps the most obvious source of unreliability in estimating school characteristics is their instability over time. When calculating the relationship between pupils' mean achievement and teachers' mean characteristics, for example, we have no way of knowing whether sixth graders who moved into their present school relatively recently had similar teachers in their previous school. Similarly, we cannot tell how closely the teachers who were in a school in 1965 resembled the teachers who had been in the school during the previous five years. If instability in the *student* population were reducing the reliability of estimates, the effects of such unreliability could be gauged by estimating separate equations for those pupils who had been in their present school since first grade. My analyses indicated that the regression coefficients of school characteristics in such equations were usually *smaller* than the coefficients in equations which included all students. The tendency was inconsistent, however. The standard errors in equations based on "one-school" students were also larger. For another similar comparison yielding equally equivocal results, see Michelson (1970).

11. Errors in measuring a school characteristic reduce the correlation between this characteristic and the social composition of the school, the mean achievement of the school, or any other school characteristic. The errors also increase the standard deviation of the school measure by a corresponding amount. The unstandardized regression coefficient (B-weight) is therefore reduced. Increases in the standard deviations also lead to increases in the standard errors of the regression coefficients and reduce the likelihood of any given variable's being statistically significant.

12. American Indians, Mexican Americans, Puerto Ricans, and Orientals were included in the estimates for the total population, but not in the estimates for black, white, poor, or middle-class students. The latter estimates were derived by weighting each school mean by the number of black, white, poor, or middle-class pupils it enrolled. For details on the classification system, see footnote 28.

13. I did not investigate within-school discrimination in resource allocation or in the application of policies at the elementary level. I have, however, begun an investigation of within-school discrimination in the allocation of teachers at the secondary level. The sample consists of the 66 Northern urban high schools in the EEOS which (a) returned teacher questionnaires, (b) had more than four teachers who reported teaching blacks and more than four who reported teaching whites, and

(c) had between 15 and 85 percent white students. The method of comparison has been as follows: (1) the mean response of all teachers in a school was computed for variables 76, 95, 96, 99, 102, 104, 108, 109, 110, 111, 113, 115, 116, 118, 120, 121, 122, 124, and 129. These means were then recomputed, with each teacher being weighted by the percentage of whites he said he taught. This gave an estimate of the characteristics of teachers of whites in the school. The process was repeated for blacks. The deviations of the black and white means from the grand means were then computed and averaged across all 66 schools, with each deviation being weighted by the approximate number of black or white pupils in that particular school. (The weight was estimated from the size of the staff, the size of the average class reported by the staff, and the percentage of whites in the average class.) This yielded an overall estimate of the difference between the teachers of blacks and whites in the same schools. The differences were almost uniformly trivial, though white students did get teachers with about a year more of professional experience than black students, and attended classes with one fewer student per classroom than blacks.

14. Coleman viewed the effects of socioeconomic background as "prior" to the effects of school, and therefore used two-stage regression equations to estimate so-called "school effects." But many verbal skills and almost all reading and math skills are acquired *subsequent* to entering school. Furthermore, affluent families are likely to move to neighborhoods with desirable school characteristics. Thus it *could* be that the relationship between family background and achievement is a result of rich families' sending their children to good schools, not of direct family influence on achievement. I thought it reasonable to assume that school characteristics account for part of the achievement gap between sixth graders from different backgrounds, but that background differences also account for part of the achievement gap between students whose schools have different characteristics. This assumption implies a single-stage regression equation, in which home and school variables have the same chance to explain the overall variation in achievement. All the analyses reported in the text were of this type.

If the relationship between family background, school characteristics, and student achievement is linear and additive, and if errors are normally distributed, regression coefficients can be understood in terms of the differences between cells in similarly constructed cross-tabulations. The following hypothetical table illustrates the principles involved:

Family Background	School Resources		
	Low	High	Total
Low	10 (8)	20 (2)	12 (10)
High	30 (2)	40 (8)	38 (10)
Total	14 (10)	36 (10)	25 (20)

The numbers in the cells represent hypothetical mean test scores. The numbers in parentheses represent the number of children in each cell. It is apparent that family background and school resources are highly correlated in this example. A single-stage regression equation estimates the "effect" of family background as 20 (the mean difference between High and Low cells in the same column). It estimates the "effect" of school resources as 10 (the mean difference between High and Low cells in the same row).

A two-stage equation which enters family background first (i.e., Coleman's equation) yields an estimated family "effect" of 26 (i.e., 38 − 12, or the overall average difference between all high and low background students, regardless of school resources). It then estimates the school "effect" as 8 (the estimate which minimizes the sum of the squared deviations of each cell from the row average).

A two-stage equation which enters school resources first estimates the school "effect" at 22 (i.e., 36 — 14, or the overall average difference between high- and low-resource schools). The background "effect" is then reduced to 16 when the family measure is entered in the second stage.

The "correct" choice among these procedures depends on one's causal assumptions.

15. The following background variables were controlled in all analyses:

Region (New England, Mid-Atlantic, Great Lakes, Plains, Far West), treated as dummy variables, with the Mid-Atlantic taken as the point of comparison;

Percentage of whites in the high school to which sixth graders would normally go, treated as a series of dummy variables, since the relationship was strongly nonlinear;

Percentage of whites in the sixth grade;

Socioeconomic level of the sixth grade (two measures, based on the two dimensions of school-wide socioeconomic status that emerged from a principal-components analysis of fourteen school-wide socioeconomic measures. The characteristics of these measures are discussed in detail in Chapter 11).

Once these variables were controlled, no other background characteristics showed a statistically significant relationship to achievement. Mean 1st-grade nonverbal scores showed a relationship to 6th-grade verbal achievement after the background variables were controlled, but it was not strong (see Chapter 11). These scores were available for only half the sample and were therefore omitted.

For reasons discussed in footnote 19, only one school policy or resource was entered in most of the final equations. Where the reported results reflect equations in which more than one school policy or resource was examined simultaneously, this will be mentioned explicitly.

16. Between-district analyses were performed in the following manner. First, the data from sample elementary schools were aggregated across districts, so as to create a district-wide mean for each variable. For reasons given in footnote 16, these means were not representative of the entire district. They were, however, presumably subject to the influence of any factor that affected an entire district. Between-district regression equations were therefore estimated, using district means as dependent and independent variables.

The within-district analysis was analogous. First, the deviation of every school from the norm for all sample schools in its district was computed for every variable. Within-district regression equations were then estimated, using schools' deviations from their district means as the dependent and independent variables.

17. If teachers with a certain characteristic selected schools primarily on the basis of 6th-grade achievement, then controlling student background, or even students' initial ability, would not reduce the teacher characteristics' regression coefficient to zero.

18. One way to describe this situation mathematically is to code all school policies, school resources, and student background characteristics so that an "advantage" has a positive sign. The resulting matrix of zero-order correlations shows a vast preponderance of positive over negative correlations. One consequence is that as new variables enter an equation, the coefficient of variables already in the equation tends to shrink, not grow.

19. I also examined the relationship of each school characteristic to achievement after controlling *both* student background characteristics *and* other school characteristics that had statistically significant coefficients and might logically be expected to influence achievement. If the school characteristics controlled in these equations affected achievement and were not affected by it, the resulting coefficients would be preferable to coefficients derived from equations which controlled only background characteristics. Since many of the school characteristics controlled in the equations seemed likely to have been affected by student achievement, however, equations that included these variables were likely to underestimate the true

"effect" of the other school (or background) characteristics. Given a choice between underestimating and overestimating "true" relationships, overestimates seemed preferable. Where the results of the two analytic methods differed in a statistically significant way, both will be reported.

20. There has been considerable controversy over whether to use mean achievement or individual achievement as a dependent variable in analyzing the EEOS data. School means have two advantages.

(1) Group means are more reliable than individual scores (see Chapter 11).

(2) Most of the variation in individual achievement lies within rather than between schools. An analysis which uses individual achievement as a dependent variable and uses individual family background as an independent variable is therefore dominated by the within-school relationship of family background to achievement. The EEOS provides no data on the extent to which the within-school relationship of background to achievement is attributable to bias in school policies or resources, but it is quite possible that this is of some importance. If this is the case, an individual-level analysis will underestimate the true regression coefficients for those resources and policies that (a) are normally allocated according to family background and (b) affect within-school achievement.

Suppose, to take an extreme example, that an extra year of father's education raises a child's verbal scores by an average of one point. Suppose that the typical school also allocates good teachers to children with well-educated fathers, so that the observed difference between children becomes two points for each extra year of father's education. Suppose that precisely the same thing is true for between-school differences in mean achievement. If we have no within-school data on teacher allocation, our equations will impute the entire two point within-school difference to father's education. If we have good data on teacher allocation between schools, our equations will impute a one-point between-school difference to father's education and will attribute the other one point to teacher characteristics. If we conduct an individual-level analysis which pools the within- and between-school differences, and if 75 percent of the achievement variance is within schools, our "best fit" regression line will be one which assumes approximately 1.75 points increase in achievement for every year's increase in father's education. Constraining the regression line in this way will leave only 0.25 points attributable to teacher characteristics. An analysis confined to school means would, in contrast, yield an estimate of 1 point for teachers and one point for father's education, which in this case is "correct."

This is equivalent to saying that there are errors in the measurement of the resources available to a given child, and that in individual analyses such errors are likely to be negatively correlated with another independent variable (family background). This will lead to an overestimate of the coefficient for family background and an underestimate of the coefficient for the school characteristic.

21. The "confidence intervals" reported in the text will nominally be such as to include the "true" value in 19 cases out of 20. Their accuracy is subject to various uncertainties.

I estimated the regression coefficients directly from means, standard deviations, and correlation coefficients based on unequal numbers of observations. This appeared preferable to filling in missing cases with regressed means, which would have artificially inflated the correlation coefficients (since regressed means correlate perfectly with one another). It also appeared preferable to filling in the sample means, which would have artificially deflated the correlation coefficients. Having adopted this procedure, I assumed that the number of degrees of freedom for any given equation derived from the smallest number of joint observations underlying any correlation coefficient in the matrix. This procedure was probably conservative and led to larger standard errors than other alternatives.

The precision of the confidence intervals is also reduced by errors in measuring school characteristics. If these errors are uncorrelated with achievement, they artificially inflate the confidence interval. If they are correlated with achievement, they may also bias the entire interval up or down. Precision may also be reduced by the loss of a third of the original sample. Another issue affecting the confidence intervals is the number of degrees of freedom. I calculated these from the number of *independent* observations, i.e., the number of schools. Others (e.g., Coleman *et al.*, 1966; Michelson, 1970) used the *total* number of observations, i.e., the number of individuals. Since the data on schools are not independent for each individual, this procedure yields artificially small confidence intervals and makes many variables look "statistically significant" when they are not.

22. Coleman *et al.* (p. 272) indicate that the difference between black and white 6th-grade verbal achievement in the urban North was approximately 18 months. The raw-score difference was nine points, which implies that each correct answer on the 6th-grade verbal test represented about two months of verbal growth. Unfortunately, the relationship between correct answers and grade-level equivalents was nonlinear, i.e., the difference between 49 and 50 correct answers represented more months of verbal growth than the difference between 29 and 30 correct answers. These differences can in theory be eliminated by rescaling student scores, as Coleman *et al.* did. The effect of this rescaling on correlation matrices is very slight, however. The analyses reported in this chapter are all based on raw scores.

23. In technical terms, I will say there was "no relationship" between a school characteristic and achievement when the t-statistic for a coefficient was less than 1.00 (not 2.00 as in most analyses), and when the 95 percent confidence interval was less than a month wide.

24. Statistically, the question is whether school characteristics had nonlinear relationships to achievement once family background was controlled. I checked this in the following manner. First, each school's achievement score was predicted on the basis of the students' family background and the school characteristic under study, on the assumption that all relationships were linear and additive. The residual errors for each school were then cross-tabulated against the value of the school characteristic under study. (All school characteristics were recoded on a scale from 1 to 9 for this purpose, with 1 representing schools that were two or more standard deviations below the sample mean, 2 representing schools that were 1.5–2.0 standard deviations below the sample mean, and so forth.) An F-test was then used to determine the likelihood that differences among the means of the residuals in the nine cells were nonrandom. This procedure was equivalent to a two-stage regression analysis, in which the first stage included the background variables and a linear variable, while the second stage included dummy variables representing the various possible values of the variable. The significance test simply indicated whether the F-ratio rose by a statistically significant amount in the second stage. Roughly 100 such tests were performed. The distribution of F-ratios was only slightly different from that expected by chance.

25. The assertions in the text are based on a transformation of the EEOS test scores into grade-level equivalents, using a formula developed by the Educational Testing Service. The formula had been empirically validated for 6th grade and above, but not for lower grades. The estimated scores of first, second, and third graders were based on linear extrapolations from higher grades (see EEOR, pp. 272–77). The formulae suggest that for sixth graders, one standard deviation was equal to about 18 months of verbal growth, 27 months of reading growth, and 22 months of math growth. These estimates may be off by a few months either way, especially since the distributions of scores on these tests would probably not be normal if a chronological metric were used.

26. For a weighted Northern urban sample of 6th-grade blacks, whites, and "others," Smith found 22.4 percent of the variation in verbal scores lay between schools, compared to 15.9 percent of the variation in reading scores and 20.9 percent of the variation in math scores. The standard deviation within the average school was therefore about 16 months for verbal scores, 20 months for math, and 25 months for reading. The standard deviations of school means were approximately 8.5 for verbal scores and 10 months for reading and math scores. These calculations were based on verbal, reading, and math scores which had been "transformed" according to an ETS scaling formula. School verbal means based on

aggregated raw scores had standard deviations about 15 percent larger (when transformed into months) than the scale-score standard deviations.

27. These inferences about different tests differ from those in the EEOR (pp. 292–95). Coleman *et al.* assumed if a test were subject to school influence the percentage of variance lying between schools would increase over time. This would not be true, however, if (a) there were a negative relationship between school inputs and initial ability, either within or between schools, and (b) school resources affected achievement. If that were the case—as Coleman and I both think it should be—school effects would *reduce* the percentage of variance lying between schools. If there were *no* relationship between school inputs and initial ability, either within or between schools, the distribution of variance would be unchanged. If the relationship were of one sort within schools and of another sort between schools, the overall effect on the distribution of the variance would depend on the relative magnitudes of all the initial relationships.

28. I defined every student reporting seven or fewer home items (Pupil Questionnaire Items 19–27) as "poor." About a sixth of the weighted sample was poor by this standard. About a sixth was black. About half the poor were black, and about half the blacks were poor. These figures correspond roughly with official estimates of the numbers of "poor" and black children in the urban North. A more sophisticated classification which used parental education and occupation as well as home items would probably show that the gap between the most socioeconomically disadvantaged sixth of the population (i.e., the "lower class") and the majority was roughly the same as the black-white gap.

29. The comparisons in the text were derived in two ways. First, schools were assigned to one of six overall socioeconomic levels. The mean scores of poor blacks and poor whites in each category of school were then tabulated. These showed an essentially linear relationship. Then a regression analysis was conducted.

The dependent variable was the mean verbal score of children who reported less than seven home items. The independent variables included the average number of home items, the average family size, the average parental educational attainment, and the percentage of white-collar fathers for these same children. In addition, the equation included the racial and socioeconomic composition of the entire school as independent variables. The regression coefficients for the school-wide racial and socioeconomic variables were used to estimate "peer effects." The coefficients for the characteristics of specifically lower-class children were presumed to represent individual background effects. This assumption appears to be conservative. If an appreciable number of students had less than seven home items, the variables which measured the socioeconomic level of these children were highly collinear with the variables measuring the level of the entire school. The coefficients for children with less than seven home items therefore measured "peer effects" as well as "individual effects," and the coefficients for the school-wide measures were artificially deflated. For a further analysis, see Smith, Chapter 6.

30. Background variables accounted for 91 percent of the variance in schools' mean verbal scores, 85 percent of the variance in mean math scores, and 80 percent of the variance in mean reading scores. The addition of all statistically significant school characteristics to the equation never boosted the explained variance more than 1 percent and reduced the regression coefficient for socioeconomic composition by only 5 percent.

The percentage of white sixth graders in a school accounted for slightly more than half the variation in the number of complaints teachers had, 20 percent of the variation in teachers' verbal scores, 12 percent of the variation in pupil attendance rates, 10 percent of the variation in the percentage of substitutes in a school, and less than 7 percent of the variation in any other school characteristic. Sixth graders' socioeconomic background accounted for more than half the variation in the number of complaints teachers had, 20 percent of the variation in the amount of preschooling and kindergarten the children reported, 18 percent of the variation in average daily attendance, 16 percent of the variation in teacher verbal scores, 15 percent of the variation in site acreage, 14 percent of the variation in the percentage of substitute teachers, 12 percent of the variation in building age, 10 percent of the variation in the percentage of children in the lowest track in their school, 9 percent of the variation in use of the National Teacher Exams to select staff, 8 percent of the variation in teacher association membership, 7 percent of the variation in library volumes per student, and less than 7 percent of the variation in the other school characteristics listed in Table 1.

31. The nonlinear relationship between *high-school* racial composition and elementary-school achievement was not a proxy for nonlinearity in the relationship of *elementary-school* racial or socioeconomic composition to achievement. These latter relationships were linear so long as I looked at *overall* school achievement. When I looked only at *white* achievement, a nonlinear relationship to the racial composition of the elementary school often emerged. Nor was the relationship a proxy for school location, as it held up consistently in different districts and states.

32. If chronic absentees had lower test scores than regular attenders, the EEOS overestimated most schools' "true" mean achievement by an unknown amount. The higher the absence rate on test day, the larger the overestimate. While schools with high and low absence rates had the same *measured* means, those with high absence rates might have had lower "true" means if all their pupils had been present. Chapter 11 discusses this issue in more detail.

33. The probability of the observed pattern occurring by chance was about one in fifty. The relationship existed only at the district level. Variations within districts were unrelated to achievement.

34. Chapter 11 indicates that pupils' reports on these matters were more accurate than one might expect.

35. There were no schools in the sample in which more than two thirds of the sixth graders reported having attended nursery school, and only 40 sample schools in which more than a third of the sixth graders reported such attendance.

36. The relationship of achievement to principals' reports about the length of the school year was slightly nonlinear, although the deviations from linearity were not readily interpretable.

37. For an interesting study that points in the opposite direction, see Hayes and Grether (1969).

38. Of 12 remaining facilities, 5 were associated with overachievement, 7 with underachievement. In no case was the difference as large as a month. One facility, namely site acreage, had a t-statistic of -2.1, but this could easily occur by chance for one variable among 12. Site acreage had a smaller but still negative relationship to reading and math scores.

39. The coefficient for free lunches in the reading regressions was just twice its standard error, which is well within the range expected on the basis of chance for one variable in 114. No other school characteristic has a t-statistic of more than 2.0 in the reading equations.

40. This relationship was significantly nonlinear. The schools with old and new textbooks did better than those in between.

41. The probability of getting six negative coefficients out of seven is about one in 16.

42. The relationship between frequency of achievement testing and EEOS verbal scores was nonlinear, with schools that reported giving very few or very many achievement tests doing worse than those in the middle.

43. See Research Division, National Education Association (1968) and Findley and Bryan (1971), for reviews of this literature.

44. See Chapter 11.

45. See Chapter 11 for a discussion of these measures. The intercorrelations among them, even after eliminating wild scores, were only 0.6–0.7. The measure which correlated best with the other two was the ratio of total enrollment to teaching staff. This seems logical if we assume that the differences between the measures represented differences in staffing patterns, not just random error.

46. Chapter 11 for details of these analyses.

47. See Research Division, National Education Association (1967).

48. The coefficient of class size was smaller when black verbal scores were used as a

dependent variable than when all pupils were examined together. This was also true when lower-class black verbal scores were used as a dependent variable.

49. For an eloquent description of several schools that conform to this theory, see Silberman (1970).

50. All six t-statistics were less than 1.00 when linear relationships were analyzed. Three of the six relationships showed statistically significant deviations from linearity, but none was readily interpretable.

51. While tenure policies normally operate on a district-wide basis, and differences between different kinds of tenure policies ought therefore to be district-wide differences, the data on tenure policies were actually gathered from principals. The data were not perfectly reliable, as indicated in Chapter 11. The differences in achievement reported in the text may therefore be partly differences between schools in the same district which reported different tenure policies, even though no such differences actually existed.

52. This was the *only* instance where separate analyses for lower-class blacks and whites yielded evidence that a resource had greater value for these students than for the majority.

53. The correlation between the percentage of white teachers and the mean percentage of white students in the teachers' undergraduate colleges was 0.90.

54. The correlation between the percentage of tenured teachers and average teacher experience was 0.46.

55. The percentage of substitute teachers was not significantly correlated with the number of days teachers reported having missed the previous year. This suggests that most of the substitutes who returned questionnaires were long-term rather than day-to-day substitutes.

56. See Chapter 11 for details.

Bibliography

Bowles, Samuel, and Levin, Henry. "The Determinants of Scholastic Achievement—An Appraisal of Some Recent Evidence." *The Journal of Human Resources*, Vol. 3, Winter 1968, pp. 3–24.

Coleman, James S., *et al. Equality of Educational Opportunity*. U.S. Government Printing Office, 1966.

Findley, Warren G., and Bryan, Miriam M. "Ability Grouping: 1970." Center for Educational Improvement, University of Georgia, 1971.

Hayes, Donald, and Grether, Judith. "The School Year and Vacations: When Do Students Learn?" Paper presented to the Eastern Sociological Association, April, 1969, available from the Urban Institute, Washington, D.C., mimeo.

Michelson, Stephan. "The Association of Teacher Resourceness with Children's Characteristics," in Alexander Mood, ed. *Do Teachers Make a Difference?* U.S. Government Printing Office, 1970.

National Education Association, Research Division. *Class Size*. Washington, D.C.: 1967.

National Education Association, Research Division. *Ability Grouping*. Washington, D.C.: 1968.

Sewall, William H., and Armer, Michael J. "Neighborhood Context and College Plans." *American Sociological Review*, Vol. 31, April, 1966, pp. 159–68.

Silberman, Charles. *Crisis in the Classroom*. New York: Random House, 1970.

Turner, Ralph, *et al.* "On Neighborhood Context and College Plans." *American Sociological Review*, Vol. 31, October, 1966, pp. 698–712.

3

On the Value of
Equality of
Educational
Opportunity as a
Guide to Public Policy*

ERIC A. HANUSHEK & JOHN F. KAIN[1]

Equality of Educational Opportunity has been part of the public record since July, 1966.[2] The best known "finding" of the *Report* is that quantity and quality of school inputs (facilities, curriculum, and personnel) have little or no bearing on achievement; home environment and the student's peers are what really count.[3] Obviously, such a finding has far-reaching implications for educational policy. At the very least, it raises serious questions about the efficacy of the billions of dollars now spent on public education. Yet in our opinion, serious doubts must be raised about this and several other "findings" attributed to the *Report*.[4] These doubts result both from the methods of empirical analysis and their interpretation. While we are not the first to raise questions about the *Report*'s analysis, we feel that the subject is both important and complex enough to merit further discus-

* Support for preparation of this paper was provided by the Harvard Program on Regional and Urban Economics. This program is supported primarily by grants from the Office of Economic Research of the Economic Development Administration in the Department of Commerce, Project Number OER–015–G–68–7, and the Program on Technology and Society conducted at Harvard University under a grant from the International Business Machines Corporation. Many of the ideas included in this paper were initially developed through participation in the Harvard Seminar on the Equality of Educational Opportunity Report (SEEOR). In addition the underlying research was partially financed by a grant from the Carnegie Corporation of New York to that seminar.

The authors take full responsibility for their views which are not necessarily those of the sponsoring organizations.

sion.[5] Our discussion of the analysis presented in *Equality of Educational Opportunity* and associated interpretative problems is preceded by a consideration of the more fundamental area of overall research strategy. Past reviews of the *Report* have concentrated on assessing the analysis and findings within the framework defined by the *Report*'s authors. We are interested, as well, in the merits of the work within the framework defined by the original Congressional directive.

I. ALTERNATIVE RESEARCH STRATEGIES —AN INTERDEPENDENT DECISION

We contend that the authors of *Equality of Educational Opportunity* made a fundamental error in confusing a responsibility for fact-finding with a mandate to carry out basic research on the educational production process. This had repercussions on all aspects of the study because the pressures of time, knowledge, and available resources were magnified by attempting the broader study in conjunction with the required fact-finding mission. The result was a failure to provide the information requested by Congress.

The *Report* was the response of the Office of Education to Section 402 of the Civil Rights Act of 1964 which stated:

> The Commissioner [of Education] shall conduct a survey and make a report to the President and the Congress, within two years of the enactment of this title, concerning the lack of availability of equal educational opportunities for individuals by reason of race, color, religion, or national origin in public educational institutions at all levels in the United States, its territories and possessions, and the District of Columbia.

There is little doubt that Congress wished to obtain an authoritative answer to the question of whether minorities were being discriminated against in the provision of public education.[6] However, this question is not as simple as it first appears. At least two possible definitions of equality of educational opportunity come to mind: (1) equality of resources or school inputs and (2) equality of achievement or output of the educational process.[7] All subsequent decisions about the research design and data needs depend on which definition is selected.

Measurement of the educational resources provided students of each minority group is the backbone of an analysis of school input inequality. Resources can be measured in either real terms (quantities of appropriately weighted homogeneous inputs) or money terms (per pupil expenditures).[8] The crucial feature of such a survey is obtaining representative samples from which population inferences can be made. There are some difficult conceptual and measurement problems of the input method, but they are not insurmountable. In fact, a major strength of this approach is simplicity (a significant consideration given the time constraint on the study). Additionally, such a study of input inequalities provides immediately usable information for initial legislative or judicial action.

For an output definition of equality of educational opportunity, the focus of the data collection should be on achievement levels of a representative sample of population groups. Again it is essential to be able to make inferences about the entire population.[9] If large inequalities in the average level of such income-related output measures are found to exist among groups in society, the policy objectives are quite clear, even if the exact means of achieving these objectives are not.

While it is conceptually a rather simple matter to equate educational inputs, it is much more difficult to devise policies that will equalize expected output. This difficulty may have been what motivated the Office of Education to commission a very broad and ambitious program of basic research on the educational production process. This larger analysis took the form of estimating a multivariate statistical model relating student and school characteristics to achievement. As is discussed in Section II of this paper, this effort was unsuccessful. The relevant issue at this point is the way in which the decision to undertake this ambitious research affected the evaluation of equality of educational opportunity.

Analysis of the educational production process requires the collection of more precise and detailed input and output data than those required for both the input and output investigations combined. These data should include information on both outside school factors (socioeconomic status, family attitudes, community environment, and similar factors) and past school inputs (longitudinal data) in addition to the levels of current school inputs (the survey of input equality) and current achievement (the survey of output equality). For a study of the educational production process, it is more important to obtain wide variation in educational practice and experience than to have a representative sample of the population of schools or students. These differences can be critical when there are time and resource constraints on the study.

We contend the Office of Education should have been less ambitious in its investigation and limited itself in the short time period available to fact-finding. We would be the last to argue against the need for more basic research on the production of educational achievement or to insist on a narrow interpretation of Congressional intent; however, we ask whether the immediate needs of public policy would not have been better served by a careful and exacting determination of the narrower question of inequality in the provision of educational resources—a question about which considerable controversy remains.[10]

Even the most permissive interpretation of the Congressional directive could not relieve the authors of the *Report* of the requirement for a systematic survey of equality in the provision of educational resources. They could do more, but not less. The clear danger of doing more was that the divergent data requirements and the different areas of emphasis demanded by the three research strategies (the input survey, the output survey, and the basic research on the educational process) would prevent them from providing an authoritative answer to any of the three questions. It appears that this is precisely what happened. Confronted with a restricted choice among three strategies, the authors chose all three. Had they succeeded in providing authoritative answers about inequalities in educational inputs, we would have had no quarrel with their decision to undertake research on the educational process. However, in attempting to do all three, the authors of the *Report* failed to provide convincing answers to the question of whether minority groups are systematically discriminated against in the provision of educational resources.

♦ The OE Survey

The following discussion of the *Report*'s data base supports our contention that the authors failed to provide satisfactory answers to the questions concerning equality of educational resources. Moreover, this section is necessary for our discussion of the conceptual model and statistical methods used by the *Report*'s authors in their research into the educational process. This data base is referred to as the *OE Survey* to differentiate it from the analysis presented in *Equality of Educational Opportunity*.

The basic sampling units used in the *OE Survey* were elementary and secondary schools attended by seven broad ethnic groups: whites, Negroes, Oriental Americans, Indian Americans, Mexican Americans, Puerto Ricans, and "others." High schools included in the *OE Survey* were selected by a stratified probability sampling technique which insured that schools attended by minorities were overrepresented. Elementary and junior high schools were sampled on a probability basis depending on the percentage of their students going to the secondary schools included in the final sample. The sample size was set originally at 900,000 students, but nonresponses reduced the usable sample to approximately 569,000 students. These students, divided among grades 1, 3, 6, 9, and 12, were given ability and achievement tests and completed a questionnaire concerning family background and attitudes. In addition, data were gathered from the teachers, principals, and school-system superintendents for the 3155 sample schools. Teachers completed an optional verbal facility test and a questionnaire on their personal histories, educational backgrounds, attitudes, and characteristics of their classes and schools. Principals and superintendents supplied information about their backgrounds and attitudes and about school facilities in their school or district.

There are several substantive problems with the *OE Survey*. Throughout the *Report*'s presentation, the reader is lulled into a false sense of security by the seemingly generous sample size (569,000 students). But, when it comes to school facilities, the relevant sample size is the number of schools, not the number of students. This reduction in effective sample size results from a failure to obtain school input data pertaining to individual students. Although the school sample is still quite large, it is reduced considerably if stratification is necessary (by grade, race, region, urban/rural). For example, the 12th-grade sample for the metropolitan South included data on only 78 schools, and only four of these had between 10 percent and 75 percent nonwhite students.[11] One is hesitant to make inferences, especially as concerns the effects of integration from an analysis of such small samples.

Nonresponse problems (which were glossed over in the *Report*) are another serious weakness of the *OE Survey*. Refusal to participate and faulty responses meant that 41 percent of the 1170 high schools included in the original random sample could not be included in the analysis. Similarly, only 74 percent of the sample of feeder schools were included in the final analysis. It is obvious from these statistics that extreme care must be exercised in making inferences about the population because analysis of the *OE Survey* data could be seriously misleading if this nonresponse were systematic. As mentioned previously, systematic nonresponse would be most serious in the case of the narrower questions relating to inequality in educational inputs or outputs, especially if the reasons for nonresponse were related to a "sensitivity" about real or believed inequalities. In fact, there are indications of such systematic nonresponse. Several large Northern central cities, where there has been considerable controversy about school discrimination, refused to cooperate.

Nonresponse to specific questions also presents serious problems. Analyses of the raw data by one of the present authors indicate that many questionnaire items are unusable because of nonresponse problems.[12] High rates of nonresponse are particularly characteristic of emotionally sensitive questions. For example, the principal's questionnaire includes three questions about the principal's attitudes concerning racial composition of the faculty, assuming student bodies of three different racial mixes. In a sample of about 300 *OE Survey* elementary schools in the northeast region, over one third of the principals failed to answer one or more of these questions. Substantial errors could be introduced by such internal nonresponse.[13]

Lying, exaggeration, and faulty responses to particular questions are a problem in any survey. However, the potential for error seems especially large for the *OE Survey*. Questions requiring numerical answers, such as school enrollment, to be coded for mechanical scoring provide the most dramatic examples of faulty response. These numerical answers entered into such traditional policy variables as class size, per-pupil expenditure, and volumes per student in the library. Cross-checking of these questions uncovered a considerable number of obvious miscodings.[14] It would appear that the computer revolution has not yet been felt fully in the nation's elementary and secondary schools. Though the possibility of error may be greatest for questions requiring self-coding of numerical answers, the frequency of such errors raises serious doubts about the reliability of the *OE Survey* in general.[15]

Serious as the problems of sample reliability may be, the fundamental weaknesses of the questionnaires are even more harmful, especially in terms of measuring school facilities. The absence of questions with any qualitative bite is particularly noticeable. There are many questions that relate to the presence of particular attributes, but few that relate to their quality. This is true of the description of physical facilities such as laboratories, gymnasiums, and textbook availability, as well as features such as curriculum and specialized classes. Measures of school facilities are very insensitive and do a poor job of differentiating schools. While these problems are not restricted to school input data, the overriding interest in school effects and the uneven quality of the data (as discussed under "Contemporaneous Errors" in Section II) suggest that the problems resulting from the inadequate measurement of school inputs are most serious for the analysis.[16]

Related to these measurement problems, the questionnaires frequently seem to stop short of asking many logical and important questions. For example, neither expenditures per school nor information on school organization were collected, except in the crudest form, and information on the educational histories of sampled students was not obtained. This omission is particularly unfortunate given the multi-tier sampling design used in the *OE Survey*. A very large proportion of high-school and junior-high-school students necessarily attended lower-tier schools in the sample. Thus, even the sketchiest historical information would provide links between elementary, junior high, and high schools.

Many of these shortcomings appear to be the result of a decision to use the same questionnaires for all grade levels. For example, the principal's questionnaire could be answered by both an elementary-school and a high-school principal, and the teacher's questionnaire could be answered by a 1st-grade teacher and a high-school guidance counselor. To an even greater degree the weaknesses of the survey instruments appear attributable to a lack of careful prior specification of hypotheses. Again, the press of time, limitations of resources, the pathbreaking nature of the research, and an unwillingness to limit the scope of the investigation appear to be responsible for these failings. Given these very real problems, the question remains whether the *Report*'s basic research finding, the no-school-effect conclusion, can be regarded as an adequate guide for public policy.

II. THE RELATIONSHIP BETWEEN INPUTS AND OUTPUTS — SOME CONCEPTUAL AND METHODOLOGICAL ISSUES

In addition to the information problems discussed previously, the *Report* employs a number of questionable procedures. These factors lead us to seriously question whether the no-school-effect finding could have arisen from data inadequacies and analytical methods rather than any underlying behavioral relationship. At the very least, it is clear that the shortcomings of the data and the analytic methods used by the *Report*'s authors in studying the educational process raise serious problems of interpretation.

There are two major sets of issues central to any discussion of the *Report*'s findings on the relationship between educational inputs and outputs. These are: (1) the conceptual and statistical models of the education process used by the *Report*, and (2) the statistical methods employed in testing these models. These two areas of concern are inextricably interrelated, and both are strongly implicated in the *Report*'s no-school-effect conclusion. Thus, no rigorous segregation of them is attempted in the discussion that follows.

It is apparent that unfamiliarity with both the terminology and methodology used by the *Report* is responsible for much of the confusion surrounding it. Because these statistical concepts are crucial to understanding both the *Report*'s findings and our critique, we have made an effort to clarify some of these concepts and to provide definitions of technical terms.

◆ The Conceptual Model

Much of the appeal of the *Report*'s analysis arises because it seems to test empirically a conceptual model of the educational process that has wide acceptance.[17] Most researchers and educational policy-makers subscribe to a general conceptual model similar to that depicted by Equation 1. This model states that the achievement of an individual (*ith*) student at time *t* [A_{it}] is some function [*g*] of his characteristics and those of *his* immediate family cumulative to time *t* [$F_i^{(t)}$]; of the characteristics of his peers [$P_i^{(t)}$]; of his initial endowment or innate ability [I_i]; and of the quantity and quality of educational (school) inputs consumed by him throughout his lifetime [$S_i^{(t)}$].

$$(1) \quad A_{it} = g(F_i^{(t)}, P_i^{(t)}, I_i, S_i^{(t)})$$

where

$A_{it} =$ Vector of educational achievement of the *ith* student at time *t*,

$F_i^{(t)} =$ Vector of individual and family characteristics for the *ith* student cumulative to time *t*,

$P_i^{(t)} =$ Vector of student body characteristics (peer influences), i.e., socioeconomic and background characteristics of other students in the school cumulative to time *t*,

$I_i =$ Vector of initial endowments of the *ith* individual,

$S_i^{(t)} =$ Vector of school inputs relevant to the *ith* student cumulative to *t*.

Two aspects of the conceptual model deserve further emphasis. Innate ability refers to a pure genetic input that should not be confused with I.Q. or any other common measure of ability. Though we do not know of any satisfactory method of measuring this elusive concept, its inclusion in the conceptual model of the educational process is nevertheless of the utmost importance. Its inclusion as a separate argument in the achievement function does not imply a fixed ability or predetermined growth theory of intelligence. In fact, the conceptual model depicted in Equation 1 hypothesizes a heredity-environment interaction.

Separate peer and family vectors are included in the model because they have different policy implications. The socioeconomic, cultural, and racial composition of schools can be modified; for example, many schemes for educational reform, such as educational parks, are attempts to achieve these ends. But to change or reduce the importance of the family background of the individual child requires much more radical surgery. It is necessary either to change the characteristics or attitudes of individual families or else to weaken their influence on the child. Both are difficult and highly controversial objectives.[18]

Although the conceptual model in Equation 1 was never presented in the *Report* in this form, it seems implied throughout the text.[19] More importantly, it appears that most readers of the *Report* accept something of this general nature as the model of the educational process tested in it. Actually, the statistical models employed in the *Report* differ considerably and in systematic ways from this conceptual model. Moreover, the divergences among them (i.e., errors in model specification) tend to bias the empirical findings toward showing negligible school effects.

◆ *The Statistical Model*

All of the *Report*'s empirical analyses assume that the conceptual model can be written in a linear form such as in Equation 2. This functional form requires that individual achievement be described by the linear addition of an array of n variables plus some random residual (error) e_i. (These n variables are elements of the four vectors included in the conceptual model.) Equation 2 hypothesizes that consistent behavioral relationships exist across individuals as represented by the parameters or slope coefficients, a_j.[20]

$$(2) \quad A_i = a_o + a_1 X_{i1} + a_2 X_{i2} + \ldots + a_n X_{in} + e_i$$

where

$$A_i = \text{achievement of the } ith \text{ student,}$$
$$X_{i1}, X_{i2}, \ldots, X_{in} = n \text{ explanatory variables corresponding to measurements of the arguments of Equation 1 for individual } i,$$
$$a_1, a_2, \ldots, a_n = \text{parameters of the educational process,}$$
$$e_i = \text{residual term or the portion of } A_i \text{ that cannot be explained by the explanatory variables.}$$

There are several ways in which this general statistical hypothesis can be tested. The procedure used in *Equality of Educational Opportunity* was to partition or allocate the variance (the average squared deviation of individual observations from the sample means) in achievement among sets of explanatory variables (roughly corresponding to the vectors in Equation 1) through a specialized analysis of variance procedure.[21] This method involves calculating the amount of explained variance of achievement resulting from inclusion of different sets of explanatory variables in a least squares regression equation, i.e., calculating increments to the variance "explained" by the regression (R^2).[22] The *Report*'s conclusions are based on an assessment of the amount of variance explained by collections of variables included in each of the vectors (family, peer, school).

◆ *Analysis of Variance in a Complex World*

The specific analysis of variance procedure used by the *Report* is completely straightforward as long as all of the explanatory variables are truly independent (are not themselves correlated).[23] This is not true of the explanatory variables used in the *Report*. For example, higher-income suburbs pay their teachers more. Similarly, well-educated parents are more likely to be strongly motivated about their children's academic achievement, will be in a better position to help them with homework, and are likely to consider school quality in choosing a place to live.[24]

When explanatory variables are intercorrelated, interpretation of the analysis of variance becomes exceedingly difficult.[25] Only a part of the explained variance can be assigned uniquely to particular variables or vectors. "Interaction" terms that measure the joint contribution to explained variance of two or more variables or vectors become very important.[26] The analysis of variance procedure used in the *Report* treats these interaction terms in a very unusual manner. Explanatory variables are entered into the model in a predetermined order and only the increment to explained variance is assigned to each new variable or vector. Thus, the proportion of variance allocated to each variable or vector depends on the order in which they are entered. If two variables or vectors are highly intercorrelated, the first entered will be assigned both its unique contribution to explained variance and its jointly explained variance with all other variables or vectors (the interaction terms). Changing the order in which explanatory variables or vectors are entered changes the proportion of explained variance attributed to each. A clear understanding of this characteristic of the statistical technique is crucial to evaluating the findings presented in the *Report* and particularly its no-school-effect finding.

The authors consistently entered family background variables first and educational inputs (school factors) last. The result of this procedure, which is referred to in the *Report* as "controlling for background factors," is to assign both the unique and disputed portions of the explained variance to background factors. The decision to enter background factors first (control for) is so critical that we feel it is necessary to consider the rationale behind this procedure. The authors state:

> Since the student's background is clearly prior to, and independent of, any influence from school factors, these background factors can and should be held constant in studying the effects of school variables. Thus, the variation in achievement and attitudes to be explained by school variables is left after variation explained by family background differences is taken out.[27]

We strongly disagree with this statement if independence of school and background factors is interpreted to mean that the spatial distribution or location of families by socioeconomic group is unrelated to the distribution of school facilities by quality. There is abundant empirical evidence to the contrary and any model of residential location that includes the provision of public services also argues otherwise. Moreover, we fail to understand the relevance of the statement if independence is intended to indicate that present school factors cannot *cause* present family background factors.

Hypothesized causal patterns among explanatory variables (at least in the models used by the *Report*) have no bearing on how the variance explained by interaction terms should be allocated. The "prior to" terminology used by the authors appears to be a temporal justification for assigning all of the interaction terms to the family background vector.

The underlying issue is how the jointly explained variance should be partitioned among explanatory variables. Despite the authors' attempts to suggest otherwise, there is no correct way of partitioning it among background and school factors within the context of the study because the samples simply do not contain the information required. These questions can only be resolved by obtaining samples with less correlated input vectors. In these cross-section samples both prior and current influences of family background are intermingled. No temporal interpretation of either the unique or jointly explained variance can be defended. Part of the disputed joint variance may be due to prior background influences, but these issues cannot be resolved within this framework. This difficulty is one major reason several critics of the *Report* have emphasized the importance of obtaining longitudinal data.[28] These questions of prior effects cannot be resolved by fiat.

◆ *The Effect of Ordering—An Illustration*

To illustrate the critical importance of the *Report*'s treatment of interaction terms, we have performed a reanalysis of the data used in the *Report* that displays the effects of reordering the input vectors. However, we wish to make it clear that this is done for illustrative purposes only. For a number of reasons, which we discuss later, we do not believe that these results are a meaningful way of looking at the educational production process.

Our reanalysis relies upon the same samples used in the *Report*'s analysis as reported in the published correlation matrices.[29] We analyzed several different samples, but only a representative case will be presented here—Negro twelfth graders in the North. Findings for the other samples that we analyzed were less dramatic but qualitatively very similar. We attempted to analyze a "median" or "composite" model constructed so as to be independent of any particular one of the many model formulations found in the *Report*. The principal innovation of this model is the inclusion of both teacher and facility measures in the vector of school inputs. The *Report* handles our school vector in what we regard as a peculiar and incorrect manner. In brief, it analyzes the effects of teachers and facilities separately, i.e., it never considers the combined effect of both kinds of school variables in the same model. This practice leads to the use of some rather odd terminology that may account for much of the confusion surrounding the *Report*'s findings about the effect of schools on achievement. In general, the authors of the *Report* do not appear to consider teaching personnel as a school input (although roughly 70 percent of current educational expenditures are accounted for by teachers' salaries).[30] The individual input vectors generally contain more elements than those found in the *Report*.[31]

The amount of variance in individual verbal achievement explained by the vectors of inputs under different ordering schemes is shown in Table 1. The results of this procedure are striking. By adding the unique contributions found in the last column, it is easily seen that only slightly more than half (.0868) of the total explained variance (R^2) is uniquely accounted for by the separate input vectors. In every instance a considerable portion of the explained variance allotted to the first vector entered is actually jointly explained variance. (This is seen by comparing the first and last columns for each input vector.) In all of the samples we reanalyzed in this way, a substantial fraction of the variance assigned by the *Report* to background

TABLE 1

Proportion of Variance Explained By Educational Input Vectors Under
Different Orderings—Verbal Achievement of Negro 12th Graders in the North
$R^2 = .1409$

| | | Order of Entry | | | |
| | 1 | 2 *After S* | 2 *After P* | 2 *After F* | 3 |
Vector					
S (school)	.0808	—	.0222	.0560	.0312
P (student body)	.0703	.0117	—	.0420	.0072
F (family)	.0777	.0529	.0494	—	.0484

Components of Input Vectors

1. S = School inputs
   Teachers' SES level
   Teaching experience
   Quality of college attended by teachers
   Degree received
   Teacher preference for middle-class students
   Teacher verbal ability score
   Teacher salary
   Science lab facilities
   Extracurricular activities
   Comprehensiveness of curriculum
   Student transfers in and out
   Attendance
   School location
   Accelerated curriculum
   Promotion of slow learners
   Per-pupil instruction expenditure

2. P = Peer effects
   Proportion white
   Proportion own encyclopedia
   Average hours homework
   Proportion read over 16 books
   Foreign language courses
   Math courses
   Proportion teachers expect best
   Average time guidance

3. F = Family background
   Reading material in home
   Items in home
   Siblings
   Structural integrity of home
   Foreign language in home
   Preschool
   Parents' education
   Urbanism of background
   Homework

factors was actually jointly explained by variables incorporated into our "composite" school vector. Though we do not attach much significance to the finding, our school vector, when entered first, explained more variance than the family vector when entered first. In fact, by all the criteria used in the *Report*, our "composite" school vector appears to be "extremely strong." [32] If the *Report*'s analysis of variance criteria is used, school factors swamp student body factors.

We do not wish to belabor a fairly simple point. It is simply not possible to determine from the sample data how much of the jointly explained variance shown in Table 1 or contained in similar samples is attributable to each of the vectors. It is conceivable, as the *Report* asserts, that all of it is attributable to background (family and student body) factors. It is just as possible that all of it is attributable to school inputs.

◆ *A Further Lesson from Reanalysis*

Equality of Educational Opportunity provides several partial pictures of education and presents distinctly different models when it examines each aspect of the educational process; for example, the model for teacher effects (page 319) and the model for school facilities effects (pages 308–09). To the extent that the various aspects of the educational process are interrelated (good facilities are found with good teachers), this procedure is improper. Instead, the estimation should be based on a single statistical model including all of the factors believed to have an influence on achievement.

Therefore, within the framework of the *Report*'s analysis, we attempted to perform a more general analysis of variance that would incorporate all of the school and teacher inputs along with family and peer variables. We quickly discovered that there was insufficient independent variation in the school factors to allow inversion of the complete matrix; that is, the variables approached having an identity relationship among them.[33] Although we are uncertain about the cause, we hypothesize that it arises from the combination of two factors. First, the nature of much of the data is such that there are relatively few dimensions of significant variation in the measures concerning schools. This results from the insensitivity of the survey instruments and possibly from a further loss of information through index creation.

Second, there are very few degrees of freedom when school factors are considered. There are a maximum of 269 schools attended by Negro twelfth graders in the North sample (the basis of the reanalysis summarized in Table 1). Nearly half, 133, of these contained fewer than 10 percent nonwhites (a more inclusive category than Negro), and an undetermined number of these had no Negro students at all. Moreover, it seems likely that not all of the sampled schools having Negro twelfth graders are included.[34] School variables (school inputs and student-body characteristics) have the same value for all students in the same school; some variables (per-pupil expenditures, number of school days, school location) are the same for the entire school district. Thus, there are relatively few observations for these explanatory variables. Unfortunately, we were unable to ascertain exactly how many separate school systems and schools are included in the sample used in the *Report* because we did not have access to these samples. When these few independent observations are coupled with the insensitivity of most of the explanatory variables used in the analysis, the likelihood of singularity of the moments matrix becomes great.[35] The swiftness with which the matrix goes singular in our generalized analysis of variance procedure causes us to be suspicious about the overall information content in the sample—a sample from which sweeping conclusions about school effects are made.

♦ Initial Endowments—Some Speculation

The most obvious discrepancy between the conceptual and statistical models is the absence of any measure of initial endowments from the latter. The reasons for omitting initial endowment or, conversely, the conceptual desirability of including it are never discussed in the *Report*.[36] Yet most conceptual models of educational achievement for individual students would include such a concept. Its omission from the statistical model may be an important source of bias.[37] If innate ability is independent of the explanatory variables included in the model, it simply will increase the size of the error term—that is, reduce the amount of variance explained by the model. But, if within the sample experience it is correlated positively with any of the explanatory variables, its influences will be represented by these included explanatory variables. We do not claim to know how initial endowment of individual students is related to the explanatory variables included within the model. However, we would note that innate ability is least likely to be correlated with school inputs which, by construction, are measured only for schools and are most likely to be correlated with individual characteristics and family variables which, by construction, relate to individual students.

There is still another way to view the issue of initial endowments. In discounting the effect of schools, the authors of the *Report* point out that within-school variation in achievement is much larger than between-school variation.[38] They contend this finding demonstrates that school inputs cannot be very important and that most of the differences in achievement are due to family (background) influences that, unlike student body and school inputs, can vary within schools. In reaching this conclusion the authors ignore their own admonition that school inputs may vary within schools even if measured school inputs cannot.[39]

Recognition of initial endowments changes the conclusions that can be reached logically from the overall within- and between-schools analysis of variance. Family background, peer influences, and school inputs interact with the constraints imposed by innate abilities. Within the same environment (family, peers, school inputs), very large differences in achievement will occur as a result of differences in innate ability. The *Report*'s analyses provide considerable support for this view. None of the published models explain more than 30 percent of the total achievement variance. Our reanalysis of the verbal achievement of Negro twelfth graders in the North, which explains only 14 percent of the variance in achievement, is not atypical. If it is claimed that the *Report*'s models are a correct representation of the educational production process and that all variables included in the model are measured without error, the unexplained variance must be attributable to innate ability. This argument would imply that between 70 and 85 percent of the differences in achievement are due to differences in innate ability. We do not set forth this extreme view as a serious proposition. However, it does raise serious questions about the *Report*'s interpretation of the meaning of the within- and between-school differences in achievement. Furthermore, it emphasizes how little we actually know about the determinants of achievement.

◆ Relative Errors of Measurement

Measurement errors always exist in research, and these are a particularly serious problem in social science research. We already have discussed some errors of measurement resulting from the shortcomings of the *OE Survey*. This discussion deals with a more subtle, but possibly more important, kind of measurement error—systematic departures of the variables actually used in the statistical models from those included in the conceptual model. These departures are regarded as errors of measurement of the independent variables. These measurement errors are important because they systematically bias the results toward the no-school-effect finding.

There are two kinds of errors of measurement of the explanatory variables: (1) historical errors of measurement and (2) contemporaneous errors of measurement. Historical errors of measurement refer to how well or how badly the cross-section data account for the intertemporal influences on achievement. Contemporaneous errors refer to imperfect measurement of influences affecting the achievement of individual students at the time of the *OE Survey*. The unifying thread of the subsequent discussion is that both kinds of measurement errors are largest for school inputs and least for individual and family characteristics. Thus, there is systematic bias of the results due to relative measurement errors.

Historical Errors

The conceptual model views education as a process and depicts achievement as being affected by the entire past history of family, student body, and school inputs. However, the data used in the *Report* relate to a particular point in time and are not cumulative. Useful insights can be obtained from analysis of cross-section data of this kind, but the results must be interpreted very carefully and the relative errors of measurement must be carefully and explicitly considered.

Individual and family characteristics are more in the form of stocks and, hence, are subject to less intertemporal variations than are school inputs, which more closely approximate flows. Thus, use of cross-section measurements of contemporaneous school factors clearly tends to underestimate the total effect of educational inputs on achievement. Better measurement of background factors at a point in time elevates the apparent significance of these factors when compared to the more poorly measured school factors. This source of bias is aggravated by the *Report*'s emphasis on the analysis of the later grades. The authors justify this emphasis on the grounds that the family and student body variables are more reliable for older students (depending as they do on self-reporting). However, this argument cuts both ways. It is equally true that school input measurement errors (in terms of viewing educational inputs over time) increase through time. A student's socioeconomic status or, at least, the relevant educational aspects of his socioeconomic status could easily remain the same throughout his years of school; however, it is virtually impossible for him to spend twelve years in the same school.

If we wish to explain current achievement, we ideally should take into account all the school experiences of students. All high-school students have attended more than one school during their lifetime, and there can be significant differences in the characteristics and quality of the feeder schools serving a large comprehensive high school. A sizable proportion of elementary-school students also have attended more than one school. Thus, even a good cross-section description of school inputs may be a poor estimate of the average quality of the schools attended by the students. The choice of the 12th grade, where family and student body variables are most accurately measured and school inputs least accurately measured, accentuates the bias against school inputs.

Contemporaneous Errors

Achievement pertains to a particular student as do the family and individual characteristics. But school inputs are aggregates, or "macro" variables, pertaining to the *school* attended by the individual student. This may be considered a measurement error for school variables when individual or "micro" relationships are analyzed. For example, well-equipped science labs may be of little value to students enrolled in a business course and extracurricular activities may provide few benefits to a student from a low-income family who must work after school. Aggregation of school inputs reduces the apparent explanatory power of such school factors (as compared to the case where school factors are measured without error). This kind of measurement error, which could be called school-input heterogeneity, is most serious for comprehensive high schools. The curricula of many of these are so segregated that they might better be thought of as separate educational institutions, except when it comes to fielding athletic teams. Tracking, within both comprehensive high schools and elementary schools, is still another cause of school-input heterogeneity. In short, students attending the same school may receive markedly different educational inputs.

♦ Peer Effects and School Quality

Given the probable magnitude of historical and contemporaneous errors in the measurement of school inputs, it is essential to consider the relationship between the average characteristics of students attending a particular school (peer effects) and the quality of that school. As Table 1 indicates, the school input and student-body (peer effects) vectors are highly intercorrelated. The school vector entered first explains 8.08 percent of the total variance. Similarly, the student-body vector entered first explains 7.03 percent. However, the incremental contribution of the student-body vector (the school input vector entered first) is only 1.17 percent and the incremental contribution of the school input vector (the student-body vector entered first) is only 2.22 percent. Between them (entered before the family background vector) they explain 9.25 percent of total variance. Of this total 5.86 percent is jointly explained by the two vectors. Only 3.39 percent (2.22 plus 1.17) is uniquely assignable to each of the input vectors.

It is not hard to justify the view that families who are more educationally concerned or who can afford to spend more on the education of their children may systematically choose to send their children to the best schools. Thus, the best schools, in terms of both broadly and narrowly conceived educational inputs, probably will have disproportionate numbers of students with well-to-do and educationally concerned parents. Under these circumstances, student body characteristics will be highly correlated with real differences in school inputs. If school inputs are measured poorly, it is possible that these student body characteristics may be the best measure of the quality and quantity of school inputs. This assertion cannot be assessed in any adequate way using the *OE Survey* data, but if it is true, part of the effect that the *Report* attributes to peer or student-body effects may be indirect measurements of the effect of school inputs.

The above argument leads to a simple conclusion: some part of the disputed variance between student body and school inputs is undoubtedly attributable to school inputs. Indeed, some part of the uniquely explained variance in Table 1 attributed to family and student body variables actually may be attributable to school inputs. Finally, it should be noted that better specification of the school vector (inclusion of both facilities and teachers at the same time) as in Table 1 considerably reduces the explanatory power (unique contribution) of student-body factors that are deemed "important" in the *Report*.

◆ Twelfth Grade?

The *Report*'s emphasis on later grades affects its analysis through more than time-related errors of measurement. First, it is likely that the independent effects of schools are strongest and most easily identified in the earlier years of schooling. Second, modeling an elementary school is a more tractable problem than modeling a comprehensive junior high or high school. It would be extremely difficult to describe exhaustively the school inputs at the high-school level, even if ideal measures of school inputs relevant to each individual student were available. No one could describe the *OE Survey* data on school inputs as ideal. These problems compound the bias against school factors.

The *Report*'s authors were obviously most interested in the 12th grade; however, they claim to have tested relationships in other grades and found that school factors had little effect on the result. At one point they conclude:

> At grades 3 and 1, little variance is accounted for either by school characteristics or student body characteristics. This result, in which no variables account for much of the variance in achievement, is true throughout the analysis for grades 3 and 1, despite the large school-to-school variations shown in Tables 3.22.1 and 3.22.2.[40]

What the authors fail to point out in this discussion (except in a footnote to Table 3.22.1) is that almost no school or student-body variables are analyzed for the earlier grades. Of the eleven school characteristics included for the 9th and 12th grades, only per-pupil expenditure (which pertains to the entire school district and is strongly affected by whether the district is simply an elementary-school district or a unified one), volumes per student in the library, school enrollment, and location (city, suburb, town, county) are included in the 6th, 3rd, and 1st grade analysis. Of the six student-body characteristics, only the proportion whose families own encyclopedias, an index of student transfers, attendance rates, and teachers' perception of student body-quality were included. We were not too surprised with the result when we discovered the limited number and scope of variables used in the analysis for earlier grades.

The selective nature of the school population (dropouts) is another difficulty associated with the *Report*'s emphasis on the 12th grade. In 1960 only 82 percent of whites aged sixteen and seventeen and 73 percent of Negroes in the same age group were enrolled in schools.[41] These figures indicate a systematic difference in nonenrollment by race. Moreover, nonenrollment almost certainly is correlated with factors such as ability, achievement, socioeconomic characteristics, and residence. Little is gained and many problems are introduced by concentrating on grades where this problem is most severe.

♦ Some New Evidence

Still another kind of empirical evidence is used in the *Report* to support its no-school-effect finding. The authors contend that, if schools did have an effect, the relative variance between schools would increase over time. Since the between-school variance remains fairly constant among grades, they conclude that schools must have little effect on student achievement. (Note that direct comparisons are only valid for grades one, three, and six where school size is roughly constant.) [42] This interpretation of the finding of approximately constant between-school variance over the years of schooling assumes the distribution of output among schools is stationary. That is, it implicitly assumes that schools with low mean achievement in the 1st grade continue to have low mean achievement in later grades; and vice versa for schools with high mean achievement. Information obtained from subsequent analysis of the *OE Survey* data is relevant to this conclusion. [43]

Analysis of mean achievement scores for a sample of schools in the Northeast and the Great Lakes region indicated that mean 1st-grade and mean 6th-grade verbal test scores were not highly correlated. For 100 schools that contained more than four Negroes, the simple correlation of the mean Negro 1st-grade verbal score with the mean Negro 6th-grade verbal score was .29. For 198 schools with over four white sixth graders, the correlation for whites was .36. This hardly supports the view that the development path is unaffected by school inputs when one considers that neighborhood schools tend to insure similarity of social and economic characteristics of first and sixth graders.

One possible explanation for this phenomenon is that the 1st-grade test is not a good test. This, among other things, would imply that the intergrade comparisons of variance are not meaningful. An alternative explanation is that schools do have an effect on students, and, while the total variance tends to be similar, the position of a given school within the distribution is altered by the inputs of the school to individual students' education. Again, the intergrade comparisons of total variance are not meaningful. Conclusions requiring time series data that are made from cross-section data are unwarranted. The *Report*'s inferences based on intergrade comparison of between-school variance are questionable.

♦ Model Specification—The Implications of Linearity

There are a number of issues relating to the model's overall specification and, in particular, to the choice of functional form. The linear, additive specification used by the authors has serious limitations. First, there is a dimensionality problem. For example, the effects of guidance counselors surely must be related to the number of students. Yet the *Report* introduces these variables in their original form. In an additive model these dimensionality problems are not accounted for by the addition of school size. Second, there are possibilities of scale problems in the economist's sense. In particular, it has been argued that scale economies are likely to exist in high schools.[44] If important economies of scale do exist, the simple linear form is incorrect. Third, it does not allow for the interaction between inputs. The effect of a given input is the same whether or not any other inputs are absent or are found in such abundance as to be superfluous. Fourth, the linear form implies that the marginal effect of a given input is the same regardless of the level of usage. Adding one guidance counselor has the same impact on student achievement when the change is from 0 to 1 as when it is from 500 to 501. Certainly few people would hold to this implicit assumption of a constant marginal product of inputs.

The principal justification (rationalization) of the linear form is that many mathematical functions look linear over a small range and all of the *Report*'s findings must be interpreted within the rather limited range of the explanatory variables. Moreover, since statistical estimation techniques are most highly developed for linear models, a linear function is generally chosen in the absence of strong a priori views favoring alternative specifications. Nonetheless, it is important to understand fully the strong implications of the functional form selected by the *Report*'s authors and its possible limitations.

♦ Analysis of Variance and Public Policy

There is one final consideration, the appropriateness of analysis of variance for studying the range of policy questions undertaken. For policy purposes, it is desirable to identify and evaluate the impact of potential policy instruments on achievement. Evaluation of alternative policies necessarily involves consideration of both the effects on output of different changes in the inputs to the production process and the costs of these changes. An analysis of variance provides almost no insight into these questions. It does not even give the direction, let alone the magnitude, of the effect that can be expected from a change in inputs. What are needed for policy purposes are estimates of the parameters of the statistical model, i.e., the a_i's in Equation 2. There is a considerable difference between the concepts and methods employed in partitioning the variance among sets of variables and those employed in estimating slope coefficients or elasticities for individual variables.[45] The latter estimates are useful in identifying potential policy, the former are of considerably less value to the policy-maker.

The closest the *Report* comes to identifying policy instruments are its estimates of the "unique" contribution of individual variables to explained variance. This procedure amounts to carrying out the specialized analysis of variance for individual variables, rather than for vectors. (The *Report* defines unique contribution when the given variable is the last one added to the regression equation.) As before, the outcome of this procedure is dependent upon the amount of intercorrelation present in the system. If high intercorrelations exist, the concept of "unique contribution" is not of much help in identifying policy instruments.[46] Instead, such an analysis is largely an indication of which variables are most orthogonal (are least highly correlated with other explanatory variables). By contrast, multiple regression analysis focuses on estimates of the independent effects of different explanatory variables. Multicollinearity tends to reduce the precision of the parameter estimates (increase the standard errors), but least squares techniques prove quite robust even when the explanatory variables are intercorrelated. The regression coefficients have remained unbiased in the presence of intercorrelations among input vectors or individual variables.[47] However, when there is a significant degree of multicollinearity present, there is no simple relationship between the regression coefficient and the amount of variance explained by the variable. Even if all explanatory variables were truly independent (not correlated with any other explanatory variable), the analysis of variance format would not be the most useful mode of analysis. The proportion of explained variance does not identify policy instruments and gives little indication of the extent of policy leverage provided by different variables. Parameter estimates are much more useful in this respect. The really interesting questions involve the effects of changes in inputs to the educational process. Explained variance, whether an orthogonal component or not, is simply not a very interesting concept either to the policy-maker or the statistician.

SUMMARY AND CONCLUSIONS.   *Equality of Educational Opportunity* has not served us well as a policy document. Distracted by the allure of basic research into the educational production process, the Office of Education failed to provide an authoritative response to the Congressional request for data on educational opportunities. The extent to which minority groups are systematically discriminated against in the provision of educational inputs is still unknown. This is a serious matter since the correction of input inequalities is a logical and necessary first step in insuring equality of opportunity for minorities.

The *Report*'s failure to provide a definitive answer to the Congressional question concerning inequality in the provision of educational inputs may be its most fundamental weakness as a policy document. Yet our evaluation of the *Report* is concerned primarily with serious flaws in its basic research into the educational production process. The reason for this is that the "findings" of the *Report*'s basic research have been widely acclaimed as its principal policy contribution. We contend that the *Report*'s analysis does not provide reasonable tests of the hypotheses attributed to it. In fact, the "findings" could have been the result of the analytic methods combined with systematic errors of measurement rather than any underlying behavioral relationship.

The large and systematic differences between the *Report*'s implied conceptual model and its actual statistical models of the educational process are its most damaging analytic shortcomings. Thus, while serious interpretative problems are raised by the specialized analysis of variance procedure used in the *Report*, its principal failing is found in its inadequate statistical models of the educational process. This inadequacy arises in large part from using poor or incomplete data that bias the empirical results toward overstating the effect of family background and student-body inputs and understating the effect of school inputs.

Although education must be viewed as a cumulative process, the *OE Survey* data contain no historical information. This weighs most heavily on school factors because contemporaneous school data are less adequate surrogates of historical influences than are contemporaneous family background measures. The emphasis on later grades exaggerates the bias toward a no-school-effect finding.

Errors also exist in the measurements of contemporaneous inputs to the production process and these are greatest for school inputs. The most critical error is the failure to collect and use data on school inputs for individuals. This omission is especially serious in later grades where the students can choose different curricula and are more completely separated. Family inputs, which are measured for the individual, necessarily have less error in a model of individual achievement and, consequently, their apparent explanatory power is raised in comparison to the more poorly measured school factors.

The neglect of innate ability in the statistical model may also bias the estimated influence of family factors upward. If innate ability is partially hereditary and social mobility exists through ability, this excluded input to the production process will be correlated with family measures, and the statistical results will be biased toward showing stronger family effects than actually exist. In any event, the *Report*'s use of differences in within- and between-school variance in achievement as prima facie evidence for the unimportance of schools in determining achievement is clearly unreasonable when the potential role of initial endowment is recognized.

In this paper we have said very little about what educational production functions actually look like. Instead our discussion is limited to a demonstration that the *Report* does not answer this question. More attention is given this question in an empirical analysis of the education process by one of the authors.[48] This analysis based on *OE Survey* data is limited by many of the data problems which hampered the *Report*'s authors. Even so, the empirical findings of that study indicate that alternative, and we contend more appropriate, models and methodology lead to important differences in empirical results. In particular, these alternative models tend to confirm the view advanced in this paper that the *Report*'s "no school effect" is due in considerable degree to its method of analysis.

Much of the preceding discussion is essentially negative. It recommends what policy-makers should not do: they should not rely very heavily on *Equality of Educational Opportunity* and in particular on its analysis of the relationship between inputs and outputs in designing educational policy. As a pioneering piece of social science research, the *Report* deserves considerable praise. However, as a policy document, it must be evaluated differently. In this guise it is potentially dangerous and destructive.

If the *Report*'s analysis of the educational process cannot be believed, what is the policy-maker to do? The one incontrovertible finding from the *OE Survey* is that the median educational attainment of blacks is considerably below that of whites. The average 12th-grade Negro in the North (who is still in school) is achieving at the 9th-grade level of his white counterpart.[49] This divergence increases when other regions are considered, reaching an apogee in the rural South where the achievement of 12th-grade Negroes lags five years behind that of Northern white twelfth graders. The existence of such sizable differentials is amply demonstrated by the *Report;* the best ways to eliminate the differentials are not.

Since we do not believe adequate knowledge for program design exists, we will not even speculate on the best mix of educational resources or programs. The authors of the *Report* have performed a valuable contribution in again reminding educational policy-makers that the production of educational output does not stop at the school door. An effective program for increasing the educational achievement of culturally deprived children, be they white or black, would almost certainly require a mix of school and nonschool programs. If publication of the *Report* has made educational policy-makers think about education in this broader framework, it will have provided an invaluable service. However, if these policy-makers conclude the *Report* provides an adequate basis for choosing among alternative programs and mixes of expenditures, it will have done a grave disservice. It simply does not provide satisfactory answers of the kind widely ascribed to it.

If, as we contend, the information does not presently exist for designing optimal or even efficient educational programs, what can be done? An admission of ignorance should not be interpreted as a plea for inaction.

Nothing would be more disastrous. The problems of low educational achievement among the culturally deprived, and particularly blacks, documented by the *Report* and other studies, will not disappear simply because the knowledge needed to design "efficient" programs is unavailable. The magnitude of these problems is so great as to demand immediate and large-scale action, even if many efforts will prove to be "inefficient."

What is demanded by a situation such as this is a process of radical experimentation, evaluation, and research. Additional large-scale research programs, similar in scope to that reported in *Equality of Educational Opportunity*, would be of considerable value in identifying promising areas for program development, experimentation, and evaluation. This is particularly true insofar as subsequent studies are able to overcome some of the most serious deficiencies of the *OE Survey*. The most prominent of these are the primitive measurements of school inputs and lack of longitudinal data.

It is beyond the scope of this paper to suggest the precise nature of the experimental activity. Indeed, it is beyond our resources and competence. However, we can identify several desirable characteristics for such a program. It is essential that the experimentation be truly radical: that is, involve a wide variety of educational practices and explore ranges of input variation in both novel and traditional educational techniques presently not found in the public schools. As is noted in the preceding discussion, the range of educational practice examined by the authors of the *Report* is exceedingly limited. This is not because the authors wanted it this way, but rather because that is the way it is. For example, the differences in student-teacher ratios examined by the *Report* were very small. Moreover, larger classes more often characterized situations where the benefits of small classes would seem greatest. We doubt that the analysis included any situations where culturally deprived students had been saturated with educational inputs over their educational lifetimes. Yet without such experience the effects of providing much higher levels of educational expenditures cannot be evaluated. It seems likely that very small changes in the level of educational inputs may have little effect, but that there may be a threshold where increased resources become effective. Similarly, the experimental program should be large-scale. Many different kinds and combinations of programs should be tried. Finally, experimental programs must last long enough to operate on the entire process of education. Massive inputs of educational resources in junior high or high school may be quite ineffective if the history has been one of neglect.

Experimentation in nonschool programs designed to increase educational achievement may be more difficult to carry out. Still, a program of large-scale experimentation such as we envisage ideally should attempt to include such programs. At minimum, the school should be construed very widely and every effort should be made to experiment with programs that are intended to extend their influence into the community. These would include preschool activities, day care, recreational and educational summer programs, after-school adult education activities, and programs designed to involve the parents to the greatest possible extent.

Evaluation is the final and most critical aspect of any well-designed program of experimentation. Without adequate evaluation, it will not be possible to determine what mix of experimental programs worked and why. Education is a highly complex process and adequate evaluation would be both expensive and difficult to design and carry out. Still, the potential benefits from high-quality evaluation, through increasing the efficiency of ongoing programs, are very great.

Notes

1. The authors would like to acknowledge the large number of constructive criticisms and suggestions on both the content and style of earlier drafts of this paper by persons too numerous to mention here. A special note of thanks is due Joseph J. Persky, John Jackson, Thomas F. Pettigrew, David Cohen, Leonard Rapping, Molly Mayo, and Frederick Mosteller, all of whom made particularly helpful suggestions. Finally we would like to express our appreciation to James S. Coleman, who was kind enough to bring to our attention several errors of interpretation of the *Report*'s analyses and findings contained in an earlier draft. Of course, any errors that remain are the sole responsibility of the authors.

2. James S. Coleman, Ernest Q. Campbell, Carol J. Hobson, James McPartland, Alexander M. Mood, Frederic D. Weinfield, and Robert L. York, *Equality of Educational Opportunity.* Washington, D.C.: U.S. Government Printing Office, 1966. This is subsequently referred to as the *Report.*

3. While there might be some doubt among those who have digested the *Report*'s tables and analysis as to whether the no-school-effect conclusion is the principal finding, it is clear that the majority of commentators on the *Report* have reached this conclusion. Moreover, the summary chapter, the major source of discussions about the *Report*, states:

> The first finding is that schools are remarkably similar in the way they relate to the achievement of their pupils when socioeconomic background of the students is taken into account. It is known that socioeconomic factors bear a strong relation to academic achievement. When these factors are statistically controlled, however, it appears that differences between schools account for only a small fraction of differences in pupil achievement. [*Report*, p. 21.]

This view of the *Report*'s findings has found its way into the professional journals as evidenced by the Editors of the *Harvard Educational Review* who state:

> . . . Coleman's analysis of the survey data suggests that the traditional remedies proposed by educators—increased expenditures, reduced class size, improved facilities, ability tracking—will make little dent, for these factors evidently exercise almost no independent effect on pupil achievement when family background variables are controlled. [*Harvard Educational Review*, Vol. 38, No. 1, Winter 1968, p. 85.]

The final demonstration of the pervasiveness of the no-school-effect finding is the fact that it was promulgated at Senate hearings by Daniel P. Moynihan. He noted that Dr. Coleman

> . . . found that the quality of schools could not explain differences in achievement, excepting of a relatively low order. For example, for Negro students in

the urban North, expenditures per pupil on instruction could only account for two-hundredths of 1 percent in the variation of achievement of ninth grade students. This is obviously nothing significant. [U.S. Senate, *Federal Role in Urban Affairs: Hearings before the Subcommittee on Executive Reorganization of the Committee on Government Operations*, Part 13, December 13, 1966, p. 2692.]

4. Although it is difficult to categorize and document the *Report's* findings, two additional views stand out. First, the *Report* is used to support the contention that schools attended by whites and minority students are not very different. This position is typified by Daniel P. Moynihan's statement that "despite our expectations, by and large the quality of school facilities available to minority children in this country are not significantly different from those available to the majority." [*Hearings before the Subcommittee on Executive Reorganization of the Committee on Executive Reorganization of the Committee on Government Operations*, 89th Congress, Second Session, December 30, 1966. Appendix to Part I, p. 2692.] This finding, we believe, is more a product of data problems (discussed in Section I, below) than of the actual distribution of facilities.

Second, close to the no-school-effect finding in terms of frequency of citation is the integration finding, i.e., integration is good because Negroes learn more in integrated schools. An example of this interpretation of the *Report* is found in Irwin Katz's letter to *Science*, May 12, 1967, p. 732. Many of the methodological difficulties discussed in this paper which seriously undermine the *Report's* no-school-effect finding apply with equal force to the integration finding. A more detailed discussion of the integration finding, particularly as it relates to the subsequent report by the U.S. Commission on Civil Rights, *Racial Isolation in the Public Schools*, Vol. 1 (Washington, D.C.: U.S. Government Printing Office, 1967), may be found in Eric A. Hanushek, "The Education of Negroes and Whites," unpublished Ph.D. dissertation, Department of Economics, Massachusetts Institute of Technology, August, 1968.

5. Samuel Bowles and Henry Levin raise many similar issues in "The Determinants of Scholastic Achievement—An Appraisal of Some Recent Evidence." *Journal of Human Resources*, Vol. III, No. 1, Winter 1968.

6. James S. Coleman reaches the same conclusion when explaining the broader construction of the mandate developed by the Office of Education. In a recent article he states:

> The Congressional intent in this section is somewhat unclear. But if, as is probable, the survey was initially intended as a means of finding areas of continued intentional discrimination, the intent later becomes less punitive-oriented and more future-oriented; i.e. to provide a basis for public policy, at the local, state, and national levels, which might overcome inequalities of educational opportunity.

James S. Coleman, "Equal Schools or Equal Students?" *The Public Interest*, No. 4, Summer 1966, p. 70.

7. James Coleman, writing eloquently on the concept of educational opportunity, identifies five kinds of inequality. These include the inequality inherent in racial segregation and that relating to a variety of output measures. James Coleman, "The Concept of Equality of Educational Opportunity." *Harvard Educational Review*, Vol. 38, No. 1, Winter 1968.

8. The expenditure measure has the advantage of providing a weighting scheme for real resources, i.e., resources are weighted by their costs. This allows an easy comparison of input quantities among schools. One of the foremost problems with this technique, however, is just this weighting scheme because, if large price differentials exist, direct comparisons are of limited value. Indeed, large input price differences are known to exist among regions, e.g., by teacher salary differences. This problem can be alleviated by either restricting comparisons to a uniform price area, such as a city, or constructing price indices. On the other hand, while real input measures avoid the problem of differences in prices, there is no

natural set of weights which can be used to create a single real resource measure. Thus, comparisons of differences in real inputs ideally require far more knowledge about the effect of these inputs on output than now exists and considerable judgment in interpreting the relative importance of various factors. (The ideal weighting scheme would account for the value of an input in producing education. If schools are operated efficiently, the expenditures on various inputs will provide such a weighting scheme.)

9. There are several ways in which these data on outputs could be obtained. First, one could sample the schools attended by various minority groups and obtain average achievement levels by schools. Alternatively, one could break away from the reliance on schools as the sampling unit and sample the population, as in the *Current Population Survey* of the Census Bureau. Finally, since many school systems conduct extensive testing programs, one could collect standardized achievement test scores already available in the schools. This would provide considerable information at a small marginal cost, especially if undertaken in conjunction with a survey of inputs. The two most populous states (California and New York) currently conduct statewide testing programs. In fact, on p. 105, the *Report* states that only five percent of the Negro and one percent of the white elementary students in the United States attend schools that do not give standardized achievement tests. Over ninety percent are tested two or more times. Similarly, less than five percent of the secondary students are not tested.

10. Chapter 2 of the *Report* contains many tables describing the schools attended by whites and the several minority groups considered by the *OE Survey*. These data have been interpreted widely as indicating the absence of all but very small differences in the quality of schools attended by whites and Negroes, at least within the same region. However, the combination of considerable fragmentary evidence to the contrary and our serious misgivings about the representativeness of the *OE Survey* and the quality of the data obtained on school inputs causes us to question this "finding." A number of expenditure studies have documented very large suburban-central city differences in per-pupil expenditures. Increasingly, central city-suburban is a euphemism for black-white. For evidence on these expenditure differences see: Dick Netzer, *Economics of the Property Tax* (Washington, D.C.: The Brookings Institution, 1966), Chapter 5; and U.S. Commission on Civil Rights, *Racial Isolation in the Public Schools* (Washington, D.C.: U.S. Government Printing Office, 1967), pp. 25–31. Several studies have produced evidence of significant expenditure inequalities by racial groups within the same school system: Martin T. Katzman, "Distribution and Production in a Big City Elementary School System," unpublished Ph.D. dissertation, Yale University, 1967; The Education Committee, Coordinating Council of Community Organizations, *Handbook of Chicago School Segregation, 1963* (Chicago: The Committee, August, 1963); Patricia Cayo Sexton, "City Schools," *The Annals of the American Academy of Political and Social Science*, 352 (March, 1964), pp. 95–106; California, Governor's Commission on the Los Angeles Riots, *Violence in the City—An End or a Beginning?* (Los Angeles, California, December 2, 1965), pp. 49–61.

11. The Southern states are: Alabama, Arizona, Arkansas, Florida, Georgia, Kentucky, Louisiana, Mississippi, New Mexico, North Carolina, Oklahoma, South Carolina, Tennessee, Texas, Virginia, and West Virginia.

12. Hanushek, "The Education of Negroes and Whites."

13. The *Report* handled internal nonresponses in two ways. If the question was to be used in an index, the sample mean was assumed to be the correct answer. If the question was to be used as a separate variable, the covariance matrix for the observations was calculated on the basis of complete observations, and individual elements were weighted in such a manner as to arrive at population figures. Cf. *The Report*, p. 572. Both corrections yield considerable errors in the face of systematic nonresponse.

14. Analysis and editing of the *OE Survey* data provide many obvious cases where teachers, principals, and superintendents coded their answers to the left rather than the right as required of such numerical responses (left justification instead of

right justification). Machine processing of these incorrectly coded answers creates a decimal point error that can lead, if not corrected, to sizable errors in any statistical analysis. The frequency of such decimal errors on student and/or teacher population questions answered by the principals in the above 300 school sample was over 10 percent. Decimal errors of this kind often can be corrected by cross-checking with other size indicators.

15. A preliminary check of the data made by comparing question responses in schools with two principals does provide a simple reliability test for different variables. As one would expect, faulty response, though not as serious on the multiple-choice answers, is an ever-present problem. The *Report* mentions one very small reliability test that the Educational Testing Service carried out. However, this seems quite inadequate.

16. For example, in terms of problems with nonschool data, each student completed a multiple-choice question concerning father's occupation that included one large category mixing traditionally blue- and white-collar occupations.

17. The basic notion of a model pertains to a simplification of reality that allows us to analyze particular aspects of a process—in this case the production of education. The conceptual model represents the theoretical backdrop for the empirical section which is the statistical testing of the hypothesized relationship. Though more will be said about the statistical aspects of the model, proper testing of a model calls for specification of all of the major influences on the dependent variable (achievement). The fact, however, that a model is a simplification of actual conditions implies that we will not be able to explain or predict perfectly the level of achievement. Statistical theory provides us with criteria for selecting models and judging their merits.

18. Proposals of the latter kind are suggested by James Coleman in an article published in the *Public Interest*. There he argues in favor of replacing the family environment of the disadvantaged child as much as possible "with an educational environment—by starting school at an earlier age, and by having a school which begins very early in the day and ends very late." Coleman, "Equal Schools or Equal Students?" p. 74.

19. The *Report* comes close to describing a very similar conceptual model on page 295. However, since the authors never refer to it in subsequent sections, it is difficult to believe that they actually attach much meaning to it.

20. The true (population) values of the a_j's are hypothesized to be the same for every individual in the population considered.

21. Variance is the average squared deviation of individual observations from the sample mean, i.e., variance $(A) = \Sigma[(A_i - A)^2]/N$ where A is the sample average of the N observations of A_i. Therefore, it is the standard deviation squared and, in a loose way, it measures the dispersion of individuals from the mean performance level.

22. Least squares regression technique is a method of estimating the parameters, a_j, of Equation 2. The basic criterion in estimation is the minimization of the sum of $e_j{}^2$. If certain conditions about properties of the e_j hold (e.g., that the e_j's are uncorrelated with the X_{ij}'s), the technique of least squares is shown to possess some desirable attributes pertaining to the estimates of the a_j's. Additionally, it is possible to relate the size of the residuals and the variance of the dependent variable in a manner that gives some feel for "how good" the model is. This measure, R^2, or the squared multiple correlation coefficient, must assume values between zero (no explained variance) and one (all of the variance explained).

23. Explanatory variables frequently are referred to as independent variables. It is important to understand that in social science research these so-called independent variables are seldom truly independent in the statistical sense of being uncorrelated with one another.

24. Relationships between the average income or social class of the school and school inputs or per-student expenditures have been found by Patricia C. Sexton, *Education and Income* (New York: Viking Press, 1961), and Martin T. Katzman, "Distribution and Production in a Big City Elementary School System."

25. The general statistical term for correlations among explanatory variables is multi-

collinearity. In the following discussions we are concerned with a specific type of multicollinearity, i.e., intercorrelations among the input vectors of Equation 1 rather than intercorrelations among the specific variables representing each vector.

26. The explained variance can be decomposed into a part that is uniquely explained by individual vectors or variables and one that is jointly explained by more than one vector or variable. This jointly explained component, which can also be decomposed into specific combinations of inputs, is referred to subsequently as an interaction term.

27. The *Report*, p. 330.

28. For example, see Bowles and Levin, "The Determinants of Scholastic Achievement," or Christopher Jencks, "Education: The Racial Gap," *The New Republic* (October 1, 1966), p. 21.

29. Supplemental Appendix to the *Survey on Equality of Educational Opportunity*. Washington, D.C.: U.S. Government Printing Office, 1966.

30. For example, James Coleman in his article published in the *Public Interest* summarizes the findings of the study as follows:

> Even the school-to-school variation in achievement, though relatively small, is itself almost wholly due to the social environment provided by the school, the educational backgrounds and aspirations of other students in the school, and the educational backgrounds and attainments of the teachers in the school. *Per pupil expenditure, books in the library, and a host of other facilities and curricular measures show virtually no relation to achievement if the "social" environment—the educational backgrounds of other students and teachers—is held constant.* [(Coleman's emphasis) Coleman, "Equal Schools or Equal Students?" p. 73.]

31. Our procedure was to include the maximum number of explanatory variables in each vector. Because of the multicollinearity among explanatory variables of each vector and the limited information contained in the sample generally, substantially fewer than all independent variables could be included.

32. This finding does not appear in the *Report* because of the separate analysis of facilities and teachers.

33. Our analysis considered white and Negro students in the North for grades six and twelve.

34. The authors did not use all of the survey data in their analysis of variance procedure. Rather, they randomly sampled 1,000 students from each of five strata included in the North sample (nonmetropolitan North, nonmetropolitan West, metropolitan Northeast, metropolitan Midwest, and metropolitan West). The probability of a school's being selected was dependent on its 12th-grade Negro enrollment; consequently the North sample was weighted heavily toward schools with predominantly Negro enrollment. It is difficult to understand why these sampling methods were used since presently available computers are unawed by large sample sizes. Whatever the reasons for the internal sampling, the procedure amplifies our earlier observations about the desirability of choosing a single research strategy and concentrating efforts on collecting the information and tailoring the analysis to answer a particular set of questions.

35. The least squares regression technique requires inverting the moments matrix of the data. (This is close to the simple correlation matrix of the variables.) Inversion is impossible if a linear identity exists among the rows or columns of the matrix. However, as a practical matter, the procedure is stopped at some point before perfect linear dependency due to the round errors in computation.

36. This is a slight overstatement. The Technical Appendix to Section 3.2 states, "they [the models] do not include differences in native endowments, *which of course must also be considered part of family background, though* an unmeasured part [Our emphasis]." We would question this assertion about the necessary link between native endowment and family background, as they certainly will not be perfectly correlated. However, this is not a serious issue since there is little evidence that the authors of the body of the *Report* acknowledge the possibility of

differences in innate abilities. A plausible hypothesis would be that the sections were written independently by different authors.

37. Bias is used throughout in the formal statistical sense (expected value of estimated coefficient $\hat{a}_i \pm$ true a_i). However, this generally implies erroneous results in the analysis of variance format used in the *Report*.

38. Cf. the *Report*, page 296, and especially Table 3.22.1.

39. The *Report*, page 295. The extreme case of within-school variance that could result from differences in school factors would be found in the comprehensive high school. However, the differences can also exist in elementary schools where there is more than one class for a given grade.

40. The *Report*, p. 304.

41. The *Report*, p. 447.

42. See The *Report*, p. 296.

43. Hanushek, "The Education of Negroes and Whites."

44. Economies of scale exist when a proportional increase in all inputs yields a more than proportional increase in output. For evidence on the existence of scale economies see: John Riew, "Economies of Scale in High School Operation," *The Review of Economics and Statistics* (August, 1966), pp. 280–7.

45. The elasticity of an independent variable is the percentage increase in the dependent variable (achievement) that can be expected from a one-percent increase in the given independent variable. The elasticity of A with respect to X is $(dA/A)/(dX/X)$. In the linear model such as Equation 2, dA/dX equals the regression coefficient for X.

46. This is especially true if, as commented on before, many different models are used to analyze different but related aspects of the educational process.

47. Note that we consider the regression coefficient, a_j, throughout the discussion. This differs from the beta or standardized regression coefficient often used by sociologists: beta equals the regression coefficient times the ratio of standard deviations of the independent and dependent variables. When the explanatory variables are orthogonal, the beta coefficient is directly related to explained variance. With multicollinearity, there is no direct relationship.

48. Hanushek, "The Education of Negroes and Whites." This analysis of the *OE Survey* data relied upon a sample of metropolitan elementary schools in the Northeast and Great Lakes regions. In order to minimize the biases due to incomplete data, the school, rather than the individual, was used as the basic observational unit. Thus, the output of the educational process is defined as the mean achievement level (of sixth graders) within a school and the inputs are aggregate student body and school characteristics. Separate functions were estimated for white sixth graders and for black sixth graders. For both blacks and whites, differences in school quality as measured by average teacher verbal score, average teacher experience, and percent of students with a nonwhite teacher during the previous year exhibit a significant influence on educational attainment.

49. The *Report*, Table 3.121.1.

4

The Evaluation of *Equality of Educational Opportunity*

JAMES S. COLEMAN

In July of 1966, the U.S. Office of Education issued a report titled "Equality of Educational Opportunity," to fulfill a provision of the Civil Rights Act of 1964 which read as follows:

> The Commissioner shall conduct a survey and make a report to the President and the Congress, within two years of the enactment of this title, concerning the lack of availability of equal educational opportunities for individuals by reason of race, color, religion, or national origin in public educational institutions at all levels in the United States, its territories and possessions, and the District of Columbia.

This request was one of the first specific requests made by Congress for social research that might provide a basis for policy. It is a kind of governmental interest in information about the functioning of society that compares to its interest that began some years ago in information about the functioning of the economy. As such, it is likely to increase as national policy becomes increasingly concerned with social institutions, an increase that is already foreshadowed by such developments as the publication of *Toward a social report* in 1970 by the Department of Health, Education, and Welfare.

As a consequence, it becomes important to examine retrospectively this attempt to address social research to social policy, as a way of learning, the problems and pitfalls of such activity, and of learning how best to carry it out. Such activity has not been the central focus of applied social research, and, as a consequence, it raises new problems of design and analysis.

I propose, then, to make such a retrospective examination. To do so as one of the authors of the report carries both advantages and disadvantages. The principal advantages are knowledge of the variety of problems that arose in the study that are not apparent in the final report, and the necessity of having given thought to various alternative designs that were not in fact used. The principal disadvantage lies in the necessity of an author to justify the work as it finally appeared. The disadvantage in this case may be reduced by the fact that I will use as a context for my examination a critical paper reviewing the report, "On the Value of *Equality of Educational Opportunity* as a Guide to Public Policy," by John F. Kain of Harvard University and Eric A. Hanushek of the Air Force Academy, published in the present volume. This is one of three papers written by economists critical of the Report, and includes many of the criticisms made by the others.* The paper by Kain and Hanushek, both economists, provides not only a check to the self-justification of an author but also the different perspective provided by a discipline that has been traditionally more closely linked to policy than has sociology, and one that has special perspectives of its own.

♦ Defining the Problem

The first question that arises in such a study as that requested by the Civil Rights Act in Section 402 is to determine precisely what the request means, and how it can be best fulfilled. In this case, the difficulty was especially great because the very concept of "equality of educational opportunity" is one that is presently undergoing change, and various members of government and of society have different conceptions of what such equality consists of. There are many such conceptions and I will not go into them here, except to say that this was regarded, as it should have been, as the major problem in the design of the survey, and a great deal of attention was paid to it. A portion of an internal memorandum discussing the varieties of concepts of "equality of educational opportunity" has recently been published elsewhere, and I will not repeat them here.† It is sufficient to say that five were discussed: first, inequality defined by degree of racial segregation; second, inequality of resource inputs from the school system; third, inequality in "intangible" resources such as teacher morale; fourth, inequality of inputs as weighted according to their effectiveness for achievement; and fifth, inequality of output as prima facie evidence of inequality of opportunity.

---

* The other papers are Samuel Bowles and Henry Levin, "The Determinants of Scholastic Achievement—An Appraisal of Some Recent Evidence," *Journal of Human Resources*, Winter 1968 and Glen G. Cain and Harold W. Watts, "Problems in Making Policy Inferences from the Coleman Report," *American Sociological Review*, V. 35, 1970, pp. 228–42.

† James S. Coleman, "The Concept of Equality of Educational Opportunity," *Harvard Educational Review*, *38*, Winter 1968, pp. 7–22.

The study as designed and executed gave evidence relevant to all five of these definitions of educational opportunity. Kain and Hanushek argue that the most serious mistake of the study was here, and that the study should have carried out a careful study of inputs, as the necessary minimum, before it could consider questions more difficult to supply definitive answers to, such as the effect of school inputs on achievement. Their charge is worth some discussion because, if indeed a mistake was made at this point, it was the most serious of the study. But I believe that to have taken the approach proposed by Kain and Hanushek would have constituted exactly this magnitude of error.

As the survey was defined and carried out, it was intended to serve three purposes: to provide an accurate description of resource inputs for six different racial and ethnic groups at elementary and secondary school; to provide an accurate description of levels of achievement of each of these groups at three points in elementary school, grades 1, 3, and 6, and two in secondary school, grades 9 and 12; and to provide the basis for an analysis of the effects of various inputs on achievement. In terms of the five definitions of educational opportunity described above, such measures of effects were necessary for the fourth, to provide weights for various inputs, so that the "effective" inequality of opportunity could be assessed, and attention could be focused on those input resources that are effective in bringing about educational opportunity, or by their unequal distribution, effective in maintaining inequality of opportunity.

As Kain and Hanushek point out, the sample design requirements and the kinds of measurement are different for each of these three purposes. In the first, the sampling variability is at the level of the *school*, even if reporting is ultimately to be done in terms of exposure of the average student to school resources, as the report did. The second and third aims, on the other hand, require measurements on students, in effect reducing the number of schools that can be included within the scope of such a study.* The third, analysis of the relation between input and output, imposes different design requirements than the second, in the way that analysis of relationships generally imposes a different sample design than does description of population characteristics, with less attention to sampling error, and more attention to the range of variability in the independent variables. Kain and Hanushek argue that the survey attempted too much; by attempting all three of these things, it failed to do well the first, minimum requirement.

This charge is a telling blow, for much of it is true. The final design *is* a compromise between three objectives, less good for any one of them than if the others had been absent. Its size is a compromise between measure-

---

* About 90 percent of the variance in student achievement lies within schools, so that the clustering effect that would be caused by sampling fewer schools and not sampling within schools (the latter of great administrative convenience) is not serious for measurement of achievement.

ment of school characteristics and of student characteristics, and its design a compromise between descriptive demands of the first two objectives and the analytical objectives of the third (for example, schools with intermediate proportions of blacks and whites had especially high probabilities of being drawn). At one time in the survey design, in fact, a design involving two samples was seriously considered: a large sample of schools to measure school characteristics, and a smaller one for measuring student characteristics, including achievement, and for analyzing the relationship of achievement to school characteristics. This design was rejected because the great effort necessary to secure cooperation of each school in releasing sensitive information would have made a much larger sample of schools difficult to achieve without sacrificing the other objectives.

The alternative, as proposed by Kain and Hanushek, was to do well the minimum necessary task: to measure carefully the input resources to school attended by blacks and those attended by whites, to show what is in fact the kind and degree of discrimination in schooling experienced by blacks. They point to a number of specific weaknesses in such measurement, attributable to the more ambitious objectives.*

The defect of the apparently simple and straightforward approach they suggest is the most serious possible: by selective attention to one of the definitions of equality of educational opportunity, that is, equality of inputs, it implicitly accepts and reinforces that definition. In effect, I suggest, it fails to see the forest because of too close attention to the trees. In contrast, the major virtue of the study as conceived and executed lay in the fact that it did *not* accept that definition, and by refusing to do so, has had its major impact in *shifting* policy attention from its traditional focus on comparison of inputs (the traditional measures of school quality used by school

---

* I will not comment on these points in the text, but some comments on specifics are useful to correct misleading impressions some of the points may leave. First Kain and Hanushek point out the levels of nonresponse.

This nonresponse of schools, together with item nonresponse on the questionnaires, is a problem that would have arisen in any of the research designs that might have been chosen, given the sensitivity of the problem. Serious biases may have been introduced, though a sample of nonresponding schools was drawn, and state records checked, showing little systematic differences on comparable items from the responding schools; but here as elsewhere, the question is whether to use data from a sample that may be biased, or to make policy decisions in the absence of data.

On the major points of nonresponse and miscoding mentioned by Kain and Hanushek (for example, nonresponse on principals' attitude questions, miscoding of school size by principal, poor coding of fathers' occupation), the problems were recognized by the staff, and the information not used in the analysis. School size, as used in the analysis, was obtained from the number of student questionnaires, because of the possible coding errors by principals, and the principals' attitude items were used only in the tabulations of school characteristics, where nonresponse was shown in the tabulation. Neither these attitude items nor the occupation of child's father were used in the analysis of effects of school inputs on achievement. Thus the points made by Kain and Hanushek on these items are not relevant to the question of biases in the analysis.

administrators: per-pupil expenditure, class size, teacher salaries, age of building and equipment, and so on) to a focus on output, and the effectiveness of inputs for bringing about changes in output.

This effect of the study in shifting the focus of attention did not come about because the study gave selective emphasis to that definition of educational opportunity that entailed examination of effects; only one section of one chapter of the report was devoted to it. The study presented evidence relevant to all five of the definitions that had been initially laid out. It was the audience who, with evidence on all of these before it rather than only the comparisons of inputs that have traditionally served as the basis for comparisons of school "quality," focused its attention on the more relevant questions of output, and effect of inputs upon output. As I indicated above, I regard this shift of attention as the most important impact on policy of the study. It raised questions where none had been before: what is the value of the new large programs of federal aid to education? (The report results indicate very little, except through improving teacher quality, which the programs are not usually designed to do.) Do smaller class sizes bring increased achievement? (The report results say no.) These and numerous other questions had been prematurely answered in the absence of facts, and if the study had taken the apparently straightforward careful approach that Kain and Hanushek propose, they would have continued to be answered prematurely, in the absence of facts. The study would have been celebrated for its careful accuracy, its measurement of inequality, and its irrelevance would have gone unnoticed, as policy-makers busily worked to eradicate those irrelevant inequalities.

I have spent so much attention upon this question of overall design because it is so important, and because one can be so easily misled. It appears most reasonable, from the standpoint of careful scientific inquiry, to limit policy-related research to that narrow definition of the problem that can give the most scientifically defensible results within the limits of time and resources available. But to do so may serve to define, and define incorrectly, the very policy questions that are addressed as a result of the research.

◆ Inputs as Disbursed and as Received

Before turning to other questions concerning the validity of the survey's results in its description of inputs and achievement outputs, and in its analysis of the relation between them, it is necessary to discuss briefly a special problem that arises in the measurement of inputs of public resources to various groups in the population. This is a problem that will arise in other studies of such resource distribution, and it is well that it be discussed in some detail.

The problem arises from the fact that inputs can be viewed in two entirely different ways: inputs as disbursed by the school system, and inputs as received by the child. The difference can be shown by numerous examples: a school board can spend identical amounts on textbooks in two different schools (or two school boards can spend identical amounts in two different systems), so that the inputs as disbursed by school boards are identical. But if texts depreciate more rapidly, through loss and lack of care, in one school or one system than the other, then the text as received by a given child (say the second year after a new text is issued) constitutes a *lesser* input of educational resources to him than if he were in the other school or the other system. The examples could be multiplied endlessly: if teacher salaries in a city and the surrounding suburban area are equal (and, as the Report shows [Table 2.34.2], they are equal for schools attended by blacks [largely in the central cities] and schools attended by whites in the same metropolitan areas [largely in the suburbs]), then the city is not competitive in salary, and loses the best teachers to the suburbs. Again, the inputs as disbursed by the school boards are equal, but the inputs as received by the children are not. As another example, if the expenditures on window glass in a city school in a lower-class neighborhood and a suburban school were equal, the child in the city school would spend much of his time in classrooms with broken windows, while the child in the suburban school would not. Furthermore, nearly all the examples in which this "loss of input" occurs between disbursement and reception go in the same direction, that is, to reduce the resources received by the average black child.

The general principle can be described by an economic concept: the black child experiences external diseconomies through living in a lower-class black neighborhood. (Sociologists often describe these as "contextual effects," but the fact that they represent real reduction of resources is better expressed through the term "diseconomies.") The fact that he himself may create external diseconomies for other black children is beside the point: those he experiences as a result of living where he does sharply reduce the resources he receives below those disbursed by the school system.

Such a difference between inputs as disbursed and inputs as received creates enormous difficulties for any research designed to measure the "amount of resource input" from a governmental unit to any group in society. The fact that different external diseconomies are ordinarily highly correlated (e.g., the school that has frequently broken windows will be the same school that cannot hire the teachers it wants without special salary or other inducements) means that if inputs are measured as disbursed, this imparts a systematic bias to the measure if viewed as inputs received. Yet certainly from one point of view—though not from all—one is interested in input resources as received by the child.

It would be possible, of course, to make a virtue out of a fault—to measure input resources as disbursed *and* received, so that one would obtain not only measures from both points of view but also, by their difference, a measure of the amount of external diseconomy in each resource (for example, in teacher quality, in teaching materials, etc.) imposed on a child as a result of his living in a given kind of neighborhood with a given group of schoolmates.

Yet to do this on a national basis would be an enormous undertaking, because of the difficulty of measuring resources as received, and would require a mixture of depth and comprehensiveness very difficult to achieve. For example, one resource never measured as an input resource is order and quiet in the classroom, presumably because it is a "free" resource. Yet one of the principal diseconomies some lower-class children impose on their classmates is the loss of this resource, the loss of order in the classroom. To measure the level of disorder carefully would be a difficult task. Another serious external diseconomy that lower-class black children impose on others in their classrooms is to depress the level of teaching that a teacher can carry out in the classroom. Thus the teaching received by a child from a teacher in a lower-class black classroom will be at a much lower level than that received from the *same teacher* in a classroom of middle-class students performing at higher levels of achievement. Such a difference in inputs as received would be very difficult to measure. Or to measure the textbook resources as experienced by a child would require an intensive examination difficult to achieve on a national basis. Clearly it is important to measure the amount of diseconomy experienced by a child as a function of the kind of classmates and neighborhood, but it is an intensive analytical study that could hardly be carried out as part of a "simple and straightforward" study of equality of input resources on a national basis.

Thus even the apparently simple study of input resources becomes a rather complex one if it is viewed as it should be—neither solely from the viewpoint of the administrator as distributor of resources, nor solely from the viewpoint of the child as recipient, but from the viewpoints of both.

It should be pointed out that this discrepancy between resources as disbursed and resources as received is and has been the cause of many disputes in the distribution of public resources generally. It can be obvious to a visitor to a ghetto school and a suburban school that the educational resources provided in the two are sharply different, ranging all the way from freshness of paint to the level of instruction in the classroom. But school administrators can then show that the same or greater resources are expended in the ghetto school than in the suburban one. The confused liberal (which many persons are on this question) often explains this as due to administrative juggling of figures to mask differences, and the administrator remains convinced *he* is right. He is right, but so is the observer who sees these sharp differences where the administrator says there are none.

This discrepancy between input resources as disbursed and as received is also very likely responsible for a large part of the confusion and disbelief attending the survey's finding of small differences or none between blacks and whites for many input resources.* Many observers "know" those inputs are different, but they know this by observations of the different schools, that is, inputs as received or experienced, not by examining the expenditures. The survey generally measured input resources as disbursed (that is, as reported by principal or superintendent) rather than as received, except in a few areas not ordinarily regarded as resources because they are not provided by the superintendent's office, such as the number of discipline problems reported by the teacher, the attitudes of teachers, and the educational backgrounds of a child's fellow students. These resources, incidentally, showed great differences between schools attended by the average black and those attended by the average white, suggesting the magnitude of the external diseconomy a black child experiences because of his neighborhood and classmates.

◆ The Analysis of School Effects

Much of the paper by Kain and Hanushek is devoted to Section 3.2 of the report, which carries out an analysis of effects of school resources upon verbal achievement. It is this section of the report that has occasioned much of the discussion surrounding it from persons concerned with school policy. This is as it should be, because as I have argued in the preceding pages, the question of effectiveness of school input resources is logically prior to the question of equality of particular inputs. To order things the other way around is reminiscent of the busy activity of southern school systems in constructing new buildings for black schools, increasing salaries of black schoolteachers, and buying new textbooks for black students in the period preceding the Supreme Court decision of 1954, to obtain an apparent equality of educational opportunity while leaving unexamined the question of whether these inputs were the important ones. As an aside, it seems to me likely that the ready acceptance by many whites of the policy of increasing the "quality" of all-black ghetto schools, whether advocated by white conservatives or by black militants, is similarly motivated: that this will solve the problem of black education without threatening the schools of the white suburbs. One might go so far as to say that the earliest cases of compensatory education for blacks were the showcase black schools in the South of the early 1950's.

Thus the examination of effects of school factors was designed as a prior step to the description of "effective" inequalities of educational opportunity. I should go into the general design in a little detail, for it did not

* This unwillingness to accept the small degree of inequality of input resources is exhibited both in the paper by Kain and Hanushek and in the paper by Bowles and Levin. They cite several studies in particular cities; but many of these studies are marked by severe selective biases, since they aim to show how great the inequality of expenditures can be in selected cases, rather than how large it in fact is on the average.

appear in the report as published, due to developments I will mention. The original intent was to carry out a regression analysis covering four general clusters of factors that might affect achievement: attributes of the child's own family background, characteristics of teachers, school resource inputs other than teachers, and social characteristics of the student body in his grade in school. The last of these is described in the report as a cluster of student-body factors, and they have been referred to elsewhere as peer factors. In effect, they are measures of some of the attributes of students in school that can exercise external economies or diseconomies upon the learning of a child in the school, through the addition or subtraction of "free" resources, and through the modification of input resources disbursed by the school administrators. The result of these regressions would then be two. The first result is the regression coefficients themselves, showing the relation of each of the teacher, school, and student-body characteristics to achievement when all the other characteristics and family background were controlled. In unstandardized form, these regression coefficients would provide an estimate of the effect of one unit of the input resource on achievement, and in standardized form (e.g., as path coefficients) they would be measures of the relative importance of different factors in affecting achievement.*

The second result of the regression analysis was to be the principal one: these regression coefficients were to be used as weights for the various inputs, so that by replacing in the regression equation the levels of input resources for the average black in the region with those of the white in the same region, the predicted level of achievement would be changed. This would produce two results: first, a measure of effective inequality of opportunity would result as the increment in achievement that would be expected for the average black if all the input resources of schools and student bodies were at the level of those for the average white in the region; second, by selectively changing in the equation some of the input resource levels to those held by whites, while keeping others at the levels held by blacks, one could see which input inequalities were the effective ones, thus indicating which input resources would be expected to produce the largest effect if the input inequality for that resource were eliminated. The final form of this

* A note should be added here concerning what is meant by "achievement." Standardized tests, constructed by Educational Testing Service, were given in areas of verbal comprehension, nonverbal classification and analogy, reading comprehension, mathematics achievement, and at grades 9 and 12, five tests of specific subject areas. These test results correlated highly, and the one showing consistently higher correlations (both zero-order and partial) with school characteristics was the verbal comprehension test (taken from the SCAT series, principally a vocabulary test). This test was used throughout in the reported regression analyses. Regressions were carried out also on reading comprehension and mathematics achievement, and these showed similar results to the verbal achievement test, except that smaller proportions of variance were explained. Thus achievement as I will use it in this discussion refers to vocabulary skills, but can stand also as a surrogate for achievement in the other areas mentioned.

analysis was to be much like that of Section 2 of the report, which showed differences in the levels of particular school input resources for the average black in a region, the average white living in the same county or metropolitan area, and the average white in the region and in the nation. The distinction of these tables would be that the inequalities of resources, rather than being expressed by a difference in units of input resources (e.g., hundreds of dollars difference in teachers' salaries), would be expressed by the difference in existing average black achievement and predicted achievement if that input resource were at the level of whites in the same county or whites in that region or in the nation.

However, this plan was never carried through to final completion, but stopped short of the final step. The reason was collinearity among the various input factors, which I will discuss in more detail.

In doing this, I want to discuss several quite general problems that arose in this research and will arise in other research that attempts to assess effects of various input factors on some performance criterion. Some of these problems are directly related to the use that has been made of the report, and to criticisms that have been made of this use, or of the report itself, including that of Kain and Hanushek.

The first problem, well illustrated by this report and its interpretations, is the problem of determining exactly what is the policy question of interest, and then developing an appropriate statistical technique to give evidence regarding it. In this case, there has been widespread confusion about exactly this question, a confusion to which the report itself contributed. The analysis was designed to answer a single question: what is the relative importance for achievement of various resource inputs into schools, including the resources provided by other students (resources which I have earlier described as external economies or, if negative, diseconomies, imposed by other students). In the conceptual model we held of the student's performance, these school inputs, together with the child's own family background and his native ability which we regarded as unmeasurable, particularly in the absence of longitudinal data, constituted the principal determinants of motivation for and attitudes toward achievement, and then, together with such motivation and attitudes, constituted the principal determinants of achievement itself. Now given this model, and given the policy interest in achievement, the overall relative effects of school factors on achievement (though not the mechanisms through which these effects occur) can be assessed by neglecting the intervening variable of motivation and attitudes. But given the differential degree of correlation of various school factors with the student's own background, and given the importance of these background factors for achievement, it is necessary to examine the relation of these school inputs to achievement when the student's own background is controlled. Otherwise, those school factors most highly correlated with the child's family background would show the strongest relation to achievement. The clearest case in which misleadingly high measures of effect would occur is for student-body factors, because the backgrounds of other students are highly correlated with the student's own. Furthermore, these misleadingly high effects of school factors associated with the child's own background would *not* be sufficiently controlled by comparing sizes of standardized regression coefficients in a regression equation that includes family background factors. The mathematics of regression analysis is such that when two variables are highly correlated and related to the dependent variable, then the multiple regression coefficients of both will include variance that is explainable by the other. However, another measure, $b^2 (1 - c^2)$, where b is the standardized multiple regression coefficient of variable x_1 and c^2 is the correlation between the two independent variables, shows only the unique variance attributable to variable x_1.* Under such conditions, the following research procedure appeared most reasonable then, as it does now: to assess the relative importance of different school factors (given their differential correlation with the child's family background), the most accurate measure of relative importance is the additional variance in achievement that can be explained by the school factor, *after* family background factors have accounted for as much variance as they are able to, that is, measures of the form of $b^2(1 - c^2)$ rather than measures of the form of b. This gives an underestimate of the absolute effects of these school factors, insofar as they are responsible for some of the variance in achievement already explained by family background, but a better estimate of the relative effects than does the standardized regression coefficient.†

It is at this point that a confusion about the goals of the analysis arose. The way the results were reported contributed to this confusion, but was in no way misleading with regard to the policy conclusions that have been drawn from the report. Many persons, including Kain and Hanushek, have responded as if the goals of the analysis were to measure the relative effects of family background factors and school factors. But as I have indicated above, this was not the case at all, since policy alternatives concerned changes in various school factors (including student bodies, by distributing the external diseconomies imposed by lower-class students among all stu-

* Kain and Hanushek describe this alternatively explainable variance as "interaction," a curious choice of words. Interaction terms in regression analysis are not this at all. An interaction term accounts for variation in the dependent variable that *neither* variable alone could account for. The terms they describe would account for variation in the dependent variable that *either* variable alone could account for. "Overlap" would have been a better choice of words.

† This statement must be qualified, because the latter half is true only under conditions that are not precisely known. I conjecture, however, that these conditions are that over half of the variance that could be alternatively accounted for by a given school factor or by family characteristics is in fact due to family. Results of numerous studies show that this condition is true for the case under consideration, that is, school and family characteristics.

dents, through school integration), but not changes in the child's own family background.

As is evident in the discussion above of the technique used to assess relative effects, the technique would in fact have given misleading results if the goal had been different, for the relative effects of family background and school factors that it shows are biased in the direction of family background. Kain and Hanushek, among others, have mistaken the goals of the analysis, and have criticized the study for exactly this bias. But if the analysis had been carried out symmetrically, as had been initially intended, the goal of the analysis, and its relevance to the policy alternatives, would have been impaired. I will show shortly specific examples of how this might have occurred.

The results of the examination of relative importance of different school factors were that the most important cluster of factors was the social backgrounds of other students, the second most important was teachers' characteristics, and the lowest level of importance, explaining very little additional variance in most regions, was school facilities and curriculum characteristics. The policy questions, of course, are which school factors have more importance for achievement, and this ordering is the result of an analysis designed to answer that question. The most crucial policy issue is the issue of school and staff integration vs. improvement of school facilities and curriculum while leaving unchanged the student bodies, and currently, under black-power pressure, leaving or bringing black teachers for black student bodies. It is worth remarking in this context that, of all the teacher characteristics, those most highly and consistently associated with student achievement were two: the verbal skills of the teacher as measured by the score on a vocabulary test, and the racial composition of the teaching staff. These two were highly correlated, white teachers scoring consistently higher than black ones.

This relation of the racial composition of the staff is not apparent in the report, because it was entered in the regression after the verbal skills were entered, and, under such conditions, explained little additional variance due to its correlation with them. Entering it in this order was based on the a priori assumption that if variance could be alternatively explained by teachers' verbal skills or teachers' race, the causal factor was more likely to be verbal skills than race. This was another example of the use of a priori assumptions rather than a wholly symmetric analysis. It was done, as in the case of family background, to prevent misleading inferences; but as in that case, interpretations should be made with knowledge of the asymmetry used in the analysis.

This high correlation between verbal skills and teachers' race, and their relation to student achievement, means that the policy alternative of improving facilities and programs of black schools and increasing the blackness of the teaching staff should, in terms of the report's results, reduce the achievement of black students, the one effect more than counterbalancing the other.

To return to the general point I wanted to make that has relevance for most policy-related research, this example of confusion about results shows clearly the importance of specifying the goal of the analysis in terms of the policy alternatives. The goal in this case affected even very technical points in the statistical analysis, and my conjecture is that it will do so in much policy-related research.

The confusion about the goals and results of the analysis has been increased in this case by several elements: first, the small amounts of additional variance accounted for by school facilities and curriculum led us as authors of the report to unduly focus attention upon the low absolute levels of additional variance explained, rather than solely upon the relative amounts explained by different factors—although we did not make specific comparisons of family and school effects, because of the bias introduced by the asymmetric analysis; second, the interests of many persons in the report's audience other than those concerned with policy alternatives were in the question of the relative effects of family and school; and third, a very elementary confusion among some readers between effects of the child's own background (the size of which was not explicitly compared to effects of school factors), and effects of the social composition of the student body on a child's achievement, *apart* from his own family background, effects that were explicitly compared to school factors.

To show the misinterpretations that can arise due to technical errors when the policy questions are not kept clearly in mind requires examining in greater detail some of the results of the study. In doing this, I will present some further analysis carried out since the publication of the report.

In carrying out the regression analysis in the report, a technical reason in addition to the intellectual decisions discussed in an earlier section prevented the use of symmetric measures such as standardized regression coefficients for comparing the relative effects of different school and student-body factors on achievement. The result was not entirely satisfactory, because it entailed the comparison of added variances accounted for by school, teacher, and student-body factors, entered in the regression equation in various orders. It is useful, then, to show symmetric measures of these factors and family background, all entered in the same multiple regression equation. The technical problem in doing so has since been overcome, and the solution of the technical problems* allows illustration of the problems that arise by the direct use of the multiple regression coefficients.

---

* The technical problem in short was this: it was desired to get a measure of the overall relation of the cluster of teacher characteristics, the cluster of school facilities and curriculum characteristics, the cluster of student-body characteristics, and the cluster of characteristics of the child's own family background. But it is not possible

Two tables are presented below, both containing symmetric measures taken from multiple regression equations in which all four clusters of variables are entered. These clusters were each entered as a single variable, an index which used as weights the multiple regression coefficients on the individual variables within the cluster, so that the total variance accounted for is the same as in the original equation, but unlike that equation, a single standardized regression coefficient for the cluster is obtained. Table 1 contains these standardized regression coefficients (which can also be regarded

TABLE 1

Standardized multiple regression coefficients (or path coefficients) as measures of the importance of each of four clusters of variables on verbal achievement at grades 12, 9, and 6. Family background (6 variables), school facilities and curriculum (11 variables), teacher characteristics (7 variables), and student-body characteristics (5 variables). Blacks and whites in North and South, grades 12, 9, 6.

Grade 12

	Black North	Black South	White North	White South
Family	.23	.22	.34	.34
Facilities & curriculum	.13	.07	.10	.07
Teacher	.13	.12	.09	.04
Student body	.23	.23	.09	.11
R^2	.15	.23	.16	.17

Grade 9

	Black North	Black South	White North	White South
Family	.26	.22	.40	.38
Facilities & curriculum	.14	.16	.10	.05
Teacher	.12	.09	.11	.09
Student body	.16	.19	.08	.07
R^2	.12	.21	.19	.20

Grade 6

	Black North	Black South	White North	White South
Family	.27	.29	.34	.41
Facilities & curriculum	.04	.14	.05	.06
Teacher	.14	.12	.07	.10
Student body	.14	.12	.12	.07
R^2	.13	.21	.16	.20

to do this by adding the multiple regression coefficients for all variables within a cluster, because the sum would be too large, containing the same variance included in the regression coefficients for several different correlated variables. The solution is to use the regression coefficients from the total equation including all variables, as weights in forming four new composite variables representing the four clusters mentioned above. Then a regression of achievement on these four composite variables gives a standard regression coefficient for each of the four clusters. In the new regression equation with four independent variables, rather than 29, exactly the same amount of variance in achievement is explained; it merely allows one to obtain a standardized regression coefficient for each of the clusters.

as path coefficients). Table 2, however, contains measures of the sort that were used in the report, except that these measures are presented for all four of the clusters at issue: the student's own background, school curriculum and facilities, teacher characteristics and characteristics of the student body. The measures are measures of the unique contribution to variance in verbal achievement, after all three of the other clusters of variables are entered in the equation. These unique contributions have been scaled up so that their sum equals the total variance explained (the square of the multiple correlation coefficient).

Table 3 summarizes these two tables over grades and regions, for blacks and whites separately, to facilitate comparison.

The major difference between these two measures is that they "control" on the other variables in different senses. When two independent variables are correlated, then the variance that may be explained by either contributes to the regression coefficients of both. In using the variance uniquely explainable by a variable, however, the variance explainable by either is not

TABLE 2

Unique contributions to variance in verbal achievement (scaled up to sum to R^2 in each regression) as measures of the importance of each of four clusters of variables: family background (6 variables), school facilities and curriculum (11 variables), teacher characteristics (7 variables), and student-body characteristics (5 variables). Blacks and whites in North and South, grades 12, 9, 6.

Grade 12

	Black North	Black South	White North	White South
Family	.067	.119	.133	.144
Facilities & curriculum	.018	.009	.014	.007
Teacher	.016	.026	.009	.002
Student body	.046	.078	.008	.013
R^2	.146	.232	.165	.166

Grade 9

	Black North	Black South	White North	White South
Family	.065	.098	.160	.183
Facilities & curriculum	.017	.046	.010	.004
Teacher	.012	.014	.010	.010
Student body	.027	.053˙	.006	.005
R^2	.121	.211	.186	.203

Grade 6

	Black North	Black South	White North	White South
Family	.086	.137	.135	.179
Facilities & curriculum	.002	.033	.004	.003
Teacher	.024	.023	.007	.011
Student body	.021	.021	.017	.006
R^2	.132	.213	.163	.199

TABLE 3

Averages of standardized multiple regression coefficients (from Table 1) and unique contributions to variance (from Table 2) for blacks and whites separately, averaged over grades 12, 9, and 6.

	Average of standardized regression coefficients		Average of rescaled, unique variance contributions	
	Black	White	Black	White
Family	.25	.37	.095	.156
Facilities & curriculum	.11	.07	.019	.007
Teacher	.12	.08	.021	.008
Student body	.18	.09	.041	.009

allocated to either variable. Thus the regression coefficients give a liberal estimate of the effect of each, and the unique contributions to the variance give a conservative measure. The question in using one or the other for purposes such as this, however, is to get a good estimate of the *relative* effects of each cluster of variables (in this study, an estimate of the relative effects of the three school-related clusters).

The problem that can arise by using regression coefficients is well illustrated by the coefficients for family characteristics and student-body characteristics. Among blacks in the South, at every grade level, the regression coefficient for student-body characteristics (which is correlated with the child's own family background) is comparable in size to the coefficient for family background, and in grade 12, it is even higher than that of family background. The unique contributions to variance in Table 2, however, show that in no cases is the unique contribution of student-body characteristics near that of family background. In grade 12, where the multiple regression coefficients are .23 and .22 for student body and the child's own family, the unique contributions are .078 and .119.

It is in cases like this that the use of multiple regression coefficients can be misleading. If such coefficients had been presented for the four sets of variables, then it would have led to the conclusion that, in the South, the characteristics of the student body in the school are as important for a child's achievement as is his own background, a conclusion that appears false on its face and a conclusion that is not drawn from the relative sizes of the unique variance contributions.

It is paradoxical that the objections to the report's use of unique variance contributions rather than regression coefficients have been by the two pairs of economists, Bowles and Levin, and Kain and Hanushek, since both of them objected also that the use of regression coefficients would have shown greater school and teacher effects relative to the student-body effects. But as comparison of these two tables shows, the variable whose apparent effect is most reduced by examining unique contributions rather than multiple regression coefficients is the student-body characteristics.*

However, apart from the extreme cases exemplified by the southern blacks, the regression coefficient and unique contributions do not give radically different results. Table 3 shows that by both measures, family background is clearly the strongest cluster, with student-body characteristics following for blacks, and both school and teacher characteristics following that, while for whites all three of the latter are smaller, and all three are nearly alike. The similarity of these two measures is more apparent if it is recalled that the unique variance is a measure that should be compared to the *square* of the regression coefficients. If the regression coefficients in Table 3 are squared, they are much more comparable in relative magnitudes to the unique contributions.

The reason for the rather good comparability between the square of the regression coefficients and the unique contributions for most of the

* Kain and Hanushek carry out a regression analysis which purports to cast doubt on our conclusions, but does so by leaving out two of the three most important Student Body variables (School Attendance and Proportion Planning to Attend College) and substituting others in their place. The major difference from our results, which is the small variance attributable to peer effects, stems directly from this omission. The table is presented here with their results and with the results obtained from using those variables that were used in the report. I have not run regressions in every order, but those that have been run are sufficient to show how the omission of these two variables emasculated any effects attributable to peers. The case of blacks in the urban North, incidentally, is hardly representative, since a number of school characteristics are negatively correlated with family characteristics for this group but for no others. This produces the increase in unique contribution shown in comparing the figures in parentheses for the third and fifth columns for family characteristics and the figures outside parentheses for the third and fifth columns on school characteristics.

An extended reanalysis of these data has been carried out in the U.S. Office of Education, showing separately the unique explanation of variance and the overlap in variance explanation, for all clusters of variables. That extensive reanalysis does not lead, as Kain and Hanushek argue from their "representative case," to any substantial revision in inferences drawn from the data. See G. W. Mayeske, *et al.*, "A Study of Our Nation's Schools," Washington, D.C.: U.S. Department of Health, Education, and Welfare, 1969.

Table 1 from Kain and Hanushek, together with comparable figures in parentheses, using variables from the report.

Added proportion of variance explained.

Variable Cluster	1	2 after S	2 after P	2 after F	3
S (Teacher, facilities, curriculum)	(.0466) .0808	— —	— .0222	(.0363) .0560	(.0185) .0212
P (student body)	(.0788) .0703	(.0487) .0117	— —	— .0420	(.0349) .0072
F (family)	(.0748) .0777	— .0529	(.0487) .0494	— —	(.0505) .0484

grade-region-race groups in Tables 1 and 2 is shown in Table 4, which gives an indication of just how highly correlated these four clusters of variables are for each grade-region-race group. Table 4 gives the total variance explained and the sum of the unique contributions to this variance. If the four clusters of variables were uncorrelated, the two numbers would be the same, and the squared multiple regression coefficients would equal the unique contributions. If they were all perfectly correlated, the unique contributions would be zero.

As Table 4 shows, it is for blacks in the South where the clusters of variables are most highly correlated.

TABLE 4

Total variance explained (R^2) and the sum of unique contributions to the variance for each grade, race, and regional group.

	Black North	Black South	White North	White South
Grade 12				
R^2	.146	.232	.165	.166
Sum of unique contributions	.111	.080	.127	.121
Grade 9				
R^2	.121	.211	.186	.203
Sum of unique contributions	.111	.097	.179	.146
Grade 6				
R^2	.132	.213	.163	.199
Sum of unique contributions	.108	.115	.119	.180

♦ Multiple Modes of Analysis

Another quite general point I want to make about policy-related research is the importance of using different modes of analysis to examine the same question. If these modes are mutually confirming, the results are considerably strengthened; if not, they are weakened. In this case, the example I want to use is the question of the absolute magnitude of school effects, for in articles subsequent to the report, I have used evidence from the study to draw strong policy conclusions from the absolute level, arguing that the low absolute level of effect means that a more radical modification of a child's environment than that provided by schools is necessary to induce achievement in children whose family environments do not insure learning.

In the present research, it would have been incorrect to base such arguments principally on the results of the regression analysis, because the techniques used there were designed to more accurately assess relative effects of school factors at the risk of underestimating absolute size of effects. For this reason, it is especially important to have several alternative grounds for such inference. And it is useful to have these other sources of evidence based on analyses as different as possible in form, so that the errors of one will not appear in the other. There were three sources of such evidence, supported by the results of the regression analysis:

1. In an analysis of variance, a generally low proportion of variance in achievement lay between schools, for each racial group: between 15 and 20 percent for blacks, and less than 15 percent for whites. This means that the major portion of the variance in achievement could never be accounted for by differences between schools, for it resides within the school itself. If schools had strong and differential impacts on achievement (and the size of the differences in impact can be expected to be proportional to the strength of impact), then children within a given school should be achieving more nearly at the same level than the study showed to be the case.

2. This analysis of variance was carried out for each of the grade levels, grades 1, 3, 6, 9, and 12. If schools have strong and differential impacts, then the proportion of variance between schools should change over the school years. The between-school variance at the beginning of grade 1 is merely due to the differences between differing entering student bodies, due solely to family backgrounds, except for variance due to the test-taking situation in the school. If school effects are strong and positively correlated with family background, as all evidence would suggest, the between-school component of variance should *increase* over the years of school. If they are strong and uncorrelated with family background, the between-school component of variance should *decrease* over the years of school, or perhaps first decrease as student input differences are washed out, and then increase as school differences make student bodies diverge in achievement.

But as it turns out (Table 3.22.1), very little happens to the between-school component of variance. It remains about the same over the years of school. The simplest explanation of this is that the initial differences with which children enter school simply continue over the years of school, unaffected by the impacts of good or poor schools. The kind of school influences that would produce such a result are those that merely carry children along at the same relative levels of performance with which they begin school.*

3. The correlation between family background and achievement is approximately constant over grades 6 to 12 for both Negroes and whites (Table 3.221.3). (For grades 1 and 3 it is lower than for the later years, but this may be due to poorer measurement of background at these levels.)

---

* Various persons have argued that this and other results of the study simply show the importance of fixed genetic differences among children. Such genetic differences, within and between schools, could produce the observed constancy of the between-school component of variance, but only if school effects were relatively weak or uniform. If school effects were strong, and different for different schools, they would magnify the between-school component of variance through interaction with the genetic factors.

The absence of a steady decline in this relation over time indicates that schools do not constitute an important enough modification of the child's environment to interrupt the family processes that in the absence of school would be expected to show the same constant correlation with achievement that they now show.*

These three modes of analysis, reinforced by the regression analyses, that show low unique variance explained by school factors (with the exception of some teachers' characteristics), provide a rather strong base of evidence for the inference that school factors constitute a relatively minor modification of the child's learning environment—a firm foundation for the argument that much more radical modifications of the environment are necessary in order to greatly increase achievement of presently low-achieving groups.

This result illustrates my more general point about policy-related research—that it should obtain evidence from analyses as technically different as possible, to strengthen the grounds for inference. It is particularly important in this case that two of the results (numbers 2 and 3) were based on comparison over grade levels from grade 1 to grade 12, since the regression analyses were necessarily carried out within the same grade level, and the inferences about small school effects were not based on trends over different grades.

♦ The Inadequacy of General Field Surveys for Answering Specific Policy Questions

The problems of interpretation of results in a massive study like this one illustrate another general point in policy research. This is the inadequacy of analysis of a general sample of institutions or students for answering very specific questions relevant to policy, when the policy-related variables of policy interest are highly correlated, and have relatively small effect on the dependent variable under study. The results of this survey show only the most general outlines of the factors affecting school achievement. For answering specific questions, it is clear that methods are necessary which empirically rather than analytically separate out the variables of policy interest. One way in which this can be done is, of course, through experimental research. This, however, has the defect that the effects occur over time, and experimental research must involve time in which the experimental variables can have their effect.

In the absence of the necessary time, it appears likely that other methods are possible, if one recognizes certain dangers inherent in them. One of the most appealing for a study like this, in which much data beyond that

---

* For some of the ethnic groups other than Negroes and whites, a decline does occur between grades 6 and 12. For technical reasons, however, less confidence should be placed in those regressions than in those for Negroes and whites.

necessary for analysis are obtained, is the use of computer procedures for selecting students within schools for which certain input variables are orthogonal and others are perfectly correlated. Regression analysis on those orthogonal sets of variables will provide estimates of the effects of the sets of perfectly correlated variables. Then further computer selection can be used to identify students for which the variables perfectly correlated in the first analysis are orthogonal, and an analysis of these students used to examine the relative effects of the newly orthogonal variables.

The details of such a procedure, the statistical problems it might introduce, and the methods for reducing these problems, are not clear. It is evident, however, that since the samples are not representative of the population of students of interest, the parameters estimated are specific to the students thus sampled, and may be in considerable error for the population of interest. Even so, some procedures, in which estimates made on the samples resulting from search were used for prediction in the unbiased sample and inferences about biases made from the errors of prediction, seem possible.

In short, it is quite evident that much work remains to be done in devising techniques that can, within reasonable time constraints imposed by policy problems, give better estimates of the expected effects of policy changes.

One aid to this, suggested by Kain and Hanushek in their critique, is the development of more fully elaborated conceptual models for use in the statistical analysis. For example, as they point out, school effects are, or should be, cumulative over time. As a consequence, the appropriate model and measurement should involve the product of the school resource times the length of time to which the child has been exposed to it. If all children remained in the same schools, were subject to the same home environmental conditions, and were in schools with the same kinds of other students, throughout their school lives, then time would be unnecessary in the model. However, if he has moved and if his peers in school have changed, both of which are true for some students, then resources have been available for different amounts of time, and time should be explicitly incorporated into the analysis.

Still another approach to these policy questions might be to examine students at different grade levels in the same schools, controlling on family backgrounds to "standardize" the student body at one level against that at another. The dependent variable in this case would be the difference in achievement levels of standardized student bodies at two grades, or the inputed "growth rates." These "growth rates" can then be related to the characteristics of the school.

More generally, it appears that the most promising possibility for policy research lies in much more systematic and careful administrative records of social institutions. These records, if they were well maintained and comparable among schools (or for other policy questions, among other institutions), would allow analyses for policy questions to be carried out regularly and at minimal cost, by local school systems, by state systems, or nationally.

Altogether, it is clear that research to examine questions of policy can be done to provide a better base for general directions of policy. I believe *Equality of Educational Opportunity* has done so principally through the way in which the problem was defined, resulting in a redirection of attention from school inputs as prima facie measures of quality to school outputs, and resulting as well in an expansion of the conception of school inputs beyond those intentionally supplied by the school board. It is equally clear, however, that policy research in social areas is only beginning, and that social scientists have much to learn about how to answer policy-related research questions.

5

School and Family Effects on Black and White Achievement: A Reexamination of the USOE Data*

DAVID J. ARMOR

The United States Office of Education data on the equality of educational opportunity, as presented in the "Coleman report," showed results that surprised many educators and researchers.[1] The surprise soon gave way to a considerable amount of controversy. Some persons discarded the findings outright, while others accepted the Coleman conclusions with complete faith and began advocating immediate changes in educational policies.[2] There must be many others who are by now totally confused about what the report actually found and what it meant for educational policy.

The first Coleman conclusion which was controversial was that, in general, blacks appear to have just as adequate school facilities as whites in most parts of the country. This finding was contrary to the popular notion that blacks suffer from inferior schools, especially in the South. The second controversial conclusion was that, aside from the distribution of school quality, the effects of school staff and facilities on achievement do not seem large for either blacks or whites, at least when the school characteristics are compared to the effects of family background. Given the finding of large differences in black and white achievement in all parts of the country, the implication of the second conclusion, if correct, was clear: equality in achievement would not be attained through an improvement of schools alone.

* Sarah Dean and Michael Useem assisted in the data analysis work. Frederick Mosteller provided many helpful criticisms and suggestions.

The major criticism of the first conclusion was that school characteristics were not adequately measured, and therefore the absence of black-white differences is not a true representation of the actual situation. The criticism of the second conclusion concerns not only the measurement problems but the data analysis procedures as well, procedures based on a particular model of educational processes adopted by Coleman. This second conclusion also seems to be the one which has led to the most confusion, since many persons do not understand Coleman's model and the methods used to test it.

This chapter will examine these two conclusions once again with a new analysis of the complete elementary-school data. We attempt this task not necessarily because we believe Coleman's original analysis to be in error, but because we believe that the importance of the issues and the complexity of the report warrant another independent assessment. We hope that our main contributions will be the selection of a realistic model of the educational process, a clear statement of it and its limitations, and a straightforward presentation of the data used to test it.

Elsewhere in this volume the main nature of the original study and its findings will be presented, so we will not attempt that here.[3] There are also other chapters which deal with some of the conceptual and methodological problems which are raised by the Coleman report. There are four such problems, however, which are sufficiently important to deserve repeated attention, particularly if one is going to draw policy conclusions from the USOE data. We shall briefly state them before we present our analysis.

I. SOME METHODO-
LOGICAL ISSUES

The investigation of the "equality of educational opportunity" presumes that one actually knows what such a concept means. Perhaps the simplest interpretation, and one followed in part of the Coleman discussion, is whether or not blacks and whites are exposed to the *same* school characteristics—facilities, teacher qualities, etc. We encounter two major obstacles in answering this question with the USOE data. First, the school data were gathered by self-administered questionnaires completed by principals and teachers. This means not only that we have to assume they filled out the questionnaire accurately, but that we are restricted to the kinds of information which can be assessed by questionnaire methods. There may be many qualities of schools (e.g., teacher warmth and understanding) which are impossible to assess by such methods. Moreover, for our reanalysis we are restricted to the questions asked; many other questions about school characteristics can be conceived which might be important for equality of opportunity.

Second, the survey procedures resulted in a loss of many schools due to failures or refusals to cooperate. Only 800, or 70 percent of the high schools in the original target sample, have usable school and teacher information, and the figure is 74 percent for elementary schools.[4] Any results, therefore, can be somewhat biased to the extent that the nonresponding schools systematically differ from those responding. When we combine this with nonresponses to individual items on the returned questionnaires, the total proportion of the target sample actually assessed with respect to a specific characteristic can become quite small.[5]

In at least one sense the answer to the question of equality of opportunity has to be in the negative. The original report clearly showed something already known, that most blacks attend schools which are predominantly black. Thus, most blacks are in black environments and most whites are in predominantly white environments, and this makes one school characteristic to which they are differentially exposed. This inherent inequality was the basis of the historic Supreme Court decision of 1954 requiring school integration. Coleman took the problem of equality of opportunity one step further. He raised the question of what students are expected to get out of school. Given a specific student output, the next logical question is what school characteristics seem to have the most impact on it. If such school features could be uncovered, and if these happened to be the ones most disparate for blacks and whites, then concrete policies could be more adequately formulated to provide for equality with respect to the output specified. It was this approach that raised the third and fourth—and much more complex—methodological problems.

The third problem is raised by the definition of school output—the effects which schools are supposed to have on students. Coleman chose as the main output the verbal achievement of students as measured by a standardized test of the paper-and-pencil type. Even assuming that such a test adequately measures academic achievement, there are many other kinds of possible school outputs which are not considered in detail—better student adjustment, motivation, good career choices, and the like. Not finding school effects on verbal achievement does not necessarily mean that schools are not having an important impact in other respects, and, in these respects, unequal impact for blacks and whites.

Fourth, to raise the question of school effects on student achievement brings about a significant methodological problem for the Coleman research design, which called for a cross-sectional survey done at one point in time. The establishment of cause-and-effect relationships generally requires an experimental, longitudinal study design. Survey data can establish, with certainty, concomitant relationships at best. Any assertions of causal order are speculative, and the basis of believing them depends upon the reasonableness of the arguments.

Our reanalysis must face these same methodological problems that were present in the first report. The questionnaires may not have asked all the important questions; the nonresponse rate may have led to a biased sample; the measures of school output may be inadequate; and the survey approach may show associations between school input and output measures which are not cause-and-effect relationships. We hope we have stated these qualifications clearly enough that the reader will understand that all of our results, like Coleman's, must be necessarily tentative.

II. A MODEL OF THE EDUCATIONAL PROCESS

Before one can evaluate the equality of educational opportunity, one must have some conception of the educational process. We shall endeavor, in this section, to spell out briefly one possible model. This model will guide us in the empirical analysis which follows. In most respects it is similar to the model adopted by Coleman, except that we hope to make it more explicit.

We start with a consideration of the main goals of schooling. American society requires children to attend school to an age which carries them almost all the way through high school. There are several quite explicit goals of this educational process. Foremost is the learning of some basic cognitive skills—reading, writing, and simple arithmetic—which are crucial for a person's full participation in modern industrial society. Second, the secondary school provides instruction in various subjects—sciences, business, languages, etc.—which helps students to decide upon and prepare for further training in a specific occupation. Third, the school at least implicitly attempts to impart attitudes to the student which help him to become an adjusted, participating citizen. These might include personal self-esteem, respect for law and the rights of others, and an understanding of and commitment to the national culture. Finally, although not necessarily part of the educational process per se, schools provide some opportunity for aiding the physical and psychological welfare of children through the existence of health clinics, physical education, free-lunch programs, and counseling services.

The major assumption of the educational process is that a child will make progress toward these goals if he is in a school setting, with facilities and staff organized to impart all of this information and training. On its face, this is a reasonable assumption; much of the subject matter—such as science and mathematics—consists of information which most parents do not possess. Moreover, it also seems reasonable to assume that if there are variations in the quality of the facilities and staff from one school to another, there might also be variations in the effectiveness of those schools in transmitting knowledge and carrying out the training.

The effectiveness of schools in imparting knowledge is without a doubt a function of many complex factors. It seems reasonable, however, to divide the characteristics of schools into two broad categories. First, we might assume that the facilities of schools will have an important effect. The existence of libraries, up-to-date textbooks, laboratories, special services such as remedial reading and the like ought to have an effect upon how much and how well a child learns.

A second category concerns the quality of the teachers. It is the teachers who carry the main burden of the knowledge transmission. A school ought to vary in its effectiveness as the quality of its teachers varies. The kinds of things which are usually assumed to make good teachers include intelligence, good professional training, and personality characteristics which generate respect and enthusiasm among their students.

While most of these characteristics of schools and their staff may seem reasonable as factors aiding children's academic progress, it must be stressed that before the Coleman research there was little evidence upon which to base any firm conclusions. Much of the field research in education fails to use specific student outcome criteria that would enable one to see which factors are the most important for various educational goals.[6]

It is probably clear to most educators today that the success of schools in attaining their goals does not depend solely on the characteristics and practices of the schools themselves. Students first enter school with a given (but not necessarily unchangeable) set of characteristics, some of which may be relevant to the progress they will make in school. Most likely to be among these are intellectual capacity for handling academic work and motivation for carrying it out. These two important characteristics of a child are originally influenced, in unknown proportions, by his genetic makeup and his preschool social environment. The genetic factors, while not fully understood today, are most likely to influence intellectual capacity. This is seen most clearly in cases of organic mental retardation, where children have difficulty in mastering even simple cognitive skills. The social environment is somewhat better understood by behavioral scientists, and we assume that it effects both capacity and motivation.

It is important to distinguish at least four major levels comprising the social environment of the child. First, there is the environment of the child's immediate family. A family's life style—their stress on education, their economic well-being, their child-rearing practices and other similar factors—is likely to have an important effect upon the child's interest in and ability to carry out academic work. This complex of factors is often referred to as the socioeconomic position of the family, although I will generally call it family life style. There has been much research in sociology, prior to the Coleman report, which has established the existence of a relationship between school achievement and family socioeconomic status or life style.[7]

The second potentially important level is the neighborhood or community in which the family resides.[8] Although the community may have an effect upon a family's life style, it is possible that the community has an independent direct effect on a child's academic orientation before school starts. One obvious example might be the existence of public facilities, such as playgrounds, which enable children to have greater contact with each other prior to the school years. Another would be the *aggregate* life style of the families in the immediate area. Much of a preschooler's time is spent playing with other children, and the play often takes place in other homes. Therefore, the orientations of the peers and the life styles of their families may directly influence a child's views toward education. A child living in an urban slum might be expected to have preschool contacts which may result in less positive attitudes toward school, compared to the results of contacts of a child in a suburban upper-middle-class neighborhood—and these results can be quite aside from the orientation of his own family.

The third level is the environment provided by the aggregate characteristics of the other students in the school, which has often been called the peer or student-body factor. There is some problem in classifying this factor as a school characteristic or a community characteristic. If the community is small and most of the students in the school live in an area close to the school, then composite student characteristics would not differ from composite community social characteristics. I have chosen to call it a community factor partly because with the USOE data one cannot separate aggregated student social characteristics from community characteristics, and partly because the aggregate student characteristics are not subject to the control of the school administration in the same way as are the school staff and facility characteristics.

The fourth level may have a bearing on both the school and the community characteristics, although not on the child directly, and this is the cultural values of the region. America is not homogeneous with respect to basic values regarding education. Rural areas may not stress education as much as urban areas, and the Deep South as a whole may be less committed to educational goals than, say, the Far West. These values are in the form of what we might term collective sentiments, and beyond this they may be manifested in public policies and procedures, such as state accrediting practices. They are not directly attributable to a single family or a single community. Rather, they are cultural characteristics of the whole region or area, similar to the cultural characteristics of a whole country.

All of these family, community, and regional characteristics no doubt continue their effect on a student throughout his school years in addition to their initial impact. But, presumably, once a child is in school the characteristics of the school facilities and staff have an additional "independent" effect on student achievement.

To this point my model stresses the effects of the social environment and school factors on the individual child. This is the approach followed by Coleman. His test of a similar (but less explicit) model involved the analysis of individual student outcomes in relation to such factors. There are several problems with this approach. Most of the USOE data gathered about school facilities and teachers applies to each school as a whole; it was not possible, for example, to relate individual teacher characteristics with the students they taught. Nor was it possible to determine which facilities were used by individual students. Since teacher quality and utilization of facilities may vary within a school, variation in student academic achievement within a school caused by these variations cannot be examined. There is, in a sense, an upper limit on the amount of achievement variance which could be explained by facility and staff variance. On the other hand, like achievement, assessment of family background was also done for individual students. Thus, such background factors have a chance, theoretically, to explain more variation of individual academic achievement than school factors, even though the effects of the latter may be equally strong.

For these reasons, we chose to consider a single school as the basic unit of analysis. We view the school as a collectivity with certain inputs from the community, in the form of aggregate student and family-background characteristics, with various school input characteristics, such as facilities and aggregate teacher qualities, and with outputs in the form of aggregate student academic achievements and attitudes.

This focus will not allow us to examine factors relating to within-school variations of achievement, nor will it be amenable to investigation of differential effects of various school and community features on individual student outcomes. Coleman has, however, already done this to a large extent (see also Chapter 6 in this volume). Moreover, we feel that our approach is a reasonable one with which to reexamine the controversial issue of school versus social background factors, especially given that school characteristics were assessed only for the school as a whole.

Figure 1 presents a schematic of the model we have outlined, as it applies when the school is the unit of analysis. We have filled in the boxes with examples of indices which might be used to assess each of the domains. We shall spell out the ones we used in more detail later. The solid arrows indicate our assumed main causal directions. The dotted arrows indicate weaker, but plausible causal directions. That is to say, families may move to or away from regions because of the differences in average life style and values, so that the causal direction is two-way. In addition, the characteristics of a school may be a factor in families moving into or out of a community, again making possible a two-way causal direction.

Figure I. A Model of Aggregate Educational Processes

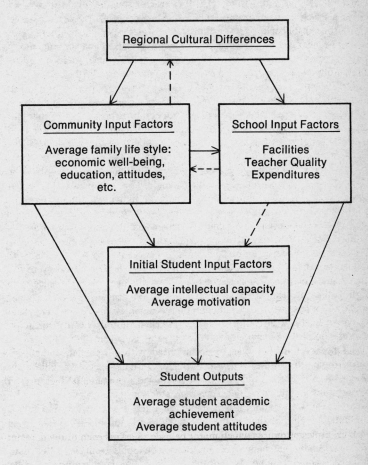

To summarize the model, regional differences may lead to different. typical life styles, as reflected in individual families. Regions may also directly affect the school systems independent of the family through such mechanisms as statewide educational policies. The community inputs to the school are twofold. First, the average family social and economic characteristics may partially determine school characteristics directly through such policies as school expenditure levels, which are decided by a publicly elected school board. Second, average family life styles result in average student academic characteristics, such as initial intellectual capacity and motivation, which in turn directly affect student output. The average family and community characteristics also continue to operate during the school career of the student. Finally, the school characteristics have an effect on student output through the mechanisms of facilities, teacher qualities, and the like. We include school expenditures in this cluster since there may be many less tangible qualities of schools due to expenditures that are not assessable directly through the available questionnaire material from principals and teachers.

There is one major issue examined by Coleman which cannot be raised with this model, and the reason stems mainly from the fact that we are using the school as the unit of analysis. At the individual student level, one might use *aggregate* student-attitude measures—which we have labeled as outputs—as potential school input factors which can affect *individual* academic achievement and attitudes. Coleman did something similar to this. He used aggregate attitudes and such measures as the percentage in the college preparatory course, and he found that such peer effects were very important. One might raise a question about this procedure, because of the high probability that such student aggregate characteristics are a consequence or at best a concomitant of student academic achievement. But at the school level, this probability makes it unreasonable for us to use aggregate attitudes and the like as predictors of aggregate achievement.

One additional problem is encountered with our model, and this involves the matter of the "ecological fallacy." In many cases we will be analyzing the relation between the *averages* of various students' measures. If we say that at the school level average student achievement is related to average family education, it is possible that such is *not* the case for individual students, or that such is the case but the relationship is not as strong. That is, average family educational background, as a community characteristic, could have the same effect on those individuals from highly educated families as those from poorly educated families. This could cause the school-level correlation to be higher than the individual-level correlation. It must be remembered that any relationships we demonstrate only hold at the aggregate level, and not necessarily for individuals. The fact that Coleman did carry out a test of a similar model at the individual level will, of course, allow such generalizations to be made if the aggregate-level analysis shows relationships which are the same as those shown by Coleman.

As a final important caution, it must be pointed out that in testing this model we will not necessarily be evaluating the absolute effect of schooling. The compulsory period of schooling is so long in this country that there are probably a minimum set of skills (reading, writing) which practically all students acquire. To this extent, then, there can be no question that schools have a definite academic effect on students. It is possible, however, that variation in school quality above and beyond a minimum level produces variation in *how much* knowledge is imparted and *how well* it is retained by students. It must be emphasized that we are interested in the effect of schools on this relative achievement variation, and that we are not questioning whether schools have any effect at all. When Coleman concludes that school facilities have little effect on achievement, he means that observed variation in achievement is not associated with the observed variation in school facilities. The additional *uniform* effect that all schools have on all students, which provides for the minimum level of achievement, would not show up as part of the variation on achievement test scores.

This concludes the outline of our idea of the major processes at work in the educational system. Our purpose has been to outline what may be regarded as current thinking of educators, rather than to speculate about new factors as yet unreported. The USOE data were gathered with current practices in mind. Hence, our approach is to test current policies—within the framework of the data available—rather than to discover new correlates of educational achievement. We move, then, to a discussion of the measures constructed to test this model.

III. ANALYSIS
PROCEDURES

Many educators would agree that the most critical years of a child's school career occur in the elementary grades. There is some important recent experimental research which indicates that experiences in these years can have important effects on achievement, and more important effects than in later school years.[9] For this and other reasons we decided to carry out our analyses on the elementary-school sample from the USOE data. This approach has several distinct analysis advantages over using the high-school sample.

First of all, there are about 2350 schools with 6th grades with usable data from the principal, teacher, and student questionnaires, which represents 74 percent of the original sample.[10] The comparable figure for the high-school sample is about 640 schools, or about 56 percent of the original sample. Not only does this imply more serious biases for the latter, but the larger number of elementary schools will permit more extensive analysis with control variables.

Another advantage is that three different grades—1st, 3rd, and 6th—were assessed in the same schools. This will enable us to compare student achievement over a six-year period. Of particular importance in these comparisons is the performance of students in the 1st grade, since the testing was done in the fall term and at this point most of the students could not have been substantially affected by the characteristics of the school.

Finally, elementary schools are likely to be more homogeneous with respect to many of our measures of community input factors, since they are more likely to draw their students from a relatively small geographical area. Student-body homogeneity is an important consideration since we are not analyzing within-school variations.

Not all of the schools with 6th grades were used for the analysis presented in the next sections. Schools which combined elementary and secondary grades (e.g., 1st through 12th) were eliminated, because it was felt that they might have different characteristics than those with only elementary grades. For example, preliminary analysis indicated that one-to-twelve schools had smaller enrollments and smaller student-to-teacher ratios than the typical elementary school. This could lead to higher per-pupil expenditure ratios without any necessary increase in school or teacher quality.[11]

Also eliminated were schools with large proportions of students with racial backgrounds other than black or white. These other groups included Oriental and American Indian. Specifically, schools were eliminated if 25 percent or more of the students indicated their race as other than black or white.

The final selected sample consists of 1623 elementary schools with a grade no higher than 8th. Since the original USOE study randomly sampled only one half of the first grades for assessment, only 880 of these schools have data for 1st grades. For each of the schools, measures were constructed for the various factors in the model presented in the previous section. Because the very large pool of questionnaire items forces one to be selective in constructing these measures, this section will be concluded with a discussion of some of the principles which guided the choices. A more detailed description of each measure will be given in later sections.

First of all, regional cultural differences will be examined using two measures: geographical region and size of place. The schools can be classified into seven regions, and, within each region, into metropolitan and nonmetropolitan areas. A metropolitan area is a Standard Metropolitan Statistical Area, as defined by the U.S. Census. Wherever possible our analyses will be carried out within these fourteen strata. We will, however, also present our results for the nation as a whole so that overall summary statements can be made.

Measures of school facilities were available from questionnaires administered to principals. For two reasons we decided to use a single index of school facilities. First, the model posits many factors, and the analysis we propose will not permit an unlimited number of variables. Second, and more important, we feel that the hypothesis that school facilities have an effect on student achievement has to be tested by considering all of the measured facilities which school administrations themselves advocate as necessary to maintain high academic standards. It does not seem appropriate in this kind of evaluation study to pick out only those facilities which do show a relationship to student achievement and then claim to have demonstrated school facility effects. If only a few of the many facilities measured show such relationships, then the hypothesis has failed. Therefore, a single index of facilities should show an effect if in fact such effects occur for most of the facilities making up the index. The index can be seen as a summary measure of school facilities taken as a whole.

Teacher quality measures were likewise derived from questionnaires administered to teachers. Three measures were constructed although only two were finally adopted. The first is an index of the quality of teachers' training and professional background. As in the case of the school-facilities index, several different items were combined in the index so as to provide for a test of the effect of professional background as a whole. The combined items were then averaged over all the teachers in a school to get a school-level measure.

The second measure of teacher quality is based on a short verbal achievement test. The test contained sentences which had to be completed by the selection of a correct word. A school-level measure was derived by taking the number of correct sentence completions for each teacher and averaging this for all the teachers in the school.

The nonresponse rates for the teacher indices were generally low. For teacher verbal achievement, it was 5 percent. The individual nonresponse rates for the teacher-background items used were also quite low, ranging from 1 to 2 percent for the sample of teachers. There were some schools, however, in which the principal's questionnaire indicated more teachers than there were teacher questionnaires. Therefore, we computed the teacher indices for a school only if more than one third of the teachers returned the questionnaire.

Given the questionnaire material, it was not possible to derive directly a more adequate measure of actual teaching ability or teaching style. To do so would have required some kind of observational study. There were, however, some questions dealing with the teacher's attitude toward teaching and toward the school's ethnic composition. Our a priori notion was that a good teacher attitude would be composed of strong commitment to teaching and to the school, and a tolerant attitude toward ethnic composition (with no objection to any racial or ethnic mixture). An index was formed using questions which seemed to tap these dimensions.[12] We found, however, that our index of good teaching attitudes was *inversely* related to average student achievement. In fact, the product-moment correlation between teacher attitude and student achievement for the nation as a whole was − .42. The higher the student achievement, the less tolerant and less committed the teachers (as measured by our index). It may be that our notion of a good teaching attitude is wrong, but we prefer to believe that for some reason the index is not adequate for assessing these attitudes. Therefore, in the following analysis we will utilize only the first two measures of teacher quality.

Since not all possible types of school facilities or teacher characteristics were assessable from the questionnaires, it was decided that some measure of school expenditures should be included. The assumption here—not an uncommon one—is that, in general, the more money spent by a school for facilities and salaries, the better trained the students. Unfortunately, total expenditures were available only for entire school systems, making it impossible to construct a per-student expenditure ratio for each individual elementary school. Since teacher salaries comprise the major portion of school budgets, per capita salaries were thought to be a good approximation to per-capita expenditures. Using data from the principal questionnaire on the number of students and teachers, and using average teacher salary from the teacher questionnaire, it was possible to construct a per-capita teacher salary figure for each school, a measure that should be strongly related to total per-capita expenditures.

The situation is somewhat more complicated when we consider the available measures for community inputs. Almost all information about students' families depends on data gathered from the student questionnaires; there was no direct assessment of family characteristics. There were three such questionnaires, one each at the 1st-, 3rd-, and 6th-grade levels. These questionnaires were administered to all of the students in each grade, except that only half of the 1st grades in the sample received questionnaires.

We say at the outset that one important family dimension was not directly assessed in the study, and that is family attitudes toward education. Although students were asked to rate their parents' interest in their schoolwork and their educational plans for the future, we did not feel that these ratings would be sufficiently independent from the students' own educational interests and motivation. In short, we viewed such ratings as student attitudes and not as family characteristics. We did not feel that students' assessment of their parents' objective social and economic characteristics presented the same kind of difficulty.

Five major family life-style indices were constructed for each grade. An index was first formed for a student from his questionnaire data and then averaged over all the students in a given grade. Thus, the indices represent aggregate family characteristics for the immediate community of the school, at least insofar as each grade represents a similar cross section of that community. The first four indices concern the family specifically: percent of the students with fathers in white-collar occupations; percent living with both natural (or legal) parents (hereinafter called the "family structure" index); average education of both parents; and the average number of household items (from a list of nine).

A fifth community index was constructed by considering the percent black in a school. It was our feeling that the proportion of black families in a town or neighborhood might indicate life-style characteristics not exhausted by the four indices above. The caste aspects of black status are such that areas which are predominantly black may have different background inputs than those which are predominantly white, aside from the objective socioeconomic factors. In particular, black families may have different attitudes toward education than white families with similar socioeconomic characteristics.

As we indicated earlier, nonresponse rates for some of the items in these community input indices have received some critical comments. It may be of some interest, therefore, to present the nonresponse rates for our indices at the individual student level. For the 6th-grade students, upon whom we carried out most of the analysis, the nonresponse rates on race, family-structure, and household-items indices were quite low, being approximately 3 percent for each. The nonresponse rates for parents' education and father's occupation were higher, being 30 percent and 26 percent, respectively. Although these two are quite high, their traditional importance in defining family life style led us to include them. Moreover, since aggregation was done over whole grades, an estimate is obtainable for every school. Preliminary analyses indicated that those students who do not know their father's education or occupation are more likely to be black; therefore, these estimates are likely to be most biased for schools which are predominantly black. The bias is probably in a direction showing higher average status than actually exists for the school.[13]

Some indication of the reliability of these measures at the school level can be gained by considering the product-moment correlations between the 6th-grade and 3rd-grade versions. For percent black and household items, the 3rd-to-6th-grade school-level correlations were .96 and .91, respectively. There seems little doubt about the consistency of these measures. For father's occupation and family structure, the correlations are .73 and .75, respectively. It is unlikely that the grades would differ on these last two indices and not on the first two; therefore, the lower correlations are most likely an indication of greater student error in answering these questions. We did not compute the parents' education index for the third grade due to a very high nonresponse rate (50 percent).

Continuing with further input factors, since the USOE data is cross-sectional, we have no direct way to assess the initial input of a student's intellectual capacity and motivation. However, since we have defined the school as our unit of analysis, average *1st-grade* achievement (as measured by standardized achievement tests) might be used in comparison to average academic achievement in a later grade of that school. We shall use this procedure in some, but not all, of our analyses. Because we are dealing in actuality with different groups of students, separated by six years, many assumptions must be made in order to use one group as the initial state of another.

Finally, we come to a consideration of school output measures. We do not have a great deal of choice here, given the USOE data. The model posited factors of academic achievement and of student attitudes. Space limitations will not permit an examination of student attitudes here. These student outputs are considered, however, in other parts of this volume.[14]

For academic achievement there are a number of standardized achievement test results for each of the grade levels. Average course grades would probably not be a good measure of achievement, since the standards of grading are no doubt different in each school. For a variety of reasons, we chose average 6th-grade verbal achievement as our measure of school output. First of all, the school-level correlation between average verbal achievement and average nonverbal achievement for all 6th grades is .92, and the correlation between the former and average math achievement is .94. It would seem in the light of these correlations that the use of any one of these tests would not give results very different from those obtained by using any other. We shall also use average verbal achievement for our 1st-grade analysis. The verbal to nonverbal school-level correlation for all first grades was .81.

These correlations set a standard which led us to reject consideration of 3rd-grade achievement test results. The school-level correlation between average verbal achievement and average nonverbal achievement was .55 for 3rd grades, and the correlation was .66 between verbal and math achievement. This is such a contrast to the correlations for the 1st and 6th grades that we suspect something may be wrong with the test for its scoring; this was mentioned in Coleman's original report.[15]

There is another analysis procedure which needs some discussion, and that is the derivation of school weights which are used in most of the analyses in the following sections. There are two reasons why weighting must be considered when analyzing the USOE data. The first reason has to do with the sampling method used in the original study, and the second has to do with the school-level analysis we plan to carry out.

The sampling design for the original survey called for oversampling of schools with predominantly minority group enrollments. Therefore, any national or regional school averages computed without regard to race will be biased to the extent that predominantly black schools differ from predominantly white schools. To correct for this possible source of bias, a weighting factor was computed for each school which varied inversely with the probability with which that school was sampled.[16]

The school-level analysis generates a second condition requiring weighting. Since a grade in a school might have an enrollment anywhere between 1 and slightly over 200 students, the variability of a mean based on aggregated individual student measures will not be constant over schools. A school mean based upon 100 students will have more stability than one based upon 2 or 3 students. Moreover, the seriousness of this latter problem for a given student variable depends upon how much of its total variation arises from school-to-school differences (among-school variance), and how much arises from student differences within schools (within-school variance). If within-school variance is small, a few students will provide as good an estimate as many students. Thus a second school weighting factor was computed for each grade which reflected the grade enrollment and the proportion of among-school variance for various student factors.[17]

The final weight for a school grade combined both weighting factors, and its form is given by $w_i = CR_ik_i$, where k_i represents the school size weight, R_i is the sampling weight, and C is chosen such that the sum of the weights is equal to the total number of 1st or 6th grades in our sample.

Table 1 gives the relationship between the sum of the 6th-grade weights and the actual number of schools in our sample, within each regional and racial stratum which will be utilized throughout most of the later analyses. The first number in each cell is the sum of the weights, and the number in parentheses is the actual number of schools. In all of our later tables we shall present only the actual number of cases in each cell.

We actually computed both weighted and unweighted versions of most of our analyses. As we expected, the only noticeable differences in the two versions occurred for the overall regional or national averages. Within the regional and racial strata, practically all differences were negligible. We shall, nonetheless, always present the weighted version of the analysis unless we indicate otherwise.

Table 1 reveals the final major research strategy utilized in following sections. Since our unit of analysis is the school, we felt it would be appropriate to differentiate *black schools* from *white schools*. By a black school, we mean one in which there are more than 50 percent black students. By a white school, we mean one in which 50 percent or more of the students are white. Since we excluded schools with majorities of other minority groups from our analysis, these labels are appropriate. About 87 percent of the elementary schools have either 80 percent or more black or 80 percent or more white in the 6th grades. Less than 3 percent of the elementary schools in the sample fall into the 40 to 60 percent black range. Further justification for this dichotomy is found in data presented in the original report. It showed, for first graders, that 87 percent of the blacks and 97 percent of the

TABLE 1

Weighted Number of Elementary Schools, by Region, Size, and Race

Size[c]	Metropolitan		Nonmetropolitan		
Racial Composition[b]	Black Schools	White Schools	Black Schools	White Schools	All Areas
Region[a]					
New England	1 (4)[e]	48 (64)		21 (10)	70[d] (78)
Mid-Atlantic	18 (57)	143 (173)	14 (8)	102 (49)	276 (287)
Great Lakes	29 (53)	243 (173)	6 (6)	53 (41)	330 (273)
Plains	10 (9)	50 (35)	5 (4)	72 (48)	138 (96)
South	71 (91)	78 (63)	62 (211)	211 (218)	423 (583)
Southwest	7 (18)	60 (17)	12 (25)	48 (54)	126 (114)
Pacific	26 (22)	128 (91)		106 (79)	260 (192)
Nation	163 (254)	749 (616)	98 (254)	613 (499)	1623 (1623)

[a] As defined in the original USOE study: New England—Connecticut, Maine, Massachusetts, New Hampshire, Rhode Island, Vermont; Mid-Atlantic—Delaware, D.C., Maryland, New Jersey, New York, Pennsylvania; Great Lakes—Illinois, Indiana, Michigan, Ohio, Wisconsin; Plains—Iowa, Kansas, Minnesota, Missouri, Nebraska, North Dakota, South Dakota; South—Alabama, Arkansas, Florida, Georgia, Kentucky, Louisiana, Mississippi, North Carolina, South Carolina, Tennessee, Virginia, West Virginia; Southwest—Arizona, New Mexico, Oklahoma, Texas; Pacific—Alaska, California, Colorado, Hawaii, Idaho, Montana, Nevada, Oregon, Utah, Washington, Wyoming.
[b] Black schools are those with more than 50 percent blacks; white schools are those with 50 percent or more whites.
[c] Metropolitan means Standard Metropolitan Statistical Areas (SMSA's).
[d] Weights in marginals may not equal sum of weights in cells due to rounding error.
[e] Numbers in parentheses are the actual number of schools.

whites in the nation are in schools in which they are the majority race.[18] For many purposes, therefore, examining the characteristics of black schools and white schools, as defined, is tantamount to examining exposure of the respective individual students to those characteristics. We shall use this dichotomy in most of the analyses which follow.

IV. CHARACTERISTICS
OF BLACK AND WHITE
SCHOOLS COMPARED

We mentioned that one of the controversial findings of the Coleman report was that the differences in the exposure of blacks and whites to important school characteristics were not as large as might have been expected:

At the same time, these differences in facilities and programs must not be over-emphasized. In many cases, they are not large. Regional differences between schools are usually considerably greater than minority-majority differences.[19]

Somewhat greater differences in exposure were found for some teacher characteristics. We can examine this issue once again at the elementary-school level with our indices.

♦ School Facilities

Chart 1 lists 26 types of school facilities and programs which were felt to be a summary of the types of characteristics important for student academic achievement.[20] Each of these items was assessed in the principal's questionnaire. The index was formed by giving a score of 1 to a school for each item it has in the manner described in the chart. If the item was not evaluated by the principal, it was assumed to be missing. A school was not scored on the index if there were more than five such missing observations. The index had a possible range from 0 to 26; a school scoring 26 would be one that had all of the facilities and characteristics listed.

Table 2 presents the means on the school-facility index within the various regions and for the nation as a whole. Data were available for 1562 schools, representing over 95 percent of all schools in our selected sample. The standard deviation of the index for the nation as a whole was 3.7; for black schools and white schools separately it was just about the same.

Within the nine size-region combinations where comparisons are possible, the differences between black and white school means seldom approach one half of a standard deviation. There does seem to be one pattern, however. In four of the six metropolitan comparisons the black schools show somewhat higher mean index scores, and in the four nonmetropolitan regions the white schools have higher means. The only large difference occurs for the nonmetropolitan Great Plains region, but the figure for black schools is only based on 6 schools. The national figures, with no control for

CHART 1

Items in the School-Facility Index

Item	Percent of Schools Having Item As Described
180 or more days in yearly session	63
Main building age 19 or fewer years old	53
No improvised rooms	79
1500 or more volumes in library	56
2 or more movie projectors	37
Free textbooks	84
Average age of textbooks 4 or fewer years	60
Copyright of 3rd-grade reader 1964 or later	26
No split sessions	91
Less than 5 percent teacher turnover	61
Regular tenure system	59
One or more art teachers	36
Speech therapist services	56
Mental health services	56
One or more remedial teachers	31
One or more guidance counselors	18
Full or part-time librarian	47
Principal with M.A. or higher degree	68
Principal undergraduate major in arts and sciences	38
Principal salary $9000 or higher	45
Accelerated program	32
School newspaper	23
Special class for low I.Q. students	45
Special class for rapid learners	17
Special talents classes	29
26 or fewer students per teacher	37

region, seem to be a good summary. They show scores of 12.2 for black schools and 12.7 for white schools.

This is not to say there are no large differences across the different regions. The mean index score ranges from a high of 15.9 for white schools in the metropolitan Pacific area to a low of 7.9 for black schools in the nonmetropolitan Great Plains and 8.9 in the nonmetropolitan South regions. But since black schools in the metropolitan Pacific area had a mean of 15.7, and white schools in the nonmetropolitan South area had a mean of 9.8, little of the difference would seem actually ascribable to the racial makeup of the school. Most of the differences are more likely due to educational practices in the regions which apply about equally to schools in those regions regardless of racial composition. The strongest overall trend seems to be that nonmetropolitan areas have considerably lower scores than metropolitan areas.

These results do not mean that black students are no worse off in edu-

TABLE 2

Mean School-Facility Index Scores For Elementary Schools[a]

Size	Metropolitan			Nonmetropolitan			All Areas			All Schools
Racial Comp. Region	Black Schools	White Schools	Difference[b]	Black Schools	White Schools	Difference	Black Schools	White Schools	Difference	
New England	c (4)[d]	14.5 (63)			11.0 (10)		(4)	13.4 (73)		13.4 (77)
Mid-Atlantic	15.1 (57)	15.5 (170)	+0.4	13.0 (7)	13.2 (46)	+0.2	14.2 (64)	14.6 (216)	+0.4	14.5 (280)
Great Lakes	14.8 (53)	13.9 (171)	−0.9	7.9 (6)	10.6 (40)	+2.7	13.6 (59)	13.3 (211)	−0.3	13.3 (270)
Plains	14.0 (8)	12.6 (35)	−1.4	(4)	10.1 (47)		11.9 (12)	11.1 (82)	−0.8	11.2 (94)
South	11.9 (82)	11.2 (63)	−0.7	8.9 (183)	9.8 (211)	+0.9	10.6 (265)	10.2 (274)	−0.4	10.3 (539)
Southwest	12.5 (17)	11.3 (16)	−1.2	9.6 (24)	10.6 (53)	+1.0	10.7 (41)	11.0 (69)	+0.3	10.9 (110)
Pacific	15.9 (22)	15.7 (91)	−0.2		12.7 (79)		15.9 (22)	14.3 (170)	−1.6	14.5 (192)
Nation	13.7 (243)	14.0 (609)	+0.3	9.5 (224)	11.0 (486)	+1.5	12.2 (467)	12.7 (1095)	+0.5	12.6 (1562)

a Range is 0 to 26; national standard deviation is 3.7 (same for black and white schools).

b Mean for white schools minus mean for black schools.

c Means are not presented if based on less than 5 actual schools.

d Numbers in parentheses are actual number of schools.

cational facilities than white students. Most black schools (and most blacks) are in the regions with the lowest means, such as the rural South. Therefore, the fact that whites in those regions are just as deprived does not alter the fact that *nationally* blacks end up with less advantages. For some policy implications, it may not be so important to ask what caused the difference as to recognize that a difference does seem to exist.

◆ *Teacher Quality*

The second set of school characteristics for our comparison concerns the quality of the teachers in a school. From the USOE data on teachers we were able to construct indices in two general areas of teaching competency which might be relevant to student academic achievement: professional background and general verbal achievement. We note again that there was no information obtainable from the questionnaires concerning teaching methods or more general personality characteristics of teachers (e.g., authoritarianism, warmth and empathy, charisma, etc.).

A professional background index was constructed for each teacher by giving him a score of 1 for each of the following conditions: (a) holding a Master's degree or higher; (b) undergraduate major in education or in the regular arts and sciences (as opposed to agriculture, business, physical education, etc.); (c) most undergraduate courses taken at a regular four-year university or college; (d) 11 or more semester hours of college work done beyond the *highest* degree; (e) having taught at least 5 but not more than 29 years; and (f) reading regularly two or more national educational journals. If a teacher did not answer 3 or more questions, his index score was treated as missing. A teacher with the highest score on this index, 6, would have a relatively high degree of training and involvement in the teaching profession. We then took an average of this index for all the teachers in each school.

Table 3 presents the average teacher-background index scores for black and white schools in the various regional combinations. For the nation as a whole the mean is 2.9, with a low of 2.5 for Great Lakes nonmetropolitan black schools and highs of 3.4 for black schools in several areas. The national standard deviation is .6, and it is the same for black and white schools separately. Again, we find that the differences between black and white schools are not consistent throughout different areas in the country. Of the 10 comparisons we can make, only 4 seem to indicate large differences between black and white schools (i.e., differences approaching a standard deviation). Surprisingly, it is the black schools with the higher average in all 4 of these comparisons. Moreover, 3 of the 4 occur in the South and Southwest regions. These differences lead to national averages of 3.1 and 2.8 for black and white schools, respectively. By our teacher-

TABLE 3

Mean Teacher-Background Index Scores For Elementary Schools[a]

Racial Comp. Region	Metropolitan			Nonmetropolitan			All Areas			All Schools
Size	Black Schools	White Schools	Difference[b]	Black Schools	White Schools	Difference	Black Schools	White Schools	Difference	
New England	[c] (4)[d]	2.6 (64)			2.6 (9)		(4)	2.6 (73)		2.6 (77)
Mid-Atlantic	2.8 (56)	2.8 (169)	0.0	2.6 (8)	2.7 (48)	+0.1	2.7 (64)	2.8 (217)	+0.1	2.8 (281)
Great Lakes	3.3 (52)	2.8 (169)	−0.5	2.5 (6)	2.7 (38)	+0.2	3.2 (58)	2.8 (207)	−0.4	2.8 (265)
Plains	2.9 (9)	2.9 (35)	0.0	(4)	2.7 (47)		2.8 (13)	2.8 (82)	0.0	2.8 (95)
South	3.4 (90)	2.7 (63)	−0.7	2.9 (201)	2.7 (210)	−0.2	3.2 (291)	2.7 (273)	−0.5	2.8 (564)
Southwest	3.3 (18)	2.8 (17)	−0.5	3.4 (24)	2.8 (51)	−0.6	3.4 (42)	2.8 (68)	−0.6	2.9 (110)
Pacific	3.4 (22)	3.3 (90)	−0.1		2.9 (77)		3.4 (22)	3.1 (167)	−0.3	3.2 (189)
Nation	3.3 (251)	2.9 (607)	−0.4	2.8 (243)	2.7 (480)	−0.1	3.1 (494)	2.8 (1087)	−0.3	2.9 (1581)

[a] Range is o to 6; national standard deviation is .6 (same for black and white schools).
[b] Mean for white schools minus mean for black schools.
[c] Means are not presented if based on less than 5 actual schools.
[d] Numbers in parentheses are actual numbers of schools.

background index, then, black schools show somewhat of an advantage when compared to white schools.

We must make at least two cautionary remarks about the interpretation of these results. First, the index we have constructed measures only one possible aspect of teacher competence; other components may be much more important for various student output characteristics. Second, in southern black schools, where most of the higher scores for black schools occur, a majority of the teachers are black, and this is not the case in many of the other regions. If most of these southern black teachers went to all-black colleges in the South, where academic quality is reputed to be very low, then their background characteristics may not be comparable to those of white teachers (or to northern black teachers). On the other hand, it may well be that the average southern white teacher is really less adequately trained than the black teacher.

To shed further light on this issue, Table 4 presents the average proportion of teachers in the elementary grades in each of the regions who are black. For technical reasons, we had to average across all teachers in a cell, without regard to the school; i.e., the percentages are of individuals, not averages of school percents. They do not differ greatly from the school averages.

As we can see, in the South and Southwestern regions the large majority of teachers in black schools are themselves black, and this is the case in only three of the remaining seven regions. These results indicate that any comparison of teacher characteristics between black and white schools in the southern regions may, in fact, be a comparison of black and white teachers.

This issue is also raised by the measure presented in the next table, teacher's verbal achievement. The USOE teacher questionnaires contained a short verbal achievement test (30 items). From this test it was possible to construct a teacher verbal achievement score by simply summing the number of correct answers. The range was 0 to 30, with 30 indicating high verbal facility. The averages are presented in Table 5. The national mean is 24, with a standard deviation of 3.6. The standard deviation of black schools is 3.6, while that of white schools is 1.7. White schools in several areas are tied for the highest average, 25, while southern nonmetropolitan black schools had the lowest mean at a little under 18.

The black-white differences are striking. In all ten comparisons the teachers in black schools have lower means, with some of them going beyond one standard deviation. The national comparison shows that the black school average is 5 less than the white school average, just about 1½ standard deviations. It is just as striking to notice that the largest differences occur in those regions which showed the largest percent of black teachers in black schools (see Table 4). In all four of the southern areas and in the nonmetropolitan Mid-Atlantic and Great Lakes, where black schools have

TABLE 4

Percent of Elementary Teachers Who Are Black[a]

Size	Metropolitan			Nonmetropolitan			All Areas		
Racial Comp. Region	Black Schools	White Schools	Difference[b]	Black Schools	White Schools	Difference	Black Schools	White Schools	Difference
New England	c	3 (1143)[d]			0 (130)			3 (1273)	
Mid-Atlantic	30 (1064)	12 (4857)	+18	99 (179)	3 (922)	+96	40 (1243)	11 (5779)	+29
Great Lakes	33 (1507)	8 (2987)	+23	100 (20)	5 (575)	+95	34 (1527)	7 (3562)	+27
Plains	98 (196)	6 (785)	+92	21 (82)	4 (718)	+17	76 (278)	5 (1503)	+71
South	99 (1945)	2 (1051)	+97	98 (3664)	4 (2922)	+94	98 (5609)	4 (3973)	+94
Southwest	78 (432)	7 (587)	+71	78 (952)	5 (1296)	+73	78 (1384)	6 (1883)	+72
Pacific	42 (360)	5 (2045)	+38		2 (1492)		42 (360)	4 (3537)	+38

[a] The percents are unweighted and are based on all individual teachers; they are not averages or school-level percentages.
[b] White school percent minus black school percent.
[c] Blank cells indicate no black schools.
[d] Number in parentheses is actual number of teachers.

TABLE 5

Mean Teacher Verbal Achievement Scores For Elementary Schools[a]

Size	Metropolitan			Nonmetropolitan			All Areas			All Schools
Racial Comp. Region	Black Schools	White Schools	Difference[b]	Black Schools	White Schools	Difference	Black Schools	White Schools	Difference	
New England	c (4)[d]	25 (64)			25 (9)			25 (73)		25 (77)
Mid-Atlantic	23 (56)	25 (169)	+2	20 (8)	25 (48)	+5	21 (64)	25 (217)	+3	24 (281)
Great Lakes	23 (52)	25 (169)	+2	20 (6)	25 (38)	+5	23 (58)	25 (207)	+2	25 (265)
Plains	22 (9)	25 (35)	+3	(4)	24 (47)		22 (13)	24 (82)	+2	24 (95)
South	19 (90)	24 (63)	+5	18 (201)	23 (210)	+5	18 (291)	24 (273)	+6	22 (564)
Southwest	20 (18)	25 (17)	+5	20 (24)	24 (51)	+4	20 (42)	24 (68)	+4	24 (110)
Pacific	24 (22)	25 (90)	+1		25 (77)		24 (22)	25 (167)	+1	25 (189)
Nation	21 (251)	25 (607)	+4	19 (243)	24 (480)	+5	20 (494)	25 (1087)	+5	24 (1581)

a Range is 0 to 30; national standard deviation is 3.6 (3.6 for black schools and 1.7 for white schools).
b Mean for white schools minus mean for black schools.
c Means are not presented if based on less than 5 actual schools.
d Numbers in parentheses are actual number of schools.

over 75 percent black teachers, the black school averages are from 4 to 5 less than white schools. In the metropolitan Mid-Atlantic, Great Lakes, and Pacific areas, where black schools have from 30 to 42 percent black teachers, the differences drop to 1 or 2 points. The only exception to this trend seems to be the metropolitan Plains region, with black schools having 98 percent black teachers, but where the difference is only 3 points. This is still a larger difference, however, than those in areas where black schools have majority white faculties.

This is convincing evidence that black teachers score lower on verbal achievement tests when compared to white teachers, even though, in some cases, their "objective" training and experience—as measured by the professional-background index—are superior to those of white teachers. The implication is that black teachers themselves have been "deprived" at some point in their background, although not necessarily by the schools they attended. The general differences in black and white student achievement which we shall document in the next section may be pervasive and lasting, extending even into the teaching profession itself.

The conclusion we draw is that black schools may be more deprived than white schools not necessarily because of formal academic characteristics of their staff, but because of race itself. The faculties of black schools may be of lower quality because most of them are mainly composed of blacks. Even though black teachers' formal training seems as extensive as that of white teachers, if not more so, their verbal scores indicate that they have far less academic achievement. It is especially ironic that, when schools are concerned with raising black student achievement, that the black teachers who have the major responsibility for it suffer from the same disadvantage as their students.

◆ *School Expenditures*

Our final school measure is annual per-student expenditures as measured by teacher salaries. As we have said, since salaries make up the bulk of school budgets, this index should vary in the same way as total per-student expenditures. As such it ought to be a partial assessment of possible school qualities not explicitly measured in the various school questionnaires. It is our assumption that schools with more funds can provide better facilities and services and attract better teachers, and can thereby be in a position to improve student academic achievement. The index was computed for each school by averaging annual teacher income from the teachers' questionnaires and multiplying by the number of teachers (principal's estimate) to get an estimate of total annual teacher salary. This total was divided by total student enrollment (principal's estimate) for the per-capita index.

The data are presented in Table 6. Missing observations occurred for about 7 percent of the sample. The national mean on the salary expendi-

TABLE 6

Mean Annual Per-Student Expenditures On Teacher Salaries For Elementary Schools, in Dollars[a]

Size	Metropolitan			Nonmetropolitan			All Areas			All Schools
Racial Comp. Region	Black Schools	White Schools	Difference[b]	Black Schools	White Schools	Difference	Black Schools	White Schools	Difference	
New England	c (3)[d]	262 (63)			208 (9)		c (3)	246 (72)		247 (75)
Mid-Atlantic	258 (54)	284 (164)	+26	219 (8)	227 (46)	+8	240 (62)	261 (210)	+21	259 (272)
Great Lakes	253 (50)	242 (164)	−11	187 (6)	222 (37)	+35	240 (56)	238 (201)	−2	238 (257)
Plains	229 (7)	222 (35)	−7	c (4)	247 (43)		200 (11)	236 (78)	+36	232 (89)
South	189 (82)	182 (61)	−7	163 (183)	177 (205)	+14	177 (265)	178 (266)	+1	178 (531)
Southwest	202 (15)	190 (16)	−12	266 (22)	222 (50)	−44	242 (37)	203 (66)	−39	209 (103)
Pacific	270 (21)	264 (87)	−6		298 (75)		270 (21)	279 (162)	+9	278 (183)
Nation	224 (232)	243 (590)	+19	186 (223)	222 (465)	+36	210 (455)	234 (1055)	+24	230 (1510)

a National standard deviation is 67 dollars (62 for black schools and 67 for white schools).
b Mean for white schools —mean for black schools.
c Means are not presented if based on less than 5 actual schools.
d Numbers in parentheses are actual number of schools.

tures index is $230 per student. The national standard deviation is $67, being $62 for black schools and $67 for white schools.

Again we find a mixed picture with respect to black-white comparisons within the various regions. In the metropolitan Mid-Atlantic region black schools average $258, lower than the white schools average of $284. Also, in the nonmetropolitan South, black schools average $163, $9 less than white schools. Yet in 6 of the 10 comparisons the black schools have the higher average, the largest difference being $44 in the Southwest nonmetropolitan region. It must be stressed, of course, that all but one of these differences is only a small fraction of the standard deviation. There is some possibility, therefore, that some of the small black-white differences are due to chance variations and would not be repeated in other samples of elementary schools.

As in the school-facilities index, there are some very large differences among the seven regions. The Pacific region has the highest average, $278, while the South is $100 lower at $178. These data seem to confirm the notion that states in the western part of the country place the strongest stress on education, while states in the South place the least stress. The Mid-Atlantic region also has a relatively high average, $258, while the Southwest is low with $209. The remaining are fairly close to the national average.

Largely because of the low South means and the large number of black schools there, at the national level black schools average $24 less than white schools for per-capita teacher salaries. This is less than one half of a standard deviation, however, so that the difference is not as large, comparatively, as that for teacher verbal ability. Nonetheless, it may be important for policy to note that blacks as a whole receive less expenditures for education.

SUMMARY.   To summarize the comparison of black and white schools with regard to school inputs, we cannot come to very different conclusions from those in the original Coleman report, even though our analytical approach has been quite different. With the exception of teacher verbal achievement, none of our measures show black schools as being far behind white schools within regions. For the teacher-background index, black schools were shown to have somewhat higher average index scores than white schools. For the school facilities index and per-student teacher salaries, there were strong regional variations, with the southern regions having the lowest averages, but no consistent black-white differences within regions. At the national level, black schools were slightly lower than white schools for facilities and teacher salaries, although it was felt that the main reason for this was a combination of the large number of black schools in the South and the lower South averages. Black schools were definitely lower than white schools on average teacher verbal achievement scores. It was concluded that all of the large differences could be explained by the facts that most teachers in those black schools with the lowest averages are themselves black, and that black teachers score lower than white teachers on the achievement test.

Our model posited that these factors were important for student output measures. If such is the case, any difference in these factors between black and white schools would tend to have serious consequences to differential student achievement. The fact that we have not observed many differences in them for black and white schools, however, does not necessarily tell us anything about black-white differences in student achievement or in community input factors. Moreover, we have not tested the basic model yet; we do not know if the school factors are empirically associated with student achievement. It is to these issues which we now turn.

V. STUDENT ACHIEVEMENT AND COMMUNITY INPUTS

◆ *Student Achievement*

One of the less controversial findings in the original USOE study was that black students scored less than whites on all achievement tests administered:

The average [black] pupil scores distinctly lower on these tests at every level than the average white pupil. The [black] pupils' scores are as much as one standard deviation below the [white] pupils' scores in the first grade. At the twelfth grade, results of tests . . . show that . . . [black] scores are further below the [whites'].[21]

The facts that large differences in black-white achievement occurred in the 1st grade, that the differences did not diminish in the later school grades, and that consistent differences were *not* found in school inputs for blacks and whites led Coleman to consider family-background factors as major factors in determining achievement. We will reexamine this issue by first considering, at the school level, black-white school differences in achievement.

We have chosen to use the results of verbal achievement tests as our major measure of student academic achievement. We have already seen that for the USOE data these results are very similar to those of other ability tests in the elementary grades. Our basic procedure will be to analyze the average 6th-grade verbal achievement scores as the student output of the elementary schools.

There is one modification of our aggregation procedure which we will follow when examining student achievement. Since this is our dependent variable, and since black and white schools do contain some students of the respective minority race, there was some possibility that black and white performance individually would not be the same within predominantly black and predominantly white schools. If it is not, then aggregating achievement scores without regard to race could obscure relations between achievement and school or community input factors. We made a refinement by aggregating achievement scores separately for blacks and whites in each school.

Figure 2 presents data bearing on our concern for differential black and white performance in schools of differing racial composition. It is a graph of average 6th-grade black and white verbal achievement plotted against the racial composition of the grade for each school. The 6th-grade verbal achievement test had a possible individual score range from 0 to 50. The national average (without regard to race) of the school averages is 33, with a school-level standard deviation of 6.2.

Although the scores generally decrease with an increase in percent black, there are several other interesting patterns which emerge. In predominantly white schools, white students score higher than black students on the average, and the differences exceed one standard deviation. But in schools where the percentage black exceeds about 65 percent, the effect is reversed: blacks score higher than whites. After this point is reached, there is also a slight tendency for blacks to score higher as the percentage black approaches 100. However, in no case does a black average in black schools surpass black averages in white schools with 1 to 25 percent black enrollment. While the majority race generally performs better than the minority race, the "best" racial composition from the standpoint of both races would be somewhere between 1 and 25 percent black. According to the graph, white scores decrease only slightly with this proportion black, while black scores are considerably higher. When we controlled for region, similar patterns emerged.[22]

We do not want to imply, of course, that the pattern of scores in the graph is due only to racial composition. Socioeconomic factors also vary with racial composition. Nonetheless, these patterns do confirm the facts that, regardless of the exact causal relationships, blacks on the average are currently performing best in majority-white environments, and that whites are not performing substantially worse in moderately integrated environments than in all-white schools. We must point out again, however, that only about 13 percent of black students are in these integrated schools.

Since we are doing a school-level analysis, and since we wish to consider black and white schools separately for the appropriate racial comparisons, the strong reversal shown in Figure 2 led us to analyze only the majority group's verbal achievement. Thus, except for what we have just pre-

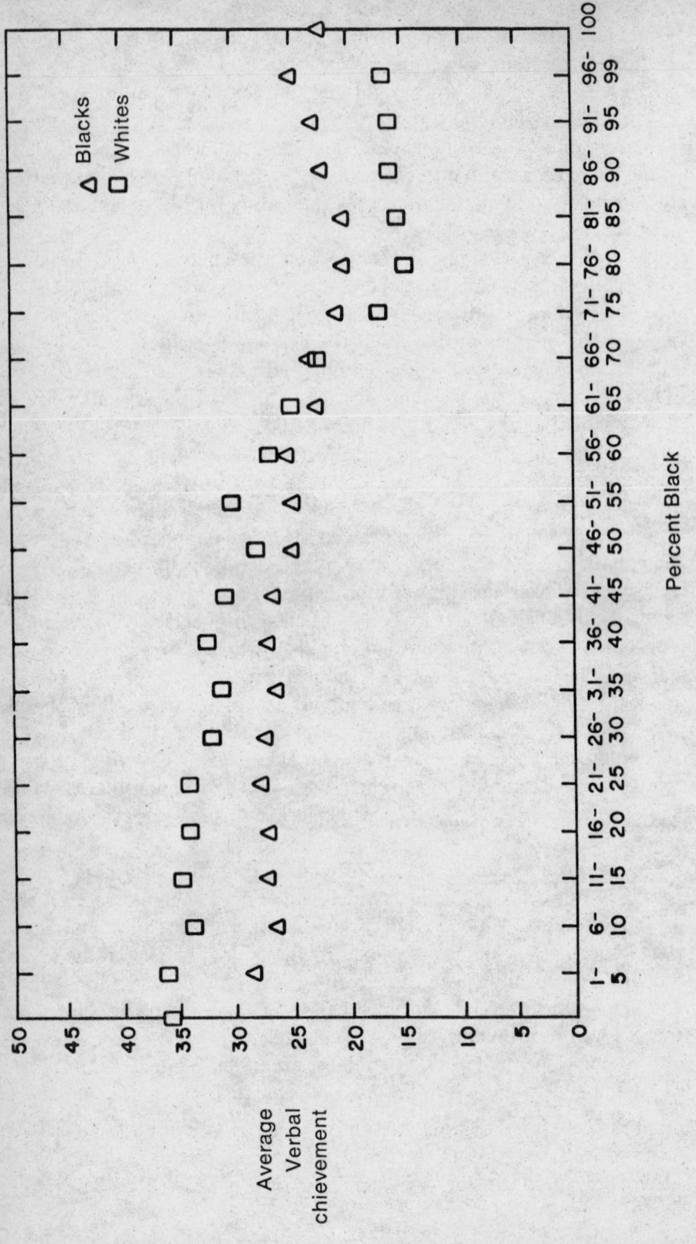

Figure II. Average 6th-Grade Verbal Achievement by Percent Black in Grade, for Blacks and Whites

sented, we will not be analyzing factors involved in the performance of each respective minority-status race. The specific effects of integration will be left to other chapters in this volume. Since, as we have seen, the vast majority of students attend a school in which they are the majority race, our approach seems to be a reasonable one for evaluating current educational processes.

Table 7 shows 6th-grade verbal achievement test averages for blacks in black schools and whites in white schools within our various regional strata. For black verbal achievement in black schools, the national standard deviation is 4.7; for white verbal achievement in white schools, it is 3.6. It is apparent from the table that black schools are far behind white schools, with most differences approaching or surpassing two national standard deviation units (6.2). For the nation, the average is 24 for black schools and 36 for white schools—a difference of almost two standard deviations. The differences are remarkably even throughout the regions, with only one difference going just barely below one and one half standard deviations. The magnitude of these differences cannot be overemphasized. In percentile terms if black schools are two standard deviations behind white schools, the white school which has an *average* score will be higher than 97 percent of the black schools!

In contrast to the strong racial differences, the regional differences seem fairly small. There seem to be no substantial differences between metropolitan and nonmetropolitan areas, when one considers black and white schools separately. For white schools, the largest regional difference is 4 points, between New England and the South; for black schools, the largest is 5 points, between the Plains and the South. The situation is just the reverse of our findings on the school measures, where regional differences were strong and racial differences slight.

Our model stated that one of the possible determinants of 6th-grade achievement output was the initial state of the student's academic achievement when he first entered elementary school. Unfortunately, the USOE data do not include any academic achievement test results for the sixth graders before they began school. However, since we are analyzing the school as a unit, we can examine the average 1st-grade verbal achievement scores. If there have not been too many changes in the school and community over the six-year period prior to the USOE study, or if whatever changes that occurred affected the two grades in about the same way, then the 1st-grade results can serve as a reasonable baseline comparison for the 6th grade.

Table 8 presents the average 1st-grade verbal achievement scores for black and white schools within each geographical region. The averages again are computed only for blacks in the black schools and only for whites in the white schools. Data were available on 880 elementary schools. As we said earlier, of the elementary schools in the original USOE sample, only half

TABLE 7

Mean Verbal Achievement Scores For 6th Grades[a]

Size	Metropolitan			Nonmetropolitan			All Areas			All Schools[c]
Racial Comp. Region	Blacks in Black Schools	Whites in White Schools	Difference[b]	Blacks in Black Schools	Whites in White Schools	Difference	Blacks in Black Schools	Whites in White Schools	Difference	
New England	d (4)[e]	38 (64)			37 (10)		(4)	38 (74)		37 (78)
Mid-Atlantic	26 (57)	37 (173)	+11	23 (8)	36 (49)	+13	25 (65)	36 (222)	+11	34 (287)
Great Lakes	26 (53)	37 (173)	+11	28 (6)	36 (41)	+8	26 (59)	37 (214)	+11	35 (273)
Plains	29 (9)	38 (35)	+9	(4)	38 (48)		27 (13)	38 (83)	+11	36 (96)
South	24 (91)	36 (63)	+12	20 (211)	33 (218)	+13	22 (302)	34 (281)	+12	29 (583)
Southwest	24 (18)	35 (17)	+11	24 (25)	36 (54)	+12	24 (43)	36 (71)	+12	33 (114)
Pacific	26 (22)	36 (91)	+10		38 (79)		26 (22)	37 (170)	+11	35 (192)
Nation	25 (254)	37 (616)	+12	22 (254)	36 (499)	+14	24 (508)	36 (1115)	+12	33 (1623)

a Range is 0 to 50; national standard deviation is 6.2 (4.7 for blacks in black schools and 3.6 for whites in white schools).
b Mean for white schools minus mean for black schools.
c Computed using average verbal scores aggregated for all students in a school.
d Means are not presented if based on less than 5 actual schools.
e Numbers in parentheses are actual number of schools.

TABLE 8

Mean Verbal Achievement Scores For 1st Grades[a]

Size	Metropolitan			Nonmetropolitan			All Areas			All Schools[c]
Racial Comp. Region	Blacks in Black Schools	Whites in White Schools	Difference[b]	Blacks in Black Schools	Whites in White Schools	Difference	Blacks in Black Schools	Whites in White Schools	Difference	
New England	[d] (4)[e]	19 (35)			19 (5)		(4)	19 (40)		19 (44)
Mid-Atlantic	15 (32)	19 (81)	+4	15 (5)	19 (22)	+4	15 (37)	19 (103)	+4	18 (140)
Great Lakes	16 (25)	19 (83)	+3	(2)	20 (19)		16 (27)	19 (102)	+3	19 (129)
Plains	17 (5)	20 (14)	+3	(4)	20 (29)		17 (9)	20 (43)	+3	20 (52)
South	16 (56)	19 (34)	+3	16 (124)	18 (122)	+2	16 (180)	18 (156)	+2	18 (336)
Southwest	16 (13)	19 (6)	+3	16 (15)	19 (31)	+3	16 (28)	19 (37)	+3	18 (65)
Pacific	16 (14)	19 (50)	+3		19 (50)		16 (14)	19 (100)	+3	19 (114)
Nation	16 (149)	19 (303)	+3	16 (150)	19 (278)	+3	16 (299)	19 (581)	+3	18 (880)[f]

a Range is 0 to 25; national standard deviation is 2 (2 for black schools and 1.6 for white schools).

b Mean for white schools minus mean for black schools.

c Computed using average verbal scores aggregated for all students in a school.

d Means are not presented if based on less than 5 actual schools.

e Numbers in parentheses are actual number of schools.

f The original USEO study tested only a 50% random sample of the 1st grades in the school sample.

of the 1st grades were selected (randomly) for achievement test administration. The possible individual test score range was 0 to 25. The national 1st-grade school-level average is 18, with a school-level standard deviation of 2.0. The standard deviation was 2.0 for black schools and 1.6 for white schools.

The table quite clearly shows that the average black 1st-grade verbal achievement is less than that for white 1st grades, and that the difference is again very even across the regions. The difference ranges from one to two standard deviations. Nationally, blacks in black schools average 16, and whites in white schools average 19, one and one half standard deviations higher.

Before blacks even start school, therefore, it appears they are considerably far behind whites in verbal achievement. Moreover, black students are still far behind in the 6th grade. As we cited above, Coleman claims that blacks actually fall further behind whites as they advance from 1st grade through high school. Our 1st- to 6th-grade differences seem to indicate this trend. There are two conditions, however, which make such comparisons tenuous at best. First, the 1st and 6th grades in the USOE data represent two cohorts at one point in time, not one cohort measured at two times. We do not know if the present sixth graders actually had a pattern of verbal achievement scores like the present first graders. Second, and more serious, the two grades were given different verbal achievement tests. Therefore, one standard deviation on the 1st-grade test may not mean exactly the same thing as one standard deviation on the 6th-grade test. Keeping these qualifications in mind, it may be instructive to consider the black-white differentials in more detail.

Table 9 is a better illustration of the relative gaps between black and white schools at the two grade levels. The relative differences between black and white schools are shown by expressing the differentials in standard deviation units. First, we computed the 1st-grade black-white gap as a proportion of one standard deviation on the 1st-grade verbal achievement test. We did the same thing for 6th-grade differentials, expressed as a proportion of the 6th-grade standard deviation. The entries in Table 9, therefore, are the number of standard deviations that black students average behind whites in verbal achievement. For example, consider the summary figures for all schools in the nation (lower right-hand corner of the table): in the 1st grades, the average black school was 1.5 standard deviations behind the average white school. In the 6th grade, black schools were 1.9 standard deviations behind, making an estimated *increase* in the black-white gap of almost one half of a standard deviation.

Inspection of the table shows that in only one area, metropolitan Mid-Atlantic, does the black-white differential diminish from 1st to 6th grade. In another, metropolitan Plains, there is no change, and all the other areas show increases in the differential. It is most distressing to see that the larg-

TABLE 9

Number of Standard Deviations in Verbal Achievement That Blacks Average Behind Whites[a]

	Metropolitan		Nonmetropolitan		All Areas	
Grade	1st Grades	6th Grades	1st Grades	6th Grades	1st Grades	6th Grades
Region						
New England	[b]					
Mid-Atlantic	2	1.8	2	2.1	2	1.8
Great Lakes	1.5	1.8		1.3	1.5	1.8
Plains	1.5	1.5			1.5	1.8
South	1.5	1.9	1	2.1	1	1.9
Southwest	1.5	1.8	1.5	1.9	1.5	1.9
Pacific	1.5	1.6			1.5	1.8
Nation	1.5	1.9	1.5	2.3	1.5	1.9

[a] In standard deviation units relative to each grade.
[b] Blank cells indicate insufficient number of cases for computing differential.

est increases in the gap occur in the southern regions, the regions where the largest number of blacks live. The increase in the gap even reaches a full standard deviation in the nonmetropolitan South region.

Because of the qualifications we have stated, we cannot flatly agree with Coleman's conclusion. Nevertheless, it is clear that blacks perform dramatically lower on verbal achievement tests than whites, and the large initial difference at the 1st-grade level probably does not decrease over the six-year elementary-school period. These results show that schooling as a whole does not close the achievement gap for blacks, regardless of what school factors we measure and regardless of how good or bad schools are. If we combine this with the fact that black and white schools did not differ substantially on most of our measured school input factors, a case can be made that school factors similar to those above will not be sufficient to close the gap in the future.

♦ Community Input Factors

We have shown large differences between the races in our student output measure, achievement, and we have failed to find large racial differences for most of the school input factors. It now remains for us to test for racial difference on the other major set of inputs specified in our model: community input factors.

Before discussing the indices, there are three points about our procedure here which need additional clarification. First, the term "community inputs" actually covers only aggregated characteristics of students' families. As such, they may reflect only the composition of the immediate neighborhood of the school, and even then only insofar as the 6th-grade class is a representative cross section of that neighborhood. Moreover, our school-level analysis does not allow us to differentiate the effects of individual family characteristics on their own children from the effects of families in general on children not their own (neighborhood effects). Therefore, our "community input" measures combine both "family" and "neighborhood" effects.

Second, because of this combination we will aggregate community input measures over both races in a school. Although they will of course be heavily weighted by the majority race for a given school, we still want our community input measures, as independent variables, to reflect all environmental conditions. Minority race characteristics are an important part of this community environment.

Third, in this section we will present the community input indices for the 6th grades only. Since the 6th-grade achievement is our output measure, we are most interested in sixth graders' aggregate family background. We did carry out the analyses on the 1st grades, however, and we can report that they are in substantial agreement with the findings on the 6th grades. The main difference was that the averages on some of the indices were lower for first graders than for sixth graders, no doubt because first graders' parents represent a younger population. But all of the relative racial differences which we report in the next four tables were replicated for 1st grades.

The first community input measure concerns the structure of the family. There has been much discussion of the claim in Moynihan's report on the black family that blacks have less intact family structure than whites.[23] Our index was constructed by taking the percentage of sixth graders who had both natural (or adoptive) parents living at home. It is our assumption that an intact family structure is more likely to lead to better initial and continuing academic achievement of children than a family characterized by a missing parent or a similar family problem.

The results for black and white schools are presented in Table 10. The national mean is 76 percent, with a standard deviation of 15 percent. The standard deviation for black schools is about 14 percent, and for white schools 10 percent. The black and white school differences are substantial. While white schools have an average, nationally, of almost 80 percent with both parents, the black school average is 55 percent. The differences in the averages stay very large within all of the regions, ranging between 17 and 31 percentage points, or one to two standard deviations. As in the case of verbal achievement, these large cross-racial differences are not matched by any substantial regional variations. Other data indicate that most of the missing parents are fathers. Confirming the Moynihan report, therefore, our data show that almost half of black students live in families without their own father.

TABLE 10

Mean Percent of Sixth Graders Living With Both Original Parents[a]

Size	Metropolitan			Nonmetropolitan			All Areas			All Schools
Racial Comp. / Region	Black Schools	White Schools	Difference[b]	Black Schools	White Schools	Difference	Black Schools	White Schools	Difference	
New England	c (4)[d]	82 (64)			80 (10)		(4)	81 (74)		81 (78)
Mid-Atlantic	58 (57)	83 (173)	+25	59 (8)	81 (49)	+22	58 (65)	82 (222)	+24	79 (287)
Great Lakes	56 (53)	83 (173)	+27	52 (6)	82 (41)	+30	55 (59)	82 (214)	+27	80 (273)
Plains	51 (9)	82 (35)	+31	(4)	83 (48)		51 (13)	83 (83)	+22	79 (96)
South	53 (91)	79 (63)	+26	54 (211)	80 (218)	+26	54 (302)	80 (281)	+26	72 (583)
Southwest	47 (18)	76 (17)	+29	56 (25)	75 (54)	+19	53 (43)	76 (71)	+23	70 (114)
Pacific	58 (22)	75 (91)	+17		78 (79)		58 (22)	77 (170)	+19	75 (192)
Nation	54 (254)	80 (616)	+26	55 (254)	80 (499)	+25	55 (508)	80 (1115)	+25	76 (1623)

a Including adopted parents; national standard deviation is 15% (14% for black schools and 10% for white schools).
b White school percent minus black school percent.
c Percents are not given if based on less than 5 actual schools.
d Number in parentheses is actual number of schools.

The second community input measure concerns the average occupational status of the father. We generated an occupational social-class index by considering the percentage of sixth graders whose fathers are in white-collar occupations. For our purposes, white-collar occupations include salesmen, officials, managers and proprietors, technicians, and the professions. The non-white-collar occupations include unskilled, semiskilled, and skilled workers, farmers, and clerical and service workers.[24] The means on this measure are given in Table 11.

Again, large and consistent differences are found between black and white schools. The national average is 29 percent. The standard deviation for all schools, and for white schools as a group, is about 18 percent; for black schools, it is about 9 percent. About 31 percent of the students in the average white school have white-collar fathers, compared to 16 percent for black schools. This is almost one standard deviation. Black schools are less white collar than white schools within all regions where comparisons are possible, but the differences seem smaller and there seems to be more variation than for the family structure index. The difference ranges from 6 percent in one region to 21 percent in three regions. Nonetheless, these differences are all larger than those found for all but one of the school measures.

The third index was formed from a set of nine questions on household items as another measure of family life style. It was felt that this index may be a somewhat better economic indicator than some of the other indices we are using. The nine items were television set, telephone, record player or hi-fi, refrigerator, dictionary, encyclopedia, automobile, vacuum cleaner, and daily newspaper. Each student answered these by indicating whether they did or did not have each one. To form the index, the number of items possessed was taken for each student in the 6th grade and averaged over the whole grade. If a student did not indicate yes or no for four or more items, he was counted as having a missing observation on the index score. To the extent that this index reflects the economic well-being of a family, then, it is our prediction that it will lead to better academic achievement on the part of the children.

Table 12 gives the means on the household-items index, and it shows consistent differences for black and white schools, with the black schools having a lower mean index score in every case where comparisons are possible. The national average is 7.6 with a standard deviation of 1.1. The black and white schools separately have standard deviations of 1.2 and .8. The means for black and white schools are 6.1 and 7.9, respectively—well beyond one standard deviation apart. The differences are greater than or equal to one standard deviation in all but the metropolitan Pacific region, where it is .9. There also seem to be some geographic differences on the index scores, with lower means in nonmetropolitan areas than in metropolitan areas for both black and white schools.

Our final community input measure is based on the education of the

TABLE 11

Mean Percent of 6th Grades With White-Collar Fathers[a]

Size	Metropolitan			Nonmetropolitan			All Areas			
Racial Comp. Region	Black Schools	White Schools	Difference[b]	Black Schools	White Schools	Difference	Black Schools	White Schools	Difference	All Schools
New England	[c] (4)[d]	40 (64)			32 (10)		(4)	37 (74)		37 (78)
Mid-Atlantic	21 (57)	38 (173)	+17	10 (8)	24 (49)	+14	16 (65)	32 (222)	+16	30 (287)
Great Lakes	11 (53)	30 (173)	+19	15 (6)	21 (41)	+ 6	12 (59)	28 (214)	+16	27 (273)
Plains	18 (9)	37 (35)	+19	(4)	21 (48)		18 (13)	27 (83)	+ 9	26 (96)
South	17 (91)	38 (63)	+21	13 (211)	23 (218)	+10	15 (302)	27 (281)	+12	23 (583)
Southwest	25 (18)	36 (17)	+11	18 (25)	39 (54)	+21	21 (43)	37 (71)	+16	35 (114)
Pacific	19 (22)	40 (91)	+21		34 (79)		19 (22)	37 (170)	+18	35 (192)
Nation	17 (254)	36 (616)	+19	14 (254)	26 (499)	+12	16 (508)	31 (1115)	+15	29 (1623)

[a] White collar means professional, technical, managerial, proprietor, and sales occupations (excludes clerical); national standard deviation is 18% (18% for black schools and 9% for white schools).
[b] White school percent minus black school percent.
[c] Percents are not given if based on less than 5 actual schools.
[d] Number in parentheses is actual number of schools.

TABLE 12

Mean Household-Items Index Scores For 6th Grades[a]

Size	Metropolitan			Nonmetropolitan			All Areas			All Schools
Racial Comp. Region	Black Schools	White Schools	Difference[b]	Black Schools	White Schools	Difference	Black Schools	White Schools	Difference	
New England	c (.4)[d]	8.4 (64)		(10) 7.9	7.9 (10)		(4)	8.2 (74)		8.2 (78)
Mid-Atlantic	6.8 (57)	8.2 (173)	+1.4	5.8 (8)	8.0 (49)	+2.2	6.4 (65)	8.1 (222)	+1.7	7.9 (287)
Great Lakes	7.0 (53)	8.3 (173)	+1.3	5.8 (6)	7.7 (41)	+1.9	6.8 (59)	8.2 (214)	+1.4	8.0 (273)
Plains	6.9 (9)	8.2 (35)	+1.3	(4)	7.8 (48)		6.5 (13)	7.9 (83)	+1.4	7.8 (96)
South	6.1 (91)	8.0 (63)	+1.9	5.0 (211)	7.0 (218)	+2.0	5.6 (302)	7.3 (281)	+1.7	6.7 (583)
Southwest	6.5 (18)	7.8 (17)	+1.3	5.6 (25)	7.5 (54)	+1.9	6.0 (43)	7.6 (71)	+1.6	7.4 (114)
Pacific	7.4 (22)	8.3 (91)	+0.9		7.8 (79)		7.4 (22)	8.1 (170)	+0.7	8.0 (192)
Nation	6.6 (254)	8.2 (616)	+1.6	5.3 (254)	7.5 (499)	+2.2	6.1 (508)	7.9 (1115)	+1.8	7.6 (1623)

a Range is 0 to 9 items; national standard deviation is 1.1 (1.2 for black schools and .8 for white schools).
b White school mean minus black school percent.
c Percents are not given if based on less than 5 actual schools.
d Number in parentheses is actual number of schools.

students' parents. For each student in the 6th grade, the education of his mother and father was trichotomized into these categories:

Score 0   less than high-school graduate
      1   high-school graduate, including post-high-school business or technical training
      2   some college or more education

An education index score for a student was then obtained by adding the scores for his mother and father. If no information was available for one parent, it was assumed that the education level of the other parent was the same for both, on the grounds that there is generally a high correlation between education levels of husbands and wives. A score of 0 would indicate both parents had less than a high-school education; a score of 4 would indicate both parents had some college education. An index was formed for a school by averaging the scores for each student over the whole 6th grade.

As can be seen in Table 13, the national average is 1.7. The national standard deviation was .7, and it was about the same for black and white schools nationally. As was the case for the fathers'-occupation index, black schools are generally lower than white schools, although no difference quite reaches one standard deviation. Nationally, black schools average 1.3 and white schools 1.8—almost one standard deviation apart.

Although we have examined some 40 black-white comparisons on four different measures of socioeconomic life style, in Table 13 we see the first case of a black school average being higher than a white school average. In the metropolitan Southwest, black schools average .1 higher than white schools on the education index.

SUMMARY.   We have seen large differences in our school output measure, 6th-grade achievement, when predominantly black schools are compared to predominantly white schools. The differences show clearly that black achievement is behind white achievement. At the same time, we saw that black and white 1st-grade achievement showed a similar gap. Also, for aggregate family life-style factors, we have documented black-white differences of the same order of magnitude. Recalling our results from the previous section, we could not find consistent differences of the same magnitude on 3 of the 4 school input measures. Thus, it seems relatively clear at this point that if we are to find factors to explain the large achievement differences between black and white schools in the various regions, the family-background factors would be far better prospects than the school input factors, with the exception of teacher verbal achievement.

We arrive, therefore, at the reconsideration of the second controversial Coleman conclusion stated at the outset of this chapter, that school factors do seem to have less effects on achievement than family background (or community input) factors. If we take the achievement differential between the races as the main effect or criterion to be explained, then the evidence

TABLE 13

Mean Parents'-Education Index Scores For 6th Grades[a]

Size Racial Comp. Region	Metropolitan Black Schools	Metropolitan White Schools	Metropolitan Difference[b]	Nonmetropolitan Black Schools	Nonmetropolitan White Schools	Nonmetropolitan Difference	All Areas Black Schools	All Areas White Schools	All Areas Difference	All Schools
New England	[c] (4)[d]	2.2 (64)		(10)	1.7 (10)		(4)	2.0 (74)		2.0 (78)
Mid-Atlantic	1.6 (57)	2.1 (173)	+0.5	1.1 (8)	1.7 (49)	+0.6	1.4 (65)	1.9 (222)	+0.5	1.8 (287)
Great Lakes	1.5 (53)	2.0 (173)	+0.5	1.2 (6)	1.6 (41)	+0.4	1.5 (59)	1.9 (214)	+0.4	1.9 (273)
Plains	1.9 (9)	2.2 (35)	+0.3	(4)	1.8 (48)		1.4 (13)	2.0 (83)	+0.6	1.9 (96)
South	1.3 (91)	1.8 (63)	+0.5	0.8 (211)	1.3 (218)	+0.5	1.1 (302)	1.4 (281)	+0.3	1.3 (583)
Southwest	1.7 (18)	1.6 (17)	−0.1	1.2 (25)	1.8 (54)	+0.6	1.4 (43)	1.7 (71)	+0.3	1.6 (114)
Pacific	1.7 (22)	2.3 (91)	+0.6	(79)	2.0 (79)		1.7 (22)	2.2 (170)	+0.5	2.2 (192)
Nation	1.5 (254)	2.0 (616)	+0.5	0.9 (254)	1.6 (499)	+0.7	1.3 (508)	1.8 (1115)	+0.5	1.7 (1623)

a Range is 0 to 4; 4 means both parents with some college or higher education. National standard deviation is .7 (same for black and white schools).

b White school mean minus black school mean.

c Percents are not given if based on less than 5 actual schools.

d Number in parentheses is actual number of schools.

presented so far is in overwhelming agreement with the Coleman finding.

However, it is possible that the educational process model we have presented works differently for black schools and for white schools. If so, we need to look at variation in black school achievement, and at variation in white school achievement, and relate each of these separately to our various school and community input factors. At the same time, we can utilize a somewhat more appropriate and compact analytic method, based on correlation and regression techniques, in our final tests of Coleman's conclusion and the educational process model we postulated.

VI. THE PREDICTION OF ACHIEVEMENT

There seem to be two somewhat independent sets of evidence that led the Coleman team to conclude that school effects on achievement were much smaller than family-background effects. One set was similar to what we have already presented, and it consisted of the findings of large black-white achievement differences at the 1st-grade level which persisted at all higher grade levels. The second set was the result of an individual student-level correlation and regression analysis, whereby estimates were computed for the effects of various school and family input factors on verbal achievement variation.

It is this second set of findings which has come under considerable attack. The main basis of the criticism involves the particular way the regression analysis was computed:

The survey made the arbitrary choice of first "controlling" for student background and then introducing school resources into the analysis. Because the student background variables . . . served to some extent as statistical proxies for school resources, the later introduction of the school resource variables themselves had a small explanatory effect. The explanatory power shared jointly by school resources and social background was thus associated entirely with social background.[25]

Therefore, correlations between school and family inputs, due to the tendency of higher socioeconomic status communities to have better school resources, caused the Coleman procedure to underestimate the school input effects on student achievement.

We can apply a similar analysis using the measures developed for our elementary-school sample. We shall, however, attempt to carry out the regression analysis in a way that avoids the Coleman assumption of a particular causal sequence for family and school factors. The educational model presented earlier does not contain any such assumptions, and our analysis must be consistent with this.

There are two procedures followed in our analysis which should be noted. First, when we refer to black and white achievement, we will mean average black achievement in black schools and average white achievement in white schools. Whenever all schools are combined, we will present the average achievement of all students in a school. Second, we shall use the percentage black in a grade as a fifth community input variable in these analyses. As we said earlier, it seems reasonable to assume that percentage black is a community characteristic which may not be fully accounted for by the other four family life-style indices.

The most straightforward way to begin this analysis is to consider the uncontrolled correlations between 6th-grade verbal achievement and the nine school and community measures. These correlations are presented in Table 14 for the nation as a whole and for the various racial and regional strata.[26] The seven regions used in previous sections have been collapsed into North and South categories so that the correlations and later regressions will be based upon a sufficient number of schools in each area.

Considering the overall national correlations at the far right of the table, a picture emerges similar to what we have seen earlier in our tables of means. The four community input indices have uniformly strong correlations with total achievement, ranging from .51 for percent white collar to .80 for the household-items index. Also, consistent with the graph given in Figure 2, we see that percent black has a very strong negative correlation, −.76, with achievement. Of the four school measures, only teacher ability has a strong correlation, .63, with achievement. The per-capita salaries and school-facilities indices have relatively low correlations of .25 and .21, respectively. The teacher-background index actually has a slight negative correlation, −.08, with achievement. This is consistent with our earlier finding that black teachers are somewhat more likely to have better backgrounds and to be in black (i.e., lower-achieving) schools.

The pattern of correlations does appear to be different for black and white schools. The pattern for white schools as a whole is similar to the overall national pattern. Three community inputs—white collar, household items, and parents' education—still have strong correlations, ranging from .51 to .67. The family structure index drops to .31. This seems to indicate that while it is an important differentiating characteristic for black and white schools, it may not be as strong a determinant of achievement if we consider white schools as a group. A similar drop occurs for teacher verbal achievement; it is only .28 when white schools are considered alone. The correlations do not change much for the salaries and facilities indices, but the teacher background now has a slight positive correlation of .13. The

TABLE 14

Correlations of 6th-Grade Verbal Achievement With School and Community Input Factors[a]

Input Factors	All Areas	Metropolitan Areas		Nonmetropolitan Areas		All Schools
		North[b]	South[c]	North	South	
Black achievement in black schools						
Family structure	.14	.30	.19		.09	.65
White collar	.16	.27	.16		.02	.51
Household items	.60	.59	.54		.39	.80
Parents' ed.	.52	.39	.50		.25	.61
Teach. verbal	.46	.00	.46		.32	.63
Teach. background	.21	.02	.30	e	.18	−.08
Salaries	.42	.08	.53		.25	.25
Facilities	.33	.01	.22		.03	.21
Percent black	.04	.03	.41		.21	−.76
	(455–508)[d]	(135–145)	(97–109)		(205–236)	(1510–1623)
White achievement in white schools						
Family structure	.31	.49	.16	.20	.14	
White collar	.51	.60	.58	.30	.56	
Household items	.67	.71	.66	.38	.72	
Parents' ed.	.66	.64	.62	.56	.64	
Teach. verbal	.28	.25	.21	.06	.29	
Teach. background	.13	.05	−.01	.08	.20	
Salaries	.22	−.05	.34	.16	.21	
Facilities	.25	−.10	.17	.09	.23	
Percent black	−.22	−.35	−.04	−.30	−.07	
	(1055–1115)	(513–536)	(77–80)	(210–227)	(255–272)	

a Product-moment correlations, uncontrolled.
b North combines New England, Mid-Atlantic, Great Lakes, Plains, and Pacific regions.
c South combines South and Southwest regions.
d Numbers in parentheses are the ranges of the number of actual schools on which the correlations are based.
e Insufficient number of schools.

percent black factor has a correlation of —.22 for white schools, again consistent with the graph in Figure 2.

Within the different regional strata the white school pattern does not seem to vary too much. The same three community input factors have the strongest correlations with achievement for all regions except the nonmetropolitan North, where the white-collar and household-items correlations drop to .30 and .38, respectively. All the correlations, except that for percent black, seem to be lower in this region. In both of the North areas the salaries and facilities correlations are less than they are in the two southern areas, although even in the South these correlations are much smaller than those for the family-background measures.

The correlations for black schools are most different from white schools in the relative strength of school and community factors. Family structure and white collar have low correlations, .14 and .16, with black achievement. Thus, contrary to the Moynihan finding, family structure does not seem to be a strong correlate of either white or black achievement. The national-level correlation drops considerably once a control is made for race. Household items and parents' education still show strong correlations of .60 and .52, but all of the school factors have stronger correlations than they did for white schools, ranging from .21 for teacher background to .46 for teacher verbal achievement. Moreover, the same pattern seems to occur for both of the southern areas, although all of the correlations are generally low for the nonmetropolitan South region. The pattern for the metropolitan North black schools, however, looks more like the white school pattern. All the school factor correlations are close to 0.

The final relationship we note in the table is that for percent black in black schools. Although it is only .03 in the North, it is .41 and .21 in the South metropolitan and nonmetropolitan regions, respectively. This is what was observed in the graph in Figure 2, where in predominantly black schools there was an upswing in black achievement as the curve approached 100 percent black. It may be that in the South, unlike the North, segregation patterns have led to a situation where relatively higher status blacks are found in the segregated schools rather than the integrated (but predominantly black) schools. This seems to be borne out by the fact that, for example, the household-items index is correlated .29 with percent black (for black schools) in the metropolitan South, and .18 in the nonmetropolitan South.

Two general conclusions can be drawn from Table 14. First, the household-items and parents'-education indices seem to be the strongest correlates of achievement throughout most of the race and region groupings, and for white schools percent white collar is also a strong correlate. Family structure does not seem like an important variable for achievement when black and white schools are separated. Second, for both black and white schools in the northern areas, the school factor correlations are practically insignificant. The highest correlation of all the school factors in these areas is .25 between achievement and teacher verbal achievement in metropolitan white schools.

On the other hand, for schools in southern regions, the correlations between some of the school factors and achievement are uniformly moderate. This is particularly true for black schools. Therefore, it may be that the importance of school factors for achievement depends on what region is being considered. They may be more important in the South, even though they do not attain the strength of most of the community input factors.

Before making any final statement about these relations, we should examine a multiple regression analysis using the same variables. This analysis enables one to find the relationship between a given input factor and achievement with all other factors controlled. We shall present the regressions within each of the race and region combinations shown in Table 14. The technique of linear regression analysis was chosen both because there were no a priori reasons for assuming any particular curvilinear relationship among the various factors. Three regression measures are shown in the following tables: (1) standardized regression coefficients, which permit comparisons among the coefficients; (2) the predicted increase or decrease in achievement, given an increase of one standard deviation in a given input factor; and (3) the squared multiple correlation coefficient, which is a measure of the total amount of variation in achievement "explained" by the 9 input factors.

Table 15 presents the regression figures for all schools combined and for black and white schools separately. For all schools, our model of 9 variables accounts for almost 80 percent of the school-level variation in average achievement. Most of this variation is explained by 3 community input factors: household items, parents' education, and percent black, with coefficients of .34, .18, and −.35, respectively. The strongest school factor, on the other hand, is teacher verbal achievement, with a coefficient of only .08.

Each coefficient can be interpreted as the predicted change in achievement (in fractions of one achievement standard deviation) due to an increase of one standard deviation of a given factor, and given that all other factors are held constant. Therefore, with each of the other 8 factors held constant, an increase of one standard deviation of the household-items index would be associated with an increase of a little over one third of a standard deviation of average school achievement (about 2.1 points). For a standard deviation increase of teachers' verbal achievement, however, controlling for the other 8 factors makes the predicted increase in school achievement less than one tenth of a standard deviation (about .5 points).

Therefore, for the nation as a whole, 6th-grade achievement is better predicted by family-background variables than by school factors, even when no particular causal ordering of variables is assumed. Although the criti-

TABLE 15

Regression of 6th-Grade Verbal Achievement On School and Community Input Factors[a]

| | All Schools | | White Achievement in White Schools | | Black Achievement in Black Schools | |
Regression Measure Factor	Regression Coefficient[b]	Predicted Change in Achievement[c]	Regression Coefficient	Predicted Change in Achievement[d]	Regression Coefficient	Predicted Change in Achievement[e]
Family structure	.11	+ .7	.08	+ .4	.02	+ .7
White collar	.04	+ .2	.04	+ .2	−.03	+ .1
Household items	.34	+2.1	.38	+1.8	.36	+1.3
Parents' ed.	.18	+1.1	.36	+1.7	.27	+1.0
Teach. verbal	.08	+ .5	.06	+ .3	.13	+ .5
Teach. background	−.02	− .1	−.06	− .3	.05	+ .2
Salaries	.07	+ .4	.11	+ .5	.13	+ .5
Facilities	−.08	− .5	−.13	− .6	−.12	− .4
Percent black	−.35	−2.1	−.07	− .3	.12	+ .4
Achievement variation explained[f]	79%		56%		45%	

a Linear regression; the number of schools for each regression is the same as that shown in Table 14.
b Standardized coefficient (beta weight).
c Given a one standard deviation increase in the factor; +means increase, —means decrease. Achievement s.d. = 6.2.
d Achievement s.d. = 4.7.
e Achievement s.d. = 3.6.
f Squared multiple correlation.

cism of the Coleman method cited earlier is technically valid, it is not correct to further assume that Coleman's causal ordering was the *sole* reason that family background factors showed stronger association with achievement than school inputs. The uncontrolled correlation between achievement and the input variables is also of critical importance in determining the predictive ability of a given variable. And, as we saw from Table 14, the uncontrolled correlations were generally lower for the school factors than for the family background factors.

In view of the controversy raised by this problem in some of the discussions of the Coleman report, an example may help make the point clearer. At the same time, it will show how some of the factors which had positive uncontrolled correlations ended up with negative regression coefficients.

Considering household-items and school-facilities indices for our example, we found an uncontrolled correlation between them of .4. From Table 14, the uncontrolled correlations are .8 and .21 between achievement and household items and school facilities, respectively. So, although the two indices share some common variance, their uncontrolled correlations with achievement are quite different, and the result is that the regression coefficients will also be different. The regression of achievement on these two factors alone results in a coefficient of −.13 for facilities and .85 for household items. Even if we adopted the unlikely model that school factors were prior to and "caused" family background factors, and controlled for facilities first, we would still conclude that family background factors were more important (.85 compared to .21). The negative coefficient for facilities in this example occurs because of the relatively small correlation between facilities and achievement and the relatively large correlations between household items and achievement, and between the two input factors.[27]

Another interesting result for all schools in Table 15 is the size of the coefficient for percent black. It is the largest of the community input factor coefficients. Thus, percent black explains more variation in achievement even when 4 other socioeconomic factors are controlled. This tends to confirm the notion that black families (or communities), on the average, may be more disadvantaged vis-à-vis whites than can be determined by objective social-class measures alone.

The pattern of coefficients for white achievement in white schools in Table 15 does not differ much from the pattern for all schools, with the understandable exception of the coefficient for percent black. It is now only −.07, indicating a very small effect. White achievement in predominantly white schools does not seem to be affected by an increasing percent black, provided that social class does not change. Because of the grouping of schools by race, which eliminates race as a major factor, the 9 variables now account for only 56 percent of the achievement variation. The strongest predictors of achievement are still the household-items and parents'-education indices, with coefficients of .38 and .36. The strongest positive school factor is per capita salaries, with a coefficient of .11.

The last two columns of Table 15 show that the highest coefficients for black achievement in black schools are, again, household items and parents' education, with values of .38 and .26. Overall, the model explains less variance, 43 percent, than for white schools. It does appear, however, that three of the school factors have stronger positive coefficients than for white schools. They are .10, .07, and .14, respectively, for teacher verbal achievement, teacher background, and per capita salaries. Thus, with all other factors controlled, per capita salaries is the third strongest positive predictor. Nonetheless, all three of these combined have less than half the predictive strength of the combination of the two strongest family background factors.

Table 16 gives the regression results for white schools within the four regional strata. Similar patterns are observed in most of the regions. The community inputs generally have the highest coefficients, with household items and parents' education sharing the strongest predictive power. In the metropolitan North, percent white collar has a coefficient of about .17. In the metropolitan South, the family structure index has a negative coefficient of −.16. This resulted from the low uncontrolled correlation with achievement, and a series of moderate correlations with the other community input factors.

Of the school input factors, the teacher-background and school-facilities indices have consistently negative coefficients in all but the nonmetropolitan South region, where they are close to zero. On the other hand, moderate coefficients are observed in both metropolitan regions for teacher verbal achievement (.12 in the North and .17 in the South), and in both nonmetropolitan regions for per capita salaries (.14 in the North and .10 in the South). The model explains between 56 and 60 percent of the variance in all but the nonmetropolitan North, where it drops to 39 percent. The main reason for the drop there appears to be the moderately low coefficient for household items (.12). It is interesting to note that, for all but this latter region, with all other factors controlled, the percent black has coefficients of zero or close to it.

Table 17 presents the same regional breakdown for the black school regressions. Generally, the results are somewhat more mixed than was the case for white schools, although some similar patterns emerge. In the metropolitan North, household items and parents' education have the highest positive coefficients, .59 and .18, respectively. Also, teacher background and facilities have negative coefficients (−.15). Only one school measure has a positive coefficient, and that is per capita salaries (.10).

As we can see from the other regions, per capita salaries is always positive, reaching a maximum of .37 in the metropolitan South. In that

TABLE 16

Regression of Sixth-Grade Verbal Achievement On School and
Community Input Factors, For Whites in White Schools, By Region[a]

Size	Metropolitan		Nonmetropolitan	
Regression Measure	Regression Coefficient	Predicted Change in Achievement[b]	Regression Coefficient	Predicted Change in Achievement[c]
Factor				
North				
Family structure	.10	+ .3	.11	+ .4
White collar	.17	+ .6	.03	+ .1
Household items	.43	+1.4	.12	+ .4
Parents' ed.	.20	+ .7	.47	+1.5
Teach. verbal	.12	+ .4	—.04	— .1
Teach. background	—.12	— .4	—.01	.0
Salaries	.02	+ .1	.14	+ .5
Facilities	—.10	— .3	—.07	— .2
Percent black	.00	.0	—.15	— .5
Achievement variation explained	60%		39%	
South				
Family structure	—.16	— .5	.07	+ .3
White collar	—.01	.0	.02	+ .1
Household items	.59	+1.7	.50	+2.1
Parents' ed.	.27	+ .8	.22	+ .9
Teach. verbal	.17	+ .5	.03	+ .1
Teach. background	—.22	— .6	.04	+ .2
Salaries	.08	+ .2	.10	+ .4
Facilities	—.05	— .1	.01	.0
Percent black	—.01	.0	—.01	.0
Achievement variation explained	58%		56%	

a Refer to appropriate notes in Table 15.
b North achievement s.d. = 3.3; South achievement s.d. = 2.8.
c North achievement s.d. = 3.2; South achievement s.d. = 4.2.

region it is the second highest coefficient, the highest being parents' education (.40). The facilities index has a large negative coefficient (—.22),
and it is also negative in the other two regions. We note that percent black
has a moderate *positive* coefficient in both Southern regions, reaching a
high of .20 in the metropolitan areas. Even after controlling for all the
other factors, black achievement in the South is higher as percentage black
increases.

The model does poorest in the nonmetropolitan South, accounting for
only 26 percent of the variation in black achievement. The strongest coefficient is that for household items, being .31. The second highest is .17 for
teacher background. We note, however, that the combined net effect of all

TABLE 17

Regression of Sixth-Grade Verbal Achievement On School and Community Input Factors, For Black Achievement in Black Schools, By Region[a]

Size	Metropolitan		Nonmetropolitan	
Regression Measure	Regression Coefficient	Predicted Change in Achievement[b]	Regression Coefficient	Predicted Change in Achievement[c]
Factor				
North				
Family structure	−.01	.0		
White collar	.04	+ .1		
Household items	.59	+1.9		
Parents' ed.	.18	+ .6		
Teach. verbal	−.15	− .5	d	
Teach. background	−.17	− .5		
Salaries	.10	+ .3		
Facilities	−.08	− .3		
Percent black	−.03	− .1		
Achievement variation explained	43%			
South				
Family structure	.09	+ .5	−.10	− .5
White collar	−.01	− .1	−.10	− .5
Household items	.10	+ .5	.31	+1.4
Parents' ed.	.40	+2.0	.15	+ .7
Teach. verbal	.10	+ .5	.11	+ .5
Teach. background	.04	+ .2	.17	+ .8
Salaries	.37	+1.9	.08	+ .4
Facilities	−.22	−1.1	−.09	− .4
Percent black	.20	+1.0	.12	+ .5
Achievement variation explained	56%		26%	

[a] Refer to appropriates notes in Table 15.
[b] North achievement s.d. = 3.2; South achievement s.d. = 5.0.
[c] South achievement s.d. = 4.5.
[d] Insufficient number of schools.

the school factors in both this and the metropolitan South region is higher than that in the black North, and higher than schools in any region, and it comes close to matching the combined net effect of the community input factors. This is further evidence for our earlier claim, based on the uncontrolled correlations, that school factors may be more important for black schools in the South than for any other grouping of schools.

To summarize, the regression results are similar to the results of the uncontrolled correlations. First, although the model we have postulated seems to account for almost 80 percent of the achievement variation for the nation as a whole, the differences within the regional and racial subgroupings are sufficient to require some separate treatment. Second, one general trend which can be discerned across the various groups is the relative strength of household items and parents' education. One or both of these two factors are the strongest predictors of achievement in every regional and racial category.

Third, the school factors, while never quite attaining the strength of community inputs, seem to be most prominent for black schools in the South. This may be quite important for future policy planning, since the black South also shows the lowest achievement levels. This suggests that when groups are sufficiently deprived, as are southern blacks, the schools become a more important resource for raising achievement levels. Finally, after controlling for all other factors, the school factor which seems most important for southern blacks, and for blacks and whites in many of the other regions, is school expenditures (as measured by teacher salaries). It may well be that in spite of its simplicity it is the best indicator of school quality. The original Coleman study may have made a major error by not attempting to assess it at the individual school level, thereby not having it available for their achievement prediction analysis.

VII. DISCUSSION AND
CONCLUSIONS

There are two different kinds of conclusions which should be drawn from our reanalysis effort. One kind is a summary statement about the results of the data analysis, drawing conclusions about the hypotheses tested and the questions answered. The other kind concerns the evaluation of the hypotheses themselves and involves conclusions about the implications of the findings for policy-planning and decision-making. The importance of the issues raised by these data and the controversy surrounding the original report make the latter conclusions as important as the former.

THE SUMMARY. The summary of our data analysis is the easiest of the two tasks. Given the measures we have used to assess school and community inputs and student outputs; given the elementary-school sample selected; and given the analysis approach, the outcome was not ambiguous.

The main thrust of this chapter, in comparison to others in this volume, was the a priori choice of overall school measures which seemed to represent the types of variables discussed by educators (as well as the Coleman report) as important for student learning, rather than searching vast numbers of specific items for those that show empirical relationships with achievement. Also, it was decided that an aggregate school-level analysis was more appropriate to the data at hand, and that the homogeneity of elementary schools made them the logical choice as the units of analysis.

The school items selected were combined into several summary indices: school facilities, teacher's verbal achievement and professional training, and school expenditures as indicated by teacher's salaries. An important omission, of course, was a teacher's personality or teaching style. An attempt to construct a fifth school variable, teacher attitudes, resulted in a factor with a strong negative correlation with student achievement. If we had included this variable in our analysis, we would have only made the case weaker for the effect of school variables on achievement. We might interpret this negative correlation as a result of the school composition on the teacher. Those teaching in lower-achieving schools, attended by lower socioeconomic students, may have chosen those schools because of their commitment and more tolerant attitudes, or else the fact of being in that kind of school may tend to increase a teacher's tolerance. An alternative interpretation would be that the teacher-attitude items were not adequate for assessing this dimension.

Systematic differences along one or more of the four school measures among various groupings of schools should show up when comparing the average index scores among the groupings. In order to ascertain whether black students were less advantaged than white students with regard to school characteristics, we compared the averages of these indices for predominantly black and predominantly white elementary schools within several regions of the country. The comparisons can be summarized as follows:

1. There were no large and consistent school-facility differences between black and white schools. There were large regional differences, with both black and white schools in the South lagging behind the rest of the country by almost a full standard deviation.
2. Black schools were generally higher than white schools in teacher's professional preparation. The largest differences were in those regions with predominantly black faculties in the black schools.
3. Black schools were substantially and consistently behind white schools in teacher verbal achievement. Again, the large differences were in these regions where black schools had predominantly black faculties.
4. No consistent within-region differences emerged between black and white schools for per-capita expenditures on teachers' salaries, but there were strong regional differences, again with the South showing lower expenditures than the rest of the nation. Because of the low South averages and the large number of black schools there, the national averages showed black schools with expenditures of $24 less per student than white schools.

In short, although many regional variations were found, black schools were consistently behind white schools only in the case of teacher's verbal achievement. The other consistent result was that black schools had somewhat higher average scores on the teacher-background index in most regions. Both of these findings can be explained by the fact that there are more black teachers in black schools, especially in the South. Black teachers in our sample generally have lower verbal achievement and higher background index scores than white teachers.

Although black schools were not more disadvantaged than white schools on 3 of the 4 school factors, they were definitely more disadvantaged with respect to student verbal achievement. This output, as measured by a standardized test, was found to be very highly correlated with other standardized tests at the 6th-grade level, including nonverbal and mathematics achievement, so that we can extend the findings for verbal achievement to academic performance in general. The findings can be summarized as follows:

5. In the 1st grades average black achievement in black schools is far behind white achievement in white schools, approaching 1½ standard deviations in many regions.
6. In the 6th grades, the national averages show that black achievement is two standard deviations behind white achievement.
7. The 6th-grade black achievement within majority-white schools is higher than black achievement in majority-black schools, but it is still almost 1½ standard deviations behind white achievement.
8. Although there are few whites in majority-black schools, they show the lowest achievement of any group. They have scores over 3 standard deviations lower than whites in majority-white schools.

Another way of putting these differences is that the *average* white 1st grade is achieving as well as the *upper 7 percent* of black 1st grades. Therefore, even before the schools have a chance to affect achievement, blacks are far behind whites in performance. Black students start disadvantaged, and the schools are apparently unable to close the gap. If we had found significant differences between black and white schools with regard to our school input measures, we might conclude that the schools' failure to close the gap was due to inferior schooling for the black student. Given the measures we had available, we could not draw this conclusion; instead, we had to search further for possible determinants of academic achievement.

Four indices of aggregated family life style were constructed as summary measures of community input to the school: percent of families with both natural or adoptive parents living at home (family structure); percent with white-collar occupations; average education of parents; and the average number of certain household items (e.g., appliances). Measures of this type have been traditional sociological indicators of socioeconomic status. The following summarize the findings:

9. Nationally, the black schools show an average of only 55 percent with both parents living at home, compared to 80 percent for white schools (about 1½ standard deviations). The absent parent was generally the father.

10. Black schools average 16 percent white-collar fathers compared to 31 percent for white schools (almost 1 standard deviation).
11. Black schools are almost 2 standard deviations behind white schools on an average household-items index. Out of nine items, white schools average about 8 and black schools about 6.
12. Black schools are almost 1 standard deviation behind white schools in the parents' education index.

Unlike most of the school input indices, therefore, all of the family measures showed large differences between black and white schools in the same direction and of the same order of magnitude as the differences in achievement. Throughout all regions of the country the differences averaged between 1 and 2 standard deviations. The average black family is less likely to have both parents present or a white-collar father, and is more likely to have less educated parents and fewer household possessions, when compared to the average white family. These results are strongly suggestive of the conclusion that the determinants of student achievement variation are more likely to be found in the home than in the school.

As a final test for the relative strength of family and school measures, and as a test for our overall model, correlation and regression analyses were applied to all of these variables. The dependent variable in all cases was 6th-grade verbal achievement. The analyses were carried out for the nation as a whole, and for black and white schools separately within eight geographical regions. This procedure enabled separate evaluations of the model within the racial and regional groupings. The significant findings of the correlation regression analyses are as follows:

13. The postulated model accounts for a large amount of the variation in achievement. For the nation as a whole, the 9 factors account for 80 percent of the achievement variance; within the racial and regional groupings the figures range from about 40 percent to 60 percent for all but one case.
14. For the nation, the community input factors of percent black, household items, and parents' education are far and away the strongest predictors of achievement. Percent black is the strongest predictor even when all the other community input measures are controlled. Within black and white schools separately, one or both of the household-items and parents'-education factors remain the strongest predictors.
15. The school factors were strongest for black schools in the South. The most consistently strong school factor in these areas, as well as for white schools, was per-capita expenditures for teacher salaries. The school facilities measure was the poorest predictor of achievement in most cases.

The final results of the correlation and regression analysis give no support for rejecting Coleman's basic conclusion of the relative importance of family background and school factors on achievement. This complete and independent reassessment shows that community inputs are clearly stronger predictors of student achievement.

There are, however, two major reasons why we cannot conclude that school factors are totally unimportant for student achievement. First, it must be stressed again that we are not assessing the *absolute* effect of schools on achievement, but rather the effect of schools on variation in achievement levels. We have no doubt that schools have an overall base-line effect. This base-line effect is probably fairly uniform for all schools, because school factors may be relatively equalized with respect to minimum standards. But, given variation in verbal achievement, especially that between black and white students, we are searching for factors which might reduce that difference. School factors may be important for a certain basic level of achievement, but this does not necessarily mean that *improving* those factors will help bring black achievement closer to white achievement. If one wants to reduce this differential, Coleman's and our analysis point to family-background factors as the more promising area for improvement.

Second, even given our interest in the black-white differential, our correlation and regression results did show some effects for school factors after controlling for family background. These effects were particularly strong in the South, and particularly for black students. We cannot conclude, therefore, that schools have no effect. We can conclude, given the limitations of our data and the assumptions of our analysis, that the family and community factors have a stronger effect on the observed variation in verbal achievement, and that this holds for both races either combined or taken separately.

♦ The Implications

What are the policy implications of all this? One clear implication is that government programs concerned with improving academic performance of blacks or other minority groups should give as much attention, if not more, to the environment—both family and neighborhood—in which the minority child lives. There does not seem to be any way for blacks to catch up with whites if family factors are ignored. Also, if school programs are to be initiated, they will probably be more effective as they approach the younger, preschool ages. Since blacks are just about as disadvantaged in the 1st as in later grades, and since they do not seem to be able to overcome this disadvantage, it is clear that special programs will have to concentrate on the early years, possibly even the infancy period.

Our aggregate analysis has necessarily combined the effects of a student's own family with those of his neighborhood or community. It would seem that policy implications might differ depending upon the relative importance of the individual family as compared to the neighborhood or nonfamily environment. Changing neighborhood composition, for example, might prove more manageable than attempting to modify individual family practices. The one set of policy issues which is probably the most debated in this area concerns the legislative integration of schools and neighbor-hoods. Do our data say anything about this issue?

We have to turn to a reexamination of Figure 2 for an answer. It will be recalled that it showed quite clearly that while black achievement gener-ally increased as the proportion of whites increased, it nonetheless remained about two standard deviations behind white achievement. At the time we noted that socioeconomic status probably played a role in the relationship. Figure 3 repeats the curves in Figure 2 and adds a similar graph of the household-items index. As we can see from the figure, the household-items index curves almost exactly repeat the curves of verbal achievement. Not only are integrated blacks achieving less than whites in predominantly white schools, their social class standing (as measured by the index) is also lower. Note also that, as in the achievement curves, the social-class index of whites in predominantly black schools drops below that of blacks.

In other words, even those black students in integrated and higher socioeconomic environments still achieve at a lower level than whites. The most likely explanation for this is that their *individual family background* is still more disadvantaged than that of white students in the same environ-ment. Thus, while integration may be an important factor for black achievement, blacks might still never attain full achievement equality until their individual family life style catches up to that of whites. The policy implication here is that programs which stress financial aid to disadvan-taged black families may be just as important, if not more so, than pro-grams aimed at integrating blacks into white neighborhoods and schools.

It must be stressed, finally, that the data we have analyzed do not really lend themselves to rigorous causal analysis. We have attempted to make controls for various factors in order to eliminate or reduce possible spurious correlations. But this is no substitute for carefully designed experimental field studies which can more adequately manipulate the independent vari-ables and measure achievement changes over time. Studies like this must be done before we can make any final scientific decision about the absolute and relative impact of school and family characteristics on student achievement. Moreover, even if we accept the associations between family factors and achievement as causal, we are not certain about the actual sociological and psychological mechanisms which produce the connection. Further experi-mental research could shed more light on these processes. If nothing else, the findings of this report, as well as the original Coleman report, must stimulate support of further research of an experimental nature in order to settle some of the issues raised.

It is not uncommon, however, for policy decisions to be made before final scientific proof of the "best" plan of action. In the face of such a situa-tion, the present data cannot be ignored. While the USOE data may contain many drawbacks, they still probably represent the most recent and most com-prehensive data yet gathered about educational processes. It would not seem

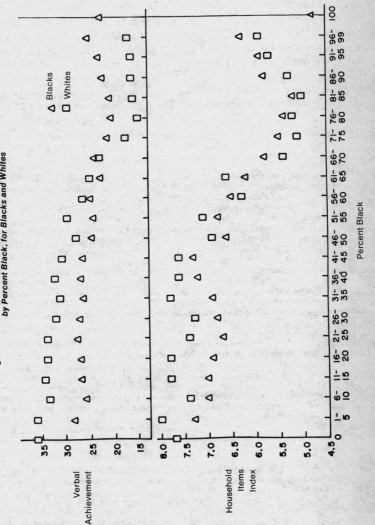

Figure III. Average Verbal Achievement and Household Items Index by Percent Black, for Blacks and Whites

to be reasonable, therefore, to totally ignore these findings, preliminary as they may be, in policy formulations. Action based on partial evidence is more desirable than action based on speculation with no evidence at all.

Notes

1. James S. Coleman, *et al.*, *Equality of Educational Opportunity* Washington, D.C.: U.S. Government Printing Office, 1966.
2. For example, Robert C. Nichols, "Schools and the Disadvantaged," *Science*, 154 (December, 1966), 1312–14, and Samuel Bowles and Henry Levin, "The Determinants of Scholastic Achievement: An Appraisal of Some Recent Evidence," *The Journal of Human Resources*, Vol. III, No. 1 (Winter 1968), pp. 3–24.
3. See Chapters 1 to 4.
4. Coleman, *op. cit.*, p. 567.
5. For example, about 71 percent of sixth graders answered the question about their father's education. Combining this with the proportion of elementary schools participating, only about 52 percent of the target population is assessed on this characteristic.
6. For example, see the review by Norman E. Wallen and Robert M. W. Travers, "Analysis and Investigation of Teaching Methods," in N. L. Gage, ed., *Handbook of Research on Teaching*. Chicago: Rand McNally, 1963.
7. Some of this work has been summarized in David E. Lavin, *The Prediction of Academic Performance*, Chapter 6. New York: Russell Sage Foundation, 1965.
8. From this point on I shall use the term "community" to stand for neighborhood environment. It should be understood that, with the USOE data, a community characteristic is computed by averaging over student characteristics in a given school; no data are derived independently for communities.
9. Robert Rosenthal and Lenore Jacobson, *Pygmalion in the Classroom*. New York: Holt, Rinehart and Winston, 1968. Teacher effect on I.Q. dropped off rapidly as the 6th-grade was approached; significant effects appeared only for the 1st-, 2nd-, and 3rd-grade children.
10. We will not use all of these schools in our analysis for reasons to be explained later.
11. A complete analysis was actually done which included all schools with a 6th grade, and although there were some differences, none was sufficiently important to change any conclusions stated in later sections.
12. The index was derived by scoring one point each for a teacher who would (1) definitely reenter teaching if they were deciding again; (2) not prefer to change schools; (3) express no preference for a particular ethnic composition; (4) express no preference for a particular racial composition; (5) expect to remain in teaching until retirement; and (6) prefer to see a black student go to a predominantly white college.
13. Blacks who did not know their father's occupation were more likely to have lower scores on the household-items index.
14. Attitudes are analyzed in Chapters 6 and 7.
15. Coleman, *op. cit.*, p. 220.
16. The actual weights used were what the Coleman report referred to as the "regression" weights, which were a "smoothed" version of the original sampling weights. See Coleman, *op. cit.*, p. 558 and p. 571.
17. The form of this second weighting factor was suggested by Frederick Mosteller. Specifically, the factor is given by $k_i = 1/(A^2 + W^2/n_i)$, where A^2 and W^2 are the among-school and within-school variance, respectively, and n_i is the enrollment in the 1st or 6th grade for school i. The proportion of among-school variance was about .25 for several student variables at both grade levels and for both races. Thus, for all variables the form becomes $k_i = n_i/(n_i + 3)$ for school i.

18. Coleman, *op. cit.*, p. 40.

19. *Ibid.*, p. 122.

20. An attempt was made to include all facility items from the principal's question-naire thought to be related to the production of academic achievement. It was de-cided to include principal characteristics in the facility index rather than combine them with teacher measures. About the only items excluded were those dealing with extracurricular activities programs and those thought to relate directly to the socioeconomic background of students or to their aggregate characteristics (e.g., percentage receiving free lunch or milk, dropout and college attendance rates, extent of discipline problems).

21. Coleman, *op. cit.*, p. 21.

22. The following summary figures, showing average verbal achievement scores by each group, can be used to make the appropriate comparisons:

	North, West		South, Southwest	
	Metropolitan	Non-metropolitan	Metropolitan	Nonmetropolitan
Whites in White Schools	37	37	36	34
Blacks in White Schools	30	30	28	25
Whites in Black Schools	25	20	14	12
Blacks in Black Schools	26	25	24	21

23. Daniel P. Moynihan, *The Negro Family: The Case for National Action.* Washing-ton, D.C.: U.S. Government Printing Office, 1965.

24. Due to an error in the USOE questionnaires, clerical workers were coded with the semiskilled category, making it impossible to separate them. For this reason, the means are much lower than they would be if we could include all white-collar occupations in the same category.

25. Bowles and Levin, *op. cit.*, p. 15.

26. The measures are Pearson's product-moment correlations.

27. The regression formula results in the following equation for the standardized coefficient for school facilities:

$$b = (.21 - .4 \times .8)/(1 - .4^2) = -.1^3$$

The interpretation is that if we control for household items, an increase in facili-ties would be associated with a *decrease* in achievement.

6

Equality of Educational Opportunity: The Basic Findings Reconsidered[*]

MARSHALL S. SMITH

Introduction

In Chapter 3 of the *Equality of Educational Opportunity Report*, data from a number of regression analyses are presented to support seven central conclusions:

1) Family background has great importance for school achievement;
2) The relation of family background to achievement does not diminish over the years of school;
3) Family background accounts for a substantial amount of the school-to-school variation in achievement and, therefore, variations in school facilities, curriculum, and staff can only have a small independent effect;
4) There is a small amount of variance explicitly accounted for by variations in facilities and curriculum;

[*] The research reported here was supported by the Carnegie Corporation of New York, the U.S. Office of Economic Opportunity (Contract CG-8708 A/O), and the U.S. Office of Education (Contract OE-5-10-239).

This research was influenced by a large number of persons. I am enormously indebted, however, to David K. Cohen and Christopher S. Jencks of the Harvard Center for Educational Policy Research and to Frederick Mosteller of the Harvard Department of Statistics for their encouragement, suggestions, and critical comments on earlier drafts of this manuscript.

5) Although no school factor accounts for much variation in achievement, teacher characteristics account for more than any other;

6) The social composition of the student body is more highly related to achievement, independently of the student's social background, than is any school factor;

7) Attitudes such as a sense of control of the environment, or a belief in the responsiveness of the environment, are strongly associated with achievement, and appear to be little influenced by variations in school characteristics.[1]

During the five years following the appearance of the Report, no one has seriously questioned the importance of family background for student achievement. Nor has the conclusion reached about the *association* of student attitudes with student achievement been controversial. Critics have, however, challenged conclusions 2–6.

This study reexamines the five controversial conclusions of Chapter 3 of the Report. Fortunately, the Supplemental Appendix to the Report contains the data from which most of the tables in the chapter were derived. I was thus able to reproduce most of the figures on which the five conclusions were based.

As my efforts progressed, five criticisms seemed especially important.

1) Coleman *et al.* made two mechanical errors in creating their tables. These errors can probably be attributed to the haste with which the authors prepared the Report. First, two "objective" measures of home background, *Parents' Education* and *Urbanism of Background*, were inadvertently replaced in the analysis by two "subjective" measures of the home background, *Parents' Interest in the Schooling of the Child*, and *Parents' Educational Desires for the Child*. Second, the student-body composition variable called *Proportion Planning to Attend College* is instead a variable measuring the *Proportion of Students in the College Track* in the school. The first error led Coleman *et al.* to over-estimate the importance of school variables. The second error led Coleman *et al.* to misinterpret the effect of student-body composition.

2) Coleman *et al.* made an error in their procedure for estimating the amount of school-to-school differences in achievement explained by individual home background. This error also led to an overestimation of the possible unique effect that school variables might have.

3) Coleman *et al.* based their conclusions on analyses of all of the groups sampled in the Survey (Puerto Ricans, American Indians, Mexican Americans, and Oriental Americans, as well as blacks and whites). Data from minority groups other than blacks, however, seem to behave differently than data from blacks and whites. There are three possible reasons for this. First, the EEOS sample included only a few students in each of the minority groups other than blacks, and these pupils were enrolled in a handful of schools. The small number of observations might have led to severe sampling fluctuations. Second, there is some evidence that students did not always ac-

curately report their race or ethnic background. For example, an amazingly large number of students in the metropolitan Northeast classified themselves as American Indians. The possibility of mis-classification together with the smallness of the samples diminished my estimate of the validity of findings about these groups. Third, the other groups may simply be different from blacks and whites. Whatever the reason, conclusions based on analyses of all of the groups may not be applicable for blacks and whites.

4) The criticisms concerning the "conceptual and methodological flaws" made by Bowles and Levin (1967) and by Hanushek and Kain (see Chapter 3) appeared in some instances to be valid. The critics argue that: a) Regression coefficients are better estimators of school effectiveness than are percentages of explained variance, and that b) the model used in the Report "consistently derogated" the role of school resources because there was an "arbitrary choice of first 'controlling' for student background and then introducing school resources into the analysis." The critics contend that an analysis of the regression coefficients and of the variance explained by the school resources prior to controlling for the individual background variables might have led Coleman *et al.* to different conclusions.

5) In their analysis and interpretation of the survey data, Coleman *et al.* completely overlooked the confounding effects that school assignment and student self-selection practices might have on inferences about the relationships between school resources and student achievement. This confounding is particularly important at the secondary level where Coleman *et al.* carried out their most extensive analyses. The authors neglected to distinguish between trade, vocational, academic, and comprehensive high schools in their analyses. Furthermore, at the 9th grade they did not distinguish between junior and senior high schools. The result of this is to put into question any findings at the secondary level about relationships between school resources and student achievement.

Taken together, the five criticisms raise doubt about the validity of conclusions 2–6. Yet, except for the last, each criticism can be tested for importance by a reexamination of the very same data that Coleman *et al.* used. The confounding effects of the assignment and selection process can be estimated, rather than eliminated, by a reexamination.

◆ *Plan of the Reexamination*

The variables and samples of students used in this analysis are exactly those used in Chapter 3 of the Report. No new variables are defined and no new samples are extracted. The study follows the general outlines of Chapter 3 of the Report. Five sections and a summary can be distinguished.

The first section is primarily methodological. In it I define the model and methodology used in the Report and present alternative approaches. The second section focuses on the relationship of student achievement to a set of variables (factor) measuring home background. Then, in succeeding sections, I examine the relationship of student achievement to three sets of school factors: the composition of the student body, the facilities and curriculum characteristics, and the teacher characteristics. The final section summarizes the findings of the reexamination.

Although the results in Sections 2 through 5 are not independent, the sections are designed to stand alone. In each I define the variables comprising the factor used by Coleman *et al.* and discuss their strengths and limitations. I then examine the overall relationship of the factor to verbal achievement. The strength of the relationship is contrasted to the strength of the relationships between the other factors and achievement. Differences between racial groups and between samples of students at various grade levels in the strength of the relationships are also examined. I conclude the study of each factor by looking at the associations between the specific variables and verbal achievement.

This format allows me to contrast my results with those of Coleman *et al.* I focus on the validity of the five controversial conclusions and on the effect that the mistakes in the original analysis had on the results. I also examine the validity of two further inferences made by Coleman: that the effects of school on achievement increase over a student's years in school and that variations in school resources have a greater effect on the achievement of minority groups than on the achievement of whites.

My intention is not simply to scrutinize the original Report but to extend it. As a result I explore various interpretations of the data as much as possible. In particular, I examine closely the possibility that the assignment and allocation processes of schools (tracking within and between schools) offer a plausible interpretation of Coleman *et al.*'s and my results at the secondary grades.

In the last section I examine the policy implications suggested by the research.

SECTION I: The Model and Methodology of the Report and of the Reexamination

Four issues preliminary to reporting the results of the reexamination are discussed in this section. First, the conceptual and statistical models used in the Report's analysis are explicated. Second, I present the general strategy of analysis used in this paper, contrasting it to the approach used by Coleman *et al.* The focus of this discussion is on the types of questions that can be answered by different approaches.

Third, I examine the overall amounts of variation in verbal achievement that lie between and within schools. The importance of these figures is discussed. Finally, I present grounds for my analyzing only two groups of students, Northern blacks and whites. In addition, reasons for carrying out analyses of these groups only for grades 6, 9, and 12 are explained.

THE MODEL AND
METHODOLOGY OF THE
REPORT

The Conceptual Model

The authors of the Report assumed that five sets of variables (factors) determine a student's achievement (A_i).[2] Each student is individually influenced by:

1) His home background experience (H_i).

He is also affected by three sets of schoolwide influences—influences which he shares in common with all other students in his school:

2) The characteristics of his student-body peers (B_i);

3) The school's Facilities and Curriculum (F_i);

4) His teacher's characteristics (T_i);

Finally, he is influenced by:

5) Other unmeasured factors of his heredity and environment (E_i).

The five factors were treated in the analysis as if they were additive; e.g., a student's relative achievement is determined by adding the effect of his home background experiences, the effect of his peers, the effect of facilities and curriculum, the effect of his teachers, and the effect of unmeasured characteristics. But even though the factors were treated as additive, they were not all expected to be equally important. The Report first examines the influence of the background characteristics. Then it assesses the magnitude of the overall effect of each of the schoolwide characteristics on achievement. Finally, it determines the relative magnitudes of the three schoolwide sets of resources.

The authors of the Report chose to carry out these tasks in a very controversial way. Two of their decisions have been especially criticized. The first was to measure the importance of a factor by the amount of independent information that it added to the prediction of the average achievement level of students in the sample. Coleman *et al.* described their second controversial decision as follows:

Before examining the relation of school characteristics to student achievement, it is useful to examine the influence of student background characteristics. Because these background differences are *prior* to school influence, and shape the child before he reaches school, they will, to the extent we have succeeded in measuring them, *be controlled* when examining the effect of school factors. This means that the achievement differences among schools which are due only to differences in student input can be in part controlled, to allow for more accurate examination of the apparent effects of differences in school or teacher factors themselves. [p. 298, (my italics)]

The home background characteristics of students were assigned both the explanatory power that they have uniquely and the explanatory power that they *share* with school resources.

The Statistical Model

The translation of these decisions into a statistical model is straightforward. The additive nature of the influences can be expressed in an equation such as the following:

$$A_i = b_o + b_H H_i + b_B B_i + b_F F_i + b_T T_i + e_i$$

where
A_i = the achievement of individual i
H_i = the Home Background experiences of individual i
B_i = the Student Body influence on individual i
F_i = the Facilities and Curriculum influences on individual i
T_i = the Teacher Characteristics for individual i
e_i = the error or residual portion of A_i that cannot be explained by the measured variables

and where b_H, b_B, b_F, and b_T are weights assigned to the various influences and b_o is a constant which adjusts the scale of the variables.

These weights are computed by a procedure which minimizes the sum of the squared deviations of the predicted students' achievement ($\hat{A}_i$) from their actual achievement (A_i). This is equivalent to minimizing the sum of squares of (e_i), since $e_i = A_i - \hat{A}_i$.

If we have no information about a particular student except that he is in our sample, the best prediction of his achievement, as measured by the criteria of minimizing the sum of the squared e_i's, is to assign to him the mean score of the sample. Then H, F, B, and T are zero. Further b_o is equal to the mean of the A_i's as is each $\hat{A}_i$. It thus follows that the size of the e_i's will depend upon how much the various A_i's differ from their mean.

For the purpose of this discussion I will call the sum of the squares of these e_i's the total sum of squares or Σe_{is}^2, where the subscript s stands for total sum of squares. As we gain information about each student (i.e., his home background, his school's facilities and curriculum, etc.), we are better able to estimate his achievement score—e.g., the $\hat{A}_i$'s will be more similar to their respective A_i's. Each new piece of information adds some more accuracy to the estimation of the scores, and reduces the sum of squares of the e_i's.

The Report's Measure of the Importance of a Factor

If a regression equation with a Home Background variable as the independent variable and achievement as the dependent variable is computed, it would look like:

$$A_i = b_o + b_H H_i + e_{iH}$$

where the e_{iH}'s are "error" terms—e.g., the unexplained differences between the actual achievement scores and the achievement scores predicted from H. The most common measure of how "good" an equation we have is based on a comparison of $\Sigma\ e_i^2$ with the sum of squares of the e_i's from the equation—in this case with $\Sigma\ e_{iH}^2$. *One minus the ratio of these figures is called the proportion of total variance "explained" by the independent variable and is equal to the square of the correlation between the independent and the dependent variables* (R^2). The proportion of variance (R_H^2) explained by an equation which includes only the Home Background variable measures the improvement in our prediction of students' scores when we know home background information over our prediction when we know nothing about the students. This is a measure of the gain in information averaged across all of the students. If we then add some information about the educational facilities and curriculum (F_i) of each student we will get a new R_{HF}^2 which will, in most cases, be larger than R_H^2. The difference between R_{HF}^2, the amount of variance explained by both Home Background and Facilities and Curriculum, and R_H^2 measures the improvement in prediction brought about by knowledge of Facilities and Curriculum after the differences in the Home Background are already taken into account.

This operation can be easily extended. More variables can be added to the equation, new R^2's computed, and estimates of the amount of added information calculated. This approach is clear except for one problem. The amount of new information—and thus the presumed importance of the new variable—often depends upon what variables are entered before it into the equation. We have seen, for example, that a measure (R_H^2) of the importance of Home Background can be computed, and how a measure $(R_{HF}^2-R_H^2)$ of the added importance of Facilities and Curriculum can also be computed. If, however, we had entered the Facilities and Curriculum measure into the equation first, we would have had another measure (R_F^2) of the importance of Facilities and Curriculum and also a second measure of the importance of the Home Background measure $(R_{FH}^2-R_F^2)$. R_{HF}^2 and R_{FH}^2 will always be equal since the total amount of information provided by two variables is the same regardless of the order they enter the equation. But the importance of the two variables may appear to depend upon the order that they are entered into the equation. The only time the information a variable adds to an equation does not depend upon the order entering the equation is when the independent variables are uncorrelated, i.e., when Facilities and Curriculum are unrelated to Home Background. This is unusual. Middle-class students usually have access to somewhat better schools than lower-class students. The Home Background measure, in other words, is positively correlated with the Facilities and Curriculum measure. And since middle-class students generally score higher than lower-class students on achievement tests, achievement scores are also likely to correlate positively with both the quality of students' homes and with the quality of their schools' resources. This means that we can explain part of a student's achievement by either the Home Background or the Facilities and Curriculum, while another part can only be explained by Home Background and still another only by Facilities and Curriculum.

When we introduce additional variables, such as teacher characteristics and student body characteristics, the problem becomes even more complex. Some of the explanatory power of a Teacher Characteristics variable may be shared with the Home Background variable, while other parts of it may be shared with the Student Body and the Facilities and Curriculum variables. Some of the explanatory power, moreover, may be unique—that is, not shared with any of the other variables.

The fact that the explanatory variables measured by Coleman *et al.* are correlated makes assessment of their relative importance difficult.[3] If placing the variables in different orders into the equations gives very different estimates of their importance relative to other variables, it is difficult to make claims about relative importance, unless we are very certain of their causal relationships.

To some extent the approach taken by Coleman *et al.* alleviated this problem in the Report. They assumed that any variation in student achievement that was associated with differences in student home backgrounds was determined prior to the children's coming to school—i.e., by the differences in student backgrounds. They therefore argued that any explanatory power of the schoolwide resources that was shared with Home Background should be assigned to Home Background, and so the student background variables were entered first in all equations. This approach substantially reduced their analytic problem, but at the cost of making their conclusions dependent on an assumption which is logically questionable.

However, there was still the problem of untangling the overlapping relationships between the three sets of schoolwide variables. One strategy for this can be explained by looking at the following table (Table 1). Although Coleman *et al.* did not present the results in the form shown below, many of the same numbers were presented.

An Example of the Report's Analysis

Table 1 presents an example of an analysis using the EEOS Report's sample of 6th-Grade Northern Negroes. For each of the three sets of schoolwide variables, five numbers are presented. The numbers in column 1 represent the amount of additional variance in verbal achievement explained by each school factor when the factor is entered in the equation directly following the Home Background factor.[4] The numbers in the second column are the amounts of additional variance explained when each school factor is entered after Home Background and Facilities and Curriculum. The fourth

TABLE 1[1]

Sixth-Grade Northern Blacks

Additional percentages of variance of verbal achievement accounted for by the introduction of three sets of schoolwide variables in different orders into regression equations. The variance accounted for by four objective and two subjective home background variables* has already been previously removed.†

	Order of Introduction into Equation				
	1	*2* (After Teacher Charac- teristics)	*2* (After Facilities and Cur- riculum)	*2* (After Stu- dent Body)	*3* (After Both Other Factors)
Factor	(Alone)				
Teacher Characteristics	2.19		1.89	1.98	1.71
Facilities & Curriculum	0.77	0.47		0.45	0.18
Student Body	2.28	2.07	1.96		1.78

[1] All of the numbers presented in this study are extracted from analyses carried out
on the data contained in the Supplemental Appendix to the EEOS Report. No numbers
were taken from the Report.

* The four objective background variables are: *Home Items; Reading Items; Number
of Siblings; Structural Integrity of Family.* The two subjective variables are: *Parents'
Educational Desires; Parents' Interest in Child's School Experience.* They are fully
described in Appendix A.

† The three sets of schoolwide factors explain 4.44 percent of the total variance after
the effect of the individual home background factors has been removed.

column shows the amount explained when each factor is entered after the
Home Background and Student Body factors. The fifth column contains the
"unique" variance explained by each of the schoolwide factors, i.e., the variance explained when it is entered after Home Background and both of the
other schoolwide factors.

Most of the conclusions in Chapter 3 of the Report were reached
through careful analysis of numbers such as those in Table 1, using ten
different samples of students at each of three grade levels. In this sample,
for example, we note that both the Teacher Characteristics and the Student
Body factors explain something over 2 percent of the variance after Home
Background has been controlled and just over 1.7 percent of the variance
uniquely. The Facilities and Curriculum factor, on the other hand, explains
about 0.8 percent of the variance after Home Background has been controlled and only 0.18 percent of the variance uniquely. From this we might
reach the conclusion that, overall, the three sets of factors do not explain
very much of the variance independently of home background (e.g., about
4.44 percent), but that the Teacher Characteristics and Student-Body factors are more important than the Facilities and Curriculum factor.

The Adequacy of the Report's Model and Methodology

Now we face the problem of considering whether this approach is right or wrong. I think that the approach described above would be defensible if the authors' intent were to carry out a static assessment of the present *independent* influence of schoolwide resources on the achievement levels of students. This is a very narrow, though important, issue. The question it responds to is *whether schools help overcome inequities with which students enter schools*. The analysis in Chapter 3 suggests that they do not. The summary statement at the end of section 3.1 speaks directly to this point:

> Taking all these results together, one implication stands out above all: That schools bring little influence to bear on a child's achievement that is independent of his background and general social context; and that this very lack of an independent effect means that the inequalities imposed on children by their home, neighborhood, and peer environment are carried along to become the inequalities with which they confront adult life at the end of school. For equality of educational opportunity through the schools must imply a strong effect of schools that is independent of the child's immediate social environment, and that strong independent effect is not present in American schools. [p. 325]

This is not to say that the schools might not someday exert a strong independent influence, nor is it to say that schools are presently ineffective in imparting information. The Report simply says that children from "advantaged" homes enter schools at 1st grade achieving at a higher level than do children from "disadvantaged" homes and that, at present, schools do not change this. It does not tell us why or whether it could be changed.

This, however, is exactly the type of question most people want tested. Both scholars and policy-makers want to know, for example, whether the Report provides information on the effects of compensatory education or integration. They want information about the possible effect of hiring better trained or smarter teachers, about the influence of small pupil/teacher ratios, and so forth. *In short, they want to know what will happen if they change the status quo.* The information collected in the survey cannot give us final answers to these questions, but if properly analyzed, it can give us some useful clues. As I have already noted, the way Coleman *et al.* chose to assess the importance of the schoolwide factors eliminated variation shared with Home Background. But an assessment of the *potential* effects of school resources would have to take into account the possibility that the apparent effects of family background are actually the results of advantaged children attending better-than-average schools.[5] In addition, the Report only gives us information about the effect of an input factor averaged over all students. We cannot estimate from the information given in the Report what the achievement of a student might be if he were exposed to a particular set of school resources and not to some others. We only know that a knowledge of the school resources available to the various students in our sample allows us to predict, on the average, students' scores more accurately by 2 or so percent.

Finally, the measures presented in the Report (percentages of explained variance) are sensitive to restrictions in the range of the distributions of the school resources being compared. A simple example should make this point. Suppose that the length of the school year is extremely important to the success of students. But also suppose that the school year is the same length for all the students in the sample. The length of the school year would explain no variance in the achievement scores of the students. Because the school year is of equal length for all students, it cannot account for any of the differences in achievement among the students. Now suppose that a few students attend school for a much shorter year than the others. Here we can compare the achievement of those with the longer school year to the achievement of those with the shorter year and determine how important the length of school year actually is. However, if the measure of importance that we are using is the percentage of variance accounted for, and if almost all schools have a long year, the length of school year may still not look as important as another resource which is available to roughly one-half of the students. All but a few students go to school for the same length of time. Only the few in the sample who do not will give evidence of the effect of the length of the year. Because the percentage of variance measure is essentially an estimate of the effect averaged across *all* of the students in the sample, the more even the split in the sample between those who have access and those who do not have access to a resource, the better chance the resource has of appearing important.

In summary, the research strategy used in the Report is defensible if the intent was only to assess whether schools now exert a strong influence on achievement which is independent of family background. Likewise it is legitimate if the aim was to measure which school characteristics have the largest present *independent* effect on achievement. But the strategy yields no information about the degree to which school influences may be masked in social-class differences, or about the potential effect of changing the distribution of any particular school characteristic.

ALTERNATIVE MODELS AND METHODOLOGY

If policy questions are to be answered, other measures of the importance of school resources must be used. First, the relationship between the schoolwide resources and student achievement should be shown without first allocating all of the shared variance to the Home Background of the student. Second, measures of the importance of the particular school resources should be displayed. Finally these measures should not be dependent on the particular distribution of a resource. This study presents measures which meet each of these criteria.

An Alternative Way of Assessing the Strength of a Factor

I have already mentioned that Home Background not only shares some of its explanatory power with the school resource factors but also that the schoolwide factors overlap one another. One way of analyzing the extent of this overlap is to divide the achievement variance explained by the three factors into seven parts. Each of the factors explains a unique share of variance, unshared with any other factor. The unique components constitute three of the seven parts. Each of the three factors can explain variance jointly with each one of the other two factors. For example, the Student Body and Teacher Characteristics factors jointly share variance—variance that is *not* also explained by the Facilities and Curriculum factor. There are three such pairs of factors, each with the share of the explained variance. Finally, all three schoolwide factors share a certain amount of explained variance. The sum of these seven parts is equal to total amount of variance explained by the three factors.

An example of this approach is given in Table 2. The data are derived from analyses of the 6th-Grade Northern White sample.

Three columns of numbers are presented in Table 2. The third column shows the seven-part breakdown and the total amount of variance explained for the three sets of schoolwide factors *without controls by a Home Background factor*. Column 1 presents the same numbers after controlling the Home Background factor used in the Report. Column 2 presents the numbers after controlling the six Home Background factors intended for use in the Report. The importance of the differences between columns 1 and 2 are discussed fully later. For purposes of this example, look just at columns 2 and 3. It is clear that the elimination of the Home Background factor makes a considerable difference in the amount of total variance accounted for by the three schoolwide factors. It is also clear why this difference arises. The Student Body factor explains three percent more variance in column 3, where the Home Background factor is omitted, than in column 2, where it is included. The variance jointly shared between the Student Body and Teacher Characteristics factors increases by over 1.5 percent when the Home Background factor is omitted. The other five parts of the variance breakdown increase only slightly. In fact, the proportion of variance uniquely accounted for by the Facilities and Curriculum factor *decreases* slightly when it is not first controlled for individual home background conditions.

Tables such as Table 2 for each of the six groups studied here are

TABLE 2

Sixth-Grade Northern Whites

Table showing the allocation of the percentages of total variance of individual verbal achievement scores for three sets of schoolwide influences (Student Body, Facilities and Curriculum, and Teacher Characteristics) into independently and jointly explained components. Three conditions are presented. The first is with four objective and two subjective Home Background variables controlled. The second is with six objective Home Background variables controlled. The third is without Home Background controls.

	With Background Controls		No Background Controls
	1 (4 obj., 2 subj.)	2 (6 obj.)	3
Student Body Uniquely	1.98	1.10	4.32
Facilities and Curriculum Uniquely	0.31	0.24	0.22
Teacher Characteristics Uniquely	0.55	0.46	0.53
Student Body and Facilities	0.00	0.01	0.16
Student Body and Teachers	0.96	0.41	2.01
Facilities and Teachers	0.07	0.08	0.00
Student Body and Facilities & Teachers	−0.09*	−0.09*	0.06
Total =	3.78	2.22	7.35

* The negative signs indicate that the total variance explained by all three variables together is greater than the sum of the amounts of variance explained by the three variables separately and in pairs. This reflects the fact that some of the factors are negatively correlated with one another.

included in Appendix B. Data are extracted from these tables (A–F in Appendix B) to form new tables for the text of this paper.

A Measure of the Importance of Specific Variables

In order to measure the relative importance of specific variables used in the regression equations, I have used standardized regression coefficients (beta weights) included in tables with the means and standard deviations of the independent and dependent variables. A beta weight measures the average change (in standard deviations) in the dependent variable (e.g., achievement) when a given independent variable (e.g., teacher salaries) is increased by one standard deviation, all other independent variables remaining unchanged. The Beta's bear a very close relationship to the *b*'s discussed earlier. A *b* weight is defined as a measure of the average or expected change in the dependent variable when the specific independent variable increases by one unit, other independent variables remaining unchanged. As such, the magnitude of a *b* weight is dependent on the units used in the analysis. The *b*'s are a good measure to use if all independent variables are assessed in the same units. But often different units are used, and thus one *b* might represent the change expected if the class size is decreased by one pupil while another represents the change if one physics laboratory is added to the science facilities. In short, the *b*'s for independent variables in the same equation often are not comparable.

Generally the Beta's are more nearly comparable. The Beta for an independent variable equals the *b* weight for that variable multiplied by the ratio of the standard deviation of the independent variable over the standard deviation of the dependent variable. A table with both the Beta's and the standard deviations of the independent and dependent variables, therefore, contains enough information to calculate the *b* weights.

Before looking at an example, it is important to realize a number of things about these measures. First of all, both Beta and *b* weights are sensitive to the relationships of a given independent variable with the other independent variables in the equation. The size of the coefficients depends on the unique contribution of the independent variable to the prediction of the dependent variable plus an apportioned amount of the influence it shares with other variables in the equation. If, for example, two variables which measure the same thing are introduced together into an equation as independent variables, the sum of their standardized coefficients will be roughly equal to the size of the coefficient of either one if it were entered in the equation alone. However, it is never entirely clear in advance just how the coefficient for one will be split between the two.

Second, the use of measures like this invite speculation about the potential effect of drastically changing some policy. For example, the Beta weight for teachers' salaries might be large and positive. Perhaps an increase of 1 standard deviation in teachers' salaries, other things remaining unchanged, is expected to produce a change of 0.2 standard deviation in student achievement. The eager policy-maker might suggest that we should raise teachers' salaries by 10 standard deviations and thereby create a generation of geniuses. Such wishful thinking is folly for at least three reasons:

1) Teachers' salaries might simply be a proxy for an influence (like teacher verbal skills) that is not included in the equation. A large weight does not insure causality.

2) The condition that "other things remain unchanged" cannot be met in the real world. A policy of raising teachers' salaries would probably change the monies spent on other educational resources —resources that might be crucial to the success of the child in the school.

3) The extrapolation of an effect of a variable beyond the range of measured observation is unwarranted. It may be that altering teachers' salaries plus or minus 3 standard deviations around the present mean will have the expected effect. But perhaps raising the salaries even more will both not buy any different teachers and

will not change the behavior of the existing teachers. We simply do not know because we have no data cases to base an opinion on.

Third, the magnitude of a Beta weight, like the percentage of variance explained, is sensitive to the distribution of the resource being assessed (one measure of this distribution is the standard deviation of the particular independent variable). As mentioned earlier the percent of variance explained is maximized when there is a large variance in the resource. Beta's are also sensitive to the variation in the allocation of the resource. One way of correcting for this sensitivity is by looking at the size of the standard deviation of the independent variable. This is equivalent to converting the Beta weight into a *b* weight. The *b*'s are not sensitive to the allocation of the resource. Therefore, when I suggest that the Beta weights are the best measures for comparing the influences of the various independent variables in an equation, the reader should remember to also check the size of the standard deviations. Also note that when comparing the relationship of the same resource to achievement in different equations for two different samples of students, the *b* weights are often the appropriate measure because they are independent of the variation in the resource.

With all of these caveats in mind, it will be useful to look at an illustrative table. The numbers in Table 3 are derived from the 6th-Grade Northern White sample. The first two columns of this table present the means and standard deviations for the independent variables used in the various analyses. The mean and standard deviation of Verbal Achievement, the dependent variable, are given at the top of the table. Column 3 shows the uncontrolled relationship between the various independent variables and the dependent variable. The last four columns of the table present standardized regression coefficients (Beta's) for the independent variables under a variety of conditions. The Beta's in column 4 were computed with all of the independent variables entered in the equation. Note that only one of the schoolwide resource variables (*Teacher Perception of Student-Body Quality*) has a Beta weight that is statistically significant, while all of the individual level background variables are statistically significant. The Beta's in column 5 are calculated by entering each of the schoolwide factors alone in an equation with the individual background factor. Thus, three separate equations were calculated to fill out this column: one with the Home Background variables and the Facilities and Curriculum variables, one with Home Background and the Student Body variables, and one with Home Background and the Teacher Characteristics variables. Column 6 shows the Beta's for a single equation with all of the variables in the three schoolwide factors and *Proportion White* in school entered in the equation but without the Home-Background characteristics entered. Column 7 is similar to column 5 except that the individual Home-Background variables have been omitted from each of the three equations.

The extraordinary thing about these final four columns is the similar-

TABLE 3

Sixth-Grade Northern Whites
Verbal Achievement Mean = 36.148, S.D. = 11.409

Means, standard deviations, and standardized regression coefficients for selected independent variables in a number of regression equations with Verbal Achievement as the dependent variable.

	Variable	1 Mean	2 S.D.	3 Zero-order r with Verbal	4 Betas for full equation	5 Betas for equations with factor & Family Bkgrd. alone	6 Betas for equations without Family Bkgrd.	7 Betas for equations with only one factor
Home Background Factor								
3	Reading Material	0.293	0.510	.23†	.12†			
4	Items in Home	0.311	0.340	.22†	.08†			
5	Siblings	0.241	0.758	.13†	.10†			
6	Structural Integrity	0.236	0.580	.11†	.06*			
39	Parents' Educ.	0.277	0.877	.28†	.19†			
40	Urbanism of Background	0.067	1.242	−.10†	−.09†			
Facilities and Curriculum Factor								
38	Per-Pupil Expenditure	492.614	174.525	.04	.01	.00	.02	.04
23	Volume/Student	4.687	5.134	.02	−.01	.00	−.01	.02
9	School Size	80.215	47.606	.01	.01	.00	−.01	.00
33	School Location	3.654	1.745	−.00	−.04	−.05	−.03	−.01
37	Promotion Slow Learners	2.696	1.451	−.03	−.01	−.02	−.02	−.04
36	Accelerated Curriculum	3.074	1.165	−.03	.00	.00	−.01	−.03
Student-Body Factor								
10	Proportion Own Encyclopedia	0.807	0.113	.21†	−.01	.01	.09*	.12†
26	Student Transfer	7.507	6.501	−.00	.03	.01	.04	.03
31	Attendance	91.132	2.520	.08†	−.01	.01	.01	.03
55	T Perception of Student Quality	−0.135	0.423	−.23†	−.10†	−.12†	−.15†	−.17†
Teacher Characteristics								
11	T SES Level	3.729	0.634	.07*	.01	.01	.01	.03
12	T Experience	11.736	4.561	−.01	.04	.04	.04	.04
13	T Localism	0.055	0.796	.07*	.03	.04	.05	.07
15	T Degree Received	3.022	0.317	.05	−.01	−.02	.01	.04
16	T Preference for Middle Class	−0.240	0.712	−.10†	−.01	−.04	−.03	−.09†
17	T Verbal Score	23.341	2.063	.05	.02	.03	.01	.04
18	T Prop. White	0.965	0.074	.09†	.03	.06*	.04	.09†
48	Prop. School White	0.877	0.143	.16†	.06		.04	

* Significant at the .05 level.
† Significant at the .01 level.

ity in the magnitudes of the Beta's for each of the variables. With only a very few exceptions the Beta's in the equation with all of the variables entered are as large as the Beta's in equations with less controlled conditions. If the Beta's were very different from column to column, we would conclude that the relationship of a schoolwide resource to achievement depends upon its relationship to the other schoolwide resources or to the individual background characteristics of the students in the school. But with the exception of the *Proportion Teacher White* variable, the only school variable seriously influenced by the removal or introduction of other controlling information into the equation are those measuring the social-class composition of the school—e.g., *Proportion Own Encyclopedia* and *Teachers' Perception of Student-Body Quality*. Such comparisons are also a way of testing the criticism about the order of introduction of the variables into the regression equations.

Without comparing this table to others, it is difficult to show how the means and standard deviations can be used. If the standard deviations for the independent and dependent variables are the same in two tables, the Beta weights can be used to compare the magnitudes of influence of the various variables. The means can also be compared to determine which sample has the greatest access to the resources. But if the ratios of the standard deviations of the dependent variables to the standard deviations of the independent variables are different from one equation to another, then *b* weights should be calculated.

Tables such as this for each of the six groups studied here are included in Appendix B. Data are extracted from those tables (G–L in Appendix B) to form new tables for the text of this paper.

In summary, two approaches for the assessment of the importance of variables in a regression equation will be used in this paper. First, the allocation of explained variation into seven uniquely and jointly explained components will allow comparisons between the explanatory power of the three schoolwide factors. Because the seven components are calculated both before and after Home Background variables are entered as controls, the manner and extent to which Home Background overlaps in explanatory power with each of the schoolwide factors also can be examined.

Second, the use of regression weights allows an assessment of the strength of individual variables. The weights, together with the means and standard deviations of the independent and dependent variables in the same tables, can be used to contrast the explanatory power of the various independent variables both within and between equations. Because weights for each variable are computed under varying conditions of control, the second technique also offers a way of examining the effect of the interrelationships among the independent variables. Finally, subject to strong caveats about the appropriateness of the models presented, a weight gives an estimate of the amount of change in the dependent variable that might be expected when an independent variable is increased or decreased.

The reason for using the two above approaches is ultimately to measure the relationships between the schoolwide resources and student achievement. These measures allow the examination of both specific individual and overall groups (factors) of variables. There is, however, another approach for estimating the overall relationship between schoolwide characteristics and individual achievement. It is to this approach that I now turn.

AN APPROXIMATE UPPER LIMIT ON THE EFFECT OF SCHOOL FACTORS ON ACHIEVEMENT

I noted earlier that one of the central tasks of Coleman *et al.* was to assess the magnitude of the overall effect of schoolwide characteristics on achievement. Differences in achievement scores among students can be thought of in a number of ways. A common way is to break down the differences into two components. One component measures how different the students are from the average student in their school. The second component measures how different the average student in a school is from the average student of all of the schools. The first component is generally called the *within*-school component and the second the *between*-school component of the total variation in student scores.

Because information about school resources was only gathered on a schoolwide basis, the school resource factors could not account for any of the differences between students within the same school. Therefore, the percent of total variance that lies *between* schools is a kind of upper limit on the amount of variance school resources could account for.

In addition, Coleman *et al.* went one step further. They computed the *between*- and *within*-school components only after separating the students within the schools into groups on the basis of racial or ethnic background. Although this probably had the effect of substantially reducing the *between*-school estimates, they claimed that such an approach was necessary. Two reasons are ordinarily given for such a decision. First, the achievement of students of different races and ethnic backgrounds may be determined by different sets of factors. Cultural differences among homes and differences in the ways that the society treats students of various groups might differentially influence the sensitivity of the student to school resources. Strong evidence exists about differences among ethnic groups in patterns of mental abilities (Lesser, Fifer, and Clark, 1965) and in the influence of social class upon the achievement of students (Wilson, 1967). If the various racial and ethnic groups differ in the determinants of their achievement and in average social class then regression analysis must be separately computed for the various groups. And if separate regressions must be computed, then separate *between-* and *within*-school components of variance must be computed for the groups to estimate "approximate upper limits of the school effects." Second, there are striking differences in the mean achievement levels of students from various groups. These differences persist even when strong social-class and schoolwide controls are introduced. They suggest that unmeasured factors influence the mean achievement levels of the various groups. If this is the case, the regression coefficients for the total sample equation will be very different from the coefficients for the separate group equations. The coefficients will be influenced by the differences in mean achievement levels among the groups.

These two reasons argue for conducting separate analyses on the various ethnic groups. Coleman *et al.* presented the *between*-school percentages of variance for 10 groups, defined by race and region, at all five grade levels. They found that for Northern blacks and whites the *between*-school variation was only 7 to 14 percent of the total variance, and that the percentage of *between*-school variation was about the same in all grades but the 3rd. There the *between*-school percentages are higher but this may be due to the inadequacies of the 3rd-grade test (see Jencks, Chapter 4). Table 4 presents the data for Northern blacks and whites at each of the five grade levels.

TABLE 4

*Percent of Total Variance in Individual Verbal Achievement
Scores that Lies Among Schools**

	Level				
	12th Grade	9th Grade	6th Grade	3rd† Grade	1st Grade
Northern Blacks	10.92	12.67	13.89	19.47	10.63
Northern Whites	7.84	8.69	10.32	11.42	11.07

* From Table 3.22.1 of the EEOS Report.
† The 3rd-grade verbal test was unreliable (see Jencks, Chapter 4).

In examining the percentages of variation, it is incorrect to compare the percentages for the elementary-school grades with the percentages for secondary-school grades. Secondary schools generally draw students from a larger, more heterogeneous population. This might well reduce the between-school percentage of variance. On the other hand, there is a greater possibility of students selecting themselves or being assigned to particular secondary schools on the basis of their elementary-school achievement. This might increase the between-school component. Because we do not know the importance of either of these differences, we should treat comparisons between elementary and secondary school skeptically. However, comparisons among the elementary grades should be less dangerous. The patterns for the two groups shown in Table 4 are similar to the patterns for the other groups. The magnitudes of these percentages, however, are somewhat lower than for the other groups.

Coleman *et al.* read these results as showing that "our schools have great uniformity insofar as their effect on the learning of pupils is concerned. The data suggest that variations in school quality are not highly related to variations in achievement of pupils" (pp. 296–7). They argued that the amount of school-to-school variation at the 1st-grade level must be due to differences among the schools in the average home backgrounds of their students. Because the tests were given in the early fall, the differences among the schools in their resources could not have caused differences among the schools in average student achievement. And because the variations among schools are roughly constant across the five grade levels, the school-to-school differences in achievement were considered to be uninfluenced by the school-to-school difference in school resources.

Earlier I noted one possible fallacy in this argument. If differences in school resources both cause the school-to-school differences in achievement and are correlated with the social-class composition of the schools, the effect of the school resources would go unnoticed. A second fallacy is that schools may carry out two competing functions which mask the effects of school resources while keeping the between-school variance constant. On the one hand, all schools, at least at the elementary level, attempt to impart the same skills and information (e.g., reading and arithmetic skills and the principal export of Saskatchewan). The uniformity of curriculum might reduce between-school variation. Competing with this might be the fact that some schools do their job well and some do it poorly. This would tend to spread schools apart increasing the between-school variance. The issue is clearly very complex.

Even so, for Northern whites and blacks, the percentages of achievement variance that lie among schools are surprisingly small. If the figures given in Table 4 are roughly accurate, a great diversity exists among children within schools and little diversity exists between schools.[6] This suggests that if the survey had gathered data on the utilization of the school resources differentially among students within schools, the conclusions of the Report might have been very different.

Rationale for the Selection of Samples

Three questions about my choice of groups and grade levels require explanation:

1) Why are only black and white students studied?
2) Why are only grades 6, 9, and 12 analyzed?
3) Why are only Northern schools studied?

At the beginning of this section, I discussed two reasons for distrusting findings in the Report about minority groups other than blacks. The first is that there is evidence of misclassification of ethnic and racial membership for the other minority groups. The second is that the method of the construction of samples of the smaller minority groups for analysis in the Report did not insure the representation of a large number of different schools which reduced the accuracy of any estimation of school effects on these students. The samples of Negroes and whites were much more massive in terms of both number of students and number of schools.

The selection of grades also was partially dictated by technical reasons. The Report's 1st- and 3rd-grade analyses used only a few school variables. Furthermore, an inspection of their correlation matrices in the Supplemental Appendix convinced me that the data were not only sparse but also contained serious errors. Finally, since the Report's conclusions are largely based on results of 6th-, 9th-, and 12th-grade analyses, I felt that my reanalysis should also focus on these grades.

The third question is more difficult. On the technical side, the overall response rate and probable accuracy of questionnaire response were higher in the North than in the South at all grade levels. In addition, I know more about Northern schools, which would make a realistic analysis easier.

But neither of these considerations is persuasive if the selection of only one region of the country covers up variations in the quality of school resources that are associated with variations in achievement outputs. The analysis of separate regions makes spurious inferences less likely. Because the South, for example, has schools with generally lower mean achievement scores than the North, any systematic difference between the schools in the two regions would be related to the achievement differences. If there were no such relationships within either region, it would be foolish to make any inferences about school factors *causing* regional differences in achievement. But some particularly important influences on achievement might not be apparent in separate regional analyses because the schools within the regions are too homogeneous.

To examine this last possibility I carried out analyses on the Northern, Southern, and Total samples of 12th-grade blacks. I selected 12th-grade blacks because the Report suggests that they are more sensitive to school resources than practically any other group. The data for these three analy-

ses are shown in Table 5. The first thing to note is that the standard deviations of the dependent variable (*Verbal Achievement*) and the standard
deviations of the independent variables (all schoolwide resources) are
roughly equal in the three samples. The standard deviations of the
independent variables are very slightly larger in the Total sample but the
differences do not suggest that there is a serious restriction in the range of
resources in either of the two regions.

A second point is more disconcerting. The R^2 for both the total
($R^2=.18$) and the Southern samples ($R^2=.19$) are almost twice as
large as the R^2 for the Northern sample ($R^2=.10$). Since only schoolwide variables are included in the analyses, the differences in the magnitudes of the R^2's might be interpreted as meaning that schoolwide resources
are more important in the South and in the country as a whole than in the
North. But comparison of the b weights in the three samples does not support this conclusion. Ignoring differences among the samples in the signs
attached to the weights, the b's in the Northern sample are equal to or
greater than the corresponding b's in both other samples for eighteen of the
twenty-three variables.

Thus we face a contradiction. Judging by the percentages of variance
accounted for by school factors, the South and Total samples are more sensitive to variations in school resources than is the Northern sample. This
was the conclusion reached by Coleman *et al.* But judging by the relative
magnitudes of the b weights, the Northern sample appears to be more sensitive than the Southern or Total samples. The Report's conclusion that
Southern students are more affected by variations in school resources may,
therefore, be wrong. Either way it appears as if regional stratification does
not seriously limit the possibility of school resources' showing strength in
this analysis.

One final point must be made. It is possible that achievement in the
North is affected by different things than achievement in the South. If this
were the case, we would certainly not analyze students from both areas in
the same sample. The data presented here suggest that there may be differences by region in the determinants of academic achievement. Nine of the
twenty-three schoolwide variables have different signs on their b weights in
the North than in the South. Although most of these differences can probably be explained by random variations, the large number of different signs
raises further doubts about combining the samples.

SUMMARY.   In this section I attempted to cover a number of issues preliminary to the presentation of the data analysis. My principal aim has been to
show that the EEOS Report's conclusions may have been influenced by the
authors' model of the educational process and by their choice of statistics. I
have argued that the alternative approaches suggested here might make

TABLE 5

Zero-order correlations, regression coefficients, and standard deviations, and R²'s for regression equations for samples of Twelfth-Grade Blacks drawn from the total country, the North and the South. Verbal achievement is the dependent variable.

		Total ($R^2 = .18$)			North ($R^2 = .10$)			South ($R^2 = .19$)		
		Zero order r	b	SD	Zero order r	b	SD	Zero order r	b	SD
		Facilities and Curriculum Factor								
38	Per-Pupil Expenditure	.21	0.00	149.09	.00	0.00	135.76	.22	−0.00	70.23
23	Volume/Student	.06	−0.00	3.99	−.06	−0.11	4.27	.16	0.11	3.70
22	Science Lab.	.19	0.01	22.46	.11	−0.00	16.45	.20	0.01	26.16
24	Extracurr. Act.	.20	0.03	14.25	.13	0.06	12.49	.16	0.02	14.84
36	Accelerated Curr.	−.11	0.05	0.94	−.10	−0.27	1.01	−.06	−0.09	0.86
25	Comprehensiveness of Curriculum	.09	−0.02	16.19	.04	−0.03	12.86	.08	−0.00	18.38
35	Tracking	−.02	0.31	0.59	.03	1.04	0.50	−.02	0.35	0.65
27	Movement between Tracks	−.03	−0.05	8.23	.05	−0.11	7.25	−.08	−0.04	8.97
9	School Size	.26	−0.00	212.77	.08	−0.01*	218.42	.31	−0.00	152.44
30	Guidance Counselor	.28	0.06	4.87	.09	0.03	4.52	.30	0.11	3.42
33	School Location	.25	0.35	2.17	.10	0.47	2.00	.27	0.30	2.12
	Student Body Factor									
10	Proportion Own Encyclopedia	.38	17.21†	0.16	.24	17.55	0.09	.38	14.24†	0.16
26	Student Transfer	.06	−0.15	4.47	−.08	−0.16	5.01	.03	0.03	3.07
31	Attendance	.05	0.08	3.67	.10	0.16	4.00	.06	0.14	3.33
52	Proportion College Track	.35	13.03†	0.16	.26	15.76†	0.15	.36	11.06†	0.16

	Total ($R^2 = .18$)			North ($R^2 = .10$)			South ($R^2 = .19$)		
	Zero order r	b	SD	Zero order r	b	SD	Zero order r	b	SD
53 Average Hours of Homework	.05	0.61	0.56	.08	−1.21	0.51	.16	1.42	0.56
Teacher Characteristics									
11 T SES Level	.19	1.34	0.55	.05	2.96	0.46	.24	1.49	0.60
12 T Experience	.13	0.14	3.21	.06	−0.06	2.99	.18	0.08	3.39
13 T Localism	.02	−0.10	0.75	−.06	−2.28*	0.78	−.11	0.08	0.60
15 T Degree Received	.25	−0.12	0.24	.12	−0.80	0.24	.20	0.65	0.18
16 T Perception of Middle-class	−.15	−0.88	0.62	−.18	−1.83	0.67	−.12	−0.71	0.58
17 T Verbal Score	.31	0.31	2.56	.13	0.25	1.96	.33	0.42	2.62
18 Proportion T White	.23	1.95	0.43	.08	−2.16	0.35	.12	0.41	0.28
Verbal Mean =		49.22			52.72			46.23	
Verbal S.D. =		14.45			14.51			13.71	

* Statistically significant at .05 level—t greater than 1.96.
† Statistically significant at .01 level—t greater than 2.57.

substantive differences in the interpretation of the data. In addition, I have presented reasons to justify my limiting the reanalysis to the examination of only Northern Negroes and whites at the 6th, 9th, and 12th grades.

In the following four sections I examine the relationships of home background and schoolwide resources to verbal achievement. Where relevant, I summarize Coleman *et al.*'s conclusions and contrast them with results from the reanalysis.

SECTION II: Individual Home Background and Achievement

The first task of the EEOS Report's Chapter 3 analysis was to examine the influence of home background on achievement. That set the stage for studying the effects of school resources on student achievement. Because a Home Background factor was used as a control in *all* later analyses, Coleman *et al.* thought it important to *first* "examine the relation of these background factors to achievement, to get a view of some of the family factors that predispose children to learn poorly in school" (p. 298). In this section I carry out a similar examination. However, my intent is to determine the effect of controlling for various background variables on the relationship between student achievement and school factors. The influence of the background variables are then examined, but they are of secondary interest.

The Variables

The survey measured twenty-five background characteristics.[7] The authors grouped these into eight variables. Six of these variables measured objective characteristics of the pupil's home. These were

1) the *Urbanism* of the pupil and his parents;
2) his *Parents' Educational* experience;
3) the *Structural Integrity* of his home: whether the pupil lived with both, one, or none of his real parents;
4) the number of *Home Items* (vacuum cleaner, TV, car, hi-fi set, refrigerator, telephone) in his home;
5) the *Number of Reading Items* (dictionary, encyclopedia, daily paper, number of magazines, books) in his home; and
6) the *Number of his Siblings* (positive score indicates few siblings).

Assessments of social class generally include measures of family income, father's occupation, and parents' education. Coleman *et al.* measured *Parental Education*. *Home Items* might be considered a proxy for family income. Coleman *et al.* assessed father's occupation but did not use the results.[8] The *Urbanism* of the family, the *Number of Siblings*, and the *Structural Integrity of the Family* indirectly assess a variety of characteristics, including ethnicity, religion, living standard, and perhaps something like the level of disorder in the home—all of which may be related to scholastic achievement. *Reading Items* in the home assesses the home educational environment. While it is unlikely that differences in students' levels of achievement cause differences in these background conditions,[9] the variables (imperfectly) reflect circumstances which are likely to strongly influence a child's readiness for school and which might facilitate or retard his progress through school.

Coleman *et al.* also created two variables assessing the "subjective" conditions of the home:

7) *Parents' Interest in the Child's School Experiences and*

8) *Parents' Desires and Expectations of the Child's Success in School.*

These variables may measure intangible characteristics of the home that motivate the child in school, but their causal relationship to student achievement is less clear than that of the "objective" factors. Most likely it is circular—the level of the student's achievement partially determines parents' interest and educational desires, and his parents' behavior partially determines the achievement level.

The Influence of Individual Background on School-to-School Differences in Achievement, and a Discussion of Two Errors Made in the Report

The EEOS Report begins its discussion of the influence of home background on school achievement by examining how much of the school-to-school variance in the student achievement is accounted for by this factor. Coleman *et al.* made two serious errors here. The data are contained in Table 6. The first row contains estimates of the school-to-school variations in achievement as percentages of the total variation in achievement. Differences in school assignment and self-selection practices between elementary and secondary schools make comparisons between grades impossible.[10] As noted earlier, at the 1st grade the numbers can be used as estimates of the upper bounds on the school-to-school differences in achievement that can be ascribed to community differences. At later grades the numbers are estimates of the percentage of total variance that could be statistically accounted for by schoolwide influences.

The other rows of Table 6 contain estimates of the amount of total variation that lies between schools and is accounted for by various combinations of the home background influences.[11] For the six objective background variables (row 2), the amount of between-school variance explained within each racial group is similar for the three grades. However, the variables explain more of the school-to-school variation for whites than for blacks.

The relationship of the "subjective" background variables to school-to-school differences in achievement is somewhat different than that of the "ob-

TABLE 6

Estimates of percentages of total variation in verbal achievement that a) lie between schools and b) are accounted for by various combinations of individual-level Home Background variables.

	Northern Whites			Northern Blacks		
	6th Grade	9th Grade	12th Grade	6th Grade	9th Grade	12th Grade
1. Among-School Variance	12.77	8.31	8.25	11.86	8.96	11.19
2. Six "Objective" Variables	6.92	5.48	5.29	4.40	2.80	3.38
3. Two "Subjective" Variables	0.33	3.29	3.78	0.16	0.76	0.80
4. Four "Objective" and Two "Subjective" Variables	4.36	4.56	4.89	3.75	2.38	2.39
5. Six "Objective" and Two "Subjective" Variables	6.64	5.54	5.68	4.18	2.64	3.30

Row 1

The numbers in the first row of this table are estimates of the school-to-school variations in Verbal Achievement as percentages of the total variation. These estimates are also contained in Table 3.221.1 of the EEOS Report. They were "obtained by regressing individual achievement on overall school mean achievement (of all groups in the school) and proportion white in the school. These two measures together (except for the presence of third groups in the school) provide an estimate of the group's mean score in the school under the assumption that differences between the white mean and the group mean are constant over all schools" (from a footnote to Table 3.221.1, p. 299). Although that assumption is wrong, the estimates for the groups studied here are nonetheless quite accurate. (Compare the figures in this table with the figures in Table 3.22.1 of the Report.)

Row 2

The six variables are fully described in the Appendix to this paper. They are: *Home Items, Reading Items, Structural Integrity of the Family, Parents' Education,* and *Urbanism of Background.* The estimates were computed by a two-step process. First, individual verbal achievement was regressed against the six background variables. This produced the percentage of *total* achievement variance explained. Second, individual verbal achievement was regressed against the overall achievement of the school, the proportion white in the school *and* all of the six background variables. The between-school percentage of variance in row 1 was subtracted from this second figure leaving the percentage of total variance that lies *within* schools and is accounted for by the background variables. This figure was then subtracted from the total percentage of variance explained by the six background items. The result of this subtraction is the amount of total variance that lies between schools and is accounted for by the six background variables.

Row 3

The two variables are fully described in the Appendix to this paper. They are *Parents' Interest* and *Parental Desires and Expectations.* The figures in this row and rows 4 and 5 were calculated in the same manner as the figures in row 2.

Row 4

The four "objective" variables are the first four listed in the footnote for row 2 and the two "subjective" variables listed in the footnote for row 3.

Row 5

The eight variables are those listed under the footnotes for rows 2 and 3.

jective" variables. Again the numbers are larger for whites than for blacks. But for both racial groups the association between the "subjective" variables and achievement is stronger in the later grades than in grade 6. Notice also that the relationship between the subjective variables and school-to-school differences in achievement is considerably smaller than that of the objective background variables for both races and at all three grade levels.[12]

The final three rows of Table 6 contain estimates of the between-school variation accounted for by various combinations of the subjective and objective background variables. Addition of the subjective variables to equations which already include objective variables explains little additional school-to-school variation. The model Coleman *et al.* adopted for their analysis required that the influence of the home background factors on student achievement be removed *before* the influence of the schoolwide factors was estimated. The between-school percents of total variance (row 1, Table 6) estimate the amount of total variation that schoolwide factors can explain. This means that the choice of different background variables affects the amount of between-school variation that is left for possible explanation by schoolwide factors. For example, if the six "objective" background variables are controlled in an analysis of 6th-grade whites, the schoolwide factors' potential unique contribution is reduced from 12.77 percent to 5.85 percent of the total variation. If, however, the background variables controlled are the four objective and two subjective (row 5, Table 6), the reduction is only to 8.41 percent. Note that the amount of between-school variance explained by the six "objective" background variables is always larger than the amount explained by the four "objective" and two "subjective" variables.

This comparison is important because the Report's authors intended to use the six "objective" variables as their home background controls and instead used the four "objective" and two "subjective" background variables. One effect of this error was to increase the amount of between-school variance available for explanation by school variables. The increase was particularly serious for 6th-grade whites (where it amounted to 2.69 percent of the *total* variance) and for 12th-grade blacks (where it amounted to 0.99 percent of the *total* variance).

Although these differences seem small (in all but one case they are less than 1 percent of the total variance), it is important to remember that the base for comparison is not the amount of total variance but the amount of between-school variance. In Table 7 the estimates for the two sets of background variables are presented as percentages of between-school variance. There the differences appear somewhat larger. In only one case is the difference less than 5 percent, and in two of the three cases for the whites the difference is greater than 10 percent. These differences led the authors of the Report to several erroneous conclusions.

The Report's authors made a second error which camouflaged the first. In order to estimate the amount of school-to-school variation in

TABLE 7

Estimated percentages of between-school variance accounted for by two combinations of student Home Background characteristics.*

		6th Grade	9th Grade	12th Grade
Northern Whites	6 Objective Variables	54.2	65.9	64.1
	4 Objective and 2 Subjective Variables	34.1	54.9	59.3
Northern Blacks	6 Objective Variables	37.1	31.3	30.2
	4 Objective and 2 Subjective Variables	31.6	26.6	21.4

* The variables are fully described in an Appendix. The six objective variables are those listed in footnote 2 of Table 6. The four objective and two subjective variables are those described in footnote 4 of Table 6. The numbers in this table were calculated directly from the numbers in Table 6. The base (denominator) in all cases was the between-school estimate in row 1 of Table 6. The devisor for the six objective variable rows in the table are taken from row 2 of Table 6. The divisor for the other numbers is taken from row 5 of Table 6. Thus the upper-left-hand number $54.2 = 100.0 \times 6.92/12.77$ and the lower-right-hand number, $21.4 = 100.0 \times 3.30/11.19$.

achievement accounted for by individual family background, they treated the school mean verbal score, controlled for percent white in the school, as a dependent variable. They tried to predict this mean with the individual-level variables. Since the students had very different backgrounds, no one of them provided a good estimate of the school's mean social class, much less its mean verbal score. Yet this clearly does not mean that if all the individuals in a school were taken together their family backgrounds would not account for most of the variation in mean achievement. Under these circumstances the obvious strategy is to average the background characteristics of all pupils in the same school and correlate the result with average achievement. But this was not acceptable because the aggregate social-class level of the school might have an additional effect over and above the individual social class of the students. An alternative approach is to find out how much of the within-school variation in achievement is accounted for by variations in family background. This can be done by computing the amount of additional achievement variance explained by family background after the mean achievement for the school has already been controlled. Subtracting the within-school achievement variance accounted for by family background from the total achievement variance accounted for by the individual background yields an estimate of the between-school achievement variance accounted for by individual family background. Comparing this to the total amount of between-school achievement variance we get the "new" numbers in Table 8. The "old" numbers are the incorrect estimates made in the Report. *The striking thing about the numbers in this table is the magni-*

TABLE 8

Two estimates of the percentages of among-school variance accounted for by six objective and two subjective Home Background variables.

		6th Grade	9th Grade	12th Grade
Northern Whites	Old Estimate*	10.99	14.42	15.99
	New Estimate †	52.0	66.7	68.8
Northern Blacks	Old Estimate	6.75	7.37	12.75
	New Estimate	35.2	29.5	29.5

* The Old Estimates were "approximated by" the proportion of mean school achievement (controlling on proportion white in school), accounted for by eight background variable factors. (See Table 3.221.2, p. 299 EEOS Report.)
† The New Estimates were computed in the same manner as the numbers in Table 7.

tude of the Report's underestimation of the percentage of between-school variance explained by the individual-level home background variables. Like the mislabeling of the individual background items this error led to an overestimate of the amount of school-to-school variation in achievement attributable to school factors.

The Influences of Home Background on Within-School Differences in Achievement

Return now to a consideration of the relationship of Home Background to achievement. Table 9 presents the amount of within-school variation accounted for by various combinations of home background variables.

TABLE 9

Estimates of percentages of total variation in Verbal Achievement that a) lie within schools, and b) are accounted for by various combinations of individual-level Home Background variables.

	Northern Whites			Northern Blacks		
	6th Grade	9th Grade	12th Grade	6th Grade	9th Grade	12th Grade
1. Within-School Variance*	87.23	91.69	91.75	88.14	91.14	88.81
2. Six "Objective" Variables	7.18	11.01	8.99	5.11	4.88	4.15
3. Two "subjective" Variables	3.05	13.82	16.57	2.08	6.24	5.33
4. Four "Objective" and Two "Subjective" Variables	6.48	15.97	18.31	5.46	8.62	6.96
5. Six "Objective" and Two "Subjective" Variables	8.93	17.24	18.88	6.07	8.77	7.66

* The numbers in this row are estimates of the within-school variation in achievement as percentages of the total school achievement. They were calculated by subtracting the numbers in row 1 of Table 6 from 100. For methods of calculation of numbers in other rows, see footnote to Table 6.

For the 6 objective variables the pattern is very similar to the pattern between schools, although the numbers are larger in this table than in Table
6. There is no consistent trend across grade level for either group.

However, the amounts of within-school variation explained by the
"subjective" variables show a distinct pattern. For both groups of students
there is a sharp rise in the "explanatory" power of the variables from the 6th
to the later grades. Note that the overall magnitude of the variation explained by these variables is *much* greater within than between schools.
These measures appear to be more effective in distinguishing among
students within schools than among schools. They are also more effective at
distinguishing among whites than they are at distinguishing among blacks.
This holds *between* as well as *within* schools.

Conclusions About the General and Specific Effects of Subjective Home Conditions on Scholastic Achievement

Summarizing the relationship between the subjective home background factor and achievement, Coleman *et al.* arrived at two sets of conclusions.

1) The increase in association of the subjective measures with
   achievement from 6th to 12th grades "indicates either that the
   older students perceive their parents' interest more accurately than
   the younger ones, or that their parents' interest has more impact
   on their achievement in the later years of school" (p. 301).

2) That the difference in explanatory power for the variables between
   the white and the black students indicates that either the black
   "children fail to perceive their parents' interest or lack of interest
   in their schooling as fully as do whites . . ."; or "the parents of
   these minority group children are less able to translate their interest into effective support for the child's learning than are white or
   Oriental parents" [13] (p. 302).

Coleman *et al.* looked at only the combined contribution of both "subjective" measures to the explanation of achievement variation. It turns out
that only the variable *Parents' Educational Expectation and Desires* increases its association with achievement between grades 6 and 12 (see
Table 10). The variable *Parents' Interest* has a relatively constant relationship to achievement for grades 6 through 12. Therefore, Coleman *et al.*'s
first conclusion should deal with the "expectations" and "desires" of parents
rather than with "parents' interest."

Further, the causal relationship between the desires and expectations
of parents and their children's achievement is unclear. A child's achievement in school may depend on whether his parents expect him to go to
college, but whether his parents expect the child to go to college also depends on whether the child is doing well in school.

TABLE 10

Zero-order correlations between Verbal Achievement and two "subjective" Home Background variables.*

| | Race | | | | | |
| | Northern Blacks | | | Northern Whites | | |
Variable	6th Grade	9th Grade	12th Grade	6th Grade	9th Grade	12th Grade
Parents' Interest	.12	.09	.03	.13	.21	.16
Parents' Desires and Expectations	.11	.26	.24	.15	.41	.45

* The correlations are transcribed directly from the Supplemental Appendix to the EEOS Report.

If parents' desires and expectations are formed independently of achievement and help to cause achievement, school-to-school differences in achievement should be as sensitive to differences among schools in the level of parents' desires as within-school differences in achievement are sensitive to within-school differences in parents' desires. But they are not, thus suggesting that a parent's perception may be determined by the child's success relative to classmates.[14] Further, the parents' desires should have a particularly strong relationship to achievement if the parents know that their expectations and desires can be translated into reality. It thus seems possible that the difference between whites and blacks in the explanatory power of the variable *Parents' Educational Expectation and Desires* reflects the problem that blacks in the society have in translating desires into action. Based on these considerations, it seems likely that the increasing association between verbal achievement and the "subjective variable" *Parents' Educational Expectation and Desires* reflects the sensitivity of parents to the achievement of their child rather than the child's increasingly accurate perception of his parents' desires or any increasing impact of these desires on the child.[15]

The variable *Parents' Interest*, on the other hand, is intended to assess the behavior of the parent before the child entered school (whether the child was read to or not) and how often the parent asks the child about his schoolwork. It seems unlikely that either of these behaviors is a direct cause of a child's success in school after 1st grade. But neither is there much increase between the 6th and the 12th grades in the (linear) relationship between *Parents' Interest* and *Verbal Achievement* (see Table 10).

In summary, the conclusions reached by Coleman *et al.* regarding the relationships between the "subjective" background variables and student achievement must be viewed with skepticism. The causal relationship between the background conditions assessed by these variables and achievement is unclear. Unlike the authors of the Report, I conclude that it is more likely that the achievement of a student causes rather than is caused by the level of his parents' expectations and desires.

Conclusions About the Overall Association of the "Objective" Home Background Variables to Student Achievement

There is no such confusion about the direction of causation for the "objective" background variables. Insofar as they accurately measure the economic and social conditions of a child's home, they can be viewed as determinants of student achievement. However, there is some confusion about the overall strength of the relationship between the "objective" variables and achievement at the various grades. In this section, I attempt to clarify this issue. Following that, I discuss the relationships between the specific "objective" characteristics and achievement.

Coleman *et al.* concluded that "family background has its greatest effect in the early years because of the decline (probably underestimated) in the relation of these conditions to achievement from grade 6 to 12" (p. 300). Yet, Tables 6, 7, 8, and 9 do not show a clear decline. One reason the discrepancy arises is because Coleman *et al.* based their conclusion not just on the Northern blacks and whites studied here but on Southerners and other minority groups. There is a dramatic decline in the explanatory power of "objective" background measures for Puerto Ricans, Mexican Americans, and Orientals, even though there is not for blacks and whites. It should be noted that a decline is what one might expect. The larger size of secondary schools (with a concomitant greater heterogeneity in social-class composition) should reduce the between-school variation in achievement explained by social-class variables.

However, there are offsetting factors. Dropouts and tracking in secondary schools confound *within*-school relationships between social class and achievement at the secondary level. The availability of special schools for academic and vocational education confounds *between*-school relationships. Apparently these factors influence white and blacks more than other minority groups.

A second reason for Coleman *et al.*'s conclusion is based on the differences between the 6th and the later grades in the validity of the social-class measures. At the 6th grade, large numbers of students did not respond or responded "don't know" to the questions about their parents' educational attainment, their family structure, and their urbanism (see Jencks, Chapter 12). At the 9th and 12th grades the problem was less acute. This led Coleman *et al.* to consider the "decline" in the effect of family background to be "probably underestimated." It leads me to think that there *is* a decline from the 6th to the secondary grades in the explanatory strength of the social-class variables for whites and blacks as well as for the other groups, although the dropout, self-selection, and school assignment processes intervening between elementary and secondary schools make it impossible to document.

It should be noted, however, that Coleman *et al.* did not find that the association between achievement and the background variables decreased over the elementary years. In a footnote to their discussion of the influence of the "objective" background variables on achievement, they said,

. . . in grades 1 and 3 these conditions (incompletely measured) show a lower relation to achievement than in any of the three grades examined here. This is true for the relation of all variables to achievement at these two grades. While this may result from incompleteness and unreliability of response at these grade levels, it may indicate that the relation does in fact increase over time [p. 300]. It should also be noted that Coleman *et al.* modified their early conclusion about the trend in the relation of Home Background to Achievement in their final summary (p. 325). There they claim that they found no trend.

Speculation About the Relationships Between Home Background and Achievement

The differences in the quality of the data at the various grade levels suggest that differences in the relations between home background and school achievement should be viewed skeptically. Nevertheless, the relationships are intriguing. They may point to important and, as yet, largely unexplored effects of schooling. It is interesting to speculate about possible reasons other than faulty data for explaining why the relationship between home background and achievement increases over the elementary-school years and then stabilizes in the secondary-school years. Suppose that the following explanation is true:

The early home-background experiences have a strong effect on the measured achievement level at which the student enters 1st grade. This helps determine the child's initial placement into fast or slow reading and arithmetic groups and affects the quality of work expected by his teachers. The initial grouping in conjunction with continued family influences helps to maintain and may in some cases amplify the early differences between the children *within* an elementary school. Since these differences are associated with social class, the relationship between social class and achievement increases *within* schools during the elementary years. An increase in the relationship *between* elementary schools might be due to better resources in the schools with more advantaged pupils and/or to continued family influence. The move to larger heterogeneous secondary schools stabilizes the amount of *between*-school variation in achievement explained by the background variables. The stabilization of the *within*-secondary-school variation in achievement accounted for by social class may be due to the joint effects of more precise measurement and the assignment of students into curricula on the basis of past achievement.

This explanation relies heavily upon the assignment and selection functions of schools. Although such an explanation might be accurate, there are no hard data to support it directly. However, sparse suggestive data do exist. At the elementary level the argument that the selection and assignment practices increase the relationship between class and achievement rests on three points: first, that practices such as grouping by "ability" exist; second, that the mechanisms used for grouping bear a relationship to social class; and third, that there is an increasing disparity between the achievement of groups. The first two parts of the puzzle are clear. In 1958–59, the Research Division of the NEA studied administrative practices in urban school districts (cities with a population above 2500). An estimated 77.6 percent of the urban districts practiced ability grouping in the elementary grades. This figure reflects only between-classroom grouping. Estimates of within-classroom grouping are even higher. Austin and Morrison found in a national survey of elementary schools that "more than 80 percent reported that they 'always' or 'often' use readiness tests for prereading evaluation (in 1st grade)" (Austin and Morrison, 1963). Most readiness tests include explicit instructions for grouping within classrooms on the basis of test results. Group assignment on the basis of measured "ability" or "readiness" is an accepted and widespread practice.

Equally strong evidence exists that readiness scores at the 1st grade are strongly correlated with home-background characteristics. In a recent survey assessing the efficacy of Headstart, for example, the data show multiple correlations of background measures with Metropolitan Readiness test scores ranging from .31 to .45 (Smith and Bissel, 1970).

The third step in the argument has less supporting data, perhaps because the educational literature is hopelessly lacking in reports of longitudinal studies. One study, Kingston (1962), reports that the multiple correlation between Metropolitan Readiness sub-test scores and Stanford achievement test scores increases from the end of the 1st to the end of the 4th grade. This suggests that the relationship between social class and achievement might also increase over the years and that the grouping practice might be a causal factor.

The relationship of social class to "ability" grouping is undergoing examination by the courts. One court has ruled that "ability" grouping in elementary schools is unconstitutional (*Hobson v. Hansen*, 1967). In that case the results of a study of a large Midwestern town by Brookover, Leu, and Kariger (1967) were admitted as evidence. The researchers analyzed seventh graders on the basis of socioeconomic status of parents and ability level and found much higher proportions of lower-class students were misclassified into low ability groups. And even though these students were initially more likely to be placed incorrectly, they also stood less of a chance to be reclassified. Although this finding does not offer direct support for the thesis that ability grouping causes an increased relationship between social class and achievement, it does suggest that lower-class students do not have the opportunities available to middle-class students, and therefore their achievement may be affected.

An argument for the effect of assignment practices on the relationship between background variables and achievement is less difficult to make at the secondary level. Although the causal mechanisms are unclear, the frequency of assignment to college and noncollege tracks within schools and to academic or nonacademic schools on the basis of standardized tests provides persuasive evidence that the effects of social class on achievement are hopelessly tangled with grouping practices. In the following sections of this paper, I return to this issue.

In summary, I have argued that the relationship between background variables and achievement is initially strong at the 1st grade and may increase over the elementary-school years and then stabilize during the secondary-school years. Three causal mechanisms might combine to cause these findings: first, there is strong evidence that the first few years of life are important in preparing the child for school and the level of preparation is correlated with early readiness and achievement; second, the family has a continuing influence on a child's achievement; and third, the selection and assignment practices carried out by the schools might well serve to exacerbate the relationship between class and achievement in the early grades while stabilizing it in the higher grades.

In the following section I pursue the relationship between the "objective" background characteristics and achievement to see whether the relation of the specific variables to achievement offers insights into the causal mechanisms.

The Separate Influences of the Six Objective Home Background Variables on Achievement

Although each of the six "objective" background characteristics is analytically distinct, separating their independent influences is a tricky business. The black family without a male head-of-household generally does not have as many home items ($r = -.09$ at the 6th grade) or as much reading material ($r = -.10$ at the 6th grade) as the family with a male head. A family with a fixed income and a large number of children cannot afford as many home items as a family with the same income and a smaller number of children. Highly educated parents are likely to receive a daily newspaper and to have a large number of books around the house. In short, the presence or absence of one of the background factors may well be associated with the presence or absence of other background factors.

This is not to say, however, that some families with poorly educated parents do not receive newspapers or have as many home items as some families with well-educated parents. And there are many large families where the child receives as much individual attention and has as much access to reading material as he would have in a smaller family. This is why six background characteristics instead of just one are included in the equations described here. To some extent, each of the indices is thought to assess a background condition which makes a unique contribution to school success. This unique contribution plus an apportioned amount of the influence shared with other indices in the equation (background and schoolwide indices) produce the numbers shown in Tables 11 and 12. The numbers are regression coefficients for the six background variables for both races at all three grade levels. The numbers in Table 11 measure the average or expected change in the dependent variable when the specific independent variable increases by 1 standard deviation, other independent variables remain-

TABLE 11

Standardized regression coefficients for six background variables[1] at grades 6, 9, and 12 for Northern whites and blacks. Each coefficient is estimated in an equation containing all other background variables, *Proportion Whites in the School*, and three sets of schoolwide variables measuring Curriculum and Facilities, Teacher Characteristics, and Student Body characteristics. Individual Verbal Achievement is the dependent variable.

	Northern Blacks			Northern Whites		
	6th Grade	9th Grade	12th Grade	6th Grade	9th Grade	12th Grade
Reading Material in Home	.11*	.08*	.04	.12*	.11*	.17*
Items in Home	.13*	.05	.02	.08*	.04	−.00
Siblings	.08*	.13*	.09*	.10*	.14*	.09*
Structural Integrity of Family	.06	.07*	.04	.06*	.08*	.03
Parents' Education	.10*	.09*	.14*	.19*	.23*	.19*
Urbanism of Background	.01	.04	.05	−.09*	.07	.01

[1] The background variables are described in detail in Appendix A.
* An asterisk next to a value signifies that this coefficient is significant at the .05 level ($t > 1.96, N = 1000$).

ing unchanged. The numbers in Table 12 measure the expected change when the independent variable increases by one unit.[16]

The first thing that stands out in both tables is that—with one exception, *Urbanism of Background*—all of the variables have statistically significant coefficients in at least two of the six equations. Two variables, *Parents' Education* and number of *Siblings*, are significant in all six of the equations, and one, *Reading Material in the Home*, is significant in five. In one equation only two of the variables are significant and in a second only three; in all of the others, four or more of the variables have significant coefficients. Overall, then, each of the components appears to contribute

TABLE 12

Regression coefficients for six background variables at grades 6, 9, and 12 for Northern whites and blacks. Each coefficient is estimated in an equation containing all other background variables, *Proportion Whites in the School*, and three sets of schoolwide variables measuring Curriculum and Facilities, Teacher Characteristics, and Student Body characteristics. Individual Verbal Achievement is the dependent variable.

	Northern Blacks			Northern Whites		
	6th Grade	9th Grade	12th Grade	6th Grade	9th Grade	12th Grade
Reading Material in Home	1.4*	1.6*	1.0	2.7*	3.2*	5.0*
Items in Home	2.2*	1.0	0.6	2.8*	1.6	−0.1
Siblings	0.6*	1.7*	1.3*	1.5*	2.4*	1.7*
Structural Integrity of Family	0.6	1.1*	0.7	1.2*	1.9*	0.7
Parents' Education	1.0*	1.3*	2.4*	2.4*	3.7*	3.2*
Urbanism of Background	0.1	0.4	0.6	−0.8*	0.8	0.2

[1] The background variables are described in detail in Appendix A.
* An asterisk next to a value signifies that this coefficient is significant at the .05 level ($t > 1.96, N = 1000$).

some independent explanatory power. There seems to be a rough tendency for the *number* of significant variables to decrease over the three grades assessed here—at grade 12 for the blacks only two variables are significant and at grade 12 for the whites only three are significant. There doesn't seem to be any difference between the two racial groups in the number of variables reaching significance, although the coefficients are generally larger for the whites. For purposes of interpretation, it is clearest to look at Table 11 when the importance of various measures within groups is being considered. When cross-race and cross-class-group comparisons of the "effect" of particular variables are being made, often Table 12 is the right place to look. The coefficients in Table 12 are independent of the distribution of home-background conditions. *Their larger magnitude for whites suggests that the stronger association between home-background conditions and achievement (greater variance explained) is not only due to a greater variation of home conditions for whites.*[17]

Parents' Education bears the strongest overall relationship to achievement of any of the background factors. Although the strength of this relationship does not increase absolutely over the years, it does become stronger relative to the other background factors, most of which decrease in strength very slightly from the 6th to the 12th grade. There is a consistent pattern of larger coefficients for the white students for the *Parents' Education* and *Reading Material in the Home* variables. The only variable for which both sets of coefficients for blacks are consistently larger is *Items in the Home*.

For the other measures, number of *Siblings, Structural Integrity of the Family*, and *Urbanism of Background*, the standardized coefficients seem equal in size for both racial groups, although the raw weights are generally larger for the whites.[18] From a *somewhat* similar analysis Coleman concluded that the achievement of whites seem particularly related to factors which relate to the educational climate of the home (*Parents' Education* and *Reading Material*) while the achievement levels of minority-group students seem to be more sensitive to factors which measure the economic level of the home (*Items in the Home*) and the utilization of resources in the home (number of *Siblings*). It is dangerous to read too much into regression coefficients because their sizes are so sensitive to the proper specification of the equations and to the validity of the questionnaire replies. However, it is not inconsistent with previous research to speculate that there may be two ways in which the family environment affects the achievement of children. One involves the disruptive input of such things as constant noise, inadequate heat, and faulty plumbing that are concomitant with economic poverty. The other involves such things as reading material, parental education, etc. Overcoming the first conditions might allow variations in educationally related factors in the home to show their effect on the child's achievement. It may be that unless the necessary economic level is attained, the energy needed to translate parents' educational advantage into an achievement advantage for children may be lost just trying to obtain minimal comforts.

SUMMARY.   With respect to the overall influences of Home Background on student verbal achievement, I find that

1) Measures of "objective" characteristics of Home Background bear a strong relationship to student achievement at all grade levels both within and between schools. However, the relationships vary from grade to grade, showing an increase over the elementary-school years and a stabilization during the secondary-school years. Because of self-selection, dropouts, and school assignment practices, the causes of these variations are impossible to accurately determine.

2) Measures of "subjective" characteristics of Home Background bear a strong relation to student achievement *within* schools. Unnoticed by Coleman *et al.*, however, was the fact that "subjective" characteristics explain little between-school variance. This suggests that the "subjective" variables are influenced by the student's success relative to his immediate peers (classmates) rather than formed by some universal criteria. A further fact unnoticed by Coleman *et al.* is that the relation between the variable *Parent Expectations and Desires for their Child's Education* increases from 3rd to 12th grade, while the variable *Parent Interest in*

Child's Schooling bears a relatively constant relation to achievement over the years. Taken together, these findings suggest that the increasing association between verbal achievement and the "subjective" background characteristics reflects the sensitivity of parents to the achievement of their child rather than, as Coleman *et al.* suggest, the child's increasingly accurate perception of his parents' desires or an increasing impact of these desires on the child.

The difference in the relation of the "objective" and the "subjective" background variables to between-school differences in achievement takes on added importance because of two errors made in the EEOS Report.

1) Instead of the six "objective" variables intended for use as the Home Background factor, four "objective" and two "subjective" variables formed the Home Background factor used in the analyses in Chapter 3 of the Report. *Parents' Education* and *Urbanism of Background* were the "objective" variables left out.

2) The authors *seriously* underestimated the amount of among-school variance "accounted" for by the Home Background factor.

The upshot of these errors is that Home Background influences were inadequately controlled in the subsequent analyses. This resulted in the *overestimation* of the effect of the school factors on achievement in the Report. The specific effects of these errors on the various school factors are considered in detail in later sections.

Finally, an analysis of the specific influences of the "objective" background characteristics suggests that:

1) Home Background characteristics have a stronger association to the achievement of whites than to the achievement of blacks. Additionally, the stronger association does not appear to be due only to the greater variation in home conditions for whites, and

2) Blacks and whites seem to be influenced differently by certain background characteristics. Specifically, whites seem to be more influenced by the educational climate of their homes, while blacks are more influenced by the economic conditions of their homes.

SECTION III: *The Influence of Student Body Characteristics on Achievement*

The summary of the EEO Report states that:

. . . it appears that a pupil's achievement is strongly related to the educational backgrounds and aspirations of the other students in the school. . . . Analysis indicates, however, that children from a given family background, when put in schools of different social composition, will achieve at quite different levels. [p. 22]

Other sources consider the problems of measuring the effect of variations in the characteristics of student bodies on the achievement of individual students.[19] The issue will not be resolved without adequately controlled experiments. Unless middle- and lower-class students are randomly assigned into middle- and lower-class schools, we will never be sure that lower-class pupils in middle-class schools are comparable to lower-class pupils in lower-class schools. Until we are sure that the two groups are comparable, we will not know whether disparities in their achievement are due to "peer effects," to unmeasured school resources, or to unmeasured individual differences. Although the EEO Survey was not an experiment, Coleman *et al.* apparently thought that their analysis adequately controlled for these alternative explanations.

This reexamination raises serious questions about the quality of these controls and, therefore, about the finding of the importance of peers for individual achievement. First, the Report substantially overestimated the amount of achievement variation uniquely explained by the aggregate student-body characteristics. Second, the Report measured peer characteristics in a way which may have confused the peer effect with the effect of student selection and school assignment practices.

The Variables

Altogether six variables were used in the *Student Body* factor.[20] Three measures were used at all three grades:

1) *Proportion Own Encyclopedia*—This is an aggregated student variable measuring the proportion of students in the school grade who reported that their families own encyclopedias. This variable was intended to assess the average educational interest in the students' families.

2) *Student Transfers*—This is a principal-reported variable assessing the overall mobility of the student population.

3) *Attendance*—This is a principal-reported variable assessing the average daily attendance of the students.

The availability of all of these variables at each of the three grades allows comparisons across the grades, although the comparisons might be misleading due to differences between the grades in the meaning of the variables. For example, a valid assessment of average encyclopedia ownership depends on the children's accurate reading of the question. Secondary-school students are likely to have less trouble reading "encyclopedia" than are 6th-grade students.

The one measure at the secondary level for which no corresponding measure exists at the elementary level is:

4) *Average Hours Homework*—This is a student-reported aggregate measure of the average hours of homework.

This is intended to measure the perseverance or dedication to academic pursuits in the student body, but it may also assess differences in curriculum and teacher style between schools.

The last two Student Body measures were intended to help assess the educational quality of the student body. The first was used in the 9th- and 12th-grade analyses and the second only in the 6th-grade analyses.

5) *Proportion Plan College*—This was intended to be a student aggregate measure of the proportion who said they definitely planned to attend college. However, an error was made and the variable was instead a measure of the *Proportion of Students in the College Track*.

6) *Student Body Quality*—This is an aggregated measure of the presence of student problems (discipline, etc.) as reported by the teachers.

As we shall see later, each of these last two variables suffers from problems of interpretation.

The Overall Relationship Between the Student-Body Factor and Verbal Achievement

In the preceding section, I noted that Coleman *et al.* made a mechanical error in the way that they controlled for Individual Home Background. Instead of using six "objective" background variables as they intended, they used four "objective" and two "subjective" variables. One overall effect of this was to *overestimate* the possible unique relation between schoolwide factors and student achievement. This mechanical error *affected the strength of the relationship between individual verbal achievement and the Student-Body factor more than any other relationship*.

The data in Table 13 show the additional variance in verbal achievement accounted for by the Student-Body factor under varying conditions. Columns 1–3 show the variation accounted for by the factor when it is entered in an equation immediately after a Home Background factor. Columns 4–6 show the additional variation accounted for when the Student-Body factor is entered after the Teacher Characteristics and Facilities and Curriculum factor.

The first thing to notice is the marked reduction in additional explained variation from the top two rows to the bottom two rows. These differences are due to the change in the home background controls. The top two rows show the figures when the Report's background factor is used. The bottom two rows show the results when the intended background controls are used. *The Report's estimates of the amount of achievement variance uniquely explained by the Student-Body factor are severely reduced when the intended background controls are used.* For whites the reduction

TABLE 13

Unique contribution to variation in Individual Verbal Achievement of Student-Body variables, controlled for two sets of individual background factors. The numbers without parentheses are the percentages of additional contribution to the explained variance. The rank order of the Student-Body factor relative to the Teacher Characteristics factor and the Facilities and Curriculum factor is shown by the numbers in parentheses.[1]

		% Explained When Student-Body Factor Entered First			Unique Contribution— % Explained by Student-Body Factor Entered After Other Schoolwide Factors Already Entered		
		6th Grade	9th Grade	12th Grade	6th Grade	9th Grade	12th Grade
Controlling Conditions as In Report[2]	Northern Whites	2.85† (1)	1.30† (1)	1.21† (3)	1.98† (1)	0.80 (1)	0.51 (3)
	Northern Blacks	2.07† (1)	2.92† (1)	6.60† (1)	1.61† (1)	1.81† (1)	2.08† (1)
Intended Controlling Condition[3]	Northern Whites	1.43† (1)	0.75 (2)	0.78 (3)	1.10* (1)	0.46 (3)	0.47 (3)
	Northern Blacks	1.70† (2)	2.63† (1)	5.59† (1)	1.34† (2)	1.58† (1)	1.78† (1)

[1] Student-Body variables are described in Appendix A.
[2] Four Objective and Two Subjective variables; see Appendix A for description.
[3] Six Objective variables; see Appendix A for description.
* Introduced at this point, the variables, taken together, are statistically significant at the .05 level.
† Statistically significant at the .01 level.

is between .25 and .50 of the original figures; for blacks the reduction ranges between .10 and .25. Thus the Report's finding that "a pupil's achievement is strongly related to the educational backgrounds and aspirations of the other students in the school" is due in part to a mechanical error made by the Report's authors.[21]

The second thing to notice is the numbers in parentheses. These numbers show the rank order of the Student-Body factor in relation to Teacher Characteristics and Facilities and Curriculum in terms of association with verbal achievement. As noted above, the first two rows give ample support for the Report's conclusion. For all but one of the six groups (12th-grade whites), the Student-Body factor ranks first in strength. When the intended background controls are used, however, the picture is not quite so clear. For whites, the factor ranks second or third in strength at the 9th and 12th grade and, in fact, is statistically significant only at the 6th grade. For blacks, the factor is stronger than the other schoolwide factors at the 9th and 12th grades but is second in explanatory strength to the Teacher Characteristics factor at the 6th grade.

Table 13 thus shows clearly that *an overall statement of strength or importance is misleading. The black and the white groups show very different patterns over the grades studied.* The relationship of the factor to student achievement decreases over the grades for the white group both in absolute amount of variation explained and in comparison to the other schoolwide factors. For the black groups the opposite holds true.

The Differential Sensitivity Hypothesis

Coleman *et al.* also noticed this difference between the white and black groups. They found, in general, that the relationship of the schoolwide variables to minority-group students' achievement increased from 6th to 12th grade, while for whites it decreased. Further, they found that the most deprived of the minority groups seemed to be the most sensitive to the school characteristics. Their interpretation was that a family background which encourages achievement reduces sensitivity to variations in schools.

The school, including the student body, apparently has less differential effect upon achievement of children from such backgrounds.

The results suggest, then, that the environment provided by the student body is asymmetric in its effects, that it has its greatest effect on those from educationally deficient backgrounds. The matter is of course more complex than this simple relation, doubtless depending on the relative number of high and low achieving students in the school, and on the other factors. [p. 304]

This might be labeled the "differential sensitivity" hypothesis. Since differences among black children's home backgrounds have less relationship to achievement, black children are more sensitive than whites to variations in factors away from the home and in particular to student peers.[22] This interpretation makes good intuitive sense. It seems reasonable that the school will have less of an opportunity to exercise an influence if home background is a strong determinant of scholastic achievement. But home background seems to influence blacks less than whites; therefore, one might expect the school to have more of a chance to affect the achievement of blacks. To conform to the data, however, the argument for differential sensitivity must account for the apparently contradictory facts that:

1) Blacks and whites are just about equally sensitive to variations in student-body composition and other schoolwide factors during the elementary-school years (note that their percentages of variation explained are about the same in the 6th grade), *but* that

2) Negro achievement is increasingly related to student-body composition after 6th grade, while white achievement becomes less related to it.

A number of studies have suggested that whites' 12th-grade scores are

influenced more by events before the student is twelve years old than by
events after twelve. The EEOS results are compatible with this research.
The pattern reported here for blacks seems, however, to suggest that blacks
are different. As Coleman *et al.* suggest, the differences between the races in
home background may cause differences in their sensitivity to school factors. This may indeed be true, but there is an alternative hypothesis to account for the greater sensitivity of blacks.

The Selection Hypothesis

The alternative is selection. This idea supposes that some older students are selected to attend particular schools on the basis of their past
achievement. We know that this is a common phenomenon in many large
cities. Students in Boston, for example, must take an examination to get into
Boston Latin. Students who fail or do not take the examination have their
choice of a number of secondary schools, though they may be "advised" to
choose a vocational school. Unfortunately, Coleman *et al.* did not account
for this selection effect in their analysis of the EEOS data. The sample of
secondary schools in their data (and the data used in this reexamination)
includes academic, vocational, and comprehensive schools.

The failure to separate the different types of schools causes serious
problems in the estimation of the relationships between schoolwide factors
and student achievement. Because teachers and facilities, as well as students, may be "assigned" (or allocated) to different types of schools, the
relationships may reflect the "assignment" process rather than the "effect" of
the teachers and facilities on achievement. For example, we might expect
that teachers with characteristics which are thought to influence verbal
achievement would be "assigned" to academic rather than vocational secondary schools. This would increase the relationship between these teacher
characteristics and student verbal achievement because these schools "select" students on the basis of their verbal achievement.

For the "selection" hypothesis to be an alternative explanation to the
"differential sensitivity," we have to postulate two things. First, the Student-
Body variables must measure things sensitive to the "selection" process.
This is certainly possible. The *Average Hours of Homework*, the *Percentage of Students in the College Track*, the *Average Attendance*, and perhaps
the *Mobility Rate* should all vary systematically between academic, vocational, and comprehensive high schools.

The second thing that we have to postulate is that somewhat different
things happen to blacks and whites after elementary school. Blacks may be
more likely than whites to be assigned to high schools (or to select them)
on the basis of their achievement. Most blacks in the Northern sample live
in large central cities (see Table 14), and city school systems often assign
students to high schools on the basis of scholastic achievement. Many of the

TABLE 14

Means and Standard Deviations for Some Schoolwide Characteristics Relevant to the "Selection" Hypothesis*

(All data from Supplemental Appendix to the EEOS Report)

	Northern Whites						Northern Blacks					
Grades	6		9		12		6		9		12	
Variable	Means	S.D.	Means	S.D.	Means	S.D.	Means	S.D.	Means	S.D.	Means	S.D.
School Location	3.65	1.75	4.00	1.70	4.11	1.80	5.12	2.12	5.18	1.86	5.11	2.00
Comprehensiveness of Curriculum			0.94	0.17	90.13	12.69			0.92	0.17	89.57	12.86
Proportion Race White	0.88	0.14	0.88	0.14	0.90	0.12	0.24	0.30	0.31	0.33	0.41	0.36
% Encyclopedia	0.81	0.11	0.85	0.08	0.85	0.07	0.64	0.15	0.76	0.11	0.79	0.09
Proportion in College Track			0.39	0.17	0.46	0.15			0.34	0.14	0.38	0.15

* All variables are fully described in Appendix A.

whites in the sample live in suburbs, and all students in a particular suburb typically attend the same high school. This should have two consequences:

1) The high schools that blacks attend would be more different in mean achievement than their elementary schools.[23] The junior high schools should fall in between. This would lead to a steady increase in the variance of mean black school achievement from the 6th to the 12th grade.

2) To some extent the same arguments should hold for whites; but because more whites than blacks are in the single high-school suburbs, the rise in school-to-school verbal variability due to selection should be at least partially offset.

Table 15 shows the standard deviations of weighted school verbal means of the black and white samples. The between-school variances for the white groups are almost equal at all three grades. The between-school variances for the blacks increase. The increase in school-to-school variation for blacks suggests that selection on verbal achievement occurs more frequently for blacks than for whites.

TABLE 15

*Measures of the School-to-School Variation in Achievement for Schools**

(From Supplemental Appendix)

	Northern Whites			Northern Blacks		
	6th Grade	9th Grade	12th Grade	6th Grade	9th Grade	12th Grade
Standard Deviation of School Means	4.46	4.81	4.62	5.40	6.74	7.51

* The Standard Deviations are computed on all students within the school. These figures are *not* analogous to those in Table 4 in that percent white is *not* taken into account here.

There are, however, problems with the hypothesis. Note in Table 14 that the increase in school-to-school variation in achievement is not paralleled by a corresponding increase in the variability in the percent of students in college tracks. If blacks are being selected into academic or vocational schools, it is reasonable to expect the variation of each of these measures to increase. In fact, the variation in these measures decreases over the years. (As I note later, however, this variable has serious problems.)

On the other hand, the percent of white students, the percent of all families with encyclopedias, and the percent who are in college tracks, all increase for blacks from 6th to 12th grades and particularly from the 9th to 12th grades. These data are consistent with what might be called a "dropout" effect. Blacks who attend suburban and middle-class schools are evidently more likely to remain in school through the 12th grade than are blacks in predominantly black and poor schools. This effect might operate in conjunction with the selection process.

In summary, the apparent difference in the sensitivity of white and black achievement to school resources may be due to a combination of "selection" (by achievement), "resource allocation," and "dropout" effects rather than to differences between the races in home background.

The Relationship Between Specific Student Body Variables and Verbal Achievement

The picture is not clarified when the contributions of the specific variables in the Student Body factor are considered. Table 16 is drawn from Tables G–L in Appendix B and shows the standardized and raw regression coefficients for the variables when home background and the other school resources are also entered. My overall conclusions from the data in this table are that there is little evidence that the composition of the student body has an independent effect on achievement and that these data constitute a poor test of the hypothesis that such an effect does exist.

Consider first the two "strongest" variables. At the 6th grade, where selection and dropout influences should be minimized and which therefore should allow the best test of the effect, only *Teachers' Perception of Student*

TABLE 16

Standardized and raw regression coefficients (raw coefficients in parentheses) for the Student-Body Composition variables calculated with Home Background, *Proportion White in school*, Facilities and Curriculum variables and Teacher Characteristics variables in the equations.[a]

		Northern Blacks			Northern Whites		
	Variable	6th Grade	9th Grade	12th Grade	6th Grade	9th Grade	12th Grade
10	Proportion Own Encyclopedia	.06 (3.5)	.05 (6.2)	.07 (11.0)	−.01 (−.75)	.01 (1.2)	.00 (.75)
26	Student Transfer	.01 (.01)	−.07 (−.14)	−.05 (−.15)	.03 (.05)	−.03 (−.10)	−.02 (−.09)
31	Attendance	.06 (.15)	.03 (.09)	.04 (.15)	−.01 (−.03)	.05 (.27)	.01 (.08)
52	Proportion College Track		−.08 (−7.1)	.12* (12.0)		−.02 (−1.8)	.06 (6.0)
53	Average Hours Homework		.07 (2.2)	−.05 (−1.3)		.01 (.35)	.00 (.13)
55	Teacher Perception of Student Body Quality[b]	−.09* (−2.2)			−.10* (−2.8)		

[a] The background variables are the six objective variables.
[b] The sign is reversed on this variable. High *Teacher Perception of Quality is* associated with high achievement.
* The coefficient is significant at the .05 level.

Body Quality enters into the equations with a significant coefficient. This variable should not have been used in the study. It is far more likely to be caused by student achievement than to cause it. Teachers are aware of their students' achievement on standardized tests. To interpret their perception as a "student-body" attribute which causes achievement is misleading.

The "strongest" variable at the secondary level is even less convincing. *The Proportion of Students in College Track* has the largest standardized coefficients for blacks at both the 9th and 12th grades and for whites at the 12th grade. For both 12th-grade groups this also is apparent with less control (see Tables K and L in Appendix B). For 9th-grade whites, it seems to bear little relationship to achievement. Two important facts about this measure should be noted:

1) Coleman *et al.* thought that this measure was the *Proportion of Students Planning to Attend College* rather than the *Proportion in the College Track*. This led them to interpret it as a measure of the aspirations in the student body. They concluded that both the background (the encyclopedia measure) and the aspirations of fellow students affect the achievement level of a student independent of his own background.

2) The controlled relationship between *Proportion in College Track* and achievement is negative in the 9th grade and positive in the 12th grade. The difference between 9th and 12th is particularly dramatic for the black students. At the 9th grade the coefficient is − .08, and at the 12th grade it is + .12.

Any interpretation of the college-track variable is dangerous due to its dubious validity.[24] Large numbers of students apparently do not know what track they are in (see EEOS Report, p. 570). However, any interpretation cannot ignore the fact that at the extremes this variable is practically a direct measure of "selection." Those schools with the largest proportions of students in college tracks are the "academic" high schools; those with the smallest proportions are the "vocational" high schools.

The remaining variables show small and inconsistent relations with achievement. They are particularly weak for whites (see Table 16). This conforms to Table 13, which showed that for whites the Student-Body factor explains very little unique variance when the six objective background variables are controlled. Even under conditions of less than full control, the student-body variables have only a small relationship to individual student achievement (see Tables G–L in Appendix B). At the 6th and 9th grades the *Proportion Owning Encyclopedia* variable is statistically significant in the equations without individual background variables included, but when the background controls are introduced the coefficients drop to almost zero. The coefficient for the variable, *Average Student Attendance*, is almost statistically significant at the 9th grade when all other factors are in the equation and is significant under two of the three other conditions. It bears little relationship to achievement at the other grades. For whites, no other student-body variable has a regression coefficient which is statistically significant in *any* of the equations in Tables G–L in Appendix B.

The picture is not very different for the blacks, although the coefficients for almost every variable are larger for the blacks than for the whites at all three grade levels. In addition, the coefficients for the variables tend to increase in size for the blacks as the grade levels rise. Even with these tendencies, only *Proportion in College Track* reaches statistical significance for the blacks at the 12th grade. None reach significance in the 9th grade, and only the *Teacher Perception* variable reaches it in the 6th grade. Of the other variables, *Proportion Owning Encyclopedia* and *Percent Transfer* are the strongest. Each of these two variables is statistically significant for blacks at the 9th and 12th grades under a variety of controlling conditions. High transfer rates seem to be associated with low student achievement in secondary schools.[25] The average *Attendance* variable is positively associated with black achievement. Although the variables are generally larger for blacks than for whites, the coefficients are not statistically significant in any of the fully controlled equations.

Taken together, these results are very different from those found in the Report. To a large extent this discrepancy is due to the different home-background controls used in the reanalysis. Consider, for example, *Proportion Owning Encyclopedia*. All coefficients for this variable are positive. However, at no grade level is the variable statistically significant when all other variables are in the equations. Of all the student-body variables, it is the most sensitive to the individual background controls, particularly to the difference between the background controls used in the Report and those intended for use in the Report. Table 17 shows the results. The difference in the variance explained by this variable with the intended and actual con-

TABLE 17

Additional percentages of variance in Verbal Achievement explained by the introduction of the school aggregate variable, *Proportion Students' Families Owning Encyclopedia*, under two conditions of control by individual background characteristics.

	Northern Blacks		Northern Whites	
	Background Control Variables			
	6 objective*	4 objective 2 subjective†	6 objective	4 objective 2 subjective
6th grade	1.10	1.36	0.40	1.18
9th grade	1.18	1.60	0.18	0.72
12th grade	2.88	3.91	0.25	0.68

* The six objective variables are described in Appendix A.
† The four objective and two subjective variables are described in Appendix A.

trols is appreciable. At all three grade levels, the variation explained when the mistaken set of background variables is in the equation is larger than when the intended set is in the equation. For blacks the reduction is about 30 percent at all grade levels; for whites the reduction is nearer 50 percent.

CONCLUSION. *I draw two main conclusions from this analysis. First, based on these data I find no evidence that characteristics of the student body have a strong independent influence on the verbal achievement of individual students. Second, although the achievement of blacks is more highly associated with the Student-Body variables than is the achievement of whites, I question whether this difference in association is caused by characteristics of the student body. The data instead suggest that student selection and school assignment policies cause the association between the student-body characteristics and achievement.*

The evidence for these conclusions is that:

1) A very large part of the explained variation in *Verbal Achievement* that was seen in the Report as being uniquely accounted for by the Student-Body factor is, in fact, shared with the individual background characteristics of the students. If the authors of the Report had controlled for the individual background variables that they intended, their case for an important independent effect of the Student-Body factor would have been weakened.

2) A careful inspection of the content of the specific variables included in this factor raises questions about what is being measured. At the 6th grade the only variable which associates with verbal achievement at a significant level after full controls are introduced is *Teachers' Perception of Student Body Quality*. Although this may be measuring the effect of aggregate student-body characteristics on the achievement of students, a more plausible hypothesis is that it is measuring teachers' sensitivity and knowledge of their students' past performance on achievement tests. At the 9th and 12th grades the variable showing the strongest overall relationship to achievement is *Percentage of Students in College Track*. Instead of directly measuring aggregate student aspirations, as the authors of the Report intended, this variable may measure school selection and assignment practices.

3) The variable which comes close to directly measuring the aggregate social-class composition of the school, *Proportion Owning Encyclopedia*, has nonsignificant coefficients when entered with all of the other variables for all six groups.

4) The authors of the Report note that the achievement of blacks is more sensitive to variations in student-body characteristics, but they fail to explain why this finding occurs at the 9th and 12th grades and not at the 6th grade. I suggest that individual selec-

tion, school assignment practices, and differential dropout rates for black students in middle- and low-class high schools offer a more plausible explanation than does a peer-influence hypothesis.

I must stress that my main conclusion is that the Report offers no evidence of an independent effect of student-body characteristics on individual achievement. *I have not concluded that this effect does not exist, but that the hypothesis is essentially untested.*

Finally, my analysis has outlined some problems in making inferences about the effect of secondary-school student-body characteristics on individuals. In addition to self-selection, at least three factors can confound any analysis at the secondary level:

1) The grade structure of the school system;

2) School selection and school assignment policies;

3) Differential dropout rates for various students and schools.

There is little chance of a successful analysis unless each of these is controlled, and such controls are only likely in a true field experiment.

SECTION IV: School Facilities and Curriculum and Student Achievement

The second school factor studied by Coleman *et al.* was Facilities and Curriculum. Its weak relationship to verbal achievement generated much of the interest and criticism of the EEOS Report. My reexamination of the relationship between this factor and achievement strengthens the original findings. Problems, however, in the interpretation of the factor preclude any strong conclusion.

The Variables

The *Facilities and Curriculum* factor contains variables that can be classified into three general categories.

1) *Descriptive School Measures:* Includes measures of the *Size** and the *Location of the School**.

2) *Physical Resource Measures:* Includes a general measure of the quantity of resources available, *Systemwide Per Pupil Expenditure,** and measures of three specific resources: *Library Volumes per Student,* Number of Science Laboratories,* and *Guidance Counselors.*

3) *Descriptive Curriculum and Program Measures:* Includes measures of the *Comprehensiveness of Curriculum Offerings* and of whether the school has an *Accelerated Curriculum**. Also includes a general measure of the school's policies about *Tracking* and a measure of the amount of *Movement Between Tracks.* At the 6th

grade a measure of the school's policy toward the *"Promotion of Slow Learners"* * is included. The last measure in this category assesses the variety of *Extracurricular Activities* offered.

With the exception of *Promotion of Slow Learners*, all variables are used in the 9th- and 12th-grade analyses. For the 6th-grade analyses only the starred variables are used.

Five Criticisms of the Variables

The variables in the Facilities and Curriculum factor have been extensively criticized (see, for example, Hanushek and Kain, Chapter 3). Five criticisms are particularly important. First, Coleman *et al.* may have left out measures of certain important facilities. It is possible that if other similar measures had been included, the factor would have shown a stronger relationship to student achievement. I do not believe this, however. As Jencks shows (Chapter 2), there are few facilities and curriculum measures which show even a strong uncontrolled relationship to achievement.[26] In fact, Coleman *et al.* went to some lengths to select the strongest of the available measures, though in so doing they opened themselves to the criticism of ignoring such a priori important measures as pupil/teacher ratio.[27] It is possible, however, that a survey is an ineffective way of measuring differences among schools in facilities and curriculum resources. It may be that data about the *quality* of science facilities are more important than data about their *quantity*. And it may be important to know whether a primary-grade reading program is geared to a sight-word or to a phonics approach, rather than knowing only whether there *is* a program.

Second, with the EEOS data there is no way of knowing which students in a school make use of a particular facility. This stops us from contrasting the achievement of students who have used a facility with the achievement of those who have not used it. Differential use of facilities may cause within-school differences in student achievement. Further, it influences our assessment of the effects of differences in facilities *between* schools. Because we are measuring the impact of a facility averaged over *all* students in a school, rather than just over those students who have access to it, we may be seriously underestimating its effect. It is easy to speculate that the Report's conclusions might have been very different if data on the differential utilization of resources within schools had been gathered.

Third, it may be important to know how extensively a facility is used. No data are available to assess what proportion of students in a school have access to or utilize any facility. If very few students make use of a facility we can expect only a small average effect at best.

A fourth criticism is that the existing differences among schools are not great enough to reveal the importance of the resources to student achievement. Since World War II a lot of effort has been made to equalize facilities. If this effort has been successful, any true causal relation between facilities and achievement will not be evident. If all schools have facilities sufficient for their students, small measured differences will show little relation to achievement. This criticism can be met partially by inspection of means and standard deviations and by the use of regression coefficients. But the effects of certain resources may not be apparent in the range of existing variation. Reducing the pupil/teacher ratio, for example, may make no difference until instruction can be really individualized, which might require a pupil/teacher ratio of less than 10:1. Because there are almost no schools in the EEO Survey with a pupil/teacher ratio lower than 10:1, however, the effect goes unnoticed.

Fifth, in the secondary grades the relationships between facilities and curriculum characteristics and achievement are confounded with assignment, selection, and dropout effects. At the 9th grade this problem is further aggravated by the fact that many 9th-grade students had been in the schools for only a few weeks when they took the achievement tests. Since those students who had just entered their first year in a four-year high school cannot be separated from other students (e.g., third-year students in a junior high), there is no way of knowing whether sampled students have even theoretically had access to the assessed resources.

It might seem as though these criticisms eliminate much of the reason for carrying out an analysis of the relationship between the Facilities and Curriculum factor and student achievement. However, while there are limits to the inferences that can be drawn from such an analysis, it may answer certain limited questions. If the measured resources strongly influence achievement, their effect should show up in the analysis. The data then might be very useful in distinguishing between the effects of the resources on children of different ages and backgrounds. If, however, the resources do not have a *very* strong relationship to the achievement measure, then the criticisms are particularly valid. The effect of the problems generally will be to dilute the relationship between the resources and achievement. If the problems are large and the "true" relationships small, then the results of the survey may be useless.

Nevertheless, the analysis is worth trying. Although the EEO Survey is one-shot, retrospective, and suffers from serious faults, it provides better data than otherwise exist to test whether gross differences between schools in facilities and curriculum have any consistent relationship to student achievement.

The Overall Relationship Between the Facilities and Curriculum Factor and Verbal Achievement

The results of this reanalysis *support* one of the Report's central conclusions: existing variations between schools in facility and curriculum resources independently explain little variation in individual achievement.

Table 18 presents the relevant results. Even without background controls (see row 1), the factor explains less than 2 percent of the total variance for the 6th- and 9th-grade groups, and between 3 and 5 percent for twelfth graders, for whom selection, assignment, and dropout effects are strongest. When controls are introduced, the factor's unique contribution to explained variance (explained variance not shared with the other schoolwide factors) is always less than 2 percent (see row 2).

TABLE 18

Additional percentages of variance in Verbal Achievement explained by the Facilities and Curriculum Factor under varying conditions of control.[1]

| | Grade | Northern Blacks | | | Northern Whites | | |
		6	9	12	6	9	12
No Individual Background Controls	Contribution Alone in Equation	1.15	1.38	5.06†	0.44	1.92	3.03*
	Unique Contribution With Other Schoolwide Factors in Equation	0.14	0.95	0.90	0.22	1.57	0.95
Six Objective Individual Background Controls	Contribution Alone in Equation	0.64	1.31	2.35†	0.24	0.68	0.81
	Unique Contribution With Other Schoolwide Factors in Equation	0.16	1.14	1.02	0.24	0.86	0.80

[1] All variables are described in Appendix A to this chapter.
* Contribution to variance explained is statistically significant at the .05 level.
† Statistically significant at the .01 level.

These figures are consistent with the coefficients in Tables G–L in Appendix B. Taking the six groups together, there are 52 zero-order correlations of Facilities and Curriculum variables with achievement (see column 3). Not one of the uncontrolled correlations has a value greater than 0.13, and 38 of the correlations have values less than 0.05. The standardized coefficients of these variables when they are entered together with the other schoolwide factors suggests that the zero-order relationships accurately reflect their weakness. Although the coefficients are changed when all factors are entered, there is no indication that any particular variable was seriously suppressed. On the contrary, when the other schoolwide factors enter, the coefficients are considerably reduced.

Furthermore, the magnitude of the means and standard deviations suggests that the lack of relationship to achievement is *not* caused by restriction of range (see Tables G–L in Appendix B). Although the *plateau levels* that some critics postulate as critical may not be attained, each of the variables shows that there are substantial differences in the allocation of resources among schools. For example, the mean *Per-Pupil Instructional Expenditure* (*PPIE*) for 12th-grade whites is \$483.50, while the standard deviation is \$173.10, suggesting that the top 20 percent of schools have a PPIE roughly \$300 greater than the bottom 20 percent. The average *Library Volumes/Student* for 12th-grade blacks is another example. The mean is about five, which is only slightly greater than the standard deviation; this suggests that some schools do not have any books, while in others, students have access to large numbers of books. In summary, it seems that between-school differences in resources are not so small as to eliminate the possibility that true effects will be apparent.

Thus, the Facilities and Curriculum factor as measured independently contributes little to the prediction of individual achievement. A plausible inference might be that the factor has little independent influence on the production of achievement.

This inference is reinforced by an inspection of the way that the factor overlaps with other factors in the explanation of achievement variance. For Northern whites, Home Background shares most of the variance explained by Facilities and Curriculum variables (see Table 18, row 3). For Northern blacks, Home Background *and* Student Body characteristics (see Tables 18 and 19) combine to explain most of the achievement variance accounted for by the Facilities and Curriculum factor.

This suggests three things. First, there may be social-class inequities in the distribution of school facilities and curriculum, particularly for whites. Middle-class students may have access to more "effective" resources than lower-class students. Second, the strength of the uncontrolled relationship between facilities and curriculum and achievement at the secondary

TABLE 19

Proportions of Total Variance in Verbal Achievement Explained by the Facilities and Curriculum Factor and Shared With the Other Schoolwide Factors Under Condition of No Controls and Controls by Six Objective Background Variables[1]

Race	Grade	Shared by F & C and Teacher Characteristics		Shared by F & C and Student Body		Shared by all three schoolwide factors	
		Con-trolled	Un-controlled	Con-trolled	Un-controlled	Con-trolled	Un-controlled
Northern Blacks	6	0.21	0.38	0.25	0.34	0.02	0.29
	9	0.03	0.25	0.63	0.65	−0.49	−0.47
	12	−0.36	−0.31	1.23	1.39	0.46	3.08
Northern Whites	6	0.08	0.00	0.01	0.16	−0.09	0.06
	9	−0.19	−0.39	0.00	0.34	0.01	0.40
	12	0.00	0.01	−0.12	0.38	0.13	1.69

[1] All variables are described in Appendix A.

grades in part may be due to selection, assignment, and dropout effects. The larger overlap in explained variance between the Facilities and Curriculum factor and the Student-Body factor for blacks suggests that these influences may be stronger for blacks than for whites.

Third, the lack of overlap between the Facilities and Curriculum factor and the Teacher-Characteristics factor suggests that few schools are "rich" enough to purchase both effective facilities and curriculum *and* "effective" teachers. In fact, the negative "shared" variance for two of the six groups indicates that school officials may choose between the purchase of "effective" teachers and "effective" facilities and curriculum.

Taken together, these three things suggest that whatever small relation school-to-school differences in facilities and curriculum have to achievement may be due to influences other than facilities and curriculum. They also indicate that the way to assess the importance of a factor is to examine its unique contributions to explained variance with home background controlled. Otherwise the effect of the factor is confounded with the effect of social-class inequities in resource allocation, with school selection and assignment practices, and with differential dropout rates.

This approach to assessing the strength of factors increases the strength of the Facilities and Curriculum factor relative to the other school-wide factors and particularly the Student-Body factor. Generally the introduction of Home Background severely reduces the *unique* effect of the Student-Body factor while only slightly reducing the *unique* relationship between the Facilities and Curriculum factor and achievement. Thus, looked at simply in terms of the amount of unique contribution, Coleman *et al.*'s conclusion that the Facilities and Curriculum factor is the weakest of the schoolwide factors does not seem substantiated. The Facilities and Curriculum factor uniquely explains more variance than the other factors for two of the groups, 9th- and 12th-grade whites, runs a close second for two groups, 9th- and 12th-grade blacks, and explains the least variance for the two 6th-grade groups. By the amount of variance explained standard for assessing the strength of a factor, Facilities and Curriculum appears as strong as either Student Body or Teacher Characteristics. However, the Facilities and Curriculum factor has eleven variables while the other factors have seven or less. Therefore, by chance we expect more variance to be explained. As Tables 1, 2, and 3 in Appendix C show, the unique variance is in fact probably due to chance. For each of the six groups, the probability that the contribution of the Facilities and Curriculum factor is greater than zero is less than for either of the other two schoolwide factors. Thus Coleman *et al.*'s conclusion is substantiated.

The Increasing Relationship Between the Facilities and Curriculum Factor and Achievement

Another way to look at the importance of a set of resources is to examine their relation to achievement across the grades. Coleman *et al.* state that "comparison between grades shows that the facilities and curriculum measures account for an increasingly larger amount of variance in achievement from the 6th to the 12th grades" (p. 313). It is not clear, however, exactly what this finding means.

Table 18 shows that the *total* variance explained by the factor does rise steadily from grade 6 to grade 12 under both controlled and uncontrolled conditions. However, there is no increase from the 9th to the 12th grade in *unique* variance explained. For both racial groups there is more variation uniquely explained by the Facilities and Curriculum factor at the 9th grade than at the 12th grade. This, combined with the fact that there is roughly equal variation in the variables at the two grades, suggests that it is unlikely that facilities and curriculum resources have a greater influence on achievement in the 12th than in the 9th grade.

There is, however, an increase in explained *unique* variation from 6th to 9th grades for both racial groups. Coleman *et al.* accounted for this increase saying that: "The absence of relation for most items at grade 6 is a result of the low variation among schools with respect to these facilities in elementary schools" (p. 313). A second possible explanation, however, is that the Facilities and Curriculum factor simply becomes more important. And a third is that the difference in the number of variables used at the two grades accounts for the extra explained variation at the 9th grade. These alternatives can be evaluated by examining the variables' means, standard deviations, and regression weights.

Tables 20, 21, and 22 contain the means, standard deviations, and two sets of raw regression coefficients for the Facilities and Curriculum variables. The first set of regression coefficients correspond to the standardized coefficients shown in column 4 of Tables G–L in Appendix B. They are the variables' weights for the full-controlled analyses. The second set of coefficients were selected to maximize the potential strength of the particular facilities and curriculum variables. For each variable, the coefficient selected was the largest one resulting from the various analyses described by columns 3–7 of Tables G–L in Appendix B. Thus, in some cases, the selected coefficient is completely uncontrolled by home background or other schoolwide variables (e.g., it corresponds to the zero-order correlation).

Inspection of the means and standard deviations of the 6th- and 9th-grade variables suggests that the first hypothesis—that less variation in facilities at the 6th grade leads to less explained achievement variance—is incorrect. The variation in facilities seems almost as great at the 6th as at the 9th grade for both blacks and whites. The second hypothesis seems

TABLE 20

*Regression Coefficients, Means, and Standard Deviations for the
Sixth-Grade Facilities and Curriculum Factor Variables*

| | | Northern Blacks | | | | Northern Whites | | | |
| | | | | Regression Coefficients | | | | Regression Coefficients | |
No.	Variable Name	Mean	S.D.	Cond.[1] Full Equation	Cond.[2] Max. Size	Mean	S.D.	Cond.[1] Full Equation	Cond.[2] Max. Size
38	Per-Pupil Instructional Expenditure	484.7	111.0	.001	0.006*	492.6	174.5	.001	0.003
23	Volume/Student	3.7	5.1	.030	0.047	4.7	5.1	−.013	0.050
9	School Size	91.9	50.8	−.002	0.005	80.2	47.6	.002	0.003
33	School Location	5.1	2.1	−.124	−0.165	3.7	1.7	−.292	−0.332
37	Promote Slow Student	2.8	1.4	−.116	−0.437*	2.7	1.5	−.065	−0.278
36	No Accelerated Curriculum	3.3	1.1	−.166	−0.337	3.1	1.2	.019	−0.334

* Statistically significant at the .05 level.
[1] This column contains the regression coefficients for the Facilities and Curriculum variables when the Home Background, the Teacher Characteristics, the Student-Body, and the other Facilities and Curriculum factor variables are all in the equation. It corresponds to column 4 of Tables G-L in Appendix B.
[2] This column contains the regression coefficients for the Facilities and Curriculum variable in the equation or zero-order form where it is largest. (Corresponds to the largest Beta Coefficient for the variable in Tables G and H, Appendix B.)

similarly incorrect; inspection of the standardized (see Tables G–L, Appendix B) and raw regression coefficients suggests that the variables are equally strong at the two grades. They have equivalent controlled relations to achievement at both grades. Thus, the greater *unique* variance explained at the 9th grade in contrast to the 6th grade appears to be due largely to the greater number of variables included in the factor at the 9th grade.

A Second Look at the Differential Sensitivity Hypothesis

The percentages of variance shown in Table 18 suggest that there is little difference in the sensitivity of blacks and whites to variations in school facilities and curriculum. At the 6th and 12th grades more variance is explained for the black groups when this factor is entered alone. When only the Home Background variables are controlled, all the black groups show larger percentages of total variation accounted for. However, when the other schoolwide factors are entered, the picture changes slightly. Without background controls, Facilities and Curriculum explains more *unique* variance for whites at all three grades. With background controls, the *unique* variance is slightly larger for the 9th- and 12th-grade black groups. Thus, the results are mixed. Using the *unique* contributions as the estimates, the

TABLE 21

Regression Coefficients, Means, and Standard Deviations for the Ninth-Grade Facilities and Curriculum Factor Variables

| | | | Northern Blacks | | | | | Northern Whites | | |
| | | | | Regression Coefficients | | | | | Regression Coefficients | |
No.	Variable Name	Mean	S.D.	Cond.[1] Full Equation	Cond.[2] Max. Size	Mean	S.D.	Cond.[1] Full Equation	Cond.[2] Max. Size
38	Per-Pupil Instructional Expenditure	512.7	142.2	0.001	−0.004	492.4	179.6	0.005	0.007*
23	Volume/Student	5.6	5.7	−0.028	−0.085	6.1	4.2	0.056	0.192
22	Science Labs	50.8	45.5	0.002	0.015	57.6	43.3	0.003	−0.022
24	Extracurricular Activities	65.0	13.2	0.037	0.051	64.4	14.6	0.003	0.056
36	No Accelerated Curriculum	2.8	1.0	−0.703	−0.738	2.6	1.0	0.064	−0.407
25	Comprehensive Curriculum	0.9	0.2	−4.786	−6.348	0.9	0.2	−6.864*	−8.808†
35	No Tracking	2.0	0.7	0.794	0.794	2.1	0.6	−0.302	−0.302
27	Movement Between Tracks	7.2	7.4	−0.133*	−0.140*	7.0	5.9	0.040	0.040
9	School Size	312.0	188.8	0.000	0.005†	289.6	157.6	0.001	0.003
30	Guidance Counselor	6.4	4.0	−0.045	0.160	4.9	3.0	−0.054	0.257
33	School Location	5.2	1.9	−0.034	0.280	4.0	1.7	0.023	0.363

* Statistically significant at the .05 level.
† Statistically significant at the .01 level.
[1] This column contains the regression coefficients for the Facilities and Curriculum variable when the Home Background, the Teacher Characteristics, the Student-Body, and the other Facilities and Curriculum factor variables are all in the equation. It corresponds to column 4 of Tables G-L in Appendix B.
[2] This column contains the regression coefficients for the Facilities and Curriculum variable in the equation or zero-order form where it is largest. (Corresponds to the largest Beta Coefficient for the variable in Tables I and J, Appendix B.)

question is whether the background controls are included or not. If background is not controlled, whites appear more sensitive—if it is controlled, blacks appear to be more sensitive to variations in school facilities and curriculum.

When the regression coefficients are investigated (Tables 20, 21, and 22 and G–L in Appendix B), the results are also mixed. Much of the reason for the ambiguity is that the signs of the variables within racial groups are often different from grade to grade and even within grades in the various equations. This makes it particularly hard to estimate the effect of a particular variable. But some generalizations can be made.

1) The School Descriptive variables are equally related to black and white achievement at all grades.

2) The Physical Resource variables are more strongly related to the achievement of blacks at the 6th grade, and have a slightly stronger relationship to the achievement of whites at the 9th and 12th grades.

TABLE 22

Regression Coefficients, Means, and Standard Deviations for the Twelfth-Grade Facilities and Curriculum Factor Variables

No.	Variable Name	Northern Blacks				Northern Whites			
				Regression Coefficients				Regression Coefficients	
		Mean	S.D.	Cond.[1] Full Equation	Cond.[2] Max. Size	Mean	S.D.	Cond.[1] Full Equation	Cond.[2] Max. Size
38	Per-Pupil Instructional Expenditure	492.9	135.8	−0.000	−0.004	483.5	173.1	0.002	0.006†
23	Volume/Student	5.0	4.3	−0.162	−0.225*	5.6	3.8	−0.141	−0.141
22	Science Labs	92.9	16.4	−0.006	0.098†	95.9	13.9	0.038	0.055
24	Extracurricular Activities	72.1	12.5	0.039	0.157†	72.4	12.6	−0.050	0.103†
36	No Accelerated Curriculum	2.8	1.0	−0.232	−1.411†	2.4	1.0	−0.711	−1.472†
25	Comprehensive Curriculum	89.6	12.9	−0.026	−0.086	90.1	12.7	−0.033	−0.082*
35	No Tracking	2.1	0.5	0.971	2.161*	2.1	0.4	−0.143	−0.955
27	Movement Between Tracks	7.2	7.3	−0.116	−0.116	7.3	5.9	0.060	0.117
9	School Size	376.6	218.4	−0.010†	−0.010†	352.8	220.2	−0.007	−0.007
30	Guidance Counselor	9.0	4.5	0.059	0.295†	7.0	3.8	0.227	0.434†
33	School Location	5.1	2.0	0.350	0.704†	4.1	1.8	0.469	0.513*

* Statistically significant at the .05 level.
† Statistically significant at the .01 level.
[1] This column contains the regression coefficients for the Facilities and Curriculum variable when the Home Background, the Teacher Characteristics, the Student-Body, and the other Facilities and Curriculum factor variables are all in the equation. It corresponds to column 4 of Tables G-L in Appendix B.
[2] This column contains the regression coefficients for the Facilities and Curriculum variable in the equation or zero-order from where it is largest. (Corresponds to the largest Beta Coefficient for the variable in Tables K and L, Appendix B.)

3) The Curriculum variables have a generally stronger relationship to the achievement of black students at all three grades.

The differences, however, are slight, and it would be foolhardy to suggest on the basis of these results that blacks and whites are differentially sensitive either to specific facilities and curriculum resources or to overall variations among schools in these items.

The Relationship of Specific Facilities and Curriculum Variables to Verbal Achievement

Until now I have examined mainly the general relationship of the Facilities and Curriculum factor to achievement. This examination has suggested that the factor has only a slight relationship to achievement that is independent of other determinants of achievement. But the general analyses have not answered the question of what effect particular changes in a school's facilities and curriculum might have. For this the regression coefficients must be examined (see Tables 20, 21, and 22 and G–L in Appendix B). I might note that strong effects should not be anticipated since the variables do not behave consistently from group to group and the *unique* contributions are tiny.

School Descriptive Variables

First consider the School Descriptive variables. At the 6th and 9th grades, for both racial groups, the *Size* and the *Location* of the school are remarkably unrelated to achievement. Neither variable has a statistically significant relationship to achievement in *any* of the regression equations. In addition, a consistent interpretation is difficult. The coefficients suggest that large schools are good for 6th-grade achievement though bad for 9th-grade achievement and that urban schools are bad for 12-year-olds but good for 15-year-olds.

However, at the 12th grade the *Size* of a school has a strong negative relationship to achievement for both groups. Although the uncontrolled correlations for both groups are positive, the regression coefficients with all other variables included in the equation are negative and of substantial size —for blacks the fully controlled coefficient is statistically significant at the .01 level. A decrease of 200 students (roughly 1 standard deviation) is associated with an increase in achievement of 2 points for blacks and 1.5 for whites.[28] The *School Location* coefficients are also larger at the 12th than at the other grades, although the difference is not so dramatic. Their signs suggest that urban schools are good for achievement.

Physical Resource Variables

On the face of it, *Per-Pupil Instructional Expenditure* is the most important of the four Physical Resource measures. But expenditure data were gathered only on a systemwide basis, and as a result some critics claim it is useless as a measure of resources. Others interpret the variable as an indicator of the community's overall monetary commitment to education. Whatever the label, the variable bears little relationship to achievement at any grade level for either racial group, although most of its coefficients are positive. Its strongest showing is for the 9th-grade whites, with a Beta of .06 in the full equation. This roughly translates into an expected .36 of a grade-level increase for an increase in PPIE of $500. It is a considerable increase, in both achievement and money. But before policy is made, two things should be remembered.

1) The Beta represents only an estimate; reasonable confidence limits for this estimate include zero as well as + 0.06.
2) The coefficients for the other five groups are considerably smaller than .06.

It is worthwhile to note, however, that had I been studying only 9th-grade whites, I might have made a great deal of the relation of PPIE to individual achievement.

Library Volumes Per Student is a complete washout. In *no* equation does it have a statistically significant coefficient, and in no case does its uncontrolled correlation exceed a magnitude of .06.

The last two resources in this category were assessed only at the 9th and 12th grades. Neither resource, *Science Laboratories* or *Guidance Counselors*, could be expected a priori to strongly influence verbal achievement and neither does. Their inclusion in this analysis only reflects the shallowness of conventional thinking about the effects of school resources. Two points in this vein should be stressed. First, if they had been strongly related to verbal achievement, I would have concluded that their effect either was due to their acting as proxies for other unmeasured resources or to selection and assignment effects. Second, on the basis of the results of this analysis little can be said about the educational significance of either resource. The importance of each lies in some other area; science laboratories might be important for students studying the methodologies of biology, chemistry, and physics; the effect of guidance counselors might be better assessed by measuring the quantity and quality of information that students have about different colleges and occupations.

Curriculum Characteristics

The final category is *Curriculum Characteristics*. Only two variables in this category were measured at the 6th grade. The first, *Promotion of Slow Learners*, was measured only at the 6th grade. For both racial groups it has a small negative relationship to achievement. Black students appear to be more affected than whites. A policy of promoting by age group rather than by achievement appears detrimental to the achievement of the 6th graders. However, the effect is small and the results are confounded by one of the alternatives which allows the principal to answer that "Pupils identified as slow learners are not enrolled or are transferred to other schools" (p. 668).

The second variable measured at the 6th grade, *(No) Accelerated Curriculum*, has insignificantly negative coefficients in all conditions. (Note that coding is such that a negative coefficient indicates that an Accelerated Curriculum is beneficial.)

At the secondary level the interpretation of the curriculum variables is more complex than at the elementary level. Two facts lend to the complexity. First, the relations of the curriculum variables to achievement should be particularly sensitive to school selection and assignment effects. Vocational and academic schools are less likely to have as comprehensive curricula as comprehensive high schools. Tracking is more likely to be important in a school with a heterogeneous student body than in a school with a specialized mission. Thus any association between the curriculum variable and achievement may be spurious.

Second, the curriculum variables highlight an important conceptual problem in the interpretation of the 9th- and 12th-grade coefficients. All of the curriculum variables assess differences between the schools presently attended by the students. For 9th grade students in their final year of junior high school (schools with grades seven to nine) the curriculum variables are arguably valid. By 9th grade the students in these schools will generally have been exposed to the various curriculum characteristics for two years. But for 9th grade students in their first year of 9th to 12th grade senior high schools, the curriculum variables are clearly not valid indicators of the effect on achievement of differences between schools in curriculum characteristics. At the time of testing, these students would have attended the senior high schools for less than one month and thus could not have felt much of the effect of the curriculum. The coefficients of the variables probably reflect the effects of selection and assignment rather than the effect of the measured characteristics. Unfortunately, in this analysis, the two types of 9th graders cannot be separated and, therefore, interpretation of the coefficients is difficult at best—the size of the coefficients being due, in part, to the effects of the curriculum characteristics and, in part, to selection and assignment.

The 12th grade coefficients are less confounded. Since 12th graders would probably have been in the same school for two or three years prior to the time of testing, the curriculum characteristics should have had an opportunity to be influential. Thus, considerably more credence may be given to the 12th grade coefficients than to the 9th grade coefficients as reflecting the effects of differences between schools in curriculum characteristics.

Yet the sizes and signs of the uncontrolled 12th grade coefficients will also be influenced by selection and assignment. A partial control for this is to include the Student-Body factor in the equation. The Student-Body factor can also be used at the 9th grade as a control for selection and assignment. If we assume that the Student-Body factor is adequate as a control, the interpretation of the coefficients is straightforward. Yet this assumption seems unlikely, particularly for the 9th grade analyses. This suggests a second strategy for interpretation. We could consider the 9th grade coefficients as mostly influenced by selection and assignment. As such, they might be used as another way of controlling the 12th grade coefficients for selection and assignment. The result of subtracting a 9th grade from a 12th grade coefficient might be thought of as a conservative estimate of the actual effect of a curriculum characteristic—since selection and assignment at the 12th grade level would be controlled for by both the Student-Body factor and by the 9th grade coefficient. The following discussion employs this strategy in addition to the more conventional approach to the interpretation of coefficients. The discussion, of course, should be thought of as speculative rather than conclusive.

The first curriculum characteristic, *Extra-Curricular Activities*, shows no relation to achievement in the 9th grade but does show some relation to achievement at the 12th grade. For both groups at the 12th grade the relation in an uncontrolled form is positive and statistically significant. The introduction of controls, however, changes the sign of the white coefficient while not affecting the black coefficient. It is difficult to conclude much from this.

Second, consider (*No*) *Accelerated Curriculum*. At each secondary grade, for both racial groups, the zero-order correlation is negative. Just as in 6th grade, students in schools with accelerated curriculum achieve at higher average levels than students in schools without accelerated curriculum. The uncontrolled relationships are particularly strong at the 12th grade. The achievement of both black and white twelfth graders is almost a grade level higher in schools with accelerated curriculum than in schools without the advanced programs. When other schoolwide and home background variables are introduced, the sizes of the coefficients drop, although they always retain a negative sign. For blacks the existence of an accelerated curriculum seems more beneficial at the 9th grade ($b = -.70$) than at the 12th ($b = -.23$) when the full controls are introduced. But the opposite is true for whites—the 9th-grade regression coefficient is .06 and the 12th grade is $-.71$. What are we to make of this?

A first interpretation would be straightforward. On the average, students learn more in schools with accelerated curricula. This is particularly true for 9th-grade blacks and 12th-grade whites. But this interpretation does not take all of the data into account.

Consider the black students first. It may be that the relationship between the *Accelerated Curriculum* variable and achievement for 9th-grade blacks is essentially unmeasured selection and assignment effects. Brighter blacks may be more likely to *attend* schools with an accelerated curriculum, but this does not mean that they benefit from the curriculum. Indeed, they may be harmed by the existence of the special advanced courses *if* they have not been placed in the advanced curriculum. The school with an accelerated curriculum may devote less of its resources to the education of those not in the accelerated curriculum. This could cause the odd results. Black students may be excluded from the accelerated curriculum.

Thus, even though they start off (at the 9th grade) and end up (at the 12th grade) smarter than their counterparts in schools without accelerated curricula, they lose some of their advantage. This explanation fits the data. Although the coefficient for blacks at the 12th grade retains the same sign, it is quite a lot smaller than the 9th-grade coefficient. Thus, 12th-grade black students in schools with an accelerated curriculum are less verbally skilled than their 9th-grade counterparts, other things being equal. The decrease in advantage from the 9th to 12th grade for black students in schools with accelerated curricula suggests that accelerated curricula are harmful for blacks.

But the same effect does not seem to hold for whites. At the 9th grade the controls remove the relationship between *Accelerated Curriculum* and achievement. But at the 12th grade there is a moderately strong controlled relationship. Therefore, the existence of an accelerated curriculum seems to be beneficial to the average achievement of white students. Perhaps this is because the students in an accelerated curriculum are predominantly white.[29]

A second curriculum variable offers similar problems in interpretation. Students in secondary schools with comprehensive curricula achieve at lower levels than students in schools without comprehensive curricula. Note that the variable is coded differently at the two grades—the standardized coefficient in Appendix B should be examined in this case. When the maximum coefficients are examined, the effects of the *Comprehensive Curriculum* variable seems to be equally as large for whites and blacks in both the 9th and 12th grades though only for 9th-grade whites is a coefficient statistically significant. When the fully controlled coefficients are examined, however, 9th-grade students appear more influenced than 12th-grade students. Thus the relationship between this variable and achievement is unclear. Although more verbally adept students may attend schools without comprehensive curricula, the *decrease* from 9th to 12th grades in the negative relationship between achievement and this variable suggests that, rather than damaging achievement, schools with comprehensive curricula may be conducive to the overall achievement of these students.

The final two curriculum variables are (*No*) *Tracking* and *Movement Between Tracks*. *Blacks* at both the 9th and 12th grades achieve higher in schools *without* tracks. For both grades, the coefficient is positive in the maximum state though it is much larger at the 12th grade. In the full equation, the regression coefficient is again larger for the 12th-grade group, though it is statistically insignificant. If the coefficient at the 9th grade is due to assignment and selection, then the important data are the difference between the 9th and 12th coefficient. Using this approach, the interpretation is that tracking has little effect on the achievement of blacks. However, if we accept the coefficients at the 9th and 12th grades as measuring the effect of tracking rather than assignment (an implausible assumption), the resulting interpretation is that *Tracking* has a substantial negative effect on the achievement of blacks. Then we might conclude, other things being equal, that schools without tracking produce *blacks* who achieve between 0.5 and 1.0 grade levels higher than schools which fully track.

Movement Between Tracks can be interpreted in exactly the same way. The coefficients for blacks are all negative and are almost equal in the two grades, though they are significant at the 9th grade and nonsignificant at the 12th grade. The amount of *Movement Between Tracks* is *associated* with lower black verbal achievement. Brookover, Lew, and Kariger (1967) found a somewhat similar result. They found that lower-class students are likely to be discriminated against in the assignment to and movement between tracks. Other things being equal, lower-class students are assigned to lower tracks and are much more likely to be moved to lower tracks. If greater amounts of verbal skills are imparted in high tracks then the more blacks moved or assigned to lower tracks (for whatever reason), the lower the overall black achievement.

For white students the relationship between achievement and the two tracking variables is just the opposite of the relationship for blacks. Whites in schools with full tracking and high levels of movement between tracks do better than whites in schools which do not follow tracking policies. This is true in the fully controlled and in the uncontrolled situations at both grades. However, all of the coefficients are much smaller in absolute magnitude than the black coefficients. Thus the "effect," if there is one, is likely to be of less magnitude for whites than for blacks.

In summary, inspection of the coefficients does not alter the preliminary finding that the measured facilities and curriculum have little influence on the production of achievement. Little new information was added by the inspection of the coefficients. One exception, however, was the analysis of the curriculum characteristics. They suggest that whites are either unaffected or are aided by the classification practices carried out in many schools, while blacks are either unaffected or harmed by employment of such classification practices.

CONCLUSIONS. The conclusion of this reexamination is that the relation between the Facilities and Curriculum factor and verbal achievement is very slight. This is similar to the conclusion reached by Coleman *et al*. It is supported both by analysis of the overall relation between the factor and achievement, and by the relationships between specific Facilities and Curriculum variables and achievement. The facts, however, that no data were analyzed on the quality of the facilities, on the overall degree of utilization of the facilities, and on the differential access of students to the facilities and curriculum components should temper any rash inferences about the effect of facilities and curriculum on student achievement. Any inferences must be restricted to applying to the effects of school-to-school differences averaged over all students within schools.

Not all of the conclusions reached in this reanalysis agree with those reached by Coleman *et al.* Specifically, I have argued that both the Home Background and the other schoolwide factors must be controlled when the schoolwide factors are compared in strength. If the *unique* contributions to explained variance are taken as the "correct" measures, two conclusions reached by the authors of the EEOS Report are challenged. First, there does not appear to be an increasing or cumulative effect of the Facilities and Curriculum factor on achievement. Second, black students do not appear to be more sensitive to variations among schools in Facilities and Curriculum than white students. Just as with the Student Body factor, the differential sensitivity hypothesis is not upheld.

Additionally, I have made more of the importance of particular Curriculum variables than did Coleman *et al.* Particularly at the secondary level, it looks as if classification practices such as tracking and accelerated curriculum may be *harmful* to the achievement of blacks while *not aiding* the achievement of whites very much.

Finally, the preceding analysis and discussion may be in some part academic. I have argued in earlier sections that the relationships between the schoolwide variables and achievement at the secondary level are seriously confounded with the effects of self-selection of schools and program of school assignment practices and with differential dropout rates. Because the Student-Body factor is essentially a proxy for these effects, it can be argued that controlling for the Student-Body factor while analyzing the schoolwide characteristics satisfies the problem. But the situation is more complex. Because the structure of the school system was not taken into account when the correlation matrices were developed, there is no way of knowing whether a 9th-grade student is in his first year of high school or his last year of junior high school. Thus, when school resources show coefficients of an interesting magnitude at the 9th grade, there is no way of knowing whether they are reflecting unmeasured assignment and selection effects or some "true" causal relationship. Similarly, when large coefficients occur at the 12th grade, it is impossible to determine whether they should be compared to corresponding coefficients at the 9th grade or accepted at face value. This issue cannot be resolved until we initiate and analyze separate samples of students in 9-to-12-year high schools and 7-to-9-year junior high schools. Until then the relationship of school resources to achievement at the secondary level must remain unresolved.

SECTION V: The Relationship Between the Characteristics of Teachers and the Verbal Achievement of Students

The final school factor studied by Coleman *et al.* was Teacher Characteristics. The EEOS Report concluded that:

Altogether, variation in school averages of teachers' characteristics accounted for higher proportion of variation in student achievement than did all other aspects of the school combined, excluding the student body characteristics. [p. 316]

Two aspects of this conclusion are particularly important. First, only characteristics averaged over all teachers in a school were included in the Report's analyses. Specific teachers were *not* associated with specific students. Therefore, the only variation in student achievement that teacher characteristics can explain is that which lies between the schools. The effect of individual teachers on particular students within schools are not represented in analyses of the EEOS data. Although this probably led to an underestimation of the "effect" that differences among teachers have on student achievement, it also makes the teacher factor directly comparable to the other schoolwide factors.

Second, the phrase "all other aspects of the school combined, excluding the student body characteristics" is misleading. It refers only to the fact that Coleman *et al.* found that the Teacher Characteristics factor explained more variation than the Facilities and Curriculum factor.

This section reanalyzes the relationship between Teacher Characteristics and student achievements. The conclusions reached here differ from some of Coleman *et al.*'s, although the differences are primarily those of emphasis. I find the relationship between the Teacher Characteristics factor and achievement to be seriously confounded with social-class-related inequities in resource allocation (for whites) and with school-assignment practices (particularly for blacks). These conclusions are in close agreement with those reached earlier about the Student Body and Facilities and Curriculum factors.

The Variables

At each of the three grades, seven aggregate teacher variables were included in the analysis. Coleman *et al.* described their selection procedure:

Several teachers' characteristics were selected for special examination, after eliminating a number of characteristics that appeared, in early regressions, to have little effect. Other variables were eliminated because they were highly correlated with one or more of those remaining, and thus their effects could not easily be distinguished. The variables which remain must be regarded in part as surrogates for other variables that are related to them. Thus, as with any investigation into a complex set of relations, the results must be interpreted with caution because of the many factors that could not be simultaneously held constant. [p. 316]

The seven variables can be grouped into three categories:

1) Ascribed Characteristics: Two variables fit this label: *Proportion of Teachers in the School Who Are White;* and *Average Educational Level of Teachers' Mothers.*

2) Achieved Characteristics: Three variables fit into this category: *Average Teacher Verbal Score, Average Teacher Educational Level,* and *Average Localism of the Teachers*—whether they had attended high school and college in the area and had lived there most of their lives.

3) Professional Commitment and Preferences: The two variables in this category are: *Average Years of Teaching Experience* and *Average Teachers' Preference for Type of Student Body.*

Overall, the seven variables comprise the strongest of the three school-wide factors. They have a breadth lacking in the selection of Facilities and Curriculum variables, and they more accurately measure Teacher Characteristics than the Student-Body variables measure dimensions of the student body. Other analyses of the EEOS data bear out this assessment. The teacher characteristics that are most often cited as being important to student achievement are all included in this selection.[30]

The Overall Relationship Between Aggregate Teacher Characteristics and Verbal Achievement

Table 23 displays percentages of verbal achievement variance explained by the Teacher Characteristics factor. Two conditions of background control are shown—none, and the six objective background variables.[31] For each condition both the total and unique contribution to explained verbal achievement variance are displayed.

The numbers present a mixed picture. The figures in the top row (no background controls, total contribution) are substantial. The total percentages of individual variance explained vary from a low of 2.65 percent for 6th-grade whites to 6.08 percent for 12th-grade blacks. The numbers also seem substantial when compared to the figures for the Facilities and Curriculum factor presented in Table 18. For only one group, 9th-grade whites, does the Facilities and Curriculum factor explain more achievement variance.

When the unique contributions (under the condition of no background controls, row 2) are examined, the contributions to explained variance are considerably reduced. The figures in the black columns suffer particularly. Only for 6th-grade blacks does the unique contribution exceed 1

TABLE 23

Additional percentages of variance in Verbal Achievement explained by the Teacher Characteristics factor under varying conditions of control for black and white, sixth-, ninth-, and twelfth-grade students.[1]

Background Controls		Northern Blacks			Northern Whites		
		6th Grade	9th Grade	12th Grade	6th Grade	9th Grade	12th Grade
No Individual Background Control	Contribution Alone in Equation	3.33†	2.26†	6.08†	2.65†	1.81*	4.00†
	Unique Contribution With Other Schoolwide Factors in Equation	1.64	0.69	0.98	0.58	0.75	0.92
Six Objective Individual Background Variables	Contribution Alone in Equation	1.82†	1.07	3.04†	0.86	0.78	1.03
	Unique Contribution With Other Schoolwide Factors in Equation	1.50†	0.62	0.92	0.46	0.68	0.60

[1] All variables are described in Appendix A.
* Statistically significant at the .05 level.
† Statistically significant at the .01 level.

percent, and the contribution to explained variance for 12th-grade blacks drops from 6.08 to less than 1 percent. The drop is least in the 6th grade—where selection and assignment effects are least—but that is small solace for those who believe in a powerful effect of teachers.

In dealing with the impact of the Student Body and the Facilities and Curriculum factors on achievement, I explored some of the reasons for the reduction in variance uniquely explained by schoolwide factors, when other schoolwide factors are included in the equations. The Student-Body factor tends to share an increasing amount of variance with both of the other schoolwide factors, as students get older. In Table 24 the variance shared by the Teacher Characteristics factor and the other schoolwide factors is displayed for each of the six groups. The numbers summarize the reductions from the total amount of variation to the unique amount of variation accounted for by the Teacher Factor under the condition of no background controls. Two sets of numbers are shown. The first shows the reduction when both the Facilities and Curriculum factor and the Student-Body factor are included in the equation. The second shows the reduction when only the Student-Body factor is in the equations with the Teacher Characteristics factor. The message is clear: the dramatic reduction in variance explained uniquely by the Teacher Characteristics factor seen in Table 23 can be almost completely attributed to an overlap with the Student-Body factor.[32]

TABLE 24

Reduction in percentages of variation uniquely explained by the Teacher Characteristics factor when both the Facilities and Curriculum factor and the Student-Body
factor are entered and when only the Student-Body factor is entered in the equation.[1]
(No background controls.)

	Northern Blacks		Northern Whites	
	Reduction in Uniquely Explained Variation When All Schoolwide Factors Are Entered in the Equation	Reduction* When Only the Student-Body Factor is Entered	Reduction in Uniquely Explained Variation When All Schoolwide Factors Are Entered in the Equation	Reduction When Only the Student-Body Factor Is Entered
Grade				
6	1.69	1.31	2.07	2.07
9	1.57	1.32	1.06	1.45†
12	5.10	5.41†	3.08	3.07†

[1] All variables are described in Appendix A.
* This includes all variance explained jointly by the Teacher Characteristics factor
and the Student-Body factor.
† For two of the six groups the Teacher Characteristics factor accounts for more
variance when the Facilities and Curriculum factor is included in the equation than
when it is not entered.

This reduction is particularly large for whites and at the 12th grade.
As we have seen in earlier analyses, the shared relationship may be due
particularly to either: 1) social-class inequities in the distribution of school
resources (here Teacher Characteristics), or 2) selection, school assignment practices, and differential dropout rates.

The numbers in rows 3 and 4 of Table 23 speak to this question.
Compare row 3 to row 1: in each row no other school factor has been entered into the equations, but in row 3 six Home Background variables were
introduced as controls while in row 1 no background controls were entered.
This comparison shows that for both groups (but particularly for whites) a
substantial amount of the relationship between *Teacher Characteristics* and
student achievement is shared with the relationship between home background and achievement. In other words, there appear to be social-class
inequities in the allocation of those teacher resources that associate positively with student achievement.

In row 4 a further reduction in the unique explanatory power of the
Teacher Characteristics factor can be seen. This reduction (from row 3 to
row 4 of Table 23) can be attributed to influence shared by the Teacher
Characteristics factor and the Student-Body factor that is not also shared
with home background. The reduction is substantial at every grade for both

groups. However, the reductions for 9th- and 12th-grade blacks over-shadow the reductions for whites. Since the Student-Body factor has been interpreted mainly as measuring selection and assignment effects, the reductions suggest that selection and assignment affect the relationship between achievement and teacher characteristics particularly for blacks.

Thus for both races a large part of the relationship between *Teacher Characteristics* and student achievement either can be attributed to social-class inequities in resource allocation or to student selection and school assignment practices. For whites the largest source of the overlap is individual social-class differences among the schools—for blacks the selection and assignment practices seem as important as the social-class differences.

For these reasons (and others presented in the sections on the Student-Body and the Facilities and Curriculum factors), I use the estimates of the uncontaminated effects of the schoolwide factors (row 4 of Table 23, unique contributions after background controls) to assess the factors' overall importance. Using these figures I conclude that the effect of the Teacher Characteristics factor is small. For only one group, 6th-grade blacks, does the factor uniquely account for more than 1 percent of the total variation in verbal achievement.

The Relative Strength of the Teacher Characteristics Factor

The argument for using unique contributions after background controls also applies to estimating the relative importance of the various schoolwide factors. Table 25 summarizes the unique contributions to explained variance for the three schoolwide factors after background controls have been introduced. The numbers in parentheses are rank orders of the three schoolwide factors by grade within race. These numbers reinforce the con-

TABLE 25

The unique percentages of Verbal Achievement variance explained by the various schoolwide factors. The six objective background variables are controlled.[1]

Schoolwide Factor	Northern Blacks			Northern Whites		
	6th Grade	9th Grade	12th Grade	6th Grade	9th Grade	12th Grade
Student Body	1.34† (2)	1.58† (1)	1.78† (1)	1.10* (1)	0.46 (3)	0.47 (3)
Facilities and Curriculum	0.16 (3)	1.14 (2)	1.02 (2)	0.24 (3)	0.86 (1)	0.80 (1)
Teacher Characteristics	1.50† (1)	0.62 (3)	0.92 (3)	0.46 (2)	0.68 (2)	0.60 (2)

[1] All variables are described in Appendix A.
* Statistically significant at the .05 level.
† Statistically significant at the .01 level.

clusion that no one of the schoolwide factors is independently strong. In no group does any factor uniquely explain over 2 percent of the variation in achievement. Although the Teacher Factor seems to exert considerable influence in the uncontrolled conditions and at the 6th grade, it explains less variation than either of the other two factors at the secondary grades when the unique contributions are examined. Only for the 6th-grade black group is the unique contribution statistically significant.

Two Conclusions of the Report—The Cumulative Effect and the Differential Sensitivity Hypotheses

Based on their analyses of the EEOS data Coleman *et al.* concluded that:

1) Teacher difference show a cumulative effect over the years in school.

2) Teacher differences show more relation to differences in achievement of educationally disadvantaged minority groups than to achievement of the white majority. The relation corresponds roughly to the general sensitivity of the minority group to variations in school environments. [p. 318] [33]

Both conclusions were drawn from an examination of contribution to variance explained with background but without other school factors in the equations. (See row 3, Table 23.) [34]

If the dip at the 9th grade is ignored, the first conclusion seems substantiated by the results in row 3. More variation is explained by the Teacher Characteristics factor at the 12th grade than at the 6th grade. Again, if we overlook the 9th grade, the second conclusion also seems reasonable. At the 6th and 12th grades, much more variation in black than in white achievement is uniquely accounted for by the Teacher Characteristics factor.

But I have argued that the numbers in row 3 are not the proper ones to look at. The right numbers are the unique contributions (see row 4)—after the effects of selection and school assignment practices have been at least partially removed. The unique contributions *do not substantiate a conclusion about an increasing or cumulative effect for teacher characteristics.* Indeed, for whites, the teacher factor shows the strongest relationship to achievement at the 9th grade (a complete switch from the numbers in row 3). However, the numbers for the whites are so similar as to make comparisons among them ridiculous; the largest of the differences is less than one fourth of 1 percent of achievement variance.

With regard to the second conclusion, at two of the three grades the explained variation is greater for blacks than for whites. Although this is the right direction, the only substantial difference is at the 6th grade. There the Teacher Characteristics factor uniquely accounts for 1.5 percent of the black achievement variance and for 0.6 percent of the variance for whites.

In summary, the data so far suggest a weak link between the Teacher Characteristics factor and school-to-school differences in student achievement. The measured variations in teacher characteristics explain only a very small *unique* amount of the school-to-school variation in student achievement. It appears that much of the uncontrolled relationship between achievement and teacher characteristics is produced by social-class inequities in resource allocation and by school selection and assignment practices. Additionally there does not appear to be a cumulative effect of the factor and only weak support for the differential sensitivity hypotheses is evident. Of course, the factor's failure to account for much variation does not rule out the possibility that a different distribution of the characteristics would have made it seem more important. If, for example, the differences among schools in the teacher characteristics are very small, we would expect little variation in achievement to be explained. Similarly, if the distributions were different across grades and between races, then comparison of unique contribution is spurious. To answer these possibilities we need to examine the means, standard deviations, and regression coefficients of the variables for the various groups.

THE RELATIONSHIP OF SPECIFIC TEACHER CHARACTERISTICS TO STUDENT VERBAL ACHIEVEMENT

Tables 26, 27, and 28 contain the means, standard deviations, and certain regression coefficients for the seven teacher variables. Two sets of regression coefficients are shown. The first are fully controlled. They correspond to the standardized coefficients in column 4 of Tables G–L in Appendix B. The equations in which they were developed contain the Home Background factor, the other two schoolwide factors, *Proportion Students White*, and all the teacher variables. The second set of coefficients are completely uncontrolled—they correspond to the zero-order correlations with achievement shown in column 3 of Tables G–L in Appendix B.

Before interpreting the regression coefficients, it is instructive to look at the means and standard deviations. At each grade blacks and whites are taught by teachers of roughly equal *SES Levels, Experience, Localism,* and

training (*Degree Received*). Teachers of black students, however, generally have lower verbal scores, are much more likely to be black, and express
a much greater preference for teaching lower-class students. On the first
two of these measures the variability of the characteristics is much greater
for teachers of black students.

These differences make direct comparisons of whites and blacks difficult. But this difficulty pales in comparison to the difficulties in interpreting
the regression coefficients in Tables 26, 27, and 28. These figures offer a
persuasive argument for a finding of no relationship between teacher characteristics and achievement. The coefficients seem almost random in direction of effects: fifteen of the forty-two pairs of controlled and uncontrolled
coefficients have different signs in the different conditions. Twelve of the
twenty-one pairs of controlled coefficients have dissimilar signs for blacks
and whites at the same grade level. Only two of the seven variables in the
controlled condition have the same sign for blacks at all three grade levels,
though six of the seven have the same sign in the uncontrolled condition.
The coefficients are somewhat more consistent for white students. Three of
the seven variables have similar signs at all three grades in the controlled condition, and six of the seven have the same sign in the uncontrolled
condition.

TABLE 26

*Regression Coefficients, Means, and Standard Deviations for the
Sixth-Grade Teacher Characteristics Factor Variables*

| | | Northern Blacks | | | | Northern Whites | | | |
| | | | | Regression Coefficients | | | | Regression Coefficients | |
No.	Variable Name	Mean	S.D.	Full[1] Equation	Uncon-trolled[2]	Mean	S.D.	Full[1] Equation	Uncon-trolled[2]
11	SES Level	3.71	0.59	−0.067	0.074	3.73	0.63	0.124	1.178*
12	Experience	11.26	3.66	0.049	0.227†	11.74	4.56	0.097	−0.037
13	Localism	0.06	0.80	−1.429†	−1.293†	0.05	0.80	0.385	1.026*
15	Degree Received	3.14	0.26	−0.701	−0.890	3.02	0.32	−0.481	1.916
16	Preference for Type of Student Body	0.21	0.66	0.069	−1.059*	−0.24	0.71	−0.218	−1.586†
17	Verbal Score	21.66	2.65	0.026	0.292†	23.34	2.06	0.088	0.255
18	Proportion Teachers White	0.56	0.36	1.053	2.714†	0.96	0.07	3.971	13.220†

* Statistically significant at the .05 level.
† Statistically significant at the .01 level.
[1] This column contains the regression coefficients for the Teacher variable when the
Home Background, the Student Body, the Facilities and Curriculum, *and* the other
Teacher Characteristics factor variables are all in the equation. It corresponds to column 4 of Tables G-L in Appendix B.
[2] This column contains the regression coefficients for the Teacher Characteristics variable calculated from the zero-ordered correlations. See Appendix B, Tables G and H.

TABLE 27

Regression Coefficients, Means, and Standard Deviations for the Ninth-Grade Teacher Characteristics Factor Variables

No.	Variable Name	Northern Blacks		Regression Coefficients		Northern Whites		Regression Coefficients	
		Mean	S.D.	Full[1] Equation	Uncontrolled[2]	Mean	S.D.	Full[1] Equation	Uncontrolled[2]
11	SES Level	3.79	0.48	1.139	1.161	3.82	0.48	−0.037	0.854
12	Experience	10.48	3.44	−0.294	0.054	9.78	3.32	−0.073	−0.182
13	Localism	0.06	0.79	−0.675	−0.501	0.03	0.81	1.274	0.789
15	Degree Received	3.41	0.21	4.534	5.180†	3.35	0.20	−1.607	3.486
16	Preference for Type of Student Body	0.28	0.75	1.223	−1.270*	−0.32	0.67	0.614	−1.648*
17	Verbal Score	22.16	2.30	0.167	0.648†	23.23	1.51	−0.055	0.016
18	Proportion Teachers White	0.62	0.35	−3.528	3.196†	0.96	0.06	7.224	17.560*

* Statistically significant at the .05 level.
† Statistically significant at the .01 level.
[1] This column contains the regression coefficients for the Teacher variable when the Home Background, the Student Body, the Facilities and Curriculum, *and* the other Teacher Characteristics factor variables are all in the equation. It corresponds to column 4 of Tables G-L in Appendix B.
[2] This column contains the regression coefficients for the Teacher Characteristics variable calculated from the zero-order correlations. See Appendix B, Tables I and J.

TABLE 28

Regression Coefficients, Means, and Standard Deviations for the Twelfth-Grade Teacher Characteristics Factor Variables

No.	Variable Name	Northern Blacks		Regression Coefficients		Northern Whites		Regression Coefficients	
		Mean	S.D.	Full[1] Equation	Uncontrolled[2]	Mean	S.D.	Full[1] Equation	Uncontrolled[2]
11	SES Level	3.73	0.46	2.730	1.651	3.77	0.48	−0.106	1.908*
12	Experience	11.75	2.99	−0.043	0.285	10.77	3.00	0.171	0.042
13	Localism	0.13	0.78	−1.747	−1.027	0.00	0.77	1.190	0.689
15	Degree Received	3.51	0.24	−1.140	7.282†	3.43	0.22	−1.833	7.427†
16	Preference for Type of Student Body	0.33	0.67	−1.867	−3.814†	−0.31	0.68	−0.737	−3.537†
17	Verbal Score	22.33	1.97	0.260	0.935†	23.13	1.30	0.520	0.347
18	Proportion Teachers White	0.69	0.35	−4.234	3.472*	0.97	0.05	1.087	8.232

* Statistically significant at the .05 level.
† Statistically significant at the .01 level.
[1] This column contains the regression coefficients for the Teacher variable when the Home Background, the Student Body, the Facilities and Curriculum, *and* the other Teacher Characteristics factor variables are all in the equation. It corresponds to column 4 of Tables G-L in Appendix B.
[2] This column contains the regression coefficients for the Teacher Characteristics variable calculated from the zero-order correlations. See Appendix B, Tables K and L.

Cumulative Effect Hypothesis

The sign differences indicate that little can be gained by contrasting the strength of particular variables across the three grades. The differences in sign from grade to grade argue against the existence of a cumulative effect. If the coefficients are at all accurate, the teacher characteristics which affect student verbal scores differ from grade to grade. This is not so absurd as it initially may sound. Effective elementary teachers may be very different from effective secondary school teachers. For one thing most elementary-school teachers are female and most secondary-school teachers are male. Thus, it is difficult to shed light on the question of a cumulative effect by examining the regression coefficients. The investigation of a cumulative effect must, therefore, depend upon the analysis of explained variation. The conclusion reached earlier holds. There is little evidence of an increasing or cumulative effect of teacher characteristics or student achievement.

Differential Sensitivity Hypothesis

The differential sensitivity hypothesis is easier to examine, because comparisons can be made within grade level. For example, the verbal achievement of both groups of sixth graders is positively influenced by teachers who have high *Verbal* scores, and by high *Proportions of White* teachers. Here, complete similarity ends. Two variables (*Experience* and *Degree Received*), however, have like-signed coefficients for both groups in the controlled condition though unlike signs in the uncontrolled condition. Whites attending schools with more experienced teachers do better than other whites—this relation decreases but remains positive after controls are introduced. Blacks, on the other hand, who attend schools with more experienced teachers score less well than other blacks. After controls are introduced, however, the *Experience* variable has a positive coefficient for blacks. Mean teacher *Degree Received* operates in an equally inconsistent fashion. For blacks in both conditions the relation is small and negative. For whites in the uncontrolled condition the coefficient is positive, but when controls are introduced the coefficient has a small negative value.

For two other variables (*SES Level* and *Teacher's Preference for Type of Student Body*) the uncontrolled coefficients for both groups have like signs while the controlled coefficients have different signs. *SES Level* has positive coefficients for whites in both conditions and, for blacks, has a positive uncontrolled coefficient and a negative controlled coefficient. Neither controlled relation is large. *Teachers' Preference for Type of Student Body* (high score signifies that teachers prefer to teach lower-class students) has a predictable set of relationships to verbal achievement. For both blacks and whites the uncontrolled relationship is negative, and for whites the relationship remains negative when controls are introduced. For blacks, however, the controlled coefficient is positive. Thus, teachers appear to help those students whom they say they prefer to teach. However, neither controlled relationship is large. The final variable, *Localism*, may well be important, though it is difficult to determine exactly what it measures. For whites both coefficients are small but positive—mobile teachers are a positive influence. The opposite holds true for blacks; both the controlled and uncontrolled relationships are strongly (statistically significantly) negative. Locally born, raised, and educated teachers who have been at their present school for most of their career have a positive influence on black achievement.

Thus, at the 6th grade we find that some teacher characteristics have a stronger influence on black achievement, while others have a greater effect on white achievement. This suggests that the differential sensitivity hypothesis might be refined. Different types of children (here blacks and whites) might be differentially sensitive to specific teacher characteristics. Such a refinement is also suggested by the data for the 9th and 12th grades. At the 9th grade, for example, only two of the pairs of controlled coefficients have the same sign. Five of the seven teachers' characteristics have influences on blacks opposite from that on whites. Three of the seven pairs of controlled coefficients have similar signs at the 12th grade. The fact, however, that the direction of a characteristic's effect on the same racial group changes from grade to grade makes me wary of any serious conclusion. It is only possible to discuss racial differences for particular variables at particular grades. These facts, combined with the earlier data, give little evidence that the *overall* influence of teachers is greater for blacks than whites.

Sixth-Grade Results

The final issue is whether individual variables in the *Teacher Characteristics* factor evidence strong relations to achievement. I will discuss only the 6th-grade results. The lack of control for differences in school structure, self-selection, and assignment practices clouds all interpretation of secondary-school results. These problems, together with the differences in signs reviewed earlier, make the 9th- and 12th-grade situation hopeless.[35]

At the 6th grade three variables have a negligible influence on achievement for both groups under all controlled conditions: *Teachers' SES Level, Degree Received*, and *Verbal Score*.[36]

The other four variables are more interesting. *Localism* has already been mentioned. Other things being equal, the 10 percent of black students exposed to the most mobile teachers achieve about four points lower (one half grade level) than the 10 percent of black students exposed to teachers who are most local. The reverse is true for whites, though to a much lesser extent. The variable, however, is difficult to interpret. Coleman *et al.* used five items from the Teachers' questionnaire to construct the variable, and their individual relationships are unclear. One possibility is that the variable does not reflect a "localism" dimension. One of its parts is a measure of the holding power of a school on its teachers (a ratio of how long the teachers had been in that school to the amount of time the teachers had been teaching); it is likely that the variable taps school "climate," "attractiveness," "spirit," or whatever it is that influences teachers to remain or leave. In this case, it might not be the simple fact that teachers stayed in some schools and not in others, but their *reasons* for staying, that account for the influence on black student achievement.

If this is the case, we also would expect the variable to have a negative relationship to the achievement of whites. However, either one of two things might be influencing the relationship for whites. First, teachers of whites (themselves almost all white) probably have access to a larger and more attractive marketplace of schools to choose from than do teachers of blacks (about 45 percent black). This might lead to a lessened holding power of any particular school on teachers of whites and, therefore, might remove the source of the relationship of *Localism* to achievement. Second, the positive relationship of the variable to white achievement might be caused by the influence of the other three items making up the variable. Particularly, given the idea of a larger and more attractive marketplace for white teachers, it is not surprising that the more parochial the teachers of whites, the less highly white students succeed.[37]

The second variable, *Experience*, has positive relationships to the achievement of whites and blacks. The positive relationship of this variable to 6th-grade achievement is well documented. Hanushek (1968) and Levin (1970), among others, have found the effect in the EEOS data. If, in these data, we accept a "true" coefficient as .10 (exactly that found for whites in the controlled condition), and roughly the midpoint of the two conditions for blacks, this means that an increase of ten years experience is associated with an increment of one verbal score point (e.g., about .15 grade levels). This is not overwhelming.

A straightforward interpretation, however, may be nearsighted. It is possible that a mean-experience variable masks the real relationship. It may be that schools with very little or very great average teacher experience do not impart as much verbal achievement as schools with a middle level of teacher experience. There may be a certain mix of experience and youth that most encourages student achievement. Suppose, for example, that the best mix is to have a number of old experienced teachers and a roughly equal number of moderately young, eager, and brash teachers. The older teachers might share their tried and true techniques with the younger, and the younger may serve as a leaven with new ideas and enthusiasm. Whatever the case the relationship of this measure to achievement clearly needs more detailed study.

The third interesting 6th-grade variable has already been discussed. The coefficients for *Teachers' Preference of Student Body* support the notion that teachers succeed if they are in a school whose social-class composition is similar to the social-class composition of the schools which they claim they prefer to teach in. Teachers who prefer to teach the middle class appear to positively influence white achievement and negatively influence black achievement. As with many other variables, however, the causal direction is unclear. The relation between this variable and achievement might well be due to teachers' rationalizing their school assignment by claiming that they *prefer* to instruct in the schools in which they teach.

The last of the 6th-grade teacher variables is *Proportion Teachers Who Are White*. For neither group is this variable statistically significant when it is controlled for *Proportion Students White*, and for blacks it never reaches significance (see Tables G and H in Appendix B). Additionally, the large coefficients for whites in Table 26 are misleading. The very small standard deviation of this variable for whites (.07) suggests that the estimates of the effect of the variable are being computed over a very narrow range of observations and may, therefore, be extremely sensitive to uncontrolled outside influences.

SUMMARY AND CONCLUSIONS.   My overall conclusion is that variations in schoolwide teacher characteristics bear little relationship to between-school variations in student achievement. I arrive at this conclusion for two reasons.

1) Taken together, the measured teacher characteristics independently (uniquely) explain very little achievement variance for any of the six groups. Although the Teacher Characteristics factor has moderately strong uncontrolled relationships to student achievement, a large part of the relationships can be attributed to social-class inequities in resource allocation for whites, and to student selection and school assignment practices for both races.

2) Taken individually, few of the teacher variables demonstrate statistically significant relationships to achievement when any controls are introduced into the regression equations. Further, few of the variables have consistent relationships to achievement within the same racial group across the three grade levels, or between racial groups within grade levels. Particularly at the secondary grades, the coefficients for most of the variables defy coherent interpretation.

This overall conclusion is consistent with the overall conclusion reached in the EEOS Report.

However, this reanalysis leads me to think that a number of the less global conclusions reached by Coleman *et al.* need to be reconsidered. Specifically, I find that:

1) The Teacher Characteristics factor does not have a stronger re-

lationship to achievement than the Facilities and Curriculum factor.

2) There does not seem to be a cumulative effect of teacher characteristics on student achievement. In fact, an argument could be made that there is a decreasing effect.

3) The differential sensitivity hypothesis is not supported. Although the Teacher Characteristics factor does explain slightly more unique variance for blacks than for whites at two grade levels, the differences are too small to deem important. However, there is a possibility that the achievement of black students may be sensitive to different teacher characteristics than the achievement of white students (although an alternative hypothesis is that the relationships of the variables to the achievement of both groups are random).

Finally, I must stress again the fact that the failure of Coleman *et al.* to control for school assignment, self-selection, and dropout effects makes conclusions reached from secondary-school results questionable.

SECTION VI: General Conclusions and Policy Implications

At the end of each of the preceding sections of this chapter specific conclusions are reached. In this section three sets of general conclusions and related policy implications are explicated. First, I discuss the validity of the overall conclusion reached in the Report with regard to the equality of educational opportunity. Second, I examine the question of whether inferences about the importance of particular school resources can be drawn from these data. Third, I focus on the research implications of this study.

The Validity and Policy Implications of the Report's Overall Conclusion

In general, the results of the reexamination affirm and strengthen the overall conclusion of the Report:

That schools bring little influence to bear on a child's achievement that is independent of his background and general social context; and that this very lack of an independent effect means that the inequalities imposed on children by their home, neighborhood, and peer environment are carried along to become the inequalities with which they confront adult life at the end of school. [p. 325]

Two sets of results lead me to this conclusion. First, a very large amount of the school-to-school variation in achievement can be attributed to school-to-school differences in individual home background. For whites, over 50 percent of the school-to-school variation in the 6th grade and over 66 percent of the variation in the secondary grades is associated with school-to-school differences in individual background. For blacks, the corresponding figures are less, averaging about 33 percent in the three grades (see Table 8). These percentages are much larger than those found by Coleman *et al.* Their analysis, which was in error, found that the average school-to-school variation in achievement attributable to home background is about 15 percent for whites and 10 percent for blacks.

The argument that can be made from these data is that much of the school-to-school variation in verbal achievement is due to sources outside of the school—specifically home background. A flaw in this argument (which existed in the Report) is that these strong relationships may, in fact, be caused by school-to-school differences in resources. If school resources are distributed among schools in the same way as home background, the school resources may cause the differences among the schools in achievement.

Secondary analyses of the EEOS data help eliminate this flaw. The correlation between the average 1st-grade verbal scores and the average 6th-grade verbal scores across the elementary schools in the North Urban region is 0.80. An even stronger school-to-school correlation (0.96) exists between mean verbal scores for 9th- and 12-grade students in Northern four-year high schools. The message is clear. On the average the school-to-school differences in resources, however measured, could not possibly have much independent influence on the school-to-school differences in verbal achievement. Although the differences in resources may maintain and, in some cases, exacerbate the differences in achievement, they are not the initial causal influence.

The policy implications of this are not clear. A first question that should be asked is whether we could have expected anything different than this result. Why should schools be expected to alter the average relative standing of the pupils who enter them? If all schools do roughly the same things, students who enter schools with advantages over their counterparts in other schools will leave school with the same advantages. There is a problem, however, with this position. While it may be argued that we cannot expect schools to, on the average, change the prospects of their students, the simple fact is that many persons view this as the central responsibility of schools. Certainly, the schools do not meet this responsibility.

My inclination in the face of this evidence is to reconsider the function of schools in society. The strong relationship between the average scores of entering and graduating students suggests that the principal function of the schools is to serve as an allocation and selection agency rather than as an equalizing agency. This is not an original thought (see, for example, Parsons, 1959, or Dreeben, 1968). To some extent this function is aided by residential patterns. The schools preserve the efficacy of these patterns by not altering the average relative achievement of their students. In secondary schools allocation and selection can be more precise by operating on an individual level leading to correlations approaching unity between the average achievement of entering and graduating student bodies.

The policy implications of this view depend, like most policy implications, upon one's beliefs. One belief is that selection and allocation are the proper functions of schools and that other institutions should be concerned with equalizing functions. A second is that the schools should be changed, so as to overcome the inequalities in achievement with which students enter. Some of the less radical school reformers believe that this change is possible without altering the essential structure of the system. The source of their belief is the idea that there are very real differences between the schools of rich and poor children. By making schools for the disadvantaged more like schools for the advantaged, they argue that we can overcome the achievement disparities. The key to this argument is that certain school resources, now inequitably distributed, might, if reallocated, reduce the achievement disparities.

Inferences About Particular School Resources

One of the strongest criticisms of the Report was that the statistics—percentage of variance explained—only allowed the authors to estimate the present importance of measured resources without estimating their *potential* importance if they were redistributed. This criticism fits with the observation that there seem to be differences in style, resources, and programs between schools which may be associated with differences in verbal achievement. In order to change the schools' impact, therefore, we have to discover which resources affect achievement and estimate the effects that changes in their allocation might have. To do this we need to look at the allocation of school resources and at the regression coefficients.

The first issue is the extent to which the resources are, in fact, allocated by achievement and social class. Tables G–L in Appendix B show that school resource variables, with few exceptions, have small zero-order correlations with achievement. They also show that schools attended by blacks and whites have roughly the same characteristics. Jencks (Chapter 2) shows similar results for a very large variety of variables. Additionally he shows that, on the whole, the resources are *not* distributed by social class. Again, with few exceptions such as race of teacher, lower-class and black children attend schools with characteristics that are measurably equivalent to those in schools attended by middle-class and white children.

In conjunction with the small amounts of variance explained, this suggests that few of the measured resources could have a very strong influence on school-to-school differences in verbal achievement even if they were reallocated. This suggestion is greatly strengthened by an inspection of the regression coefficients—again with very few exceptions, they show little promise for policy-makers. Three points, however, suggest that these results are not necessarily conclusive.

First, both in the Report and in my reexaminations, the failure to control for self-selection, school assignment, and grade structure at the 9th and 12th grades leads to hopeless confounding of the secondary-school coefficients. This criticism, however, does not apply to elementary schools. Although there is self-selection by parents of their children's schools primarily through residential patterns, it is generally selection by socioeconomic status rather than by past achievement.

Since social-class selection can probably be "controlled," the 6th-grade coefficients may reflect the "effects" of the measured resources on between-school differences in verbal achievement; therefore, policy implications about particular resources might be made. But no assessed facilities and curriculum resource was found to have other than a negligible influence on between-school differences in achievement. And if Coleman *et al.*'s assertion that the Facilities and Curriculum variables included in the analysis were selected on the basis of their showing the "most relation to achievement" is granted, then we might infer that none of the measured facilities and curriculum have important influences on achievement. With the exception of *Localism of Teachers* and *Average Teacher Experience*, the teacher variables also show little effect on the achievement of sixth graders.

The two teacher variables, however, are good examples of my second reason for distrusting the coefficients—there is no way of knowing what they mean. At least three alternative explanations are very likely for the *Localism* variable and numerous possibilities are evident for *Experience*. One problem is the way the variables were aggregated. *Average Teacher Experience*, for example, apparently has a somewhat curvilinear relation to student achievement (see Jencks, Chapter 2). Thus, it may be that the computation of a mean level of experience masks the real relationship. There may, for example, be an optimum mix of experience and youth which maximizes student achievement within a school. A second problem is that we have no way of knowing which students in a school have access to and utilize a particular resource. Since a science laboratory or a library can only contribute to the achievement of students who utilize them and since the coefficients estimate an average effect across all students in a school, the coefficients probably *underestimate* the effects of the resource on the students who utilize them.

My third reason for counseling caution is that the dependent variable, *Verbal Achievement*, may in no way be representative of the outputs that the resources are intended to affect. Science laboratories might be effective for teaching a way of thinking—experienced teachers may exercise a more acceptable form of control over potentially unruly classes. Neither "resource" may contribute to the skills tapped by conventional standardized tests of achievement. Before policy can be made about specific resources, decisions about the priorities of outputs must be reached.

Nevertheless, I believe that results from this reexamination and from other reanalysis of the EEO data give important information to policy-makers. First, these results can be viewed as corroborating the results of much past educational research. For years educational researchers have published conflicting results about a wide variety of educational practices and resources. People have criticized this literature because it was inadequate either methodologically or conceptually. Although their criticisms may often have been just, many careful people pointed out that even inadequate research is generally sufficient to discover strong effects.

It seems to me that the same is true about the results of the examinations of the EEO Survey data. By now (1970) at least a half-dozen people have carried out extensive reanalyses of these data. Although some argue that school resource effects are apparent in the data (see Levin, 1970, and Michelson, 1970), no one argues that the effects are very strong. Instead they present the same arguments that I have for not believing the coefficients—arguing that the coefficients are biased downward and, therefore, that resources probably do have an effect.

I think this is the wrong approach to take. I think that we have now milked the EEOs data dry with respect to the "determinants" of verbal achievement. The overall results should be clear to policy-makers and researchers alike. With regard to the differences among schools in resources that we conventionally measure and consider in making policy, there are few that give us any leverage over students' achievement. Within the fairly broad boundaries of existing variations, the simple manipulation of per-pupil expenditure or the hiring of more experienced teachers or the instituting of a new curriculum does not lead to dramatic changes in students' verbal achievement. The myth that the reallocation of conventional inputs will lead to a redistribution of achievement outputs can no longer be accepted.

Research Implications of the Reexamination

Many implications for research can be drawn from this study. The most important fall into three categories.

1) Individuals should be followed in a true longitudinal study. Cross-sectional matching of schoolwide aggregates is not sufficient. If a longitudinal approach were followed, two important problems with the EEO Survey would be eliminated. First, an early achievement measure could be gathered—"gain" scores would be the dependent variables. This would substantially improve the accuracy of our estimates of the effects of various influences. Second, we should gather information about dropouts, transfers, etc., such that estimates of the importance of selection or assign-

ment into schools by achievement, race, or social class could be made.

2) Measurements of the access and utilization of resources for specific individuals must be made. Within-school differences generally account for over 80 percent of the total variation in achievement scores. Estimates of class-to-class variation must be calculated—therefore, pupils must be associated with their particular teachers. The importance of within-school mechanisms for selection and assignment must be estimated on an individual level. Until some estimates can be made of the differential impact that resources have on students within schools, it will be difficult to generate reasonable policy.

3) Multiple outputs must be specified. Scores on standardized achievement tests are not the schools' only output.

Even such a longitudinal study would leave a great deal to be desired. If, however, clear and reasonable results came from such a study, we would be a lot closer to knowing something about the effects of specific school resources and policy on achievement.

Unfortunately, even that would not satisfy the major policy question. For most of the nation's students the schools are successful at least in terms of results on standardized achievement tests. Only for a minority are the schools a dismal failure. It seems unlikely that anything that we could find in a longitudinal survey of students in schools as they presently exist will give us the information that we need to increase the efficacy of schools for the children who are presently failing.

In order to solve this problem we must modify substantially our present strategies of both research and schooling. Fully controlled and large-scale experiments must be funded and carried out. Until we adopt the experimental model, we will continue to founder in the swamp of uncontrolled plausible hypotheses. Furthermore, the available evidence strongly suggests that our present thinking about the problems of education is inadequate. If the beliefs of the nation leads to a policy of equality of opportunity in terms of achievement outputs, we may need to think about ways to restructure radically the educational institution rather than about ways to reallocate ineffective resources.

Notes

1. The seven conclusions are paraphrased from p. 325 of the EEOS Report.
2. A sixth set of variables considered in the Report were student attitudes. These measures, particularly the ones labeled *Control of Environment* and *Self Concept*, have strong associations with *Verbal Achievement*. However, their causal relationship to achievement is obscure. On the one hand, high achievement by a student may cause him to feel control over his environment or to have a positive self-concept; on the other hand, the attitudes might influence his achievement level.

Even though the association of the variable with achievement is unchallenged, the causal ordering is so unclear that I have not included the attitude measures in this reanalysis. For an interesting discussion of the attitude measures, see Banys (1968).

For clarity throughout this paper I have capitalized the first letters of the names of each of the four major sets of variables (Home Background, Student Body, Facilities and Curriculum, and Teacher Characteristics). In addition, the names of particular variables are italicized and their first letters capitalized.

3. I have been speaking of only one Home Background variable, one Facilities and Curriculum variable, etc. In the Report a set of variables were used for each of the various types of influences. The arguments and problems stated above are easily generalized to sets of variables.

4. Unfortunately, for the tired reader, the numbers for the first Teacher Characteristics column are not precisely those defined by $(R_{HT}^2 - R_H^2)$. Instead they are $(R_{HT}^2 - R_H^2) / (1 - R_H^2)$. The same holds for the other two schoolwide factors. These numbers can be interpreted as the percentage of variance explained by the school resource factor after the variance explained by the Home Background factor has been removed. The idea given above, however, is correct.

5. One would also need to explain the success of the "advantaged student" on achievement tests in 1st grade.

6. Under certain circumstances, the between-school percentages of variance shown above are slight underestimates of the amount of variance possibly explained by the school-to-school factors. Such a circumstance occurred in the discussion of the breakdown of variance for the 6th-grade whites. There I noted that with background controls the amount of variance explained by the Facilities and Curriculum factor was greater than without background controls.

7. All variables in the analysis are described in Appendix A. Three problems with the Home Background variables should be mentioned. First, the very high level of *nonresponses and don't-knows* for important student background items in grades 1, 3, and 6 makes the individual measurement of social class for students in these grades difficult. These items, e.g., Mother and Father's Education and Father's Occupation, are important in the traditional assessment of social class.

Second, a readability analysis of the 6th-grade questionnaire (Overlan, 1968) reveals that the reading grade level needed to understand the average item is about 4.5. This implies that at least 50 percent of all minority-group students would have difficulty just reading and understanding the items—much less accurately knowing the information needed to answer the question. (See Jencks, Chapter 12, for a complete discussion of the first two problems.)

Third, those students who did not respond or who did not answer an item were given the population means in the construction of the index. This undoubtedly resulted in an underestimation of the predictive power of the indices. Examination of the verbal means of students who answered "Don't know" or who did not respond to certain items suggests that these students are considerably below the population mean in achievement.

8. The variable, Father's Occupation, was not included in the analyses for two reasons: the item asking about the father's occupation had eleven difficult alternatives *and* one of the alternatives included both service and clerical workers —destroying the investigators' opportunity to make a standard white-collar–blue-collar distinction.

9. Some critics have argued that the ownership of reading items such as an encyclopedia or a dictionary may be caused by the achievement of children in the family, but these items are only two fifths or two thirds of one of the six indices.

10. The percentage of between-school variance seems fairly constant from 1st to 6th grades within the same schools for both groups. For a further discussion of the sources of variation within junior and senior high schools, see Chapter 7 by Cohen, Pettigrew, and Riley. They discuss the importance of estimating the within- and between-curriculum variation.

11. The supplemental appendix does not contain the proper variables for estimation of comparable numbers at the 1st and 3rd grades.

12. However, this may be due to either or both of two causes: 1) to slight differences in the questions asked in the 6th grade from the questions asked in the later grades, and/or 2) to differences in the accuracy of the answers between the grades.

13. Two points should be noted. For both whites and Orientals, there was a substantial increase in the explanatory power of the subjective background variables from the 6th to the 12th grades. The other groups studied in the Report behaved similarly to the blacks. The second point is that Coleman *et al.* investigated the possibility that the differences between the groups were due to differences in the amount of variation in the "subjective" variables within the groups. They concluded that "almost none of the variation in achievement accounted for is related to the different variances in each group" (p. 302).

14. A corroboration of this interpretation comes from the work of James Davis. In a study of educational and occupational aspirations, Davis found that students tend to form their opinions based on evidence from their immediate surroundings. See James Davis, "The Campus as a Frog Pond," *American Journal of Sociology*, Vol. 72, July, 1966, pp. 17–31.

15. Although the conclusions reached here as to the likely causal ordering of *Parents' Educational Desires* and individual achievement are not in agreement with Coleman's, they do coincide with interpretations of the Plowden Report made by David K. Cohen. Cohen notes that a Plowden measure of Parental Aspiration for the education of a child is "less an independent measure of an attitude than a reflection of knowledge of the child's level of achievement and, therefore, a realistic assessment of his actual academic prospects," HER, Vol. 38, No. 2, 1968, p. 334. Cohen also notes that another of Plowden's measures, *Parents' Interest in School*, might well be facilitating the achievement of the English students. As in the case of the equivalent variable in the Coleman Report, the association between this measure and student achievement rises slightly over the elementary-school years but has considerably less association with achievement in the later years than does the *Parental Desires and Expectations* variable.

16. The unit is somewhat difficult to interpret. The background variables were each formed by pooling a number of questionnaire items into indices after first standardizing each item to a zero mean and unit variance. The standardization was carried out over all students in the sample at each grade level. Thus subgroups of students will have means different from zero and standard deviations different from one for each of the various items. See Tables G–L in Appendix B for the values.

17. The general finding that the magnitude of home background "effect" on Negro achievement is less than the "effect" on white achievement is well known. See, for example, Wilson (1967), who concluded that ". . . the family has much more influence on the achievement of white students than Negro students."

18. As usual, the interpretation of results is very complex. In the 6th grade, the standard deviation of the independent variable (number of *Siblings*) is smaller for whites than for blacks and the standard deviation of the dependent variable (*Verbal Achievement*) is larger for whites than for blacks. Thus, although the standardized regression coefficients are very similar (.076 *vs.* .096), the raw regression coefficients are quite different. In particular, an increase of one unit in the number of *Siblings* (as contrasted to an increase of one standard deviation) results in an increase of .64 *Verbal Achievement* points for blacks and a similar increase of one unit for the whites results in a gain of 1.5 points in *Verbal Achievement*.

19. See, for example, A. Wilson, 1967.

20. One EEOS Report analysis of the effect of the composition of the student body on individual achievement did not use any of the six cited variables. (See Table 3.23.1, p. 303, and Table 3.231.1, p. 312.) Instead, the Mean School Achievement for all students in the school was used as the measure of the composition of the student body. This approach has the questionable property of accounting for school-to-school differences in achievement with a measure of school-to-school differences in achievement. Because the groups studied are stratified and therefore

do not include all of the students in a particular school, the overall school mean does not necessarily account for all of the among-school variation. However, due to the high incidence of segregated schools, the overall school mean achievement is often almost exactly equal to the mean achievement of the predominant group in the school. Therefore, to use the overall school mean as a student-body composition measure of school-to-school differences in achievement might be very misleading. Entered with the school-resource factors it would account for a substantial portion of unique variance while allowing the other factors to account for almost no unique variance.

21. It is reasonable that the schoolwide factor most sensitive to differences in individual background controls is the Student-Body factor. Each reduction in the strength of the Student-Body factor from the uncontrolled condition to the controlling condition used in the Report to the one intended for use in the Report might be considered to be due to the removal of individual social-class influences.

22. This interpretation is consistent with other research: Wilson, for example, found that black students are "more sensitive to variations in school milieu" than are whites (A. Wilson, 1967).

23. There are reasons to believe that the measures of school-to-school variation are not comparable from grade to grade. At other points in this paper I have warned the reader not to make too much of such comparisons. The reasons I give generally are those of differences in size, school, system-assignment practices, and pupil-selection practices. In some ways this section is examining the validity of these reasons.

24. If the measure had really been college aspirations of fellow students, the coefficients' change in sign would not have occurred. One possible reason for the change in sign is that some 9th-grade students may not have been assigned to a track or curriculum at the time that the questionnaire was administered. Few junior-high-school students, for example, are formally assigned to a particular track, and these students may have left the item blank. The correlation of this with other variables at the 9th-grade level is thus based on pupils in schools which assign the students to track early in the 9th grade—e.g., four- and six-year high schools. For each group the 9th-grade zero-order correlation of the variable with verbal achievement is positive, and it is only after other Student-Body composition variables have been added to the equation that the coefficient becomes negative. When the individual and aggregate social-class controlling variables are introduced, the coefficients drop dramatically. But in the 12th-grade case, the starting point is much higher, so the coefficients remain positive and even statistically significant.

One possible reason for this is that four- and six-year high schools are more prevalent in suburbs than in cities. These schools are less likely to have selected students on the basis of achievement than are city high schools without 9th grades. The proportions of students in the college tracks in these comprehensive school are probably positively related to achievement. Now suppose that the strength of that relationship is less than the relationship between social-class composition of the schools and achievement; then the association between the *College Track* variable and achievement at the 9th grade might be reduced to zero and possibly overcorrected by the introduction of the social-class controls.

A second possibility might be different dropout rates in schools with high and low percentages of college-tracked students. It might be, for example, that the low verbal achievers in schools with high porportions of college-bound students are more likely to drop out than are low achievers in schools with a low percentage of students in the college track. Since dropouts do not ordinarily occur until after the 9th grade, the effect of this would not show up until 12th grade. Conversely, high-achieving students might be more likely to drop out of schools with a low percentage of college-bound students.

This second possibility is closer to the Report's interpretation. Differential dropout rates might indeed be heavily influenced by the aspirations and characteristics of the student bodies of the schools. But even so, the measure at best offers inconclusive support for a student-body composition effect that is independent of the individual social class of the students. Even if it measures precisely what the authors of the Report wanted it to, the fact remains that when entered with individual background and with other schoolwide factors, the variable has a significant coefficient only for 12th-grade blacks.

25. The Transfer Rate variable does *not* count dropouts as transfers.

26. In addition, see Armor (Chapter 5) and Hanushek (1968). Armor found only a very small coefficient in the Northern Urban region for an especially constructed facilities variable. Hanushek argues that he found an important set of school variables for a Northern urban sample, but he included no facilities or curriculum variable in his equations for either black or whites.

27. Coleman described this selection procedure. "The next step in the examination is to introduce certain selected facilities and curriculum measures which gave evidence in early analyses of showing most relation to achievement or appear to be intrinsically important in school policy (such as grouping or tracking). Some facilities measures, such as the pupil/teacher ratio in instruction, are not included because they showed a consistent lack of relation to achievement among all groups under all conditions" (p. 312).

28. Coleman also noted the strength of the *School Size* variable at the 12th grade and in an analysis of the effect of the variable in urban and rural populations concluded that:

> This again suggests that quite apart from facilities and curriculum, the smallest and most rural schools have lower achievement than larger and more urban schools, but the largest and most urban do not have higher achievement than those of middle size and again, that this is most true for Negroes (p. 314).

29. To complete either interpretation I must account for the increase from 9th to 12th grades in the zero-order relationship between *Accelerated Curriculum* and achievement. For whites the explanation is easy. Accelerated curricula are conducive to white achievement, *and* accelerated curricula are generally in schools with other resources, uncontrolled in the zero-order relationship, which are even more conducive to achievement. For blacks I must postulate that, although accelerated curricula have a negative effect, other characteristics of schools with accelerated curricula have positive effects.

30. In particular, see Levin (1970), Michelson (1970) and Hanushek (1968). *Average Teacher Verbal Score* and *Teacher Experience* are the two variables most favored.

31. An inspection of Tables A–F in Appendix B shows that there is little difference in the relationship between the Teacher Characteristics factor and student achievement when either the six objective or the four objective and two subjective background variables are used as controls.

32. Because the numbers in Table 24 include the three-way overlap of the Teachers Characteristics and the Student-Body factors, some of the overlap between the Teacher Characteristics and the Student-Body factor is also shared with the Facilities and Curriculum factor.

33. This second conclusion also states that: "In addition, teacher differences are over twice as strongly related to achievement of Southern Negroes as to achievement of Northern Negroes."

34. The background variables used as controls are somewhat different in this analysis, but this has little effect on the relationship between the Teacher Characteristics factor and achievement (see Tables A–F in Appendix B).

35. The reader is, of course, invited to spin a theory to explain the results that I have labeled as hopeless. The coefficients in Tables G–L of Appendix B offer a fertile field in which to plow.

36. It may be surprising that mean *Teachers' Verbal Score* does not evince a strong relationship to student achievement. Although there are a number of problems with the measure, particularly the fact the test was not supervised and there is some evidence that teachers collaborated, other investigators have found that it has a statistically significant relationship to achievement (see Hanushek, 1968; Levin, 1970; and Michelson, 1970). However, each of these investigators used somewhat

different samples than was used here. Hanushek analyzed urban schools in the New England, Mid-Atlantic, and Great Lakes regions of the country. Both Levin and Michelson studied a single SMSA in the northeast. Additionally, there are still other investigators who have found nonsignificant or conflicting results (see Armor, Chapter 5, and Jencks, Chapter 2).

37. Two interesting points might be noted. The finding that mobile teachers have a positive effect on whites and a negative effect on blacks corresponds to the finding that white students from mobile families achieve more and black students from nonmobile families achieve higher. Second, large cities are more likely to have requirements that their teachers be local products. The variable may thus be measuring a suburb-inner city difference.

Appendix A

Description of Variables in
Equality of Educational Opportunity Survey Report Regression Equations
for 6th, 9th, and 12th Grades
(Variable numbers are those used in the Supplemental Appendix.)

Home Background Factor

All variables in the factor were constructed of items from the student questionnaire. Each item was standardized to a zero mean and unit variance. Nonresponses to items were assigned a zero value. Indices were formed by summing the standard scores and dividing by the number of scores. An increment of 1 in a score is roughly equal to an increase of 1 standard deviation. All are individual level variables.

Objective Home Background Variables

39—URBANISM OF BACKGROUND.   This variable is made up of questions about the communities where the student and the mother grew up: A two-item index was used. The place where the student was born was weighted twice in forming the index. A positive score indicates an urban background. (Questionnaire items 6, and 21 in 9th and 12th grades; items 3 and 13 in grade 6.)

40—PARENTS' EDUCATION.   This variable was intended to be an index made up of the sum of a standardized measure of students' father and mother's education. Due to a processing error, however, father's education was not included in the measure. It has been estimated since the publication of the report that this error had very little effect. A positive score indicates more education. (Questionnaire items 19 and 20 in grades 9 and 12; 11 and 14 in grade 6.)

6—STRUCTURAL INTEGRITY OF THE FAMILY. This variable is made up of items about who acts as the student's mother and father—the two questions were standardized and summed after being dichotomized into measures with a *one* denoting the reported presence of the real parent and a *zero* the absence of the real parent. (Questionnaire items 16 and 17 in grades 9 and 12; 9 and 10 in grade 6.)

5—SIBLINGS. This variable is made up of one question about the number of brothers and sisters that the student has. A positive score indicates few siblings. (Questionnaire item 10 in grades 9 and 12; 8 in grade 6.)

4—ITEMS IN THE HOME. This variable is made up of six questions about if the home contained a TV, phone, vacuum cleaner, record player, refrigerator, and automobile. A positive score indicates many amenities. (Questionnaire items 31, 32, 33, 34, 37, and 38 in grades 9 and 12; 19, 20, 21, 22, 25, and 26 in grade 6.)

3—READING MATERIAL IN THE HOME. This variable is made up of five questions in the 9th and 12th grades and three questions in the 6th grade. Dictionary, encyclopedia, daily newspaper were included in all three grades and magazines and books in two. A positive score indicates many reading materials. (Questionnaire items 35, 36, 39, 41, and 42 in grades 9 and 12; 23, 24, and 27 in grade 6.)

Subjective Home Background Variables

45—PARENTS' INTEREST. This variable is made up of questions about how much the student talked with parents about school and whether or not the student was read to before he entered school. A positive score indicates greater parental interest. (Questionnaire items 26 and 30 in grades 9 and 12; 18 and 54 in grade 6.)

44—PARENTS' EDUCATIONAL DESIRES. In 9th and 12th grades this variable was made up of the answers to five items: how good a student the mother and father want the student to be; how far in school the mother and father want the child to go; and the extent of parents' attendance of the PTA. In the 6th grade only the first two items were used to form the variable. A positive score indicates stronger parental desires. (Questionnaire items 27, 28, 29, 24, and 25 in grades 9 and 12; 41 and 42 in grade 6.)

Student-Body Factor

Variables were formed from items on the Student, Principal, and Teacher questionnaires; all variables are schoolwide measures.

10—PROPORTION FAMILIES OWN ENCYCLOPEDIA. This variable was formed by aggregating responses to a question about family ownership of an encyclopedia across all students in the school. Missing data were not included in the computation. Possible Range = 0 to 1.00. (Student questionnaire item 36 in grades 9 and 12; item 24 in grade 6.)

26—STUDENT TRANSFERS. This variable is a measure of the principal's estimate of the total percentage of pupils transferring in and out of school the preceding year. Two items were used. The items were summed and divided by 2. If one was blank, the other was divided by 1. If both were blank, the variable was treated as missing. A high score means more transfers. Possible range is 0–100. (Principal Questionnaire items 44 and 45.)

31—ATTENDANCE. This variable is the principal's estimate of the average daily attendance of the students' schools. Possible range from 00 to 100. (Principal Questionnaire item 42.)

52—PROPORTION IN COLLEGE TRACK. This variable was aggregated from student records and equals the proportion of students in the school who reported that they were in the College Track. Possible Range = 0 to 1.00. Used only in the 9th- and 12-grade analyses. (Student Questionnaire item 43 in grades 9 and 12.)

53—AVERAGE HOURS HOMEWORK. This variable was formed by aggregating six student responses to a question about the amount of homework they do. The measure ranges from 1–7 (e.g., from zero to four hours/day of homework). A score of 4.5 means between 1.5 and 2.0 hours of homework averaged/day. Used only at 9th and 12th grades. (Student Questionnaire item 61 at grades 9 and 12.)

25—TEACHER PERCEPTION OF STUDENT-BODY QUALITY. This variable was aggregated from teacher responses to questions about the characteristics of their schools' students. The items were summed after being standardized to a zero mean and unit variance. A negative number means high quality. Used only at the 6th grade. (Teacher Questionnaires items 33, 34, and 37.)

Facilities and Curriculum Factor

Variables were formed from the Student, Principal, and Superintendent questionnaires. All Student and Principal variables are schoolwide measures—the Superintendent variable is systemwide.

38—PER-PUPIL INSTRUCTIONAL EXPENDITURE. This variable is an estimate of the instructional dollars per pupil averaged over the *entire* school system. (Superintendent Questionnaire item 41B.)

23—VOLUMES PER STUDENT. This variable is an estimate of the number of library volumes per pupil. It was obtained by dividing the number of volumes by the number of pupils. (Principal Questionnaire items 13B and 40.)

22—PERCENTAGE SCIENCE LAB FACILITIES. This variable is the percentage of three kinds of science laboratories in the school: biology, chemistry, physics. The range is 0 to 99.0. The variable was computed by adding 1 to numerator for Principal Questionnaire items $13k = 1$, $13L = 1$, $13M = 1$; Add 1.01 to denominator for $13K = 1$, 2, 3, for $13L = 1$, 2, 3, for $13M = 1$, 2, 3; test for blank in denominator; give blank if so— otherwise divide. Used only at the 9th and 12th grades. (Principal Questionnaire, item 13.)

24—EXTRACURRICULAR ACTIVITIES. This variable is the percentage of the nineteen extracurricular activities available at the school listed in the Principal Questionnaire. Blanks were not counted in denominator or numerator. Range is 0–99.0. The variable was used at the 9th and 12th grades. (Principal Questionnaire, item 90.)

36—ACCELERATED CURRICULUM. This variable assesses the extent to which accelerated curricula are in the school. $1 =$ Yes AC in all subjects; $2 =$ Yes in several; $3 =$ Yes in one or two; $4 =$ No. (Principal Questionnaire, item 80.)

25—COMPREHENSIVENESS OF CURRICULUM. This variable is the proportion (9th grade) or percentage (12th grade) of six kinds of curriculum available at the school (college preparatory, commercial, general, vocational, agricultural, industrial arts). It was computed in the following manner: add one to numerator for Yes on college prep; commercial and general; add 1.01 to denominator if Yes or No on same 3 curricula. Do same for only one of Voc., Agri., or Indus. Arts. Maximum is four. Range from 0 to .99 at the 9th grade and 0–99.0 at the 12th grade. The variable was used only at 9th and 12th grades. (Principal Questionnaire, item 78.)

35—TRACKING. This variable assesses the extent of tracking in the school. $1 =$ tracking for all students; $2 =$ tracking for highest achieving students only; $3 =$ tracking for lowest achieving students only; $4 =$ no tracking at all. The variable was used only at 9th and 12th grades. (Principal Questionnaire, item 80.)

37—MOVEMENT BY TRACKS. This variable assesses the extent to which there is movement between the tracks. Two items were used in the variables' construction. If one is blank, add other to itself. High score means lots of movement. Measure ranges from 0–18. Coding on the two items are, A = blank, None = 0, 1–4% = 1, 5–9% = 2, 10–14% = 3, 15 =19% = 4, 20–39% = 6, 40–59% = 8, 60% + = 9. The variable was used only at the 9th and 12th grades. (Principal Questionnaire, items 84 and 85.)

9—SCHOOL SIZE. This variable is the number of students in the particular school grade. Its value is the number of students completing a questionnaire for that school grade.

33—LOCATION. This variable specifies the demographic location of the school. 1 = rural, 2 = small town (5000 or less), 3 = city (5000 to 50,000), 4 = residential suburb, 5 = industrial suburb, 6 = residential area of larger city (over 50,000), 7 = inner city (over 50,000). (Principal Questionnaire, item 72.)

30—GUIDANCE COUNSELOR. This variable assesses the number of guidance counselors in the school. Range from 0–9. 0 = no guidance counselor; 1 = one, less than fulltime; 2 = one fulltime; 3 = 1.5; 4 = 2; 5 = 3; 6 = 4; 7 = 5; 8 = 6; 9 = 7 and 7+. The variable was used only at the 9th and 12th grades. (Principal Questionnaire, item 35.)

37—PROMOTION SLOW LEARNERS. This variable assesses the school's policy toward slow learners. The range is between 1 and 4. A high score signifies that pupils are transferred to another school; a middle score signifies that they are promoted with age group; a low score signifies that pupils must repeat grades. This variable was used only at the 6th grade. (Principal Questionnaire, item 89.)

Teacher Characteristics Factor

All variables are schoolwide. Individual teacher responses to questionnaire items were aggregated "to obtain averages for the teaching staff in that school. For grades 1, 3, and 6, aggregation was done only over teachers who taught grades 1–6; for grade 9, aggregation was done only over teachers who taught grades 7–12; and for grade 12, aggregation was done only over teachers who taught grades 9–12" (EEOS Report, p. 316).

17—TEACHER VERBAL ACHIEVEMENT SCORE. This variable is the average teacher's score on a thirty-item test of verbal skill. Range from 0–30.

15—TEACHER DEGREE RECEIVED. This variable measures the average educational level of the school's teachers. 1 = no degree; 2 = less than 4 years; 3 = Bachelor's; 4 = Master's; 5 = Specialist's; 6 = Doctorate. (Teacher Questionnaire, item 11.)

11—TEACHER SES. This variable measures the average of the teachers' mothers' education. 1 = none; 2 = grade school; 3 = some H.S.; 4 = H.S.; 5 = H.S. +; 6 = some college; 7 = B.A. or B.S.; 8 = college +. (Teacher Questionnaire, item 10.)

16—TEACHER PREFERENCE FOR TYPE OF STUDENT BODY. This variable is the average of the sum of 3 standardized items. The first item measures the type of school that teacher wishes to teach in; the second measures the type or class of children; the third measures the ability grouping of children the teacher likes to teach. Low score = teachers prefer middle-class students. High = teachers prefer lower-class students (Teacher Questionnaire, items 39, 40, 43.)

12—TEACHERS' EXPERIENCE. This variable is the average total number of years taught by teachers in the school. (Teacher Questionnaire, item 25.)

13—TEACHERS' LOCALISM. This variable is the average sum of a set of standardized items measuring the parochialism of the school's teachers. Low score = local teachers, high = outside teachers. (Teacher Questionnaire, items 3, 7, and 15 added to the ratio of item 25/26.)

18—TEACHERS' RACE. This variable measures the proportion of teachers in school who are white. Proportion white, Range = 0–1.00. (Teacher Questionnaire, item 5.)

School Racial Composition

48—PROPORTION STUDENTS WHITE. This variable is an estimate of the proportion of white students in the school grade. It was formed by dividing the number of students who responded that they were white by the total number of students returning questionnaire. (Student Questionnaire, item 5.)

Appendix B

This appendix contains two sets of tables (A–F and G–L). Full explanations of the tables are contained in Section I of this chapter. The variables referenced in the tables are described in Appendix A.

TABLE A

Sixth-Grade Northern Blacks

Table showing the Allocation of the Percentages of Total Variance of Individual Verbal Achievement Scores for Three Sets of Schoolwide Influences (Student Body Composition, Facilities and Curriculum, and Teacher Characteristics) Into Independently and Jointly Explained Components. Three conditions are presented. The first is with four objective and two subjective Individual Background variables controlled. The second is with six objective Individual Background variables controlled. The third is without background controls.

	With Background Controls		No Background Controls
	1 (4 obj., 2 subj.)[1]	2 (6 obj.)[2]	3
Student Body Uniquely	1.61	1.34	3.12
Facilities and Curriculum Uniquely	0.16	0.16	0.14
Teacher Characteristics Uniquely	1.55	1.50	1.64
Student Body and Facilities	0.27	0.25	0.34
Student Body and Teachers	0.17	0.09	1.02
Facilities and Teachers	0.25	0.21	0.38
Student Body and Facilities and Teachers	0.02	0.02	0.29
Total =	4.03	3.57	6.93

[1] The four objective variables used as controls are *Siblings*, *Items in the Home*, *Structural Integrity of the Family*, and *Reading Material in the Home*. The two subjective variables are *Parents' Interest* and *Parents' Educational Desires*. The same variables are used as controls in column 1 of Tables B–F in this Appendix.

[2] The six objective variables include the four specified in footnote 1 and *Parents' Education* and *Urbanism of Background*. The same six variables are used as controls in column 2 of Tables B–F in this Appendix.

TABLE B

Sixth-Grade Northern Whites

Table showing the Allocation of the Percentages of Total Variance of Individual Verbal Achievement Scores for Three Sets of Schoolwide Influences (Student Body Composition, Facilities and Curriculum, and Teacher Characteristics) Into Independently and Jointly Explained Components. Three conditions are presented. The first is with four objective and two subjective Individual Background variables controlled. The second is with six objective Individual Background variables controlled. The third is without background controls.

	With Background Controls		No Background Controls
	1 (4 obj., 2 subj.)	2 (6 obj.)	3
Student Body Uniquely	1.98	1.10	4.32
Facilities and Curriculum Uniquely	0.31	0.24	0.22
Teacher Characteristics Uniquely	0.55	0.46	0.58
Student Body and Facilities	0.00	0.01	0.16
Student Body and Teachers	0.96	0.41	2.01
Facilities and Teachers	0.07	0.08	0.00
Student Body and Facilities and Teachers	−0.09	−0.09	0.06
Total =	3.78	2.22	7.35

TABLE C

Ninth-Grade Northern Blacks

Table showing the Allocation of the Percentages of Total Variance of Individual Verbal Achievement Scores for Three Sets of Schoolwide Influences (Student-Body Composition, Facilities and Curriculum, and Teacher Characteristics) Into Independently and Jointly Explained Components. Three conditions are presented. The first is with four objective and two subjective Individual Background variables controlled. The second is with six objective Individual Background variables controlled. The third is without background controls.

	With Background Controls		No Background Controls
	1 (4 obj., 2 subj.)	2 (6 obj.)	3
Student Body Uniquely	1.81	1.58	2.74
Facilities and Curriculum Uniquely	0.99	1.14	0.95
Teacher Characteristics Uniquely	0.66	0.62	0.69
Student Body and Facilities	0.56	0.63	0.65
Student Body and Teachers	1.01	0.91	1.79
Facilities and Teachers	0.19	0.03	0.25
Student Body and Facilities and Teachers	−0.46	−0.49	−0.47
Total =	4.76	4.42	6.60

TABLE D

Ninth-Grade Northern Whites

Table showing the Allocation of the Percentages of Total Variance of Individual Verbal Achievement Scores for Three Sets of Schoolwide Influences (Student-Body Composition, Facilities and Curriculum, and Teacher Characteristics) Into Independently and Jointly Explained Components. Three conditions are presented. The first is with four objective and two subjective Individual Background variables controlled. The second is with six objective Individual Background variables controlled. The third is without background controls.

	With Background Controls		No Background Controls
	1 (4 obj., 2 subj.)	2 (6 obj.)	3
Student Body Uniquely	0.80	0.46	1.57
Facilities and Curriculum Uniquely	0.78	0.86	1.57
Teacher Characteristics Uniquely	0.58	0.68	0.75
Student Body and Facilities	0.05	0.00	0.34
Student Body and Teachers	0.48	0.28	1.05
Facilities and Teachers	−0.22	−0.19	−0.39
Student Body and Facilities and Teachers	−0.03	0.01	0.40
Total =	2.44	2.10	5.29

TABLE E

Twelfth-Grade Northern Blacks

Table showing the Allocation of the Percentages of Total Variance of Individual Verbal Achievement Scores for Three Sets of Schoolwide Influences (Student-Body Composition, Facilities and Curriculum, and Teacher Characteristics) Into Independently and Jointly Explained Components. Three conditions are presented. The first is with four objective and two subjective Individual Background variables controlled. The second is with six objective Individual Background variables controlled. The third is without background controls.

	With Background Controls		No Background Controls
	1 (4 obj., 2 subj.)	2 (6 obj.)	3
Student Body Uniquely	2.08	1.78	2.75
Facilities and Curriculum Uniquely	0.91	1.02	0.90
Teacher Characteristics Uniquely	1.12	0.92	0.98
Student Body and Facilities	1.20	1.23	1.39
Student Body and Teachers	2.08	2.02	2.33
Facilities and Teachers	−0.50	−0.36	−0.31
Student Body and Facilities and Teachers	1.24	0.46	3.08
Total =	8.13	7.07	11.12

TABLE F

Twelfth-Grade Northern Whites

Table showing the Allocation of the Percentages of Total Variance of Individual Verbal Achievement Scores for Three Sets of Schoolwide Influences (Student Body Composition, Facilities and Curriculum, and Teacher Characteristics) Into Independently and Jointly Explained Components. Three conditions are presented. The first is with four objective and two subjective Individual Background variables controlled. The second is with six objective Individual Background variables controlled. The third is without background controls.

	With Background Controls		*No Background Controls*
	1 *(4 obj., 2 subj.)*	*2* *(6 obj.)*	*3*
Student Body Uniquely	0.51	0.47	1.45
Facilities and Curriculum Uniquely	0.97	0.80	0.95
Teacher Characteristics Uniquely	0.68	0.60	0.92
Student Body and Facilities	0.01	−0.12	0.38
Student Body and Teachers	0.30	0.30	1.38
Facilities and Teachers	0.08	0.00	0.01
Student Body and Facilities and Teachers	0.39	0.13	1.69
Total =	2.94	2.18	6.76

TABLE G

Means, Standard Deviations, and Standardized Regression Coefficients for Selected Independent Variables in a Number of Regression Equations With Verbal Achievement as the Dependent Variable

Sixth-Grade Northern Blacks
Verbal Mean = 24.1966, S.D. = 9.1030

		1	2	3	4	5	6	7
	Variable	Mean	S.D.	Zero-Order R w/Verbal	Betas for Full Equation	Betas for Equations w/Fact. & Family Bkgrd. Alone	Betas for Equations w/o Family Bkgrd.	Betas for Equation w/Only 1 Factor
Family Bkgrd. Factor								
3	Reading Material	−0.0359	0.7018	.21†	.11†			
4	Items in Home	0.0030	0.5358	.23†	.13†			
5	Siblings	−0.1967	1.0761	.12†	.08*			
6	Structural Integrity	−0.1101	0.8097	.09†	.06			
39	Parents' Educ.	−0.0123	0.9097	.17†	.10†			
40	Urbanism of Bkgrd.	0.0315	1.2863	.02	.01			
Facilities and Curriculum Factor								
38	Per Pupil Expend.	484.7192	111.0183	.07*	.01	.04	.02	.07*
23	Volume/Student	3.6973	5.0532	.03	.02	−.01	.02	.01
09	School Size	91.9283	50.7859	.03	−.01	−.01	−.01	.01
33	School Location	5.1197	2.1169	.02	−.03	−.04	−.00	.00
37	Promotion Slow Learners	2.7988	1.4183	−.07*	−.02	−.06*	−.02	−.07*
36	Accelerated Curriculum	3.2982	1.1090	−.04	−.02	−.02	−.02	−.03
Student-Body Factor								
10	Proportion Own Encyclopedia	0.6415	0.1465	.20†	.06	.09†	.15†	.18†
26	Student Transfer	10.9076	8.5403	−.02	.01	−.01	.01	−.00
31	Attendance	93.3065	3.3833	.08*	.06	.02	.06	.03
55	T Percept. of Student Quality	0.2753	0.3676	−.12†	−.09*	−.07*	−.10*	−.07*
Teacher Characteristics								
11	T SES Level	3.7101	0.5935	.00	−.00	.01	.01	.05
12	T Experience	11.2591	3.6628	.09†	.02	.06	.03	.09†
13	T Localism	0.0632	0.8032	−.11†	−.13†	−.09†	−.13†	−.10†
15	T Degree Received	3.1438	0.2640	−.03	−.02	−.03	−.02	−.01
16	T Preference for Student Body	0.2095	0.6618	−.08*	.01	−.02	.01	−.04
17	T Verbal Score	21.6620	2.6468	.08†	.01	.00	.01	.02
18	T Race	0.5592	0.3646	.11†	.04	.05	.05	.08
48	Proportion School White	0.2431	0.3027	.15†	−.01		−.03	

* Significant at the .05 level.
† Significant at the .01 level.

TABLE H

Means, Standard Deviations, and Standardized Regression Coefficients for Selected Independent Variables in a Number of Regression Equations With Verbal Achievement as the Dependent Variable

Sixth-Grade Northern White
Verbal Mean = 36.1482, S.D. = 11.4087

		1	2	3	4	5	6	7
						Betas for Equations w/Fact. & Family Bkgrd. Alone	Betas for Equations w/o Family Bkgrd.	
	Variable	Mean	S.D.	Zero-Order R w/Verbal	Betas for Full Equation			Betas for Equation w/Only 1 Factor
	Family Bkgrd. Factor							
3	Reading Material	0.293	0.510	.23†	.12†			
4	Items in Home	0.311	0.340	.22†	.08*			
5	Siblings	0.241	0.758	.13†	.10†			
6	Structural Integrity	0.236	0.580	.11†	.06*			
39	Parents' Educ.	0.277	0.877	.28†	.19†			
40	Urbanism of Bkgrd.	0.067	1.242	−.10†	−.09†			
	Facilities and Curriculum Factor							
38	Per-Pupil Expenditure	492.614	174.525	.04	.01	.00	.02	.04
23	Volume/Student	4.687	5.134	.02	−.01	.01	−.01	.02
09	School Size	80.215	47.606	.01	.01	.00	−.01	.00
33	School Location	3.654	1.745	−.00	−.04	−.05	−.03	−.01
37	Promotion Slow Learners	2.696	1.451	−.03	−.01	−.02	−.02	−.04
36	Accelerated Curriculum	3.074	1.165	−.03	.00	.00	−.01	−.03
	Student-Body Factor							
10	Proportion Own Encyclopedia	0.807	0.113	.21†	−.01	.01	.09*	.12†
26	Student Transfer	7.507	6.501	−.00	.03	.01	.04	.03
31	Attendance	91.132	2.520	.08†	−.01	.01	.01	.03
55	T Percept. of Student Quality	−0.135	0.423	−.23†	−.10†	−.12†	−.15†	−.17†
	Teacher Characteristics							
11	T SES Level	3.729	0.634	.07*	.01	.01	.01	.03
12	T Experience	11.736	4.561	−.01	.04	.04	.04	.04
13	T Localism	0.055	0.796	.07*	.03	.04	.05	.07
15	T Degree Received	3.022	0.317	.05	−.01	−.02	.01	.04
16	T Pref. for Student Body	−0.240	0.712	−.10†	−.01	−.04	−.03	−.09†
17	T Verbal Score	23.341	2.063	.05	.02	.03	.01	.04
18	T Race	0.965	0.074	.09†	.03	.06*	.04	.09†
48	Proportion School White	0.877	0.143	.16†	.06		.04	

* Significant at the .05 level.
† Significant at the .01 level.

TABLE I

Means, Standard Deviations, and Standardized Regression Coefficients for
Selected Independent Variables in a Number of Regression Equations
With Verbal Achievement as the Dependent Variable

Ninth-Grade Northern Black
Verbal Mean = 40.8533, S.D. = 12.5671

		1	2	3	4	5	6	7
	Variable	Mean	S.D.	Zero-Order R w/Verbal	Betas for Full Equation	Betas for Equations w/Fact. & Family Bkgrd. Alone	Betas for Equations w/o Family Bkgrd.	Betas for Equation w/Only 1 Factor
Family Background Factor								
3	Reading Material	0.010	0.593	.16†	.08*			
4	Items in Home	0.014	0.544	.15†	.05			
5	Siblings	−0.253	1.017	.20†	.13†			
6	Structural Integrity	−0.184	0.856	.11†	.07*			
39	Parents' Educ.	−0.009	0.840	.16†	.09†			
40	Urbanism of Bkgrd.	0.462	1.210	.09†	.04			
Facilities and Curriculum Factor								
38	Per-Pupil Expenditure	512.695	142.116	.00	.01	−.04	.04	−.00
23	Volume/Student	5.581	5.735	−.04	−.01	−.01	−.02	−.03
22	Science Lab.	50.752	45.549	.02	.01	.05	−.01	.03
24	Extracurr. Act.	65.009	13.155	.04	.04	.01	.05	.03
36	Accelerated Curr.	2.830	1.041	−.06	−.06	−.04	−.06	−.05
25	Comprehensiveness of Curriculum	0.919	0.168	.00	−.06	−.01	−.08	−.02
35	Tracking	1.996	0.662	−.00	.04	.03	.03	.02
27	Movement Between Tracks	7.210	7.423	−.06	−.08*	−.06	−.08*	−.06
9	School Size	312.015	188.776	.08†	.01	.06	.01	.06
30	Guidance Counselor	6.426	3.975	.05	−.01	−.02	−.03	−.02
33	School Location	5.181	1.858	.03	−.01	−.04	.04	.01
Student-Body Factor								
10	Proportion Own Encyclopedia	0.758	0.107	.18†	.05	.11†	.12*	.19†
26	Student Transfer	7.558	6.087	−.09†	−.07	−.07*	−.08*	−.07*
31	Attendance	91.367	4.041	.10†	.03	.05	.01	.03
52	Proportion College Track	0.339	0.136	.08*	−.08	−.04	−.08	−.04
53	Average Hours of Homework	4.113	0.380	.09†	.07	.06	.07	.06

* Significant at the .05 level.
† Significant at the .01 level.

TABLE I Continued

	Variable	Mean	S.D.	Zero-Order R w/Verbal	Betas for Full Equation	Betas for Equations w/Fact. & Family Bkgrd. Alone	Betas for Equations w/o Family Bkgrd.	Betas for Equation w/Only 1 Factor
		1	2	3	4	5	6	7
Teacher Characteristics
11	T SES Level	3.790	0.480	.04	.04	−.01	.07	.04
12	T Experience	10.483	3.441	.01	−.08	−.01	−.08	−.02
13	T Localism	0.061	0.790	−.03	−.04	.00	−.04	−.03
15	T Degree Received	3.414	0.213	.09†	.08	.04	.08	.06
16	T Preference for Student Body	0.280	0.749	−.08*	.07	−.04	.06	−.05
17	T Verbal Score	22.158	2.300	.12†	.03	.08*	.04	.09*
18	T Race	0.624	0.348	.09†	−.10	.00	−.10	.00
48	Proportion School White	0.311	0.329	.14†	.22†		.20*	

* Significant at the .05 level.
† Significant at the .01 level.

TABLE J

Means, Standard Deviations, and Standardized Regression Coefficients for Selected Independent Variables in a Number of Regression Equations With Verbal Achievement as the Dependent Variable

Ninth-Grade Northern White
Verbal Mean = 55.4182, S.D. = 13.8927

	Variable	Mean	S.D.	Zero-Order R w/Verbal	Betas for Full Equation	Betas for Equations w/Fact. & Family Bkgrd. Alone	Betas for Equations w/o Family Bkgrd.	Betas for Equation w/Only 1 Factor
		1	2	3	4	5	6	7
Family Background Factor
3	Reading Material	0.242	0.477	.27†	.11†			
4	Items in Home	0.290	0.319	.17†	.04			
5	Siblings	0.375	0.801	.21†	.14†			
6	Structural Integrity	0.267	0.572	.14†	.08†			
39	Parents' Educ.	0.253	0.850	.33†	.23†			

† Significant at the .01 level.

TABLE J Continued

Variable	1 Mean	2 S.D.	3 Zero-Order R w/Verbal	4 Betas for Full Equation	5 Betas for Equations w/Fact. & Family Bkgrd. Alone	6 Betas for Equations w/o Family Bkgrd.	7 Betas for Equation w/Only 1 Factor
40 Urbanism of Bkgrd.	0.138	1.192	.12†	.07			
Facilities and Curriculum Factor							
38 Per-Pupil Expenditure	492.378	179.586	.07*	.06	.02	.08*	.06
23 Volume/Student	6.106	4.172	.06	.02	.02	.02	.03
22 Science Lab.	57.552	43.255	−.02	.01	−.00	−.02	−.07
24 Extracurr. Act.	64.388	14.637	.05	.00	.01	.02	.06
36 Accelerated Curr.	2.633	1.014	−.03	.00	−.00	.00	−.02
25 Comprehensiveness of Curriculum	0.940	0.167	−.08	−.08*	−.07*	−.11†	−.10†
35 Tracking	2.073	0.582	−.01	−.01	.00	−.00	.01
27 Movement Between Tracks	6.991	5.904	.00	.02	−.00	.01	.00
9 School Size	289.594	157.617	.04	.02	−.03	.03	−.00
30 Guidance Counselor	4.904	3.019	.06	−.01	.01	.02	.04
33 School Location	4.005	1.705	.04	.00	−.03	.02	−.03
Student-Body Factor							
10 Proportion Own Encyclopedia	0.851	0.079	.17†	.01	.05	.10*	.17†
26 Student Transfer	5.069	4.223	−.02	−.03	−.03	−.01	.01
31 Atttendance	94.272	2.442	.08*	.05	.06*	.06	.07*
52 Proportion College Track	0.393	0.170	.06*	−.02	−.04	.00	−.00
53 Average Hours of Homework	4.072	0.410	.01	.01	−.00	.02	−.00
Teacher Characteristics							
11 T SES Level	3.820	0.477	.03	−.00	−.03	.01	−.01
12 T Experience	9.776	3.324	−.04	−.02	−.01	−.03	−.05
13 T Localism	0.031	0.807	.05	.07	.06	.07	.05
15 T Degree Received	3.348	0.201	.05	−.02	−.01	−.02	.06
16 T Preference for Student Body	−0.316	0.672	−.08*	.03	.00	.00	−.06
17 T Verbal Score	23.226	1.511	.00	−.01	−.00	.01	−.00
18 T Race	0.959	0.059	.07*	.03	.07*	.04	.08†
48 Proportion School White	0.881	0.137	.12†	.06		.05	

* Significant at the .05 level.
† Significant at the .01 level.

TABLE K

Means, Standard Deviations, and Standardized Regression Coefficients for Selected Independent Variables in a Number of Regression Equations With Verbal Achievement as the Dependent Variable

Twelfth-Grade Northern Black
Verbal Mean = 52.7150, S.D. = 14.5147

	Variable	Mean	S.D.	Zero-Order R w/Verbal	Betas for Full Equation	Betas for Equations w/Fact. & Family Bkgrd. Alone	Betas for Equations w/o Family Bkgrd.	Betas for Equation w/Only 1 Factor
		1	*2*	*3*	*4*	*5*	*6*	*7*
Family Background Factor								
3	Reading Material	−0.007	0.597	.15†	.04			
4	Items in Home	0.020	0.541	.13†	.02			
5	Siblings	−0.258	1.018	.18†	.09†			
6	Structural Integrity	−0.170	0.835	.07*	.04			
39	Parents' Educ.	−0.045	0.830	.21†	.14†			
40	Urbanism of Bkgrd.	0.394	1.198	.14†	.05			
Facilities and Curriculum Factor								
38	Per-Pupil Expenditure	492.917	135.759	.00	−.00	−.03	.01	.01
23	Volume/Student	5.001	4.275	−.06*	−.05	−.06	−.03	−.07
22	Science Lab.	92.906	16.446	.11†	−.01	.10†	−.01	.11†
24	Extracurr. Act.	72.103	12.488	.13†	.03	.10*	.06	.14†
36	Accelerated Curr.	2.800	1.014	−.10†	−.02	−.08*	−.01	−.07*
25	Comprehensiveness of Curriculum	89.576	12.856	.04	−.02	−.06	−.03	−.08
35	Tracking	2.074	0.501	.03	.03	.07*	.04	.07*
27	Movement Between Tracks	7.153	7.254	.05	−.06	−.03	−.05	−.02
9	School Size	376.594	218.422	.08*	−.15†	−.04	−.13*	−.03
30	Guidance Counselor	8.988	4.524	.09†	.02	−.02	.02	−.02
33	School Location	5.110	1.999	.10†	.05	−.01	.08	.05
Student-Body Factor								
10	Proportion Own Encyclopedia	0.794	0.087	.24†	.07	.09*	.09	.13†
26	Student Transfer	7.154	5.012	−.08†	−.05	−.08*	−.05	−.07*
31	Attendance	90.987	3.995	.10†	.04	.06	.05	.04
52	Proportion College Track	0.381	0.148	.26†	.12*	.15†	.15†	.18†
53	Average Hours of Homework	4.672	0.508	.08*	−.05	−.02	−.03	.00

* Significant at the .05 level.
† Significant at the .01 level.

TABLE K Continued

	Variable	Mean	S.D.	Zero-Order R w/Verbal	Betas for Full Equation	Betas for Equations w/Fact. & Family Bkgrd. Alone	Betas for Equations w/o Family Bkgrd.	Betas for Equation w/Only 1 Factor
		1	2	3	4	5	6	7
Teacher Characteristics								
11	T SES Level	3.733	0.459	.05	.09	.05	.10	.08*
12	T Experience	11.746	2.988	.06	−.01	.01	−.02	−.01
13	T Localism	0.129	0.783	−.06	−.09	−.03	−.12*	−.08
15	T Degree Received	3.505	0.236	.12†	−.02	−.01	−.01	.05
16	T Preference for Student Body	0.332	0.670	−.18†	−.09	−.16†	−.07	−.17†
17	T Verbal Score	22.335	1.965	.13†	.04	.09*	.03	.10*
18	T Race	0.692	0.353	.08†	−.10	−.06	−.10	−.07
48	Proportion School White	0.413	0.359	.15†	.09		.06	

* Significant at the .05 level.
† Significant at the .01 level.

TABLE L

Means, Standard Deviations, and Standardized Regression Coefficients for Selected Independent Variables in a Number of Regression Equations With Verbal Achievement as the Dependent Variable

Twelfth-Grade Northern Whites
Verbal Mean = 67.6352, S.D. = 14.0792

	Variable	Mean	S.D.	Zero-Order R w/Verbal	Betas for Full Equation	Betas for Equations w/Fact. & Family Bkgrd. Alone	Betas for Equations w/o Family Bkgrd.	Betas for Equations w/Only 1 Factor
		1	2	3	4	5	6	7
Family Background Factor								
3	Reading Material	0.233	0.480	.29†	.17†			
4	Items in Home	0.278	0.295	.13†	−.00			
5	Sibling	0.401	0.761	.16†	.09†			
6	Structural Integrity	0.239	0.594	.08*	.03			
39	Parents' Educ.	0.245	0.834	.32†	.19†			
40	Urbanism of Bkgrd.	0.196	1.227	.13†	.01			

* Significant at the .05 level.
† Significant at the .01 level.

TABLE L Continued

	1	2	3	4	5	6	7
Variable	Mean	S.D.	Zero-Order R w/Verbal	Betas for Full Equation	Betas for Equations w/Fact. & Family Bkgrd. Alone	Betas for Equations w/o Family Bkgrd.	Betas for Equation w/Only 1 Factor
Facilities and Curriculum Factor							
38 Per-Pupil Expenditure	483.526	173.104	.08†	.03	.02	.04	.05
23 Volume/Student	5.593	3.843	−.03	−.04	−.03	−.03	−.02
22 Science Lab.	95.943	13.931	.06	.04	.03	.04	.02
24 Extracurr. Act.	72.397	12.630	.09†	−.05	−.03	−.04	.02
36 Accelerated Curr.	2.444	0.994	−.10†	−.05	−.07*	−.04	−.09*
25 Comprehensiveness of Curriculum	90.128	12.693	−.06	−.03	−.05	−.03	−.07*
35 Tracking	2.125	0.442	−.03	−.00	−.00	.00	.01
27 Movement Between Tracks	7.337	5.907	.05	.03	.02	.03	.03
9 School Size	352.804	220.169	.07*	−.10	−.09	−.10	−.04
30 Guidance Counselor	7.013	3.827	.12†	.06	.05	.09	.10*
33 School Location	4.108	1.798	.07*	.06	.02	.06	−.01
Student-Body Factor							
10 Proportion Own Encyclopedia	0.850	0.072	.17†	.00	.02	.06	.08*
26 Student Transfer	4.400	3.608	−.01	−.02	−.00	−.03	.00
31 Attendance	94.275	2.473	.04	.01	.02	.01	.02
52 Proportion College Track	0.464	0.152	.21†	.06	.08*	.12*	.17†
53 Average Hours of Homework	4.395	0.532	.10†	.00	−.00	.01	.00
Teacher Characteristics							
11 T SES Level	3.772	0.476	.06*	−.00	−.00	.01	.03
12 T Experience	10.770	2.995	.01	.04	.02	.04	.00
13 T Localism	0.002	0.773	.04	.07	.04	.07	.03
15 T Degree Received	3.431	0.218	.11†	−.03	.02	−.03	.09*
16 T Preference for Student Body	−0.312	0.679	−.17†	−.04	−.08*	−.06	−.15†
17 T Verbal Score	23.125	1.301	.03	.05	.04	.05	.03
18 T Race	0.966	0.050	.03	.00	.02	.01	.03
48 Proportion School White	0.899	0.122	.06*	.03		.03	

* Significant at the .05 level.
† Significant at the .01 level.

Appendix C

Tables 1–3: F = Ratios for Contribution to Explained Variance

TABLE 1

F-ratios corresponding to contributions to explained variance in total Verbal Achievement for three schoolwide factors. No background controls are used. Both unique and unique + joint contributions are tested. Main numbers in cells are computed F-ratios. Numbers in parentheses indicate numerator and denominator degrees of freedom.

	Northern Blacks			Northern Whites		
Schoolwide Factor	6th Gr.	9th Gr.	12th Gr.	6th Gr.	9th Gr.	12th Gr.
UNIQUE						
	(4/982)	(5/976)	(5/976)	(4/982)	(5/976)	(5/976)
Student Body	8.23†	5.73†	6.04†	11.45†	3.24†	3.04†
Facilities and Curriculum	(6/982)	(11/976)	(11/976)	(6/982)	(11/976)	(11/976)
	0.25	0.90	0.90	0.39	1.47	0.90
Teacher Characteristics	(7/982)	(7/976)	(7/976)	(7/982)	(7/976)	(7/976)
	2.47*	1.03	1.54	0.88	1.10	1.38
UNIQUE + JOINT						
	(4/995)	(5/994)	(5/994)	(4/995)	(5/994)	(5/994)
Student Body	10.77†	9.83†	20.99†	17.44†	6.91†	10.24†
Facilities and Curriculum	(6/993)	(11/988)	(11/988)	(6/993)	(11/988)	(11/988)
	1.93	1.28	4.79†	0.73	1.76	2.81*
Teacher Characteristics	(7/992)	(7/992)	(7/992)	(7/992)	(7/992)	(7/992)
	4.88†	3.21†	9.17†	3.78†	2.61*	5.90†

* Statistically significant at the .05 level.
† Statistically significant at the .01 level.

TABLE 2

F-ratios corresponding to contributions to explained variance in total Verbal Achievement for three schoolwide factors. Background controls are the four objective and two subjective measures described in Section 3 and Appendix A. Main numbers in cells are computed F-ratios. Numbers in parentheses indicate numerator and denominator degrees of freedom.

Schoolwide Factor	Northern Blacks			Northern Whites		
	6th Gr.	9th Gr.	12th Gr.	6th Gr.	9th Gr.	12th Gr.
UNIQUE						
	(4/967)	(5/970)	(5/970)	(4/976)	(5/970)	(5/970)
Student Body	4.53†	4.17†	4.89†	5.63†	2.01	1.34
Facilities and Curriculum	(6/976)	(11/970)	(11/970)	(6/976)	(11/970)	(11/970)
	0.30	1.04	0.97	0.59	1.80*	1.16
Teacher Characteristics	(7/976)	(7/970)	(7/970)	(7/976)	(7/970)	(7/970)
	2.49*	1.09	1.88	0.09	1.04	1.28
UNIQUE + JOINT						
	(4/989)	(5/988)	(5/988)	(4/989)	(5/988)	(5/988)
Student Body	5.77†	6.70†	15.52†	8.13†	3.29†	3.16†
Facilities and Curriculum	(6/989)	(11/982)	(11/982)	(6/987)	(11/982)	(11/982)
	1.28	1.30	2.90†	0.77	0.66	1.98*
Teacher Characteristics	(7/986)	(7/986)	(7/986)	(7/986)	(7/986)	(7/986)
	3.16†	2.25*	6.40†	2.38*	1.45	2.71†

* Statistically significant at the .05 level.
† Statistically significant at the .01 level.

TABLE 3

F-ratios corresponding to contributions to explained variance in total Verbal Achievement for three schoolwide factors. Background controls are the six objective measures described in Section 3 and Appendix A.

Schoolwide Factor	Northern Blacks			Northern Whites		
	6th Gr.	9th Gr.	12th Gr.	6th Gr.	9th Gr.	12th Gr.
UNIQUE						
	(4/976)	(5/970)	(5/970)	(4/976)	(5/970)	(5/970)
Student Body	3.78†	3.49†	4.04†	3.15*	1.10	1.09
Facilities and Curriculum	(6/976)	(11/970)	(11/970)	(6/976)	(11/970)	(11/970)
	0.30	0.62	1.05	0.47	0.93	0.84
Teacher Characteristics	(7/976)	(7/970)	(7/970)	(7/976)	(7/970)	(7/970)
	2.81†	0.99	1.49	0.75	1.16	1.53
UNIQUE + JOINT						
	(4/989)	(5/988)	(5/988)	(4/989)	(5/988)	(5/988)
Student Body	4.73†	5.99†	12.47†	4.19†	1.79	1.81
Facilities and Curriculum	(6/987)	(11/982)	(11/982)	(6/987)	(11/982)	(11/982)
	1.17	1.29	2.33†	0.46	0.73	0.85
Teacher Characteristics	(7/986)	(7/986)	(7/986)	(7/986)	(7/986)	(7/986)
	2.89†	1.65	4.79†	1.49	1.29	1.71

* Statistically significant at the .05 level.
† Statistically significant at the .01 level.

Bibliography

Austin, Mary C., and Morrison, Coleman. *The First R: The Harvard Report on Reading in Elementary Schools*. New York: The Macmillan Company, 1963.

Banys, Peter. "Fate-Control and Academic Self-Concept: Motivational Determinants of Negro Scholastic Achievement." Undergraduate thesis, Social Relations Department, Harvard University, April 1, 1968, 115 pages.

Bowles, Samuel, and Levin, Henry M. "The Determinants of Scholastic Achievement—An Appraisal of Some Recent Evidence." *Journal of Human Resources*, Vol. 3, Winter 1968, pp. 3–24.

Brookover, Wilbur B., Leu, Donald J., and Kariger, Hugh. "Discrimination in Tracking." Unpublished paper, Michigan State University, 1967.

Central Advisory Council on Education. *Children and their Primary Schools:* Vol. 1, *The Report;* Vol. 2, *Research and Surveys*. London: Her Majesty's Stationery Office, 1967.

Cohen, David K. "Children and Their Primary Schools: Vol. II." *Harvard Educational Review*, Vol. 38, No. 2, Spring, pp. 329–340.

Coleman, James S., *et al. Equality of Educational Opportunity*. Washington: U.S. Government Printing Office, 1966.

Davis, James. "The Campus as a Frog Pond." *American Journal of Sociology*, Vol. 72, July, 1966, pp. 17–31.

Dreeben, Robert. *On What Is Learned in School*. Reading, Mass.: Addison-Wesley Publishing Company, 1968.

Hanushek, Eric. "The Education of Blacks and Whites." Unpublished Ph.D. dissertation, Department of Economics, Harvard University, 1968.

Hayes, Donald, and Grether, Judith. "The School Year and Vacations: When Do Students Learn?" Paper presented to the Eastern Sociological Association, April, 1969, available from the Urban Institute, Washington, D.C., mimeo.

Hobson v. Hansen, 269F, Supp. 401 (D.C.D.C. 1967).

Jencks, Christopher. "Some Natural Experiments in Compensatory Education." Paper prepared for Conference on Pre-School Education, 1969.

Kingston, Albert J., Jr. "The Relationship of First-Grade Readiness to Third- and Fourth-Grade Achievement." *The Journal of Educational Research*, Vol. 56, No. 2, October, 1962.

Lesser, G. S., Fifer, G., and Clark, D. H. "Mental Abilities of Children From Different Social-Class and Cultural Groups." Monograph on Child Development. Cooperative Research Project No. 1635, funded by the Office of Education. New York: Hunter College, City University of New York, 1964.

Levin, Henry M. *Recruiting Teachers for Large-City Schools*. The Brookings Institution, Washington, D.C., June, 1968.

Michelson, Stephan. "School Resource Allocation and Equal Protection," in *Inequality in Education*, No. 2. Center for Law and Education, Harvard University, 1970.

Overlan, Frank. "Out of the Mouths of Babes: The Accuracy of Students' Responses to Family and Educational Background Questionnaires." Harvard Graduate School of Education, 1968, xeroxed.

Parsons, Talcott. "The School Class as a Social System: Some of Its Functions in American Society," *Harvard Educational Review*, Vol. 29, Fall 1959, pp. 297–318.

Smith, Marshall S., and Bissell, Joan. "Report Analysis: The Impact of Head Start," *Harvard Education Review*, Vol. 40, No. 1, February, 1970, pp. 51–104.

Wilson, Alan. "Educational Consequences of Segregation in a California Community," in *Racial Isolation in the Public Schools*, U.S. Commission on Civil Rights Report, Appendix C3, Washington, D.C.: Superintendent of Documents, Government Printing Office, 1967.

7

Race and the Outcomes of Schooling

DAVID K. COHEN, THOMAS F. PETTIGREW,
& ROBERT T. RILEY

In research on matters of great public interest and political delicacy, the ability to pose searching questions is more highly developed than the capacity to provide solid answers. A host of such questions arises in any consideration of education and race. How can the racial disparity in school achievement be eliminated? In what part is it caused by the schools? Does racial integration affect students' achievement? Does parent participation? The *Equality of Educational Opportunity Survey* (EEOS) demonstrated that in most cases the available data provide a basis for only tentative answers to such queries, and the Survey's reception has shown something less than perfect agreement on the validity and meaning of those answers it did provide.

The research problems may be divided into three categories, along lines given by the chief policy issues: Are there racial disparities in school resources? How can racial disparities in school achievement be eliminated? What are the dynamics and consequences of interracial interaction in the schools?

The third group of research questions—those related to the dynamics of interracial interaction in schools—involves a range of policy issues. Some have to do with the racial contexts and conditions often thought to influence the academic achievement of Negro students (does integration improve performance? does interracial "hostility" damage it?). Others have to do with the relationship between students' interracial experience and somewhat less conventional outcomes of schooling (do interracial schools have a positive effect on racial attitudes? does tracking with schools nullify these effects?).

Our chapter is directed at this group of issues; it comprises two areas of work. First is the question of relationship between racial contexts and achievement; here we shall investigate the impact of racial composition and schools' interracial climates upon student achievement. But schools' interracial climates are worthy objects of attention in their own right; common observation tells us that the character of interracial situations varies and common sense suggests it would be worth knowing what produces the differences. The second part of our inquiry is addressed to this issue.

A. ACHIEVEMENT AND RACIAL COMPOSITION

Since the Supreme Court decided the *Brown* case, schools' racial composition has been the center of attention in most matters concerning education and race. The single most important reason for this has been the idea that Negro students' academic performance was shaped by their schools' racial composition. The Court's position in the 1954 decision was based in some measure on its view that segregated schools damaged Negro students' achievement by adversely affecting their motivation to learn.[1] Much speculation and debate centered around this point in subsequent years, and the Court's view gained greater acceptance in the following decade. But direct evidence was sparse; data for even minimally satisfactory tests of the notion did not become available until the EEOS *Survey*. Its conclusion was that:

. . . the apparent beneficial effect of a student body with a high proportion of white students comes not from racial composition per se, but from the better educational background and higher educational aspirations that are, on the average, found among white students. The effects of the student body environment upon a student's achievement appear to lie in educational proficiency possessed by that student body, whatever its racial or ethnic composition.[2]

As a practical matter, since the probability of having a "better educational background" is dramatically lower for Negroes than whites, the only way to provide many schools with a majority of advantaged students would be to integrate them racially. But the Survey's conclusion on this point appeared to undercut earlier ideas about the existence of a direct causal relationship between schools' racial composition and Negro students' achievement. The academic benefits of racial integration suggested by the EEOS *Survey* report appeared to be a consequence of racial differentials in the distribution of social class.

The U.S. Commission on Civil Rights undertook to analyze the data upon which the Survey's conclusions were based, but its work did not disturb the earlier findings.[3] These analyses did, however, suggest the existence of a relationship between the racial composition of 9th-grade Negro students' classrooms and their achievement. The Commission concluded on this basis that racial composition was an important determinant of students' achievement.[4]

Two questions can be raised about these findings. One has to do with the adequacy of efforts in the EEOS report to disentangle class and race in the schools' composition and to accurately assess their separate impact upon performance. The authors of the Survey report were evidently uncertain on this question, for in addition to the passage quoted just above they elsewhere pointed out that school social class "largely accounted for" the effects of proportion white on achievement.[5]

The second question has to do with causal priority, or selection, and it applies at both the school and classroom level. For schools, what causes higher Negro performance in those which are more advantaged and predominantly white? The more stimulating student body, or the fact that Negro children in such schools come from more advantaged homes? It is widely assumed that white parents with the necessary motivation and wherewithal seek to enroll their children in the best schools available— should not identical assumptions be made about Negroes? Similarly, do higher Negro scores in mostly white classrooms result from classroom interaction, or from schools' internal selection routines? In biracial* schools we would expect selection for ability groups and curricula to result in more able Negro students being placed in mostly white classes.

1 ◆ The Effect of School Racial Composition at Grades 9 and 12

The evidence for the EEOS report's findings concerning the relative importance of schools' race and class composition arose from regression analyses of individual students' verbal achievement. The unique contribution to percentage of explained variance in individual verbal ability accounted for by school percent Negro diminished to the vanishing point when variables measuring the social-class composition of the student body were entered into the regression.[6] (Coleman considered the five student environment measures indicators of school social class; all references to the effect of school social class for grades 9 and 12 in this section refer to the effect of the five student environment measures. See Coleman *et al.*, page 307.) Replicating these analyses failed to reveal any discrepancies in the proportion of total variance explained (R^2); in our replication the unique contribution to the variance explained by schools' percent Negro also was reduced to a vanishingly small amount by the introduction of school social-class measures. But the unique proportion of variance explained is not the only relevant statistic in regression analysis; consideration of other aspects of the results might have led to another interpretation.

*In this analysis, biracial schools have at least five whites and five Negroes.

Table I presents the results of our EEOS replication (for which we used the EEOS correlation matrices) for the 9th-grade Northern Negro stratum.[7] It reveals that the standardized regression coefficients (Beta

TABLE I

Regression of individual Negro verbal ability on percent Negro, six individual background measures, and five student environment measures for grades 9 and 12 in the Urban North

Variables in Regression	Grade	Unique Contribution to the Variance Explained of Percent Negro	Beta Weight of Percent Negro	t's of Percent Negro
Percent Negro* controlling for six individual background measures †	9	2.14%	−.147	−4.94
	12	2.14%	−.147	−4.80
Percent Negro controlling for six individual background and five student environment measures ‡	9	0.68%	−.212	−2.80
	12	0.12%	−.100	−1.97

* The *School Percent Negro* takes as its base only Negro and white students within a school; thus the *Percentage White* and the *Percentage Negro* sum to 100.0. In order that the sum of these two percentages equal 100.0, all Mexicans, Puerto Ricans, American Indians, and Orientals were excluded from this entire analysis, both at the individual level and in the formation of school-level measures. Second, only schools in which the Percentage White and Percentage Negro with all students in the school as its base exceeded 89.9 percent for a given grade level were included in the analysis. On this basis schools that are 75 percent Negro and 25 percent Puerto Rican fail to meet the criteria for inclusion in the analysis.

† The six individual background measures employed by Coleman are:
   1. *Urbanism Index* (questions 6 and 21, grade 12)
   2. *Parents' Education* (questions 19 and 20, grade 12)
   3. *Structural Integrity of the Home* (questions 17 and 18, grade 12)
   4. *Family Size* (question 10, grade 12)
   5. *Home Items Index* (questions 31, 32, 33, 34, 37, and 38, grade 12)
   6. *Reading Materials Index* (questions 35, 36, 39, 41, and 42, grade 12)

See Coleman, p. 298, for the details in the construction of these measures, and Smith, Chapter 6, for a critical appraisal of their construction.

‡ The five student environment measures employed by Coleman are:
   1. *Percent of Families Owning Encyclopedias*
   2. *Transfers In and Out of School*
   3. *Average Daily Attendance* (as percentage of the total enrollment)
   4. *Percentage of Students in the College Curriculum*
   5. *Average Hours Spent on Homework*

See Coleman, p. 306, for the details in the construction of these measures and Smith, Chapter 6, for a critical appraisal of their construction.

weights) for percent Negro (controlling for the effect of the six individual background characteristics: 1) Urbanism, 2) Parent's Education, 3) Structural Integrity of the Home, 4) Family Size, 5) Home Items Index, 6) Reading Materials Index), are as large as or larger than those of the five student environment measures: (1) Percent of Families Owning Encyclopedias, 2) Transfers In and Out of School, 3) Average Daily Attendance, 4) Percent of Students in College Curriculum, 5) Average Hours Spent on Homework). Two points are particularly worth noting in this connection. Comparing the unique contribution to the variance explained of percent Negro before and after the addition of the five student environment measures estimates the effect that student environment measures have on percent Negro.* The introduction of the five school social-class measures *increases the size of the Beta weight for percent Negro*, from −.147 to −.212. This can be interpreted to mean that schools' social class as measured by the five student body characteristics mediates the effect of school percent Negro: once variation in schools' social class has been taken into account, the regression coefficients for percent Negro increase. This certainly does not support the contention that the percent Negro in a school becomes insignificant when school social class is controlled. Rather it suggests that a moderate proportion of the variance attributed to school social class is, in fact, shared with the school percent Negro, and cannot be uniquely decomposed into either its racial composition or social-class components.

Entering percent Negro in the regression in conjunction with the six student background *and* the five student environment measures reduces the magnitude of the beta weights and the unique contribution to the variance explained of the five student environment measures. (Table II.) The largest reduction occurs in the specific school social-class measure, *percent owning encyclopedias*, from .134 to .069. This finding adds further doubt to the validity of the original explanation.

The above interpretation of the effect of percent Negro in the 9th-grade Negro stratum relying on regression coefficients offers an alternative to the interpretation based solely upon unique contributions to the variance explained. In fact, it suggests *that the original interpretation—based only on the unique contribution to the variance explained—might have been different had it been based on the evidence just presented*. The authors of the EEOS report could not have concluded that the effect of schools' racial composition was actually the effect of their social-class composition, but would have concluded that schools' racial and social-class composition were confounded.

The results of a similar procedure with the same measures for grade 12 are presented in Tables I and III. Although they are not nearly as dramatic as those for grade 9, they are fundamentally the same. Comparing the unique contribution of percent Negro before and after controlling for the effect of school environment indicates a sharp reduction in the unique contribution of percent Negro (from 2.14 percent to 0.12 percent); but once again this is not paralleled by a reduction of similar magni-

* In both cases the original six background variables are controlled.

TABLE II

Regression of individual Negro verbal ability on five student environment measures, controlling for six individual background measures before and after the entry of percent Negro for grade 9 in the Urban North

Variables in Regression	Unique Contribution to Variance Explained		Beta Weight		t's	
	#B	#A	#B	#A	#B	#A
Six individual background variables with:						
1. Percent of families who own encyclopedias*	0.81	0.17	0.134	0.069	3.05	1.38
2. Percent of transfers in and out of school	0.52	0.33	−0.091	−0.073	−2.45	−1.95
3. Percent average daily attendance	0.07	0.05	0.035	0.032	0.88	0.79
4. Percent of students in college curriculum	0.27	0.34	−0.068	−0.077	−1.74	−1.97
5. Average hours spent on homework	0.11	0.19	0.043	0.056	1.14	1.49

#B = Before the entry of percent Negro
#A = After the entry of percent Negro

* Separate analyses were carried out such that each student environment variable entered the regression equation alone with the six individual background measures before and after the addition of percent Negro.

TABLE III

Regression on individual Negro verbal ability on five student environment measures, controlling for six individual background measures before and after the entry of percent Negro for grade 12 in the Urban North

Variables in Regressions	Unique Contribution to Variance Explained		Beta Weight		t's	
	#B	#A	#B	#A	#B	#A
Six individual background variables with:						
1. Percent of families who own encyclopedias*	0.20	0.12	0.081	0.012	1.51	1.16
2. Percent of transfers in and out of school	0.19	0.14	−0.058	−0.050	−1.43	−1.24
3. Percent average daily attendance	0.10	0.05	0.053	0.055	0.75	0.78
4. Percent of students in college curriculum	0.64	0.47	0.140	0.128	2.54	2.30
5. Average hours spent on homework	0.16	0.08	−0.061	0.048	−1.26	−0.97

#B = Before the entry of percent Negro
#A = After the entry of percent Negro

* Separate analyses were carried out such that each student environment variable entered the regression equation alone with the six individual background measures before and after the addition of percent Negro.

tude in the regression coefficients for percent Negro, which change from −.147 to −.100 (Table I) Adding percent Negro to the set of predictors of individual verbal ability decreases the effect of student environment both in terms of the Beta weights and the unique contributions to the variance explained (Table III). In fact, the Beta weight of the only specific school social-class measure (percent owning encyclopedias) drops from .082 before the entry of percent Negro to .012 after its entry.

These regression analyses indicate that racial composition is less important at grade 12 than at grade 9, but they also indicate that racial composition was not simply a disguised effect of school social class at grade 12. An interpretation based on the regression coefficients as well as the unique contributions to the variance explained would have been different from the one which appeared in the EEOS report, and would have stressed that school social class and racial composition share much of the same variance.

Decisive conclusions about the effect of racial composition, then, are not possible with either set of results. Can a reanalysis produce more conclusive results than the original EEOS analyses?

The SEEOR replications previously presented are not a suitable alternative for two reasons. As Smith shows in his chapter, some of the original variables were mistakenly chosen or misformed. But even if these were corrected, we would be hesitant to proceed with the 9th and 12th grades. Results for grade 12 are likely to be biased—to an indeterminate degree—by selective attrition: the results would be open to unanswerable questions about the effect of dropouts. Results for grade 9 would be subject to other problems: many of the Northern urban 9th grades in the EEOS were the lowest grade in their school (nine-to-twelve high schools). Since the survey instruments were administered within a few days after school opened in September, 1965, this would cast doubt upon the validity of any student environment measure in the "grade-9 lowest" schools. Therefore, a valid analysis of the effect of school environment measures could only be carried out for the 9th-grade schools which had grades lower than 9. The only difficulty with this, of course, is its limited scope: at best, the results could apply to junior high schools and the few grade-7-to-12 high schools. To provide greater scope, the only alternative is the 6th-grade schools. They provide the necessary breadth of coverage in the urban North, without posing problems resulting from school organization and unmeasurable student selection.

The Effect of Racial Composition at Grade 6

Since the racial composition of schools has been such an important policy issue, we decided to proceed with the analysis at grade 6. The students for this analysis were the sixth-grade sample described in C. S. Jencks's chapter, elsewhere in this volume.[8] Since our concern is with school-to-school differences in achievement and racial composition, the work was carried out at the school (aggregate) level, with school averages or percentages defining all measures.

Table IV presents the results of a regression analysis of school average 6th-grade Negro verbal achievement, in which measures of school average social class and the school quality were controlled.

TABLE IV

The impact of school percent white on black verbal achievement, grade 6, Urban North

Simple Correlation of Percent White and School Average Negro Verbal Ability	.406
Standardized Regression Coefficient, After School Average Social-Class Measures Entered the Equation	.144
Standardized Regression Coefficient After School-Quality Measures Entered the Equation	.094

Comparing the effect of racial composition before and after the addition of the school social-class measures reveals that at grade 6 controlling for school social class effectively eliminates the influence of percentage white (Table IV). Adding further controls for school quality reduces the effect of schools' racial composition still further, but the reduction is far less than that which occurs with the addition of the school social-class measures.

Selection Processes and the Effect of Racial Composition

One can argue that this analysis fails to take into account differences among schools in the initial quality of their students. Two types of selection processes might produce such an effect. In one, children are assigned to schools (chiefly secondary) as a result of demonstrated academic ability. The other is initiated by parents, whereby residence (or school assignment irrespective of residence) is determined on the basis of the schools' social or academic attributes. The two are not mutually exclusive. Direct knowledge of the extent to which either process operates among the schools in the EEOS sample is not available; neither was taken into account in the original regression analyses, and it appears that direct efforts to estimate the extent of selection were lacking.

Without any doubt, the selection issue is crucial. Measuring the impact of any influence upon student achievement—whether it was teachers, school facilities, or social-class composition—would be uncertain until initial differences among students were taken into account. Or at least it would be uncertain until it could be shown that students' initial abilities are randomly distributed across the school attributes whose impact is in question.

This certainly is not the case; consider measures of parent-initiated selection among elementary schools. Students' social class has repeatedly been shown to be an important predictor of school ability; Table V reveals systematic differences between the average social class of those Negro and white students attending mostly white and mostly Negro schools.[9] The stability of the correlations at both grade levels implies that the influence of these processes does not diminish over time; in fact for whites the influence of selection processes of this type appears more pronounced as the correlation between percent Negro and school social class increases absolutely from $-.442$ at grade 1 to $-.668$ at grade 6. The difference in the mag-

TABLE V

Correlations of school percent Negro with school social class by race for grades 1 and 6 in the Urban North

	Negroes	Whites
Grade 1* (N = 208)	−.136	−.462
Grade 6* (N = 208)	−.154	−.668

* In this case the measure of School Social Class resulted from the school mean on the Home Items Index. See Jencks, Chapter 11, for the details of its construction.

nitude of the correlations for whites and Negroes at both grade levels may reflect the lower level of residential mobility generally possible for Negro families, and consequently the greater social and economic heterogeneity within mostly Negro schools. These correlations coincide with results reported by Alan Wilson from research in Richmond, California; there, Negro students in mostly advantaged and mostly white schools came from more advantaged homes, and began first grade with higher I.Q.'s than their peers in mostly Negro schools.[10]

Evidence of this type suggests that the much publicized EEOS finding that schools' race-class composition has an important influence upon achievement may result from earlier selectivity. The most effective way to pursue this relationship directly would be to collect data on grade-1 I.Q. from a wide variety of students in a wide variety of schools; add to it data on the quality of the schools' program, their student bodies' composition, and the students' later achievement; and then assess the impact of the first three sets of factors upon the last. But although they present a wide variety of schools and students, the EEOS data are cross-sectional and not longitudinal; on the other hand, the data which are longitudinal (Wilson's) represent only one small community. It remains unclear what would emerge if data from many different communities—as are available in the EEOS— were combined with longitudinal data on initial differences such as those employed by Wilson.

Our findings on the school racial composition issue, then, are mixed. Although the initial EEOS analysis overstressed the impact of school social class, it would not be profitable to perform a complete reanalysis at both the school and student level at grades 9 and 12, given the problems of unmeasured school selection processes. When the issue is probed at grade 6, a small independent effect of schools' racial composition appeared, but its significance for educational policy seems slight. The evidence suggests that student-body racial composition at grade 6 acts more as a "proxy" than a "mediator" of the school social-class effects. Until the breadth of the EEOS data can be combined with sufficient longitudinal information on students and their schools, stronger results on this point will not be forthcoming.

2 ♦ Classroom Racial Composition and Curricular and Track Assignment at Grade 9

A second problem of selection arises in the Civil Rights Commission's analysis of the data on classroom composition. The fact is that students' prior achievement typically is used as a basis for assignment to ability groups and tracks, especially within secondary schools. Is the apparent effect of classroom racial composition actually the result of selection processes? [11] The Civil Rights Commission's analysis of classroom composition focused on 9th-grade students in the urban Northeast and Mid-Atlantic regions, so our efforts will follow this group of pupils. Since the measure upon which the analysis was based is the proportion white which students reported in their classes "last year," there is not as much need to be concerned with variations in school organization as in the analysis of schools' racial composition.*

The main issue is whether classroom racial composition is related to the curricular and ability group selection processes. But we should establish how widespread these practices are. As Table VI shows, ability grouping is

TABLE VI

School racial composition and the frequency of ability grouping* for grade 9 in the Urban North

| | School Percent Negro | | | |
	0–5	6–50	51+	Total
Ability grouping present*	83.1 (59)†	93.6 (76)	86.2 (25)	88.4 (160)
Ability grouping absent	16.9 (12)	6.4 (5)	13.8 (29)	11.6 (21)

* The *Presence or Absence of Ability Grouping* within a given school was ascertained from the questionnaire completed by the school's principal (question 80 of the Principal's Questionnaire). If a principal failed to return his questionnaire, the school was not included in the table.
† N's refer to schools.

almost universal in the secondary schools we have under scrutiny. The presence of such grouping practices occurs with a little greater frequency in biracial schools than in the majority Negro or almost all-white schools. In addition, more than seven in every ten of our schools are multicurricular,

* The question read: In your classes last year, how many students were white? 1. None, 2. Less than half, 3. About half, 4. More than half, 5. All.

comprehensive institutions; the remainder are mainly academic schools. Internal selection is virtually universal in these schools.

As might be expected, the relationship between achievement and assignment to curricula is strong. Curricular assignment is the largest single correlate of individual Negro student achievement; $r = .384$ at grade 9, and .399 at grade 12. It also is worth noting that the correlation between Negro students' curricular assignment and their parents' education is about .250 at both grades. This suggests that curricular selection also depends upon Negro students' social status. This also finds support from the frequencies in Table VII. They show that curriculum assignment is highly related to verbal achievement. At both grade 9 and grade 12, at all social-class levels, students in the academic curriculum obtain the highest verbal-ability scores. The differences in verbal achievement among curricula are consistently larger than those among social-class strata.

A relationship also exists between students' assignment to ability groups and their verbal achievement—the correlations are moderate: .238

TABLE VII

Mean individual Negro verbal achievement* by parents' education and curriculum assignment, for grades 9 and 12 in the Urban North

	Grade 9			Grade 12		
Parents' Education†	Academic ‡	General	Vocational, Industrial Arts, Commercial, Other, Don't Know Yet	Academic	General	Vocational, Industrial Arts, Commercial, Other
Less than High School Graduate	264.0 (358)	257.7 (353)	253.9 (2009)	279.5 (159)	264.9 (264)	265.1 (463)
High School Graduate	267.3 (984)	260.2 (646)	256.9 (2464)	283.3 (689)	267.3 (607)	265.6 (1201)
More than High School Graduate	272.9 (752)	265.0 (276)	258.7 (903)	286.1 (658)	271.4 (214)	270.0 (365)
Curriculum Mean	268.7 (2094)	260.5 (1275)	256.6 (5554)	284.1 (1506)	276.6 (1085)	266.3 (2029)
	Overall Mean = 259.67 (8923)			Overall Mean = 272.27 (4620)		

* *Verbal Achievement* is measured by the Verbal Scale. See Coleman, p. 273.

† *Parents' Education* refers to the highest level of education reported for either parent, if information is available for both, or to the educational level of the parent for which it is available, if not available for both (questions 19 and 20, grade 12). If it is available for neither, the student is not included in the analysis. For the purposes of this table, the eight original categories have been collapsed to three.

‡ *Curriculum Assignment:* Students in both grades 9 and 12 responded to the following question: Which of the following best describes the program or curriculum you are enrolled in? (question 43, grade 12) The response categories were: 1. General, 2. College Preparatory, 3. Commercial or Business, 4. Vocational, 5. Agricultural, 6. Industrial Arts, 7. Other, 8. Don't Know Yet (Grade 9 only).
N's refer to students.

at grade 9, and .249 at grade 12. At the same time, ability-group placement relates to curricular assignment; students in an academic curriculum are more likely to be in a high-ability group than those in a nonacademic curriculum. When students in academic curricula undergo analysis, the relationship between ability-group assignment and verbal achievement remains moderate at both grade levels (r > .200). Thus, even in the academic curriculum, further selection occurs in the verbal ability groups.

Do these selection processes relate to the racial composition of classrooms? Are Negro students in academic curricula more likely to have white classmates than their peers in general or business curricula? Table VIII suggests an affirmative answer.[12] It shows that in both grades 9 and 12 students in an academic curriculum were likely to be in classes with more white students than those in other curricula. This is not, however, true of

TABLE VIII

Mean classroom racial composition* by curricular assignment
for grades 9 and 12 in the Urban North

	Academic	General	Commercial	Other Categories Combined
Grade 9	4.0 (2094)†	3.4 (1275)	3.2 (1514)	2.9 (1683)
Grade 12	3.1 (1506)	2.7 (1085)	2.9 (1267)	2.7 (782)

* *Classroom Racial Composition.* All students responded to the following question: In your classes last year, how many students were white? (question 50, grade 12). The following values were assigned to each response category: 1. None, 2. Less than half, 3. About half, 4. More than half, 5. All. The higher the score, the greater the proportion of white students in the responding student's classroom tends to be. A higher mean in one curriculum compared to another indicates that students in the first curriculum were in classrooms with a greater proportion of white students than students in the second.
† N's refer to students.

ability groups, once curricular assignment is controlled.

We have shown that selection processes are related to both verbal ability and classroom racial composition. Does the relationship between students' assignment to curricula and their classrooms' racial composition account for the relationship between achievement and classroom composition?[13] The issue was explored in a series of regression analyses of 9th- and 12th-grade students' achievement.

Table IX presents the first analysis for 9th-grade Negro students.[14] Inspection of the beta weights for the classroom racial composition measure shows that track and curricular assignment reduces its effect (.156 to .112) and thus its impact upon achievement, but the addition of selection and class controls does not totally eliminate the original relationship between individual verbal achievement and classroom racial composition.

TABLE IX

Regression of individual Negro verbal ability on classroom racial composition, parents'
education, curricular assignment, and track assignment for grade 9 in the
Urban North (N = 8,261)

		Variables in Regression			
	1	1, 2	1, 2, 3	1, 2, 3, 4	t's‖
(1) Classroom Racial Composition*	.156	.138	.123	.112	11.2
(2) Parents' Education†		.237	.159	.157	15.4
(3) Curricular Assignments‡			.331	.300	29.0
(4) Track Assignments§				.167	16.4
Total Variance Explained:	2.4%	8.1%	16.7%	21.2%	

* *Classroom Racial Composition* was defined in Table VIII.
† *Parents' Education* was defined in Table VII, but this time the full range of categories from "none or some grade school" with a value of 1 to "attending graduate or professional school" with a value of 8 was used. "Don't know" responses were not included or recoded to a usable value (questions 19 and 20, grade 12).
‡ *Curricular Assignment* is a "dummy variable" such that score of 1 was given to a student if he reported his curriculum assignment as college preparatory; otherwise he received a score of 0 (question 43, grade 12).
§ *Track Assignment* resulted from the following question: What ability group or track are you in, in your English class? Responses were: 1. Highest group, 2. Middle group, 3. Lowest, 4. School does not track, 5. Don't know (question 86, grade 12). Only those students who gave responses 1, 2, or 3 were included (89.9 percent at grade 12, 91.3 percent at grade 9); all others were eliminated. With this subset of students a "dummy variable" was formed such that students in the highest track received a score of 1 and students in other tracks received a score of 0.
‖ For last step in the regression.

Yet the criterion for such individual track and curricular assignment varies among schools, and this source of variation could affect the influence of the individual assignment variables on verbal ability. Such school-to-school differences among curricula should be held apart from consideration of the impact of classroom composition, since by definition it only involves a mechanism which operates within schools.

Table X presents the results of an effort to eliminate the influence of such extraneous school effects. The approach employed here statistically equalizes all schools on their average Verbal Achievement; our reasoning is that this equalization would eliminate the variation among schools in the achievement criteria for assignment to track and curriculum. Schools with a high verbal achievement level presumably would have higher entry standards for the academic curriculum than those with a low average, and controlling school-to-school variations in average verbal ability would eliminate the differences. As a comparison of Tables IX and X shows, the effect of classroom racial composition becomes only slightly less (from .112 to .088) with the addition of the school mean for Negro verbal ability.

Another approach to the same problem involves replicating the analyses presented in these two tables *for only students within the academic curriculum*. This has the effect of removing all variance lying among curricula

TABLE X

Regression of individual Negro verbal ability on classroom racial composition, parents'
education, curricular assignment, track assignment, and school mean Negro verbal
ability for grade 9 in the Urban North (N = 8,261)

Variables	Variables in Regression	t's
	(1, 2, 3, 4, 5)	
(1) Classroom Racial Composition	.088	9.1
(2) Highest Parent Education	.115	11.5
(3) Curriculum Assignment	.281	28.0
(4) Track Assignment	.166	16.9
(5) School Mean* Negro Verbal Ability	.236	23.9
Total Variance Explained	26.5%	

* *School Mean Negro Verbal Ability.* This is the mean on the individual verbal ability scale for all Negroes within a school.

for a selected subsample. The results of this replication do not differ from the overall results; the beta weight for classroom racial composition is .098, slightly larger than the overall beta weight of .088.[15]

These findings support the Commission on Civil Rights' finding that proportion white classmates was positively related to Negro students' achievement, even after selection processes are controlled. The Commission's results, however, were reported for all 9th-grade schools—and the question remains whether they hold up when schools of different racial compositions are distinguished. Table XI reveals that in fact they do not. The results are almost reversed in mostly white and mostly Negro schools. In the former schools, the results parallel those in Table X, but in the mostly Negro schools classroom racial composition has a slight negative effect (−.020) on Negro students' verbal ability. But its uncontrolled magnitude (−.065) was reduced by taking account of curricular track assignment and social class.

At grade 9, then, the relationship between classroom racial composition and Negro students' verbal achievement occurs in opposite directions for mostly Negro and mostly white schools. The source of this is not at all clear. Perhaps school and classroom composition interact, so that there is a positive effect only in mostly white schools. Perhaps it results from differences in the quality of white students in schools of different racial compositions. If white students in mostly Negro schools were systematically less able than those in mostly white schools, the level of performance in mostly white classrooms might impede Negro students' academic progress.

Whatever the causes of these unexpected results may be, they are not apparent from the EEOS data. We can, however, repeat the analysis at grade 12. Data from this grade are better suited to exploration of the classroom composition issue; very few students change schools between grades 11 and 12 as compared with between grades 8 and 9, since there is no

TABLE XI

Regression of individual Negro verbal ability on classroom racial composition, parents' education, curricular assignment, track assignment and school mean Negro verbal ability by school racial composition for grade 9 in the Urban North

| | Schools Less than 60% Negro (N = 2386)* Variables in Regression | | | | | Schools More than 60% Negro (N = 5740)* Variables in Regression | | | | |
Variables	(1)	(1,2)	(1,2,3,4)	(1,2,3,4,5)	t's	(1)	(1,2)	(1,2,3,4)	(1,2,3,4,5)	t's
(1) Classroom Racial Composition	.244	.221	.185	.165	12.1	−.065	−.070	−.038	−.020	−1.4
(2) Highest Parent Education		.224	.151	.119	8.4		.250	.162	.105	7.3
(3) Curriculum Assignment			.288	.273	19.4			.302	.278	19.4
(4) Track Assignment			.139	.147	10.6			.197	.198	14.1
(5) School Mean Verbal Ability, Negro				.222	16.0				.242	17.2
Total Variance Explained	5.9%	10.9%	21.9%	26.6%		0.4%	6.7%	21.9%	27.3%	

* N is the number of students.

organizational break. This means that there is a greater likelihood of congruence beween the classroom racial composition measures (". . . classmates *last year* . . ."), and other measures—such as ability grouping or curricular assignment—which were derived from attributes of the school or student body current at the time of the survey.

Table XII presents the results of the analysis with 12th-grade Negro students. In some respects they parallel those for the 9th grade. The curriculum and ability group measures were introduced *after* achievement variance lying among schools was taken into account. These selection variables

TABLE XII

Regression of individual Negro verbal ability on classroom racial composition, parents' education, curricular assignment, track assignment, and school mean Negro verbal ability for grade 12 in the Urban North (N = 4,135)

	Variables in Regression				
Variables	1	1,2	1,2,3	1,2,3,4,5	*t's*
(1) Classroom Racial Composition	.196	.112	.107	.078	7.7
(2) School Mean Verbal Ability		.654	.637	.628	61.5
(3) Parents' Education			.139	.049	4.7
(4) Ability Group				.175	16.7
(5) Curriculum Assignment				.266	24.6
Total Variance Explained	3.8%	46.0%	49.1%	59.8%	

reduced the impact of classroom racial composition upon verbal ability (from .196 to .078), but they did not eliminate the relationship. Further analyses showed that the reversal of effects in 15–60 percent as against 60+ percent Negro schools did not occur at grade 12; rather, the classroom racial composition effect remained at approximately the same level for both types of schools.

SUMMARY.   Taken together, then, the results from grades 9 and 12 provide no basis for seriously modifying the Commission on Civil Rights' overall conclusion that there is a positive relationship between Negro secondary-school students' verbal achievement and the proportion white of their classrooms.

But if the relationship is significant from a statistical point of view, its absolute magnitude must also be kept in mind. As Table XII shows (assuming relationships to be linear), an increase of 1 standard deviation on the class white variable would produce .078 of a standard deviation increase in individual verbal achievement at grade 12. This implies that assigning Negro students to mostly white classes would raise their verbal ability about 1.94 points. That is less than one sixth of the difference between average Negro and white achievement in these schools at grade 12.

In summary, then, it appears that the modest relationship between classroom racial composition and verbal ability for Negro secondary-school students is not purely a result of those selection processes which can be measured with the EEOS data. Of course, it is possible to hypothesize other unmeasured selection processes, and in the absence of data on students' early I.Q., such a possibility can hardly be dismissed. But a survey which combines the breadth of the EEOS with longitudinal depth will not soon be undertaken.

B. INTERRACIAL CLIMATES AND ACHIEVEMENT

These results (and others in this volume) which relate achievement to racial composition may not be convincing. After all, interracial contact in schools can range from acceptance to hostility; some schools are effective settings for intellectual development and others are ineffective. Racially mixed schools can be either "desegregated" or "integrated." A desegregated school includes both Negro and white children, but contact between races is minimal and tense; an integrated school also is interracial, but there is considerable cross-racial interaction and friendship.

We sought to investigate the notion that these differences among biracial schools are systematically related to achievement. Our basic hypothesis was that *the academic achievement of Negro children in biracial schools would be highest in integrated settings*. This hypothesis derives directly from the findings of extensive laboratory research on Negro performance in biracial situations, conducted over the past decade by Professor Irwin Katz.[16] He found in one experiment after another that black subjects performed best in interracial situations free of stress and threat, moderately well in all-Negro situations, and worst in interracial situations characterized by stress and threat. Katz concluded:

The psychological evidence that I have presented is consistent with a definition of racial integration which emphasizes the beneficial effects to Negro pupils of attending racially balanced classes *when an atmosphere of genuine respect and acceptance prevails*.[17]

The *Equal Educational Opportunity Survey* presents the first opportunity to pursue Katz's findings outside the laboratory. The questionnaires contain two items which may tap the integration-desegregation continuum. The first item asked teachers to judge the extent of racial and ethnic hostility in their schools; the second item asked students to estimate the extent to which their friendship groups were interracial. The latter serves as a direct measure of the interracial climates of schools, as called for by our hypothesis. Although it turned out that neither measure was really suitable for analysis, it is worth briefly recounting the reasons for this.

Intergroup Hostility

The intergroup-hostility item appears in a list of twenty-one statements about their schools with which teachers were asked to agree or disagree. The statement reads: "The different races or ethnic groups don't get along together." This wording has serious deficiencies for our purposes. Since it refers to both racial and *ethnic* hostility, it raises issues about intergroup conflict among whites that obscure our emphasis upon racial climates. Preliminary analysis revealed a number of all-white schools in which teachers reported that groups "don't get along together." Since the hostility item leaves the referent unclear, it lacks the necessary specificity to measure a school's interracial climate accurately. Neither the item nor its context specify whether the "groups" refer to segments of the student body, the faculty, the school's community, or all of them together. Our concern, however, is with students, though the interracial climate of student bodies would probably be influenced by the staff and community. The hostility item correlates positively ($r > .450$) with teacher ratings of such matters as whether the students create a discipline problem or come from poor home backgrounds; and this suggests that it reflects teacher ratings of the general intergroup conditions present within the school as a whole.

The item has two further limitations. Our primary interest is the effect of interracial climates upon student achievement. Hence, measures taken directly from the students are clearly preferable. Moreover, since there are far fewer teachers than students, the teacher ratings may be less stable and reliable than indices of interracial climates formed from the responses of all students within a school.

It should not be surprising, then, that schools' hostility levels are not identical to their cross-racial friendship levels. Table XIII provides results for grades 6 and 9. Although the school average cross-racial friendship (both Negro and white) and teachers' perception of interracial hostility are negatively related, the correlations are not large. In other words, while there is a tendency for the schools having high perceived intergroup conflict (more teachers agreeing that hostility between ethnic groups exists) to have less cross-racial student friendship, it is weak.

Interracial Friendship

Prediction of higher Negro achievement in integrated settings involves schools and not individuals. We are not testing how individual friendship relates to individual Negroes' achievement, but how schools'

TABLE XIII

Correlations between teacher's perceptions of "ethnic group hostility" * and school mean cross-racial friendship, Negro and white, for grades 6 and 9 in the Urban North

Grade	Negroes Having White Friends†	Whites Having Negro Friends
6 (N = 208)	−.257	.315
9 (N = 109)	−.258	.190

* This is the Percentage of Teachers within a school who agree with the statement, "The different races or ethnic groups do not get along well together" (Teacher's Question 47-C). The greater this percentage, the higher the perceived level of intergroup hostility within a school.

† *School Mean Cross-Racial Friendship:* These are School Means on the Cross-Racial Friendship Measure computed separately for each race. The difference in the signs of the correlations for Negroes and whites between the Cross-Racial Friendship measure and the Percentage of Teachers reporting "Ethnic Group Hostility" is an artifact of the scoring procedure, and does not represent a true reversal in the direction of the relationship by race.

For Negroes a score of 4 indicates that a student's friends are mostly or all white, while a score of 1 indicates that a student's friends are all Negro. (Response categories 4 and 5 of question 64, grade 12.) Thus, a high score for Negroes points to a high level of cross-racial friendship.

For whites, a score of 4 indicates that a student's friends are all white, while a score of 1 (response categories 1 and 2 of question 64, grade 12) indicates that a student's friends are mostly or all Negro. Thus, a high score for whites points to a low level of cross-racial friendship.

The school means on cross-racial friendship computed separately for each race reflect this scoring difference, and in turn the differences in the signs in the above correlations for Negroes and whites are expected. Both correlations suggest that the greater the percentage of teachers that reported "Ethnic Group Hostility," the lower the level of cross-racial friendship tends to be.

interracial climates (as measured by levels of cross-racial friendship) affect schools' average achievement. *The question is whether differences among schools' climates relate to differences in their average student achievement.* Under these conditions the friendship index must reflect how common cross-racial friendship is in each school. The wording of the EEOS item, however, is not a direct measure of within-school friendship choices; it asked students how many of their friends were white, not how many of their *school* friends were white. Thus, to the degree that the respondents have friends of the other race entirely outside of school, ambiguity is present. But it is not crucial for the hypothesis that the interracial friendship be exclusive to schools: the question is not whether schools or neighborhoods *cause* interracial friendship, but whether levels of interracial friendship—whatever their cause—relate to schools' achievement levels. As long as residential and school segregation maintain their close relationship, it would be impossible to separate their contribution to schools' levels of interracial friendship.

The concept of "interracial climate" raises other issues. Is such a climate best conceived as a single measure of interracial interaction, established proportionately by white and Negro students, or should it be racially specific, requiring separate measures of white acceptance of Negroes and Negro acceptance of whites? We decided to employ racially specific indices for two reasons. Most important, since our basic hypothesis concerns white acceptance of Negroes, racially specific measures are necessary. Second, only modest relationships ($r = -.300$) exist between average white and Negro cross-racial friendship across schools, pointing to the lack of symmetric friendship choices, and raising doubts about attributing a unitary property to each school.*

At this point, however, we noted a rather high correlation between the school average of interracial friendship and the school percent Negro ($r \cong .800$). Since this suggested that most of the variation in friendship might be associated with schools' racial composition, a table was run to determine whether there was adequate variation in the friendship climate variable to test its effect on achievement, once racial composition was controlled. Table XIV displays the results for Negroes in grade 6. It classifies the grade-6 schools by their levels of interracial friendship and racial composition. The entries reveal that *there are virtually no predominantly white schools in*

TABLE XIV

School mean white cross-racial friendship by school racial composition for grade 6 in the Urban North

School Average Whites Having Negro Friends	School Percent Negro					
	80+	60–80	40–60	20–40	0–20	Total
Mean Cross-Racial Friendship (None or less than half, 3.01–4.00)	—	16.7 (2)	73.7 (14)	87.0 (20)	100 (34)	64.2 (70)
Mean Cross-Racial Friendship (About half, 2.01–3.00)	57.1 (9)	83.3 (10)	26.3 (5)	13.0 (3)	—	27.5 18
Mean Cross-Racial Friendship (More than half, 1.01–2.00)	42.9 (9)	—	—	—	—	8.3 (9)
Mean Cross-Racial Friendship (All, 0.0–1.00)	—	—	—	—	—	—
Overall Mean Cross-Racial Friendship Choice: Whites Having Negro Friends	2.57	3.17	3.74	3.87	4.00	3.56

which the average of white friendship with Negroes was "half," "more than half," or "all." This means that the range of variation among schools' interracial climates was insufficient (once racial composition was controlled) to provide a meaningful test of our hypothesis. As long as variation in interracial friendship remains so constrained, survey research on the problem of interracial climates will be impossible.

* The minus sign of this correlation is an artifact of the scoring procedure. See footnote to Table XIII.

Sources of Variation in Climates

The same problem also made it impossible to explore the predictors of schools' interracial climates. Among the schools selected for this sample, the collinearity of interracial climates with racial composition precludes the investigation of other school attributes which relate to schools' interracial climates, independent of a school's racial composition.

Notes on Future Studies

Post-EEOS experimentation can be much more valuable than similar work might have been earlier. In this sense, EEOS represents a watershed in educational research. It raised fundamental questions for more thorough testing, and challenged some long-held beliefs. It forces us to place results from the typically isolated situations in which experiments are performed in a national perspective, and it has generated enthusiasm for fundamental educational research. One of the chief vehicles for future work should be longitudinal field research, conducted directly in the schools.

Some field research meeting this description has been conducted. To illustrate our hopes concretely, we shall describe two of the more interesting studies. The first, by St. John and Smith[18] of ninth graders in Pittsburgh, explicitly sets out to test racial composition hypotheses stemming from EEOS, using longitudinal independent variables and an array of achievement and aspiration measures as dependent variables. The second, by Veroff and Peele,[19] investigates the effect of one year of elementary-school desegregation on achievement motivation. Both studies focus upon the effects of school desegregation on Negro children; both employ longitudinal data and a variety of dependent variables; each exploits research opportunities in the field rather than in the laboratory. In short, these two investigations typify what we envision as an especially important approach for future educational research.

St. John and Smith selected eight Pittsburgh schools, varying from 2 to 99 percent Negro. Limiting their work to 1400 ninth graders, they obtained four dependent variables: 1) reading, 2) arithmetic achievement scores from school records, 3) occupational, and 4) educational aspirations obtained directly from the children by questionnaire. These are static indicators, but longitudinal data were employed for two of the racial-composition variables. St. John and Smith improved on the Coleman procedures by forming a measure of each child's *cumulative school racial experience* by averaging the racial percentages of previous schools attended. In addition, they formed a discontinuous "pattern" indicator with five types of Negro pupils: those with experience only; those with experience only *in* schools; "resegregated" children with majority-white primary-school experience followed by majority-Negro junior highs; "desegregated" children with majority-Negro primary-school experience followed by majority-white junior highs; and those with experience only in majority-white schools. One nonlongitudinal predictor, the Negro percentage for each school's 9th grade, also was used. Finally, they employed several control measures: school mean parent education and school mean occupational status; the average social-class level of each school's district, sex, and school-recorded I.Q.

The results are straightforward. For all three of the racial composition indicators, percent Negro was negatively related with arithmetic achievement and positively related with educational aspirations,[20] with full controls applied. Negro children tended to attain higher arithmetic scores in desegregated schools, and report higher educational aspirations in segregated schools. The achievement advantage for interracial education was strongest when *present* (grade 9) racial composition was the independent variable; the aspiration advantage for segregated education was strongest when the cumulative, longitudinal indicator was used. However, the "pattern" variable proved to be the strongest predictor of achievement scores. And, while not generally attaining statistical significance, the other dependent measures gave similar results: reading achievement tended to be highest in desegregated, and occupational aspirations highest in segregated schools. In short, educational desegregation for Negro ninth graders in Pittsburgh appears to elevate achievement and lower aspirations.

The results on aspirations are open to a number of interpretations. The explanation that comes first to mind is simply that majority-white schools discourage high educational aspirations among most of their Negro students. This could take the form of blatant racism and paternalism on the part of teachers and peers. A second possibility is put forward by Irwin Katz.[21] He maintains that the high aspirations of lower-status Negro children in overwhelmingly Negro schools tend to be rigid and unrealistic. Katz has experimentally demonstrated how such high aspirations can doom their victims to serious learning difficulties and ultimate failure. In his view, integration benefits learning among Negro children by lowering their aspirations to more effective and realistic levels. Our second example of a longitudinal field investigation bears directly on these possibilities.

Veroff and Peele seized an unusual research opportunity presented by a public school system of a small midwestern city. In order to overcome racial segregation in the system's elementary schools, the city closed the predominantly Negro facility and required its students to attend overwhelmingly white facilities. Attendance at one elementary school whose student body was approximately one half white was not altered, and it served as a convenient control group. The majority-white receiver schools shifted from an average of 3 percent to 7 percent Negro. The bused Negro children were largely lower status, the unchanged school was intermediate in social status, and the receiver schools were generally middle class. The study tested for changes in achievement motivation among approximately 1000 Negro children over the first year of desegregation. Two measures of achievement motivation were employed, together with an aspiration indicator: *autonomous achievement motivation* tests individually for a child's avoidance of achievement challenges within his own ability range; *social comparison achievement motivation* tests individually for a child's avoidance of achievement when he knows how well others have done on the task at hand.

Critical to this investigation is the well-known psychological fact that achievement motivation and aspiration level are *not* identical. Following Atkinson,[22] Veroff and Peele define extremely low and high aspirations as avoiding risk—opting out of the achievement challenge. Thus, they judge moderate, realistic levels of aspiration as indicating the highest and most effective motivation for excellence and achievement—a view for which there is considerable supporting evidence. Hence, in measuring autonomous achievement motivation they had children perform a series of graduated tasks until they failed two in a row. Then they were asked to select one of four tasks to try again—the easiest, the last he was able to do correctly, the first he failed, or the second he failed (the most difficult in his series). The choice of either the first or last of these tasks reveals low autonomous achievement motivation, choice of either of the two moderate tasks reveals high autonomous achievement motivation. Social-comparison achievement motivation was measured by having the child select one of three visually identical tasks to do: the first is described as one that is easy for children his age to do; the second as one some children his age can do and others cannot do; and the third as one that most children his age cannot do. Once again, selection of the moderately difficult task indicates high achievement motivation. Veroff and Peele also employed as an indicator of aspiration level the absolute level of the social comparison desired, which is the most comparable of their measures to the aspiration measures found by St. John and Smith to be highest for Negro ninth graders in Pittsburgh's predominantly Negro schools.

The results of this longitudinal field experiment help clarify both the aspiration and sex findings of the Pittsburgh study. All of the Veroff and Peele analyses controlled for initial achievement scores and I.Q. while varying race, grade, sex, and minority status in school. For Negro *boys* bused to majority-white schools, compared to Negro boys who remained in the racially balanced school, achievement motivation—especially autonomous achievement motivation—significantly increased after a year of desegregation. This trend occurs largely because the majority-white school lowers unrealistically high aspirations of the Negro boys, depressing them to moderate risk-taking levels and stronger achievement motivation. Negro girls, however, do not evince similar trends.

As in the St. John and Smith study, then, Veroff and Peele find desegregation tends to depress aspiration levels of Negro children, particularly those of Negro boys. But these data further suggest that this process actually increases effective achievement motivation—a finding which is also consistent with the higher Negro achievement scores which generally accompany school desegregation. This study bears out Katz's original contentions regarding the rigid overaspiring which acts to retard learning among many Negro children in majority-Negro schools. Moreover, Veroff and Peele believe that there is a critical "sensitive period" around grades 3 through 5 for shaping social-comparison goals to effectively moderate levels.

SUMMARY.   These two studies nicely illustrate the potential and limitations of field research on educational experiments. The Ann Arbor research reveals some of the opportunities for studying changes in attitude consequent upon desegregation; direct work on aspirations in the later elementary and secondary grades would be equally useful, as would research on the influence of deliberate desegregation on friendship patterns. It is, however, difficult to imagine school systems which will systematically try to affect children's friendship patterns directly, and even more difficult to imagine biracial systems which would abandon internal ability grouping or tracking at the secondary level.

If our suspicions prove to be correct, then it should be possible—in theory, at least—to learn a good deal about the influence of desegregation on children's attitudes, achievement, and aspirations, but relatively little about the impact which changes in schools' interracial climates or classroom compositions have on these domains.

Notes

1. 347 U.S. 483. The Court quoted, with approval from the opinion of an appellate court, to the effect that:

   Segregation of white and colored children in public schools has a detrimental effect upon the colored children. The impact is greater when it has the sanction of law; for the policy of separating the races is usually interpreted as denoting the inferiority of the negro [sic] group. *A sense of inferiority affects the motivation of children to learn. Segregation with the sanction of law, therefore, has a tendency to* [retard] *the educational and mental development of negro* [sic] *children.* . . . [emphasis added]

2. J. Coleman *et al.*, *Equality of Educational Opportunity Survey* (henceforth EEOS), Washington: 1966, pp. 307–8.
3. U.S. Commission on Civil Rights, *Racial Isolation in the Public Schools* (henceforth USCCR), 2 vols., Washington, D.C.: 1967, Vol. 2, Tables 5.1, 5.2, pp. 86–7.
4. *Ibid.*, Vol. 1, pp. 113–4.
5. EEOS, p. 330.
6. For an explanation of this procedure, see EEOS, pp. 328–9.

7. Readers will notice a peculiarity in the results at grades 9 and 12 for one of the student environment variables (percent in college curriculum); it is mildly negative at grade 9 and mildly positive at 12. There are two problems with this. First, the variable was mislabeled: the authors thought it was the percent of students planning college whereas actually it was the percent saying they were in the college curriculum (see Smith, Chapter 6). Second, at grade 9 roughly one quarter of the students responded that they did not know yet what their curriculum was (at least Negroes in the urban Northeast and Mid-Atlantic regions so responded). Their verbal mean was 255.8, whereas the verbal mean for those saying they were in a college curriculum was 268.7, and those in a general curriculum 260.5. The procedure of assigning such "don't know" responses to the mean value of the available response categories thus resulted in artificially distorting the relationship between the percent in the college curriculum and individual achievement, which probably accounts for the negative value at grade 9. No such response category was available at grade 12.

8. Jencks, Chapter 11.

9. The results in this table are based on all Northern urban elementary schools. For a description of this group of schools, see Smith, Chapter 6.

10. A. Wilson, "The Consequences of Segregation in a California Community," in USCCR, Vol. 2, p. 136, Table 13.

11. This question was taken up in part by the Commission on Civil Rights; in cross tabulations of individual Negro students' verbal ability, their ability group placement at grade 9 was controlled. A residual effect of white classmates remained (USCCR, Vol. 1, pp. 100–3). J. McPartland, in *The Desegregated Negro Student in Segregated High Schools* (Center for the Study of the Social Organization of Schools, The Johns Hopkins University, 1968), pursued these issues in greater detail. Successive controls were applied for ability group, classroom social class, and curricular placement, but a residual effect of proportion white classmates remained in each case. However, since the controls were applied successively rather than simultaneously, a suspicion that the results were spurious also remains.

12. Table VIII was computed from 9th grades in the urban Northeast, Mid-Atlantic, and Midwest, but the data on curricula arise from only some of these schools— namely, those with 12th grades. Principals in 9th-grade schools without 12th grades were asked *not* to respond to the question on curricula. Since the table thus excludes junior high schools, it probably overstates the extent of curricular tracking at grade 9.

13. This is not easy to investigate. We know, for example, about the racial composition of each student's classroom and the ability group and curriculum to which he was assigned. Unfortunately, however, the latter items were current as of the date of the survey, whereas the former referred to the previous academic year. This introduces some problems which can be resolved only by faith—the facts required for an empirical solution are not available. We must assume that what was true for classes "last year" (which may have been an elementary school) also was true of curricula and ability groups in September, 1965. There is no way of knowing how mistaken this assumption is, although the greater mobility between grades 8 and 9 (due to organizational changes) makes us more uneasy about the data for 9th-grade students than for those in grade 12.

Another problem with the investigation of anything involving classmates white last year is the question of whether there are differences between students who entered their school in the fall of 1965 and those who had been there in previous years. We might expect there to be, but the answer for ninth graders is doubtless confounded with the fact that in many schools (those that begin with grade 9) all students transferred in the fall of 1965; it is therefore difficult to compare high-mobility with low-mobility students. Comparisons of the verbal achievement of grade-12 students, between those who changed schools in 1965 and those who did not, were therefore carried out; in this grade there is no problem of an organizational break in schooling. The difference between the verbal achievement of those who changed school "last year" and those who did not was 1.3 points (in favor of those who did not change).

14. The analysis was undertaken for all 9th-grade Negro students in the urban Northeast and Mid-Atlantic regions. Curricular assignment is a dummy variable, in which assignment to an academic curriculum had a value of one, and assignment to all other curricula a value of zero.

15. The results for academic curricula are as follows:

TABLE XV

Regression of individual Negro verbal ability on classroom racial composition, parents' education track assignment, and curriculum mean Negro verbal ability for Grade 9 academic curriculum in the Urban North

$$(N = 2029)$$

Variables	Variables in Regression				t's
	(1)	(1, 2)	(1, 2, 3)	(1, 2, 3, 4)	
(1) Class White	.145	.122	.124	.098	4.9
(2) Highest Parent Education		.231	.208	.124	6.1
(3) Track Assignment			.206	.182	9.2
(4) Curricular Mean Negro Verbal Ability				.358	17.6
Total Variance Explained	2.1	7.4	11.6	23.5	

16. Katz has summarized and discussed his research in three papers, the first of which is especially relevant to our hypothesis. See: Irwin Katz, "Review of Evidence Relating to Effects of Desegregation on the Intellectual Performance of Negroes," *American Psychologist*, Vol. 19, 1964, pp. 381–99; Irwin Katz, "The Socialization of Academic Motivation in Minority Group Children," in D. Levine, ed., *Nebraska Symposium on Motivation, 1969*, Lincoln, Nebraska: University of Nebraska Press, 1969, pp. 133–91; and Irwin Katz, "A Critique of Personality Approaches to Negro Performance, with Research Suggestions," *Journal of Social Issues*, Vol. 25, No. 3, 1969, pp. 13–27.

17. Katz, "Review of Evidence Relating to Effects of Desegregation on the Intellectual Performance of Negroes."

18. Nancy St. John and M. S. Smith, "School Racial Composition, Achievement, and Aspiration," unpublished paper, Graduate School of Education, Harvard University, 1969.

19. J. Veroff and S. Peele, "Initial Effects of Desegregation on the Achievement Motivation of Negro Elementary School Children," *Journal of Social Issues*, Vol. 25, No. 3, Summer 1969, pp. 71–91.

20. A procedure used by St. John and Smith needs to be mentioned, as it would be a useful practice for such research. As in the EEOS, missing data and lost cases pose special problems of sampling bias and selection errors. St. John and Smith constructed, out of their almost 1400 total cases, a "clean" sample of 650 for which all data were available. Then they provided a complete analysis on each set of data and checked for differences. Remarkably, the "dirty" and "clean" results were identical as to conclusions, and generally of the same as to orders of magnitude. But such will not always be the case; such a procedure is absolutely essential for research.

21. Katz, "The Socialization of Academic Motivation in Minority Group Children."

22. J. W. Atkinson, *An Introduction to Motivation*. Princeton, N.J.: Van Nostrand, 1964.

IMPLICATIONS FOR
THE FUTURE

8

The Urgent Need for Experimentation [*]

JOHN P. GILBERT & FREDERICK MOSTELLER

To get better schooling for our children, we must find out how to strengthen our educational system. This will require study and especially, as we shall explain, experimentation.

When we speak of experiments, we are not talking about innovation in the "let's first try this and then try that" sense. Instead we mean large-scale field experiments with honest controls. To show how the methods tested work in different places and under different conditions, the size must be large. Few great gains having wide application will be made in the educational process without such large-scale experiments, even though the ideas to be tested may arise from the most delicate laboratory work or from the most abstruse theories. Innovation, while essential, cannot strengthen the educational system unless its gains are confirmed by extensive trial and evaluation.

The nation is currently redefining the goals and reordering the authority structure of its school systems. We do not discuss these issues, though we recognize that political changes can make great differences. No matter how these issues are resolved, society will still need to know how to teach children well. Although some experiments cannot be carried out in the midst of upheaval, the type of investigations we recommend need not delay any particular change in school systems.

Furthermore, the educational process must be related to the larger process of the community. For example, school milk and lunch programs long ago recognized how important physiological factors were to children. Evidence grows that better nutrition much earlier may prevent damage to a child's mental processes. How much earlier? Before birth? We are slow to find out about this because we don't do enough genuine experiments. Similarly, we need to appraise other physical, economic, and social factors not

[*] This work was facilitated by a grant from the National Science Foundation (GS-2044X).

only in the school but also in the family and community for their effects upon children's education. How important is father's employment to success in school? We need not limit the experiments to the confines of the school-yards, for one way to strengthen the schools is to strengthen the students.

◆ *Experiments Are Convincing*

Nearly everyone writing about the Coleman Report has emphasized that it was based on a survey taken at one moment of time and not on an experiment. Thus, even though we can compare groups of pupils who were exposed to somewhat different conditions, we have difficulty in arguing that those differences in conditions largely or even importantly contributed to the differences in performance of the various groups. Everyone sees why. Let us take a neutral example. If we see that one group of people has bigger dwellings than another, we can spend the rest of our lives arguing the reasons. Were they richer to begin with? Did they have more children and need the space? Were they rural people at heart who just appreciated space more than city-lovers? Or all of these? However, suppose that we take a large group of people, give a randomly chosen half of them $1000 a year and give the other half nothing. If at the end of two years we find that the half with the extra money have increased the size of their dwellings considerably more than the others, few will argue that the increased income was not a cause. The random assignment of the experimental treatment triumphs over all the little excuses for not attributing the effect to the difference in treatment. To summarize, an experiment is a strong way to find out the effect of a treatment. George Box said it well: "To find out what happens to a system when you interfere with it, you have to interfere with it (not just passively observe it)."

◆ *Other Ways to Knowledge*

Admittedly, experimentation is not the only way to find the effect of a treatment. Much of what we have learned and act on in life comes from observation—studies that systematically gather facts about what is happening, but do not actively interfere with the process. If we observe that children with less food do not learn as much in school as those who have more, we are inclined in the twentieth century to suppose that families with more food will produce healthier children and that healthier children will learn more quickly, rather than that hunger sharpens the wits.

Consider the Coleman Report's suggestion that school variables have little effect and let us misunderstand that claim to mean that schools don't matter to learning. Then we can do a mental experiment by thinking about how much algebra will be learned if students do not go to school, but just stay home and sop up learning by themselves. After all, isn't that the best way? Self-motivated learning? Surely, but we all see that only a very few people will learn any algebra.

In a sense, we also have observational evidence on this as well as a mental experiment. Many college-educated people today had fathers who did not go past the 6th grade. By and large they know that their fathers didn't learn any algebra by themselves, however clever they may have been with numbers. Studies of adult education don't show people learning mathematics by themselves until they have learned a great deal of it. Even self-taught heroes like Abraham Lincoln made no progress in algebra and calculus. Both mental experiment and observation tell us that mathematics beyond arithmetic would not be learned if schools were abolished. Therefore, the notion that school variables have little effect does not in the least mean that schools don't matter to learning. Rather, given that we have school systems, the objection has been that the presence or absence of certain school features does not seem to make large differences in performance by the pupils. Insofar as it is true, this is important because the schools have not educated certain groups as well as society wishes, and we do not see how to improve their education by modest changes in the school variables available for adjustment. The argument is a bit queasy here because 1) of lack of experimentation, 2) of not pairing a facility with its special trainees (swimming pools don't teach much French), 3) previous successful equating of important variables may have concealed their effect, and 4) reports for school systems rather than schools also suppress effects.

When we find that an observational study suggests that certain variables produce effects of a given sort, we are usually correct in assuming that they do. Once in a while, a more controlled study will give a different answer.

Still another difficulty is that many different causal schemes can usually be proposed to "explain away" the results of an observational study. The number of alternative explanations should certainly be weighed, but it is well to put one's faith in simple direct explanations rather than elaborate circuitous ones. Our own experiences with observational studies and related experiments have been that the controlled study usually does not contradict the observational study, but it does clarify matters and make them firmer. Let us give a concrete example of the sort of thing this experience suggests until better evidence appears. We know that richer people are better educated, and so we conclude for the moment that if poorer families get more money their children will later be better educated than they would otherwise have been. But this conclusion will always be tantalizingly and endlessly arguable. Therefore, where we, as a society, care about a causal relation, we need substantial experiments to settle some of the arguments— arguments that cannot be put to rest by observational studies or mental experiments.

♦ Facts Help

Firm facts now and again clear the air in remarkable ways, and they are needed because we are so good at speculating. If a rumor circulates that disease A is soon going to become a public health problem, facts such as that only 1 death per 100,000 relates to this disease and that no increase in the rate has been observed in ten years rather chill further speculation. But without such facts, we can worry about building special hospitals to take care of the patients, perhaps think of creating a medical speciality for it, consider what antipollution measures may be effective against it, and at the very least organize a study. The Coleman Report has done a great deal to supply firm facts.

For example, almost no one tries to argue in the face of the Coleman Report that rural areas produce the best students. Yet prior to the publication of the report, it would have been easy to find proponents of this position.

Let us note that we have got rather good at fact-gathering through sample surveys and observational studies over the last forty years. The improvement has come from the increased use of quantitative methods in a variety of fields: public health, sociology, psychology, and economics, and from new statistical developments that have strengthened the theoretical and practical bases of these surveys and studies. The result is that we have become better at measuring how things are now, and even at measuring how they have changed recently in the general population. The development of this statistical ability has been most important, and we now have several facilities for carrying out such studies. Such facilities must have know-how in the practice and theory of sampling, in question-wording, in interviewing, and in the construction of questionnaires. They must also have field staffs ready and waiting, technical staffs and equipment to code and check and analyze the questionnaires, and fiscal groups to handle costing and accounting. Such organizations take years to create and shake down, and we are most fortunate to have a variety of them. These organizations are found in the commercial field, in universities, and in the government, where the Bureau of the Census has been an exceptionally able leader. Large-scale investigations of any kind require large and complicated facilities to carry them out, and we see that in the area of sample surveys we now have great resources.

Our progress in national sample surveys has not been matched by corresponding progress in large-scale controlled social investigations nor in the evaluation of large social programs. We have large-scale experimental research organizations in the agricultural experiment stations of the nation, and we have mounted large medical experiments, such as the nationwide trials of the Salk vaccine for polio, but nothing comparable* is available in the social field.

◆ Large-Scale Controlled Investigations

If we are to move into large-scale experimentation we shall have to have the facilities for it. In 1967 Manning Pattillo suggested that in the future private foundations would be more interested in evaluating their programs and that they therefore would need more staff qualified to make appraisals. He even suggested that private foundations might be able to offer government an impartial appraisal of its programs. Such ideas must in the end lead to controlled experimentation in social programs.

Haven't we done controlled experimentation in the past in the field of education? We have. The literature is full of it. We have not been very successful with such experimentation, but not for want of trying. Our attempts have been frequent, usually in the tradition of the small tight experiment of the laboratory psychologist rather than the broader large-scale field study, with repetition in a variety of places: repetition suited to the place and personnel. For example, to improve the teaching of students handicapped by poverty, language, and indifference, research will have to be done in schools where such conditions apply rather than among the rich or middle class alone.

We have not done these large-scale experiments partly because the money has not been available, and partly because we have thought that the tightly controlled classroom study would tell us what we wanted to know. Such studies have generally been disappointing in practice. Some possible reasons are that organizations, families, teachers, students, and their backgrounds vary a great deal from one part of the country to another and even from neighborhood to neighborhood, and so any investigation is bound to have a great deal of background noise in it. Indeed, after half a century of tightly controlled studies of optimum class size, we have made practically no progress toward answering the question (perhaps nature is hinting that the question is a poor one as customarily phrased). It is not that we haven't done controlled investigations, but rather that the studies have been too small and specialized for their implications to have much chance of holding in new situations.

To spell out a difficulty with the tightly controlled experiment, one might note that an experiment involving 600 pupils sounds good-sized, but if classrooms rather than students were what was important, we might be down to 20 classrooms for classes of 30 students. If, further, schools were important, the 20 classes might be distributed among only 4 schools, say,

* Perhaps the nearest to an example of such a facility would be the University of Michigan's Research Center for Group Dynamics.

and a sample size of 4 is small, indeed. But the final blow may be that all schools are from 1 school system in 1 county in 1 state in 1 region of the county, and so from many points of view such experiments are based on samples of size 1, a very small sample for choosing a national program.

When the same treatment under controlled conditions produces good results in many places and circumstances, then we become confident that we have found a general rule When the payoff is finicky—gains in one place, losses in another—we are wary because we can't count on the effect. A nice experiment like the Hartford busing study reported in Dyer's chapter on future studies has a partial replication from grade to grade. But we dare not press whatever generalization we draw beyond "communities like Hartford" until other places can show similar gains.

♦ *The Obligation to Experiment*

We have many social programs, and these programs are often repeated in place after place. Yet we seldom take any advantage of the existence of these automatic repetitions, which are just what one needs for controlled investigation. When such programs exist in parallel for community after community, we owe it to society and the taxpayer to take advantage of these repetitions to strengthen our inferences about what aspects make them better.

People often think that if we are to experiment, then we are going to abuse or mistreat. They may even say that we must not experiment with people, especially children, because they are too precious to be so abused. Since we change the educational system frequently and arbitrarily, and cannot profitably record the results of these haphazard adjustments, the abuse is that while "experimenting" in this casual way we are learning little. Since planned variation can tell us something, frittering away the opportunities to learn from operational changes devalues the experiences of the participants by neglecting to use them for society's benefit.

We want to find better ways of teaching where we are not doing as well as we would like. Living in ignorance, we have an opportunity, even an *obligation*, to experiment. The purpose of the experimentation is to aid innovation. Much has been said and written lately against experimentation, but little or nothing about the obligation to experiment. When we are spending huge sums on programs that have little theoretical or empirical grounds for success in improving society, we should evaluate and experiment as we go to find out how the programs can more fully carry out their missions. To find out more, we will have to change our attitude toward the word "experiment" or perhaps get ourselves a new word.

Experimentation need not affect a large portion of the program, indeed often not much more than the informal sort of changes that are so often made and explored in every school system. But it does require planning, careful execution, data-gathering, and analysis. We need not expect the first few to be carried out very well; we need experience.

Since we are involved in distributing scarce resources, we need to evaluate new programs carefully to see first how to strengthen them and then second whether to maintain them, or try an alternative development. We should be continually planning alternative programs to replace those that do not work out.

The position of the administrators of experimental programs needs to be clearly understood. Their careers should not depend upon the success or failure of a particular program but rather upon their skill in exploring the virtues and shortcomings of the program. This point has been eloquently discussed by Donald Campbell (1969) who has pioneered in the development of statistical methods for quantifying the effects of changes in policy.

One of the compelling reasons for educational experiments is the importance for society of every improvement in the learning process. The lives of large numbers of people are appreciably improved by every such advance. In addition, how successfully our society functions relates directly to the extent that people have acquired the skills we need to achieve our goals and individuals need to achieve theirs.

No matter how much experimentation we do, controversy will still be the order of the day. Every part of science and engineering has its prizes. When they are as large as those resulting from a huge new program in education, we can expect controversy even in the presence of good data. Conflicting advice will be available from highly regarded experts. This calls for some innovations in the appreciation of science for policy decisions, and we might hope that political scientists would suggest and appraise some ways that administrators could use to help choose between competing programs. Until now an administrator mainly relied upon his own intuition, the "consensus" found in the journals, the advice of wise friends or of special commissions created to study specific programs. In the fall of 1968, both McGeorge Bundy, in an address at the American Academy of Arts and Sciences, and Harvey Brooks, in conversation, have called our attention to the possibility of developing an adversary procedure so that an administrator could fairly hear the sides of a difficult question argued by prepared experts, with the help of his own experts to guide some part of the questioning. We believe that exploratory studies should be undertaken to find ways to help administrators make good use of science and scientists.

◆ What If We Don't Experiment?

First, without experimentation we are dependent upon the natural selection and evolution of programs to strengthen and improve the system. The social process is too complex and educational institutions are too rigid for us to expect speedy unaided evolution. The appraisal of results from informal variation is too difficult, in the face of so many uncontrolled variables, to guide policy. We need experiments to get some firm results. Without them, we will discard fine programs along with the poor ones.

Second, a great many innovations will be tried in one or two places each, and each will be declared the solution to our educational problems. Then as others try them, they will usually fail. If these were the only losses, they could be borne. We expect many failures. Furthermore, every new plan has to have some pilot studies before we try it out on a larger scale. But unless studies are carried out in a systematic way, we will not have learned about conditions when a method may be of use and when it may not, or what features of the program still show promise in spite of general failure. These are the losses that matter, for without systematic effort, we stumble on generation after generation, learning little and fooling ourselves that we are learning something about the process because we are busy doing new things. Thus, by never getting firm facts, we are always in the position of believing that "the" solution is contained in the new program just being tried.

The controversies about the Coleman Report show that we still are ignorant of what makes education tick for children and of why what works for some doesn't seem to for others. For whom is laissez faire wise, and for whom a lockstep program? Naturally we do not expect that only one sort of program is workable, because children can adapt to or resist most things. Our point is that when a big national effort is as little understood as education now is, we are obligated to experiment.

Third, without experimental studies we can expect continual arguments like those that surround the present Coleman Report. Do school variables matter, and if so, how much? If we care about questions of this sort, and they seem to be of general interest, we need experiments. Actually, the controversy here is as much over the definition of a school variable as over the magnitude and importance of its effect. Designing and executing an experiment or two will go far toward clarifying these issues.

The more general sorts of methodological squabbles on which many papers about the Coleman Report focus can be partly cured by carrying out some actual experiments. As long as these are not done, we have no solid foundation to build upon. Much of science makes its progress by discovering a few firm facts, then moving up a level and building on these. Once one gets three or four layers high, the discipline is on its way to an era well removed from its earlier primitive state. We have received a few firm facts from the Coleman Report; now we need some experiments to build on them.

◆ Innovations Are Often Ineffective

Here again we have to face the music. Most innovations will do little or no good. In reviewing a recent survey reported by Jack Elinson at the

Ross Pediatric Conference, we concluded that among ten substantial programs designed to improve the welfare or health of the people involved, the control group in seven did about as well as those receiving the new treatment. The most valuable lesson here is that we find this out only because we had controlled investigations. Had experiments not been done, we would have had little way of knowing that the programs were not improving the performance that they were intended to advance. Instead, encouraged by the originality, progressiveness, and plausibility of the programs, we might have initiated them at great expense throughout the nation. Now, at least we know that the particular techniques do not work well and in some instances why not.

The second valuable lesson is that most innovations don't work, even when they are introduced with the best will in the world, are carefully thought out, and vigorously and expertly executed. This shouldn't surprise anyone. There must be hundreds of new mousetraps invented for every one that catches on in the marketplace. Building a better society is not easy.

Why are educational innovations frequently ineffective? A great effect occurs when we introduce a school or a school system into a region that has none. Those who go to school are going to learn arithmetic and spelling better than they would have if they had not had systematic schooling. Indeed, one of Elinson's exceptions to the lack of effect in social programs had to do with starting new programs of training.

Introducing a brand-new program where none existed before can have enormous specific effects. However, when someone looks at a going school system and suggests that it be changed to make it better—let's be specific, to make the students learn arithmetic better—he has two strikes against him. First of all, the system is running now, and the proposed innovations can possibly reduce its effectiveness. Second, the people who formerly ran and are now running the school will have put a strong effort into doing what they can to make the system pay off well. So at best the change is only going to take up part of the slack between how well the system works now and the best it could do. When one has a choice, as a manager may have in a plant, between trying to produce a product more cheaply and thinking of a new product that may bring in additional profit, he is very likely to opt for the latter because he will usually have done the obvious and the customary things to improve the process of manufacturing for the old product. Beyond this, he cannot expect hard effort to pay many percent. This does not mean that a new insight, material, or machine might not come along that would make a tremendous difference in profit, but until it does, he is justified in putting his effort and investment of capital into a new product line.

This is, of course, one possibility for education. Perhaps new product lines are what we need. We are not arguing this point, but about the need to notice that when one has a going concern, improvement isn't easy. In spite of all the discussion about the feebleness of our school system, we are putting more students into college than ever before both absolutely and per-centagewise; this is true of every race, color, and creed; and we lead the world in this effort. Nevertheless, we are called upon to make changes. We have noted that improving a going concern is not likely to pay off as well as introducing the concern in the first place did. So in innovating we are likely to be in for disappointments, but we may pick up an acorn once in a while, occasionally even find a pot of gold. Just as we won't readily make great gains, we also aren't likely to suffer big losses.

We emphasize this appreciation of the frequent failure of innovation because it alerts us to the need for experimentation both to secure the gains already made and to identify the successful ventures. Ideas are easy to come by in social areas, but hard, expensive, and risky to introduce on a broad scale, and hence the necessity for realistic appraisal based on sound experi-mental procedures.

In addition, verifying that ideas work, finding when they work, and training people to make them work, are also hard and expensive. For ex-ample, Skinnerian training programs for young children attract investiga-tors in many areas of education, as well they should. The descriptions of Hamblin *et al.* (1969) in teaching young abnormally aggressive children and autistic children are on the one hand most encouraging, but on the other illustrate how hard it is to train teachers and mothers in this skill. Even after training, the responses required are hard to choose and execute. Con-sequently, hidden observers had to use radios to direct the teachers and mothers, who received their instructions through small earplug receivers. We need to see whether other investigators can make the process work, whether the cures can be maintained through the years, and whether ag-gression is reduced by persons untrained in handling the children, as well as for those who are. One can readily see the great need for repeating and extending such promising experiments, and one can also see that the verifi-cation will be costly. But preventing individuals from spending their lives in prison or in an asylum offers society financial rewards as well as satisfac-tion.

♦ Experimentation Without Regimentation

If we are to find out whether some new ideas do produce a substantial gain, then we shall have to be prepared to measure the effects carefully. And this means experimentation. We need to know where we instituted what programs, and where what others, and then we need to find out what was achieved. This is the main feature of experimentation. The programs need to be introduced randomly, or nearly so in a large variety of places. One way is to find a number of places that are willing to introduce either of a pair of new programs and then randomly assign the program. If the school or the school district has agreed to take the one that it is assigned of the two, and if the school is offered some financial support for it, then the school will be encouraged to institute the program assigned to it. If it is a wild success, compared to its competitor, very likely others will want it, too.

We need to make clear here that it is not necessary to press distasteful experiments down the throats of reluctant school-board members. Experimentation can be a most attractive thing, and most of what are regarded as the best schools do experimentation in the sense of innovation. But usually only in the sense that Princeton's Harold Gulliksen deprecates when he says, "They didn't use any controls because it was only an experiment."

Experimentation, then, is not distasteful but attractive when properly considered. It is not necessary for us to impose new treatments on some schools and withhold them from others. We can in principle offer new treatments to many schools in the same experimental system. It is only necessary that a reasonable number of institutions be willing to institute either one of a pair of programs.

Naturally, we are not proposing that there be large-scale experimentation on programs that have not been carefully worked out and that don't have promise. We all understand that new therapies have their preliminary tryouts before moving into practical programs. What we are pressing is that when they move into large-scale use, they be assessed, given a fair chance to show their worth, and expanded if they work, revised if they don't.

◆ Educational Goals

In improving the atmosphere for educational experimentation, we will find ourselves regimented in a different way. We have to know just what it is that we want improved. The ambitious goal of creating a modern version of the Renaissance Man is not going to be successfully met by any program. If we want something better than we have now, we need to specify it and key our program to accomplishing it. (See Henry Dyer's article.) We seldom make progress of much account in unexpected directions. It is hard enough to make gains in directions we are working toward. If we want verbal facility improved, then we should make that clear and concentrate on that. If we want to combat prejudice, then let's make very clear what it is that we want taught and see how effective we are at communicating it. If we teach Latin in hope that it will improve our English vocabulary, then we must spend plenty of time on this latter aspect, and we can expect less Latin to be learned. Similarly, let's not teach logic or mathematics to discipline our minds, let's teach mathematics in hope that the student will learn mathematics. Perhaps team sports can teach the need for teamwork. Construe nothing in the above to suppose that the authors have any specific subject or goal they wish to push as far as the general experimental program is concerned; rather, we are discussing some of the atmosphere that is required if we are to try to develop a systematic effort at improving schools. We believe that experimentation may be part of the answer.

Dyer discusses the educational goals set by a commission for the Commonwealth of Pennsylvania. The general attitude is that every student should make the most of himself in every possible direction. Without restriction, this set of goals is not achievable. Given the limitations of the 24-hour day, no one can make the most of himself in many directions. The most that he can hope to do is to achieve some minimum goals in a number of desirable directions and then distribute the rest of his effort in ways that he, his parents, his teacher, the school, the state, and the nation find rewarding.

Setting many desirable maxima makes it hard to know what program might possibly lead to achievement of the goals. A well-known mathematical theorem states that one cannot ordinarily maximize two or more variables simultaneously. Consequently, it would be vain to hope to maximize the achievement of each child in several different subjects. If we set minimum standards to be achieved by each group, we can offer goals capable of achievement, while leaving time for individual preferences and excellences.

♦ The Hawthorne Effect

Some will have heard of the Hawthorne effect and be worried about it in the presence of all the innovations being discussed. Since this is the most widely cited effect in the field of social science according to David Sills, editor of the new *International Encyclopedia of the Social Sciences*, let us take a moment to deal with it. It is true that if a program is introduced and if people like the idea of participating in the experiment, then they will respond well. That is, people respond well to attention. This effect, apart from any intended effect of the program itself, is called the Hawthorne effect. It is analogous to the placebo effect in medicine which is the relief given the patient by a pill or a treatment having no medicinal value. The existence of these effects is well documented and at least in the case of the placebo has been frequently measured with repeatable results on many populations of patients. Beecher (1959) reports about 35 percent of patients were satisfactorily relieved of severe postoperative wound pain by a placebo, and a similar percentage were relieved of other discomforts in other conditions (headache, pain from angina pectoris, cough, cold, anxiety and tension). What then shall we say of experimental programs subject to such effects? We say that it is important that they be compared with competing experimental programs. Then the portion having to do with the Hawthorne effect will presumably be somewhat comparable.

SUMMARY.   The United States has rarely studied the educational process at a national level. Consequently, when the Coleman Report offered, on a large scale, measures of performance for various groups of pupils, educational critics, both pro and con, attacked this fresh meat enthusiastically, having little else to get their teeth into. Although the Coleman Report gives a fine start by illustrating the need for and value of large-scale investigations, we must think of it as a *first* study—not last, not definitive.

After figuring out what immediate actions may be sensible in view of the Coleman Report, we must resolve not to freeze these policies but to prepare for the long run by mounting systematic large-scale research programs. Furthermore, we can begin thinking of research, including experimentation, in education as a necessary continuing process, just as it is for many other important national institutions.

If we are to improve the educational system, we need to acquire a different attitude toward experimentation and to develop new facilities for large-scale experimentation. We do not have such facilities now. Inevitably many experimental programs will fail because the gain from improving a program is small compared to that from starting it. Nevertheless, if we want to improve educational methods we shall need experimental evaluation, the more so because few new programs will make material improvements. At the same time we must clarify our goals, since we can hardly expect that any program will improve many aspects of a school's educational output.

References

Beecher, Henry K. *Measurement of Subjective Responses*. New York: Oxford University Press, 1959, pp. 66–7.

Campbell, Donald T. "Reforms as Experiments." *American Psychologist*, Vol. 24, 1969, pp. 409–29.

Eichnwald, H. F., and Fry, Peggy C. "Nutrition and Learning." *Science*, Vol. 163, No. 3868, February 14, 1969, pp. 644–8.

Hamblin, Robert L., Buckholdt, David, Bushell, Donald, Ellis, Desmond, and Ferritor, Daniel. "Changing the game from 'get the teacher' to 'learn.'" *trans*action Vol. 6, No.3, January, 1969, pp. 20–9.

Pattillo, Manning M. *Annual Report 1967*, The Foundation Library Center, 444 Madison Avenue, New York, New York 10022.

9

Some Thoughts
About Future Studies[*]

HENRY S. DYER

Fore-Thought

The purpose of this essay is to identify some research questions suggested
by the Coleman Report and to indicate the kinds of studies that are needed
to provide answers to them. I conceive of these future studies in three broad
and fairly arbitrary categories: descriptive studies, analytical studies, and
experimental studies. Descriptive studies include the kind of wide-ranging
surveys of American education that make up most of the Coleman Report.
They are the studies that have as their goal the accumulation of data to
depict as accurately and comprehensively as possible what the schools of the
nation are like, what their operating conditions are, and what is happening
to various kinds of pupils who pass through them. Analytical studies are
those that typically hunt for the important relationships among the components of the educational system and its products, the principal purpose being to locate possibilities for improvement that appear worth exploring. The
studies in sections 3.2 and 3.3 of the Coleman Report are examples of this
type. Experimental studies are the kind in which interventions of some sort
are made into the processes of an educational system in order to see whether
they produce changes for the better in pupils. The Coleman Report contains
no studies of this kind, but the literature of educational research teems with
thousands of them—most of which are remarkably inadequate and inconclusive.

These three categories of studies form a hierarchy of sorts. Descriptive studies collect and organize information about the system; analytical
studies use the information to generate hypotheses about it; experimental

* In putting down these "thoughts," I have drawn heavily from ideas developed in the
Harvard Seminar on the Equality of Educational Opportunity Report. However, I have
twisted and expanded on the ideas in so many ways that the members of the Seminar
cannot be held responsible for the thoughts that have finally emerged in this essay.

384

studies test the hypotheses by introducing new information. It is clear that as one goes up the hierarchical ladder the studies can become increasingly neat and elegant. It should be equally clear, however, that more and better studies *of all three types* are absolutely indispensable to any program for upgrading and equalizing educational opportunities for all groups in American society.

It is common knowledge that research in education has usually failed to produce results leading to improved practice. A major reason for this state of affairs is that so much of the work has been fragmentary and lacking in continuity. This piecemeal character of the effort has had two unfortunate effects that are particularly serious : (1) the research has been unable to take into account important interactions among the many variables, inside and outside the schools, that may influence pupil development, and (2) because of the disparity in the designs, methods, and measures employed by different studies, their findings have tended to be noncumulative. A persistent theme, therefore, in much of the discussion below is the need for greater coordination in the planning and execution of all types of studies (descriptive, analytical, experimental) that bear on the conditions and processes of the educational enterprise.

♦ Descriptive Studies

Anyone who has been involved in a study yielding disappointingly low relationships between school-system characteristics and pupil achievements or attitudes or outlook on life should seriously entertain the explanatory hypothesis that the measures used to describe the schools and their functioning are simply too crude to yield any useful amount of meaningful variance. This deficiency is pervasive. It envelops even the most mundane educational statistics in clouds of doubt. It has several sources: inadequate definition of the fundamental variables, inconsistencies in the data supplied by different school systems and often by different persons within the same system, confused record-keeping, a tendency to fill up the informational gaps with impressionistic or fictional data, and unwillingness to supply facts, either because they are hard to obtain or because they may reflect unfavorably on the schools or on the respondents.[1] As a consequence, many of the numbers that look like hard data may give a picture of the educational scene that is at best superficial and at worst illusory. A few examples will highlight the problems.

Even a simple statistic like total enrollment can be troublesome. The total enrollment of a school is a quantity that fluctuates from day to day because of the continual movement of pupils from one school or school district to another. Moreover, the amount of fluctuation may vary considerably from school to school. In the urban ghettos it tends to be high, in rural communities low. As a result, when a school principal is asked the seemingly straightforward question, "What is the total enrollment in your school?" [2] he may be hard put to find a straightforward answer. If he follows the procedure required by the New York State Education Department, he will put down the number of pupils registered in his school on October 31 and leave the matter there. If his school is in another state, he may use some other formula for arriving at "average daily membership." Whatever the formula, the single number he provides will conceal some unknown amount of variance in the day-to-day enrollment of his school, and anyone who aggregates such numbers over a national sample of schools will inadvertently bury additional variance generated by the variety of formulas used, not to mention the variety of errors principals can make in the use of any given formula. As a result, when one looks at the "average total enrollment" for one section of the country as compared with another, one can have no idea of how much the difference reflects a genuine regional difference in enrollments, how much might be attributed to errors of sampling, and how much arises from at least two degrees of wobbliness in the underlying units.

An index like "average per-pupil expenditure" is another case in point. Since it is customarily figured by taking the ratio of total instructional expense to total enrollment, it suffers from hidden variance in both the numerator and the denominator. The error variance in the numerator can be very large indeed because of the differing combinations of components school systems use in breaking out instructional expense from overall expense—if indeed they pay any attention at all to such breakdowns. Moreover, as far as I know, there is not a single school system in the country with a cost accounting system capable of identifying how much is spent on any particular pupil or group of pupils for any particular purpose. Within the same district, for instance, the amount spent in two schools of equivalent size may differ considerably because of differences in programs, salary levels, quality of equipment, and supplies consumed. Yet such differences are generally unaccounted for, and, because of the way accounts are ordinarily kept, cannot be accounted for.[3] This sort of deficiency in the basic data is especially serious since school-to-school or pupil-to-pupil differences in educational expenditure clearly have much to do with what is implied by the term "equal educational opportunity."

Assessing the quality of school plant and facilities, irrespective of cost, raises other problems that are not dissimilar. The Coleman study asked the principals for data on the age of their school building, the number of classrooms, the number of makeshift classrooms, etc., on the assumption that combinations of these numbers with one another and with total enrollment would provide suitable indices of the quality of the school plant.[4] But again, because of imprecision in the terms used, it is hard to see how these data can add up to numbers capable of extracting truth from confusion. What, for instance, is the age of a school building that was originally built in 1920, completely renovated in 1940, and further remodeled in 1963? Or how many "makeshift" classrooms are there in an up-to-date building with movable walls that enable teachers to enlarge or reduce classroom space at will depending on the purpose for which they want to use it? Information on the presence or absence of facilities like science laboratories or on the number of books in school libraries is similarly vulnerable.[5] A biology laboratory may be well-equipped or ill-equipped, large or small, up-to-date or out-of-date. One school library may have 5000 volumes largely unrelated to the interests and educational needs of the children; another may have a collection half the size which is geared into every aspect of the educational program.

One could cite hundreds of other types of "basic" data in common use that fail to add up to meaningful or dependable indices descriptive of the quality of schools and their operations: for example, the use of teacher credentials as an index of teacher competence, the number of specialized personnel on the staff, the frequency with which standardized tests are given, the copyright dates in textbooks, the number of paraprofessionals and teacher aides a school employs, the rate of pupil absenteeism, and so on. The point is not that the kind of information such measures are reaching for is unimportant, but that the measures themselves are generally too gross and indirect to convey a true image of the shape and quality of the educational enterprise. There is, therefore, urgent need for a whole host of what might be called micrological studies aimed at developing feasible procedures for constructing educational index numbers sufficiently sensitive to detect small but possibly important differences in (1) the quality and adequacy of school facilities and personnel, (2) the level and distribution of instructional expenditures, and (3) the demography of school populations.

Such studies should begin by examining the smallest possible observable units and then should try out various methods for aggregating them so as to ascertain what sorts of indices at any of several levels of generality filter out the least amount of fundamental information. In working out the best method for securing an index of total enrollment, for example, one might collect data on the daily enrollments of a diversified sample of schools and determine what particular slices through the total accumulation would yield (1) an index of average daily membership having the smallest amount of within-school variance over all the schools, and (2) an index of the variability of enrollment in any one school during the school year. For it seems clear that usable information on enrollment requires at least two numbers of known reliability from each school: an estimate of the average enrollment for the year and an estimate of the variability around the average. The same tack might be taken to develop methods for computing indices on pupil attendance, teacher absenteeism, use of substitute teachers and teacher aides, school visits by parents, and any other items involving fluctuations in the number of personnel connected with the school.

Micrological studies of a somewhat different nature are needed for investigating indices of many other aspects of educational systems. The planning of such studies need not start from scratch. For many years a number of individuals and organizations have given considerable attention to the quantity and quality of school offerings, operations, facilities, personnel, instructional materials, and the like.[6] These studies, taken together, provide a reasonably comprehensive classification of the items to be examined; their weakness is that they usually fail to analyze each item into the kinds of irreducible elements that must be isolated and recombined to furnish descriptive measures that usefully differentiate one school or school system from another.

The same can be said of the many studies of educational expenditures.[7] In this case the tendency of most investigators is to leap from gross categories of expenditure (e.g., total salaries, material costs, maintenance costs) to correlations with similarly gross categories of pupil performance (e.g., retention rate, college-going rate, etc.)—all because more refined indices for each side of the cost-benefit equation are unavailable. I shall come back to this point in the section on analytical studies, but I wish to emphasize here that expense factors in national surveys of education are not likely to be understandable or appropriately summarized until the elements of differential expense by program, by school, and by pupil have been incorporated into educational accounting procedures. In light of the present confused condition of such procedures, the task will be one of massive proportions. All one can suggest is that pilot studies of considerable depth be undertaken in a number of school systems to see what problems are encountered in adapting to educational accounting some of the management information systems that appear to work well in some private industries.[8] The emphasis, however, has to be on the word *adapt* (not *adopt*), since educational systems differ from industrial systems in some very fundamental ways. Even in industry the nature of the product and the distinction between producer and consumer are not always clear. In education they are even less so. In education the "product" consists of the knowledge, skills, attitudes, and values that pupils choose to build into *themselves*. These products are not readily specifiable, nor, in a pluralistic society, is it altogether clear who should do the specifying. Furthermore, the producer and the consumer are essentially one and the same person, namely, the pupil. These circumstances make an accounting system designed for the management and control of production in education uniquely different from that required for the same purpose in most industrial enterprises.

Studies concerned with equality of opportunity in education have to be peculiarly concerned with the question: *Equal for whom?* And this question raises a whole set of problems having to do with demographic characteristics of the pupil population and how the data for describing them are to be obtained and organized. These problems are far from solved. Despite a good deal of research that has been done on indices of social stratification, there is still much to be learned. Most such research up to now has been done on samples of whites. It has produced consistent findings which show that, for whites, such variables as occupation, family income, educational attainment, and household possessions can be converted into internally consistent indices that accurately reflect the prestige in which the social groups described by them are held.[9] One of the important questions that still remains to be answered is whether socioeconomic indices developed on whites are meaningfully descriptive of the class structure of Negroes and other ethnic groups. It is conceivable that, because of cultural differences, the variables involved may require a different set of weights for each group. A pilot study of Negroes and whites in a Northern city is now going forward with the purpose of opening up this problem,[10] but many more such studies will be needed before we can have assurance that the socioeconomic indicators currently in use are capable of yielding dependable comparisons across ethnic or regional groups in the school population.

There is another aspect of the school population, which, in view of its obvious relevance to the schools, is remarkable by the fact that it has received no sustained attention whatever from national surveys of education: namely, the abilities and the accomplishments of pupils in the sorts of things schools are supposed to teach. Only two one-shot studies of this kind preceded the Coleman survey. In 1960 Project Talent took the first look in history at the academic ability and achievement of a national sample of high-school students,[11] and in 1964–65 the Department of Defense surveyed the basic skills of 18-year-old males.[12] Thus, the Coleman survey was the first to provide any kind of countrywide data on the school-related performance of elementary—as well as secondary—school children. Yet it too was planned and executed as a one-time study.

It seems obvious that if the policy-makers and managers of American education are ever to have the information necessary for informed long-term planning, they require at a minimum some indices from which it will be possible to discern *trends* in pupil performance at the national, state, and local levels. In the nation as a whole, for instance, has the reading ability of 13-year-olds gone up or down in the last twenty-five years? And how does the trend in County X or School System Y compare with the national trend? Or how does the trend for Negroes compare with that for whites? It seems incredible that at the present time there is simply no way of answering questions like these. Thus, the thought is inescapable that plans should be made now for a series of continuing and coordinated studies that will provide at the end of the next twenty-five years, preferably sooner, some useful answers.

The groundwork for such an undertaking has already been laid in the project for a National Assessment of Educational Progress,[13] but at this writing the question is still moot whether continuing support and sponsorship can be found so as to prevent the project from becoming just another single-shot survey. The National Assessment will secure performance data on a probability sample of individuals in each of four age groups: 9, 13, 17, and young adult (ages 26–35). The sample of each age group will be divided into two subgroups by sex, two by the socioeducational status of the family, four according to geographical region (Northeast, Southeast, Central, and West), and four according to type of community (urban, suburban, small city, and rural). Some attention will also be given to the racial composition of the samples by noting how many in each are white, Negro, or "other." Thus, the National Assessment will provide a set of educational indices for the nation as a whole and for various combinations of a large number of subgroups at each of four age levels. The sampling plan purposely avoids the possibility of providing descriptive indices for state and local school systems, although any system, if it wished, could presumably develop such information about itself for comparative purposes by using similar instruments and following the same procedures with enlarged samples in its own area.

Three features of the National Assessment Project are of particular interest: the nature of the instruments to be used, the manner in which they will be administered, and the form the resulting indices will take. The instruments will consist of exercises embracing pupil performance in ten areas: reading, writing, mathematics, science, social studies, citizenship, music, literature, vocational education, and art. The educational objectives on which the exercises are based have been worked out in detail for each area and each age group by panels of teachers, scholars, and lay persons so as to tap all the major facets of individual learning that, in the judgment of the panels, American education ought to encompass or has been encompassing in these areas. The objectives cover not only the knowledge, understanding, and skills with which the schools have been traditionally concerned, but also many that are characteristic of the new curricula being adopted by many schools. In some of the ten fields they give attention as well to the kinds of interests, attitudes, and values that one hopes a student would acquire from his learning experiences—e.g., "*interest* in reading for pleasure and information," "*responsiveness* to aesthetic qualities of mathematics and *awareness* of its significance in modern life," "*concern* for the welfare and dignity of others," "listening to music with *understanding* and *enjoyment*." [14] (Italics added)

To test the degree to which all objectives are being met requires more exercises than one individual can reasonably be asked to take. Since neither individuals nor local systems are being assessed, there is no reason not to divide the total set of exercises into a number of subsets—"packages"—of appropriate length and to give each person only one of the packages. The packages at each age level will be assigned to random clusters of individuals to be tested—whether a random selection from a school or, in the case of adults and dropouts, a random selection from a neighborhood.

As a consequence of this sampling technique, the results of the survey will provide meaningful indices for various groups of individuals but not for any single individual nor for the group in any one local or state school system that happens to be in the sample. The indices by which the results will be expressed will be in terms of percentages of persons succeeding on any specific exercise. It may be possible to say, for example, that x percent of 17-year-old boys from poor families in urban areas can comprehend material of the type found in comic books; another y percent of them can comprehend material of the type in weekly news magazines; and z percent of the type in periodicals like the *Scientific American*. Or, by aggregating across the subsamples, it would be possible to make a statement of the form, a percent of all young adult females in the nation can listen to a recording by the Beatles with enjoyment while only $\frac{a}{3}$ percent of adult males get the same bang out of the stuff—if indeed such a recording were included in any package. Such statements will be highly useful in making the performance characteristics of the population concrete. The directors of the National Assessment Project have thus far been silent on how this mass of data might be aggregated over each content area. The construction of index numbers capable of yielding trend data is a problem for the future.[15]

Without in any way deprecating the value of the National Assessment Project, one can argue that its resulting indices will tell only one side of the story that needs to be told about progress in education. Its focus, quite properly, is on the kinds of learning with which the schools as presently constituted are presumed to be concerned. The educational objectives and the exercises into which they have been translated grew out of the subjective wisdom of scholars, educators, and others who have thought deeply about what the schools ought to be doing for children. This is all to the good, but as a counterpart to the National Assessment of the Progress of Education per se, we require similar periodic surveys at a similar level of specificity of the talent *needs* of the national economy. Such a survey is indispensable as a basis for checking on the *relevance* of the kinds of knowledge, skills, and attitudes that the National Assessment, as presently conceived, will presumably find in the process of development in the American population. There have, of course, been many studies and projections of manpower requirements,[16] but their findings have been expressed in such general terms that they have provided little help in specifying concretely the kinds of competence and behavior required to move the economy and the social system it supports into a healthy condition. What particular *kinds* of proficiency in reading or mathematics, for instance, are required of a fully competent garage mechanic, or the manager of a cast iron pipe company, or a labor economist, or a voter? Such questions are seldom asked and never answered in any precise way. Nor has enough continuing attention been given to another kind of question and its implications for education locally as well as nationally: for example, what is the level of citizen participation in local politics, or what kinds of TV programs absorb how much of the citizen's attention? A large number of indices of this sort need to be fed regularly into the thinking of educational policy-makers and curriculum constructors if the operations of educational systems are to be kept in touch with the rapidly changing needs of the times.

It might be objected that, in view of the rate of social and technological change, periodic surveys of the kind here suggested would yield information of only limited value for the schools. Such information could reflect only the proficiency requirements for no more than a few years in the future, but in the nature of the case they could not give projections needed to indicate what 5-year-olds or 10-year-olds ought to be learning now in order to be ready to participate effectively in the social system as it will be ten or fifteen years from now. This argument has some merit, but it seems unlikely that long-range forecasts of proficiency requirements will ever become feasible until we have learned how to assess short-range requirements with a degree of specificity well beyond anything that is now available. Furthermore, such a short-range picture could have immediate usefulness in raising fundamental questions about the relevance of offerings in the later years of schooling. In the case of the community colleges and technical institutes particularly the problem of relating instruction to the immediate needs of the job market is still far from solved.[17]

Another important question that the National Assessment as presently planned will not answer is one that has been raised by Stodolsky and Lesser in their study of the learning patterns of disadvantaged children.[18] They found striking differences in the patterns of mental abilities exhibited by the children in four ethnic groups—Chinese, Jews, Negroes, and Puerto Ricans. They also found that although *within* each group the *level* of performance on each of four measures varied significantly with the social class of the children, the *pattern* of performance was roughly the same for both middle-class and lower-class youngsters.

These findings are of considerable importance, but, as is so often the case, they raise a host of troubling questions for which the data provide no clear answers: questions having to do, first, with the psychosocial genesis of the group differences observed and, second, with the far-reaching implications they may have for social and educational policy. The authors consider both types of questions in some detail and have sketched a line of future studies that will be needed to answer them. Such studies are urgent, for the thought persists that, until the dimensions of the situation are more clearly defined, there is a very real danger that the present incomplete picture could lead to seriously mistaken policies concerning the education of a number of ethnic groups in American society.

◆ *Analytical Studies*

The Stodolsky-Lesser study is an example of one that stands somewhere between purely descriptive studies and what I am choosing to call analytical studies. Analytical studies generally entail some form of multivariate analysis of the characteristics of educational systems and the social systems in which they are embedded. In this section I shall discuss some of the substantive problems associated with such analyses that require concentrated attention if the functioning of the schools is to be better understood.

In the recent past there has been a considerable amount of interest in applying to education, as well as to other public services, the methods of economic analysis (variously called operations analysis, systems analysis, input-output analysis, cost-quality control, cost-benefit analysis, and the like) which have worked more or less effectively in the management of industry. In government the efforts along these lines that have probably received the most public attention have been those associated with the Department of Defense.[19] In barest essentials, this type of analysis is addressed to three kinds of questions that any executive of any enterprise, including education, ought to be asking himself: (1) Given a certain amount of money (or other resources) to spend, how much of each of several kinds of benefits will it buy? (2) Given a particular desired benefit, what among several methods for achieving it will each one cost? And (3) how much of an increase in any benefit is likely to be produced by changing by any given amount some identifiable component of the system? This last question has to do with the economist's concept of "value-added." In an educational system it might take the form: How much of an increase in the reading test scores of 4th-grade children is likely to result from any given reduction in the size of 4th-grade classes, all other things being equal?

It is this final proviso, *all other things being equal*, that is troublesome, since in any analyses of educational systems as they currently exist it is never possible to take account of all the "other things" that might be unequal. The findings of any kind of systems analysis are therefore necessarily always probabilistic. Even so, well-based probabilistic statements about "What would happen if—?" are likely to lead to far wiser decisions about educational policies and programs than the kinds of uninformed hunches on which educational decision-makers usually rely. Hence, theoretically, there is every reason to suppose that systems analysis should be highly useful in helping educators get some idea of how to deploy available funds, facilities, and personnel so as to maximize the educational benefits pupils will receive, or to arrive at informed judgments about what trade-offs might be made among several kinds of benefits. A high-school principal, for instance, would find it useful to know what might be the consequences (other than political) if he were to transfer a sizable amount of funds from his athletic department to his science department. How many defeats in interscholastic contests might buy how much of a gain in student competence in science? (The availability of such information might even help him to damp down the political consequences of such a decision if he were actually moved to make it.)

As matters now stand, however, the systems theorists have not been able to provide even good probabilistic answers to educational questions like these. In a recent report on an input-output analysis of a number of school systems, Burkhead, Fox, and Holland observe that the most that can be expected from their studies

is to suggest a way of looking at public schools as a mechanism for the production of education. It is believed that this approach will yield some fruitful insights; *it cannot be expected to yield final answers on questions of resource allocation for public education.*[20] [Italics added]

A paper by Mood and Powers,[21] while recognizing the ultimate importance of cost-benefit analysis in educational decision-making, nevertheless sketches in agonizing detail the many difficulties that will have to be overcome before the full possibilities of such analysis can be realized. It outlines the many unsolved problems, particularly in data collection, that stand between systems theory and its practical application. One is the complex relationships that exist among the enormous number of factors that affect pupil learning—factors associated not only with the structure and operations of the school, but also with the home background of the pupil, the influences of the community in which he lives, and the imperfectly understood genetic determiners of his temperament and physical and cognitive development. Another is the extraordinary diversity in the amorphous collectivities of people, facilities, and procedures that we choose to call educational "systems." A third is the lack of clarity about what the multiple outcomes of the educational experience ought to be. And a fourth, as suggested in the preceding section, is the primitive condition of the measures available for sorting out the variables in all these phenomena.

In reviewing the inconclusive findings from their studies of two large-city systems and 206 systems in small communities, Burkhead and his collaborators conclude that part of the difficulty in comparing one school system with another, especially when the communities they serve are in different states, is that

school outputs will be conditioned by far more factors than can be indexed in a regression equation. Post high school education will be influenced not alone by the average family income of the community, but by its educational traditions, the local labor market, and the availability of opportunities for education beyond the high school. School dropouts will be influenced by differences in school leaving laws and practices among the states and by employment opportunities that may be available. Even test scores will be influenced, not alone by the educational attainment added by the school, but by the experience of the students in test-taking.

But the more pervasive difficulty in the application of an input-output framework to a cross-section of small-community high schools is that the student input measured in terms of the socioeconomic background of the students has a very different meaning than for large cities . . . The deviations around the mean family income are likely to be much greater in the small community than in the school attendance area of the large city.[22]

It seems to me that none of the difficulties here described is ultimately insuperable. If the educational traditions of a community, or the condition of the local labor market, or opportunities for post-secondary education, or other similar matters are likely to be important variables in the regression equation, it is reasonable to suppose that, with sufficient funds and effort, measures of them could be obtained and entered. If there are likely to be school-to-school differences in heterogeneity of family income or other socioeconomic variables, then these, too, can be accounted for if one is willing to go beyond census tract data and get the needed information on the individual students in each school. Indeed, Kiesling, working with some of the same data used by Burkhead *et al.*, was able to do just this with some interesting though not definitive results.[23]

In brief, the problem is not one of being confronted with "more factors than *can* be indexed in a regression equation," but of getting measures of the factors that *ought* to be so used. If the result of such an effort turns up too many variables relative to the number of observation units (usually schools), then one obvious way around the difficulty is to reduce the number of variables, not by throwing some of them away (as too often happens), but by employing some appropriate form of factor analysis.[24] To get beyond the stage of theory and inconclusive demonstrations thereof based on any data that happen to be lying around, systems analysis in education must become far more sophisticated in gathering and processing the kinds of data that are particularly relevant to the operations of educational systems as contrasted, say, to missile systems or manufacturing systems or monetary systems. We need to be sure that the educational numbers are saying something intelligible about education per se before feeding them into regression equations. Clearly, a vast amount of preliminary work must be done before we shall be able to get off the level of systems theory and down to the level of its practical application in the rational management of educational systems. Until this quantum jump is accomplished, the allocation of educational resources is unlikely to have any discernible connection with the equalization of educational opportunities.

Accordingly, it is hardly to be questioned that studies looking to the practical application of systems theory should be energetically pursued to provide, eventually, a firmer basis than we now have for dealing with broad questions of educational policy. There is, however, just as great a need for another kind of analytical studies to help toward a better understanding of the collection of human activities that go by the name "educational process." The Coleman survey touched on this domain to some extent by giving attention, as best it could, to the relations of academic achievement to environmental conditions and certain attitudes of pupils, parents, teachers, and principals. In some instances the attitudinal variables turned out to be some of the most interesting in the entire Report. For example, student attitudes toward themselves, toward learning, and toward their environment "showed the strongest relations to achievement at all school levels. The zero-order correlations of these attitudes with achievement were higher than those of any other variables, in some cases as high as the correlation of some test scores with others (between .4 and .5)." [25]

The Coleman results in this area are provocative, but there are severe limits on how far a survey of such broad scope can go in probing for those chains of variables that begin in the school and home environment, have an impact on pupil attitudes, and terminate in the pupil's performance in school. There is, therefore, an urgent need for many small-scale, but intensive, studies directed at identifying such chains—studies that can secure data on factors related to individual children's educational development which go well beyond the kinds of data that massive surveys can reach. The set of relationships to be explored in greater depth are shown perhaps too simplistically in the following diagram:

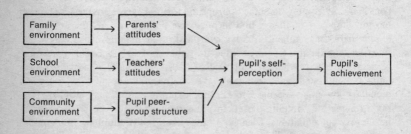

There have, of course, been many isolated studies of the various elements involved in this total process, but they have tended to focus on only a few aspects of the process at a time and have employed such a miscellany of measures and methods of analysis, that attempts to tie them together into some well-supported generalizations have been considerably less than satisfactory. To get around this difficulty one might envision a *network* of five interlocking studies, so planned and so organized that their findings will be cumulative and will embrace as many as possible of the factors that, in their numerous combinations, have important effects on what the child gets out of his education. The pattern of the network should be such that some part of the pupils and schools participating in any one of the five studies would also participate in others so that there would be enough linkages in the data to permit tenable inferences about the interrelationships of the variables in all five studies.

The pattern could look something like the scheme in Figure I. Each of the ten samples in the scheme might consist of perhaps 300–500 pupils in six to eight schools concentrated at three grade levels, say 1st, 6th, and 11th. The arrangement by which each study involves four of the samples and each sample participates in two of the studies should provide for the necessary linkages across all the studies. These linkages would be reinforced by making provision for a number of observations common to all the studies in the network—e.g., indices of the socioeconomic status of the pupils' families, level of wealth of the community served by each school, type of community, current per-pupil expenditure for each school at each grade, proportion of nonwhites in the school, size of school, pupil mobility rate, pupil absenteeism, scores on achievement tests. In respect to such variables each of the ten samples would be as diverse as possible and as nearly the same in composition as each of the other nine. The schools involved in any one sample might well come from widely scattered school districts in order to produce the diversity required. The emphasis on diversity is to ensure that the variables to be analyzed in each study would have the best possible chance to become visible in the data, for the purpose in this instance is to try to discern those psychosocial forces that make a difference for different

FIGURE I

Scheme for a Pattern of Studies with Overlapping Samples of Pupils and Schools*

	Study I	Study II	Study III	Study IV	Study V
Sample A	x	x			
Sample B	x		x		
Sample C	x			x	
Sample D	x				x
Sample E		x	x		
Sample F		x		x	
Sample G		x			x
Sample H			x	x	
Sample I			x		x
Sample J				x	x

* I am indebted to Robert L. Linn for suggesting this design.

kinds of pupils, not to secure normative information on schools in general.

Study I, which is central to the scheme, would focus primarily on pupils' perceptions of themselves, their parents, and their teachers. It would take off from previous research that has been devoted to the measurement of self-concept and its relation to performance in school.[26] It would also have the benefit of a number of recent studies in this area that have been especially concerned with the self-perception and self-acceptance of black children.[27] The notion of self-concept covers a broad territory and is not without problems in the definition of the variables used to define it and measure it.[28] Nevertheless, the fact that the Coleman survey, as noted above, found a reasonably strong relationship between verbal achievement and what looks like a somewhat-less-than-adequate measure of the degree to which a child feels he has control over his environment suggests how important some of the self-concept variables may be. Other variables in this category that need deeper exploration with more refined measures are the child's perception of how he stands relative to his classmates in his interests, his aspirations, and his accomplishments in both academic and nonacademic pursuits.

A second set of variables on which Study I would focus are those having to do with the child's perceptions of his parents. The Coleman study found that for certain groups of pupils the child's perception of what his parents expect of him in school had a sizable correlation (.4 or higher in some cases) with his test performance, even though, again, the perception measure was crude.[29] In fact, the crudity of the measure may account, at least in part, for some of the low correlations found with some of the minority and younger children where language difficulties may have had a masking effect.[30] It is reasonable to suppose that a measure based on a more comprehensive array of questions, validated for internal consistency and individually administered if need be, would have produced stronger relationships with achievement in these groups. Such questions might take the form: How often do your parents inquire about your school work? help you with your homework? disagree with the way your teacher says it ought to be done? discuss your school work with your teachers? etc. There are a number of recent studies that point to the educational importance of pupils' perceptions of parental concern.[31] It must be remembered, however, that such questions can reflect only the pupil's perceptions of his parents' concern for him; they may not reflect his parents' actual concerns. The amount of discrepancy between these two data sources in those cases where it is obtainable, could turn out to be a significant variable in itself. This is one reason why the overlap in the studies would be important (see Study II below on parents' perceptions).

A third set of variables to be treated in Study I would derive from the pupil's perception of his teachers. Much can be learned about the important variables in the teaching-learning process by assessing the pupil's perceptions of such matters as (1) the teacher's knowledge of the subject matter being taught, (2) her ability to get the subject matter across, (3) her effectiveness in coping with the human situation of the classroom, (4) her interest in the pupil, (5) her readiness to give attention to pupils with learning difficulties, (6) her willingness to let pupils explore subjects of their own choosing, (7) her concern for individual differences in ability to learn, (8) her fairness in marking and administering discipline, (9) her readiness to let the pupil show what he can do, and (10) the pattern of the teacher's likes and dislikes for pupils in her class. There is good reason to believe that, by use of appropriate techniques, it is possible to elicit consistent responses on many such items from children at least as early as the 1st grade.[32] The possibilities in the upper grades are fairly obvious, though, with some exceptions, they have not been much explored below the college level.[33] The practical difficulties are equally obvious: because of the threatening nature of the exercise, teachers tend not to be favorably disposed to being rated by their pupils. However, these difficulties have been overcome in the past, and there is no reason to believe that, with adequate preparation, they cannot be overcome again.[34] In any case, there can be little doubt that pupils' observations of their teachers' classroom behavior—granting the inevitable distortions in such observations—are likely to be far more informative of the quality of the teaching-learning process than such remote measures as teacher training, credentials, and length of experience which are so frequently used as proxies for the real thing.

Study II would focus primarily on the parents' perceptions of the child-as-pupil and of the school he attends. Any number of studies, including the Coleman survey, have consistently reported that the family socioeconomic variable is associated with the major portion of the predictable variance in pupil achievement as measured by tests and other indices. Sexton, for instance, has shown that the children from families with incomes over $7000 average considerably higher on achievement tests than those from families where the income is below $7000.[35] In the jargon of regression analysis, it is usually said of this phenomenon that socioeconomic status "explains" most of the variation in pupils' academic performance, but of course, in the ordinary usage of the verb "explains," it does nothing of the sort. That is, it tells nothing whatever about why the children of low-income families tend to do worse in school than the children of high-income families. Many explanatory hypotheses have been proposed, but few have been adequately investigated: high-income families tend to live in communities where schools are good; low-income families tend to live in communities where schools are poor; the homes of high-income families tend to be culturally "richer" than those of low-income families; high-income families tend to exert more pressure on their children to "make it" to a good college than is the case with low-income families. And so on. These are some of the suggested mechanisms by which differences in family income get translated ultimately into differences in pupil achievement. The actual operation of these mechanisms, however, is not likely to be well understood until one goes directly to the parents themselves to assess their perceptions of the situation in relation to their children.

Some of the variables of interest here would be much the same as those suggested above in connection with Study I. How much attention do parents say they give to the pupil's school work? How frequently do they visit the school on the child's behalf, and not just to participate in ceremonial occasions? What is their opinion of the competence of the child's teachers? What are their aspirations for the child as compared with their actual expectations of how he will do in school and beyond? What is their attitude concerning control over their own and their child's environment? Numerous small studies have dealt with these and other intrafamily influence variables. The effects of maternal attitudes and behavior on the cognitive development of preschool children in the ghetto have lately received considerable attention, for instance.[36] However, an adequate understanding of how these variables operate will not be forthcoming until such studies (1) are designed to sample pupils in all types of schools concurrently—inner-city and suburban; public, private, and parochial; conventional and highly innovative, (2) include children all the way from preschool through high school, and (3) are conducted within a framework that makes it possible to relate the family influence to the many other influences that presumably affect the child's development.

As a control on the parental attitude variables vis-à-vis the school, it will be important to get, in addition, an assessment of the parents' *factual knowledge* of the school and its operations. An attitude, whether favorable or unfavorable, may mean one thing when it rests on reasonably accurate information and something quite different when it rests on ignorance. For example, do the parents know the names of their child's teachers? the school principal? Do they know anything about the condition of the classroom? the extracurricular opportunities afforded by the school? whether the school has a nurse? a psychologist? In the aggregate the answers to questions of this sort should begin to throw some light on the meaning of the currently popular but ill-defined notion of "community involvement" and what relation it may in fact have with pupil achievement under a variety of circumstances.

Study III would be concerned primarily with the teacher's attitudes toward her pupils, her fellow teachers, and her supervisors. The Coleman Report touches briefly on these variables.[37] The only one, however, that got into the regression analysis was based on a single question having to do with the teacher's preference for teaching middle-class children. In this case, the zero-order correlations with pupils' verbal achievement, although generally low, are almost uniformly negative. That is, the greater the teacher's preference for teaching middle-class children, the worse the children do in verbal achievement. The tendency is slight, and of course complicating factors are at work. Much more needs to be known about the impact of teacher attitudes on pupils' learning.

There has recently been a considerable amount of impressionistic discussion of this matter,[38] and there is a considerable history of studies addressed to the measurement and evaluation of teacher attitudes per se.[39] But, as Stern has pointed out, not much has been done to relate teacher attitudes to pupil achievement, and the little that has been done has produced only meager results.[40] A good part of the difficulty, as noted above, is that the studies in this area pay attention to too few variables at a time and tend to deal with samples that are too homogeneous to bring some of the important variables to the surface. The way teachers perceive their pupils and their preferences for teaching various kinds of students (bright vs. dull, well-dressed vs. poorly dressed, white vs. black, noisy vs. quiet, etc.) need to be seen against (1) their perceptions of the pupil's parents (interested vs. uninterested, threatening vs. nonthreatening, intelligent vs. unintelligent, etc.), (2) their perceptions of their colleagues (cooperative vs. uncooperative, competent vs. incompetent, etc.), and (3) their perceptions of their principals.

Teachers' perceptions of their principals may be particularly important, since there is good reason to believe that these perceptions may have a good deal of influence on classroom atmosphere and the quality of instruction. A pioneering study by Gross and Herriott[41] suggests that teachers' perceptions of their principals as educational leaders may bear some fairly strong relationships to the level of both teacher and pupil performance (pp. 48–57). However, many more studies of the same type are needed to get a better fix on the interactions among the variables having to do with teachers, principals, and pupils. The Gross-Herriott study explored such matters as (1) the principals' ability to offer constructive criticism to teachers in coping with their major problems, (2) their concern for upgrading the educational program, (3) their ability to make teachers believe that they can contribute significantly to improving the performance of pupils, (4) their support of experimentation in the schools, (5) their ability to obtain parental support for and cooperation with the school, (6) their ability to establish a professional climate in the school, and (7) their ability to establish an esprit de corps among the members of the faculty.

If we assume that teaching in a school in the slums is an especially difficult and complex task (as most of the current evidence indicates), then the type of leadership and support teachers in such schools feel they are getting from their principals may be a critical variable in accounting for variations in teacher performance which may in turn account for at least some of the variation in the pupil's own attitudes and performance. At the same time, however, it should be important to examine how this network of relationships in ghetto schools compares with that in schools operating under more favorable conditions.

Study IV would concentrate primarily on the peer-group structure of the student body in each school and the relation of interpersonal attitudes to pupil achievement. The Coleman Report gives some attention to this matter in terms of the interaction of average achievement level with the ethnic composition of the schools surveyed. It shows that, in schools where the achievement level is relatively high and the ratio of Negroes to whites is low, Negroes tend to score higher on verbal achievement than they do in the reverse situation. This finding, however, leaves to conjecture what social and psychological forces are actually at work to produce the difference. In view of the very important bearing that this question has on such matters as school district reorganization, the retention or rejection of neighborhood schools, the busing of minority groups out of the ghetto, and the like, mere conjecture on the basis of such problematic evidence seems hardly adequate. Studies in far greater depth are needed, first, to identify the actual subgroups that exist in a given school's population; second, to describe the value system of each such subgroup; and third, to determine insofar as possible what effects these values may be having on the performance of its individual members and on their relationships with one another.

There are well-known sociometric devices for accomplishing the first and second of these purposes.[42] With respect to the third purpose, it appears that peer ratings, when obtained from groups of students who have come to know each other well, tend to be considerably superior to self-ratings as measures of noncognitive traits predictive of academic success. In a recent study of the subject, Smith found that "(1) peer ratings of personality, properly elicited and evaluated, can provide information of high reliability and predictive validity; (2) the factor analytic structure of . . . personality variables studied with the peer rating technique is highly stable from sample to sample within and across populations; and (3) the peer variables belonging to the 'strength of character' factor are important nonintellective correlates of academic success." [43] Smith has recently produced further evidence in support of the same conclusions in a study of 798 student nurses and a study of 1,022 Spanish-speaking students in San Juan, Puerto Rico.[44]

One of the significant advantages of the peer-rating technique is that it provides a basis for getting at the all-important interracial attitudes that may be having a negative effect on the achievement of minority groups in mixed school populations. Direct questioning on the subject by means of ordinary self-report devices is likely to elicit responses that are overly contaminated with social pretense or self-deception. Asking students to rate each other on behavior traits, where the focus is on the specific characteristics of the individual other than his race, avoids this defect. If one infers a white child's attitudes toward Negroes, or a Negro child's attitudes toward whites, not by what he *says* he feels or thinks, but rather by how he responds to his classmates as individuals, the chances are that a more accurate assessment of the prejudicial climate of a classroom could be obtained and its effect on academic achievement estimated.

In a series of studies designed to assess the effects of integration on the interracial attitudes of children in the early grades of school, Koslin and her collaborators[45] have been developing some ingenious techniques for measuring such attitudes in a manner that is "(1) situationally relevant for children in school settings (2) simple enough for first graders (3) group administrable with a minimum of verbal instruction and no reading requirements (4) sufficiently disguised to minimize the likelihood of eliciting socially desirable responses and (5) sufficiently structured to permit unambiguous scoring." [46] In essence, the technique relies on the child's responses to pen-and-ink sketches of various types of classroom situations in which there are differing combinations of white and black pupils and teachers. In one approach, the "social distance" between the child and each of several classroom figures is determined by measuring the distance between each of the target figures and the point on the page at which the child pastes a picture representing himself. In other approaches, the child expresses in somewhat similar fashion his preference for each of a series of pictured classroom activities in which the composition of the groups pictured is varied.

By these means Koslin *et al.* have been able to show a number of striking and statistically significant differences in the racial attitudes of Negro and white children under a variety of conditions. She plans to use these techniques in further research to investigate the relationship between this attitude variable and various types of cognitive development in the children. In most of her work, however, she regards the attitude measures as *dependent* variables—i.e., outcomes of the school experience that are educationally and socially important in their own right—not merely as mediators of academic achievement. This shift away from the usual fixation on academic achievement as the only educational outcome of prime concern is one that needs far greater emphasis in educational research than it has had in the past if we are ever to reach a better understanding of the role that the schools can play in undoing the divisiveness that currently plagues all of our social institutions.

Study V would focus on controlled observations of the classroom process as perceived by trained observers. This outside look at the content and quality of the transactions that occur between teacher and pupil and pupil and pupil is needed as a corrective of the several kinds of perceptual data accruing from the previous four studies. In their classic paper on methods for systematic observation of classroom behavior, Medley and Mitzel [47] begin with the following sage comment:

Certainly there is no more obvious approach to research on teaching than direct observation of teachers while they teach and pupils while they learn. Yet it is a rare study indeed that includes any formal observation at all. In a typical example of research on teaching, the research worker limits himself to the manipulation or study of antecedents and consequents of whatever happens in the classroom while the teaching itself is going on, but never once looks into the classroom to see how the teacher actually teaches or the pupils actually learn.[48]

The reasons for the nearly universal failure to lift the lid of the black box are fairly obvious: direct and reasonably objective observations of this sort are difficult, time-consuming, and expensive. Moreover, they require trained observers who are in short supply. Over the years, however, enough research has been done on the development of classroom observational techniques to bring them to the point where they yield highly objective and reasonably reliable time samples of various categories of classroom behavior. One instrument developed for this purpose by Medley and Mitzel, the Observation Schedule and Record, measures fourteen behavior variables that the authors have reduced to three orthogonal factor scales which they have named emotional climate, verbal emphasis, and social organization.[49] One advantage of this technique is that an intelligent adult, with no background in psychology or pedagogy, can be trained in three or four hours to use it effectively. Indeed, the less knowledge of educational or psychological theory the observer has, the less observer bias is likely to contaminate the measures.

A different approach to the direct observation of the teaching-learning process has been successfully demonstrated by Taba and Elzey in connection with a study of an elementary-school social studies program aimed at developing specific logical processes through well-defined teaching strategies.[50] For this purpose, they needed a running account of teacher-pupil interactions that would "depict the flow of the classroom discussion by charting the sequences of transactions between the teacher and the children, the changes in level of thought during the discussion, and the effect of these strategies upon the level and direction of thought" (p. 532). In order to secure the data required, they obtained tape-recordings of the classroom discussions at four critical points during the course of the year. These recordings were later transcribed and analyzed in accordance with an elaborate code descriptive of the cognitive tasks involved. From a preliminary analysis of these detailed data they were able to conclude that there is an "enormous influence of teacher behavior on the thinking of students" (p. 533).

From the foregoing, it seems clear that the analysis of teacher-pupil and pupil-pupil interactions is not only possible but imperative if we are to achieve useful insights into the difference between what the schools *are* doing for pupils as contrasted with what, under optimal conditions, they *can* do.

What has been lacking up to now in research on the classroom process is any major attempt to view it in the context of the many other variables that are assumed to influence pupil achievement. This is why Study V should help to fill a serious void in our understanding of the relationship between classroom operations and the conditions in the home, the community, and the schools that bear upon those operations.

The network of five interlocking studies briefly described above are bound to entail not only many very complex theoretical and technical problems, but some serious political and logistical problems as well. Problems of the latter type are well described in the Stodolsky-Lesser report mentioned above.[51] Clearly, however, the problems are not insoluble, and some such strategy as those hitherto suggested seems essential if we are to have in-depth studies that are small enough to be manageable and at the same time capable of furnishing information on the large number of interacting elements that seem likely to condition the learning and growth of pupils—boys and girls, white and black, bright and dull, advantaged and disadvantaged. For all such subgroups must be studied simultaneously before we are likely to get any really useful clues about what changes are needed to maximize the educational opportunities for each of them.

The overlapping feature of the interlocking studies has another advantage of considerable importance. By making possible a series of comparisons of the perceptions of several different groups of observers of the conditions, operations, and effects of the educational process, we should make some much needed advances in establishing the construct validity of the variety of measures that are commonly based on such perceptions. For example, pupil perceptions of teacher behavior (Study I) could be interrelated with teachers' perceptions of their own behavior (Study III), and both sets of perceptions could be interrelated with the perceptions of outside observers (Study V). It is only as we are able to find some consistencies in interrelationships like these that we shall be able to get a firmer handhold than we now have on the variables involved in affective and interpersonal behavior which are ordinarily considered of paramount concern in understanding pupil development.

Nevertheless, the five interlocking studies have at least one fundamental weakness that needs mentioning: these studies envisage analyses of data that are primarily cross-sectional. Although the limitations of such data are well-known, their relatively high feasibility, in comparison with studies of a longitudinal nature, makes them attractive as a way of generating hypotheses concerning the many variables in the school-home-community situation that need to be examined in greater depth before they can be seriously considered in the determination of educational policy. One of the principal weaknesses of the Coleman Report is that it failed to put sufficient emphasis on the fact that its findings, being based only on cross-sectional data, could be regarded as no more than highly tentative hypotheses and therefore highly inadequate grounds for any firm decisions about the future direction that American education ought to take. Rational decisions on long-term educational policy must rest on nothing less than long-term studies of educational practices which follow samples of the same children through large segments of their school experience—say four or five years. For only so is it possible to get a reasonably dependable check on the relative importance of the innumerable factors that are in fact shaping pupil development.

Longitudinal studies are not without a history of considerable interest. Notable examples of them are Terman's studies of gifted children,[52] Gesell's normative studies of young children and youth,[53] and those of the Fels Institute.[54] The emphasis in these studies has been on the growth of the child as an individual apart from his school experiences. A study begun in 1961 at Educational Testing Service[55] has had the opposite emphasis; it has focused primarily on the academic progress of a sample of children as they have moved from grade 5 to grade 12 in a variety of schools.

A study currently being launched by Educational Testing Service under the auspices of the Office of Economic Opportunity[56] will attempt to combine these two emphases in following children over the period age 3 to age 8 in four urban school systems. A major concern of this study will be to observe the impact of Project Headstart and other in-school and out-of-school experiences on the early learning of socially disadvantaged children. This study, though limited in scope, nevertheless exemplifies the massive effort that is required for the planning, development, and application of techniques adequate to the task of monitoring all the elements in both the school and the home that are likely to have a bearing on children's growth over any considerable period of time. It also exemplifies the enormous difficulties that must be overcome in securing the willing and continuing cooperation of school officials, teachers, parents, and community organizations concerned about the urban poor. Even so, the study can be regarded *only as a prototype* of the many additional highly complex longitudinal studies that ought to be continually going forward with all types of pupils in all types of schools in order to provide a flow of information of sufficient scope to help differentiate successful from unsuccessful educational practice at all grade levels and to suggest promising new approaches to be examined by means of controlled experimentation wherever possible.

♦ Experimental Studies

It will be recalled that in this essay I am making a rather arbitrary distinction between analytical studies and experimental studies. Since the methods of dealing with data in the two kinds of studies are often similar, it may be well at this point to spell out somewhat more specifically wherein the two types are alike and wherein they differ. Both types, if properly done, may use some form of multivariate analysis: regression analysis, analysis of variance, analysis of covariance, factor analysis, multiple discriminant analysis, and variants and combinations thereof. Both types are concerned with getting as good an assessment as possible of the factors in the educational scene, including the influence of the home and the community as well as the school, that appear to account for what pupils learn and for how much they learn. Both types try to take account of the *conditions* under which the learning of various kinds of pupils takes place and also of the educational *processes* that may or may not facilitate such learning.

There are two fundamental differences, however, between an analytical study and an experimental study. First, an analytical study investigates the variables in the educational system as they exist in their "natural state" while the latter investigates what happens when new variables are introduced into the system for the express purpose of *changing* the outcomes in student learning in certain ways hypothesized in advance. These new variables—e.g., a change in the number of hours per year devoted to reading, a change in the methods for teaching mathematics, the introduction of Afro-American studies, the introduction of a program of providing hot breakfasts for pupils from disadvantaged homes—are the *experimental variables or treatments*. The other difference between analytical studies and experimental studies is that the groups of pupils involved in the latter type of study are assigned *at random* to any of several treatments. The purpose of this randomization is to eliminate from the results the effects of variables that have been unmeasured or overlooked. As a consequence, the singular advantage that experimental studies have over analytical studies is that they can bring us considerably closer to an understanding of the factors that actually *cause* differences in pupil performance. A pair of studies—one analytical and one experimental and both addressed to the same general question—will illustrate these points.

One section of the Coleman Report consists of an analytical study of the probable effect of student-body characteristics on the achievement of individual pupils.[57] This section has attracted a good deal of attention because of the implications it has for educational policy on the matter of integration. In the words of the Report, "Attributes of other students account for far more variation in the achievement of minority group children than do any attributes of school facilities and slightly more than do attributes of staff." [58]

This conclusion was reached through a series of regression analyses performed on data from eight subgroups in the pupil population at five grade levels: 1, 3, 6, 9, and 12. The following table gives the results from part of the elementary-school sample.

Four sets of variables are involved in this analysis: (1) *verbal achievement* as measured by a test of verbal ability (the dependent variable), (2) *school characteristics* as measured by current staff expenditure per pupil, size of school, number of books in the library, and location

*Percentage of Incremental Variance in Verbal Achievement Predictable Successively from School Characteristics and Student-Body Characteristics after Controlling for Home Background**

(Northern Negro Sample)

	Grade 1	Grade 3	Grade 6
School characteristics	2.38%	2.96%	0.77%
Student-body characteristics	0.90%	2.17%	1.96%
Both combined	3.28%	5.13%	2.73%

* Adapted from Table 3.23.2 in the Coleman Report.

(urban-suburban-rural), (3) *student-body characteristics* as measured by proportion of students whose families own encyclopedias, number of students transferring in and out of the school, average attendance, and teachers' perception of student-body quality, and (4) *home background* as measured by parents' education, structural integrity of the home, size of family, items in the home, reading material in the home (the control variables).

This particular segment of the Coleman data does not support the general conclusion stated above, but the findings are nevertheless usefully illustrative of the kind of information an analytical study can provide. The manner in which the table is to be interpreted can be seen by examining the percentages in the Grade 1 column as an example: (1) After taking into account the percentage of variance in verbal test scores predictable from a knowledge of home background, we find that if we then take into consideration the differences in the characteristics of the schools that the children attend, we increase by 2.38 percent the accuracy with which we can predict how well these Negro first graders will do on a test of verbal ability. (2) If, on top of this, we consider the differences in the student-body characteristics of these same schools, we increase the accuracy of prediction by 0.9 percent. (3) If, finally, we consider the differences in both the school and student-body characteristics, we find that the total improvement in accuracy of predicting the verbal test scores becomes 3.28 percent.

By looking only at the amount of accuracy added by taking the student-body characteristics into account, we arrive at the inference that the more favorable the student-body characteristics are, the better the chances are that the children will do well on verbal tests. This, however, is an inference concerning the way things *are* for these children, not what they *might be* under different circumstances. That is, it raises, but does not answer, the question: If we actually *moved* the Negro children in the early grades from schools where the student-body characteristics are unfavorable to schools where the student-body characteristics are more favorable, would the change in schools bring about a rise in the children's verbal scores?

An experimental study now under way in the Hartford, Connecticut, area is addressed to this last question among others.[59] Although at this writing the study is not yet finished and the available data not yet fully analyzed, the strategy of the study and the interim results illuminate some of the possibilities of an experimental study.

Known as Project Concern, the experiment began in September, 1966, by busing 266 children beginning grades kindergarten through 5 from five predominantly Negro schools in the northend of Hartford to 35 elementary schools in five suburban towns outside the city. The children to be bused were selected on a random basis from the schools in the northend district. No more than three of these children were placed in any one class in any of the suburban schools. A group of 305 nonbused children was similarly selected from the same five sending schools to remain there and serve as controls.[60] The experimentals and controls entering grades 3 to 5 were further divided into two subgroups each. Provision was made to give the individuals in one of these subgroups special compensatory support as needed; those in the other two received only regular instruction. Thus, in the upper three grades the experiment consisted of four groups to be observed and compared: Group I (nonbused, nonsupported), Group II (nonbused, supported), Group III (bused, nonsupported), and Group IV (bused, supported).

As mentioned above, the analyses of the data have not yet been completed. But some of the raw data suggest that moving elementary children out of the ghetto into suburban schools does indeed tend to improve their level of accomplishment. One set of data, for instance, provides a comparison of the mean gains in I.Q. scores during the period from the spring of 1967 to the spring of 1968. The following table suggests what is happening:

*Gains in I.Q. of Four Groups at Six Grade Levels**

Grade completed in Spring 1968	Controls		Experimentals	
	Group I	Group II	Group III	Group IV
Grade 1	3.0	—	8.2	9.3
Grade 2	2.0	—	5.0	2.6
Grade 3	3.3	0.5	5.4	6.7
Grade 4	−0.5	−4.2	6.4	6.2
Grade 5	6.7	−7.0	−2.2	2.6
Grade 6	3.3	−0.5	4.6	1.9

* Adapted from Table 5 (p. 23) of the report on Project Concern.

From these data it seems clear that in grades 1 through 4, the bused children made gains in I.Q. that were consistently greater than those made by the nonbused children. The results for grades 5 and 6 are not similarly consistent, but the general trend here also favors the experimentals.

Further analyses of these and other similar data from this experimental study are obviously needed to sort out the factors that are at work in the results. The effects of the home background variables have presumably been eliminated as a factor by means of the random process by which the four samples of children were selected, but there is still much to be learned about possible differential effects arising from qualitative differences in the schools to which the experimental pupils were sent. Furthermore, one needs to know (following Coleman) whether the greater gains of the experimentals are to be explained by reason of the quality of the schools per se, by the characteristics of the pupils in those schools, or possibly even by the fact of catching and riding the bus every school day, which for these young children has no doubt been an important learning experience in itself.

By appropriate analytical techniques, these and other factors presumed to be causative of cognitive improvement can be teased out of the data in the Hartford study. There are, however, other aspects of this study that make it something of an exemplar for experimental studies having to do with broad-scale changes in school operations designed to have a favorable impact on minority children. The study is concerned not only with the direct impact of busing and compensatory support on the cognitive development of such children; it is concerned also with other effects of the enterprise—on the children themselves, and on their schoolmates, their teachers, their families, the families of their schoolmates, and the attitudes of the general citizenry in the several participating communities. This attention to what might be called the "ripple effects" of the experimental treatments seems extremely important for two reasons. The first and most obvious is that it can serve to identify negative attitudes which, despite favorable outcomes for the pupils themselves, could conceivably prevent the experiment from becoming a regular part of the educational program. The second reason is perhaps somewhat more subtle, but possibly just as important to a full understanding of the educational process: it is that the attitudes such an experiment generates in the school, the homes, and the surrounding community may react upon the children directly involved in such a way as to reinforce or inhibit the first-order effects of the experimental treatment.

In view of the importance of the issue of integration and the promising results of the Hartford experiment thus far, it seems clear that we urgently need first of all replications of the same experiment, *under similarly controlled conditions*, in several different parts of the country where busing pupils out of the inner city is logistically feasible. "Experiments" in busing are under way in a number of places. As far as I know, however, the Hartford experiment is the only one that can be considered a true experiment—that is, one that yields reasonably dependable information on the actual effects of the busing operations by themselves.

It is admittedly difficult to organize true experiments in the schools, particularly when the treatments involve administrative or personnel changes of any fundamental kind. Most of the difficulty arises from the fact that the participants (administrators, teachers, parents, children) generally do not understand the need for randomization and may be unwilling to submit to it. At the same time, however, a number of educational innovations *could* have become true experimental studies if those in charge of them had given sufficient thought and energy *in advance* to the problems of experimental design and data analysis. The More Effective School Program in New York City is a case in point.[61] This program got under way in the fall of 1964 in 10 inner-city elementary schools with "a set of eight schools designated as 'control' schools . . . selected because of their similarity to an ME school in terms of their location and pupil population." [62] In the following year 11 more ME schools were added to the program. The principal experimental variables consisted in reductions in class size and pupil-teacher ratios. Other variables that concerned the investigators were the provision of teacher specialists, team teaching, heterogeneous grouping, and emphasis on school-community relationships. As matters turned out, however, these were more in the nature of hopes than well-monitored experimental treatments.[63] Because of the apparently disappointing outcomes of the study in terms of pupil achievement, the report cited above has generated no small amount of controversy.[64] The social and political tensions that had much to do with bringing the project into being and that have hardly abated since the last report was issued have perhaps made much of this controversy inevitable. On the other hand, one cannot help but wonder whether at least some of the controversy would not have been alleviated if more earnest attention at the outset had been given to advance planning and monitoring of the treatments, to the manner in which the sample of schools (experimentals and "controls") had been selected, and to the specific types of multivariate analyses that would be needed to extract meaning from the data. It is not inconceivable that, had all this been done, the outcomes of the project would have taken on a more favorable aspect, or at least would have provided some strong hints as to what adjustments might have improved the program.

In "real-life" experiments of this kind, compromises with scientific purity will no doubt always have to be made to make the experiments at all feasible. But the compromises are likely to be a good deal less disastrous if they are made grudgingly and with full awareness of the ideal that is being compromised. Anyone responsible for a "real-life" experiment should be aware of the respectable strategies for compromise that have been spelled out by Campbell and Stanley in their article on experimental and quasi-experimental designs.[65]

In view of the flood of innovations proposed and under way in American education these days, there is need for a great many different kinds of "real-life" experiments to bring us somewhat closer to an understanding of what the new programs, devices, and administrative arrangements are actually doing for children—especially minority-group children. One set of such experimental studies should focus on the abilities and attitudes of teachers of the disadvantaged. The authors of the Coleman Report admit that the circumstances of their survey prevented them from getting adequate information on the relation of these teacher variables to pupil achievement.[66] The main reason was that it was not possible to tie together the data on teachers with those on the pupils whom they had actually taught. The consequence is that the amount of pupil achievement variance "explained" by these teacher variables is vanishingly small. Common sense, however, insists that the way teachers feel about the children they teach and the amount of skill they possess in adapting instruction to individual pupil needs *must* be strong factors in determining what the children learn. The reanalyses of the Coleman data by Hanushek and Kain (see Chapter 3) tend to support the notion that the quality of teaching does indeed make for differences in the quality of pupil learning. The Taba-Elzey study previously cited reinforces the point.

It is this commonsense assumption that lies back of the innumerable programs for in-service training and the organization of summer institutes for the teachers of disadvantaged children that have been offered in various parts of the country during recent years. The theory is entirely straightforward: if one can bring about positive changes in the abilities and attitudes of these teachers, such changes will be accompanied by a positive change in the achievement of their pupils. Support for the theory, however, has usually been hortatory rather than experimental. Little solid information has been forthcoming on the amount and kinds of change that the training programs have produced in the teachers, and practically nothing of any consequence is known about the effects such changes, if any, have had on their students. With reasonably sophisticated planning it should be possible to correct this situation by designing a series of feasible experimental studies tied in closely and simultaneously with the teacher training projects and the schools where the teachers teach. Until this is done, we shall never get more than an inkling of whether the considerable effort going into these projects is producing any real educational payoff or what might be done to increase it.

In view of the extensive and diverse efforts during the last decade to bring about major improvements in elementary and secondary school curricula,[67] it is unfortunate that the Coleman survey was apparently unable to give more than superficial attention to curriculum and instructional variables. The Report considers only four of them: (1) the comprehensiveness of the curriculum measured in terms of the number of different courses offered, (2) the presence or absence in the curriculum of any opportunity for acceleration, (3) the number of mathematics courses offered, and (4) the number of foreign-language courses offered. In the elementary grades only the first two of these variables were used in the regression analyses.[68] Any noticeable relationships between level of pupil achievement and such generalized curriculum measures as these would be surprising; in this respect the Coleman Report contains no surprises.*

The Coleman results notwithstanding, it seems reasonable to expect that the quality and content of school curricula can and do make a substantial difference in what and how much pupils learn. But well-controlled studies of this question are scarcer than they ought to be or need to be. A small study comparing three preschool programs for disadvantaged children is one of the exceptions that illustrate the power and some of the possibilities in true experiments on the curriculum.[69] In this study, Karnes, Teska, and Hodgins divided a sample of 59 disadvantaged preschoolers into three groups according to I.Q. and then randomly assigned the children in each I.Q. group to three different preschool curricula. One was the *traditional* preschool program in which the emphasis is on socialization through free play and on incidental and informal cognitive learning through activities involving art, music, and stories. The second curriculum, labeled the *ameliorative* program, required the children during part of the school day to engage in a series of gamelike activities focused specifically on making up deficits in language, sense of number, and grasp of elementary social and scientific concepts. In the third curriculum, called *direct verbal*, the children received concentrated drill in language, arithmetic, and reading in accordance with the procedures described by Bereiter and Engelmann in their book *Teaching Disadvantaged Children in the Preschool*.[70] The children assigned to the first two curricula—traditional and ameliorative—attended a regular public-school kindergarten and 1st grade in the second and third years of the experiment, but those in the ameliorative program were given some supplementary "ameliorative" instruction during the kindergarten year following the regular school sessions. The direct verbal curriculum covered *both* the preschool and kindergarten years, following which the children assigned to it entered a regular public-school 1st grade.

The investigators responsible for this study looked at several types of cognitive and perceptual development that occurred over the three-year period under the three types of treatment and found some interesting as well as statistically significant differences in their developmental patterns. The next table gives a rough indication of what happened to the three groups in respect to their general cognitive development as measured by increments in I.Q. While this is only a sample from the data produced by the study, some of the results are nevertheless rather striking: (1) all groups gained in I.Q. during the preschool year, but those following the two experimental curricula gained more; (2) in the kindergarten year only the direct-verbal group continued to gain, but this gain was entirely wiped out during the 1st-grade year; (3) at end of the 1st grade, the

---

* Except for the one in which Northern white sixth graders turn up the remarkable correlation between verbal achievement and curriculum comprehensiveness of 8.6597! (See Supplemental Appendix, p. 401.)

*Mean Gains in Binet I.Q. for the Three Groups**

Curriculum	N	During preschool	During kindergarten	During 1st grade	Over the 3-year period
Traditional	25	+ 9	− 3	0	+ 6
Ameliorative	24	+14	− 1	− 5	+ 8
Direct verbal	10	+13	+11	−11	+13

* Adapted from Table 2 of the report by Karnes *et al*.

overall gain of the direct verbal group was nevertheless greater than that of either of the other two.

Small experimental studies like this are of very great importance for identifying and testing the specific effects of specific instructional programs on specific kinds of pupils. We need thousands of such studies with children of all ages if we are ever to come reasonably close to an understanding of the causal connections to be found at the point where the materials of the curriculum, the performance of teachers, and the activities of pupils are supposed to intersect. Up to now, however, small studies of this sort have suffered from two kinds of isolation that have tended to weaken if not to vitiate their usefulness in advancing knowledge of the educational process and in opening up practical possibilities for increasing its effectiveness.

The first kind of isolation has to do with the limited focus of most such studies: they usually deal with only one or a few of the many dependent variables of interest in human development. The study by Karnes *et al*. exemplifies this defect in that, while it throws important light on certain curriculum strategies for stimulating some aspects of the cognitive development of disadvantaged children, it gives little or no information on the *side effects* that such stimulation may be having on the children's emotional and social development. One might ask, for example, as a consequence of the "direct verbal" treatment, what is happening to the children's feelings about themselves, about each other, and about the whole idea of going to school. This is a question that has generated considerable argument among the adherents of various theoretical positions concerning child development. *But there are no clear answers one way or the other because too many of the critical dependent variables have gone unobserved or inadequately observed in the individual isolated studies that have attempted to deal with the problem.* The result is a running debate that appears to be going nowhere.

The second kind of isolation is of a different order. The typical experimental study in education, even though otherwise well designed, tends to employ treatments, samples of children, and observational techniques that are unique to itself. As a result the findings from most such exercises are seldom, if ever, cumulative. The "review of the literature" with which they usually start off is for the most part little more than scholarly window-dressing. There is hardly ever any systematic examination of all the "plausible rival hypotheses" that might account for earlier experimental observations or any effort to develop an integrated series of further studies to test their plausibility. We have plenty of "exploratory studies" that take interesting peeks at disparate segments of the teaching-learning process, but no truly coordinated research programs capable of mapping and explaining the whole terrain. In a word, the bits-and-pieces character of educational research to date has hardly contributed to the growth of what Platt has called the "logical tree" of consecutive inference.[71] The construction of such a tree in any of the social sciences—especially those related to education—is peculiarly difficult for the well-known reason that both the sources and objects of the necessary observations, being human, tend to be intractable.

There is, however, at least one corner of the weedy garden of educational research where the logical tree might be firmly planted and, if properly fenced about and nurtured, might grow into a useful theory of instruction. This is the corner that has been preempted by computer-assisted instruction (CAI).

CAI as an instrument for instruction in itself, rather than as a tool for *research* in instruction, has generated a good deal of excitement—so much indeed that it is in danger of being buried in controversy and of becoming a discredited miracle before it gets the chance to fulfill its promise as a basis for orderly experimentation. Two recent series of articles give a good idea of the flavor of the controversy.[72] It centers on such matters as the speed with which CAI will become technologically feasible on a large scale, the quality of its impact on the minds and social behavior of pupils, the resistance it will encounter from teachers who see it as a threat to their jobs, and the pressure tactics of the promoters who operate out of what one polemicist calls the "educational hardware stores." [73] The situation is well summarized in the introduction to a sober paper by Atkinson who is himself a serious worker in the vineyards of CAI research:[74]

In recent years there has been a tremendous number of articles and news releases dealing with computer-assisted instruction . . . One might conjecture that this proliferation is an indicant of rapid progress in the field. Unfortunately, I doubt that it is. A few reports about CAI are based on substantial experience and research, but the majority are vague speculations and conjectures with little if any data or real experience to back them up. I do not want to denigrate the role of speculation and conjecture in a newly developing area like CAI. However, of late it seems to have produced little more than a repetition of ideas that were exciting in the 1950's but, in the absence of new research, are simply well-worn clichés in the late 1960's . . . Important and significant research on CAI is being carried on in many laboratories around the country, but certainly not as much as one is led to believe by the attendant publicity. The problem for someone trying to evaluate developments in the field is to distinguish between those reports that are based on fact and those that are disguised forms of science fiction . . . [p. 225]

The research effort Atkinson describes is one part of a program that he and Suppes organized at Stanford University in 1964.[75] Its goal is to develop programs via computer for three modes of instruction: (1) a drill-and-practice mode aimed at increasing facility in routine skills, (2) a tutorial mode in which the computer leads the individual pupil, step by step, to new concepts, and (3) a dialogue mode in which the pupil learns by querying the computer for information and being queried by the computer in return. The drill-and-practice mode is the most well-developed and operational; the dialogue mode exists only in crude prototypes.

The technological problems are of course enormous, especially for the tutorial and dialogue systems, but the point of interest in Atkinson's paper is that apparently the curriculum development problems are even more severe. He develops a computerized reading program (tutorial mode) for 1st-grade children. In the process of working out the minute step-by-step procedures required by computer programming, he demonstrates how little we really know empirically about the complex behavior involved in learning to read and how lacking we are in any but the most primitive and tentative theories for guiding the operation—this despite four decades of "research" in reading. He also demonstrates, though, how rich a resource computerized teaching can be in producing, organizing, structuring, and continually restructuring the vast quantities of the sort of minute behavioral data required if we are to achieve increasingly accurate insights into the different ways different children learn best.

Some of the results Atkinson obtained in the first year of the experiment are shown in the following table:

Some End-of-Year Scores on Reading Tests*

Test	Experimental group	Control group	p value
California Reading (total)	46	40	<.01
Hartley Reading			
Vocabulary	19	17	<.01
Word pronunciation	10	6	<.01
Word recognition	20	17	<.01

* Adapted from Atkinson, p. 236.

The experimental and control groups were made up of some 100 socially disadvantaged first graders. The experimentals had the CAI reading course, the controls a CAI course in beginning mathematics. This arrangement presumably eliminated any Hawthorne effect resulting from coping with the devices at the computer terminals. Both experimentals and controls had a mean I.Q. of 89, and both were at the same reading levels at the beginning of the program.

The numbers above suggest a conventionally neat experiment with encouraging if not startling results. What they fail to show is the wealth of developmental data behind the numbers for the experimental group—data that, when appropriately analyzed, should at least begin to provide clues as to *why* some children learn faster than others and how the materials of learning might conceivably be altered to maximize the learning of each child. Atkinson's study makes only a first small dent on the fundamental problems involved in curriculum research, but it is an extremely important dent because it makes a beginning at specifying the sequences of hypotheses that need testing and the kinds of data required to test them. Thus, CAI, at least for the present, might better be regarded as a means of learning how to put together effective curricula than as a device for prepackaging curricula for sale on the educational market—i.e., a tool for programing instructional *research* rather than a tool for programing instruction.

One aspect of CAI that quite properly worries the skeptics is the influence that it may possibly have on the interpersonal behavior of the children exposed to it. There have been impressionistic reports on this matter but few that are based on hard data. An exception is a small side study by Sears and Feldman that looked at the changes in the classroom behavior of some of the same children who participated in Atkinson's study.[76] The effects they were able to find were small, but nevertheless of sufficient size to indicate that there may be behavioral correlates of CAI that need attending to. In any event, any program of curriculum research, whether or not it is centered on CAI, will be incomplete unless it examines affective as well as cognitive development. It is conceivable that some pupils can be turned off by computers just as effectively as by live teachers.

One very great advantage of CAI as a strategy for curriculum research, which has not yet been adequately exploited but which should be, lies in the fact that it is capable of reaching highly diverse samples of pupils *simultaneously* in a number of different school systems throughout the country—rural, urban, suburban; public and private; North, South, East, and West. It could not only provide a communication network for the schools involved in some such scheme of interlocking analytical studies as has been sketched above (pp. 396–405); it could also provide the means for a common series of controlled experimental studies within and among the same schools. There has recently been a considerable proliferation of "consortia" of school districts, and of schools within districts, with terminals connected to a single computer.[77] The emphasis in these undertakings, however, has thus far been primarily on developing prepackaged computerized curricula for immediate use rather than on serious experimentation aimed at coming closer to a set of general principles that govern the why and how of pupil learning under the variety of conditions that affect it. As a consequence, there is a real danger that the spread of CAI will tend to freeze into educational systems the myths and materials that have characterized instructional procedures of the past instead of opening the way to a sounder understanding of the causal connections between teaching and learning that could and should lead to better education for all segments of the population in the future.

After-Thought

It should be obvious that the thoughts about future studies contained in this essay scarcely constitute a definitive program for the future of all research in education, nor were they intended to do so. Specialists in the several disciplines (psychologists, sociologists, economists, statisticians, computer scientists, etc.) related in one way or another to research on the educational enterprise will find many gaps that need filling, especially those having to do with such fundamental matters as the nutritional and neurological factors that affect children's growth.[78] Nevertheless, it should be equally obvious that the ideas presented here are extraordinarily ambitious ideas—ambitious because they envisage a vast amount of cooperation within and among researchers and school people, and ambitious also because, taken together, their implementation will require more money for the support of educational research than has hitherto been dreamed of. The current national outlay for such research, which admittedly is higher than it has ever been before, is probably something less than one tenth of 1 percent of the gross national product. Even this amount is scattered so widely among so many unrelated and unrelatable projects and programs that the outlook for compiling any really useful body of information on how to improve schools and school systems is dubious if not totally bleak. In view of this situation and of the overriding importance of better education to the health of American society, the next two items on the agenda of educational research ought to be (1) research on how to organize the researchers for more productive research and (2) research on how to persuade taxpayers to provide funds commensurate with the need for it. If we could solve the first of these two problems, we might have a much better chance of solving the second one.

Notes

1. See Chapter 3 by Hanushek and Kain in this book for a discussion of these matters in connection with the Coleman Report.
2. This is question 40 of the Principal Questionnaire used in the Coleman study.
3. See Part IV of the Superintendent Questionnaire used in the Coleman study. The experience of that study was that in most cases the expense data called for were not or could not be supplied. Even had they been, it is difficult to see, from the questions asked, how it would have been possible to break down the figures in the manner here suggested.
4. Questions 9–12 in the Principal Questionnaire.
5. Question 13 of the Principal Questionnaire.
6. See, for instance, *Evaluative Criteria*, Washington, D.C.: National Study of Sec-

ondary School Standards, 1960; F. G. Cornell, C. M. Lindvall, and J. L. Saupe, "An Exploratory Measurement of Individualities of Schools and Classrooms," *University of Illinois Bulletin*, Vol. 50, No. 75, 1953; P. R. Mort and F. G. Cornell, *American Schools In Transition*, New York: Bureau of Publications, Teachers College, Columbia University, 1941.

7. See, for instance, T. H. James, J. A. Thomas, and H. J. Dyck, *Wealth, Expenditures, and Decision-Making for Education*, Stanford, Calif.: Stanford University, School of Education, 1963; D. H. Ross, *Administration for Adaptability*, New York: Metropolitan School Study Council, Teachers College, Columbia University, 1958.

8. A few efforts along this line are in the early planning stage, but attempts to wrestle with reorganizing the real data of real school systems are at most only tentative. See, for example, William H. Curtis, *Project to Develop a Program Planning-Budgeting-Evaluation System Design*: First Year Final Progress Report (Project No. 8-0 290, Grant No. OEG-0-8-080290-3315), Chicago: Research Corporation of the Association of School Business Officials, 1968.

9. E.g., K. R. Atherton, "A Comparison of Solutions Obtained in Factor Analyses of Socio-economic Variables," *Psychological Reports*, Vol. 11, 1962, 259–73; J. A. Kahl, *The American Class Structure*, New York: Rinehart, 1957; A. B. Hollingshead, *Elmstown's Youth*, New York: Wiley, 1949; W. L. Warner, Marchia Meeker, and K. Eells, *Social Class in America*, New York: Harper, 1960.

10. It is being conducted by Lawrence J. Stricker, Educational Testing Service, Princeton, N.J.

11. J. C. Flanagan, J. T. Dailey, Marion F. Shaycoft, D. B. Orr, and I. Goldberg. *Studies of the American High School*. Washington, D.C.: Project TALENT Office, 1962.

12. B. D. Karpinos. *The Mental Test Qualification of American Youths for Military Service and Its Relationship to Educational Attainment*. Washington, D.C.: Proceedings of the Social Statistics Section, American Statistical Association, 1966, pp. 92–111.

13. See R. W. Tyler, "Assessing the Progress of Education," *Phi Delta Kappan*, Vol. 27, 1965, pp. 13–6; N. J. Higgins and J. C. Merwin, "Assessing the Progress of Education: a Second Report," *Phi Delta Kappan*, Vol. 29, 1967, pp. 378–80.

14. Quoted from the article by Higgins and Merwin cited above.

15. John W. Tukey. Personal communication.

16. E.g., Leonard A. Lecht, *Goals, Priorities, and Dollars: The Next Decade*, New York: The Free Press, 1966; also, Donald N. Michael, *The Next Generation: The Prospects Ahead for the Youth of Today and Tomorrow*, New York: Random House, 1965.

17. See K. Patricia Cross, *The Junior College Student: A Research Description*, Princeton, N.J.: Educational Testing Service, 1968.

18. S. S. Stodolsky and G. Lesser. "Learning Patterns in the Disadvantaged." *Harvard Educational Review*, Vol. 37, No. 4, pp. 546–93.

19. C. Hitch. *Decision Making for Defense*. Berkeley, Calif.: University of California Press, 1965.

20. J. Burkhead, T. G. Fox, and J. W. Holland. *Input and Output in Large City High Schools*. Syracuse, N.Y.: Syracuse University Press, 1967, p. 13.

21. A. M. Mood and R. Powers. "Cost Benefit Analysis of Education," in M. Alfandary-Alexander, editor, *Analysis for Planning Programming Budgeting*. Potomac, Md.: Washington Operations Research Council, 1968.

22. Burkhead, *et al.*, *ibid.*, pp. 84–5.

23. H. J. Kiesling. *High School Size and Cost Factors*. Washington, D.C.: Office of Education, 1968. (Project No. 6-1590, Contract No. OEC-3-7-061590-0372.)

24. Kiesling in another study has taken precisely this approach. See his study, "The Relationship of School Inputs and Community Characteristics to Public School Performance" (mimeo, undated).

25. Coleman Report, p. 319.

26. E.g., R. C. Wylie, *The Self-Concept*, Lincoln, Nebraska: University of Nebraska Press, 1961; P. S. Sears and V. S. Sherman, *In Pursuit of Self-Esteem*, Belmont,

Calif.: Wadsworth Publishing Co., 1965; P. H. Coombs and V. Davies, "Self-conception and the Relationship between High School and Scholastic Achievement," *Sociology and Social Research*, July, 1966, pp. 468–9.

27. E.g., M. Deutsch, *et al.*, *The Disadvantaged Child*, New York: Basic Books, 1967; H. H. Davidson and J. W. Greenberg, *Traits of School Achievers from a Disadvantaged Background*, New York: City College of the City University of New York, May, 1967; A. F. Pouissaint and C. O. Atkinson, "Negro Youth and Psychological Motivation," *Journal of Negro Education*, Vol. 37, 1968, pp. 241–51.

28. D. P. Crowne and M. W. Stephens. "Self-Acceptance and Self-evaluative Behavior: a Critique of Methodology." *Psychological Bulletin*, Vol. 58, 1961, pp. 104–21.

29. A. M. Mood and F. C. Massetta. *Supplemental Appendix to the Survey on Equality of Educational Opportunity*. Washington, D.C.: U.S. Government Printing Office, 1966, pp. 75, 117, 189. The questions on which the measure is based are 24, 25, 27, 28, and 29 in the 9th- and 12th-grade questionnaire; 41 and 42 in the 6th-grade questionnaire; 30 and 31 in the 3rd-grade questionnaire.

30. *Ibid.*, pp. 19, 61, 359, 461.

31. W. H. Sewell and V. P. Shah. "Social Class, Parental Encouragement, and Educational Aspirations." *American Journal of Sociology*, Vol. 73, 1968, pp. 559–72; R. Q. Bell, "A Reinterpretation of the Direction Effects in Studies of Socialization." *Psychological Review*, Vol. 75, 1968, pp. 81–95.

32. E.g., S. R. Cohen, "An Exploratory Study of Student Attitudes in the Primary Grades," in *A Plan for Evaluating the Quality of Educational Programs in Pennsylvania*, Vol. II, Harrisburg, Pa.: State Board of Education, 1965, pp. 61–130.

33. W. E. Coffman, "Determining Students' Concepts of Effective Teaching from Their Ratings of Instructors," *Journal of Educational Psychology*, Vol. 45, 1954, pp. 277–86; C. A. Gibb, "Classroom Behavior of the College Teacher," *Educational and Psychological Measurement*, (1955) Vol. 15, 1955, pp. 254–63; D. M. Medley and A. A. Klein, *Studies of Teacher Behavior: Inferring Classroom Behavior from Pupil Responses*, New York: Board of Education, 1956 (Research Series No. 30); D. C. Neale and J. M. Proshek, "School-related Attitudes of Culturally Disadvantaged Elementary School Children," *Journal of Educational Psychology*, Vol. 58, 1967, pp. 238–44; L. K. Conn, C. N. Edwards, D. Crowne, "Perception of Emotion and Response to Teachers' Expectancy by Elementary School Children," *Psychological Reports*, Vol. 22, 1968, pp. 27–34; M. L. Jackson and F. F. Fuller, "Influence of Social Class on Students' Evaluation of Their Teachers," Proceedings of the 74th Annual Convention of the American Psychological Association, 1966, pp. 269–70.

34. E.g., David J. Fox, *Expansion of the More Effective School Program*, New York: Center for Urban Education, 1967 (mimeo). Elementary-school children in this study filled out a questionnaire with questions like the following (p. B37):

The teachers in this school won't help you.	Yes—No
The teachers in this school are really interested in you.	Yes—No
The teachers in this school are fair and square.	Yes—No

35. P. C. Sexton. *Education and Income*. New York: Viking Press, 1961.

36. R. D. Hess and V. C. Shipman, "Maternal Attitude Toward School and the Role of the Pupil: Some Social Class Comparisons," paper prepared for the Fifth Work Conference on Curriculum and Teaching in Depressed Urban Areas, Columbia University Teachers College, June 20–July 1, 1966; H. F. Clarizio, "Maternal Attitude Change Associated with Involvement in Project Headstart," *The Journal of Negro Education*, Vol. 37, pp. 106–13.

37. See Teacher's Questionnaire: perception of student quality—questions 33, 34, and 47; perception of school quality—questions 38, 44, 47; attitude toward integration —questions 46a, 46b, 46d, 46f; preference for middle-class students—questions 39, 40, 43; preference for white students—question 42.

38. R. D. Strom, editor, *The Inner-City Classroom: Teacher Behaviors*. Columbus, Ohio: Charles E. Merrill Books, Inc., 1966. See especially, the following; J. H. Niemeyer, "Importance of the Inner-city Teacher," pp. 1–20; R. D. Strom,

"Teacher Aspiration and Attitude," pp. 21–39; A. H. Passow, "Diminishing Teacher Prejudice," pp. 93–109.

39. J. W. Getzels, and P. W. Jackson. "The Teacher's Personality and Characteristics," in N. L. Gage, editor, *Handbook of Research on Teaching*. Chicago: Rand McNally, 1963, pp. 506–82.

40. G. B. Stern. "Measuring Noncognitive Variables in Teaching," in Gage, *op. cit.*, pp. 422–25.

41. Neal Gross, and Robert E. Herriott. *Staff Leadership in Public Schools: A Sociological Inquiry*. New York: John Wiley, 1965.

42. H. H. Remmers, "Rating Methods for Research in Teaching," in Gage, *op. cit.*, pp. 343–60; A. Anastasi, *Psychological Testing*, 3rd edition, New York: Macmillan, 1968, pp. 539–42.

43. G. M. Smith. "Usefulness of Peer Ratings of Personality in Educational Research." *Educational and Psychological Measurement*, Vol. 27, 1967, pp. 967–84. Quoted from abstract in *Psychological Abstracts*, Vol. 42, June, 1968, p. 8844.

44. G. M. Smith. "Progress Report on Analysis of Peer Ratings of Personality." Paper presented at the Interamerican Congress of Psychology, Montevideo, Uruguay, 1969.

45. S. C. Koslin, M. Amarel, and N. Ames, "A Distance Measure of Racial Attitudes in Primary Grade Children: An Exploratory Study," in *Psychology in the Schools* (in press); ———*The Effect of Race on Peer Evaluation and Preference in Primary Grade Children: An Exploratory Study*, Research Bulletin RB-69-12, Princeton, N.J.: Educational Testing Service, 1969; S. C. Koslin, B. L. Koslin, J. Cardwell, and R. Pargament, "A Quasi-disguised and Structured Measure of Schoolchildren's Racial Preferences," paper prepared for presentation at the American Psychological Association, 1969 (mimeo); ———"Measuring Schoolchildren's Racial Preferences," paper prepared for presentation to the Eastern Psychological Association, 1969 (mimeo).

46. Koslin, *et al.*, APA paper, 1969.

47. D. M. Medley, and H. E. Mitzel. "Measuring Classroom Behavior by Systematic Observation," in Gage, *op. cit.*, pp. 247–328.

48. *Ibid.*, p. 247.

49. D. M. Medley, and H. E. Mitzel, "A Technique for Measuring Classroom Behavior," *Journal of Educational Psychology*, Vol. 49, 1958, pp. 86–92; and "Some Behavior Correlates of Teacher Effectiveness," *Journal of Educational Psychology*, Vol. 50, 1959, pp. 239–46.

50. H. Taba and F. E. Elzey. "Teaching Strategies and Thought Processes," *Teachers College Record*, Vol. 65, No. 6, pp. 524–34.

51. *Ibid.*, p. 525.

52. Lewis M. Terman, editor. *Genetic Studies of Genius*. Stanford, Calif.: Stanford University Press, 1925.

53. Arnold L. Gesell, *The First Five Years of Life*, New York: Harper, 1940; ——— and F. L. Ilg, *The Child from Five to Ten*, New York: Harper, 1946; ———, ———, and L. B. Ames, *Youth: The Years from Ten to Sixteen*, New York: Harper, 1956.

54. J. Kagan, and H. A. Moss. *Birth to Maturity*. New York: Wiley, 1962.

55. Educational Testing Service. *The Growth Study: A Brief Description of "A Study of Academic Prediction and Growth."* Princeton, N.J.: Educational Testing Service, 1966.

56. S. Anderson, A. Beaton, W. Emmerich, and S. Messick. *Disadvantaged Children and Their First School Experiences*. Princeton, N.J.: Educational Testing Service, 1968. (OEO Contract 4206; OEO Grant C6-8256.)

57. Coleman Report, section 3.23, "Student Body Characteristics," pp. 302–12.

58. *Ibid.*, p. 302.

59. T. W. Mahan. *Project Concern—1966–1968: A Report on the Effectiveness of Suburban School Placement of Inner-City Youth*. Hartford, Conn.: Board of Education, 1968.

60. The author of the study is careful to point out that, because of logistical considera-

tions, the randomization of experimentals was in some respects not "ideal." However, it is worth pointing out that the families of only twelve of the children originally assigned to the experimental group refused to let their children participate. (See page 14 of the Report.)

61. D. J. Fox, *op. cit.*

62. *Ibid.*, p. 1.

63. J. Abramson, *et al. Evaluation of the More Effective Schools Program, Summary Report.* New York: Board of Education of the City of New York, Bureau of Educational Research, 1966 (mimeo), pp. 66–7. See also Fox, *op. cit.*, pp. 69–80.

64. N. Aldrich, D. J. Fox, S. Schwager, H. Gottesfeld. "The Controversy over the More Effective Schools: A Special Supplement." *The Urban Review*, Vol. 2, May, 1968, pp. 15–34.

65. D. T. Campbell and J. C. Stanley. "Experimental and Quasi-experimental Designs for Research in Teaching," in Gage, *op. cit.*, pp. 171–246.

66. Coleman Report, p. 311.

67. For a comprehensive account of these efforts see J. I. Goodlad, R. V. Stoephasins, and E. F. Klein, *The Changing School Curriculum*, New York: Fund for the Advancement of Education, 1966.

68. Coleman Report, pp. 572–75.

69. M. B. Karnes, J. A. Teska, and A. S. Hodgins. *A Longitudinal Study of Disadvantaged Children Who Participated in Three Different Preschool Programs.* U.S. Office of Education, Bureau of Research, Grant 5-1181, Contract OE 6-10-235 (mimeo, undated).

70. C. Bereiter, and C. Engelmann. *Teaching Disadvantaged Children in the Preschool.* Englewood Cliffs, N.J.: Prentice-Hall, 1966.

71. John B. Platt. "Strong Inference." *Science*, Vol. 146, No. 3642, pp. 347–53.

72. See the articles in the *Phi Delta Kappan*, Vol. 48, No. 8, April, 1968, pp. 420–44, by Patrick Suppes, Robert F. Bundy, Richard S. Barrett, David A. Thatcher, and Marianne Trippon. See also the series in the *Harvard Educational Review*, Vol. 38, No. 4, Fall 1968, pp. 697–755, by Anthony Oettinger and Sema Marks, Maurice Belanger, Allan B. Ellis, Patrick Suppes, Warren G. Bennis, Robert Glaser, and James W. Becker.

73. Thatcher, *op. cit.*, p. 435.

74. Richard C. Atkinson. "Computerized Instruction and the Learning Process." *American Psychologist*, Vol. 23, No. 4, pp. 225–39.

75. For a general discussion of this research program see Patrick Suppes, "The Uses of Computers in Education." *Scientific American*, Vol. 215, September, 1966, pp. 207–20.

76. P. S. Sears, and D. H. Feldman. *Changes in Young Children's Classroom Behavior After a Year of Computer-Assisted Instruction: An Exploratory Study.* Stanford, California: Stanford Research Center for Research and Development in Teaching, 1968 (mimeo).

77. For a summary account of these developments see Albert E. Hickey, *Computer-Assisted Instruction: A Survey of the Literature*, third edition, Newburyport, Mass.: Entelek, Inc., October, 1968, pp. 37–41.

78. For a good summary of the basic research needed in areas like these see National Institute of Child Health and Human Development, *Perspectives on Human Deprivation: Biological, Psychological, and Sociological*, Washington, D.C.: National Institutes of Health, 1968.

10

Toward Defining Equality of Educational Opportunity

EDMUND W. GORDON

One of the traditional roles of education in the U.S.A. has been to broaden opportunities for productive, influential, and rewarding participation in the affairs of the society by developing those skills and entry credentials necessary for economic survival and social satisfaction. The idea of education for all grew gradually. In this country we extended this opportunity to more and more of our people, by a steady increase in the quantity of educational experiences available and the quality of the educational product. While the quantity of available educational experiences has grown, there also has been a marked increase in the quality of the skills and competencies demanded of those who would achieve much. Similarly, the individual's goals are higher. He wants to be productive in the sense that the society sees his effort as resulting in a valued product; influential in the sense that his participation is viewed as having some influence on outcomes; and rewarded for his effort both materially *and* psychologically.

Increased perception of this role of education makes us want to equalize access to basic education of high quality. Spurred on by the civil rights movement of the 1950's and 60's, equal opportunity in education has become an issue of crucial national concern. By many, it is regarded as the base for all the rights, privileges, and responsibilities of membership in this modern democratic society.

Our country's desire to equalize educational opportunities is in part a product of advances in the organization and development of human societies during the past six centuries. In earlier periods when neither the need nor the resources for wide access to education existed, the ideal of universal equalization of education opportunities also did not exist, certainly not in the public policy sphere. The concept itself and the concern for its implementation could not have emerged as an important issue, even now, if we had not earlier developed an awareness of the universality of educability. Human societies have always considered educable those categories of persons thought to be needed in the maintenance of the social order. Consequently, as the human resource requirements of social orders have changed, concepts of educability have changed. Educability in human subjects has been defined less by the factual potentials of persons and more by the level of society's demand for people capable of certain levels of function. In more simplistic and exclusive social systems most people were considered uneducable and effort was not "wasted" on their formal training. As long ago as the early Christian period and as recently as the early nineteenth century, it was only the religious and political nobility who were thought to be capable and worthy of academic learning. The social order was maintained by the machinations of these elite groups and the simple and routine gaming, farming, and crafting skills of illiterate masses. Under the triple pressures of the reformation in religion, mechanization in industry, and institutionalization in commerce, categories of persons thought to be capable of academic learning were greatly expanded. Opportunities for active participation in religious activities and rituals made reading and writing more widely usable and salable skills. Similarly, the emergence of collective machine production in shops and the expansion of commerce and trade through institutions made necessary the broader distribution of these skills. The combined impact was a greatly increased societal need for computational and communicative skills in larger numbers of people. As a corollary, previously illiterate people were drawn into the small body of literates and the mass of "uneducables" was reduced.

In the United States, where religious freedom and diversity became widespread, where democracy in government became the ideal, and where industrialization and economic expansion advanced most rapidly, more and more literate persons were required. In mid-nineteenth-century U.S.A., society's view of who could be educated quickly expanded to include all people in this country except for slaves. With the end of slavery and the incorporation of ex-slaves into the industrial labor force, ex-slaves gradually came to be regarded as educable. Through the exercise of briefly held political power, together with uneducated poor whites, they literally forced increased access to public education as a vehicle for their education. These indigenous poor were later joined by waves of immigrants who also saw the public school as their major route to economic and social salvation. In the metropolitan areas of the period, the school also became the major vocational training resource that prepared semiskilled and commercial workers for rapidly expanding industries. Although the school did not succeed in educating all of these new candidates, the once narrowly defined concept of educability was now nearly universal in its inclusiveness.

Our conception of education has also changed over the years. In Thomas Jefferson's view the school was expected to provide the technical skills and basic knowledge necessary for work and economic survival. It was from newspapers, journals, and books and from participation in politics that people were to be really educated. In reviewing Jefferson's position on education, Cremin (1965) has concluded that it never occurred to Jefferson that schooling would become the chief educational influence on the young. However, changes in the number and variety of persons served by the school, changes in the functioning of the society, and changes in the nature of the skills and competencies required by the social order have also changed the nature of education.

By the middle of the nineteenth century in this country, public schools serving the upper classes had developed curriculums basic to a liberal education. In this period the secondary school was quite selective and was designed to prepare a relatively few young people for entrance into college where most of them would pursue studies leading to one of the professions. While this trend continued through the latter half of that century, the first half of the twentieth century was marked by a high degree of proliferation in the development of technical and vocational training programs. Preparation in the liberal arts was considered a luxury and was thought by some to be relatively useless. It was the Jeffersonian concept of utilitarian education which prevailed. And it was this utilitarian education which came to be the mode in the growing acceptance of universal educability. "Everyone can and should be taught to do useful work and to hold a job" was the prevalent view.

The wide acceptance of this view contributed to the salvaging of education for Negroes following the betrayal of the Reconstruction Period and its leadership. In the great debate symbolized by verbal conflict between Booker T. Washington and William E. B. DuBois, the real struggle was between those who stood for the narrow but practical training of the hands of Negro and poor children so that they could work and those represented by DuBois who believed in the broad and somewhat less immediately practical education of the mind through the liberal arts and sciences. Those favoring the training of the hands won that debate. Educational facilities for Negroes and other poor people slowly expanded under the banner of technical and vocational training. This may have been a victory for expanded access to education, but the neglected concern for the "liberating" study of the arts and sciences made this a victory from which true equality in education has yet to recover. We will return to this point concerning the function of liberal arts and sciences in education later in this paper. At the moment our concern is with the protean nature of educability and education.

In this country the battle for equality of educational opportunity was first waged to establish public responsibility for the education of children in states where public education did not exist. This was followed by the struggle for adequate educational facilities and diverse educational programs. The twentieth century was one third spent before the struggle for equal though separate schools was engaged. By midcentury it was legally determined that in our society separate schools are intrinsically unequal. However, even before the 1954 Supreme Court school desegregation decision was promulgated, it was becoming clear that racially mixed school systems do not automatically insure education of high quality. This observation was supported by data on minority group children from schools in the North where varying degrees and patterns of ethnic mix were extant. Although the performance of minority-group children in some of those schools was superior to that of such children in segregated systems in the South, differences in achievement and in the characteristics of their schools were notable.

The early 1960's brought campaigns for education of high quality provided in ethnically integrated school settings. Some school systems responded with plans for the redistribution of school populations in efforts to achieve a higher degree of ethnic balance. Some of those along with other schools introduced special enrichment and remedial programs intended to compensate for or correct deficiencies in the preparation of the children or the quality of the schools. Neither these efforts at achieving integrated education nor at developing compensatory education resulted in success. Ethnic balance and educational programs of high quality proved impossible to achieve instantaneously. Confronted with the failure to obtain ethnic integration and high quality in education, and given the recalcitrant presence of segregation in schools North, South, and West, the goals for many minority-group parents shifted. In the late 1960's the demand is made for education of high quality, where possible, on an ethnically integrated basis. However, where segregation exists (and it does exist for the great majority of ethnic minorities in this country), the demand increases for control of those schools, serving such children, by groups indigenous to the cultures and communities in which they live. Hence the demand for "black schools run by black people."

Alongside this growing acceptance and promotion of ethnic separation, there continues to be concern for ethnic integration in education and compensatory education as complementary strategies in the equalization of educational opportunity. The introduction of the concept "compensatory education" grew out of the recognition that learners who did not begin from the same point may not have comparable opportunities for achievement when provided with equal and similar educational experiences. To make the opportunity equal, it is argued, it may be necessary to make education something more than equal. It may be necessary to compensate for the handicaps if we are to provide education of equal quality. It may be necessary to change the educational method and create new models in order to meet the learning need and style of the youngster who comes to school out of a different background of experiences.

Out of this concern for equalizing educational opportunity, some thoughtful persons have begun to think about what the criterion is to be. This became a problem of critical importance when Congress placed on the Office of Education the responsibility for determining the status of equal opportunity for education in the U.S.A. James Coleman, the principal investigator for that study, used equality of educational achievement as his criterion. Coleman argued that it is one of the functions of the school to make academic achievement independent of the social background of its pupils. This view holds that the adequate school experience should enable groups of youngsters from different backgrounds to reach the same levels of academic achievement. When the schools do not compensate for the variations in the background experiences of their pupils, they are failing to provide equal educational opportunity. This position assumes general comparability of potential for learning and has not been advanced as applicable in cases of actual intellectual incompetence.

There have been several attempts at defining equality of educational opportunity or at suggesting criteria for assessing its degree. Havinghurst (1944) has advanced a position based upon a match between measured intelligence and length of guaranteed educational experience. "We might speak of equality of educational opportunity if all children and young people exceeding a given level of intellectual ability were enabled to attend schools and colleges up to some specified level." Following this position, if all youth with I.Q.'s higher than 100 were assured of a high-school education up to the age of 18 and all young people with I.Q.'s over 110 were able to attend college for four years, "we could say that equality of educational opportunity existed to a considerable degree."

Equal education does not mean the same education, according to Tumin (1965), but it does mean equal concern

that each child shall become the most and the best that he can become . . . equal pleasure expressed by the teacher with equal vigor at every child's attempt to become something more than he was, or equal distress expressed with an equal amount of feeling at his being *unable* to become something more than he was . . . and equal *rewards* for all children, in terms of time, attention, and any symbol the school hands out which stands for its judgment of worthiness . . . Equal rewards mean . . . the elimination of competitive grades . . . One simply takes the child and teaches him for a given period of time what one thinks it is important to teach. When he learns that, he then goes on to the next thing . . . The maintenance of the highest standards in public education is achieved by getting out of children the most that each child has in him. Any other notion of high standards fails to take into account the different capacities for development and growth of large numbers of children. Equality of education . . . is the only device that I know of for the maintenance of high standards, as against the false measure that relies on the achievements of the elite minority of the school.

Tyler (1967) argued that since children come to school with different abilities the criterion should be that the learning process continue even though one child's rate may exceed another's. He feels that children do not have equal educational opportunity until the meaningfulness, the stimulation, and the conditions for learning are equal among the various children in the school. One measure of equality is that every child is learning. Tyler holds the teacher responsible for insuring that some learning takes place as long as the child remains in school. Negatively, equal educational opportunity is not provided simply by having materials there and time available for learning. Rather, the child himself must perceive the opportunities, feel confident that he can do something with them, and find them within his ability to carry on. Furthermore, according to Tyler, learning should promote a broader range of choice rather than continually narrowing the youngster so that after several years of education he has only one possible direction that he can go.

Lesser and Stodolsky (1967) have advanced a view of the equality of educational opportunity which is based in part on Lesser's finding of differential patterns of intellective function distributed by ethnic group identification. These investigators argue that equal opportunity is provided if the school makes maximum use of the distinctive pattern of ability the child possesses. The school would be held responsible for providing differential education experiences designed to build upon the special abilities the child brings to the learning experience. Thus, if adequate achievement is demonstrated in that special abilities area, the school can be judged to have provided an equal opportunity to learn.

Kenneth Clark (1965) has advanced a more simplistic view. He feels that it is possible to identify certain essential features of good education. Education which includes the best expressions of those features should be made available to all children alike. Clark argues that if just that goal were achieved, we would have moved a long way toward providing equal educational opportunity. He rejects as destructive the search for deficiencies and special characteristics in Negro children. Rather, his focus is on the deficiencies and special negative characteristics in the schools and the teachers who inhabit them. For Clark, equalizing the opportunity involves the removal of the burdens of poor teaching, negative teacher attitudes, and inadequate educational resources from the shoulder of minority-group children.

All of these views have definite merit, and the adoption of any one or a combination would significantly improve the quality of educational opportunities. Each view, however, has critical limitations. The mechanical approach advanced by Havinghurst is probably the least complicated to implement. Since the schools already have I.Q. measures on all children above the 6th grade, it would only require that educational resources be made available to insure specified years in school or college for every child in each designated I.Q. range. The major problems involved would be financial and logistic, if it were not for the fact that the number of those who share this implied confidence in I.Q. tests is rapidly decreasing. The fact that these scores often misrepresent the functional capacities of the persons studied and that it is the functional capacities of the very groups who are the target of our concern in equalizing educational opportunities that these tests underestimate, make the Havinghurst position unacceptable. It would not insure equality of opportunity except in a very limited sense. Everybody with the same I.Q. would be treated the same. However, it has been demonstrated that I.Q. is greatly influenced by social and school experience (Klineberg). The school and its society would then be providing education in relation to its success in providing previous education. If it did not provide good and adequate early education, it would be freed of responsibility for providing education at a later stage of development. This is the situation with which we are currently confronted and one which is strongly associated with inequality in educational opportunity. The Havinghurst position simply insures a certain period of schooling for those whom the school now succeeds in educating.

The Tyler position places a greater responsibility on the school and teacher, insisting that some learning occur as long as the child continues in school. However, this position allows for too little from the school and the child. If the school's function is simply to insure that the child learns at his own rate and functions in his own way, whose estimate of the child's potential shall be used? Whose definition of the child's functional level shall be accepted? This laissez-faire approach to education lends itself to gross underestimation of the potential of youngsters from backgrounds unfamiliar or unappealing to the teacher and the school. Like the Havinghurst position, the Tyler position places too great a reliance on inadequate measures of intellectual potential. There are, nonetheless, excellent features in the Tyler position. His concern that the learning experience be meaningful for the learner, that the stimulation be effective, and that the conditions be appropriate are important and lead to the kind of individual consideration which may be necessary to the equalization of opportunity.* Similarly, his concern that learning should promote a continuing broader range of choices is directed at a key problem in democratic education. The acceptance of the

---

* For current developments in individually prescribed instruction applied in public school settings see S. Bolvin and C. M. Lindvall, "Individually Prescribed Instruction: One Approach to the Problem of Individual Differences," Pittsburgh, Pa.: Learning Research and Development Center, University of Pittsburgh, 1965. The following are also pertinent: C. Braddock, "Computer Fits Teaching to Individual Student," *Southern Educational Report*, January–February, 1968; T. Esbensen, "Individualizing the Instructional Program," Duluth, Minnesota: Duluth Public Schools, 1966; and J. C. Flanagan, "Project Plan: A Program of Individualized Planning and Individualized Instruction," Washington, D.C.: Project ARISTOTLE Symposium, December, 1967.

Tyler model would do much to improve education and to broaden educational opportunities. Unfortunately, it too does not form a basis for equalizing educational opportunity.

In his effort at identifying equal education, Tumin also takes a laissez-faire approach in which individualization is stressed. He adds a concern with getting the most from each child, and avoids judging individual achievement on group norms. Competition is deemphasized. Teacher concern and reward are stressed. Despite the very humane elements in the Tumin position, he does not take into account the possibility of underestimation of potential or the fact of performance requirements in the real world against which achievement must be measured. He rejects sameness in educational method but accepts a common approach, sameness in reward or pattern of reinforcement. Like Tyler's position, Tumin's approach should improve education but will hardly equalize opportunity.

The Lesser-Stodolsky view of differential patterns among ethnic groups may lead some educators to as limited a definition of potential as those positions advanced by Havinghurst and Tumin. Further, this position could lure many people into a racial and ethnic-group-determined view of behavioral characteristics and developmental expectations. Educators have too often assumed that because certain patterns occur in high frequency in certain groups, intrinsic or genetic factors are the best or sole explanation. Insufficient attention has been given to the facts that the racial or ethnic groupings utilized are by no means pure, to the wide variation in functioning within these identified groups, or to the overlap in quality and character of function between the several groups studied. Nonetheless, we have used these factors and evidence from psychological performance and achievement data to assign individuals and groups to certain categories of educational service and anticipated achievement. Our determination of these assignments has been based upon stereotypes of status rather than analyzed educational need. There remain questions as to whether these differences in the characteristics of children are genetically determined, are peculiar to certain groups due to their cultural history, or are simply environmental-determined characteristics commonly encountered. No matter how these questions are answered, however, the data showing how children with these characteristics function could be used to prescribe the kinds of educational experiences necessary to improve development learning. The possibility that certain characteristics may be intrinsic to the learner and that these characteristics are different from those of other learners leads to no clear conclusion relative to the modifiability of the characteristics. It is quite possible, even likely, that humans from different family stocks vary with respect to behavioral characteristics just as they do with respect to physical characteristics. It may also be true that certain behavioral characteristics are of greater value in the mastery of certain tasks. What is not known is the extent to which specific characteristics can be adapted or utilized under varied conditions. Questions related to the genetic basis of characteristics are important to our understanding of origin but are considerably less crucial to our understanding of mechanisms for change.

Happily, the Lesser-Stodolsky position has not been used to advance the case for genetically determined patterns of functioning. To the contrary, Lesser and Stodolsky proposed education which would maximize achievement in areas of special ability. For example, Lesser found that children from Oriental backgrounds tend to show good performance on tasks requiring mastery of spatial relationships; thus he would argue that the schools should be trying to build upon this special ability and possibly produce more architects or draftsmen among these youngsters. It would be even more appropriate if, following models from Special Education, the differential characteristics identified by Lesser and Stodolsky were used as a basis for optimizing total intellectual functioning. For example, the special spatial abilities of certain children could be used in the design of individualized learning experiences through which reading, writing, compositional skills are developed and humanities and science concepts are communicated.

Clearly, some children come to the school situation with a pattern of strengths and weaknesses and styles that may be somewhat atypical to the pupil ability patterns the school is most accustomed to work with. This may mean that the school is now more greatly challenged to design learning experiences that build upon these particular patterns. Opportunity is enhanced when we build upon these patterns in the formal learning experience. We move toward equalization of opportunity when these special patterns become guideposts around which learning experiences are designed to achieve common standards as well as unique achievements.

The Clark position would be more acceptable if we knew that all children learned in much the same manner, and if we had achieved a higher level of pedagogical competence. It is dangerous to settle for the best we currently practice when that practice is so often unsuccessful even with large numbers of children. In addition, the Clark definition is only concerned with alleged input and takes no cognizance of output. He says that we have some good schools in this country, "let's make all of our schools good schools." Now, we embrace this as an idea, since everybody favors good schools, but if one is concerned about equalizing educational opportunity and compensating for the background variations that youngsters bring to school, then simply taking the best available model may not be enough.

Let us return to the purpose of education in a democratic society. If that purpose is to broaden opportunities for meaningful participation in the mainstream of society through the development of necessary skills and credentials, then educational opportunity is unequal unless it serves that purpose for all learners. At any point in the history of a society, the minimum educational goals are defined by the prerequisites for meaningful participation or for economic, social, and political survival. The educational experience can and should enable many persons to go far beyond the development of such survival skills, but it cannot be considered to have provided equality of opportunity unless it enables nearly all to reach the survival or participation level. The survival or participation skills (Gordon and Wilkerson, 1966) likely to be required in the emerging period include:

1. *Mastery of Basic Communication Skills*

While physical strength and manual skill represented man's basic tool of survival in years past, it is increasingly clear that communication skills have emerged as the survival tool of the future. Education for all in our society must be built upon the mastery of basic skills in symbolic representation and utilization. Such skills include speech, reading, writing, and arithmetic computation.

2. *Problem-Solving*

A second tool of survival, somewhat less critical than the basic skills, is skill in the movement from anxiety, confusion, and disorder to problem formulation. This involves competence in problem identification and problem-solving.

3. *The Management of Knowledge*

Knowledge of the physical, biological, and social sciences is so vast as to preclude complete content mastery by any single person. Knowledge of the dimensions of these fields, mastery of their principles, skill in the creation or discovery of order or pattern in their data, and competence in the management and utilization of this knowledge are urgently needed survival tools.

4. *Employment, Leisure, and Continuing Education*

Theobald sees the world of the future as one where achievement through physical work will no longer be a prime requirement in society. Utilization of leisure will emerge as a central problem. Rapidly changing technology is destroying the lifetime career in a single vocation (Harrington). Today's children may as adults often change not only jobs but kinds of work and will be required to make quick adaptation to radically different work situations. The demand will be for trainability and continuing education throughout one's life span in the labor force. However, if some of the projections hold true, many of today's young people as adults will live in a society which no longer rewards physical work. The new society may reward instead self-expression through art, through interaction with nature, through social interchange, and through symbolization and ideation as art forms. Creative self-expression may become important for vocational utilization as well as for aesthetic purposes.

5. *Self Management*

The achievement of goals such as these will involve the schools in activities more explicitly directed at personal, social, and character development. It may require a more adequate understanding of self and others than is usually achieved. It may mean that we give greater attention to the use and control of one's self in interpersonal relations. It may make essential, wider adaptations to multiethnic and multicultural societies. It may give added urgency to conflict resolution through avenues of nonviolence and the development of appreciative and respectful relationships with the world of nature, of man-made objects, of ideas, and of values.

With education defining its concerns in such broad terms, it seems obvious that the school must speak to the academic, emotional, and social developmental needs of pupils. Some children will be better at learning some of these things than at others. Differential levels of achievement will certainly result. But these differences need not be solely determined by cultural, economic, or ethnic origins. Rather, achievement should reflect variations in the quality of intellect found in all groups and variations in the adequacy of the learning experiences to which they are exposed. Democratically administered educational programs combined with enlightened educational practices should insure that basic competencies are universally achieved.

Equality of educational opportunity would mean the achievement of at least these basic competencies in all pupils save the 3 percent to 5 percent who are truly mentally defective. To make the opportunity equal, the school would have to develop and use whatever methods, materials, or procedures are required by the special style, special ability, or special background the child may bring. That the school may not yet know what and how to do this is a part of the problem. That it accept the challenge to pose the question and actively pursue solutions is the issue at hand.

Equal educational opportunity demands that, where what children bring to the school is unequal, what the school puts in must be unequal and individualized to insure that what the school produces is at least equal at the basic levels of achievement. Equalization of educational opportunity in a democracy requires parity in achievement at a baseline corresponding to the level required for social satisfaction and democratic participation. It also demands opportunity and freedom to vary with respect to achievement ceilings. It is in the reconciliation of these sometimes conflicting requirements that equality of opportunity is tested. At some points in the development of a society it may be necessary to favor universality to the disadvantage of uniqueness. At other times universality may need to be sacrificed in the interest of unique achievement. If preferential position is continuously given to one, equality of opportunity is precluded. However, the more optimistic among us claim that this country can well afford to allocate the necessary resources to give greater priority to health, to education, and to welfare to more nearly insure equal opportunity for basic educational achievement without limiting the freedom of individuals to rise above that baseline. For those of us who are critical of the current priorities at this time in the history of our nation, the vastness of these resources indicates that the conflict simply need not exist.

References

Clark, Kenneth B. *Dark Ghetto.* New York, N.Y.: Harper and Row, 1965.

Cremin, Lawrence A. *The Genius of American Education.* Pittsburgh, Pa.: University of Pittsburgh Press, 1965.

Gordon, Edmund W., and Wilkerson, Doxey A. *Compensatory Education for the Disadvantaged.* New York, N.Y.: College Entrance Examination Board, 1966.

Harrington, Michael. *The Other America.* New York, N.Y.: Macmillan, 1962.

Stodolsky, Susan S., and Lesser, Gerald S. "Learning Patterns in the Disadvantaged." Presented at the Conference on Bio-Social Factors in the Development and Learning of Disadvantaged Children, commissioned under U.S. Office of Education contract, Syracuse, N.Y., April, 1967.

Theobald, Robert. *Free Men and Free Markets.* New York, N.Y.: Crown Publishing, Inc., 1963.

Tumin, Melvin. "The Meaning of Equality in Education." Presented at the Third Annual Conference of the National Committee for Support of Public Schools, Washington, D.C., April, 1965.

Tyler, Ralph W. Personal correspondence, October 9, 1967.

Warner, William, Havinghurst, Robert, and Loeb, Martin. *Who Shall Be Educated?* New York, N.Y.: Harper and Brothers, 1944.

APPENDICES:
THE PROBLEM
OF MEASUREMENT:
Survey & Measurement

11

The Quality of the
Data Collected by
The Equality of
Educational
Opportunity Survey [*]

CHRISTOPHER S. JENCKS

Introduction

Chapter 2 of this volume reached two somewhat surprising conclusions, namely that:

(1) The policies and resources of Northern urban elementary schools are only slightly related to the socioeconomic and racial backgrounds of their pupils; and

(2) Once the weak relationship of policies and resources to student background has been taken into account, the independent relationship of policies and resources to student achievement is pedagogically insignificant.

These conclusions are vulnerable to attack on a wide variety of grounds. Some maintain that if the data are correctly analyzed they do not support these conclusions. Others maintain that the data are defective and that these defects account for the surprising conclusions. This appendix is

[*] The research reported in this appendix was supported by the Carnegie Corporation of New York and the U.S. Office of Economic Opportunity (Contract CG-8708 A/O).

I am indebted to David Cohen, Stephan Michelson, and Marshall S. Smith of the Harvard Center for Educational Policy Research, Samuel Bowles of the Harvard Department of Economics, and Frederick Mosteller of the Harvard Department of Statistics for suggestions about the problems discussed here and for critical comments on earlier versions of the manuscript. Steve Chilton, Christine Schmahl Cowan, Martha Kay, Carol Ann Moore, and Randall Weiss assisted at various stages in the data processing.

concerned exclusively with the second group of objections. Specifically, it takes up the following hypotheses that have been advanced to explain the survey's findings:

1. *The Invalidity Hypothesis*

According to this theory, the EEOS data on schools are both inaccurate and inadequate. Were we to collect accurate and relevant data about schools and students, stronger relationships might emerge.

2. *The Nonresponse Hypothesis*

According to this theory, selective participation in the EEOS makes the final sample an inadequate microcosm of the nation's public schools. Again, if data were available for a truly representative sample, stronger relationships between school and student characteristics might emerge.

Section I of this appendix deals with the validity hypothesis. It is divided into three parts. Section I-A examines the reliability of the data collected from principals about the policies and resources of their school and their district. Section I-B looks briefly at the reliability of the data collected from teachers about their characteristics. Section I-C evaluates the information collected from students about their family backgrounds and academic competence.

Section II of this appendix deals with nonresponse. It too covers three areas, but not in discrete sections. It takes up:

(1) The characteristics of missing school systems, schools, and pupils;

(2) The likely effects of selective participation on inferences about the distribution of school resources to students from different racial and socioeconomic backgrounds;

(3) The likely effect of selective participation on inferences about the relationship of school characteristics to student achievement.

Throughout the appendix, I will make a distinction between "school characteristics" and "student characteristics." When I speak of "student characteristics" I will mean the racial and socioeconomic backgrounds of individual children, as well as their attitudes and academic achievement. I will also include the attributes of any given child's classmates under this broad rubric. When I speak of "school characteristics" I will exclude the attributes of the pupils, even though they are a school's most important single attribute, and will refer exclusively to school facilities, programs, and staff. In many instances I will further subdivide "school characteristics" into "school resources" and "school policies." By "school resources" I mean those facilities, programs, and staff characteristics which can be purchased. I will subsume the diverse ways in which resources are utilized in a given school under the heading "school policies." [1]

I will refer continually to "the relationship between school characteristics and student achievement." Unless the context clearly indicates the contrary, this phrase refers to the relationship between school characteristics and student achievement when students' socioeconomic and racial backgrounds are controlled. In this context the word "relationship" will be synonymous with the regression coefficient of a given school characteristic when it is entered along with other relevant variables in an equation predicting student achievement. For reasons discussed in Chapter 2, I will not normally make any assumptions about whether such coefficients represent the effect of school characteristics on achievement, the effect of achievement on school characteristics, the effect of unmeasured extraneous variables on both school characteristics and achievement, or a combination of these three.

I will confine my analyses to Northern metropolitan 6th-grade schools. My definition of "Northern" follows Coleman *et al.* (1966, p. 9), and includes the entire United States except for the Southeast and Southwest. My definition of "metropolitan" also follows Coleman *et al.*, and includes Standard Metropolitan Statistical Areas (SMSA's) which had more than 50,000 inhabitants in 1962.[2] The "6th-grade schools" are those which the district superintendent or the principal said enrolled sixth graders. There were approximately 1,196 such schools in the original Northern metropolitan EEOS sample,[3] enrolling about 740,000 pupils.[4] Their locations are shown in Table 1.

In many instances I will further limit my inquiry to what I will call "Northern urban elementary schools." This reduced sample excludes all schools whose principals said they were "rural," [5] all schools whose principals said they had no 1st grade, and all schools whose principals said they had a 9th grade or higher. There were approximately 1,030 Northern urban elementary schools in the original EEOS sample,[6] enrolling about 630,000 pupils.[7] In a few instances I will limit my sample still further, to Northern urban elementary schools in "major cities," i.e., the largest city in any given SMSA.[8]

I will confine most of my analyses to the metropolitan North, and to elementary schools for reasons given in Chapter 2. The reader should bear in mind, however, that Northern urban schools had slightly better response rates than Southern or rural schools.[9] Their principals, teachers, and pupils probably also furnished more accurate data. Had I analyzed Southern or rural schools, I might therefore have reached slightly gloomier conclusions than those reported here.

TABLE 1

Locations of Northern Metropolitan Schools with Sixth Grades in EEOS[a]

Districts Testing Students	Number of School Districts[b]	Schools with Sixth Grades in Sample[c]	Schools with Sixth Grades Returning No Data[d]	Schools with Incomplete Data[e]	Schools with Complete Data but "Rural" Location or Nonelementary Grade Structure[f]	Final Samples
Atlantic City	1	12	0	2	0	10
Bakersfield	1	28	5	10	10	3
Bakersfield—Suburbs	1	1	0	0	0	1
Baltimore	1	8	0	0	0	8
Baltimore—Suburbs	1	4	0	0	1	3
Boston—Suburbs	5	12	0	0	4	8
Bridgeport	1	7	1	0	0	6
Bridgeport—Suburbs	1	1	0	0	0	1
Buffalo—Suburbs	6	22	0	0	6	16
Canton, Ohio	1	12	5	0	0	7
Canton—Suburbs	1	9	0	1	0	8
Chicago—Suburbs	6	33	4	2	5	22
Cincinnati—Suburbs	2	3	0	2	0	1
Cleveland—Suburbs	2	8	0	0	0	8
Detroit	1	42	0	2	3	37
Detroit—Suburbs	4	31	0	1	1	29

	A	B	C	D	E	F
Evansville (Ind.)	1	23	0	1	3	19
Evansville—Suburbs	2	11	3	0	1	7
Fall River (Mass.)	1	26	0	2	1	23
Fall River—Suburbs	2	8	0	2	2	4
Gary-Hammond-E. Chicago	2	5	0	0	1	4
Gary-Hammond-E. Chicago—Suburbs	1	8	0	0	1	7
Green Bay (Wis.)	1	7	0	0	0	7
Green Bay—Suburbs	1	5	0	2	3	0
Hartford—Suburbs	1	3	0	0	0	3
Honolulu	1	7	0	1	3	3
Indianapolis—Suburbs	2	3	0	0	1	2
Johnstown (Pa.)	1	16	0	0	0	16
Johnstown—Suburbs	2	3	0	0	2	1
Kansas City—Suburbs	1	2	0	1	1	0
Las Vegas	1	13	1	0	0	12
Los Angeles—Suburbs	2	19	0	1	0	18

a See text for definitions.

b See footnote 26 for sources of possible error.

c See footnotes 3 and 33 for sources of possible error. Includes schools which returned no 6th-grade questionnaires and no principal questionnaire.

d See footnote 33 for sources of possible error.

e Includes schools which returned either principal or 6th-grade questionnaires, but either did not return both but did not return teacher questionnaires.

f See text for definitions. See footnote 5 and Tables 2 and 4 for possible sources of error.

g Final sample used for analyses reported in Chapter 2.

TABLE 1 (continued)

Districts Testing Students	Number of School Districts[b]	Schools with Sixth Grades in Sample[c]	Schools with Sixth Grades Returning No Data[d]	Schools with Incomplete Data[e]	Schools with Complete Data but "Rural" Location or Nonelementary Grade Structure[f]	Final Sample[g]
Milwaukee	1	31	0	2	0	29
Milwaukee—Suburbs	3	15	0	0	0	15
New Haven	1	13	0	1	0	12
New Haven—Suburbs	1	5	0	0	0	5
New York City	1	49	0	6	1	42
New York—Suburbs	8	33	0	7	6	20
Newark-Patterson	1	8	2	0	0	6
Newark-Patterson—Suburbs	2	9	0	0	0	9
Ogden	1	12	0	0	2	10
Omaha	1	23	0	0	0	23
Omaha—Suburbs	1	2	0	2	0	0
Peoria—Suburbs	3	13	4	5	3	1
Philadelphia	1	38	0	2	0	36
Philadelphia—Suburbs	6	23	1	0	4	18
Portland (Maine)	1	6	0	1	1	4
Portland—Suburbs	1	6	1	0	1	4
Racine (Wis.)	1	11	0	2	0	9
Racine—Suburbs	1	5	2	0	1	2
Sacramento	1	16	0	2	1	13
Sacramento—Suburbs	3	29	7	0	1	21

St. Louis	1	8	0	1	1	6
St. Louis—Suburbs	4	10	1	1	5	3
Salem (Oregon)	1	11	0	0	3	8
Salem—Suburbs	1	1	0	0	1	0
San Francisco	1	26	2	1	0	23
San Francisco—Suburbs	3	22	2	3	1	16
Scranton	1	2	0	0	0	2
Scranton—Suburb	1	3	0	0	1	2
Sioux City (Iowa)	1	14	0	1	2	11
Sioux Falls—Suburbs	1	2	0	1	0	1
Steubenville-Weirton—Suburbs	1	1	0	0	1	0
Syracuse—Suburbs	3	5	0	3	1	1
Trenton (N.J.)	1	14	0	4	2	8
Trenton—Suburbs	2	11	0	7	2	2
Washington, D.C.	1	26	13	2	0	11
Washington—Suburbs	2	11	0	0	2	9
Wilmington—Suburbs	3	13	0	2	3	8
Totals for Districts Testing Students	124	919	54	86	95	684

Districts Not Testing Students

Atlantic City—Suburb	1	2	1	1		
Baltimore—Suburb	1	3	0	3		

TABLE 1 (continued)

Districts Not Testing Students	Number of School Districts[b]	Schools with Sixth Grades in Sample[c]	Schools with Sixth Grades Returning No Data[d]	Schools with Incomplete Data[e]	Schools with Complete Data but "Rural" Location or Nonelementary Grade Structure[f]	Final Samples
Boston	1	5	5			
Boston—Suburb	1	2	0	2		
Buffalo	1	12	0	12		
Canton, Ohio—Suburbs	2	13	8	5		
Chicago	1	21	21			
Cincinnati	1	13	0	13		
Cincinnati—Suburb	1	1	1	0		
Cleveland	1	5	0	5		
Cleveland—Suburbs	2	5	3	2		
Columbus	1	23	23			
Columbus—Suburbs	2	4	3	1		
Detroit—Suburb	2	7	3	4		
Hartford	1	3	3			
Hartford—Suburb	1	1	1			
Indianapolis	1	17	0	17		
Indianapolis—Suburb	1	7	7			
Kansas City	1	5	0	5		
Kansas City—Suburbs	2	7	6	1		

Los Angeles	1	32	32	1		
Los Angeles—Suburbs	3	18	17	1		
Milwaukee—Suburb	1	1	1			
New York City—Suburb	1	3	0	3		
Ogden—Suburb	1	1	1			
Omaha—Suburb	1	1	0	1		
Peoria	1	8	2	6		
Philadelphia—Suburb	1	12	12			
San Francisco—Suburb	1	4	0	4		
Sioux City, Iowa—Suburb	1	2	2			
Sioux Falls, South Dakota	1	12	10	2		
Steubenville, Ohio	1	8	0	8		
Steubenville, Ohio—Suburb	1	1	1			
Syracuse	1	3	0	3		
Syracuse—Suburbs	2	10	0	10		
Wilmington	1	5	5			
Totals For Districts Not Testing Students	44	277	168	109		
Totals For All Northern Metropolitan Districts	168	1196	222	195	95	684

I. THE VALIDITY OF THE
EEOS DATA

A ♦ *Principal Data*

One of the most common objections to inferences based on the EEOS has been that principals of predominantly lower-class and/or black schools must have exaggerated the resources available to their pupils. How else, the critics ask, can one explain the survey's failure to find substantial discrimination in the allocation of school resources? Unfortunately, no visits were made to check the accuracy of principals' descriptions of their schools. Furthermore, while USOE asked state departments of education for certain kinds of information about some of the high schools which *failed* to return principal questionnaires (see Coleman *et al.*, section 9.6), it sought only one item of information (racial composition) about schools which *did* return questionnaires. We therefore have no independent check on the accuracy of principals' reports and must depend on internal consistency checks and a priori reasoning to evaluate them.

I can see no a priori reason for assuming that principals distorted their reports in a particular direction. It is true that school boards and superintendents had a vested interest in showing that they treated black and white pupils alike. But the superintendent and school board had no way of knowing what the principal said about his school, since his questionnaire was mailed directly to ETS. While some principals may have been sufficiently paranoid to suppose that the superintendent or school board would go to ETS and try to determine whether he had told the lies they might have wanted him to tell about his school, it is hard to believe such fears were widespread. Furthermore, principals knew their pupils were being tested. Most principals with large numbers of black or low-income pupils must also have known that their pupils would not score high. Many presumably wanted to justify the school's poor performance by showing that their school had inadequate resources: too few teachers with too little experience, crowded buildings with inadequate facilities, and so forth. This would lead them to understate rather than exaggerate their resources. Thus, while we cannot rule out misrepresentation a priori, neither can we automatically assume that misrepresentation took any consistent form or direction in ghetto schools.

When we turn from a priori reasoning to empirical evidence, we encounter a serious problem. Since we cannot make on-site visits to determine the accuracy of principals' reports, the only way to evaluate principals' reports is to see whether they are internally consistent, either with other data provided by principals or with data provided by teachers and students. Yet if principals deliberately distorted their reports, and if they were sufficiently shrewd in doing so, they would presumably do so in such a way as to avoid inconsistency with other data they knew the survey was collecting. Thus a check on internal consistency offers only an estimate of the maximum possible accuracy of a particular variable, not an unbiased estimate of its actual accuracy. Furthermore, evidence of internal inconsistency tells us nothing about the *direction* of bias in data; it only tells us that the data contain a certain amount of error.

There are a variety of ways to estimate internal consistency in survey data, but wherever possible I will report what psychologists call a "reliability coefficient." This coefficient is the proportion of the variation in a given variable that is accounted for by the actual characteristics of the individual or the school under study. When, for example, I say that an estimate of the number of preschool grades in a specific school has a reliability of 0.87, this means that 87 percent of the variation in EEOS data is accounted for by the actual variation among schools, and that 13 percent is accounted for by principals' response errors. The reader should bear in mind that while the "unreliable" portion of the variable is by definition uncorrelated with the reliable portion, it may be highly correlated with other school or pupil characteristics. The correlation between the observed value of a variable and its true value is equal to the square root of the reliability coefficient. Principals' estimates of the number of preprimary grades in their schools, for example, correlate 0.93 with the actual number of grades if the reliability is 0.87.[10] The remainder of this section is devoted to estimating the reliability of data supplied by principals of Northern metropolitan 6th-grade schools.

1. *Lowest Grade*

The first item on the principal questionnaire asked for the lowest grade in the school. This is a straightforward question which would be hard to misunderstand. Yet Table 2 shows that 4 percent of the principals' responses to this question were inconsistent with other items of information about the school. The effect of such errors can be judged by comparing two estimates of the number of preprimary grades in each school. My first estimate was based exclusively on the principal's report of the lowest grade in his school (questionnaire item 1). My second estimate was based exclusively on his reports about the existence and cost of a kindergarten (item 3) and a nursery (item 4). The two estimates correlated 0.865 with one another. If we assume that errors were equally common in both indices (which I doubt), we would ascribe a reliability of 0.865 to both indices and would assume that each index correlated 0.93 with the "true" value of the variable. If we were to assume that the index based on direct questions about kindergarten and nursery programs was completely accurate, we would attribute a reliability of 1.00 to it and a reliability of 0.75 to the index based on lowest-grade reports. All sorts of other combinations of assumptions would also be reasonable, subject only to the constraint that the geometric mean of the two reliability coefficients be 0.865.

TABLE 2

Inconsistencies in Reports of Lowest Grade From 949 Northern Metropolitan Principals Reporting a Sixth Grade

Principal reports kindergarten (Q3) but says lowest grade is first or higher (Q1)	13
Principal reports no kindergarten (Q3) but says lowest grade is kindergarten or nursery (Q1)	1
Principal reports nursery (Q4) but says lowest grade is kindergarten or higher (Q1)	19
Principal reports no nursery (Q4) but says lowest grade is nursery (Q1)	7
Principal reports no 1st grade but school returned 1st-grade data	2
Principal reports lowest grade which is higher than highest grade	3
Number of principal reports of lowest grade (Q1) inconsistent with other data	38[a]

[a] Total does not sum to 38 because some principals had more than one inconsistency.

2. *Location*

Principals were asked (item 72) to classify the location of their schools. Of 449 principals whose schools were in cities of more than 50,000, 17 said the school was "in a rural area," 3 said it was "in a small town" (5,000 or less), 19 said it was "in a city of 5,000 to 50,000," and 18 said it was in "a residential suburb" (as distinct from "a residential area of a city of over 50,000") or in an industrial suburb. In a few cases there were enough reports of "rural" location from the same city to suggest that the district boundaries really included rural areas. In most cases, however, the principals simply appear to have misread or mismarked the question. The accuracy of this kind of data cannot be readily summarized in a single reliability coefficient, but we can say that 13 percent of all principals gave apparently erroneous answers. If these answers were random with respect to the correct answer, the reliability would be 0.87. If the answers were viewed as having only two possible values, one for "correct" and one for "incorrect," then "incorrect" answers are nonrandom and the reliability coefficient falls to 0.74.

3. *School Size*

About 2 percent of all principals filled in implausible numbers of teachers and pupils for their schools. If these errors had been strictly random and had had the same distribution as accurate responses, the resulting reliability would have been 0.98. But the situation was worse than that. The range of possible answers was from zero to 9,999, while the range of accurate answers was from about 30 to about 2,200 in the case of enrollment and from 1 to about 80 in the case of staff. Random erroneous answers therefore tended to be well above the true mean, and the reliability of the uncleaned responses was considerably less than 0.98.

4. *Libraries*

Principals were also asked two questions about their library:

a. *Does your school have a room set aside as a centralized school library?*

 (A) *Yes*

 (B) *No*

b. *How many catalogued volumes are there in your school library?*

(A)	*None or less than 249*	(62.4 percent)
(B)	*250–499*	(5.0 percent)
(C)	*500–749*	(5.8 percent)
(D)	*750–999*	(4.5 percent)
(E)	*1,000–1,499*	(5.0 percent)
(F)	*1,500–2,499*	(6.6 percent)
(G)	*2,500–4,999*	(7.0 percent)
(H)	*5,000–7,499*	(2.1 percent)
(I)	*7,500–9,999*	(None)
(J)	*10,000 or more*	(1.7 percent)

The numbers in parentheses after responses (A–J) of question (b) give the distribution of responses for the one principal in four who said that his school had no central library room. While some principals may, of course, have kept the books they reported in *de*centralized libraries, some probably did not have as many volumes as they said, while others probably had a library and mismarked their answer sheet. If we were to assume that all schools with more than 2,500 catalogued volumes had a library, we would get a reliability for the library question of about 0.80. My guess, however, is that the library question has a reliability greater than 0.80, and that errors are concentrated in the question about library volumes. There is no way to test this or estimate the reliability of the question about volumes.

5. *Racial Composition*

Principals were asked (item 43) the proportion of their students who were white. The multiple correlation of the principals' answers with the cumulative percentage of first, third, and sixth graders whose questionnaires indicated they were white was 0.90. If we assumed that the combined students' reports were absolutely correct, we would estimate the reliability of the principal's response at 0.81. If we make the more realistic assumption that students' reports have a reliability of 0.98, the reliability of the principal's response is 0.83. The overall mean proportion of whites reported by principals was the same as the overall mean reported by 6th-grade pupils.

Principals' estimates of racial composition seem to have been slightly less accurate than state departments of education estimates for high schools. The percentage of ninth graders who said they were white correlated 0.982 with the percentage of twelfth graders in the same high school who said they were white (using a national urban sample rather than a Northern urban sample), and the (unweighted) mean percentages of whites in 9th and 12th grades differed by only 2 percent, so we can probably assume that the mean of the 9th- and 12th-grade student reports for a given high school correlates at least 0.98 with the actual percentage of whites in the school. Because USOE reduced the state estimates of racial composition to a five-category code, the maximum possible correlation between state and student estimates turns out to be 0.98. The observed correlation is 0.915, indicating that if we had the original state estimates, they would correlate 0.934 with the student estimates. If we impute a reliability of 0.98 to the student estimates, we get a reliability of 0.87 for the state estimates.

Estimates of the proportion of white students in a high school based on state data exceed estimates based on 12th-grade student data by an average of 4 percent and estimates based on 9th-grade data by an average of 2 percent. This may be an artifact of the way in which I decoded the five-category USOE code, or a by-product of the states' having outdated or erroneous information. Or it may reflect the failure of some white students to report their race. State estimates for high schools exceeded principals' and pupils' estimates for elementary schools in the same districts by an average of 5 percent. Again, it is impossible to determine to what extent this was an artifact resulting from the five-category code, to what extent it was a by-product of the changing racial composition of Northern metropolitan school systems, to what extent it was a reflection of inaccuracies in the state departments' original estimates, and to what extent it indicated errors by elementary-school principals and pupils.

6. *Socioeconomic Background*

Principals were asked (item 73):
Which Best Describes the Pupils Served by This School?
A) All Children of Professional and White-Collar Workers (0.5 percent)
B) Mostly Children of Professional and White-Collar Workers (13.7 percent)
C) Children from a General Cross-Section of the Community (48.5 percent)
D) Mostly Children of Factory and Blue-Collar Workers (26.4 percent)

E) All Children of Factory and Blue-Collar Workers (7.9 percent)

F) Children of Rural Families (2.9 percent)

The numbers in parentheses indicate the distribution of responses among Northern metropolitan 6th-grade principals. It is clear that most principals preferred to describe their school as serving "a general cross section of the community," rather than giving more specific information. Two thirds of the principals who had reported that their school was in a rural area, for example, described its clientele as "a cross section of the community" rather than as "rural families." Given the vagueness of the question, it is hardly surprising that the principals' reports correlate only 0.684 with the best measure derived from the pupils' reports about themselves. Since this latter measure has a reliability close to unity (see section 2.3), it is probably necessary to assume that the principals' responses explain less than half the variance in true socioeconomic status.

7. *Tenure System*

Principals were asked (item 28):

Is there an official tenure system for teachers in your school system?

A) Contracts are on a yearly basis—no tenure (7.8 percent)

B) Tenure is awarded to teachers on the recommendation of school officials (13.7 percent)

C) If they meet all the qualifications for the position, teachers are automatically placed on tenure after a certain fixed period of time established by school system or state regulations (78.4 percent)

In theory, all the principals in any given district should have given the same answer to this question. In point of fact, there was tremendous variation in responses from the same district. If we create dichotomous variables which correspond to the responses "No Tenure," "Conditional Tenure," and "Automatic Tenure," we can then estimate the reliability of these three variables by looking at the percentage of the total variation in each variable that lies within districts. (All within-district variance is presumably error variance.) Using this procedure we find that the reliability of the "No Tenure" variable is 0.778, the reliability of the "Conditional Tenure" variable is 0.293, and the reliability of the "Automatic Tenure" variable is 0.426. I conclude that principals have a fair idea whether tenure exists in their system, but do not agree how it works.

8. *Accreditation*

Principals were asked (item 5):

Is your school accredited by the state accrediting agency?

(A) *Yes* (56.0 percent)

(B) *Yes, provisional* (0.4 percent)

(C) *Yes, probational* (none)

(D) *No* (4.0 percent)

(E) *State accreditation is not available for schools at this grade level in this state* (39.6 percent) [11]

There were only three (small) states where all principals agreed about whether there was accreditation in their state. Indeed, if we make the reasonable assumption that all within-state variance is error variance, we must conclude that principals' reports about whether their state has elementary-school accreditation have a reliability of 0.33. This is not especially surprising. Elementary schools are not in fact accredited in many states. It is easy to imagine that some principals in such states supposed that their school must be accredited, since nobody had ever said it wasn't. Conversely, accreditation is so nearly automatic in some states that some principals might easily not know it took place at all.

9. *Tracking*

Principals were asked (item 80):
Does your school carry out grouping or tracking of students according to ability or achievement?
(A) *Yes, for all students* (40.7 percent)
(B) *Yes, for highest achieving students* (4.0 percent)
(C) *Yes, for lowest achieving students* (4.6 percent)
(D) *No* (50.7 percent)

The sensitivity or ambiguity of the question is suggested by the unusually high nonresponse rate: about 11 percent. The inaccuracy of the answers is indicated by comparing the principals' responses to those of teachers, who were asked (item 57):
Because of ability grouping of students in some schools, some teachers teach students at predominantly one ability level. Which of the categories below best fits your classes?
(A) *All high ability groups*
(B) *All low ability groups*
(C) *Combination of various ability groups*
(D) *Ability grouping is not used in this school*

Table 3 compares the percentages of teachers who gave answer (D) in schools whose principals said they had no tracking and in schools whose principals said every child was tracked. Table 3 suggests that many teachers believe there is ability grouping even though their principal denies it. Some teachers also deny ability grouping even though the principal claims it takes place. Discrepancies may reflect the fact that some teachers use grouping within their classes, even though (or because) these classes are heterogeneous. But the discrepancy is also consistent with Coleman *et al.*'s finding (1966, p. 569) that 9th- and 12th-grade pupils often considered themselves to have been ability grouped when their school denied the practice. If we correlate principal with teacher reports, we get an estimated

TABLE 3

Proportions of Teachers Who Say There Is No Ability Grouping in Schools
Where Principals Say There Is or Is Not Grouping

| | Percentage of Schools Where Indicated Proportion of Teachers Say No Grouping | |
Proportion of Teachers Saying There Is No Grouping	Schools Where Principal Says No Ability Grouping	Schools Where Principal Says All Are Grouped By Ability
0	8.3	45.4
.01 to .100	9.9	18.2
.101 to .200	11.7	15.0
.201 to .300	18.7	9.6
.301 to .400	17.4	5.4
.401 to .500	14.4	3.9
.501 to .600	8.3	0.4
.601 to .700	6.1	1.1
.701 to .800	2.9	0.7
.801 to .900	1.3	0.4
.901 to .999	—	—
1.00	0.8	—
Total	99.8 (N = 365)	100.1 (N = 273)

mean reliability of about 0.55 for the two measures. Which one is more reliable is difficult to say, since they are not precisely comparable in form.

10. *Teacher Exams*

Principals were asked (item 29):
Are the National Teacher Examinations or equivalent local examinations used for appointing teachers to your school?
(A) *Yes, used for all positions*
(B) *Yes, used for some positions*
(C) *No*

I transformed the principals' answers to this question into a dichotomous variable, "Exams for All Teachers," which had a value of 1 if the principal answered (A) and 0 if he did not. In all districts with which I am familiar, the use of such exams is a matter of districtwide policy rather than a matter of discretion for individual principals. I therefore estimated the reliability of principals' answers on the assumption that all variation within districts was error variance. The resulting reliability was 0.769. This figure probably understates the actual reliability of the principals' answers, however, since principals who answered (B) are ambiguous cases.

11. *Class Size*

Principals were asked the number of rooms in their school, the number of teachers, and the enrollment. The difficulties that arose from principals' gridding their answers have already been mentioned. Once unreasonable and inconsistent responses are eliminated, however, principals' responses should yield accurate estimates of the number of pupils per room and the number of pupils per teacher. In addition, teachers were asked the average number of teachers in their classes. Their responses were also gridded, and contained a very large proportion of wild scores. After cleaning and averaging their answers, however, this question yields plausible estimates of average class size in a school. Pupils per teacher, pupils per room, and average class size are not precisely comparable measures, but one would expect them to be highly correlated. It is therefore depressing to find that the actual correlations among them are only 0.62 (pupils per room with class size), 0.68 (pupils per room with pupils per teacher), and 0.70 (pupils per teacher with class size). This suggests that if a single measure must be used, pupils per teacher is the best of the lot, but it also suggests that none of the three measures is very reliable. I am inclined to assume reliabilities of about 0.80 for the three cleaned measures.

12. *Textbook Costs*

Principals were asked (item 16):
How are textbooks provided to your students? Check the response which best decribes your program.
(A) *All textbooks are free*
(B) *Rental Plan with no waivers on rental fees*
(C) *Rental plan with fees waived or reduced for certain students*
(D) *All students buy their own books*
(E) *Certain students receive their books free, but all others buy their books*
(F) *Students buy some books, receive others free*

Eighty-five percent of all Northern metropolitan 6th-grade principals said that all textbooks were given out free. Since this is normally a matter of district policy, I again estimated the reliability of the principals' reports by examining the amount of variance within districts on a dichotomous variable "Free Textbooks for All." This procedure yielded an estimated reliability of 0.876.

13. *Teacher Turnover*

Principals were asked (item 27) what proportion of their teachers had left during the previous year for reasons other than death or retirement. Teachers were asked (item 26) the number of years they had been teaching in their present school. The two statistics are not precisely comparable. The teachers' average number of years in their present school would, for example, be higher in a school where half the teachers left every year and the other half had been there thirty years each than in a school where 20 percent of the teachers had left every year for a generation. Nonetheless, it is disturbing to discover that the principals' estimates of turnover correlate only −0.30 with the teachers' reports of their experience in their present school. At the very least, this argues against using turnover and experience as synonymous concepts, and it may also imply that one or both variables is quite unreliable.

14. *Perception of School Problems*

Principals were asked a number of questions about problems in their schools (items 48a–g). Teachers were asked a number of similar questions (items 47a–u). Principals' perceptions of racial tension correlated 0.40 with the percentage of teachers who reported such tension. Principals' reports that there was a problem of physical violence against teachers correlated 0.51 with the percentage of teachers who reported having to spend too much time on discipline. These correlations suggest that principals' reports tell more about a principal than about a school. If we arbitrarily assume that since teachers' reports come from many individuals, they are twice as reliable as principals' reports, we get estimated reliabilities for the two principal variables of 0.28 and 0.36 respectively.

SUMMARY.   Table 4 lists the estimated reliabilities of variables derived from the principal questionnaire, subject to a variety of caveats already mentioned. It seems that principals' responses are fairly reliable when they are asked unambiguous questions about resources, that they are much less reliable when asked about policies, and that they are least reliable when asked about school "climate." Whether this situation could have been improved by more carefully worded questions is not clear. While I can see no reason for assuming that principals deliberately gave erroneous or misleading answers, this possibility cannot be ruled out with presently available information.

B ♦ *Teacher Data*

If it is difficult to determine the accuracy of principals' responses to questions, it is doubly difficult to determine the accuracy of teachers' responses. Teachers were mostly queried about their personal characteristics and attributes, rather than about their school, so there is no reason to expect consistent answers to most questions from teachers in the same school.

TABLE 4

Estimated Reliabilities of 15 Variables Derived From Questionnaires Returned By 949 Northern Metropolitan Sixth-Grade Principals[a]

Free Texts for All	.88
Number of Preprimary Grades	.87
Type of Community	.87
Racial Composition	.83
Class Size	.80
Library/Library Volumes	.80
No Teacher Tenure	.78
Exams for All Teachers	.77
Tracking	.55
Socioeconomic Composition	.50
Automatic Tenure for Teachers	.43
Disciplinary Problems with Pupils	.36
No Accreditation in State	.33
Conditional Tenure for Teachers	.29
Racial Tension among Pupils	.28

[a] See text for descriptions of variables and methods of estimating reliabilities. Figures cited in Table are for illustrative purposes and are often very approximate.

1. Tracking

As already indicated, teachers in the same school had quite different views about whether or not ability grouping took place in that school. To what extent this represented real differences in the way teachers handled their own classrooms is hard to say. It is notable, however, that even where the principal said all students were grouped by ability, 11 percent of the teachers denied the practice. Nonetheless, the percentage of teachers who said there was ability grouping might be a pretty good estimator of the prevalence and importance of such grouping in a particular school. This percentage might, indeed, be a better indication of the extent of ability grouping than a "Yes" or "No" report from the principal, even if the principals' reports were accurate in some literal sense.

2. Tenure

Another indication of the accuracy of teachers' reports can be obtained by examining their reports about whether they had tenure. There were 15 districts in which all or all but one of the principals said there was no teacher tenure. Fifteen percent of the teachers in these districts reported that they had tenure. They were presumably misinformed—though in some cases the courts might have held they were right despite the contrary consensus of administrators.

3. School Problems

One approach to estimating the reliability of teachers' reports about school problems is to examine the ratio of within-school to between-school variance in such reports. One way to estimate the reliability of teachers' reports about problems in their school is to calculate the correlation between responses given by different teachers in the same school. These correlations are generally low. Teachers' reports that their students have home problems (Q.47a) have a reliability of 0.46 using this method. Reports of racial tension (Q.47c) have a reliability of 0.16. Reports of disciplinary trouble in the school (Q.47j) have a reliability of 0.33. Reports of ineffective leadership from the school administration (Q.47l) have a reliability of 0.17. Reports that the teachers do not work well together (Q.47n) have a reliability of 0.08. Reports of excessive teacher turnover (Q.47t) have a reliability of 0.28. Reports of inadequate equipment (Q.47r) have a reliability of 0.27.

An alternative approach is to compare teachers' reports to those of students and/or principals. As already indicated, the percentage of the teachers who felt there was racial tension in their school correlated 0.40 with the perception of the principal. The figure was 0.51 for perceptions of disciplinary trouble. The percentage of teachers who complained about the inadequacy of their students' home environments correlated −0.76 with the mean number of home items reported by sixth graders and −0.68 with the mean nonverbal score of first graders. The percentage of teachers who complained about excessive teacher turnover correlated 0.201 with the turnover rate reported by the principal. All these correlations are subject to diverse interpretations, but none suggests that teachers' complaints yield "objective" information about actual conditions in a school.

4. Racial Composition of Classrooms

Teachers were asked to report the racial composition of their classrooms. The school-wide average of their answers to this question correlated 0.96 with the percentage of sixth graders who said they were white. This is considerably higher than the correlation between sixth graders' self-reports and the principal's estimate of his school's racial composition. It supports the assumption that averaging teachers' responses to "objective" questions usually yields a more reliable data than a single principal's answer to a similar question. This is encouraging.

C ✦ Student Data

This section is divided into two parts. Part 1 deals with the student questionnaires, and especially with the information students provided about their family backgrounds. It examines both the reliability of this information and its adequacy as a measure of the overall effect of nonschool influences on student achievement. Part 2 deals with the tests administered by the EEOS. It examines their reliability and also their validity for predicting subsequent student performance in school and in the job market.

1. *Student Questionnaires*

My discussion of the information collected in the EEOS student questionnaires is divided into four parts. Part (a) discusses the reliability of individual students' reports about their family backgrounds. Part (b) discusses the reliability of schoolwide averages computed from the reports of all pupils in the same grade of the same school. Part (c) discusses the adequacy of the background measures for appraising the overall influence of family background on student achievement, with particular emphasis on unmeasured differences among families of the same socioeconomic stratum. Part (d) attempts some empirical estimates of the consequences of not measuring the factors discussed in (c).

a. THE RELIABILITY OF INDIVIDUAL STUDENTS' REPORTS ABOUT BACKGROUND.   Coleman *et al.* (1966, section 9.7) reported a small validity check on EEOS student questionnaire responses. This was carried out by classroom teachers in both urban and rural Tennessee. The teachers examined school records and called or interviewed parents to determine whether the pupils' responses had been accurate. One must obviously be cautious about generalizing from Southern urban and rural students to the rest of the country, but the study is nonetheless worth some attention.

Unfortunately, Section 9.7 of Coleman *et al.* is deficient in two respects. First, the authors reported the percentage of agreements between each item of information collected by teachers and each comparable item of information supplied by the students. They did not report the magnitude of the disagreements, so we cannot tell whether the pupils whose replies disagreed with their parents mostly gave answers that were close to their parents' answers or mostly gave random answers that had no relation to their parents' answers. Without this information we cannot translate the published results into reliability coefficients, nor into any other useful statistic. Second, the authors counted a student who omitted an item or said he did not know the answer as being in agreement with his teacher/parent.

Overlan (1968) reanalyzed the data collected by Coleman *et al.*, counting all students who answered "Don't Know" or who failed to answer at all as "disagreements" if the teachers succeeded in obtaining information from the parents, but as "agreements" if the teachers failed to obtain the information. He did not investigate whether students who disagreed with their teacher/parent made large or small errors.

The correct procedure in my judgment would be to compute correlations between students' and teachers' reports, coding student "blanks" and "don't knows" in the same way that they were coded in subsequent analyses of the data. Unfortunately, I have not been able to locate the original data for the study, and have therefore not been able to follow this procedure. Instead, I have had to estimate the likely results of such an analysis from Overlan's paper.

Table 5 shows the percentages of agreement between parents/teachers and students reported by Overlan. Let us assume that the data supplied by parents to teachers are completely accurate, and that every disagreement therefore represents an erroneous reply (or a nonreply) by a student. This assumption will probably overstate the actual number of student errors, but probably not by much. If students who gave erroneous replies had simply

TABLE 5

Comparison of Percentages of Agreement in Coleman Report and in Overlan* Reanalysis

	3rd Grade		6th Grade		9th Grade		12th Grade	
	Cole-man et al.	Over-lan	Cole-man et al.	Over-lan	Cole-man et al.	Over-lan	Cole-man et al.	Over-lan
Sex	99	99	100	98	99	99	100	100
Age	98	97	88	85	98	97	96	95
Race	98	98	100	99	95	99	100	100
Puerto Rican	98	98	100	98	98	98	100	100
Mexican American	98	98	100	99	98	98	100	100
No. people in home	91	89	90	89	98	97	95	95
No. children in family	92	91	87	84	92	91	96	96
Does mother work	99	97	92	90	98	94	97	96
Read to before going to school	92	72	60	45	82	66	78	61
Foreign language in home	97	97	97	94	98	97	100	99
Do you speak foreign language outside school	96	95	98	97	97	95	86	85
No. rooms in home	82	79			96	95	93	92
Television	99	99	98	98	100	99	99	98
Telephone	100	99	92	93	99	98	100	100
Record player, etc.	96	96	92	92	99	98	99	97
Refrigerator	98	98	100	99	99	99	100	100
Automobile	96	95	95	95	97	97	100	100
Vacuum cleaner	98	99	97	95	96	95	97	96
Daily newspaper	97	95	88	85	100	99	98	97
Dictionary			95	94	98	97	100	99
Encyclopedia			96	93	95	95	98	97
Different schools gone to	92	93	85	86		83		76
Nonwhite teacher last year	96	96	98	95				
Go to kindergarten	95	95	92	93	95	95	99	98

* Source: Overlan, 1968, p. 21.

TABLE 5 (continued)

	3rd Grade		6th Grade		9th Grade		12th Grade	
	Cole-man et al.	Over-lan	Cole-man et al.	Over-lan	Cole-man et al.	Over-lan	Cole-man et al.	Over-lan
Go to nursery school	98	86	98	87	98	93	98	90
Grade in last year	98	99	100	99				
Where born			88	87	100	99	99	98
Father's education			79	38	87	70	84	78
Father's work			84	58			90	79
Where mother born			90	83	97	94	97	96
Mother's education			79	52	90	77	86	81
White students in class last year			83	80				
Time on homework			64	60				
Area spent most of life					97	95	98	97
Type of community					84	81	67	66
How many older brothers & sisters					95	94	96	96
Brother and sister dropouts					96	94	94	95
Grade average					94	73	84	78
Type of school attended in 8th grade					99	97	100	100
Type of community mother lived in at pupil's age					91	78	79	70
Parent attendance at PTA meetings					84	71	86	78
No. magazines gotten regularly					81	77	86	81
No. books in home					82	79	85	79
Curriculum enrolled in					84	75	77	70
Last time changed school					88	87	76	73
Days absent					80	78	78	75
Ability group or track					69	56	64	60
Repeating English course					99	98	97	97

marked their answer sheets randomly, the correlation between students' replies and the true value of a given variable would be equal to the percentage
of agreements between students and their parents. But erroneous replies are
seldom truly random. Instead, the answer given by a student who is
"wrong" tends to be correlated with the "true" answer for that student.
Whether the correlation is positive or negative depends mostly on the
number of categories into which students' answers have been divided. The
reliability implied by any given percentage of agreements between students
and their parents is therefore quite different for questions with large numbers of alternatives and questions with only two alternatives.

If we are willing to make some arbitrary assumptions, however, we can calculate crude reliabilities for student questionnaire responses from Table 5.[12] For sixth graders I get an estimated reliability of 0.96 for reports of sex, 0.81 for reports about the presence of a vacuum cleaner in the home, 0.59 for reports about mother's education, 0.38 for reports about father's education, and 0.63 for reports about father's occupation. The corresponding figures for ninth and twelfth graders are considerably more satisfactory. Overlan's analysis also showed that the figures for whites were better than those reported in Table 6, while the figures for blacks were less so. Finally, Overlan found a modest upward bias in sixth graders' reports about parental education and occupation, but not in ninth or twelfth graders' reports.

These estimates of the reliability of individual responses to the EEO survey are so low for sixth graders as to raise serious questions about the wisdom of analyzing the determinants of individual achievement. As indicated in Chapter 2, there are also other reasons for avoiding such analyses. I turn, therefore, to the reliability of schoolwide measures of mean socioeconomic status.

b. THE RELIABILITY OF SCHOOL MEANS FOR BACKGROUND MEASURES. Shaycroft (1962) gives the following formula for estimating the reliability of the group means:[13]

$$r_{\overline{aa}} = I - \left[\frac{I - r_{aa}}{n}\right]\left[\frac{S^2_a}{S^2_{\overline{a}}}\right]$$

where $r_{\overline{aa}}$ is the reliability of the group mean, r_{aa} is the reliability of individual responses to the same item, S^2_a is the variance of the individual responses, $S^2_{\overline{a}}$ is the variance of the group means, and n is the number of individuals in the group. (If n varies from group to group, the reliability must in theory be computed separately for groups of varying size.)

While I have not calculated reliabilities for each measure of schools' socioeconomic level, a single illustration suffices to show that they are much higher than the reliabilities for individual measures. The variance of the mean level of mothers' education for Northern urban elementary schools is about 8 percent of the variance in individual mothers' education for the urban North. Let us suppose that the reliability is 0.59—the figure derived from the Tennessee study. The mean number of sixth graders in a Northern urban school is about 70. Substituting in Shaycroft's formula we get:

$$r_{\overline{aa}} = I - \left(\frac{I - 0.59}{70}\right)\left(\frac{1.00}{.08}\right) = 0.93$$

A group reliability of 0.93 seems quite satisfactory, even though the individual reliability of 0.59 was considerably less so. Two caveats must be mentioned, however.

First, my estimate of 0.93 assumed that each school in the sample tested 70 sixth graders. In fact, some schools tested more and some tested fewer. This would cause no problems if the reliability of mean scores increased in direct proportion to the number of children tested; but Shaycroft's formula shows that it does not. An increase from 5 to 10 sixth graders will yield a much larger increase in the reliability of a school mean than will an increase from 65 to 70 sixth graders. The use of the average number of sixth graders per school in Shaycroft's formula therefore leads to some upward bias in estimating the average reliability of school means. Computing the precise reliability for a sample of varied size would be extremely laborious, however, and I did not attempt it.

Second, these estimates assume that the sources of unreliability in a measure are independent of the way pupils are grouped for analytic purposes. This is not always true. If, for example, the direction of pupils' errors depends on their race, reports from all-white schools will have one bias while reports from all-black schools will have another. Grouping will do nothing to reduce the magnitude of such errors. On the contrary, since there is less variation in school means than in individual scores, the relative importance of correlated errors, and hence of bias, will often *increase* as a result of grouping. The ratio of correlated to uncorrelated errors in schoolwide estimates is unknown.

Taking all these factors into account, it is probably reasonable to assume that schoolwide estimates of the number of items in children's homes have reliabilities in excess of 0.95 for Northern metropolitan 6th-grade schools, and that schoolwide estimates of the educational and occupational level of parents have reliabilities of at least 0.8 and probably closer to 0.9 for such schools.

c. THE ADEQUACY OF STUDENT DATA FOR ASSESSING VARIATIONS IN FAMILY BACKGROUND. Variations in family background are known to explain a very large fraction of the variation in individual performance on tests of academic competence. If we compare identical twins reared in the same home, for example, we find that their scores on both individual and group intelligence tests correlate better than 0.90 in most studies.[14] This resemblance reflects both the fact that such twins have the same genes and the fact that home environment is likely to be very similar for both twins. If we compare ordinary siblings reared together, we find more variation within families: first, because siblings share only about half their genes and second, because they are often treated rather differently at home (and in school). Yet siblings' scores on intelligence tests correlate better than 0.50 in almost every sample with which I am familiar.[15] Siblings' scores on school achievement measures correlate even higher, with Burt (1966) reporting figures between 0.75 and 0.85.[16] These correlations indicate that family background could explain as much as 50 percent of the variation in individual performance on group I.Q. tests and 75–85 percent of the variation in school achievement.[17] Unfortunately, we have no data on family resemblances for the EEOS tests, but judging by the character of the tests I would anticipate a correlation between siblings around 0.60.

Socioeconomic, racial, and geographic factors measured in the EEOS explain almost 30 percent of the variation in sixth graders' performance on the EEOS verbal tests.[18] I will refer to these as "demographic" factors. The remaining 30 percent of the between-family variation must be attributable to differences between parents from the same socioeconomic stratum, geographic area, and racial group. I will refer to these as "intraclass, interfamily" factors.

The EEOS questionnaire contained a number of items which might be expected to explain intraclass, interfamily variation in achievement. The survey asked whether a student's parents had read to him before he entered school, whether they talked to him about school now that he was enrolled, whether they cared about how well he did in school, whether they wanted him to graduate from high school and/or enter college, and whether they attended PTA meetings. Sixth graders were queried only on the first three of these areas, and their answers did not explain an appreciable fraction of the intraclass, interfamily variation in their achievement. Ninth and twelfth graders were queried about all five areas, but only one set of answers showed an appreciable relationship to their achievement after demographic factors had been controlled. Ninth and twelfth graders' answers to about how far they thought their parents wanted them to go in school explained almost 10 percent of the variation in the students' achievement, over and above that explained by demographic factors. Unfortunately, a student's success in school probably affects his parents' expectations and hence the student's perception of these expectations. This makes it hard to tell how much of the intraclass, interfamily variation in achievement is attributable to variations in parental expectations and how much of the relationship works the other way around.

Another nondemographic source of family resemblance in achievement is the similarity of the schools children attend. Siblings do not always attend the same schools, but the schools they attend are certainly more alike than the schools attended by random pairs of children with the same geographic, racial, and socioeconomic background. And while we cannot estimate the effect of schooling on family resemblance directly, we can calculate an upper limit on the proportion of family resemblance that could conceivably be attributed to similarities in school experience.

If we weight the EEOS data so as to create a representative national sample of sixth graders, we find that 26 percent of the variation in their verbal scores, 19 percent of the variation in their reading scores, and 24 percent of the variation in their math scores lie between schools. The rest is within schools. If we eliminate the effects of race, socioeconomic level, and geographic background, differences between schools explain only about a tenth of the remaining variation in individual achievement. If we confine ourselves to intraclass, interfamily variations in achievement (30 percent of the total) we cannot possibly impute more than about a quarter of it to schools.

Let us therefore reverse the question and ask whether intraclass, interfamily variations in background might provide a sufficient explanation for variations in schools' mean achievement. Demographic differences accounted for about half the variation between families and about three quarters of the variation between schools.[19] Since nondemographic differences between families also account for half the variation between families, it is obviously possible that they account for the remaining quarter of the variation between schools. Whether this possibility is in fact a reality depends on whether the relevant nondemographic variables really differ substantially from one school to the next.

Demographic differences between families can explain a large fraction of the variation in schools' mean achievement because schools are quite segregated with respect to race, social class, and the geographic origins of their pupils. Were this not the case, the demographic variables would explain variation within schools rather than variation between them. The question, therefore, is whether schools are also segregated with respect to the variables that cause intraclass, interfamily variations in achievement. If schools were even half as segregated with respect to these variables as they are with respect to demographic ones, we could explain *all* the variation in schools' mean achievement in terms of differences between the families who send their children to various schools.

The nondemographic differences between families measured in the EEOS were almost randomly distributed among schools. But this proves relatively little, since these are not the variables that account for intraclass, interfamily differences in achievement. Until we can define and measure such variables, we can never be very sure whether schools differ with respect to them. We can, however, make some educated inferences from available data. These are presented in the next section.

d. THE RELATIONSHIP BETWEEN SCHOOL CHARACTERISTICS AND ACHIEVEMENT WITH FULL BACKGROUND CONTROLS. Unmeasured family background differences between students in different schools could have two distinct effects. First, they could lead to differences between the students entering various schools. Second, they could affect students' development after they had entered a given school.

At least in principle, differences that exist at the time pupils enter a school should be detectable by testing the pupils at the time of entry. If the children are very young, however, it is extremely difficult to devise tests of academic achievement. Even among older children, it is hard to be sure that any given test really taps the same skills as another test designed for students of a different age.

The sixth graders tested by the EEOS in 1965 mostly entered 1st grade in 1960. We have no data on their test performance at that time, nor at any time prior to the 1965 survey. We can, however, approximate the mean 1960 scores of sixth graders in a given school by looking at the mean 1965 scores of first graders in the same school.

At first glance this may seem absurd, since the test scores of students entering a given school often rise or fall appreciably in a five-year period. The problem is more apparent than real, however. When the characteristics of the students entering a school change, the characteristics of the other students in the school usually change in much the same way. Suppose, for example, that a neighborhood turned black between 1960 and 1965 and that the neighborhood school's 1st-grade test scores fell as a result. This would not normally produce a discrepancy between 1st- and 6th-grade scores, because if the percentage of whites in first grade fell, the odds would be high that whites had also withdrawn from the higher grades and that blacks had moved in.[20]

Nonetheless, even if the ratio of black to white families remained perfectly stable in every neighborhood, the ratio of black to white births in the neighborhood would fluctuate slightly from year to year. This kind of random variation would not be significant if every neighborhood were infinitely large, but the typical Northern urban elementary school enrolled only 80 first graders in 1965. Modest annual fluctuations in racial composition, socioeconomic status, and mean academic aptitude are therefore inevitable. These fluctuations imply a qualification on my earlier assertion that we can estimate the scores of 1960's first graders from the scores of first graders in the same school in 1965. Random annual variation sets an upper limit on the accuracy of our estimates. In order to estimate the "true" correlation between 1st- and 6th-grade mean scores for a given cohort of pupils, we must correct the observed correlation between the two cohorts so as to eliminate the "noise" generated by random annual fluctuations.

The observed correlations between 1st-grade nonverbal and 6th-grade verbal scores for Northern urban elementary schools are 0.808 for all children, 0.638 for the whites, and 0.428 for the blacks. Correcting these correlations for random annual fluctuations, we obtain "true" correlations between the mean nonverbal scores of entering pupils and their mean verbal scores five years later of 0.839 for all children in a school, 0.707 for the whites, and 0.530 for the blacks.[21] Schools' first grade scores thus account for 70 percent of the variance in their sixth grade verbal means.

These correlations provide a crude estimate of the extent to which family background differences prior to children's entering different schools determine the schools' 6th-grade achievement. We can now ask how much additional influence family background has *after* children enter 1st grade. The answer is that it explains an additional 21 percent of the variance. There are two alternative explanations for this.

(1) The 1st-grade EEOS nonverbal test was an inadequate measure of overall initial ability. The EEOS 1st-grade verbal test did not explain any additional variance in 6th-grade scores, but a better test, such as the Metropolitan Readiness Test, might have done so. Good noncognitive measures in 1st grade might also have explained some of the variance that now seems attributable to the influence of socioeconomic factors between first and sixth grades.

(2) While demographic and nondemographic background differences clearly have a major influence before a child enters school, demographic background factors may also have a substantial additional influence thereafter. Schools with unusually low socioeconomic levels or small percentages of whites certainly have lower 6th-grade verbal means than we would expect on the basis of their 1st-grade nonverbal scores, while schools with unusually high socioeconomic levels or high percentages of whites have higher 6th-grade verbal means than we would expect on the basis of their 1st-grade scores.

We must also ask to what extent 1st-grade nonverbal tests are measuring nondemographic variations in family background that may influence children before they enter school. The answer is that the 1st-grade tests do not seem to capture much of the nondemographic variation in family background. Socioeconomic, racial, and regional factors can account for 89.7 percent of the variance in 6th-grade verbal achievement in those schools which tested first graders. Even after correcting the 1st-grade scores to take account of annual fluctuations in ability, they only explain an additional 1.5 percent of the variance. This could be interpreted as meaning either of three things:

(1) The nondemographic differences between families that explain so much of the variation in individual children's achievement are almost randomly distributed between schools, so that mean 1st-grade scores pick up almost nothing but demographic differences between families.

(2) Nondemographic differences between families only begin to exert a substantial effect after the children enter school—perhaps because they involve "attitudes" and "motivation" rather than "ability."

(3) Nondemographic differences between families exert an important influence on children's development even before they enter 1st grade, and are not at all randomly distributed across schools, but the tests used in the EEOS were too crude to pick up the effects of these differences.

While the nondemographic background variation captured by the 1st-grade nonverbal test is not large in absolute terms, it can affect estimates of the relationship between school characteristics and 6th-grade achievement. Table 6 shows the results of nine different regression equations for a sample of Northern urban elementary schools that tested first graders. All nine equations include the school characteristics that show the strongest independent relationship to achievement in the full Northern urban sample, as well as regional controls, but each equation uses different background measures. A comparison of equation 8 with equation 9 shows that the inclusion of even a bad measure of initial ability can affect the coefficients appreciably, and that the effect is more often to shrink than to inflate them.[22]

Variations in initial ability are more important at the high school than at the elementary level. While I have not had an opportunity to analyze the relationship between high-school characteristics and student achievement fully, an initial investigation showed that the relationship between mean 9th- and 12th-grade achievement was much stronger than the relationship between 1st- and 6th-grade achievement. This is what one would expect on the basis of the conventional wisdom about the importance of early cognitive development. It probably also reflects the fact that psychologists have had considerably more success devising comparable tests for 14- and 17-year-olds than for 5- and 11-year-olds.

More important than the absolute magnitude of the 9th–12th-grade correlations, however, is the fact that 9th-grade achievement accounts for a considerable fraction of the variation in 12th-grade achievement that is *not* accounted for by socioeconomic status. This is quite different from the elementary-school situation. Racial and socioeconomic composition account for about 83 percent of the variance in schools' mean 12th-grade achievement. Ninth-grade scores explain an additional 10 percent of the variance.[23] This means that demographic variables are inadequate proxies for overall differences in the background and prior schooling of students entering different high schools. This is hardly surprising, for, while students seem to be allocated among elementary schools on the basis of demographic characteristics, they are often allocated among high schools on the basis of prior achievement too. If we estimate the relationship between high-school characteristics and 12th-grade achievement without measuring 9th-grade achievement, we may therefore be badly misled.

Failure to measure all the relevant background factors may also help explain differences between findings reported by various analysts of both the EEOS and other comparable data. Most social scientists have recognized the importance of background differences, but many have failed to appreciate the importance of measuring them really well. Many analyses have therefore been content to use one or two demographic measures, eliminating the others as redundant. Table 6 presents the results of a series of analyses in which demographic measures were successively "improved." A comparison of the regression coefficients of school characteristics in these successive analyses suggests that the choice of background measures can in fact be quite important. The use of too few measures can lead both to overestimates of the relationship between school characteristics and achievement and to underestimates of the statistical significance of these relationships. Table 6 also indicates, however, that there is a law of diminishing returns to the accumulation of additional demographic information about schools' mean

TABLE 6

Regression Coefficients of Selected School Characteristics With Varying Student Background Controls For Northern Urban Elementary Schools

	Variables	Means (Standard Deviations)	Regression Coefficient (Standard Errors in Parentheses)									
			I*	II*	III*	IV*	V*	VI*	VII*	VIII*	IX*	X†
111	Teacher Years Experience This School	5.262 (2.870)	.068 (.073)	.082 (.064)	.140 (.054)	.115 (.050)	.076 (.050)	.017 (.048)	.014 (.044)	.026 (.044)	.016 (.046)	.036 (.029)
122	Teacher Mean Preparation Time	2.414 (.527)	.246 (.392)	.084 (.342)	−.350 (.294)	−.266 (.272)	−.406 (.270)	−.352 (.250)	−.461 (.233)	−.268 (.231)	−.222 (.240)	.208 (.157)
50	Library Volumes/Student	6.342 (5.218)	.001 (.036)	.010 (.031)	−.007 (.026)	−.005 (.024)	−.015 (.024)	−.006 (.022)	−.026 (.021)	−.028 (.021)	−.022 (.022)	.012 (.016)
62	Hours Homework	.587 (.431)	−.465 (.388)	−.179 (.339)	−.239 (.289)	−.093 (.265)	−.090 (.259)	−.003 (.239)	−.095 (.223)	−.074 (.228)	.010 (.236)	.200 (.180)
76	Teacher Estimate Mean Class Size	29.153 (2.816)	.064 (.067)	.023 (.059)	−.052 (.050)	−.070 (.047)	−.074 (.046)	−.060 (.042)	−.007 (.040)	−.016 (.041)	−.040 (.042)	−.060 (.027)
108	Teacher Percent Tenured	52.688 (20.074)	−.011 (.010)	−.018 (.009)	−.016 (.007)	−.013 (.007)	−.015 (.007)	−.008 (.006)	−.008 (.006)	−.006 (.006)	−.006 (.006)	−.068 (.004)
143	Principal Estimate: PTA Attendance	30.208 (16.911)	.038 (.011)	.035 (.010)	.016 (.008)	.010 (.008)	.008 (.008)	.012 (.007)	.015 (.007)	.015 (.007)	.017 (.007)	.011 (.004)
—	Automatic Promotion	.483 (.501)	−.186 (.346)	−.122 (.301)	−.226 (.256)	−.183 (.236)	−.124 (.231)	−.195 (.214)	−.190 (.200)	−.013 (.203)	−.118 (.211)	−.166 (.144)
110	Teacher Percent Substitutes	2.672 (6.294)	−.043 (.032)	.035 (.029)	−.008 (.025)	−.036 (.024)	−.051 (.023)	−.033 (.022)	−.029 (.021)	−.018 (.020)	−.027 (.020)	−.037 (.014)
—	Teacher Years Experience Other Schools	5.472 (2.396)	.015 (.071)	−.018 (.062)	.038 (.053)	.051 (.049)	.059 (.048)	.085 (.044)	.077 (.041)	.065 (.042)	.073 (.044)	.078 (.028)
130	New England	.078 (.268)	.453 (.710)	.743 (.618)	.898 (.526)	1.073 (.484)	1.427 (.484)	1.098 (.451)	1.067 (.420)	.955 (.416)	1.083 (.432)	.882 (.283)
132	Great Lakes Region	.220 (.415)	−1.384 (.499)	−.849 (.439)	.118 (.387)	.313 (.366)	.575 (.369)	.483 (.341)	.638 (.319)	.755 (.310)	1.118 (.311)	.565 (.208)
133	Plains Region	.045 (.208)	−3.811 (.898)	−2.559 (.795)	−1.534 (.684)	−.562 (.657)	−.108 (.668)	−.065 (.618)	−.160 (.576)	−.149 (.557)	.645 (.547)	.137 (.329)
134	Far West	.379 (.486)	−2.160 (.519)	−2.003 (.451)	−1.493 (.388)	−.967 (.369)	−.713 (.410)	−.749 (.379)	−1.010 (.362)	−.897 (.323)	−.669 (.331)	−1.180 (.233)

* The first nine equations are based on schools in the final sample which have first-grade nonverbal data (weighted N = 315).
† The last equation is based on schools in the final sample (weighted N = 658).

No.	Variable											
—	First-Grade Nonverbal	.316 (.811)	4.887 (.247)	3.086 (.301)	2.343 (.268)	1.882 (.255)	1.586 (.277)	1.148 (.266)	1.113 (.247)	1.029 (.239)	—	—
—	Durable Items in Home	92.740 (7.386)	—	.282 (.033)	.219 (.029)	-.001 (.048)	.027 (.048)	.065 (.044)	.058 (.042)	—	—	—
268	Sixth-Grade Percent White-Collar	38.036 (21.355)	—	—	.079 (.009)	.041 (.012)	.039 (.011)	.036 (.010)	.036 (.010)	—	—	—
—	Cultural Items in Home	86.367 (9.964)	—	—	—	.192 (.039)	.133 (.042)	.074 (.040)	.081 (.038)	—	—	—
269	Sixth-Grade Mean Father's Education	4.952 (.726)	—	—	—	1.327 (.377)	1.506 (.371)	1.276 (.345)	1.393 (.321)	—	—	—
270	Sixth-Grade Mean Mother's Education	6.236 (.553)	—	—	—	-.494 (.359)	-.621 (.353)	-.152 (.335)	-.256 (.319)	—	—	—
271	Sixth-Grade Percent Family Intact	75.117 (13.716)	—	—	—	—	.013 (.016)	-.001 (.015)	-.006 (.014)	—	—	—
272	Sixth-Grade Mean Family Size	5.984 (.591)	—	—	—	—	-1.038 (.290)	-.712 (.274)	-.841 (.254)	—	—	—
149	Sixth-Grade Percent White	75.236 (30.570)	—	—	—	—	—	.038 (.006)	.024 (.006)	.031 (.006)	.039 (.006)	.043 (.004)
—	High School 0-25% White	.031 (.174)	—	—	—	—	—	—	-3.260 (.545)	-1.044 (.640)	-.941 (.665)	-.632 (.438)
—	High School 25-50% White	.042 (.200)	—	—	—	—	—	—	-1.573 (.461)	-3.238 (.556)	-3.321 (.640)	-2.348 (.391)
—	High School 50-75% White	.059 (.235)	—	—	—	—	—	—	-.566 (.556)	-1.150 (.452)	-1.165 (.577)	-.549 (.385)
—	High School 75-90% White	.076 (.266)	—	—	—	—	—	—	-1.373 (.629)	-.361 (.371)	-.324 (.470)	-.303 (.253)
150	Sixth-Grade SES 1st Principal Comp.	3.313 (7.344)	—	—	—	—	—	—	—	.347 (.027)	.405 (.024)	.422 (.016)
151	Sixth-Grade SES 2nd Principal Comp.	-.347 (1.251)	—	—	—	—	—	—	—	-.499 (.095)	-.513 (.098)	-.433 (.063)
171	Sixth-Grade Verbal	35.000 (4.995)	—	—	—	—	—	—	—	—	—	—
	R^2	—	.771	.828	.876	.898	.904	.918	.931	.926	.920	.918

background characteristics. Finally, it indicates that the information embodied in large numbers of separate measures of socioeconomic background can be compressed into two principal components without substantial loss of information or predictive power.[24]

2. *Student Tests*

Psychometricians make a useful if sometimes elusive distinction between "reliability" and "validity." A test's "reliability" is said to depend on how much variation there is between an individual's test score on one day and the next, or between one form of the test and another. A test's "validity" is said to depend on its correlation with some external criterion, like school grades or occupational success. Tests obviously predict some things better than others, and the validity of a test therefore varies according to the criterion. Reliability, in contrast, is presumably constant for a given population under specified testing conditions. The validity of a test can never exceed the square root of its reliability and is usually much less.

a. THE RELIABILITY OF THE EEOS TESTS. Table 7 shows the estimated reliabilities of the tests used in the EEOS for individual pupils. Although no data are available on the characteristics of the pupils for whom these reliabilities were estimated, it is probably reasonable to assume that they were predominantly white and very likely middle-class. The reliability for black and/or lower-class students might be lower.

TABLE 7

Estimates of Reliability of Individual Scores on Tests Used in the EEOS

Grade	Verbal Ability	Nonverbal Ability	Reading	Math
1	.78	.77	—	—
3	.72	.62	.88	.80
6	.94	.78	.90	.80
9	.93	.85	.82	.72
12	.92	.88	.85	.73

Estimates were kindly supplied by the Educational Testing Service. They were based on data reported for the original tests, not on EEOS data. The Spearman-Brown correction was applied to EEOS tests which varied in length from the original tests.

ETS reports that the methods of computation were as follows:
Grade 1   Verbal: mean of 2 reported r's between forms C and D: .83 and .73.
Grade 1   Nonverbal: mean of 2 reported r's between forms C and D: .72 and .83.
Grade 3   Verbal: mean of 2 reported r's between forms C and D: .70 and .74.
Grade 3   Nonverbal: mean of 2 r's reported between forms C and D: .53 and .72.
Grade 3, 6, 9, 12   Reading: KR-20
Grade 3, 6, 9, 12   Math: KR-20
Grade 6, 9, 12   Nonverbal: Odd-Even
Grade 6, 9, 12   Verbal: KR-20

If we use Shaycroft's formula to estimate the reliability of Northern urban elementary-school means, we find that they all exceed 0.98 and all but one exceeds 0.99. The reliabilities for groups within schools (e.g., all whites, all lower-class blacks, all girls, etc.) are somewhat lower, but probably still exceed 0.90. The two caveats mentioned in connection with estimating the reliability of schools' socioeconomic level also apply to mean achievement. Nonetheless, it would be surprising if more than 2 or 3 percent of the variation in the mean 6th-grade achievement of Northern urban elementary schools were attributable to random errors.

b. FACE VALIDITY OF THE EEOS TESTS.   All the tests used in the EEOS were developed by the Educational Testing Service (ETS) in Princeton. In theory, the EEOS battery can be divided into two different kinds of tests. The first kind measures "aptitude" ("verbal" and "nonverbal"). The second kind measures "achievement" ("reading," "arithmetic," and five kinds of "general information"). In practice, however, the two kinds of tests seem to measure pretty much the same thing.

"Aptitude" tests are supposed to have what psychologists call "predictive validity." That means they are supposed to discriminate between students who will do well at some task and students who will do badly at it. In theory, the nature of the aptitude test is adapted to the nature of the task. A test which measures "scholastic aptitude" (i.e., predicts subsequent grades in school or college) may not measure "vocational aptitude" (i.e., predict success in a particular job or the kind of jobs a man can succeed in). The EEOS aptitude tests were designed to predict scholastic success—though we shall see that they also have some value in predicting vocational success.

Scholastic aptitude tests were originally created to help schools and colleges predict which applicants would do well if admitted and which would do badly. The items which proved most useful for discriminating between promising and unpromising applicants were not, by and large, items which required highly specific knowledge of the kind that appears in one textbook but not another or gets taught in one school but not another. Instead, the most efficient items turned out to be those which tested general knowledge of vocabulary, numerical relationships, spatial relationships, and other things that can be picked up from almost any school curriculum, from a wide variety of books and magazines, from parents, from television, or from a dozen other sources. The results of such tests were presumed to reflect some combination of native ability and overall environmental influence. They were not supposed to be much influenced by the quality of the applicant's school or college preparation.

In theory, achievement tests are quite different. Whereas aptitude tests are meant to have "predictive validity," achievement tests are usually supposed to have what psychologists call "face validity." Instead of predicting a student's future accomplishment in a particular area, they are supposed to evaluate his present competence. Their purpose and character are thus similar to a regular school examination. They are meant to determine whether the student has acquired certain skills or information that educators regard as intrinsically important and legitimate. The only difficulty is that educators seldom agree on what students should learn in the first year of chemistry, American literature, or even 6th-grade arithmetic. ETS therefore employs educators from diverse backgrounds to invent and screen proposed items. Such people tend to settle on items which represent the lowest common denominator of their particular subject, i.e., items which will be covered by almost every school, be it good or bad. This procedure tends to make the "achievement" tests rather like the "aptitude" tests.

In addition, ETS is anxious to create tests which combine brevity with high reliability. The easiest way to do this is to select items which correlate highly with one another. If a test begins with a high proportion of items measuring "aptitude," the quest for reliability tends to mean that the proportion of such items steadily increases. Any item which is not highly correlated with aptitude tends to get eliminated as "unreliable." This may reduce the predictive validity of the test under certain circumstances. But in most cases the predictive validity of an "aptitude" test is higher than that of an "achievement" test, so the search for reliability tends to introduce the same biases as the search for a predictive validity. Only face validity suffers.

These considerations suggest that tests such as those used in the EEOS are all likely to measure pretty much the same thing. Table 8 shows the correlations among individual students' scores on the various EEOS tests for a full national sample, inflated to take account of unreliability. The correlations are quite high for sixth, ninth, and twelfth graders. The third graders'

TABLE 8

Correlations Among Individual Scores on EEOS Tests for National Sample*

Type of Test	Twelfth Grade					Correlations With Principal Components	
	1	2	3	4	5	1st	2nd
1. Nonverbal Ability	1.000	0.675	0.671	0.699	0.681	0.82	−0.51
2. Verbal Ability		1.000	0.907	0.734	0.882	0.94	0.25
3. Reading Comprehension			1.000	0.709	0.830	0.92	0.25
4. Mathematical Computation				1.000	0.848	0.88	−0.16
5. General Information					1.000	0.94	0.11
Percent of total variance in all tests explained by Prin. Comp.						81.2	8.5

* Taken from Mayeske *et al.* (1968), Table 2. Correlations reported by Mayeske *et al.* were corrected for unreliabilities shown in Table 7 of this Appendix. Since no reliability estimate was available for the General Information test, I used the reliability of the test it was being correlated with for both.

TABLE 8 (continued)

Correlations Among Individual Scores on EEOS *Tests for National Sample**

Ninth Grade

	1	2	3	4	5		
1. Nonverbal Ability	1.000	0.679	0.707	0.787	0.701	0.83	−0.55
2. Verbal Ability		1.000	0.878	0.842	0.914	0.93	0.21
3. Reading Comprehension			1.000	0.849	0.857	0.93	0.12
4. Mathematical Computation				1.000	0.980	0.97	−0.01
5. General Information					1.000	0.97	0.16
Percent of total variance in all tests explained by Prin. Comp.						85.8	7.9

Sixth Grade

	1	2	3	4		
1. Nonverbal Ability	1.000	0.697	0.702	0.755	0.87	−0.50
2. Verbal Ability		1.000	0.717	0.850	0.90	0.18
3. Reading Comprehension			1.000	0.860	0.90	0.15
4. Mathematical Computation				1.000	0.96	0.14
Percent of total variance in all tests explained by Prin. Comp.					82.3	8.2

Third Grade

	1	2	3	4		
1. Nonverbal Ability	1.000	0.622	0.580	0.642	0.84	0.30
2. Verbal Ability		1.000	0.580	0.618	0.83	0.37
3. Reading Comprehension			1.000	0.700	0.84	−0.43
4. Mathematical Computation				1.000	0.88	−0.22
Percent of total variance in all tests explained by Prin. Comp.					71.8	11.5

First Grade

	1	2	
1. Nonverbal Ability	1.000	0.828	0.91
2. Verbal Ability		1.000	
Percent of total variance in all tests explained by Prin. Comp.			82.8

scores are less closely correlated, despite substantial corrections for unreliability, probably because the 3rd-grade tests were too easy for many of the children in this sample who took them. Table 8 also shows the correlation of each test with the first and second principal components of variation in individual scores. The first principal component seems to represent a general ability factor and explains more than 80 percent of the variance in scores on the 6th-, 9th-, and 12th-grade tests. The second principal component represents an independent nonverbal dimension of ability, but it is very weak, accounting for a quarter of the variance on the nonverbal tests in 6th grade and above, but not for much of anything else.

Table 9 shows selected correlations among schoolwide averages on various tests, uncorrected for attenuation. The first principal component explains 92–95 percent of the variance in these tests. The second principal component is statistically insignificant for both 12th and 9th grades, and does not explain any of the variance in schools' nonverbal scores. The second principal component is intrinsically meaningless for 6th grades, since only three scores were used at this level.

It seems reasonable to conclude that while the EEOS tests may measure

TABLE 9

Correlations Among School Means on Achievement Tests

Variables	Twelfth Grade									Correlation With First Principal Component
	1	2	3	4	5	6	7	8	9	
1. Verbal Ability	1.000	0.931	0.968	0.930	0.890	0.950	0.933	0.913	0.948	0.982
2. Nonverbal Ability		1.000	0.935	0.887	0.883	0.899	0.898	0.884	0.909	0.954
3. Reading Comprehension			1.000	0.922	0.882	0.940	0.923	0.910	0.921	0.975
4. Mathematics Achievement				1.000	0.903	0.897	0.891	0.883	0.892	0.952
5. General Information 1					1.000	0.889	0.864	0.879	0.861	0.934
6. General Information 2						1.000	0.911	0.905	0.926	0.965
7. General Information 3							1.000	0.883	0.916	0.954
8. General Information 4								1.000	0.881	0.944
9. General Information 5									1.000	0.958

Percent variance accounted for by First Principal Component: 91.7%

Variables	Ninth Grade									Correlation With First Principal Component
	1	2	3	4	5	6	7	8	9	
1. Verbal Ability	1.000	0.927	0.966	0.956	0.932	0.956	0.956	0.936	0.962	0.987
2. Nonverbal Ability		1.000	0.930	0.909	0.871	0.887	0.897	0.886	0.899	0.942
3. Reading Comprehension			1.000	0.949	0.922	0.938	0.830	0.942	0.932	0.977
4. Mathematics Achievement				1.000	0.928	0.936	0.926	0.928	0.924	0.971
5. General Information 1					1.000	0.934	0.918	0.943	0.937	0.959
6. General Information 2						1.000	0.937	0.943	0.937	0.973
7. General Information 3							1.000	0.921	0.942	0.968
8. General Information 4								1.000	0.909	0.966
9. General Information 5									1.000	0.965

Percent variance accounted for by First Principal Component: 94.7%

Variables	Sixth Grade			Correlation With First Principal Component
	1	2	3	
1. Verbal Ability	1.000	0.937	0.940	0.979
2. Reading Comprehension		1.000	0.944	0.980
3. Mathematics Achievement			1.000	0.981

Percent variance accounted for by First Principal Component: 96.0%

two distinct dimensions of individual ability, they measure only one dimension of school output.

If I am right that the EEOS tests measure only one dimension of school achievement, and if the tests are designed in such a way as to reward kinds of achievement that are unrelated to the specific content of a school's curriculum, nobody should be too surprised by the weak relationship between students' scores on the EEOS tests and the characteristics of the schools the students have attended. A generation of psychologists worked to design tests which would yield these results, and they seem to have been moderately successful. Had the EEOS used different tests, it might well have found stronger relationships between school characteristics and students' scores. Suppose, for example, that the EEOS had tested students' ability to swim. The survey would almost certainly have found a strong independent relationship between students' mean time in the 100-yard breaststroke and the presence of a swimming pool in their school. Or suppose Coleman *et al.* had asked ten leading historians to select the "best" American history textbook used in the public schools in 1965. Suppose they had then asked the author of this textbook to write 25 questions which he thought a student ought to be able to answer about American history. It seems likely, though admittedly not certain, that students' performance on this test would have been substantially better in schools that used the author's textbook than in schools that did not.

We do not know, of course, whether such tests would have had any predictive validity for other behavior we care about. We do not know, for example, whether students who have studied one high-school history text rather than another are more likely to go to college as a consequence, more likely to study history when they get there, more likely to do well if they study it, more likely to become historians, more likely to become good citizens, more likely to vote Democratic, or anything else. If we *assume* that the school's choice of a text is unimportant, however, and that a test measuring mastery of one text rather than another is therefore invalid, we have assumed away the lifework of many educators. More generally, by assuming that our measures of school output should measure skills and knowledge available to students in almost every school, we have reduced the chance of finding major differences between schools.

c. THE PREDICTIVE VALIDITY OF THE EEOS TESTS. The primary reason for using tests like those in the EEOS to evaluate schools is that such tests allegedly predict the subsequent success of the students who take them. This section provides a cursory review of the evidence for this assumption.

i. *School and College Grades.* David Cohen and Robert Riley have analyzed the relationship between EEOS high-school seniors' verbal scores and their reports of their high-school grades. After correcting for school-to-school differences in test scores and grading practices, they found correlations of 0.48 for white girls, 0.34 for white boys, 0.30 for black girls, and 0.13 for black boys. Whether this means that blacks are awarded grades on a different basis from whites, that they respond to tests such as the EEOS in different ways, that their test scores are less correlated with other factors like motivation, or all three, is unclear from the available data. These correlations might be higher if we had fully accurate data on students' grades instead of self-reports (though the latter are not as bad as one might expect). The correlations would be lower if we were predicting high-school grades from 6th-grade test scores instead of 12th-grade scores. As a guess, I would predict an overall correlation of around 0.40 between sixth graders' EEOS scores and their high-school grade-point average.

We have no direct evidence about the correlation between EEOS tests and college grades, but we do have evidence about the correlation between the Scholastic Aptitude Test (SAT) and college grades. Since the EEOS verbal and nonverbal tests and the SAT were both developed by ETS, using similar items, it seems likely that they measure much the same thing. The relationship between SAT scores and college grades has been shown to depend on the character of the college. Some colleges seem to reward the same skills that the SAT rewards. Other colleges grade students on some other basis. Whitla (1968, p. 459) reviewed more than 125 different studies of the relationship between SAT scores and college grades and found that the correlation between SAT verbal scores and grades in liberal arts colleges ranged from 0.05 to 0.67, with a median of 0.36. For engineering schools the range was from 0.01 to 0.46, with a median of 0.22. The correlation of the SAT mathematical test with liberal arts college grades ranged from 0.04 to 0.62, with a median of 0.30. For engineering schools the range was from 0.10 to 0.52, with a median of 0.30. For the verbal and mathematical tests together, the multiple correlation ranged from 0.10 to 0.71, with a median of 0.45 for men in liberal arts colleges, 0.39 for women in liberal arts colleges, and 0.35 for engineering colleges. In general, then, the skills measured on the EEOS high-school tests can probably account for between 10 and 20 percent of the variation in the grades of those students who attend college.

It would be dangerous, however, to infer that raising students' scores on the EEOS tests above the level predicted from their background would raise their probable school or college grades. It hardly seems likely that scores on the EEOS tests have much direct effect on grades. Rather, they are probably imperfect proxies for things like genetic endowment, family background, interest in words and ideas, and so forth. School characteristics may influence test scores without influencing the traits for which test scores are a proxy. If, for example, test scores were related to college grades only insofar as the scores were proxies for genetic differences, a school might boost students' test scores but it would not thereby improve their college grades.

ii. *Survival in School and College.* The EEOS provided no data on the relationship between students' test scores and their chances of completing high school, entering college, or completing college. Nor have I found any studies of the relationship between SAT scores and subsequent attainment. There are, however, a number of suggestive studies using the Army General Classification Test (AGCT) and the Armed Forces Qualification Test (AFQT). These are similar to the EEOS tests in that they are primarily verbal paper-and-pencil tests with good reliabilities. I would anticipate a correlation of around 0.80 between the army tests and the EEOS tests if both were given to the same people at the same time.

Tuddenham (1948) found a correlation of 0.73 between AGCT scores and the number of years of schooling completed by a more or less representative sample of enlisted men. Fulk and Harrell found correlations of 0.66 for whites and 0.67 for blacks in a large sample of Air Force men. Interestingly, Fulk and Harrell found *no* relationship between AGCT scores and years of schooling for those who quit school very early in life (before 6th grade for blacks and before 8th grade for whites). With the early leavers eliminated, the correlations rose to 0.75 for whites and 0.72 for blacks. These correlations would be somewhat reduced if a single age-group were examined. Duncan (1968), for example, estimated the correlation between Armed Forces Qualification Test (AFQT) scores and years of school completed at 0.59 for a sample of whites born in 1939–48. In part, the difference between Duncan's and earlier results may reflect differences between the AGCT and the AFQT, though the two are very highly correlated.

Since all the aforementioned studies are retrospective, the observed correlations are presumably attributable in part to the fact that staying in school leads to high AFQT or AGCT scores, rather than the other way around. This impression is supported by Lorge (1945), who conducted a twenty-year longitudinal study of a small and probably unrepresentative sample of New York City eighth graders. He reports that a weighted combination of Thorndike-McCall Reading scores and I.E.R. Arithmetic scores in 8th grade correlated 0.36 with the number of years of schooling the eighth graders eventually completed. Otis I.Q. scores at age 33 correlated 0.67 with the number of years of schooling completed. Benson (1942) followed up a larger and more representative sample of Minneapolis sixth graders. She found a correlation of 0.57 between the Haggerty Intelligence Examination scores and their eventual educational attainment. This correlation would presumably have been slightly higher if a national sample had been available. I have no data on the correlation between any of the foregoing tests and the EEOS battery, but it was probably fairly high in each case.

Taking all sources into account, my best guess is that scores on the full EEOS sixth or ninth battery probably correlate around 0.6 with the number of years of school students will eventually complete. This is substantially higher than the correlation between demographic background measures and eventual educational attainment ($r = 0.4$ to 0.5). Given the moderate correlation between background measures and EEOS scores, we can assume a strong independent relationship between test scores and educational attainment for both blacks and whites. This conclusion is supported by studies of the factors that influence college attendance. Sewall and Shah (1967), for example, followed up a representative sample of Wisconsin students. They found that high-school seniors' scores on the Henmon-Nelson Test of Mental Maturity showed a stronger relationship to both college entrance and college graduation than did socioeconomic background. Flanagan *et al.* (1966) also found that their test battery explained slightly more of the variation in college attendance than did their background measures, and that both had strong independent effects.

iii. *Adult Success.*   I have not been able to discover data on the relationship between any ETS test and adult success, so again I turn to other similar tests. Duncan's analysis (1968) is the best currently available. He found a correlation of 0.45 between veterans' AFQT scores and their subsequent occupational status. The correlation between their AFQT scores and their subsequent incomes was 0.31. Since the correlation of income with occupational status increases with age, it is probably reasonable to assume that the correlation of income with AFQT scores does likewise. A study of older workers might therefore have yielded a correlation between AFQT scores and earnings closer to 0.4 than 0.3. A good part of this relationship is clearly attributable to the relationship between AFQT scores and years of schooling completed, but AFQT scores also show a moderately strong independent relationship to both occupational status and income.

Sewall, Haller, and Portes (1969) report somewhat different results from a follow-up of Wisconsin high-school graduates. Eleventh graders' scores on the Henmon-Nelson Test of Mental Maturity correlated only 0.33 with their occupational status seven years after finishing high school. The difference between Sewall's 0.33 and Duncan's 0.45 presumably reflects the youth of Sewall *et al.*'s respondents, the absence of regional differences among them, and perhaps also differences between the AFQT and the Henmon-Nelson test.[25] Nonetheless, there is a significant independent relationship between Henmon-Nelson scores and the occupational status of 25-year-olds in the Sewall sample, even after controlling both their father's occupation and their own educational attainment.

Once a man has gained entry to a particular occupation, the relationship between his scores on tests like the EEOS battery and his success on the job varies according to the job (Super and Crites, 1962, Ch. 6). Duncan (1968) found a modest but significant relationship between income and AFQT scores after he had controlled the occupational status, educational attainment, and family background of veterans. But several other unpublished studies have suggested that the relationship between test scores and income was attributable to the relationship between test scores and years of schooling completed.

I have not been able to locate any data on the relationship between test scores and either occupational success or marital prospects for women.

Overall, it appears that tests such as those used in the EEOS (1) predict grades in most schools and colleges moderately well; (2) predict the number of years of school and/or college an individual will complete quite well; (3) largely in consequence of (2) predict men's occupations and incomes moderately well; and (4) predict differential success within occupations quite poorly. All of the caveats mentioned in connection with inferring the effect of test scores on college grades also apply to inferences about their effect on other forms of attainment. We simply do not know whether a school that boosts students' scores on the EEOS is also developing the traits for which EEOS scores are a proxy and which really cause variation in later attainment. In the absence of evidence to the contrary, it is reasonable to assume that schools which boost scores also improve life chances, but we cannot be sure until we measure the relationship between school characteristics and life chances directly.

D ♦ The Effects of Invalid Data on Estimates of the Relationship between School Characteristics and Achievement

Invalid or unreliable estimates of either school characteristics or student achievement will normally lead to an underestimate of the relationship between the two. Specifically, if we are estimating the true correlation (R_{as}) between a school characteristic (s) and an achievement measure (a), and if the reliability of the school characteristics is r_{ss}, the reliability of the achievement test is r_{aa}, and the observed correlation between the school characteristic and the achievement measure is r_{as}, we will find that:

$$R_{as} = \frac{r_{as}}{\sqrt{r_{aa'} \, r_{ss'}}}$$

The observed correlation between the percentage of teachers who say they have tenure and a school's mean verbal score, for example, is -0.050. The reliability of the mean verbal score is probably 0.99, and the reliability of the tenure measure is perhaps 0.75. The "true" correlation between tenure and achievement is then

$$\frac{-0.050}{\sqrt{(.75)(.99)}} = -.058$$

Unreliable measurements also increase the standard deviation of a variable, since the variance is then based on the true measurements plus or minus an error, instead of being based solely on the true measurement.

This has two results. First, it reduces the apparent statistical significance of observed relationships and leads to overestimates of the likelihood that such relationships could occur by chance alone. Second, if school characteristics are unreliably measured, the apparent effect of these characteristics on achievement will diminish. If achievement is unreliably measured, and if the errors are random, the increase in the standard deviation of achievement offsets the decrease in the correlation between achievement and the school characteristic under study, leaving the regression coefficient unbiased.

The situation is perhaps most easily explained by examining a simple case in which achievement (A) is predicted from a single school characteristic (C). If S_A is the standard deviation of achievement, S_C is the standard deviation of the school characteristic, r_{AC} is the correlation between achievement and the school characteristic, and e is an error term, then

$$A = (r_{AC}) \frac{(S_A)}{(S_C)} (C) + e$$

If we make unreliable estimates of A, we will underestimate r_{AC} and overestimate S_A. If, on the other hand, we make random errors in measuring C, which is more likely in the EEOS, we will underestimate r_{AC}, and overestimate S_C. These two errors compound one another. The magnitude of the bias is readily calculated when only one school characteristic is used to predict achievement. It is more difficult to calculate when a number of school characteristics are used simultaneously to predict achievement, and each has a different unreliability. If each reliability is known, the simplest procedure for correcting the estimates is probably to generate an "observed" matrix of means, standard deviations, and correlations among variables. One can then correct the relevant standard deviations and the relevant vector of correlations for each unreliability estimate. The new standard deviations and the new matrix will then produce unbiased regression coefficients. This is, however, rarely possible with available data, because no empirical evidence of reliability is usually available.

The foregoing observations about unreliable measures hold only so long as measurement errors are random. If measurement errors are correlated with school characteristics—as they are likely to be—there may be either an upward or downward bias in the regression coefficients, according to the correlation. When the reliability of a measure is very low, moderate correlations between the errors and the achievement measures can produce substantial biases in the coefficients. Extreme caution is therefore required when interpreting the coefficients of EEOS variables with low reliabilities. Since the reliability of most EEOS school measures is unknown, caution ought to be exercised in dealing with them all.

II. SELECTIVE
PARTICIPATION AND
RESPONSE IN THE EEOS

There were unusually high levels of nonparticipation and nonresponse in the EEOS, first by entire districts, then by schools in participating districts, then by individuals in participating schools, and then for particular questionnaire items among participating individuals. As a result, many critics (e.g., Bowles and Levin, 1968) have suggested that the results of the survey may have been significantly biased in some way. This section of this appendix investigates the likelihood of such biases.

As indicated at the outset, I will attempt to determine the extent of various kinds of nonparticipation, the effect of nonparticipation on the apparent relationship of students' family backgrounds to the characteristics of their schools, and the effect of nonparticipation on the apparent relationship of school characteristics to student achievement. As in section I, the analyses in this section will be confined to the 1,196 Northern metropolitan 6th-grade schools in the original EEOS sample. Part A will deal with nonparticipation of districts and schools, and Part B will deal with nonparticipation by individuals and nonresponse to particular questions.

A ◆ Selective Participation by Districts and Schools

My discussion of nonparticipation by districts and schools will be divided into three sections, dealing with three of the four levels of district participation.

UNCOOPERATIVE DISTRICTS.   These were districts that returned no principal or student questionnaires from any school with a 6th grade. Thirteen percent of the 168 Northern metropolitan districts fell in this category.[26]

SEMI-COOPERATIVE DISTRICTS.   These are districts that returned no 6th-grade student questionnaires but eventually returned principal questionnaires for one or more 6th-grade schools. Fourteen percent of the Northern metropolitan districts fell in this category.

SELECTIVELY COOPERATIVE DISTRICTS.   These were districts that returned 6th-grade questionnaires from one or more schools, but not for all schools. Twenty-eight percent of the Northern metropolitan districts fell in this category. Eleven percent of the 6th-grade schools in these districts returned no data whatever, while another 11 percent returned principal but not student data. Student data is available for 78 percent of the schools in these districts.

COOPERATIVE DISTRICTS. These were districts in which every school with a 6th grade returned 6th-grade student questionnaires. Forty-five percent of the Northern metropolitan districts fell in this category.

Though my discussion is organized around different *district* policies, it will also be necessary to examine categories of *schools*. I will classify schools in the same way as districts.

UNCOOPERATIVE SCHOOLS. These were schools that returned no 6th-grade questionnaires and no principal questionnaire. There were 145 such schools in uncooperative districts, 23 in semi-cooperative districts, and 54 in selectively cooperative districts. Overall, they constituted 19 percent of the initial Northern metropolitan 6th-grade sample.

SEMI-COOPERATIVE SCHOOLS. These were schools that returned no 6th-grade questionnaires but returned principal questionnaires. There were 109 such schools in semi-cooperative districts and 55 in selectively cooperative districts. Overall, they constituted 14 percent of the Northern metropolitan 6th-grade sample.

COOPERATIVE SCHOOLS. These were schools that returned 6th-grade questionnaires. There were 397 such schools in selectively cooperative districts and 413 in cooperative districts. Overall, they constituted 68 percent of the Northern metropolitan 6th-grade sample. Thirty-one of these schools failed to return principal questionnaires, teacher questionnaires, or both, but for analytic purposes they are nonetheless deemed "cooperative" because they returned student questionnaires.[27]

1. *Uncooperative Districts*

The 21 Northern metropolitan school districts which refused to participate in the EEOS included Boston, Chicago, Columbus, Hartford, Los Angeles, Wilmington, and 15 suburbs. These 21 districts contained 12 percent of the 6th-grade sample schools. Half the missing schools were in Chicago, Columbus, and Los Angeles. The 21 districts' reasons for refusing to cooperate appear to have varied. A number were under fire from civil rights groups, either for segregating black children, failing to provide segregated schools with adequate resources, or both. Several were being sued in federal court for failure to desegregate, and allegedly feared that the survey's results might be subpoenaed as evidence against them. Then too, the survey asked teachers and students a number of questions about "sensitive" subjects, and officials in several districts seem to have thought that such probing might stir up racial trouble in the schools. Finally, there was some feeling that the survey might presage a serious federal effort to eliminate de facto segregation in Northern cities, and hostility to this kind of federal intervention may have made some districts uncooperative even though they felt they had nothing to hide.

Districts were less likely to participate if they had large numbers of nonwhite pupils. Or perhaps it would be more accurate to say that districts which were asked to provide information about nonwhite or integrated schools were less likely to participate than those which were asked to provide information about white schools.[28] State department of education reports indicate that high schools in uncooperative districts averaged 60.3 percent white, compared with 73.2 percent for the Northern metropolitan sample as a whole.

It would be natural to assume that the 21 uncooperative districts were those which had the most to hide, i.e., those in which the differences between black and white schools were greatest. There does not, however, seem to be any empirical evidence to support such a conjecture. I have not been able to locate any adequate data regarding the distribution of resources in either Los Angeles or Columbus, but Burkhead (1967, pp. 57–8) provides figures on resource allocation in Chicago secondary schools. He found that expenditures per pupil were highest for the poorest districts, lowest for the middle-income districts, in-between for the upper-income districts. He did not report racial disparities. At the elementary level, Michelson (forthcoming) reports that Chicago spent ten percent less on black than on white pupils; this is comparable to the disparity he reports for San Francisco. The only other data I have located on resource allocation in an uncooperative district are for Boston. Katzman (1966, 1969) found that Boston spent slightly more on elementary schools in low-income than in high-income neighborhoods.[29] While data from 2 out of 21 uncooperative districts are hardly definitive, they do cast doubt on the theory that nonparticipating districts allocated resources less equitably than participating districts. Indeed, the data from these two districts suggest—though they certainly do not suffice to prove—that if all 168 districts had cooperated, the EEOS would have found the same modest relationship between school resources and student characteristics reported by Coleman *et al.* (1966, Chapter 2).

For the sake of argument, however, let us suppose that selective participation led to an underestimate of the actual relationship between family background and school resources in the urban North. It would not follow that selective participation also led to an underestimate of the independent relationship between resources and student achievement once family background was taken into account. Alternatively, let us suppose that the EEOS findings on the relationship of school resources to family background were broadly representative of the actual situation in the urban North. Again, this would not prove the correctness of the EEOS findings about the relationship of resources to achievement once background was taken into account. The two issues are both logically and empirically distinct.

Chapter 2 showed that the relationship between school characteristics and student achievement was somewhat different in the five major cooperative or selectively cooperative districts, even though policies and resources were always of minor importance compared to family background. It seems reasonable to assume that there were also differences between cooperative and uncooperative districts. The question, however, is not whether nonparticipating districts were different, but whether they were systematically different. More specifically, the question is whether the relationship between school characteristics and achievement was consistently stronger in uncooperative districts like Boston, Chicago, Columbus, and Los Angeles than in cooperative or selectively cooperative districts like New York, Detroit, Milwaukee, and San Francisco. If there were consistent differences of this kind, analysis of the EEOS data for the urban North would lead to an underestimate of the relationship between resources and achievement.

I can see no a priori reason for assuming that resources had more effect on achievement in uncooperative than in cooperative districts. Indeed, a priori reasoning seems to me to support the opposite expectation. If there were any pattern to nonparticipation, one would expect it to be more common in poorly managed school districts than in well-managed districts. One characteristic of a well-managed system is presumably its capacity to utilize additional resources effectively. Poorly managed systems presumably utilize additional resources wastefully or even destructively. If this is true, additional resources would boost achievement in well-managed systems more than in badly managed systems, and school characteristics would have bigger coefficients in cooperative than in uncooperative districts.

Katzman's Boston study provides our only empirical evidence about the relationship between elementary-school characteristics and student achievement in an uncooperative EEOS district. Katzman's data differ in a variety of important respects from those collected in the EEOS, but he nonetheless found raw correlations between school characteristics and student achievement in the same range as those I found in the five largest cities in the EEOS. Yet his regression equations indicate stronger relationships between some school characteristics and student achievement than I found in any of the five largest EEOS cities. This may be a result of inadequate data on the initial ability and socioeconomic background of students in his schools.[30] Nonetheless, it lends some support to those who maintain that school characteristics could have been more closely related to achievement in uncooperative than in cooperative districts.

2. Semi-Cooperative Districts

In addition to the 21 Northern metropolitan districts which returned no EEOS data, another 23 districts refused to test pupils but eventually returned some or all of their principal questionnaires. These districts included Buffalo, Cincinnati, Cleveland, Indianapolis, Kansas City, Peoria, Sioux Falls, Steubenville, Syracuse, and 14 suburbs. The 23 semi-cooperative districts included 132 6th-grade schools (11 percent of the Northern metropolitan sample). One hundred and nine of these schools returned principal questionnaires, while the other 23 returned no data whatever.

When I compared the responses of the 109 principals in semi-cooperative districts who returned questionnaires with the responses of the 840 principals in fully or selectively cooperative districts who returned questionnaires, I found statistically significant differences for about a third of the 100-odd items I analyzed.[31] A selection of these 100 items is presented in Table 10. The first 21 items in Table 10 were included on a priori

TABLE 10

Means, Standard Deviations, and Correlations for Selected Principal Responses From Districts Returning Student Data vs. Districts Returning No Student Data[1]

| | | | | Correlation With Principal Estimate | |
| | | | | of Percent | of Pupil |
Var. No.	Variables[2]	Mean	Standard Deviation	White	SES
9	Hold Back Slow Learners	0.422	0.494	.022	−.025
		0.308	0.465	.127	.012
10	Transfer Slow Learners	0.029*	0.168	.045	.076
		0.090*	0.288	−.005	−.026
16	Free Kindergarten	0.855	0.352	−.197	.011
		0.852	0.357	−.262	.040
20	Free Nursery	0.050	0.218	−.212	−.170
		0.029	0.167	−.075	−.018
24	State Accreditation	0.072	0.259	.069	.068
	Refused or Provisional	0.077	0.268	.104	.020
28	Students/Room	27.880	8.269	−.143	.010
		27.379	5.785	.000	.059

[1] Results for schools returning principal data (N = 840) in districts returning student data are given above; results for schools returning principal data (N = 109) in districts returning no student data are given below.
[2] Variables 9, 10, 16, 20, 24, 28, 32, 48, 50, 59, 61, 69, 105, 112, 129, 147, 241, 245, 266, 267 were included a priori; other variables were selected for significance of mean differences from an overall list of 80 other school characteristics. For sources of variables, see Table 2.1 in Chapter 2.
* Alpha level of T-tests: .05–.001.

TABLE 10 (continued)

Var. No.	Variables[2]	Mean	Standard Deviation	Correlation With Principal Estimate of Percent White	of Pupil SES
32	Building Age	28.438	18.233	−.181	−.222
		27.907	18.165	−.055	−.352
48	Enough Texts	0.940*	0.237	.048	.012
		0.991*	0.096	−.054	.062
50	Library Volumes/Student	5.322*	5.476	.219	.042
		4.044*	4.500	.307	.385
53	Teacher Specialization	0.358	0.480	.128	.038
		0.396	0.491	−.117	.250
59	Number of Prior Intelligence Tests	2.053	0.864	−.034	−.012
		1.949	0.596	−.125	−.089
61	Accelerated Courses	0.406	0.491	.176	.192
		0.410	0.495	.040	.255
69	Principal Says No Tracking	0.515	0.500	.149	−.047
		0.427	0.498	−.007	−.362
105	No Teacher Tenure	0.082	0.275	.152	.021
		0.046	0.210	−.080	−.231
112	Percent Teacher Turnover	8.972	11.086	.013	−.026
		9.009	9.388	.009	−.080
129	Principal Percent Gripes	33.453	8.537	−.454	−.312
		32.077	7.720	−.252	−.125
147	School Size in 100's	6.103*	3.670	−.382	−.030
		6.896*	3.503	−.280	.180
241	Principal Data: Percent Blanks	10.135*	16.842	−.042	−.043
		14.884*	8.867	−.092	−.030
266	Principal's Estimate: Pupil Percent White	69.321	37.122	1.000	.401
		73.853	37.943	1.000	.100
267	Principal's Estimate: Pupil SES	3.643	0.930	.401	1.000
		6.602	0.963	.100	1.000
245	High Grade	6.490	1.032	.186	−.106
		6.596	1.046	−.016	−.069
14	Length of School Day	5.546†	0.538	.114	−.007
		5.778†	0.565	−.036	−.055
26	No Elementary Accreditation in Area	0.392*	0.488	.047	.022
		0.257*	0.439	−.063	−.019
34	Cafeteria	0.258*	0.438	−.067	−.013
		0.398*	0.492	−.109	−.088
35	Gymnasium	0.263*	0.440	−.138	−.001
		0.370*	0.485	.021	.174
36	Athletic Field	0.585*	0.493	.124	.124
		0.475*	0.502	.428	.335
40	Language Facilities	0.107*	0.309	−.003	−.025
		0.040*	0.197	.123	.251

* Alpha level of T-tests: .05–.001.
† Alpha level of T-tests: .001.

TABLE 10 (continued)

Var. No.	Variables[2]	Mean	Standard Deviation	Correlation With Principal Estimate	
				of Percent White	of Pupil SES
42	Movie Projectors	1.975†	1.167	−.158	−.024
		2.528†	1.315	−.189	.027
43	Infirmary	0.782*	0.413	.015	.151
		0.890*	0.314	−.162	.260
47	Text Copyright Age	3.594†	3.044	.020	.011
		4.780†	3.876	−.206	−.053
51	Library	0.727†	0.446	.104	.167
		0.495†	0.502	.273	.375
52	Free Texts	0.858*	0.349	−.140	−.002
		0.769*	0.424	−.284	.259
60	Number of Prior Achievement Tests	3.464†	1.380	.044	.025
		2.749†	1.219	−.079	.013
62	Hours Homework	0.623†	0.527	−.104	−.064
		0.944†	0.509	−.081	−.124
63	Percent in Special English	4.980†	6.370	−.294	−.148
		2.594†	3.970	.082	.085
64	Percent in Special Math	2.592*	4.840	−.164	−.130
		1.196*	2.387	.008	.131
66	Behavior Problem Classes	0.191*	0.393	−.073	.059
		0.085*	0.280	.103	.131
67	Verbal Extracurricular Activities	1.079†	1.079	−.103	.014
		0.667†	1.017	.096	.006
68	Nonverbal Extracurricular Activities	2.382†	1.650	.007	−.008
		3.051†	1.646	.194	.090
80	Speech Therapists/1000 Students	0.573*	0.661	.166	−.096
		0.427*	0.281	.246	.033
82	Remedial Reading Teachers/1000 Students	0.744*	1.220	−.111	−.045
		0.455*	0.817	−.178	.134
83	Counselors/1000 Students	0.446*	0.949	−.164	−.001
		0.194*	0.461	−.031	.055
84	Librarians/1000 Students	0.609*	0.814	.104	.050
		0.387*	0.599	.201	.234
87	Nonteaching Staff/1000 Students	8.794*	5.154	.217	−.049
		7.533*	3.699	.132	−.100
107	Conditional Teacher Tenure	0.126*	0.333	.048	.048
		0.220*	0.416	−.169	.041
119	National Teachers Examinations for Teachers	0.188*	0.391	−.272	−.102
		0.110*	0.314	.042	−.102
130	New England	0.098*	0.298	.150	.071
		0.018*	0.135	.077	.205

* Alpha level of T-tests: .05–.001.
† Alpha level of T-tests: .001.

TABLE 10 (*continued*)

Var. No.	Variables[2]	Mean	Standard Deviation	Correlation With Principal Estimate	
				of Percent White	of Pupil SES
132	Great Lakes Region	0.298*	0.458	.010	−.120
		0.560*	0.499	−.086	−.055
134	Far West Region	0.194†	0.396	−.007	.008
		0.046†	0.210	.134	.188
140	Small Town Location	0.047*	0.211	.066	.049
		0.0	0.0	.0	.0
142	Neighborhood School	0.530†	0.499	.105	.051
		0.750†	0.435	−.006	.130

* Alpha level of T-tests: .05–.001.
† Alpha level of T-tests: .001.

grounds. The means for these 21 items were significantly different ($p > .05$) in only three cases, which is not impressive. In particular, the principals' estimates of the elementary schools' socioeconomic and racial composition were similar for semi-cooperative and more fully cooperative districts, as were the state department of education estimates for high schools. The next 30 items were selected *because* there were significant differences between semi-cooperative and other districts. Semi-cooperative districts were more likely to be in the Midwest and more likely to assign children to schools on a neighborhood basis. They were slightly larger and had fewer specialized personnel per pupil. They had smaller sites and fewer athletic fields, but compensated for this with more cafeterias, infirmaries, movie projectors, and gymnasiums. The semi-cooperative districts had longer school years, longer school days, and assigned more homework. They were much less bookish, however, with fewer libraries, fewer librarians, fewer library books, older textbooks, and less likelihood of giving texts to children free. They had fewer children in remedial classes and gave fewer achievement tests (though no fewer I.Q. tests).

Table 10 also shows the correlation between each school characteristic and two family background measures for semi-cooperative and for selectively or fully cooperative districts. The estimate of the students' mean socioeconomic level is derived from the principal's questionnaire and is not very reliable. The measure of racial composition is derived from the same source and is fairly good. The correlations between school characteristics and student background measures show no consistent tendency to be either stronger or weaker in the semi-cooperative districts. Nor are any of the correlations very large.[32] When the two samples are pooled, the resulting correlations are naturally quite close to the correlations for the selectively and fully cooperative districts, and they remain generally low.

These findings suggest that neither class nor race had a predominant influence on school policies or resources in either semi-cooperative or selectively and fully cooperative districts. It must be remembered, however, that we have been looking only at those school policies and resources reported by principals, and have been ignoring teacher characteristics. At least in cooperative districts, teacher characteristics show stronger relationships to both student background and student achievement than do school characteristics reported by principals. Some caution is therefore required in generalizing about similarities between semi-cooperative and other districts.

Generalizations about semi-cooperative districts are nonetheless important, not only for what they tell us about the schools in these districts but for what they imply about schools in uncooperative districts. It seems logical to suppose that there is some sort of continuum running from complete lack of cooperation to full cooperation, and that the semi-cooperative districts fall toward the middle of this continuum. This view is supported by state department of education estimates of high-school racial composition, which show that the uncooperative districts have the fewest whites, the cooperative districts have the most, and the semi-cooperative districts fall between. If this assumption is correct, we would expect that:

(a) The differences found in Table 10 between schools in semi-cooperative and other districts would be even larger if we could compare uncooperative and other districts.

(b) The similarities found in Table 10 between semi-cooperative and fully cooperative districts with respect to their overall racial and class bias in allocating resources and determining policies would also recur if we could compare uncooperative and cooperative districts.

(c) The differences found in Table 10 between semi-cooperative and fully cooperative districts with respect to the relationship between race, class, and specific school characteristics would probably diminish in many cases if we were to compare both uncooperative and semi-cooperative districts to fully cooperative ones, since this would reduce the importance of random sampling differences.

These inferences, while hardly airtight, seem to support the general conclusion that the omission of uncooperative districts probably did not substantially bias EEOS estimates of the relationship between school characteristics and student background.

Evidence about the relationship between school characteristics and student background does not, unfortunately, tell us much about the independent relationship of school characteristics to student achievement. We know from Chapters 2, 5, and 6 that this relationship is weak in selectively and fully cooperative districts. One can make a variety of a priori arguments about the likely situation in semi-cooperative districts, based on one or another assumption about the reasons for their recalcitrance, but such reasoning is unlikely to persuade skeptics. I have not been able to find empirical studies of the relationship between school characteristics and student achievement in any of the 23 semi-cooperative districts.

3. Selectively Cooperative Districts

There were 47 selectively cooperative districts which failed to return 6th-grade questionnaires for one or more of the schools which the superintendent had originally described as having a 6th grade and feeding a sample high school.[33] These districts had 506 6th-grade schools, 54 of which returned no data and 55 of which returned only principal data. What is the most reasonable explanation for the loss of these schools?

One theory is that the superintendents of these districts knew that the schools in question would do poorly when tested, so they told the principal not to test the pupils and perhaps not to return any data whatever. I find this theory implausible, however. If a superintendent was really worried about what the tests would show, why not invent a plausible reason for officially pulling the whole district out of the survey instead of covertly pulling one school out? Or if selective participation seemed more politically convenient, why not provide a selective list of feeder schools to the U.S. Office of Education and then tell all these schools to cooperate instead of admitting the existence of a bad school and then telling its principal not to cooperate? I find it much easier to blame the principals of the missing schools than the superintendent. Some principals undoubtedly thought the survey a waste of everybody's time, and didn't want to disrupt the school day with another round of tests and questionnaires. Other principals were doubtless offended by the whole survey for ideological reasons. Still others may simply have lost the questionnaires either before or after administering them, may have shipped the questionnaires to the wrong place, and so forth. Some presumably thought their students would perform badly on the tests and preferred not to let them perform at all.

Selective participation could have introduced two distinct biases. First, uncooperative or semi-cooperative schools might have differed significantly from the average school in the district in which they were located. Second, uncooperative and semi-cooperative schools might have been quite representative of their districts, but the districts as a whole might have differed appreciably from the Northern metropolitan norm.

Table 11 shows the extent of such differences for the 55 semi-cooperative schools that returned principal but not pupil questionnaires. The variables in Table 11 were selected in the same way as those in Table 10. Column 1 shows the characteristics of the 55 semi-cooperative schools in selectively cooperative districts, while column 2 shows the means for the

TABLE 11

Characteristics of Semi-Cooperative Schools in Selectively Cooperative Northern Metropolitan Districts Compared to All Schools in Selectively Cooperative Districts and to All Schools in Metropolitan North

Var. No.	Variables	Means and S.D.'s for Semi-Cooperative Schools in Selectively Cooperative Districts[a]	Means and S.D.'s for Semi-Cooperative Districts[b]	Means and S.D.'s for Entire Sample
9	Hold Back Slow Learners	0.326	0.416	0.410
		(0.474)	(0.298)	(0.492)
10	Transfer Slow Learners	0.043	0.033	0.035
		(0.206)	(0.068)	(0.184)
16	Free Kindergarten	0.792	0.736*	0.855
		(0.409)	(0.353)	(0.353)
20	Free Nursery	0.0	0.029	0.047
		(0.0)	(0.057)	(0.213)
24	State Accreditation Conditional or Refused	0.158	0.197	0.073*
		(0.037)	(0.318)	(0.260)
28	Students/Room	29.682	27.769	27.820
		(21.634)	(9.606)	(8.013)
32	Building Age	24.527	25.409	28.377
		(16.264)	(10.758)	(18.217)
48	Enough Texts	0.982	0.955	0.946
		(0.135)	(0.060)	(0.226)
50	Library Volumes/Student	6.152	6.223	5.186
		(7.924)	(5.046)	(5.393)
53	Teacher Specialization	0.364	0.397	0.362
		(0.485)	(0.328)	(0.481)
59	Number of Prior Intelligence Tests	1.939	1.839	2.041
		(0.806)	(0.672)	(0.838)
61	Accelerated Courses	0.471	0.427	0.406
		(0.504)	(0.282)	(0.491)
69	Principal Says No Tracking	0.385	0.528*	0.507
		(0.491)	(0.292)	(0.500)
105	No Teacher Tenure	0.071	0.110*	0.078
		(0.260)	(0.278)	(0.269)
112	Percent Teacher Turnover	6.339	7.230	8.976
		(7.707)	(3.870)	(10.901)
129	Principal Percent Total Gripes	34.193	32.865	33.295
		(10.258)	(4.960)	(8.455)
147	School Size in 100's	7.496	6.191*	6.193*
		(6.852)	(2.947)	(3.658)

[a] Includes 55 schools that (1) returned principal but not student data and (2) were located in districts where at least one other school returned complete data.
[b] Mean for all schools in districts where schools in column (1) are located. District means weighted by number of schools in district returning principal but not student data.
* Difference from column (1) significant at .05 level.

TABLE 11 (continued)

Var. No.	Variables	Means and S.D.'s for Semi-Cooperative Schools in Selectively Cooperative Districts[a]	Means and S.D.'s for Semi-Cooperative Districts[b]	Means and S.D.'s for Entire Sample
241	Percent Principal Blanks	8.555 (6.335)	10.484 (6.155)	10.667 (16.213)
245	High Grade	7.268 (1.421)	6.891* (0.651)	6.503† (1.033)
266	Principal Estimate: Student Percent White	66.429 (36.801)	74.263* (24.937)	69.842 (37.225)
267	Principal Estimate: Student SES	3.852 (0.656)	3.617* (0.594)	3.638 (0.933)
11	Admission of Only High IQ Students	0.018 (0.134)	0.009 (0.016)	0.003* (0.056)
14	Length of School Day	5.750 (0.580)	5.766 (0.378)	5.572* (0.546)
15	Years of Preschool	0.429 (1.438)	0.229 (1.082)	0.783* (1.012)
30	Teachers/Room	1.151 (0.754)	1.072 (0.321)	1.011† (0.257)
35	Gymnasium	0.364 (0.485)	0.271* (0.330)	0.275 (0.447)
37	Biology Laboratory	0.182 (0.389)	0.137 (0.177)	0.073* (0.260)
38	Chemistry Laboratory	0.109 (0.315)	0.072 (0.158)	0.047* (0.213)
39	Physics Laboratory	0.073 (0.262)	0.030* (0.091)	0.030 (0.171)
40	Language Facilities	0.179 (0.386)	0.152 (0.195)	0.100* (0.300)
41	Typing Laboratory	0.143 (0.353)	0.035† (0.081)	0.022† (0.145)
42	Movie Projectors	2.255 (1.364)	1.997* (0.843)	2.039 (1.197)
43	Infirmary	0.661 (0.478)	0.673 (0.297)	0.794* (0.404)
56	Physics Courses	0.127 (0.336)	0.069* (0.107)	0.063* (0.242)
57	Typing Courses	0.446 (0.502)	0.303* (0.255)	0.178† (0.383)
58	Language Courses	0.554 (0.502)	0.494 (0.382)	0.394* (0.489)
62	Hours Homework	0.798 (0.659)	0.755 (0.270)	0.655* (0.534)

* Difference from column (1) significant at .05 level.
† Difference from column (1) significant at .001 level.

TABLE 11 (continued)

Var. No.	Variables	Means and S.D.'s for Semi-Cooperative Schools in Selectively Cooperative Districts[a]	Means and S.D.'s for Semi-Cooperative Districts[b]	Means and S.D.'s for Entire Sample
64	Percent in Special Math	3.778 (7.445)	2.822 (2.933)	2.444* (4.662)
67	Verbal Extracurricular Activities	1.623 (1.350)	1.251* (0.767)	1.035† (1.080)
68	Nonverbal Extracurricular Activities	3.000 (1.925)	2.860 (1.113)	2.456* (1.662)
70	Principal Says All Tracked	0.519 (0.505)	0.385* (0.265)	0.407 (0.492)
75	Students/Teacher	25.669 (6.529)	25.930 (4.149)	27.594* (4.741)
78	Art Teachers/1000 Students	0.792 (1.440)	0.616* (0.812)	0.596* (0.756)
79	Music Teachers/1000 Students	1.171 (1.242)	1.290 (1.126)	0.883* (0.912)
80	Speech Therapists/1000 Students	0.349 (0.321)	0.551* (0.607)	0.557* (0.631)
83	Counselors/1000 Students	0.904 (1.126)	0.549† (0.466)	0.418† (0.911)
94	Principal Salary in 100's	122.273 (33.080)	114.478† (23.541)	117.503 (23.622)
137	Medium-Size Town	0.143 (0.353)	0.098* (0.216)	0.111 (0.315)
141	Rural Location	0.054 (0.227)	0.186† (0.266)	0.082 (0.274)

* Difference from column (1) significant at .05 level.
† Difference from column (1) significant at .001 level.

33 districts in which these 55 schools are located. A comparison of columns 1 and 2 indicates that out of nearly 100 potential comparisons, about a fifth showed statistically significant differences. In particular, semi-cooperative schools reported fewer white but more middle-class children than the norm for their districts. In general, principals who did not test their pupils reported more resources than principals who did test their pupils. Column 3 shows the means for the entire Northern metropolitan sample. Comparison of these regional means with the means for semi-cooperative schools reveals statistically insignificant differences in racial and socioeconomic composition. Again, principals who failed to test their pupils report more resources than other Northern metropolitan principals.

Unfortunately, we cannot generate a Table 12 which compares unco-

operative schools to either district or regional norms, because we have almost no information about uncooperative schools. We do have one clue,
however. State department of education reports on high schools indicate
that districts with uncooperative schools had the same percentage of whites
as districts without uncooperative schools. But when we look at schools
which actually returned questionnaires in the two sets of districts, we find
about 10 percent fewer whites than there ought to be in the districts with
missing schools. This suggests that schools with large numbers of blacks
returned data, while schools in the same district with few or no blacks did
not.

None of the foregoing findings supports the idea that schools which
failed to test pupils had "something to hide." Instead, it suggests that they
simply "couldn't be bothered."

4. *Overall Effects of Selective Participation by Districts
   and Schools*

The EEOS provides data on the background and achievement of the
sixth graders in 810 of the 1,196 Northern metropolitan sample schools.
What can we say about the overall bias introduced by losing one school in
three? A rigorous answer to this question would be extremely complex and
speculative, but a crude answer is fairly easy.

Suppose we want to estimate the average effect (E_t) of some school
characteristic on student achievement for all 1,196 Northern metropolitan
6th-grade schools. Suppose that we divide the 1,196 schools into two subsamples, one of which includes the 810 schools which tested pupils while
the other includes the 386 schools which did not test them. Suppose that the
school characteristic produces a difference in mean achievement between the
two groups of schools of E_b. Suppose that the characteristic has an average
effect of E_1 in the subsample of 810 schools and E_2 in the subsample of
386 schools. Then

$$E_t = \frac{E_b + \dfrac{810}{1,196}E_1 + \dfrac{386}{1,196}E_2}{2}.$$

Admittedly, this formula has relatively little to do with the real world.
To begin with, we do not know the E's for *any* sample of schools, including
those for which we have complete data. All we know are the regression
coefficients that give the most accurate predictions of achievement after we
have made various unlikely assumptions about the nature of the variables
that affect achievement and the relationships between these variables. Since
these assumptions are seldom accurate, regression coefficients seldom combine in precisely the way suggested by the above formula. The formula
does, however, yield tolerable approximations in most of the instances I
have examined.

A second difficulty is that even if we equate the E's with regression coefficients, we have no way of estimating either E_b or E_2. So we have to make more assumptions. One seemingly reasonable assumption is that most school characteristics have the same effect on differences between groups of schools as on differences between schools within these groups. This is equivalent to saying that E_b is equal to the weighted mean of E_1 and E_2, and reduces our equation to:

$$E_t = \frac{810E_1 + 386E_2}{1,196}.$$

A second assumption is that the effect of a school characteristic in the missing schools (E_2) may be two or three times the effect in schools which returned data (E_1), but it will not be 20 or 30 times as great. A little experimentation will show that, if these assumptions are correct, E_t will not differ dramatically from E_1. If, for example, the effect of a school characteristic were three times as great in schools which returned no student data as in schools which did so, an estimate derived solely from schools which returned data would be 39 percent lower than the true value. This is hardly surprising. It is really just a complicated way of saying that if you have data on two thirds of a sample, and if the missing third isn't too different from the available two thirds, then the overall sample won't differ much from the two thirds for which you have data.

B ♦ Selective Participation by Individuals

This section deals with five kinds of selective participation and nonresponse.

Missing Principal Questionnaire Items. The typical Northern metropolitan 6th-grade principal omitted about 5 percent of the questionnaire items applicable to his school.

Missing Teachers. In schools that returned teacher questionnaires, an average of one teacher in ten appears to be missing.

Missing Teacher Questionnaire Items. The teachers who returned questionnaires failed to answer about 3 percent of the items.

Missing Students. In schools which tested their pupils, an average of one pupil in eight seems to be missing.

Missing Student Questionnaire Items. Among sixth graders who returned questionnaires, the proportion of blank or "Don't know" answers ranged from 2 to 40 percent, according to the question.

1. *Missing Principal Questionnaire Items*

The questionnaire for principals included 158 items grouped into 100 questions. Some of these items touched on sensitive subjects, some were not applicable to all schools, and some forced principals to categorize their opinions in ways which would probably not have occurred to them spontaneously. Only four Northern metropolitan principals with 6th grades answered every item applicable to an elementary school, but half answered 95 percent of such items, three quarters answered 90 percent, and nineteen out of twenty answered at least three quarters of the relevant items.

Principals who omitted large numbers of items had the same kinds of pupils and reported the same resources as other principals. They were less likely to report either ability grouping or automatic promotion, but they reported similar policies on other matters. They were more likely to come from New England, to be women, and to be older than average.

A priori reasoning suggests that principals who omitted large numbers of items may have had a generally casual attitude toward the survey, and may therefore have given less accurate as well as less complete answers. If this were the case, however, school policies and resources reported by low-response principals should show unusually weak relationships both to one another and to student characteristics, since data provided by these principals should contain a disproportionately large number of errors. No such pattern was detectable.

A priori reasoning also suggests that principals who failed to answer particular items may have been concealing something about their school. If a given resource had an effect on achievement, and if principals who lacked the resource were reluctant to answer questions about it, then schools which provided no information about the resource would have had unusually low achievement scores after all other factors had been taken into account. There were a few questionnaire items which seemed to follow this pattern, but there did not seem to be any regular or meaningful trend in this direction. Indeed, the overall pattern of relationships between missing principal items and student achievement was within the range expected on the basis of chance alone.[34] If a given school characteristic did *not* affect student achievement, there would be no reason to expect achievement differences between respondents and nonrespondents. But in that event there would also be little reason to worry about nonresponse.

A second and subtler possibility is that principals might have answered questions about a given resource or policy so long as they thought it had no effect on their students' achievement, but that they might have felt reluctant to answer if they thought that the resource or policy was affecting their students' achievement either for better or for worse. I can see no empirical way to investigate this possibility, but it is probably safe to ignore it simply on a priori grounds. In order for such a pattern to arise we must assume that: (1) the resource or policy in question has substantially more effect on achievement in some schools than in others; (2) principals know which of their resources or policies have an effect and which do not; and (3) principals' reluctance to answer a question depends not on whether the school has a given resource but on whether the resource affects student achievement. I find it hard to imagine many such cases.

All in all, principals' failure to answer certain questions does not seem likely to affect estimates of the relationship between school characteristics and either student background or student achievement.

2. Missing Teachers

Each principal was asked the number of "fulltime equivalent" teachers on his staff. After eliminating completely implausible replies, I compared the principals' estimates of their teaching staff with the number of teachers actually returning questionnaires. Table 12 shows the frequency of various response rates.

Low response could be explained in several ways. First, the principal could have distributed questionnaires selectively (e.g., to regular full-time teachers but not to part-timers, substitutes, etc.). Second, after teachers received the questionnaire, they might have failed to return it either because

TABLE 12

Frequency of Various Teacher Response Rates in Northern Metropolitan 6th-Grade Schools[a]

Response Rate	Percentage in Category
Less than 25 percent	0.7
25–49 percent	3.5
50–74 percent	6.1
75–84 percent	10.7
85–94 percent	28.7
95–100 percent	37.4
More than 100 percent[b]	12.9
Total	100.0

[a] Based on 689 schools which returned principal and teacher questionnaires, for which the principal's estimate of the number of teachers was compatible with his report of enrollment and of the number of rooms, and for which Armor (see Chapter 5) had counted all teacher questionnaires.

[b] Estimates in excess of 100 percent can be explained in several ways. First, principals were asked to estimate the size of the teaching staff in "fulltime equivalents." This meant that if a man taught part-time and served part-time as a librarian, guidance counselor, or whatever, only the fraction of his time devoted to teaching was supposed to be included in the principal's estimate. Teacher questionnaires, on the other hand, were supposed to have been returned by anyone who taught at all, however small the fraction of his time devoted to teaching, and by anyone who spent five or more hours as a guidance counselor. In schools where a number of specialized personnel taught part-time, these rules should have produced an appreciable excess of teacher questionnaires over full-time equivalent teachers. In addition, of course, some principals may simply have forgotten to count one or more teachers, particularly persons who taught specialized subjects, did not have a regular classroom, and so forth. These people could nonetheless have received and returned teacher questionnaires.

they disapproved of the whole survey or because they found specific questions embarrassing or offensive. Yet given the general atmosphere of most schools, it does not seem likely that many teachers would have failed to return a form which the principal had asked them to fill out—unless he made it clear he did not really care. Failing that, it seems likely that teachers would simply have failed to answer those questions which they found irritating. The fact is, however, that the response rate for specific items on the teacher questionnaire exceeded 95 percent for almost every item. This suggests, though it certainly does not prove, that teachers who failed to return questionnaires were probably careless rather than anxious or hostile. Low response, therefore, seems best explained by assuming that certain principals failed to distribute questionnaires to all teachers or else failed to get them back from all teachers.

A comparison of schools with above-average and below-average teacher response rates failed to uncover statistically or pedagogically significant differences in mean achievement, socioeconomic composition, racial mix, or most teacher characteristics. (Schools with low response rates did have more substitutes and less experienced teachers—both of which are significantly related to achievement.) Low teacher response rates might nonetheless have led to unusually inaccurate estimates of the characteristics of the teachers to whom the average sixth grader had been exposed. The relationship of teacher characteristics to student achievement in these schools might therefore have been underestimated. In order to check on this, I calculated separate regression equations for schools with high and low teacher response rates. The overall difference was statistically significant ($p < .05$) for an equation using teacher characteristics that had a significant relation to achievement for the overall sample.[35] But the coefficients for the teacher variables were no smaller on the average in low-response than in high-response schools, and slightly more teacher variables were statistically significant in low-response schools than in high-response schools. The hypothesis that low-response schools returned less accurate data is therefore not supported.

All in all, it seems unlikely that estimates of the relationship between teacher characteristics and student achievement would have been very different if complete teacher data had been available.

3. *Missing Teacher Questionnaire Items*

Even when a teacher returned his questionnaire, he did not always answer every question. Fortunately, this is less of a problem than with principals, since most schools had more than one teacher. Estimates of teacher characteristics which affect 6th-grade achievement are necessarily based on means for a number of teachers. When computing such means, most EEOS analysts (including myself) have ignored teachers who failed to answer a given question. This has the same effect as assuming that the average teacher who did not answer was like the average teacher who did answer. A few analysts have rejected this assumption. The best procedure would probably be to fill in each missing answer on the basis of the teacher's answers to other questions. The time and money required to do this, however, seem excessive. The typical Northern metropolitan 6th-grade school had about 20 teachers, and at least 19 answered any given item. The twentieth teacher would have had to be extraordinarily deviant for his absence to have had a significant effect on schoolwide averages for all teachers. For this reason I made no detailed analysis of the problem.

4. *Missing Students*

Principals in EEOS schools were supposed to test every third, sixth, ninth and twelfth grader in their school. Half were also asked to test first graders. Unfortunately, the survey neglected to ask principals the number of students in each grade of their school. This makes it quite difficult to determine whether every eligible pupil was really tested. Nonetheless, the question seemed important, so I devised a crude technique for estimating the number of sixth graders, based on the principal's report of total enrollment and the number of grades in his school. While my estimates were often inaccurate for a given school, the errors which they embody seem likely to be more or less random. This means that we can estimate the response rate for the entire sample more accurately than we can estimate it for any specific school. The estimated distribution of response rates for Northern metropolitan 6th-grade schools is shown in Table 13.

The existence of an appreciable number of schools which did not test all their pupils suggests that some schools may only have tested those pupils who they thought would do well. This suspicion is supported by the fact that response rates are particularly low in poor, black, low-achieving, inner-city schools. It could be, however, that these schools simply had a harder time getting children to take the tests, had more defaced or lost score sheets, had higher absence rates on test day, and so forth.[36]

If low student returns reflected deliberate efforts to make the school "look good," we would expect schools to select students for testing primarily on the basis of achievement and only secondarily on the basis of race, class, and similar factors. Schools with low response rates would then have higher achievement scores than schools with high response rates, even after factors like race and social class had been taken into account. This does not turn out to be the case. Once other factors are controlled, the relationship between the response rate and mean achievement is well within the range that could be explained by chance alone, and is not in the direction predicted by the "deliberate selection" hypothesis. This suggests that while disadvantaged schools were less likely to test all their students, the students they failed to test were not underachievers relative to their family background.

Failure to test all students, while not affecting the apparent relation-

TABLE 13

Frequency of Various Sixth-Grade Pupil Response Rates in Northern Metropolitan Sixth-Grade Schools[a]

Response Rate	Distribution of Raw Estimates[b]	Distribution of Corrected Estimates[c]
40 or less	2.4	1.6
40.1 to 50	4.6	3.9
50.1 to 60	6.2	3.7
60.1 to 70	7.7	3.9
70.1 to 80	13.9	8.4
80.1 to 90	18.5	2.0
90.1 to 100	16.9	76.5
100.1 to 110	16.5	—
110.1 to 126	5.5	—
126.1 to 147	3.8	—
147.1 to 177	2.5	—
177.1 to 220	0.7	—
Over 220	0.8	—
Total	100.0	100.0

[a] Based on 745 Northern metropolitan schools which returned 6th-grade questionnaires and in which the principal provided plausible estimates of total enrollment and the number of grades in the school. Roughly one principal in fifty failed to report enrollment, and another one in fifty reported an enrollment that was clearly inconsistent with his reports about the number of teachers and rooms in his school. One percent failed to return plausible information on the highest and lowest grades in their schools. The number of sixth graders in these schools could not be estimated.

[b] Column 1 shows "raw" response rates (R_r). They were estimated from the principal's report of total enrollment (E), the number of 6th-grade questionnaires returned (Q), the number of grades reported in the school (G), and the ratio of 6th-grade enrollment to mean enrollment per grade (K), using the formula:

$$R_r = \frac{(Q)(G)(100)}{(E)(K)}$$

Schools only provided data on Q, G, and E. K was assigned a constant value of 0.94. This was a national average, derived from Simon and Vance (1967, Table 26), and led to a number of errors, as indicated by the fact that 30 percent of the estimates of R_r exceeded 100 percent. (These errors are attributable to local variations in both birth rates and school assignment practices.)

[c] Column 2 estimates the "true" distribution of response rates (R_c), employing a better procedure for estimating K. The distribution of K was inferred by examining the number and magnitude of the R_r's which exceeded 100 percent. The true mean response rate $(\overline{R_c})$ of schools with R_r's in excess of 100 percent was presumed to be 94 percent. (I assumed that attendance early in the fall, when morale is above average and colds few, would be above the annual average of 94 percent, but that a few of the schools with R_r's over 100 would have R_r's lower than attendance on test day, leaving a mean of 94.) Thus if $R_r = 113$, $K = 1.13$. (The equivalence of R_r and K is a by-product of the coincidence that $K = \overline{R_c}$ for schools in which $R_c > 100$.) The distribution of K was presumed to be symmetrical around a geometric mean of .94. Thus for every K of 1.13, I assumed another K of .78 (since $\sqrt{(.78)(.113)} = .94$). I then assumed that the distribution of R_c for R_r's in excess of 100 lay entirely within the 90–100 range—a reasonable assumption if one accepts the initial premise of a 94 percent mean and a 100 percent maximum. The result of assigning all these R_r's (59.6 percent of the total) to the 90–100 interval is the distribution in column 2. This entire procedure involves a number of oversimplifications, but the additional labor involved in developing better procedures seemed disproportionate to the problem.

ship between background and achievement, might nonetheless have affected the independent relationship between school characteristics and achievement. One can imagine several ways in which this might happen.

(1) Some schools might have failed to test underachievers while other schools failed to test overachievers. The net effect of nonresponse would then have been to reduce the reliability of estimated school means without affecting the average level. Regression equations predicting achievement from the characteristics of schools with low response rates would then have lower coefficients and explain less of the variation in achievement than similar equations derived from schools with high response rates.

In order to test these hypotheses, I divided Northern urban elementary schools into those with estimated student response rates above 90 percent and those with estimated response rates below 90 percent. As indicated in Table 12, about two fifths of the schools with estimated response rates below 90 percent probably had actual response rates between 90 and 100 percent, but there is no way of determining *which* two fifths. The true differences between schools with high and low response rates may therefore be greater than the observed differences.[37] Using the present classification system, however, the differences between regression equations derived from the two samples were not statistically significant.[38] The absence of statistically significant differences between equations does not, of course, prove that the two sets of schools were identical in every respect. It does, however, suggest that neither of the two hypotheses outlined above about nonresponse is strongly supported by the evidence, and that we should probably direct our search for serious flaws in the data elsewhere.

5. *Missing Items on Student Questionnaires*

The overall item response rate for sixth graders throughout the nation was 97.3 percent, but the response rate for certain critical questions was much lower (see Mayeske, 1968). Only 94 percent of the nation's sixth graders answered the question about their father's occupation. Of those who did answer, 15 percent said they could not classify their father's occupation into any of the EEOS categories. Only 3 percent failed to answer the question about their mother's education, but 31 percent said they didn't know how much education she had. Five percent failed to answer the question about their father's education and 36 percent said they didn't know. Nonresponse was considerably more common among those with low verbal scores and among those whose other responses indicated low socioeconomic status.

The importance of these missing observations depends on the way in which the EEOS data are analyzed. Some analysts have sought to estimate the effects of *all* determinants of individual achievement. For reasons given in Chapter 2, I think this strategy wrong and have not used it in my own work. Nor have I explored the effect of missing student background data on estimates of the relationship between school characteristics and either individual background or individual achievement.

Missing student background data pose far fewer problems when one analyzes the relationship between school characteristics and the average characteristics of all students in a school. To begin with, there is a high correlation between the percentage of students who fail to answer questions about family background and the average background of those who do answer. This means that there is also a high correlation between school means based only on students who answer a given question and school means derived by imputing an average value to nonrespondents. Furthermore, the most powerful predictors of mean 6th-grade achievement are those derived from the questions about the presence of various items in the students' homes. The response rates on these questions average 98 percent. Once these questions have been used to estimate a school's average socioeconomic level, schoolwide data derived from the questions about parental education, father's occupation, family size, and the intactness of the family add a little more precision, but the treatment of missing cases in computing these averages turns out to make no difference whatever.

As a result, I decided not to analyze item nonresponse on the student questionnaires in much detail.

C ♦ Conclusions

Several general conclusions about nonresponse in the EEOS seem warranted.

(1) There was a lot of it. Out of 168 districts in the original Northern metropolitan sample, only 77 returned student data for every school and only 67 returned student, teacher, and principal data for every school. Out of 1,196 schools in the original sample, only 779 returned student, teacher, and principal data. As many as a fifth of all principals failed to answer certain rather straightforward items with clear applicability to their school (e.g., promotion policy, amount of homework assigned), and as many as two fifths of sixth graders did not know the answers to certain questions about their family background.

(2) The evidence presented in this Appendix does not indicate that the final EEOS sample was seriously unrepresentative of the urban North. But neither is the evidence presented here sufficient to rule that possibility out entirely.

(3) This Appendix has given primary attention to the question of whether the relationship between school characteristics and student achievement in the final EEOS sample was different from the relationship in the target population. It has given secondary attention to the question of whether the relationship of school characteristics to students' backgrounds

was different in the initial and final samples. It has found relatively little evidence that selective response led to underestimates of either relationship.

(4) The most controversial conclusion drawn from the EEOS was that school resources had surprisingly little relationship to students' background and even less independent relationship to students' achievement. The validity of these assertions does not depend on obtaining *precise* estimates of the relationships in question. It does not matter much, for example, whether race accounts for 1 percent of the variation in per-pupil expenditure or 5 percent; both relationships are "weak" by conventional standards. Nor does it matter much whether schools with 20 students per classroom have verbal scores that are one month above schools with 30 students per classroom, or whether the true difference is two months. Neither difference will suffice to persuade legislators that a 33 percent reduction in class size would be worthwhile. In order to reject the major policy conclusions of the EEOS, we have to assume that our estimates were off by factors of five, ten, and twenty, not a fifth, a half, or one. *There is no likelihood that selective participation could have introduced errors large enough to affect the policy implications of the survey.*

(5) There are a lot of serious problems in the EEOS data. Much of the data is probably inaccurate. Even when the data are accurate in their own terms, they often provide inadequate evidence about both the present state of the schools under study and the likely future lives of their alumni. In my judgment those who want to discredit inferences from the EEOS ought to concentrate on these defects and forget about selective participation, which is a rather minor problem by comparison. Conversely, those who wish to defend inferences based on the EEOS ought to deal more satisfactorily with doubts about the accuracy, adequacy, and relevance of the information collected, and not waste any more time proving that 65 percent response is adequate for most practical purposes.

Notes

1. These distinctions are further developed in Chapter 2.
2. A few SMSA's (e.g., Washington, D.C.; Evansville, Indiana; Steubenville, Ohio) are spread across two states which are in different regions. I have followed Coleman *et al.* in assigning all schools in such SMSA's to the region in which the principal city of the SMSA was located.
3. The EEOS 6th-grade sample was derived from the high-school sample. USOE asked each superintendent to identify all schools which fed pupils into the sample high schools. Nine of the twenty-one uncooperative Northern urban districts initially failed to provide this list of feeder schools, though several did so later. I estimated the number of feeders in the nine uncooperative districts from other information. Some initially uncooperative districts were sent test instruments, and in these cases I used the total number of schools sent test instruments to estimate the number with 6th grades. If no test instruments were sent to a district, and if it was located in the main city of an SMSA, I assumed that there were seven 6th-grade schools for every high school in the sample. (This was the average number of 6th-

grade schools per high school for the main cities of Northern SMSA's.) If the district was suburban, I assumed that it had the same number of 6th-grade schools per high school as other suburbs in its SMSA. Because these estimation techniques were subject to error, and because the information supplied by local districts was sometimes erroneous, my estimate of 1,196 6th-grade schools in the original sample should be presumed to have a standard error of at least five.

4. My enrollment estimate of 740,000 pupils is based on estimates provided by the 906 principals of Northern metropolitan 6th-grade schools who returned plausible answers to this question. It assumes that the 290 schools which returned no usable enrollment data had about the same mean enrollment as the 906 that did so.

5. The existence of "rural" schools within SMA'S of more than 50,000 is a by-product of the fact that the Census Bureau defines SMSA's in terms of political jurisdictions. If the bulk of a jurisdiction falls within an SMSA, the Census assigns the entire jurisdiction to the SMSA. This means that some rural areas are part of SMSA's. There may also have been some response error among principals on this item.

6. The estimate of 1,030 Northern urban elementary schools is based on the fact that 13.8 percent of the Northern metropolitan 6th-grade schools which returned principal questionnaires were either "rural" (8.2 percent), were not elementary schools (6.8 percent), or were both (1.2 percent). I assumed that the percentages were the same for Northern metropolitan 6th-grade schools which did not return principal questionnaires.

7. The estimate of 630,000 pupils is based on enrollment reports from those urban elementary schools which returned usable principal questionnaires and plausible data. Again, I assumed that the schools which did not return such data had the same mean enrollment as those which did.

8. The Census Bureau usually refers to these as "central cities" rather than "major cities." Unfortunately, the term "central city" has come to imply the social disorganization and physical decay of the "inner city," so I have eschewed the term.

9. Coleman, *et al.*, 1966, Table 9.6.4, which gives response rates for 6th-grade feeder schools, is based on erroneous estimates of the initial sample size; Tables 9.6.1–9.6.3, which give response rates for high schools, appear to be essentially correct.

10. There are several different methods for estimating the reliability of a given statistic. One method is to administer the questionnaire twice and compute a correlation between the first set of responses and the second. Another method is to ask the same question in two ways in the same questionnaire. In achievement tests, where many items are included to measure a single factor, we can compute correlations between large numbers of different pairs and then use these correlations to predict the correlation between two different administrations of the test.

If r_{ts} is the correlation between the first set of scores and the second, r_{1t} is the correlation between the first set of scores and the true scores, and r_{2t} is the correlation between the second set of scores and the true scores, we can usually assume that $r_{ts} = r_{1t}r_{2t}$ and that $r_{1t} = r_{2t} = \sqrt{r_{ts}}$. If the correlation between observed scores and true scores is $\sqrt{r_{ts}}$, the proportion of the variation in the first set of scores explained by the true scores is r_{ts}. When the variables in the question are dichotomous (i.e., have only two values), the use of correlation coefficients and reliability can be somewhat misleading, and other statistics (e.g., gamma) have certain advantages. But since virtually all the analyses in this book employ correlation and regression, and reliability coefficients are the most appropriate statistics for correcting such analyses, I have stuck to the reliability coefficient wherever possible.

11. Unfortunately, ETS coded both principals who answered (E) and principals who did not answer at all as blanks, so that I could not distinguish the two types of response. The question appears at the beginning of the questionnaire, however, and the response rate on all prior questions had been 98–100 percent. It therefore seems safe to assume that most of the principals who were coded as blank actually gave answer E.

12. Answers which are "wrong" cannot, by definition, be randomly distributed with

respect to the "right" answer, because they cannot be equal to it. If, for example, we ask students whether or not their families own vacuum cleaners, and if 5 percent give the wrong answer, the correlation between the replies given by this 5 percent and the true answers for this 5 percent will be —1.00, not o. If, on the other hand, we ask students the precise number of years of schooling completed by their fathers, they have perhaps twenty alternatives. The chances that they will give the correct answer are lower than if they had only two alternatives. But since most students have *some* idea how much education their fathers have had, their replies are only likely to be off by a couple of years one way or the other. As a result, there is likely to be a positive correlation between erroneous student answers and parental answers to the same question. When the number of alternatives is large, I will assume that this correlation is equal to the percentage of agreements between students and their parents.

Since the reliability coefficient ought to estimate the amount of variance in the true value of a variable that can be explained from the observed value, it ought to include an estimate of the effect of missing data. To obtain such an estimate we must assign some value to students who omit a question or do not know the answer and must correlate this value with the true value. The socioeconomic and academic data available for students who did not answer specific questions about parental education, occupation, and home items, show that these students are mostly at the bottom of the socioeconomic scale. Indeed, the data suggest that if we impute a value to students who fail to answer socioeconomic questions, our imputed values will explain as much of the variance in the true values as do other "erroneous" answers. For questions such as sex, where no reasonable procedure is available for imputing values to missing cases, I will assume a correlation between missing values and true values of zero.

If the percentage of correct student answers is p, if the correlation between erroneous student answers and true answers is r, and if we ignore missing cases, the overall reliability of the students' answers is $(p + r - pr)^2$. If a variable is binary, so that $r = -1.00$, the reliability becomes $(2p - 1)^2$. If $p = r$, as I have assumed for variables with large numbers of alternatives, the reliability is $(2p - p^2)^2$. If p is the percentage of genuine agreements, q is the percentage of cases for which no student data are available, r is the correlation between disagreements and true values, and s is the correlation between the value assigned to missing cases and their true value, the reliability is $(p + r - pr - qr + qs)^2$. If $r = s$, as I have assumed for variables measuring socioeconomic level, the reliability becomes again $(p + r - pr)^2$. As an example, take father's education in the sixth-grade. Table 5 shows that 38 percent gave correct answers, 21 percent gave incorrect answers, and 41 percent gave no answer. Thus p = 0.38. If we assume that for this multi-category variable r = s = p, then the reliability is $(2p - p^2)^2 = 0.38$.

13. This formula applies when all members of each group have been tested. For formulae that apply when all have not been tested, see Shaycroft (1962). Note that if individuals are assigned to groups randomly,

$$\frac{S_a^2}{S_{\bar{a}}^2} = n, \text{ and } r_{\overline{aa}} = r_{aa}$$

14. See, e.g., Burt (1966) and sources cited there.
15. See Ehrlenmeyer-Kimling and Jarvik (1963) and the bibliography available from these authors.
16. The precise character of Burt's school achievement measures is unclear from the articles in which I have seen his results reported.
17. Readers not familiar with studies of family resemblance may find it useful to think of the correlation between two relatives as resembling the correlation between two forms of the same test. This correlation estimates the percentage of variation in each sibling's scores explained by their common background. It is *not* squared to estimate explained variance.

18. The figures in the text are estimated from Coleman *et al.* (1966, *Supplemental Appendix*). The estimation technique was as follows. First, I compared the means and standard deviations for the total white and total black samples. These indicated that about 11 percent of the overall achievement for a representative American sample would be explained by race. Next, I compared the means and standard deviations for Northern and Southern blacks and whites. These indicated that an additional 1 percent of the national variation could be explained by a two-way regional split. I assumed that a more refined regional split would explain another 1 percent of the total variance. I then computed the percentage of variance within each regional/racial group explained by a linear combination of mother's education, reading items, home items, number of siblings, structural integrity of the home, parental education, and urbanism of background. The weighted average for these six background factors was 15 percent. The overall variance explained by race, region, urbanism, family size, and socioeconomic level thus summed to about 28 percent. Allowing for the omission of occupational and other variables from these matrices, I concluded that one could explain about 30 percent of the total variance if one used all the EEOS family background data. (This figure exceeds estimates from most other studies because it pools racial and regional groups rather than separating them.)

19. The 75 percent estimate differs from my 85–90 percent estimates in Chapter 2 because it includes only school-to-school variance explained by *individual* background differences, not variance explained by differences in school social context, i.e., mean social class. It differs from Smith's estimates in Chapter 6 because it includes variation in overall achievement attributable to race and region.

20. The percentage of black pupils in the 3rd grade correlates 0.932 with the percentage of blacks in the 1st grade and 0.933 with the percentage in the 6th grade. The 1st-6th correlation, instead of being lower than this, is 0.939. This pattern of correlations means that when a school's racial composition changes, it changes all at once, rather than from the bottom up or from the top down.

21. In order to estimate the amount of annual variation in samples of 80 pupils drawn from a stable underlying population, I used an analogue of test theory. I first divided every school's first graders into two random samples: the "odds" and the "evens." I then computed the correlation between the nonverbal means of these two subsamples. I then used the Spearman-Brown formula to estimate the correlation that would have been obtained from two samples twice as large, drawn from the same hypothetical underlying population. The resulting estimate was equivalent to the expected correlation between the mean nonverbal scores of successive entering 1st grades in the same schools, assuming no change in the population from which the first graders were drawn. For my sample of Northern urban elementary schools, the estimated interannual correlations were 0.963 for the entire class, 0.902 for all the whites in each class, and 0.807 for all the blacks in a class. For urban secondary schools, the interannual correlation for 9th-grade verbal means was 0.976 for the entire class. The differences between the entire class, the whites, and the blacks at the elementary level do not reflect underlying differences between racial groups. Rather, they reflect the fact that the average number of pupils involved in the interannual comparison is largest when all students are used and smallest when only blacks are used. The larger the number of pupils sampled each year, the less the mean for the year is likely to deviate from the true mean for the underlying population and the more closely the means for successive years correlate with one another. For a full exposition of the relevant formulae, see, e.g., Gulliksen (1950), Chapter 8.

22. Coefficients derived from equations which include 1st-grade scores are subject to an unknown amount of distortion when the 1st-grade scores are not derived from the same children as the 6th-grade scores. Dyer, Linn, and Patton (1969) have demonstrated that when the unit of observation is a school district, residuals derived from cross-sectional data like the EEOS have extremely low correlations with residuals derived from longitudinal data on the same districts. The same may well be true if the unit of observation is the school. The reasons for the low cor-

relations are unclear to me, since the absolute correlations reported by Dyer *et al.* are comparable using the two methods. Nonetheless, extreme caution should be used in interpreting coefficients of school characteristics which are in part determined by the relationship between 6th-grade scores derived from one sample and 1st-grade scores derived from another sample.

23. Coleman *et al.* (1966, Table 9.6.3.) reported that they received 12th-grade student data from 780 schools throughout the United States. I found 621 schools that returned both 9th- and 12th-grade data. The correlation between these schools' 9th- and 12th-grade mean verbal scores was 0.926. After correcting for annual fluctuation, this implies a "true" correlation between 9th-grade verbal means and the verbal mean of the same class four years later of 0.96 for the nation as a whole. The correlation would presumably be still higher if we could also eliminate the effects of selective dropout. For the 130 four-year high schools in Standard Metropolitan Statistical Areas, the correlation between 9th- and 12th-grade achievement composites was 0.956. Correcting for annual fluctuations, I estimated the "true" correlation at 0.98.

For comparative purposes, it may be useful to note that the correlation between 9th- and 12th-grade school means exceeds not only the correlation between 1st- and 6th-grade means, but also the correlation between 3rd- and 6th-grade means. The latter correlations may be artificially lowered by the poor quality of the 3rd-grade tests. The observed correlations between 3rd- and 6th-grade means in the urban North are 0.77 for 3rd- and 6th-grade verbal scores, 0.81 for 3rd- and 6th-grade math scores, and 0.85 for 3rd-grade math and 6th-grade verbal scores.

24. The principal components of schools' mean socioeconomic level were derived from a factor analysis of fourteen measures: the mean educational attainment of fathers, the mean educational attainment of mothers, the percentage of white-collar fathers, the percentage of intact families, the mean size of families, and the mean percentage of families having each of the nine home items on which the EEOS collected data. The first principal component accounts for 61 percent of the variation in the fourteen measures; the second accounts for another 10 percent; the third is insignificant. The first seems to be a general affluence index, dominated by the home items. The second captures a certain amount of residual "cultural" variance and is dominated by parental education and occupation.

25. The AFQT correlates 0.29 with father's occupational status in Duncan's sample whereas the Henmon-Nelson correlated 0.21 in Sewall's. The correlation between fathers' and 25-year-old sons' statuses in Sewall's data is only 0.14, compared to 0.39 in Duncan's data.

26. My estimate of 168 districts is based on a list of the high schools in the original sample, kindly supplied by Dr. James McPartland of Johns Hopkins University. This list had been derived from the U.S. Office of Education's list of American high schools, by techniques described in Coleman *et al.* (1966), pp. 550–4. Unfortunately, the original Office of Education list seems to have contained a number of errors. The correct figure was certainly between 165 and 170, but it may not be exactly 168.

My estimate of 21 uncooperative districts is based on an examination of 6th-grade principal and student data. Conceivably one or two of these districts returned high-school data, elementary-school teacher data, 3rd-grade student data, or 1st-grade student data.

27. Twenty-one schools returned student and teacher but not principal questionnaires. It seems unlikely that any principal who had gone to the trouble of testing his students would deliberately have failed to return teacher or principal data. The main cause of missing principal data in schools with student data seems to have been a mixup at ETS, as a result of which a number of principal questionnaires could not be matched to other data from the same school (see Coleman *et al.,* [1966], p. 557). The mean socioeconomic status and the mean achievement in these schools were roughly the same as in the rest of the 6th-grade sample. The correlation between mean achievement and mean socioeconomic background was

also about the same in both sorts of schools. Schools of this sort constituted less than 3 percent of the 6th-grade sample, and in my judgment they can be safely presumed to resemble schools with both student and principal data.

28. Although the EEOS schools were meant to be representative of the urban North once appropriate weighting procedures had been applied, the schools in a given school district were not meant to be representative of that district. On the contrary, since integrated and all-black schools were oversampled, many districts were represented largely or entirely by such schools, even though the majority of their schools were white. It is therefore risky to relate the characteristics of sample schools in a particular district to the characteristics of the district as a whole. Thus, one cannot tell whether the districts which refused to participate were disproportionately black or whether districts simply refused to participate when the EEOS sampled their black or integrated schools.

29. Katzman has reported (1969) that his previous work on resource allocation (1966) was erroneous because of a computing error. He was, however, kind enough to make his revised correlation matrices available to me, and these showed a small negative correlation between family income and per-pupil expenditure.

30. Katzman had no data on individual pupils or schools. Instead, he had data on Boston's 56 elementary-school "districts," most of which contain several schools. Nor did he have socioeconomic data on the sixth graders in his districts. He estimated their mean socioeconomic level from Census tract data for the district. Such estimates were subject to several kinds of error. (1) Census tracts do not precisely overlap with elementary district boundaries. (2) Families with children are not a random sample of families in a Census tract. (3) Families with children in public school are not a random sample of families with children. (4) There is random annual fluctuation in the socioeconomic level of students entering any given public school.

Katzman measured academic productivity by comparing each district's mean 6th-grade performance on the Stanford Intermediate Achievement tests of word meaning and paragraph meaning (translated into a grade-level equivalent) with its mean 2nd-grade performance on the Gates Primary Reading Test of sentence and paragraph reading (translated into a grade-level equivalent). He did *not*, however, use 2nd-grade scores as a control variable in his regression equations. Instead, he subtracted the 2nd-grade scores from the 6th-grade scores and treated the residual "gain score" as his dependent variable. Variation in grade level is inevitably more restricted among second than among sixth graders, since second graders have had less time to get ahead or fall behind. Thus, while variation in 2nd-grade scores might *predict* the variation in 6th-grade scores perfectly in a regression model, 2nd-grade scores cannot reduce 6th-grade variation much when they are scaled into grade-level equivalents and subtracted from 6th-grade scores. Katzman's procedure was equivalent to assigning 2nd-grade scores an arbitrary regression coefficient equal to the ratio of the 2nd-grade standard deviation to the 6th-grade standard deviation. The limitations of this procedure are underlined by his report (1966) that Metropolitan Readiness Tests administered in the 1st grade explained 42 percent of the variance in his 2nd–6th-grade gain scores. This suggests that inclusion of an initial ability measure in his equations might have substantially altered his estimates of the independent relationship between school characteristics and student achievement.

31. The skeptical reader may question the accuracy of the answers supplied by principals whose questionnaires were often extracted only after much delay and were not subject to cross-validation against teacher or student questionnaires. Such suspicions are encouraged by the fact that principals in semi-cooperative districts omitted significantly more items than principals in cooperative districts.

32. The correlation of 0.10 between the principals' estimates of racial and socioeconomic composition in semi-cooperative districts is so low as to cast doubt on the validity of these principals' answers to these questions. The relatively good correlation between principals' racial estimates and state department estimates in semi-cooperative districts suggests that the problem in these districts is probably with the principals' socioeconomic estimates rather than with their racial

estimates. For validity estimates for principals in selectively or fully cooperative districts, see section I-A of this appendix.

Skeptical readers may suspect that the correlations in Table 10 would be larger if they were based on more accurate student background measures. Good background measures were available for selectively and fully cooperative districts, however, and the correlations between school characteristics and student background turned out to be about the same when background was estimated from student questionnaires as when it was estimated from principal questionnaires.

33. My estimate of 47 selectively cooperative districts is subject to error for several reasons. First, it is based on an early USOE count of feeder schools at each grade level in each district. This count appears to have been revised at a later date in the light of additional information, but no final count could be located. The initial count contained many inaccuracies. Sixteen districts returned principal and/or student questionnaires from more 6th-grade schools than appeared in the initial count. In a few districts these excess schools were represented only by principal questionnaires, and the principals may simply have misreported their school's grade structure (see section I-A). In most instances, however, we must assume that USOE's initial count omitted one or more of the feeder schools which subsequently received questionnaires. If the initial count was lower than the actual number of returns in 16 districts that returned full data, it was probably also low in some districts where certain 6th-grade schools returned no data. If the number of schools omitted from the original list equaled or exceeded the number which eventually received but did not return questionnaires, the district in question ended up looking as though it had returned data on every 6th-grade sample school when in fact it had not. There were probably several such "pseudo-complete" districts.

On the other hand, if the initial count was too low in 16 or more districts, it was probably too high in others. Six superintendents reported only one more 6th-grade school than returned data, and four reported only two more. Perhaps half a dozen of these discrepancies should be attributed to errors in the original count rather than selective participation.

The estimate of 47 selectively cooperative districts should therefore be read as 40–60.

34. Tests of statistical significance are, of course, unlikely to yield impressive results when the number of nonrespondents is extremely low, as it was for most principal questions. But the absolute differences were also small. Among Northern urban elementary schools which returned principal, teacher, and student data, only one principal failed to answer the question about the cost of his kindergarten. This school's verbal scores were almost half a year below the norm for students of the kind it enrolled, but this could easily happen by chance. The two schools whose principals failed to answer the questions about physics, chemistry, biology, and typing programs and facilities, as well as the eight principals who failed to answer questions about the number of I.Q. and achievement tests their students had taken, had pupils who averaged one to two months below the norm for students of their background. The seven principals who refused to report their sex or the amount of experience they had had as principals had similarly disadvantaged pupils. Principals who failed to report site acreage and libraries had pupils who slightly overachieved relative to their race and class, as did principals who failed to report on extracurricular activities. Failure to answer the other principal items in Table 1 of Chapter 2 was not significantly associated with either overachievement or underachievement.

35. Two equations were compared: one using statistically significant school characteristics, and one using random school characteristics. Both used family background controls. The random variable equation yielded indistinguishable results for high- and low-response schools. For the method used in comparing this and other regression equations, see Chow (1960).

36. The tests were supervised by untrained personnel. One possible result of this is that students who found the test difficult simply failed to hand in answer sheets and that the loss of these sheets was not detected. Another possible result

is that some students handed in completely blank answer sheets. Given the paucity of zero scores in the final data, it seems possible that some teachers discarded blank sheets, or else that ETS did so. If, as seems likely, the number of pupils who scored zero was highly correlated with the mean of those who scored above zero, elimination of all zero scores would lead to roughly the same rank order of schools as the inclusion of zero scores. But if some teachers discarded blank sheets while others did not, the reliability of school means would be appreciably reduced.

37. True mean differences are likely to average 60 percent larger than the observed mean differences, assuming the latter are really related to nonresponse.

38. Two equations were used for this comparison, identical to those described in footnote 35.

References

Benson, Viola E. "The Intelligence and Later Scholastic Success of Sixth Grade Pupils." *School and Society*, February 7, 1942, pp. 163–7.

Bowles, Samuel, and Levin, Henry. "The Determinants of Scholastic Achievement—An Appraisal of Some Recent Evidence." *The Journal of Human Resources*, Winter 1968, Vol. III, pp. 3–24.

Burkhead, Jesse. *Input and Output in Large-city High Schools*. Syracuse: Syracuse University Press, 1967.

Burt, Sir Cyril. "The Genetic Determination of Differences in Intelligence: A Study of Monozygotic Twins Reared Together and Apart." *British Journal of Psychology*, Vol. 57, 1966, pp. 137–53.

Chow, Gregory C. "Tests of Equality Between Sets of Coefficients in Two Linear Regressions." *Econometrica*, July, 1960, Vol. 28, pp. 591–605.

Cohen, David. "Report Analysis: Children and their Primary Schools." *Harvard Educational Review*, Spring 1968, Vol. 38, pp. 329–40.

Coleman, James. *The Adolescent Society*. Glencoe, New York: Free Press, 1961.

Coleman, James J., Campbell, Ernest Q., Hobson, Carol J., McPartland, James, Mood, Alexander M., Weinfeld, Frederic D., and York, Robert L. *Equality of Educational Opportunity*. Washington, D.C.: U.S. Government Printing Office, 1966.

Duncan, Otis Dudley. "Ability and Achievement." *Eugenics Quarterly*, Vol. 15, March, 1968, pp. 1–11.

Duncan, Otis Dudley, Featherman, David L., and Duncan, Beverly. "Socio-economic Background and Occupational Achievement: Extensions of a Basic Model." Ann Arbor, Mich.: Center for Population Studies, University of Michigan, 1968 (offset).

Dyer, Henry S., Linn, Robert L., Patton, Michael J. "A Comparison of Four Methods of Obtaining Discrepancy Measures, Based on Observed and Predicted School System Means on Achievement Tests." *American Educational Research Journal*, Vol. 6, November, 1969, pp. 591–606.

Erlenmeyer-Kimling, L., and Jarvik, Lissy F. "Genetics and Intelligence: A Review." *Science*, Vol. 142, December, 1963, pp. 1477–9.

Flanagan, John C., *et al. The Talents of American Youth, Vol. 1, Design for a Study of American Youth*. Boston: Houghton Mifflin, 1962.

———. *Studies of the American High School*. Cooperative Research Project 226, Project Talent, University of Pittsburgh, 1962.

———. *The American High School Student*. Cooperative Research Project No. 635, Project Talent, University of Pittsburgh, 1962.

———. *Project Talent One-Year Follow-up Studies*. Cooperative Research Project 2333, Project Talent, University of Pittsburgh, 1966.

Fulk, Byron E., and Harrell, Thomas W. "Negro-White Army Test Scores and Last School Grade." *Journal of Applied Psychology*, Vol. 36, 1952, pp. 34–5.

Gulliksen, Harold. *Theory of Mental Tests*. New York: Wiley, 1950.

Kapel, David E. *Effects of Negro Density on Student Variables and the Post High School Adjustment of Male Negroes*. Project Talent, American Institutes for Research, 1968.

Katzman, Martin. "Distribution and Production in a Big City School System." Ph.D. Dissertation, Yale University, Department of Economics, 1966.

———. "The Political Economy of Urban Schools." Draft manuscript, Cambridge, 1969.

Lavin, David. *The Prediction of Academic Performance*. New York: The Russell Sage Foundation, 1965.

Lorge, Irving. "Schooling Makes a Difference." Teachers College Record, Vol. 46, 1945, pp. 488–92.

Mayeske, George W., Weinfeld, Frederic D., Beaton, Albert E., Jr., Davis, Walter, Fetters, William B., Hixson, Eugene E. "Item Response Analyses of the Educational Opportunities Survey Student Questionnaires." Technical Note 64, U.S. Office of Education, April, 1968 (mimeo).

Michelson, Stephan. "The Association of Teacher Resourceness with Children's Characteristics," in Alexander Mood, ed., *Do Teachers Make a Difference?*, U.S. Government Printing Office, 1970.

Michelson, Stephan. "The Political Economy of Public School Inequalities," in Martin Carnoy, ed., *The Political Economy of Education: New Approaches to Old Problems*, David McKay, (forthcoming).

Overlan, Frank. "Out of the Mouths of Babes: The Accuracy of Students' Responses to Family and Educational Background Questionnaires." Harvard Graduate School of Education, 1968 (xeroxed).

Owen, John D. "The Distribution of Educational Resources in Large American Cities." Johns Hopkins Center for the Study of the Social Organization of Schools, 1969 (xeroxed).

Peaker, Gilbert F. "The Regression Analyses of the National Survey," in Central Advisory Council for Education, *Children and Their Primary Schools*, Vol. 2: Research and Surveys, London: Her Majesty's Stationery Office, 1967 (also known as "The Plowden Report").

Rosenthal, Robert, and Jacobson, Lenore. *Pygmalion in the Classroom*. New York: Holt, Rinehart and Winston, 1968.

Sewall, William H., Haller, Archibald O., Portes, Alejandro. "The Educational and Early Occupational Attainment Process." *American Sociological Review*, February, 1969, Vol. 34, pp. 82–92.

Sewall, William H., and Shah, Vimal T. "Socio-Economic Status, Intelligence, and the Attainment of Higher Education." *Sociology of Education*, Winter 1967, Vol. 4, pp. 1–23.

Shaycoft, Marion. "The Statistical Characteristics of School Means," in John C. Flanagan *et al.*, *Studies of the American High School*. Cooperative Research Project 276, Project Talent, University of Pittsburgh, 1962.

Simon, Kenneth, and Grant, W. Vance. *Digest of Educational Statistics*. Washington, D.C.: U.S. Office of Education, 1967.

Super, Donald E., and Crites, John O. *Appraising Vocational Fitness*. New York: Harper & Bros., 1962.

Thorndike, Robert. "Review of *Pygmalion in the Classroom*." *American Educational Research Journal*, November, 1968, Vol. 5, pp. 708–10.

Tuddenham, Read D. "Soldier Intelligence in World Wars I and II." *American Psychologist*, Vol. III, 1948, pp. 54–6.

Whitla, Dean K., *et al. Handbook of Measurement and Assessment in Behavioral Sciences*. Reading, Pa.: Addison-Wesley, 1968.

12

The Measurement of Educational Opportunity

HENRY S. DYER

To speak of equality of opportunity in education implies that one has some method of measuring the opportunities for learning that an educational system provides. The methods that have traditionally been used for this purpose are typically half-measures. They rest on a number of implicit assumptions that are at best questionable and at worst wrong. In this essay, I shall first examine two of these traditional methods of measuring educational opportunity and shall point out why I believe them to be inadequate or misleading. I shall then consider what the goals of education might be, and in light of these, suggest a different approach to the measurement of opportunity which, although somewhat complicated, strikes me as more nearly acceptable.

This new approach has much in common with the approach taken by Coleman in his analysis of the factors related to school achievement.[1] The Coleman approach, however, seems to me to have two deficiencies for this purpose: it takes too narrow a view of the goals of education, and it fails to account for pupil development over time. The approach I am suggesting will attempt to define a set of standards by which schools may be legitimately compared with one another in the amount of pupil development that is attributable to the school's efforts on behalf of the children. How far a school falls short of any given standard becomes the measure of its failure to provide its pupils with its maximum potential of educational opportunity.

I shall make the point that there are a number of different kinds of standards to be defined for this purpose, each kind being associated with one of several goals that an effective educational system should be helping pupils achieve. This is to say that educational opportunity is to be regarded as multidimensional rather than one-dimensional. No single measure of it is sufficient. A school may be giving its pupils an excellent opportunity to grow in one direction, but may be deficient in providing equivalent opportunities for growth in other directions that are just as important for their well-being.

I

Probably the oldest and still the commonest method of measuring educational opportunity mistakes means for ends; a more recent one, conversely, mistakes ends for means. As far back as 1849, Charles Sumner argued before the Massachusetts Supreme Court that the racially segregated schools in Boston provided unequal opportunities for Negroes and whites, on the ground that his client, a Negro girl, had to walk 2100 feet to her school while a white school was only 800 feet away from her home.[2] He lost the case, but the same kind of reasoning has pervaded the thinking of educators, the courts, and the public ever since. Up to 1954, innumerable attempts were made to prove that the separate education of Negroes in the South was either equal or not equal to white education by comparing schools in respect to their location, the quality of their buildings, the adequacy of facilities, the number of courses in the curriculum, the length of the school term, the paper credentials of teachers, and most importantly, the amount of capital outlay and annual expenditure per pupil.[3]

The counting of dollars and cents is still the most commonly used method of measuring educational opportunity. The notion is implicit in the formulas for allocating state aid to local school districts and in state laws that put a floor under teachers' salaries. The theory is very simple, in fact oversimple. It says that equalizing per-pupil expenditure from one school district to another tends to equalize the educational opportunities available to the pupils in each district.

The weakness in this method of measuring educational opportunity is that it rests on two highly questionable assumptions. The first assumption is that there is a one-to-one relationship between the cost of what goes into the running of a school and the quality of the goods and services bought for the purpose. The second is that the quality of the goods and services, thus measured, bears a similar relationship to the effectiveness of the school in meeting the developmental needs of the children. Consider, for example, the case of a school that installs a language laboratory. There is no guarantee that a more expensive installation is inherently better, if only as a piece of machinery, than a less expensive one. There is also no guarantee that a more expensive laboratory is capable of producing more language learning than a less expensive one, or indeed no language laboratory at all. Furthermore, even if a language laboratory has such a capability, its potential can not be realized unless it is actually used, and used appropriately. (During the period of excitement over the possibilities for audio-lingual instruction, many schools bought language labs that are now gathering dust.) Finally, the question remains whether the kind of learning envisaged by the laboratory is the kind of learning that the pupils who use it really need. It is the frequent failure of educational authorities to consider matters of this kind that results in the fallacy that equivalence in the means of education is synonymous with equivalence in the opportunities they provide.

The opposite fallacy is just as serious: it rests on the assumption that if certain end results of the educational process are the same for two school systems, the opportunities for learning in both are *ipso facto* equal, or that any difference in the results constitutes a measure of the degree to which they are unequal. According to this conception, the results of schooling fall into two broad categories: (1) those that have to do with when the pupil leaves school and what happens to him thereafter, and (2) those that rely on standardized achievement tests administered at various points in his school career.

In the first case, it is assumed, for instance, that a school system with a low dropout rate is in some sense better than a school system with a higher dropout rate, or that one with a high percentage of students going on to college is better than one with a lower percentage of students going on. The difficulty with measures like these is that they assume the quality of instruction to be perfectly related to retention rate or college-going rate when, as a matter of fact, the relationship may be considerably less than perfect. A student may drop out of school for many reasons that have little or nothing to do with what he has learned there; he may indeed have legitimate aspirations and opportunities that make further formal schooling inadvisable for him. And whether a student goes to college may depend more on his family's status and desire for reflected prestige than on anything the schools may have done or failed to do for him.

The same sorts of considerations apply to achievement test scores. The tendency is to assume that if on a reading test the 6th-grade pupils in a slum school average X points lower than those in a school in white suburbia, then X is the measure of the difference between the two schools in the effectiveness of reading instruction. The case may be quite the opposite: the slum school may be *more* effective than the suburban school in upgrading reading competence, especially in light of the deficiencies it has had to overcome. Thus, the pupils' level of performance as they emerge from any phase of the educational system tells nothing in itself about how well the system is functioning. One needs to know, in addition, what the pupils have *gained* during the time they have been under instruction, how much of the gain may be reasonably attributed to the instruction, and how much to factors beyond the reach of the school.

An interesting and important feature of the Coleman study is that it challenges the ends-means confusion in both of these traditional ways of measuring educational opportunity. What Coleman tried to do was to identify those characteristics of schools (plant, facilities, personnel, programs) that bear an empirically determined relationship to pupil achievement and to assess educational opportunity in light of these relationships. Those characteristics having a high relationship to such achievement were to be weighted heavily in the assessment, and those with a low relationship would carry a smaller weight. There is no question in my mind that this general approach is the right one. The main difficulty with the Coleman study is that it, too, oversimplifies the problem. In the search for school correlates, for instance, Coleman settled for measures that, on the face of it, are too gross and insensitive to reflect those characteristics of a school that might actually be having an impact on pupil learning. This grossness of the data is what concerns Sheldon White when he suggests that we must look for causal relationships "at a deeper level" than that represented by such items as teacher credentials, number of books in the school library, age of school building, and the like.

The grossness of the measures is indeed a weakness, but there are others as well. Coleman did not, and in the circumstances of his study could not, pay attention to student *gains* in performance under various learning conditions. And he was in no position to allow for the fact that an ideal system will have to provide for different kinds and rates of growth, depending on the differing needs and aspirations of the individual pupils.

I I

The Coleman approach has still another weakness that I think warrants fairly detailed attention because a number of recent investigations have not recognized it.[4] Coleman conceives of educational opportunity far too narrowly. He concentrates on a single kind of educational achievement, namely, the acquisition of verbal ability. This is the one measure he uses as a basis for determining the relative utility of various aspects of educational systems. To be sure, verbal ability is basic to most forms of achievement in school and in a symbol-oriented society like ours. It is paramount among the so-called basic skills, and it correlates so highly with measures of achievement in reading, mathematics, and factual information that it serves as a useful surrogate for the measurement of these other forms of learning. Even so, the basic skills alone hardly encompass the full range of children's developmental needs that an educational system might be expected to serve, especially those having to do with the affect of the learner. Coleman recognizes three such aspects of development—self-concept, interest in school and reading, and sense of control over the environment—all of which are of obvious importance. He treats them, however, not as ends to be achieved through the educational process, but merely as means to academic achievement as measured by verbal ability.[5] That is, he treats them not as important in their own right, but as mediators in learning how to read, write, and figure. One might reasonably argue that the approach is upside down, that what is of ultimate importance in the life of a human being is how he feels about himself, how he feels about his world, and whether he finds rewards in learning. His ability to read, write, and figure is more appropriately regarded as the means to these larger ends.

This is to say that educational opportunity should mean the opportunity, provided by the community, through its schools and otherwise, for many kinds of personal and social, as well as intellectual, growth. An educational system, furthermore, has the obligation not only to help pupils learn, but to get them to *want* to learn, and to choose wisely among the opportunities for different kinds of learning that good schools should make available to them. Education has too frequently been thought of as a one-dimensional enterprise for schools and pupils alike.

Any appropriate effort to measure educational opportunity is thus confronted with the problem of defining a multiplicity of educational goals. And the first question to be considered in this connection is: *Whose* goals shall be determinative—the goals of society, the goals of the disciplines, or the goals of the pupils themselves? The answer is, of course, that the claims of all three must be taken into account, and not least the goals of the pupils. Indeed, a case can be made for the proposition that the prime goal of education is to help children in the search for their own goals, while taking note of the fact that there are certain minimum levels of competence necessary for their survival and the survival of society generally.

To avoid semantic confusion at this point, it is important to make a distinction between two terms: *educational goals* and *educational standards*. I am using the term educational *goals* in an inclusive sense to designate those areas of pupil functioning with which all schools should be concerned. A goal is not to be thought of as a specific target, that is, as a particular level of accomplishment that children should reach at some point in their school career. Educational *standards*, on the other hand, do indeed refer to definite levels of accomplishment within any goal area. They are those levels of accomplishment that, all things considered, the pupils in a given school *ought* to reach if the school is doing its job properly. As I shall point out in the next section of this paper, reasonable and workable educational standards will necessarily vary from pupil to pupil and from school to school. The goals of education, however, are to be thought of as the same for *all* schools, for they represent the kinds of things that *all* children should have an opportunity to know and do and become as a consequence of going to school.

It is easy enough to reel off any number of abstractions that purport to state the goals of education. It is not so easy to express these abstractions in the form of acceptable measures for assessing how pupils and schools are meeting educational standards. The problem of educational goals is, thus, in the last analysis, a problem in measurement—that is, a problem not only of naming the categories of pupil behavior that are, or ought to be, of interest to society and to the disciplines and to the pupils themselves, but equally importantly, of finding valid methods for ordering the real behavior of real pupils within these categories. There has been at least one attempt on a statewide basis to cope with this problem.

In 1965 the State Board of Education in Pennsylvania tackled the problem of goals in a series of discussions among its own members and with behavioral scientists, professional educators, and the general citizenry. It arrived at tentative agreements on ten broad categories of pupil behavior that should constitute the goals of education.[6] Three of these goals dealt with intellectual processes; the remaining seven focused on attitudes, social outlook, self-esteem, and the like. The goals, having been described in general terms, were then translated into actual measures that school administrators, local school-board members, and PTA's agreed *looked* as though they measured some important aspect of pupil progress. More often than one would have liked, the measures of the noncognitive processes depended on self-report data that in most instances gave only superficial indications of the attitudinal outcomes in which the Board was particularly interested. Nevertheless, so the argument ran, pending the development of ways to observe how youngsters "really" think and feel about themselves and their world, it is better to observe how they *say* they think and feel than to let the "noncognitive" objectives of education go by default.

One such noncognitive goal, Goal 1, was stated and elaborated as follows:

Quality education should help every child acquire the greatest possible understanding of himself and an appreciation of his worthiness as a member of society. Self-understanding should increase as the child matures. That is, he should become increasingly aware of his strengths and weaknesses, his values and interests and aspirations, so that the decisions he makes about his educational and occupational future will be informed, reasonable, and rational. He should be helped to know the strengths in himself that he should exploit and the weaknesses that he should try to overcome or that he must learn to live with.

On the other hand, regardless of the level and pattern of his particular talents, the school experience should be such that it will strengthen, not damage, his self-esteem. The school should be operated in such a way that children at all levels of talent can achieve a growing awareness of their worth as persons in a society that claims to have an equality of concern for all its members.[7]

The effort to get a measure of how well pupils are progressing in this particular goal area resulted in eleven questionnaire items suitable for both elementary- and secondary-school pupils. Two of these items may give some idea of the nature of the attempt to translate the abstract goal into observable pupil responses:

Please think about the Reading test you took as part of these tests. Can you guess the mark you got on that test?
Please circle one of the letters in front of the answer.
   A. My mark was *lower than most* in the class.
   B. My mark was a little lower than the middle of the class.
   C. My mark was *around the middle* of the class.
   D. My mark was between the middle and the top of the class.
   E. My mark was *near the top* of the class.
How are you at *making good friends easily?*
   A. I am better than most others.
   B. I am about the same as most others.
   C. I am not as good as most others.
How sure do you feel your answer is right? (Circle one letter.)
   A. I am sure.
   B. I am not very sure.
   C. I have not thought about it before and I don't know.
Do you think that most people in your classroom would agree with your answer about yourself? (Circle one letter.)
   A. Yes.
   B. No.
   C. I don't know what others in my class think about me.[8]

These questions, and others of a similar nature, were keyed by a group of judges and then the aggregate was scored to provide a measure of attainment with respect to Goal 1. Although this procedure yields admittedly "soft" data, nevertheless, when the average of the scores of a given school suggests that most of the pupils in a school *admit* to a strong feeling of inadequacy or that they lack a sense of self-worth, the outcome is not to be taken lightly.

In the Pennsylvania project, the goals, both cognitive and noncognitive, were regarded as tentative. They have, however, been to some extent authenticated by the fact of their public acceptance, by the fact that it was possible to develop face-valid measures of their attainment, and by a preliminary examination of their construct validity through factorial methods. Thus, they are something more than "pious platitudes." They give schools a reasonably definite picture of what they and their pupils should be working at. This does not mean, of course, that the goals as stated are definitive.

They will become better clarified and better understood as the whole exercise is repeated and as research turns up more and better measures to define them.

III

Having decided on what the goals of education ought to be and on the measures by which standards of attainment can be defined, one requires some sort of scheme for relating the measures to those variables that characterize an educational system, so as to determine how well the system *is* doing for its pupils as compared with what it *could* be doing. For the difference between the *is doing* and the *could be doing* is what I regard as the amount of educational opportunity *not* being provided by a given school or school system.

The scheme I am proposing is summarized in what I call the "student-change model of an educational system" (see Figure I). I do not pretend that this is a model in the strict scientific sense of the word; it is, rather, merely a convenient way of thinking about what measures might be regressed on what other measures to arrive at a reasonable approximation of the amount of educational opportunity a school is providing as compared with other schools in similar circumstances.

The student-change model conceives of four types of factors operating in an educational system: input, educational process, surrounding conditions, and output. The *input* of the system consists of all the measured characteristics of pupils as they enter any particular phase of the educational program at a given time (t_1): their mastery of cognitive skills, their health and physical makeup, their knowledge, attitudes, interests, social behavior, aspirations, and so on. The *output* of the system consists of all the same measured characteristics as they finish any particular phase of the educational program at a later time (t_2). For purposes of illustration, I shall let the period t_1 to t_2 stand for any of four phases of schooling: the primary-school phase, the elementary-school phase, the junior-high phase, and the senior-high-school phase. *Educational process* consists of all the observable activities in a school system that are expressly designed to bring about changes in pupils during any particular phase of the program. These activities may include a wide variety of things—lessons in arithmetic, organized athletics, the way teachers converse with children in the cafeteria, PTA programs, home visits, vocational counseling, and the like. The *surrounding conditions* are all of the influences in the educational environment that are likely to affect for better or worse what teachers teach and pupils learn. There are three kinds of conditions that must be measured and statistically

**Figure I. Factors in the Student-Change Model
of an Educational System**

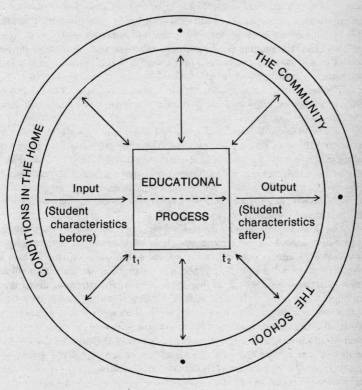

controlled if the student-change model is to make sense: home conditions, school conditions, and community conditions. An important dimension running through all the conditions that surround the educational process is the degree of their modifiability. Are they easy or hard to change? The importance of this dimension will be apparent presently.

In applying the student-change model to the measurement of educational opportunity one may think, provisionally, of four output measures corresponding to four goals of education: (1) self-understanding and self-acceptance, (2) mastery of the basic skills, (3) social and vocational competence, and (4) the student's physical well-being. Since output measures will be needed for each of the four phases of the educational process— primary, elementary, junior high, senior high—the total number of output measures will come to sixteen, i.e., four for each of four phases. To simplify the illustration of how the model works, I shall consider the school as the unit of observation and deal only with the mean attainment of the pupils in any one school as they finish any particular phase of their educational experience.

In addition to measures of output, I shall also require measures of input which I shall define as measures of the same pupils as they enter any phase of the system. These input measures will include the four measures of output from the previous phase. Thus, the output measures at grade 6, for example, become the input measures for the next phase beginning at grade 7. For convenience, I shall again deal only with school means as measures of input at any particular phase.

I will now consider how the student-change model would work for the junior-high-school phase (grades 7–9) in measuring the opportunity a school provides its pupils for attaining Goal 2, the basic skills. The task is to get for each school the best possible estimate of its *mean output* in the basic skills as a basis for classifying the schools in accordance with the level of pupil input and the hard-to-change conditions within which they have had to operate during the three-year period. To do this I use ordinary regression techniques. First, a diverse sample of, say, 1000 junior high schools—or indeed school systems from which the grade 7–9 block can be conveniently extracted—must be found, whether or not the grades are organized and labeled as junior high schools. Then the means of pupil performance at the end of grade 9 are regressed on the means of all four input measures and measures of all the hard-to-change conditions that have obtained over the three-year period (amount of bilingualism in the homes, average wealth of the community served, etc.). In actual practice one would probably want to look at other parameters than just the means so as to take account of certain subgroups in the pupil population (e.g., those with high, average, or low inputs, or those from families with high, average, or low socioeconomic status) in order to see whether a school may be having differential effects on different kinds of pupils. For illustrative purposes, however, I shall omit this complication. In any case, the results of the regression analysis makes it possible to wrap up all the inputs and hard-to-change conditions into a single weighted predictive composite expressed in terms of an estimated mean output for each of the 1000 schools. It should be noted that the estimated mean output is not to be confused with a *standard* of output that the schools in any category ought to reach. The development of standards will be discussed presently.

Given the estimated mean output for each of the 1000 junior high schools, together with their actual outputs, how does one arrive at a measure of the amount of educational opportunity with respect to Goal 2 that each school fails to provide? The chart in Figure II may help with the answer. To simplify the picture, I shall consider only 27 hypothetical schools from among the 1000 schools. Each dot in the chart represents one school. In the case of the hypothetical 27, the schools fall into two groups—Group X and Group Y. If one were to take account of the entire 1000 schools, there would be more than two groups, possibly as many as ten or more. The group in which any school is placed is determined by the number that expresses its estimated output. Thus, the twelve schools in Group X form a category having an estimated output of 4; the thirteen schools in Group Y form another category in which the estimated output is 7.

In Group X there are two schools (Schools A and B) that turn up with an *actual* output of 6.2 and 5.8 respectively. *These two schools set the standard for all the schools in Group X.* Since the average of the two gives an actual output of 6, I take 6 as the standard for Group X. By a similar procedure I arrive at 9 as the standard for the schools in Group Y. The rationale for setting standards in this way is quite straightforward: in a group of schools working with equivalent pupil inputs and in similar hard-to-change conditions (the two together being indicated by the estimated output), every school in the group should be able to do what the most productive schools in that group have done. School C, with an actual output of 2, is 4 points off the standard; the measure of its failure to provide opportunity for its pupils to learn the basic skills is thus—4. School D is a special case. Having an actual output of 1, the measure of its failure is—5. This brings it below the dashed line marked "minimum," which indicates that its output is below the point at which *any* school in any category should be allowed to operate. The establishment of this minimum level for all schools will depend on expert judgment that takes cognizance of the barest essentials that an individual requires to function in American society.

It might be objected by schools falling below the standard set for their category that their inferior position may reflect either unreliability in the measures or failure to take into account special circumstances beyond the schools' control. There has been at least one study with real data from tests of the basic skills which suggests that the low reliability argument may not stand up. In an input-output analysis using several basic skills scores ob-

Figure II. Method of Measuring Educational Opportunity

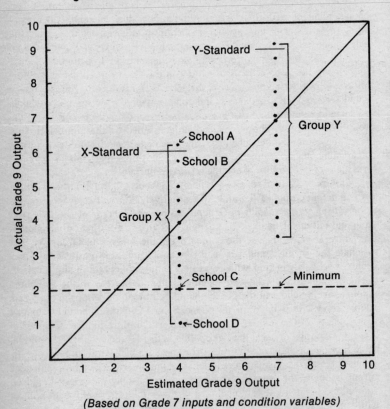

(Based on Grade 7 inputs and condition variables)

tained on pupils first tested at grade 5 and retested at grade 8, Dyer, Linn, and Patton found that correlations between two sets of residuals computed on random halves of the pupils in 64 school districts ranged from .73 to .88.[9] The argument that special circumstances may have been overlooked, however, carries some weight. It is conceivable that School C is as far off the standard as it is because, during the three-year period of junior high, the school was afflicted with an influenza epidemic, a series of teacher strikes, a fire, and various other "Acts of God." One can think of any number of good reasons to explain why School C has not reached the standard and should probably be excused because of its special difficulties. It is, nevertheless, of interest to know how much such "Acts of God" may have deprived the pupils of School C of the educational opportunities afforded the pupils in Schools A and B.

There are two significant advantages in this approach to the measurement of educational opportunity. One is that it can help show the way by which deficient schools may improve themselves. It is at this point that the educational process variables and measures of the more readily modifiable surrounding conditions come into play. Referring again to the chart in Figure II, we may ask a whole series of questions about the characteristics of Schools A and B that may differentiate them from Schools C and D—questions about school organization, courses offered, methods of instruction, teacher attitudes and behavior, special services, community involvement, quality of facilities, level of financial support, and the like. All such matters are the sorts of things that educational systems can presumably *do* something about in order to help their schools move up toward the standard. The difficulty with most surveys of school effectiveness is that they have failed to provide the kind of focus on the most likely specifics for improvement that the framework I am suggesting provides. It is not enough merely to label a school deficient; it is necessary to show what deficiencies might be worth correcting by pointing out what successful schools in similar circumstances are doing.

The second advantage of the approach is that it highlights the fact that educational opportunity is multidimensional. A school system may be succeeding at some points and failing at others. The use of the student-change model in a set of school systems could provide each school in the set with a picture of itself showing where it is doing a good job and where it should be worrying about how to do a better job. The matrix in Figure III illustrates what such a picture might look like. School System S, according to this hypothetical picture, is generally weak in helping its pupils to attain Goal 1, and especially so in its primary grades. It is a pacesetter on Goal 2 except at grades 4–6 where it is 2 points off the standard. Its junior and senior high schools are well below standard in giving students social and vocational competence, but in the early grades it does somewhat better. With respect to Goal 4, however, it is at the top of the heap at all levels.

FIGURE III

Hypothetical Strengths and Deficiencies in School System S

Phases of Education	Educational Goals: 1 *Self-understanding and self-acceptance*	2 *Mastery of the basic skills*	3 *Social and vocational competence*	4 *Student's physical well-being*
Grades 10–12	−2	0	−3	0
Grades 7–9	−1	0	−3	0
Grades 4–6	−3	−2	−2	0
Grades 1–3	−4	0	−1	0

Key
0 = top performance
−1 = one point below standard
−2 = two points below standard, etc.

It is unlikely that in actual practice a chart as neat as the one shown in Figure III could be wholly realized. Nevertheless, the State Education Department of New York has, over the years, developed somewhat similar charts for schools participating in its Quality Measurement Project.[10] So presumably the notion of charting multiple measurements of educational opportunity in some such fashion is practicable.

Anyone who examines closely the method I am proposing for assessing the educational opportunities provided by the schools will find plenty of problems in it, some theoretical or technical and some practical. There is no space here to discuss these problems, but I am convinced that, possibly with some modifications in the basic model, they can be solved, and I am even more deeply convinced that, in view of the desperate need for better information about what American education is doing to and for children, they are very much worth trying to solve.

Notes

1. James S. Coleman *et al. Equality of Educational Opportunity.* Washington, D.C.: U.S. Government Printing Office, 1966, pp. 290–330.
2. Harry S. Ashmore. *The Negro and the Schools.* Chapel Hill: The University of North Carolina Press, 1954, p. 4.

3. *Ibid.*, pp. 109–10.
4. E.g., Herbert J. Kiesling, *High School Size and Cost Factors*, Washington, D.C.: U.S. Office of Education, 1968.
5. It is only fair to say that Coleman recognizes that the "causal sequence" *could* be in the opposite direction (see Coleman, p. 230). My point is that he does not so treat the noncognitive variables in the analysis.
6. Henry S. Dyer, John Hemphill, *et al. A Plan for Evaluating the Quality of Educational Programs in Pennsylvania*. Harrisburg, Pa.: State Board of Education, 1965, Vol. I, pp. 1–4.
7. *Ibid.*, Vol. I, p. 1.
8. *Ibid.*, Vol. III, pp. 259 and 262.
9. Henry S. Dyer, Robert L. Linn, and Michael J. Patton. "A Comparison of Four Methods of Obtaining Discrepancy Measures on Observed and Predicted School System Means on Achievement Tests." *American Educational Research Journal*, Vol. VI, No. 4, November, 1969.
10. William D. Firman. "The Quality Measurement Project in New York State." *Science Education*, Vol. 50, April, 1966, pp. 259–79.

13

Models of the
Educational Process:
A Sociologist's
Perspective

JAMES M. BESHERS

Models of the educational process can guide educational research and policy. To see how, we must consider strategic elements in model-building. Efforts to clarify and to formalize alternative assumptions and descriptions of the nature of the educational process must be continually revised in the light of the pragmatic purposes that the model is to serve. Thus basic theory, research strategy, and policy will influence the model-builder as he proceeds. The model-builder seeks to make clear the reasonable alternatives that may be posed.

Here we describe some models in conventional terms and bring out the strategic elements in the model-building process as well. Let us initially accept a global policy purpose, then refine when necessary. At the outset we assume that we seek to improve the educational system, and that our criteria will be based on characteristics of the students produced by that system. We shall use social theory that bears on the national and regional social context of education as well as social theory that relates characteristics of the family, the community, and the school to the social psychological processes within the school itself.

To make more explicit how we might improve the educational system, we should indicate objectives that the educational system might reasonably pursue. To make evaluation relevant, we must indicate how the attainment of these objectives is revealed in the resulting characteristics of students. To define policy implementation, we must specify the components of the educational system and define the relationships among these components in the system in such a way that a change in these relationships has implications that can be traced out to the resulting characteristics of students.

In order to assure a nontrivial character to our solutions we shall require that they be relevant to the Negro population, but we do not limit the benefits of these solutions to this group alone. This means that we shall carry our analysis through at two levels, Negro students and all students. For specificity we shall consider the Negro case in detail, but we shall use system descriptions of more general applicability.

Let us consider three objectives that might be proposed for educational systems: (1) imparting skills in language and mathematics (to be measured by student performance on tests and in subsequent situations, e.g., performance in higher education); (2) imparting skills in social participation and leadership (to be measured by student performance in subsequent roles, such as nurse, teacher, doctor, foreman, committee member, or social worker, that require effective social participation); and (3) imparting innovative and creative capacities (to be measured by performance in subsequent situations, as well as display or products where possible, such as art work).

One might argue that a single school system should perform well on all three. Are the three, however, fully compatible? If a school system is designed to perform very well on any one, can it also serve the others well? To determine compatibility we might consider each objective separately and design systems accordingly. Then the three resulting systems can be compared.

One could also argue that the performance of a school system with respect to all three objectives is largely conditional on its performance on a prior objective, the inculcation of attitudes of self-confidence and self-respect that enable the student to identify with the objectives of the school. The school system could be designed to perform well in this regard.

Now, however, another difficulty emerges. It is especially clear that self-attitudes are strongly influenced by experiences in the home and in the larger community, and that even within a school there could be several different kinds of influence operating—from teachers, from other students, from administrative procedures, and so on. The components of the educational system must be defined broadly enough to encompass these possibilities. Further, the same argument could be made for the other objectives—the relevant educational processes are far broader than those contained within the school system. With more educational television the processes will be broader yet.

One can accept this argument and then seek to isolate the influences of the school component on the grounds that this component is the only one legitimately subject to the implementation of policy. Such a view often leads to an input-output analysis—one measures students before school experiences begin and after the conclusion of school experiences in hopes of isolating a school effect by subtraction. The weakness of this view is that frequently home and community continue to influence the child during the time that the school influences him; complex and significant interactions among these several influences may be obscured by this kind of input-output analysis.

Let us retain an open mind on the mutual effects of home, peer group, community, and school. There is every reason to suspect that the conflict relations among races, religions, classes, and ethnic groups exercise strong influences over the educational system in any given community, and that the precise nature of these influences varies considerably according to the historical situation in each community.

In general, the personnel and the dominant ideologies of the school system are middle-class in the U.S. today. To some degree (variable) the school system will express a lack of sympathy for a lower class, perhaps a symbolic repudiation, perhaps an open hostility. Sociologists widely hold that, in this situation, lower-class children tend to withdraw from participation in the school system and its goals with the result that their performance on tests is relatively low and perhaps deteriorates until they drop out. To what extent is this generalization contingent upon other special effects, stemming from family situation, peer-group situation, or school?

The relevant home effects are often viewed in three categories: (1) emotional support; (2) attitudes towards the school system; and (3) specific preschool training. The first is viewed as provided best by a stable family with husband and wife present, with lack of stability reducing the capacity of the family to provide support. The second is viewed as ranging from enthusiasm to hostility with a lower-class emphasis on discipline, that is, their children should play it safe and stay out of trouble, an essentially negative attitude. The third is viewed as certain types of experiences provided directly by the parents, such as reading to children, passing on language skills, or as nursery or kindergarten experience.

Thus the relatively poor performance of lower-class children might be charged off to any one or all three of the factors above operating to their detriment. But these three as stated are ambiguous in essential details, and perhaps even mutually contradictory. The first category overlooks the possibility that the parents might dislike the child and optimistically assumes that strong emotions are kindly emotions; further, it leaves clouded the quality of the relationship between husband and wife—perhaps a stable single parent is sometimes better than certain combinations of parents. The second category becomes entangled with the first if the parents are strongly hostile to school; the child might be better off to have a remote relationship with such parents rather than a close one. The third point again overlooks the parents' basic motivation in providing such experiences; if the parents' intention is to manipulate the child so as to satisfy some peculiar ambitions of their own, then the child may permanently reject such experiences (the piano lessons of another day). This list of ambiguities is not exhaustive, but perhaps suggestive.

Next, consider peer-group effects. They are hardly independent from the home effects; indeed, most theorists argue that the strength of peer-group effects is in direct relation to the rejection of the parents, the peer group serving as an alternative source of emotional support and values. The role of the peer group, for instance the corner gang, has been especially emphasized for the second-generation children of immigrant parents. In this instance, the parents are not simply rejected on personal grounds but on the grounds that their way of life is not relevant to the child's needs. Such rejection would also be expected in times of rapid social change, insofar as the parents' values seemed no longer relevant. Whether the peer-group effects are necessarily opposed to scholastic achievement (note fraternities among upper-middle classes); or whether peer-group effects are essentially unrelated to the school system but perhaps create competitive goals; or whether peer-group effects can be used to support the school system is an unclear area of social theory. Likely all are possible, but the conditions under which they might occur are not so easily spelled out. Lower-class children with parents hostile to school might find the peer-group influences relatively favorable to school. Authoritarian parents, however, even those sympathetic to school, might lead to nihilistic peer groups.

Now consider school effects. These are often simplified to teacher effects plus teacher-pupil ratio plus curriculum plus per-pupil school expenditures. That this is a mixed bag should be clear enough. If the teacher effect is negative, then the more pupils per teacher, the more diluted the negative effect. If the manner and method of teaching are not sensitive to the number of pupils per teacher, then the results should be independent of the number. Curriculum effects are hardly independent of teacher effects. School expenditures may have a variety of emphases irrelevant to scholastic achievement, or even possibly opposed to it. It is quite possible that many students would perform better on tests if they had less of teacher rather than more, especially if the dominant teacher effect is annoying or "bugging" the students. Even if we assume that lower-class children are most often found in "poor" school systems, we cannot be certain which aspects of these systems are most detrimental, nor which might, if modified, produce the greatest change.

The pertinent community effect is the proportion of types of people in the vicinity of a particular school, as expressed in the student population and in the range of experiences the children have with various social groups. Here we have apparent "multipliers" in peer-group effects that may be either positive or negative to scholastic objectives. If the students are initially positive in a majority, say over 70 percent, then the minority may be influenced to become more positive, whereas if the students are initially negative in a majority, the minority may become more negative. The multiplier effects might not be so strong, however, if there were sharp social cleavages among the peer-group structure of the students. One must observe the effect of cleavages in the larger community upon the peer-group cleavages, as well as effects within the school, such as tracking and differential participation in extracurricular activities. One might expect that a predominantly lower-class school would have difficulty in maintaining extracurricular activities with a positive outlook on scholastic achievement.

Let us now turn to the additional effect of race upon educational achievement in a traditional sense. Here we can utilize the evidence from the Coleman Report as well as sketch out alternative analyses and research that might better answer our questions. Since the Coleman Report was organized around traditional educational objectives, we shall have to defer the other two until later.

It is not easy to show the additional effects of race upon class in the Coleman Report. This is partly due to features of the Coleman research design and its implementation, especially in the analysis; partly due to features in the original sponsorship, e.g., the emphasis on race; and partly due to sticky technical issues, especially surrounding the quality of the measures of class within the school system and class in the larger community.

Here I shall state by fiat three additional effects of race upon class revealed by the Coleman Report. These are: (1) a strong regional effect, South as compared to other regions, and metropolitan as compared to non-metropolitan; (2) an intensified peer-group "multiplier" as suggested by the effects of integration, for example; and (3) an intensified effect of self-attitudes, especially lack of control over events.

The regional effect is so strong that it must attract our attention first. Not only is Negro achievement everywhere lower than white, ranging from nonmetropolitan South to metropolitan non-South, but the effect increases dramatically with grade level; the Negroes appear to drop back drastically in the higher grades in all regions save the metropolitan Northeast. Two types of explanation can be offered, one based on the psychological character of the Negroes' status in the South, and one based on the notion of urban immigrants from a traditional, or peasant, society. The former suggests that the drift North is associated with a psychological transformation, one of escaping a slave mentality; the latter suggests that the drift North is associated with the acquisition of literacy and therefore of becoming a part of broader trends toward modernization and social change. Both are undoubtedly at work, but there remains the policy question of how best to accelerate the change. Research of two kinds would be helpful in establishing these points: one is to use the experience of migrants as a key to the transformation, and the other is to concentrate on the metropolitan Northeast as the region in which the transformation has gone farthest.

The peer-group "multiplier" effect complicates the regional effect. The multiplier effect should result in a relative drop in achievement in predominantly lower-class schools that in addition are predominantly Negro. Such a "sink" effect, if felt widely, would depress Negro achievement below levels that one might otherwise expect. In particular, this effect should be revealed in large central-city school systems. Would recent Negro migrants reflect a "sink" effect in the same way as longer residents of the urban North?

The peer-group effects are not readily disentangled unless the social psychology of the classroom can be related to the community context of the school. Negro subcommunities within large central cities vary widely; the role of a classroom teacher is not easily measured in this context; the extent to which street gangs interpenetrate the peer-group structure of the school system is not clear. The social-psychological significance of racial segregation for the lower classes is a very subtle issue, especially in its implications for peer-group dynamics.

Now let us turn to self-attitudes. To a degree, they have been discussed in the other two effects above. In effect, alternative views have been offered: one, that demoralization and self-hatred are lessened by the drift north; the other, that demoralization and self-hatred are increased by sink effects of the urban ghetto. One reconciliation of these views might be the argument that the first positive effects of escape from the South are followed by a period of testing. Those Negroes who establish themselves in the job and housing markets maintain a middle-class identification that carries them along on conventional lines of social mobility, and those who fail may ultimately repudiate such middle-class aspirations (perhaps to rationalize their situation), leading to a widening cleavage within the Negro community itself. Here we have to distinguish demoralization and apathy as a response from self-hatred and repudiation as a response, for the latter could lead to goal substitution and an active response of the type that we suspect in the peer-group case whereas the former is more often associated with withdrawal from groups of any kind.

Here again we can make little headway without a full appreciation of the social psychology of the classroom in the context of the larger community. From the discussion above the special study of the metropolitan Northeast might be productive, including study of the migrants into the region. The distinction between apathy and repudiation must be maintained in the measurements of personality and self-attitude; the meaningful comparative measures are within the same social-psychological system, e.g., the classroom, and in the context of the group structure of that system.

From the above discussion we see that reanalysis of the Coleman data and the design of future studies could well be influenced by a desire to reconstruct the social-psychological dynamics and climate of the school as seen in the context of community characteristics. Thus a smaller sample with more intensive study might be valuable, especially if follow-up measures and alternative policies can be included in the study design.

Let us recapitulate where we stand. We have discussed class and race effects on students' progress towards conventional educational goals. Two points have been emphasized. First, a very complex system of components is at work in the lower-class situation, especially due to the presence of negative effects within social relationships. Second, many of the issues turn on the formation of negative self-attitudes in the social-psychological context of home, peer group, and school; factors in the formation of these attitudes are poorly understood; how the school might change these attitudes or learn to work more constructively with them is barely suggested.

Policy issues might influence the tactics appropriate for a school. Previously two nontraditional educational objectives were posed as alternative goals for overall educational systems. Let us consider the significance of these goals for the design of the schools themselves. In particular, let us concentrate on the role of the teacher in relation to the students' activities.

Even with respect to traditional objectives it is possible that too much teacher is present, especially if teaching methods are insensitive to the gains in opportunity presented by small classes; in general, if the teachers' role is defined as authoritarian, then the students may best be served by a highly impersonal relationship—television, teaching machines, and large lectures.

Now consider relevant social roles as the objective of education. Here we might expect the use of role-playing techniques to extend insight into the relations between oneself and others, and we might expect activities and experiences of leadership in a variety of tasks, where the tasks should be as realistic as possible. Much of this work might best be done in rather small groups, with the teacher's participation always subtle, and perhaps tending to withdraw. The conventional classroom is oriented to the wrong size of group and to inappropriate activities. It is an open question whether conventional teacher training can support this kind of teaching. Possibly retraining of present teachers is a proper initial goal.

To have any lasting merit such teaching must face up to the real issues in the community that dominate the lives of the students, but to do so is to risk rather exciting situations that are typically deplored by the older and wiser members of the community. Two tactics are obvious, to extend the drama program to incorporate some of the more exciting aspects, and to shorten the conventional school day to allow optional participation in a variety of community-related activities, perhaps sponsored by civic organizations or professional artists' organizations. Possibly more imaginative use of television could help here; children could produce programs for other children, and wider community involvement could be sought, e.g., the parents might be more effectively involved. In general, blurring the boundaries between the classroom and the community might make more possible the kind of teaching and therefore the kind of objective that we advocate here.

Now consider creative or innovative persons as the objective of education. Here we might expect the teacher to get out of the picture after providing supplies and equipment, with an absolute minimum of suggestion and relatively subtle indication of the work of others that might provide comparisons. Most teachers could not leave the student alone. They are accustomed to the busyness and the routine in the teaching situation as providing rituals throughout the day; to them teaching method is a ritual. Thus the whole idea that they might do a better job by doing less is not conceivable, especially if doing less is a subtle activity that requires detailed observation of the work of each student as an individual.

These new objectives would place great strain on teachers, facilities, and equipment. Quite novel administrative skills would be required to implement either one. Would it be possible to implement all three in one educational system?

We return now to the question of the compatibility of these three objectives within a single educational system. The skills of the administrators and the teachers would clearly be a major limiting factor. The major obstacle, however, would seem to be the way in which traditional educational objectives were sought. If the spirit of achieving traditional goals were contrary to the spirit of the others, and if in particular the notion of evaluation (say, grading) were organized in such a way as to downgrade the others, then there would be no gains along the lines of the other two objectives discussed above, or of many other worthy objectives that one might pose.

Therefore we return to the previous suggestion that healthy self-attitudes (not platitudes) be viewed as a prior objective to the attainment of other objectives. If the traditional objectives were restructured in this way, possibly other objectives would also be compatible. This view, however, must be tempered by the complexities of the community context, especially in terms of class and of race. Self-hatred and negative multipliers are not likely to be diminished by activities in the school alone. Broader programs of a supportive character must reach out to involve the larger community, to gain its recognition of these goals, to involve parents and others directly in the educational process.

Now let us face up to model-building issues at a more technical level. A verbal sketch has covered many issues of system components, system interrelation, and of system outputs. It is clear, however, that these issues should be expressed in a less diffuse way, in particular in a way that lends itself to computer representation. The alternative assumptions that generate alternative models must become more clear. The models must serve to guide research design and research analysis in a more explicit way; and the models must serve as policy instruments.

My own view of the general system representation for such social systems is that of a nonstationary stochastic process, a probabilistic model that generates a time series. The heart of the problem is defining the rules (or transformations) that update the probabilities; the probabilities themselves are then applied to a description of the population and update that description. In effect, this is a population projection, where the probabilities are not fixed, but are subject to change by quite complicated functions. My previous work is described in a number of sources. (See especially Beshers and Reiter, "Social Status and Social Change," in *Behavioral Science*, Vol. 8, No. 1, January, 1963; and two papers in Beshers [ed.], "The Social Theorist" and "Substantive Issues in Models of Large Scale Social Systems," in *Computer Methods in the Analysis of Large Scale Social Systems*, revised edition, Cambridge, Mass.: MIT Press, 1968.)

It is clear that some of the relevant descriptions of the population may include psychological characteristics of the individual, as well as the relation of the individual to groups. The updating transformations may be selected to represent learning, or other psychological processes. There are three very subtle issues that arise in defining the relevant description of the population (states of the system) and in defining the updating transformations.

First is the problem of negative relations, such as hatred, that we may represent with minus signs. The solutions for lower classes or for Negroes clearly involve quite complex negative factors. There is very little guidance in previous social theory or in previous model-building for this task. Some original work at an abstract level may be necessary before this aspect of the work can proceed.

The second problem is the definition of output characteristics in terms of which to measure the improvement of the system and to evaluate the system. Suppose the definition of improvement is that each student gets better, rather than the class average. Then suppose the standards of getting better are multidimensional, so a student might be better in some ways and worse in others. Finally, suppose that progress is not defined as a single path through the multidimensional standards, but is defined as a variety of paths, with different paths relevant for different students. These differing trajectories and targets will place great strains on the model-builder.

Third, the model-builder must retain a reasonable relationship between the psychological processes and the social context, including the continued response of the school system to effects from the home and the community. Thus the initial characteristics cannot simply be taken as those at age five or six with all other parameters of change residing in the school system; other dynamic factors enter in, including some apparently idiosyncratic to the larger historical context—wars and depressions, for example.

Let me provide a highly simplified example of such a model, then indicate how to extend it to the issues discussed above. We take as our problem the extent to which the child's feelings of control over environment can be enhanced as he passes through the school system. We assume that increased feelings of self-control will lead to other improvements in the educational achievement of the students individually as well as in the educational potential of the school itself as a social environment. Our key theoretical parameters will represent the effects of the students upon each other, so-called peer-group pressures. We shall represent the school and community effects as parameters to be empirically estimated.

We shall consider a single school. Within it we consider one group of students from 1st to 12th grade (ignoring migration, dropouts, and students held back). The students, at any year, may be classified into four states representing the combinations of two social classes (say middle and lower) by two psychological states (say control of environment and no control of environment). We wish to study the change in feelings of control as children pass through the school system.

Thus for each grade we have a distribution vector with four elements, say

$$m(T) = (m_1(T), m_2(T), m_3(T), m_4(T)),$$

where:

state 1 $\equiv$ Middle Class $\wedge$ Control,
state 2 $\equiv$ Middle Class $\wedge$ No Control,
state 3 $\equiv$ Lower Class $\wedge$ Control,
state 4 $\equiv$ Lower Class $\wedge$ No Control,

and T runs from 1, 2, . . . , 12.

We also have a transition matrix $P(T)$, but we shall assume no social mobility (since it depends on father's status).

		Middle Class		Lower Class	
		Control	No Control	Control	No Control
Middle	Control	P_{11}	P_{12}	0	0
Class	No Control	P_{21}	P_{22}	0	0
$P(T) =$					
Lower	Control	0	0	P_{33}	P_{34}
Class	No Control	0	0	P_{43}	P_{44}

Suppose we assume no segregation within grade in school, i.e., equal probabilities of contact among students in different states. Then we can simplify our representation of peer-group pressures.

To define the updating equations for the (P_{ij}) values, consider: Two "sink" parameters based on peer-group effects:

$$d_1 = \frac{m_3 + m_4}{m.}$$

(the proportion lower-class) Where

$$m. = \sum_{i=1}^{4} m_i$$

$$d_2(T) = \frac{m_2 + m_4}{m}$$

(the proportion with no sense of control).

These parameters represent alternative ways in which gain or loss of control may occur.

Then some simple updating equations are:

$$\begin{cases} P_{12}(T+1) = a_{12} + b_{12} \cdot d_1 + c_{12} \cdot d_2(T) \\ P_{21}(T+1) = a_{21} + b_{21} / d_1 + c_{21} / d_2(T) \\ P_{34}(T+1) = a_{34} + b_{34} \cdot d_1 + c_{34} \cdot d_2(T) \\ P_{43}(T+1) = a_{43} + b_{43} / d_1 + c_{43} / d_2(T) \end{cases}$$

Net loss of control results from large d_1 and $d_2(T)$, while net gain of control results from small d_1 and $d_2(T)$.

These equations thus depend upon two parameters that represent "environmental" effects: one of them, d_1, is independent of time under the present restrictive assumptions, while the other, $d_2(T)$, depends upon the initial distributions and values of the constants (if you like, you may view $d_2(T)$ as a feedback parameter).

The system then follows a time path defined by the two equations:

$$(1) \quad m(2) = m(1) P(1)$$
$$(2a) \quad P(2) = f(d_1, d_2(2)) \text{ or}$$
$$(2b) \quad P(2) = f(d_1, d_2(1))$$

If (2a) is used, then both $m(1)$ and $P(1)$ must have initial values, while if (2b) is used then $P(1)$ can be calculated from it.

The substance of these models is that gain or loss of control depends on the linear constants A_{ij}, b_{ij}, and C_{ij}, and upon the initial distributions and probabilities. If the empirical adequacy of this model could be established, then we could predict net gains or losses of control according to the estimates of these parameters.

To indicate methods of solution let us consider even simpler equations:

$$\begin{cases} P_{12} = P_{34} = d_1 \\ P_{21} = P_{43} = 1 - d_1 \end{cases}$$

or

$$\begin{cases} P_{12}(T) = P_{34}(T) = d_2(T) \\ P_{21}(T) = P_{43}(T) = 1 - d_2(T) \end{cases}$$

The first case reduces to a stationary process with the fixed vector $(1 - d_1, d_1, 1 - d_1, d_1)$ starting in equilibrium.

The second case is not so simple. If $P(1)$ is the identity matrix and if $d_2(1) = 0$, then

$$P(2) = \begin{pmatrix} 1 & 0 & 0 & 0 \\ 1 & 0 & 0 & 0 \\ 0 & 0 & 1 & 0 \\ 0 & 0 & 1 & 0 \end{pmatrix} = P(T) \text{ for } T > 1$$

This is an optimistic situation. If $P(1)$ is the identity matrix and $d_2(1) = \frac{1}{2}$, then

$$P(2) = \begin{pmatrix} \frac{1}{2} & \frac{1}{2} & 0 & 0 \\ \frac{1}{2} & \frac{1}{2} & 0 & 0 \\ 0 & 0 & \frac{1}{2} & \frac{1}{2} \\ 0 & 0 & \frac{1}{2} & \frac{1}{2} \end{pmatrix} = P(T)$$

for $T > 1$ and

$$m(T = 1) = \left(\frac{m_1 + m_2}{2}, \frac{m_1 + m_2}{2}, \frac{m_3 + m_4}{2}, \frac{m_3 + m_4}{2} \right)$$

Other cases can be examined. The point here is that such systems can be solved.

In using these models we may engage in an interplay of theory and research. On the basis of our prior knowledge we may choose several alternative equations to represent several types of school systems. Thus the constants A_{ij}, b_{ij}, and C_{ij} might be given somewhat extreme values in order to bring out the contrast of several situations. Then we may solve these equations to obtain their consequences through the twelve years of school.

The solutions may be used to compare schools on "expected" outputs, given our prior knowledge. If we have appropriate data available we may compare them with our theoretical calculations and then choose to modify our equations. We might go through several cycles of recalculation in a manner analogous to Bayesian statistical procedures.

Our study of the theoretical calculations with the model might also be guided by a "sensitivity" perspective. The alternative equations might be selected to represent alternative policies. Then we would like to determine the amount of change—that is, amount of increase in feelings of control over environment—that is associated with each policy. Perhaps we could pinpoint the crucial differences among alternative policies.

With either a "Bayesian" perspective or a "sensitivity" perspective we might be able to identify and pinpoint our needs for further empirical information. Thus these models can be used to guide research design.

Let us now consider ways in which to relax the restrictive assumptions. One might wish to introduce family effects and school effects as exogenous influences upon these equations. Here one must decide whether the equations have the same form at all levels of family and school effects (e.g., can the constants be expressed as functions of family effects and/or school effects). The school effects might influence segregation within schools, and thus bias the peer-group effects insofar as they depend upon probabilities of contact.

If we consider a set of schools and allow migration among them, then we can treat our "sink" parameters as variables in the larger systems. Thus, various policies of mixing students might be examined in the light of particular equations.

We could augment the set of states by race. Then we must decide how to represent the effects of integration or of ghetto schools upon the transitions among psychological states. This could be done by introducing further environmental parameters, but we have a further problem. Do the environmental effects depend upon the rate of change, say $[m(T + 1) - m(T)]$? Also, is there a positive effect associated with long stay in integrated schools and long stay in segregated schools, but not with changes resulting from a particular student going from one kind of school to another, or aggregated changes to a particular school influencing students who remain in that school?

Finally, we may augment the set of states with output variables, such as test scores or grades. Then we would have to decide how the psychological states relate to the output variables. In particular, we would have to decide whether the relation between the psychological states and the output states was independent of the race and class states. If they are not independent, then we must specify the form of the dependence. Much of the earlier discussion in this paper was addressed to the possibility that peer-group effects might yield a relation such that (relatively) optimistic lower-class children might reject or ignore the goals of the school, and therefore perform poorly on these output variables.

It should be clear that we have relaxed assumptions in order to become more relevant to policy.

Let me conclude by reiterating my general argument. The strategy of model construction is to state the reasonable alternatives in such a way that the implications of these alternatives are clarified. In particular, the clarification should extend to the interpretation of new information, e.g., new research, and the clarification should aid in the framing and the resolution of policy questions.

14

The Two–Year Compensatory Program of the College of Basic Studies: Implications of a Successful Model*

GENE M. SMITH

Coleman *et al.* (1966) report that about 85 percent of 12th-grade Negroes are below the white average in academic achievement (p. 219). Automatically, this precludes admission of most Negroes to most colleges. Of course, the ultimate aim is to remove this gap before it develops. But what can be done to relieve this inequity for twelfth graders who find themselves excluded? How can current resources be redirected to help such students catch up?

The present section discusses an ongoing program, the College of Basic Studies (CBS) of Boston University, which offers an educational model relevant to the problem just posed. CBS admits marginal students and presents them with a unique academic experience which appears surprisingly successful in salvaging their academic careers.

CBS admits applicants who are denied admission into four-year programs at Boston University because of poor high-school records, shortages in prerequisites, low academic aptitude scores, or some combination. Despite initially poor academic promise, approximately 36 percent of the entering students complete the two-year program at CBS and then transfer, with full status as juniors, into four-year programs at Boston University. An additional 28 percent transfer to other universities offering baccalaure-

* Supported in part by a grant from the Esso Education Foundation, in part by the Spaulding-Potter Charitable Trusts, and in part by Public Health Service Grant GM–15904.

ate programs. The significance of the 64 percent transfer figure at CBS is seen when compared with Medsker's finding of a 33 percent transfer rate for a national sample ($N = 17,627$) of students in two-year collegiate programs (Medsker, 1960).

More importantly, Medsker found that only 40 percent of transferees from two-year programs throughout the nation received baccalaureate degrees; whereas, by contrast, 84 percent of CBS transferees within Boston University receive the baccalaureate degree. These and other indications of the success of the CBS plan are discussed in further detail below.

Features of the CBS Plan

The CBS plan, which began in 1952, employs team teaching, a core curriculum, extensive guidance counseling, and a highly student-centered orientation. These four features combine to produce a unique administrative and social structure designed to strengthen the motivation of teachers as well as pupils and to increase the per-hour efficiency of teacher-pupil contact. The CBS plan is similar, both philosophically and structurally, to more recent plans designated variously as "cluster colleges," "living-learning" units, and "residence college" programs (Woodring, 1967).

An entering class of approximately 550 freshmen is divided into twenty sections of 25–30 students each, four sections of which are assigned to a team of five instructors who represent the five divisions which make up the core curriculum of the College—Humanities, Science, Social Science, Rhetoric (Communications), and Psychology and Guidance. The team, which has full responsibility for the academic education of 100–120 students, meets regularly in formal and informal sessions, reviewing common concerns and problems, teaching techniques, and, above all, their knowledge of the students assigned to them.

The team system attempts to involve a small group of faculty more completely and more intimately in the education of their students than more traditional systems permit. It is as though the College were divided into a number of small colleges, each with a faculty of five. Except for the guidance member, who is assigned an individual office to protect a formal counselor-counselee relationship, the instructors forming a team share a common office suite. The resulting high frequency of informal interaction among team members is intended to promote interchange of ideas regarding methods of instruction, content and integration of curriculum, transdepartmental projects, and the educational progress and problems of individual students.

Development and implementation of the CBS plan was based on three assumptions: (1) Many rejected applicants to four-year programs at Boston University *do* have the potential to complete such programs, and this potential can be realized if appropriate educational advantages are made available. (2) Team teaching, a core curriculum, extensive guidance counseling, and a highly student-centered orientation can provide such "appropriate educational advantages." (3) Student enthusiasm, interest, and motivation to learn are stimulated by opportunity for active student participation in group discussions and tutorial sessions, and by sincere faculty interest in each student's individual needs, scholastic effort, and academic achievement.

Evidence of Success of the CBS Plan

As already stated, 64 percent of the students admitted to CBS transfer to four-year programs and 84 percent of those who transfer within Boston University receive their baccalaureate degree. (Currently we do not know the corresponding percentage for students who transfer *outside* of Boston University but data on this question are now being collected.) These conclusions are based on data collected from students of three CBS classes: those who completed the program in 1962, 1963, and 1964. (See Table 1.)

TABLE 1

Follow-Up Data on Three Classes of CBS Students ($N = 1656$)

Year of Graduation	Entering Freshmen	Transfers Outside BU	Transfers Within BU	Transfers Within BU Getting B.A. Degree
1962	577	186 (32%)	211 (37%)	177 (84%)
1963	566	155 (27%)	203 (36%)	175 (86%)
1964	513	128 (25%)	180 (35%)	147 (82%)

For one class of CBS students, success of the plan has been evaluated in terms of scores on standardized tests of academic achievement. The Graduate Record Examinations tests of Achievement (hereafter abbreviated GRE) in the areas of Social Science, Humanities, and Natural Science were administered to students at CBS at the beginning of the freshman year (October, 1958) and again at the end of the sophomore year (April, 1960). Parallel forms were used. Each student's growth score on a particular test was obtained by subtracting his pre-score from his post-score.

Table 2 indicates that, as first semester freshmen, the members of the class of 1960 at CBS were below the national freshman average on the GRE, but that as second semester sophomores, they were above the national sophomore average. Table 2 also shows that the change in status of the CBS students, relative to the national norms, was not due to a difference between

TABLE 2

Graduate Record Examination Area Test Data for the College
of Basic Studies Class of 1960

	All Entering Freshmen			"Surviving" Freshmen			Sophomores		
	N	Raw Score	Per-centile*	N	Raw Score	Per-centile	N	Raw Score	Per-centile
S.S.	603	308	37	252	314	40	289	432	65
Hum.	602	348	27	252	356	31	293	461	68
N.S.	597	398	47	252	402	50	292	486	62

* Percentile scores are based on norms supplied by Educational Testing Service, Princeton, New Jersey. Norms are based on scores of 2,591 freshmen and 5,611 sophomores.
S.S. = Social Science
Hum. = Humanities
N.S. = Natural Science

TABLE 3

Comparison of CBS "Growth" Data with Reported "Growth" of 996 Students
Studied by Educational Testing Service GRE Area Tests

	Norm Group Freshman*		CBS Freshman†		Norm Group Sophomore*		CBS Sophomore†		"Growth" Norm Group*	"Growth" CBS Group†
	Mean	S.D.	Mean	S.D.	Mean	S.D.	Mean	S.D.		
S.S.	350	80	314	64	410	92	431	73	60	117
Hum.	395	67	356	55	456	83	459	68	61	103
N.S.	401	70	402	48	457	75	487	63	56	85

All mean differences between CBS growth and norm group growth were statistically significant at the 0.001 level.
* 996 students, taking area examinations as freshmen and as sophomores reported by G. U. Lannholm and B. Pitcher (1957).
† 252 College of Basic Studies students taking area examinations as freshmen and as sophomores.
S.S. = Social Science
Hum. = Humanities
N.S. = Natural Science

mean GRE scores of freshmen who subsequently "survived" the two-year program at CBS and mean scores of the entire entering freshman class.

Table 3 provides a different standard for evaluating the GRE growth scores. The data reported there show that the CBS growth scores are from $1\frac{1}{2}$ to 2 times as great as those found with 996 college students studied by Lannholm and Pitcher. All mean growth scores in the CBS sample are significantly greater ($p < 0.001$) than the mean growth scores of the Lannholm and Pitcher sample. Concerning their sample, Lannholm and Pitcher (1957) say:

. . . scholastic ability of the combined groups from these three colleges was similar to that of the typical four-year college in the 1952 norms for the American Council on Education Psychological Examination.

We considered the possibility that the greater-than-average growth of the CBS students might be due to the fact that their low pre-scores gave them greater-than-average "room to grow"; however, that interpretation was rejected because the correlations between pre-scores and growth scores were found to be very low for all three areas tested. The correlation coefficients were $+ 12$, $- .04$, and $- .09$.

Efficiency of the CBS Plan

Because of the combined use of team teaching and a core curriculum, most of a student's contact with the CBS faculty is with *his* five instructors. He may have only a nodding acquaintance with most other faculty members, but he knows *his* five and they know him. It is this feature of the program that provides the unusual combination of economy of teaching and extensive individual student attention. Upon first learning of the CBS plan, many educators mistakenly infer that this plan requires a large investment of faculty time per student taught. As just stated, this is not the case. The student-faculty ratio at CBS is about twenty to one. This point is emphasized because its recognition is crucial for understanding the *practical* value of the CBS plan. Indeed, as an educational model, perhaps the most provocative aspect of the CBS plan is that it provides increased student-faculty contact by modifying the use of currently available resources rather than by allocating new resources. Thus it generates increased educational excellence without increasing the cost of education.

Implications for Education

The success of the CBS plan has implications for educational theory and practice which go beyond the specific problem of providing compensatory education for marginal high-school seniors desiring a college education. New educational models are needed to permit the ever-increasing population of college students to be served without sacrificing the benefits of frequent face-to-face interaction between student and instructor. CBS offers such a model.

There is a growing awareness that the impersonal atmosphere of the large university has adverse effects on student morale and motivation (Katz, 1962; Katz and Sanford, 1962; Riesman and Jencks, 1962; Kerr, 1963; Kauffman, 1966). Furthermore, with anticipated growth in the future college population, the problem of "academic anonymity" and lack of meaningful student-faculty interaction is likely to grow worse (Wilson, 1966; Newcomb, 1966). As emphasized by Kerr (1963), we need ". . . to make the university seem smaller, even as it grows larger." The recent advent of "cluster college plans" and "living-learning" units (see Stickler, 1964, and Woodring, 1967) seems directed precisely at the accomplishment of such a change, and the success of the CBS program, documented here, augurs well for the success of similar efforts elsewhere.

References

Coleman, J. S., Campbell, E. Q., Hobson, C. J., McPartland, J., Mood, A. M., Weinfeld, F. D., and York, R. L. *Equality of Educational Opportunity.* Washington, D.C.: U.S. Department of Health, Education, and Welfare, U.S. Government Printing Office, 1966.

Katz, Joseph. "Personality and Interpersonal Relations in the College Classroom," in *The American College: A Psychological and Social Interpretation of Higher Learning*, edited by Nevitt Sanford. New York: John Wiley and Sons, 1962, pp. 365–95.

Katz, Joseph, and Sanford, Nevitt. "The Curriculum in the Perspective of the Theory of Personality Development," in *The American College: A Psychological and Social Interpretation of Higher Learning*, edited by Nevitt Sanford. New York: John Wiley and Sons, 1962, pp. 418–44.

Kauffman, Joseph F. "The Student in Higher Education," in *The College and the Student*, edited by Lawrence E. Dennis and Joseph F. Kauffman. Washington, D.C.: American Council on Education, 1966, pp. 141–62.

Kerr, Clark. *The Uses of the University.* Cambridge, Mass.: Harvard University Press, 1963.

Lannholm, G. U., and Pitcher, B. *Achievement in Three Broad Areas of Study During the First Two Years of College.* Educational Testing Service Report presented to American Educational Research Association Convention, Atlantic City, N.J., February 20, 1957. Princeton, N.J.: Educational Testing Service.

Medsker, L. L. *The Junior College: Progress and Prospect.* New York: McGraw-Hill, 1960.

Newcomb, Theodore M. "Research on Student Characteristics: Current Approaches," in *The College and the Student*, edited by Lawrence E. Dennis and Joseph F. Kauffman. Washington, D.C.: American Council on Education, 1966, pp. 101–16.

Riesman, David, and Jencks, Christopher. "The Viability of the American College," in *The American College: A Psychological and Social Interpretation of Higher Learning*, edited by Nevitt Sanford. New York: John Wiley and Sons, 1962, pp. 74–192.

Stickler, W. Hugh. *Experimental Colleges: Their Role in American Higher Education.* Tallahassee: Florida State University, 1964.

Wilson, Logan. "Is the Student Becoming the 'Forgotten Man'?" in *The College and the Student*, edited by Lawrence E. Dennis and Joseph F. Kauffman. Washington, D.C.: American Council on Education, 1966, pp. 59–66.

Woodring, Paul. "The Idea of Cluster Colleges," *Saturday Review*, January 21, 1967, p. 64 ff.

Index

Ability, innate, 123, 129–130, 137, 155, 172, 182, 467, 471; and nonenrollment, 134; and student output, 176; and ethnic differences, 248

Ability grouping, 54, 96–97, 345; at first-grade level, 263; and social class, 264; and racial composition, 352–354. *See also* Tracking

Accreditation, school, 10; as crude index of expenditures, 91–92; in principal's questionnaire, 451–452

Achievement, academic, 6–7, 70–71, 86–88, 104–105, 148, 182; and facilities, 8, 34, 36, 37, 93–94, 150, 157, 160, 168, 176, 178–179, 281–297; ethnic, racial, and regional groups, 14–15, 35, 168, 247; and variation of resources, 15–16, 247–249, 313; and social composition, 17–20, 37, 39, 154; and social class, 22–24, 248, 262–264, 532–534; and socioeconomic status, 22–24, 37, 39, 70–71, 87–88, 105, 226, 399–400; and sense of control of environment, 25–27,

231, 398, 517; EEOR findings, 27, 29, 31, 33; and integration, 36, 42–43, 50–51, 197–199; and racial composition, 41, 43, 70, 71, 82–84, 86–88, 344–359; and interracial climate, 41, 45, 343, 359–363; and expenditures, 42, 90–92, 281, 285, 291–292; of similar students under different policies or resources, 82, 129–130; and variation in school characteristics, 82–84; and family background, 86–88, 125–126, 154, 155, 168–228, 230, 232, 249, 254–269; and regional and community characteristics, 88–90, 196–212, 214–215, 221, 224; and PTA attendance, 89–90; and pupil-teacher ratio, 91, 94, 97, 154, 282, 283; and pre-schooling, 92–93; and students' access to books, 94–96, 254–255, 265–266, 322, 346; and curriculum, 96–97, 157, 160, 230, 233, 234, 281–297, 300, 352–353, 412–413; and personnel, 97–99, 168; and teacher selection devices, 99–100; and teacher background and train-

Achievement (*continued*)

ing, 100–102; and teacher professional standing, 102–103; and teacher morale, 103–104; and inputs, 116, 150–153; conceptual model, 122–124; statistical model, 124–126; and innate ability, 129–130; and nonenrollment, 134; and no-school-effect finding of Report, 134, 168, 177, 239; among culturally deprived, 138–139; and nonschool programs, 139; and class size, 150; and school effects, 153–163, 168–228, 464–470, 479–480, 484; and teachers, 154, 157–158, 160, 162, 165, 212, 231, 234, 298–311, 412; and background factors, 155–158, 160–162, 174, 249, 254–269, 408, 464–470; and facility and staff variance, 174; elementary school, 177–178; and students' family structure, 204, 212, 214, 218, 223, 254, 262, 265, 268–269; prediction of, 206, 211–221, 235–236; and percent black, 217; and Report's errors in estimating school-to-school differences, 231; and schoolwide resources, 241, 247–254; unmeasured factors influencing, 248; individual background, and school-to-school differences in, 255–259; influence of background on within-school differences, 259–260; and parents' expectations, 260–261; influence of student-body characteristics on, 269–281, 300–302, 407–408; and teacher localism, 299,

304, 308–309; and teacher attitudes, 400–402; and peer-rating technique, 402–403; and questionnaire response rate, 499–501; and effect of race upon class, 532–533. *See also* Verbal ability

Achievement tests, 96, 316; black-white differences in score, 196; and racial composition of school, 197–202; class differences in scoring, 236–237; in EEOS battery, 471; "face validity" of, 471–473; as measure of educational opportunity, 515

Adjustment, student, 170

Administrators, school, 62, 410–411, 535

Absenteeism: teacher, 104, 387; pupil, 387

Adult education, 373

Advisory Committee on Government Programs in the Behavioral Sciences, National Research Council, 42

Aid, federal and state, 514; to education, 150; to disadvantaged, 228

Alabama, 60

Alexander v. Holmes County Board of Education, 60

Ambition, 26. *See also* Motivation

American Academy of Arts and Sciences, 377

Analysis, 63, 163–165, 169, 384–385, 393–406; need for weighting, 182–183; and interlocking studies, 405, 417. *See also* Reanalyses

Ann Arbor, 366

Aptitude tests, 471. *See also* Testing

Arithmetic, *see* Mathematics

Arkansas, 60

Armed Forces Qualification Test (AFQT), 477, 478

Armor, David J., 8n, 24, 38, 39, 40, 42, 43

Army General Classification Test (AGCT), 477

Art teachers, 98

Aspirations, 278, 364–365, 366; career, 26, 170; parents', 399–400. *See also* Goals; Motivation

Assignment, school, 232, 249, 255, 262–265, 281, 298, 300–302, 314; on basis of achievement, 274; and facilities-achievement relationship, 283, 286, 297; and curriculum characteristics, 292; and classroom racial composition, 352–359

Atkinson, J. W., 365

Atkinson, Richard C., 415–418

Attainment, and test scores, 476–478

Attendance, 162n, 270, 274, 278, 323, 347, 387, 395, 408; compulsory, 171, 177; and black achievement, 279

Attention, span of, 54

Attitudes: student, 25–26, 181, 396; regional differences in, 88; family, 118, 125, 180, 399–400, 466; teacher, 153, 179–180, 222, 400–402; toward achievement, 155, 231; imparted by school, 171; and academic orientation, 172–173; in Coleman's analysis, 176, 396–398; of black family toward education, 181; and desegregation, 363–366; analysis of, 396–397; racial, 402–403; community, 410; and model of educational process, 530

Austen, Mary C., 264

Authority structure, of schools, 371

Background factors, 86–88, 125–128, 131, 234–238, 241, 271, 300, 311–312, 321–322, 394, 410; and achievement, 155–158, 160–162, 174, 249, 254–269, 408, 464–470; Coleman quoted on, 234–235; apparent effects of, 239; and schoolwide characteristics, 241, 247–254, 257, 489; and school-to-school differences, 255–259; and within-school differences, 259–260; and reading readiness, 264; and differential sensitivity hypothesis, 273; reliability of students' reports about, 458–461; reliability of group mean for measures of, 461–462; assessment of variations in, 462–464; and school resources, 483. *See also* Family

Baltimore, 89

Basic skills, 520, 522

Bayesian statistical procedures, 539

Beecher, Henry K., 382

Behavioral and Social Science Survey, National Academy of Sciences, 42

Benson, Viola E., 477

Bereiter, C., 413

Beshers, James M., 536

Beta weight, 242–246

Bias, 13, 70; and omission of measure of initial endowments, 129; and relative measurement errors, 130–131; and observational study, 404; due to nonresponse to survey, 481

Birthrate, 46

Bissell, Joan, 264

Black power, 157

Blacks, *see* Negroes

Books, access to, 71, 77, 94–96; as
    response to nonachievement,
    95; in home, 95, 254–255, 322,
    346; and family structure, 265–
    266. *See also* Textbooks

Border states, 62

Boston, 274, 482, 483, 484

Boston University, *see* College of
    Basic Studies, Boston Univer-
    sity

Boulding, Kenneth, 3, 53

Bowles, Samuel, 33, 38, 147n, 153n,
    161, 232, 437n, 481

Box, George, 372

Bronfenbrenner, Urie, 57

Brookover, Wilbur B., 264, 296

Brooks, Harvey, 377

Brown, Dr. Nathan, 27

*Brown v. Board of Education of To-
    peka,* 30, 31, 70, 344

Buffalo, 485

Buildings, school, 27, 514. *See also*
    Facilities

Bundy, McGeorge, 377

Bureau of the Census, U.S., 374

Burkhead, J., 394–395, 483

Burt, Sir Cyril, 17, 462

Busing, 50–51, 62, 364–365, 410.
    See also Hartford busing ex-
    periment

Cafeterias, 9

CAI (computer-assisted instruction),
    415–418; and child's interper-
    sonal behavior, 417

Cain, Glenc G., 147n

California, 62, 89

Campbell, Donald T., 51, 53, 377,
    411

Campbell, Ernest Q., 5; on provision
    of school facilities, 10

Career aspirations, 26, 170

Certification, teachers', 102. *See also*
    Teacher training

Characteristics: school, 71, 169,
    172–176, 438; regional and
    community, 72–73, 88–90, 173,
    176, 178; student-body, 74, 83,
    160, 172; of principals, 79, 99;
    and achievement, 82–85, 160;
    and student background, 84–
    85, 176; and survey measure-
    ment design, 148–149; teacher,
    160, 165, 172, 174, 231, 237,
    238, 271–272, 299–311, 325–
    326; family, 180–181; of black
    and white schools, compared,
    185–196; curriculum, 292–296;
    of individual student, 438–439

"Cluster colleges," 542, 546

Charlotte, North Carolina, 62

Chicago, 482–484

Chilton, Steve, 437n

Chinese American, 392. *See also* Ori-
    ental Americans

Cincinnati, 485

Citizenship, 391–392

Civil Rights Act of 1964, 4, 7, 8, 10,
    30, 31, 33, 117; preoccupation
    with Negro, 9; and provision of
    school facilities, 11; and con-
    duct of EEOS, 146, 147

Civil Rights Commission, *see* Com-
    mission on Civil Rights, U.S.

Civil-rights movement, 27, 28, 62;
    and response to EEOR, 29–30,
    482; and equality of educational
    opportunity, 423

Clark, D. H., 248

Clark, Kenneth, 428, 431

Class, social, 36, 49, 345, 347, 364,
    388–389; and Grade Level
    Equivalent, 23; and achieve-

ment, 22–24, 248, 262–264, 532–534; and ability grouping, 264–265; and facilities and curriculum, 285; relationship to teacher characteristics, 300–302; and allocation of resources, 313; as predictor of school ability, 350–352; and level of performance, 392. *See also* Status, socioeconomic

Class size, 83, 93, 94, 97, 139, 150, 375; in New York ME schools, 411; in principal's questionnaire, 454. *See also* Student-teacher ratio

Classmates, *see* Peer influence

Cleveland, 485

Cognitive development, 171, 172, 410, 414, 467; and maternal attitudes and behavior, preschool, 400; and preschool programs, 413

Cohen, David K., 25, 36, 40, 41, 43, 50, 230n, 437n, 475–476

Cohen, Wallace M., 22, 23

Coleman, James S., 5, 25, 34, 37, 38, 168–169, 182, 221, 427, 513; on differences in school facilities, along racial lines, 8, 185, 195; on achievement and racial or ethnic background, 19–20, 234; and future policy, 41–42; and policy research, 146–166; and definition of school outputs, 170; his model, 171, 172, 174, 176–177; and family-background factors, 196, 217, 224, 262–263; and black's verbal achievement scores, 202–203; underestimation of school input effects on achievement, 211; and social-class composition, 345; and

child's school racial experience, 363

Coleman Report (Report on Equality of Educational Opportunity; EEOR)

NONRESPONSE FACTORS, 36, 120, 149n, 170, 171, 481–502; for teacher indices, 179; and community-input indices, 181; selective participation by districts and schools, 481–495; selective participation by individuals, 495–502

QUESTIONNAIRES, 120, 149n, 169, 171, 176, 250; and assessment of teacher characteristics, 178–180; and family-characteristic information, 180–181; and student error, 181; principal's misrepresentation of resources, 446–447; principal's response, 447–455; lowest grade (Item 1), 447–448; school location, 448; school size, 448–449; libraries, 449; racial composition, 449–450; socioeconomic background, 450–451; tenure system, 451, 456; accreditation, 451–452; tracking, 452–453, 456; teacher exams, 453; class size, 454; textbook costs, 454; teacher turnover, 454–455; principal's perception of school problems, 455; teachers' responses, 455–457; teachers' response concerning school problems, 457; student data, 457–470, 495, 499–502; participation and response, 481–502; importance of missing observations, 501–502

REPORT: origins of, 4–5; and def-

Coleman Report (*continued*)
inition of equality of educational opportunity, 6; *Summary Report*, 8–9, 10, 29; and achievement by ethnic, racial, and regional groups, 14–15, 247, 541; and analysis of achievement by class, 22–24; findings on integration, 24–25; findings on sense of control of environment, 25–27, 231, 398; general appraisal, 27–28; response to, 28–32; challenges to, 32–34, 378; reanalyses of, 34–43; social value of, 43–45; findings on effect of school characteristics, 48, 134, 138, 311, 372–373; four major points of, 69; Coleman's major conclusions concerning, 70–71; as guide to public policy, 116–140 *passim*, 311–313; models, 122–126, 128, 137; treatment of interaction terms, 126–129, 137; and relative errors of measurement, 130–132, 137; emphasis on later grades, 131, 133–134, 137; evidence to support no-school-effect finding, 134, 138; and implications of linearity, 135; and identification of policy instruments, 136; failure as policy document, 136–140; and divergence in black-white median educational attainment, 138; Coleman's evaluation, 146–167; reconsideration of basic findings, 230–340; possibility of ethnic and racial misclassification, 232, 250; measures of importance of a factor, 235–237, 239, 349; adequacy of model and methodology, 239–241; computation of between- and within-schools components, 247; choice of statistics, 250–254; variables used, 254–255, 298–299; errors in, 255–259; conclusions concerning home conditions and achievement, 260–263, 271, 399–400; conclusions on student-body characteristics, 273, 278, 280–281, 407–408, 410, 483; and differential sensitivity hypothesis, 273–274, 288–290, 304, 307–308, 311; and selection hypothesis, 274; conclusions on facilities and curriculum, 281, 282, 286, 287, 296, 297, 314, 386; findings on teacher characteristics, 298–304, 308, 310–311, 412; and supplying of facts, 374; and educational experimentation, 372, 378, 382–383; and research, 384, 389; and student attitudes, 396; and teacher attitudes, 400; and peer-group structure, 402; and use of cross-sectional data, 405–406; and curriculum and instructional variables, 412–413; definition of "Northern," 439; validity check on student questionnaire responses, 458; weaknesss of, 513, 516; narrow conception of educational opportunity, 516–517; and effects of race on class, 532; and effects of race on educational achievement, 532–533

SURVEY (OE *Survey;* EEOS), 4, 27, 119–122, 132, 134, 343, 372; presumes inferior facilities for

minorities, 8, 11, 136; and
measurements, 12–13, 148–149,
170; challenges to, 32; Northern
urban sample, 72; and teacher
training, 83–84; participants,
119–120, 231, 485; problems,
120–121; question of reliability,
121, 130; problems of interpretation, 122; data on school inputs, 133, 168–169; failure as
policy document, 136, 137, 139;
problems in definition, 147–148,
170; purposes of, 148; overall
design, 148–150; shift in focus
of attention, 149–150; and disbursement of input resources,
153; confusion about goals, 158;
need for weighting data, 182–
183; possibility of ethnic and
racial misclassification, 232,
250; conclusions on racial composition, 344–345, 349, 350–
352, 356, 359; and racial
climate-achievement correlation,
359–360, 361–363; as watershed in educational research,
363–366; quality of data collected by, 437–503; validity of
data, 446–480; student tests administered by, 458, 470–479;
participation and response problems, 481–502
College, 6, 26, 57–58, 162n; as social goal, 58, 380; tracking,
271, 274, 276, 278, 323, 347,
515; in EEOS student-test data,
476–478; Negro admission precluded by lower achievement,
541
College of Basic Studies, Boston University, 541, 546; features of
plan, 542–543; evidence of

plan's success, 543–545; efficiency of plan, 545; implications
for education, 545–546
Color, 5, 146
Columbus, Ohio, 482, 483, 484
Commission on Civil Rights, U.S.,
344–345, 352, 356, 358
Commitment, professional, of teachers, 102, 103, 179–180, 299,
307–310
Communication skills, mastery of,
432
Community, 39, 72–73, 88–90, 394;
environment, 118, 173; input
factors, 176, 180, 203–209, 212;
and homogeneity of elementary
school, 178; and achievement,
196–211, 212, 221, 224; in government policy, 225; and educational process, 371–372; and
schools, relationship, 411; and
self-attitudes, 529–530. *See also*
Neighborhood
Community control, 25, 89, 426
Compensatory education, 54–57, 239,
426; and Boston University's
College of Basic Studies, 541–
546
Computers, 4, 166, 415–418. *See also*
CAI
Conceptual models, 122–124, 128,
155, 166, 233–235; and initial
endowments, 129; of the education process, 171–177
Congress, U.S., 5, 28, 117, 118, 119,
136; and definition of equality
of educational opportunity, 6;
and EEOR, 146, 427
Continuing education, 432
Cost-benefit equation, 388, 393–394
Counselors, 98, 171. *See also* Guidance counselors

Cowan, Christine Schmahl, 437n

Creativity, 534

Cremin, Lawrence A., 425

Crites, John O., 478

Cultural deprivation, 138–139

Cumulative effect hypothesis, 303–304, 307, 311

Curriculum, 10, 29, 40, 72, 77–78, 121, 158, 236, 241, 249, 323–325, 514; and achievement, 83, 96–97, 157, 160, 230, 233, 234, 281–297, 300, 352–353, 412–413; and school social composition, 96; and student-body factors, 271–272; and differential sensitivity hypothesis, 288–290; and verbal achievement, 290–297; characteristics, 292–296; accelerated, 292, 294–295; and classroom racial composition, 352–359; research, 416–417; mid-nineteenth century, 425; in model of educational process, 531; at Boston University's College of Basic Studies, 542–543, 545

Data, 72–73, 386–387, 388, 390; collection problems, 394

Day care, 140

Dean, Sarah, 168n

Decentralization, 89

Demography, of school populations, 387, 388; and differences between families, 464; and verbal ability, 466–467

Dentler, Robert A., 5, 29

Department of Commerce, U.S., Office of Economic Research of the Economic Development Administration, 116n

Department of Defense, U.S., 389, 393

Descriptive studies, 384, 385–392; classification of items to be examined, 387–388

Desegregation, 30, 41, 60–63; and interracial climate, 359; effect on Negro children, 363–366. *See also* Integration

Detroit, 72, 89, 484

Deutsch, Karl, 4

Differential sensitivity hypothesis, 273–274, 288–290, 539; and teacher differences, 303–304, 307–308, 311

Discipline: problems, 153, 314; lower-class emphasis on, 530

Discrimination, 5, 117; and facilities provided, 5, 10; in schooling of blacks, 149

Diseconomies, external, 151–153, 155

Disorder, *see* Order, classroom

District of Columbia, 62, 89

Districts, and response to EEOS, 481–495

Dreeben, Robert, 312

Dropouts, 133, 262, 276–277, 281, 300, 315, 515; and relationship between facilities and achievement, 283, 286, 297

Du Bois, William E. B., 425

Dugan, Dennis J., 48

Duncan, Otis Dudley, 47–48, 477, 478

Dyer, Henry S., 50, 53, 376, 381, 382, 524

Eckland, Bruce K., 17

"Ecological fallacy," 176

Educability, universality of, 424; and the Negro, 425

Education, 59–60, 172; of parents, 22, 24, 36, 47, 101, 181, 209, 212, 214, 218, 221, 223, 254, 262, 266–267, 321, 346, 364, 389; and occupation and income, 46–48; recommendations for establishment of goals for, 52–63; family, 176; and methods of economic analysis, 393–394; changing concept of, 424–426, 431–432; and survival or participation skills needed, 432–433

Educational opportunity, equality in, 117, 423–434; definition of, 6, 147–148, 427–431; as national goal, 45, 52; and periodic assessment of schools, 55–56; output definition, 118; and shift in focus of survey, 150; examination of effects of school factors, 153–163; and Northern *de facto* segregation, 170; studies concerned with, 388; as national concern, 423; and educability, 424; and achievement of basic competencies, 433; measurement of, 513–526; and multiplicity of educational goals, 517; multidimensional aspect of, 525

Educational process, 171–177, 396; goals of, 171; need for experimentation in, 371–383; need for future studies of, 384–418; in student-change model, 520; models of, 528–540

Educational research, *see* Research programs

Educational television, 529. *See also* Television

Educational Testing Service (ETS), 154n, 406, 446; and EEOS student tests, 471–472, 476; and attainment, 476–478; and adult success, 478–479

EEOR (Report on *Equality of Educational Opportunity*), *see* Coleman Report

EEOS (Survey on Equality of Educational Opportunity), *see* Coleman Report

Elementary and Secondary Education Act, 11n, 31; Title I programs, 51, 52

Elementary school, 9, 38, 177, 248–249; enrollments (1970–1974), 46; Coleman's analysis, urban North, 72–105; in OE *Survey*, 119; relationship between home background and achievement in, 262–265

Elzey, F. E., 404, 412

Elinson, Jack, 378–379

Employment, 432. *See also* Occupation

Employment-training programs, 56

Encyclopedia, student-owned, 270, 278, 279, 280, 323, 347, 408. *See also* Books, access to

Engelmann, S., 413

Enrichment programs, 426

Enrollment, school, 46, 121; fluctuation in, 385–387

Environment, 234; sense of control of, 25–27, 231, 398, 517; parents' attitudes toward, 400; in model of educational process, 536–539

Equality, educational, 45, 52; defined, 6; Faulkner's definition of, 7; of output, 11; conclusions concerning, 11–12. *See also*

Equality (*continued*)
  Educational opportunity, equality in

Ethnicity, 14–15, 17, 21, 23–24; and mental abilities, 248; and balanced school populations, 426; separation, and community control, 426

Evaluation, 139, 140

Examination, teachers', *see* National Teacher Examination

Executive branch, U.S. Government, 6, 60

Expectations, educational, 6, 26, 40. *See also* Aspirations; Goals

Expenditure, instructional (PPIE), 16, 19–20, 59, 71, 74–75, 90–92, 180, 324, 407, 514; and neighborhood school, 24–25; in New York, 31–32; and achievement, 42, 90–92, 281, 285, 291–292; and class size, 98, 139; and OE *Survey*, 121; in Report, 133, and discrepancy between disbursement and reception of inputs, 150–153; and community life style, 176; black school and white school compared, 193–195; descriptive studies of, 386, 388; in model of educational process, 531

Experimental studies, 406–418; "ripple effects," 410; isolation of, 414–415

Experimentation, educational, 63, 139–140, 363–366, 371–383, 384; in nonschool programs, 139; in research, 165; alternatives to, 372–373, 377–378; large-scale controlled, 375–376; funding of, 375; as social obligation, 376–377; administrators

of, 377; and identification of successful ventures, 380; unregimented, 380–381

Exposure, to school, 71, 75–76, 93

Extracurricular activities, 97, 131, 282, 294, 324

Facilities, school, 5, 6, 8–12, 29, 40, 71, 76–77, 236, 241, 323–325, 514; and achievement, 8, 34, 36, 37, 93–94, 150, 157, 160, 168, 176, 178–179, 217, 218, 230, 233, 234, 281–297, 300; regional and racial differences, 8–10, 11, 31; variations in, and achievement, 15–16, 34, 36, 37, 93–94; and statistical "variance," 19; reanalyses of, 36; and OE *Survey*, 121; in Report models, 128; and effectiveness of imparting knowledge, 172; utilization of, 174, 282; in Armor's model, 178; black school and white school compared, 185–188, 195; and student-body factors, 271–272; and differential sensitivity hypothesis, 288–290; and verbal achievement, 290–297; assessment of quality of, 386–387

Facts, gathering of, 374–375. *See also* Data

Family, 17–19, 48, 56, 209; and achievement, 19–21, 37, 43, 86–88, 154, 158, 160–165, 168–228 *passim*, 230–231, 466–470; and verbal ability, 39; as input characteristic, 39–40, 123, 125–126, 128–131, 137, 155, 174; size, 47, 346; attitudes, 118, 125, 180, 181, 399–400, 466; and school quality, 132; in child's social environment, 172, 174; data concerning, 180–181; structure, 181, 204, 212, 214, 218, 223, 254, 262, 265, 268, 322, 346; as community input factor, 203–204; in government policy, 225; income, 254, 389, 395, 399–400; and self-attitudes, 529–530; in model of educational process, 530–531, 534. *See also* Background

Family-income programs, 56. *See also* Income

Faulkner, William, 7

Feldman, D. H., 418

Fels Institute, 406

Fifer, G., 248

First National City Bank, its report, *Public Education in New York*, 31–32

Flanagan, John C., 27, 478

Florida, 60

Fortune magazine, 30

Foundations, private, 375

Fox, T. G., 394–395

Friendship, interracial, 359–362

Froomkin, Joseph, 24

Fulk, Byron E., 477

Galton, Francis, 34–35

Genetics, 17–19, 164n, 394, 430–431; and child's predisposition toward learning, 172

Georgia, 60

Gessell, Arnold L., 406

Gilbert, John P., 51, 53

Ghettos, Northern, 30–31; schools, 45–46, 152, 153, 385, 401–402; principal's misrepresentation of resources in Survey response,

446; "sink effect," 532–533, 540. *See also* Slums

Gittell, Marilyn, 25

Goals, educational, 171–172, 381–382, 513, 517–520; redefinition of, 371; and student-change model, 522

Gordon, Edmund W., 53, 432

Government, U.S., 3, 26; aid to education, 150

Grade Level Equivalent (GLE) index, 22–24

Graduate Record Examination tests of Achievement (GRE), 543–544

Great Lakes, 88, 134

Green v. New Kent County Board of Education, 60

Grether, Judith, 48

Gross, Neal, 401

Gross national product, 59–60

Grouping, *see* Ability grouping; Heterogeneous grouping; Tracking

Guidance counselors, 135, 281, 292, 325; at Boston University's College of Basic Studies, 542

Gulliksen, Harold, 381

Gymnasiums, 121

Haggerty Intelligence Examination, 477

Haller, Archibald O., 478

Hamblin, Robert L., 380

Hanushek, Eric A., 34, 37, 38, 41–42, 232, 282, 309, 412; Coleman's criticism of analysis of, 147–150 *passim*, 153n, 155–157 *passim*, 161, 166

Happiness, as school output, 6

Harlem, 30

Harrell, Thomas W., 477

Harrington, Michael, 432

Hartford, 482

Hartford busing experiment (Project Concern), 50–51, 376, 408–410; "ripple effects," 410

Harvard Program on Regional and Urban Economics, 116n

Havighurst, Robert J., 11n, 427–430

Hawthorne effect, 382, 416

Hayes, Donald P., 48

Headstart, *see* Project Headstart

Health, Education, and Welfare, U.S. Department of, 28, 60–61; *Toward a social report*, 146

Health clinics, 171

Henmon-Nelson Test of Mental Maturity, 478

Heredity, 17–19, 137, 234

Herriott, Robert E., 401

Heterogeneous grouping, 411

High school, 72, 467; racial composition, 89; and scale economies, 135

Hobson, Carol J., 5

Hobson v. Hansen, 264

Hodgins, A. S., 413

Holland, J. W., 394–395

Home, *see* Family

Homework, 125; assignment of, 96, 232; average hours of, 271, 274, 323, 347

Hostility, interracial, 360. *See also* Race relations

Household items, 181, 206, 212, 214, 217, 221, 223, 226, 254, 322, 346, 389; as predictor of achievement, 218; correlation with family structure, 265, 267

Ideology, middle-class, 530

I.E.R. Arithmetic Scores, 477

Income, 52, 59; of graduates, 6; effects of improvements in education on, 46–48, 50; racial differences, 47; family, 254, 389, 395, 399–400; and AFQT scores, 478–479

Indian Americans, 14, 22, 24, 46, 59, 178, 231, 232; in OE *Survey*, 119

Indianapolis, 485

Initial endowments, 129–130, 137

Initiative, 57

Inner city, 8, 72; teachers' salaries, 151

Innovation, 63, 371, 376–378; ineffective, 378–380; as educational objective, 534

Input-output analysis, 394–395

Inputs, school, 6, 8, 27, 38; defined, 6; and regression analyses, 35; and achievement, 116, 150–153; inequalities in, 117–119, 147, 154–155; measurement of, 121, 130–132, 149–150; relationship to outputs, 122–140; reanalyses of, 126–129, 154–155; and amount of variance, 127; within-school variation, 129; peer influence, 132–133; and linearity in models, 135; disbursement and reception of, 150–153; effectiveness of, 153–163; community, 176, 180, 203–209, 212; black school-white school comparisons, 185–195; in student-change model, 520

In-service training, 412

Integration, 6, 41, 228, 239, 343; EEOR findings, 24–25; and benefits to Negro child, 36, 50–51; effects on white child, 39; socioeconomic, 42–43; and

Supreme Court, 69–70; and results of verbal achievement tests, 197–199; and racial climate, 359; and interracial attitudes of younger children, 403

Intelligence, 17–19; of teacher, 172. *See also* Ability, innate

I.Q. (intelligence quotient), 351, 364, 365, 427–429; testing, 96; and Project Concern trends, 409; and preschooling for disadvantaged, 413

Interaction: interracial, 359; pupil-pupil, 402–404; teacher-pupil, 403–404; student-faculty (at college level), 545–546

International Business Machines Corporation, 116n

International Encyclopedia of the Social Sciences, 382

Interpersonal relations: and pupil achievement, 402–403; and CAI, 418

Interracial climate, *see* Race relations

Invalidity hypothesis, *see* Validity hypothesis

Jackson, Philip W., his *Life in Classrooms*, 54

Jefferson, Thomas, 424–425

Jencks, Christopher S., 9n, 36n, 37, 40, 42, 43, 230n, 282, 313, 314, 349, 545

Jews, 30–31, 392

Journal of Human Resources, The, 33

Journals, professional, 102, 103

Junior high schools, 119, 276, 364; and student-change model, 522–525

Kagan, Jerome, 49

Kain, John F., 34, 37, 38, 41–42, 232, 282, 412; Coleman's criticism of analysis of, 147–150 *passim*, 153n, 155–157 *passim*, 161, 166

Kansas City, 485

Kariger, Hugh, 264, 296

Karnes, M. B., 413, 414

Katz, Irwin, 359, 364, 366

Katz, Joseph, 545

Katzman, Martin, 483, 484

Kauffman, Joseph F., 545

Kay, Martha, 437n

Keppel, Francis, 5

Kerr, Clark, 545, 546

Kiesling, H. J., 395

Kindergarten, 92, 447. *See also* Preschool programs

Kingston, Albert J., Jr., 264

Klineberg, Otto, 429

Koslin, S. C., 402

Laboratories, 121, 172. *See also* Language laboratories; Science laboratories

Language, facility in use of, 51, 529

Language laboratories, 9, 35, 83, 514–515

Lannholm, G. U., 544–545

Leadership, 529

Leisure, 432

Lesser, Gerald S., 248, 392, 393, 405, 428, 430–431

Leu, Donald J., 264, 296

Levin, Henry M., 33, 38, 43–44, 147n, 153n, 161, 232, 309, 315, 481

Librarians, 9, 94–95, 98

Libraries, 9, 94–95, 172, 387, 407; volumes per student in, 281, 292, 324; utilization of, 314; in principal's questionnaire, 449

Life style, 172, 174, 176, 223; indices of, 180–181; racial differences, 196–209, 228. *See also* Social environment

Linearity, 135

Linn, Robert L., 525

Localism, of teacher, 299, 304, 308–309, 314, 326

Location, school, 281, 291, 325, 408, 514; in principal's questionnaire, 448

Lorge, Irving, 477

Los Angeles, 482–484; County, 62

Louisiana, 60

Lower class, 72, 236–237, 392; and ability grouping errors, 264–265; and assignment and tracking, 296; teachers of, 304, 307; and withdrawal from hostility, 530; emphasis on discipline, 530; and peer-group effects, 531–533; and effects of race, 532–533; and negative social relations, 534. *See also* Class, social

Lunch programs, 94, 171, 371

McPartland, James, 5

Males, as teachers, 100

Mann, Horace, 30

Mathematics, 15, 21–22, 46, 50, 73, 372–373, 381; early disadvantage for minority child, 49; test scores, and school's social composition, 70; within-school test score variation, 86–88; and desegregation, 364; skill in, 529

Mayeske, George W., 22, 23, 501

Measurement, 63; relative errors of, 130–132; differences in design requirements, 148–149; "ecological fallacy," 176; of background factors, 466–467; of educational opportunity, 513–526. *See also* Statistics

Medical care, 51. *See also* Health clinics

Medley, D. M., 403–404

Medsker, L. L., 542

Mencken, H. L., 13

Methodology, 4, 232; and Coleman research design, 170–171; of Smith's reexamination, 233–247; of Report, 239–240

Metropolitan Readiness test, 264, 466

Mexican Americans, 14, 22, 24, 46, 59, 231; in OE *Survey*, 119; and "objective" background measures, 262

Michelson, Stephen, 315, 437n, 483

Michigan, 89

Mid-Atlantic region, 88

Middle class, 72, 87–88, 236–237, 310, 392, 400–401; and ability grouping, 265; access to resources, 285. *See also* Class, social

Midwest, U.S., 9, 71, 72

Migration, of Negro to North, 38, 532–533, 537, 540

Milwaukee, 72, 89, 484

Minneapolis, 477

Minority groups, 5, 426; presumption of inferior facilities for, 8, 11, 136; and achievement scores, 14; early educational disadvantage of, 49; as part of community environment, 204; effect of variations in school resources on, 233

Miscoding, 121, 149n

Mississippi, 60

Mitzel, H. E., 403–404

Mobile, Alabama, 62

Models, *see* Conceptual models; Statistical models

Mood, Alexander M., 5, 394

Moore, Carol Ann, 437n

Morale, 93; teachers', 72, 81, 103–104, 147

Morrison, Coleman, 264

Mosteller, Frederick, 51, 53, 168n, 230n, 437n

Motivation, 54, 84, 155, 170, 172, 182, 363; parents', 125, 255, 260–261, 268, 466, 530–531; and school segregation, 344; and integration, 364–365

Moynihan, Daniel P., 204, 214

Music teachers, 98

Myrdal, Gunnar, his *American Dilemma*, 5; compared to EEOR, 29

National Assessment of Educational Progress, Education Commission of the States, 55–56, 389–392

National Education Association, Research Division, 264

National Institute for Advanced Research on Public Policy, recommended, 42

National origin, 5, 7, 146

National Schools Survey, H.E.W., 61

National Teacher Examination, 99; in principal's questionnaire, 453

NEA, *see* National Education Association

Negative income tax, 50

Negro, 7, 8, 14, 46, 59, 149, 392; and Civil Rights Act (1964), 8–9; and social class, 22–24; and grade level, 24; and career aspirations, 26; benefits of integrated school for, 36; teachers, 100–101; in OE *Survey*, 119; divergence of median educational attainment of, 138; and disbursement and reception of resources, 151; and external diseconomies, 151; in Armor's community index, 181; and differential sensitivity hypothesis, 273; and selection hypothesis, 274; and curriculum characteristics, 294–295; and tracking, 295–296; and school's racial composition, 344, 359–363; effects of desegregation on, 363; and universal educability, 424–425

Neighborhood, 89–90, 239; schools, 19, 24–25, 134; external diseconomies of, 151–153; in social environment of child, 173; and community input factors, 203–204

New England, 88

New York City, 25, 27, 71, 72, 89, 477; Master Plan, 45; demands for black teachers and administrators, 62; The More Effective School Program (ME), 411

New York State, 89; Education Department, 386, 526; response to EEOS questionnaire, 484; Quality Measurement Project, 526

Newcomb, Theodore M., 546

Nichols, Robert C., 29

Nonresponse, 481–503; hypothesis, 438; areas covered, 438–439. *See also Coleman Report*, Questionnaire

North, U.S.: school facilities, 10; response to EEOR, 30, 482–483; bias in allocation of resources

North, U.S. (*continued*)
in, 70; Coleman's analysis of
schools in, 69–105
North Carolina, 60
Northeast, metropolitan, 14–15, 50,
71, 72, 134; response to EEOR,
30
Nursery school, 92, 447. *See also*
Preschool programs
Nurses, 98
Nutrition, 51, 371, 372. *See also*
Lunch programs

Observational study, 372–373, 403–
406
Occupation, 52, 59; of graduates, 6,
26; of father, 22, 36, 47, 149n,
181, 206, 212, 214, 223, 254,
372, 389; and effects of improvements in education upon,
46–48, 50; training for, a goal,
171
Office of Economic Opportunity,
11n, 406
Office of Education, U.S., 4, 5, 8, 28,
63, 117, 146, 168, 427; response
to EEOR, 26; on need for public
policy, in education, 44–45;
research on educational production process, 118–119; *Survey*,
119–122
Okada, Tetsuo, 22, 23
Order, classroom, 152
Oriental Americans, 14, 22, 59, 178,
231; career aspirations, 26; in
OE *Survey*, 119; "objective"
background measures, 262; and
special ability in spatial relationships, 431
Orientation, academic, 172–174; and
regional cultural values, 173

Otis I.Q. test, 477
Outputs, school, 6, 8, 27; equality
of, 11, 147; and regression
analyses, 35; as measured by
verbal achievement, 38–39;
relationship with inputs, 122–
140; focus of Survey, 150;
problems of definition, 170;
analysis of, 182, 196–203,
394–395; measured by EEOS
student tests, 474; in student-
change model, 520
Overachievement, 82–83, 501; defined, 82; and teacher's experience, 82, 85; and teacher's
salary, 91; and frequency of
I.Q. testing, 96
Overlan, Frank, 458, 459

Paraprofessionals, 11n, 49, 387
Parents, 140, 343, 463; education of,
22, 24, 36, 47, 101, 181, 209,
212, 214, 218, 221, 223, 254,
262, 266–267, 321, 346, 364;
occupation, 22, 36, 47, 149n,
181, 206, 212, 214, 223, 254,
364, 372; motivation, 125, 255,
260–261, 268, 322, 530–531;
student's perception of, 260,
398; impact on older child's
achievement, 260; and school
selection process, 350; school
visits by, 387, 400; perception
of child-as-pupil, 399–400;
factual knowledge of school,
400. *See also* Family
Parsons, Talcott, 312
Paternalism, 364
Pattillo, Manning, 375
Patton, Michael J., 525

Peele, S., 363, 364, 365, 366

Peer-group structure, 402–403; "multiplier" effect, 532–533

Peer influence, 40, 69, 116, 153, 176, 530; and achievement, 17–20, 37, 39, 154, 234, 239, 270; at secondary level, 72; as input characteristic, 123, 128, 130; and school quality, 132–133; and child's academic orientation, 173; in model of educational process, 531–534, 540. *See also* Social environment

Pennsylvania, 382; State Board of Education in, 518–519

Peoria, 485

Personality: teachers', 172, 188, 222; peer ratings, student, 402

Personnel, 72, 78–79, 410–411; and achievement, 97–99, 168 (*see also* Teachers); nonteaching, 98; as school input, 126–127; specialized, 387; middle-class dominance, 530

Pettigrew, Thomas F., 25, 36, 40, 41, 43, 50

Philadelphia, 71, 72, 89

Physical education, 171

Physiology, 371

Piccariello, Harry, 51

Pitcher, B., 544–545

Pittsburgh, 363, 365

Placement, school, 40. *See also* Ability grouping; Tracking

Plains states, 88

Planning, long-range, 53

Platt, John B., 415

Playgrounds, 173

Plessy v. Ferguson, Supreme Court decision, 69

Policy, educational, 37–38, 73, 85, 116–140, 176; and reanalyses, 41–43, 155; and social value of EEOR, 43–45; to equalize expected output, 118; and analysis of variance, 135–140; impact of study on, 150; confusion about goals, 158; multiple modes of analysis, 163–165; and general field surveys, 165–167; and family and community factors, 225; and validity of Report's overall conclusions, 311–315; and models of educational process, 528–540 *passim*

Politics, 26, 27; education for citizen participation in, 391–392

Population, school, 46; redistribution of, 426. *See also* Enrollment

Portes, Alejandro, 478

Powers, R., 394

Prediction, of achievement, 211–221, 235–236; and facilities and curriculum factor, 284–285

Prejudice, 381

Preparation time, teachers', 103–104

Preschool programs, 26, 53, 71, 75, 140, 413; and achievement, 92–93; and social environment (life style), 173; and parents' interest, 261; and early readiness and achievement, 265; and maternal attitudes and behavior, 400; and model of educational process, 530

Principals, 323; characteristics of, 79, 99; salary, 91; in OE *Survey*, 120; teachers' perception of, 401; response, and EEOS data validity, 446–455, 484–490; perception of school problems, 455; reasons for selective re-

Principals (*continued*)
sponse to EEOS questionnaire,
490–494; and missing questionnaire items, 495–497

Priorities, national, 69–70

Problem-solving, 432

Professional standing, teachers', 72,
81, 102–103

Program development, 139

Program on Technology and Society,
Harvard, 116n

Project Concern, *see* Hartford busing experiment

Project Headstart, 26, 49–50, 92,
264, 406

Project Talent, 27, 389

Promotion, of slow learners, 282,
292, 325

Psychologists, 98

PTA, 89–90, 322

Public facilities, 173

Puerto Ricans, 14, 22, 24, 46, 59,
231, 392; in OE *Survey*, 119;
and "objective" background
measures, 262

Pupil, individual, *see* Student

Quality, 13, 282; and neighborhood
school, 24–25; student body,
271, 277, 279, 280, 323

Quality Measurement Project, New
York State Education Department, 526

Questionnaire, EEOS, *see Coleman
Report*, Questionnaire

Quiet, classroom, 152

Race, 4, 7, 36, 59–60, 146, 437;
separation by, 7, 61; and
achievement, 71, 88, 217, 532–
533; nonenrollment by, 133; of
teacher, 313, 326; and outcome
of schooling, 343–368

Race relations, 41, 45, 343, 359–363,
364; and peer-rating techniques,
402–403

Racial composition (mixture), 6,
73, 326; and achievement, 41,
43, 70, 71, 82–84, 86–88, 344–
359; in Southern schools, 60–
62; and verbal ability, 89,
196–197; in OE *Survey*, 120,
446; of faculty, 120, 157, 179–
180, 326; and outcome of
schooling, 343–368; effect at
Grade 6, 349–350; and selection processes, 350–352; and
curricular and track assignment, 352–359; and interracial
climate, 362–363; in principal's
questionnaire, 449–450; in
teachers' response to questionnaire, 457

Randomization, 407, 410, 411

Reanalyses, and regression methods,
34–43

Reading, 517; readiness testing,
264–265; materials in home,
265–267 (*see also* Books);
computerized program, 416

Reading level, 32, 50, 70, 73, 389;
and Title I programs, 51; variation within school, 86–88

Region, 14–15, 17, 21, 38, 72–73,
88–90, 178; cultural values, and
child's academic orientation,
173; and difference in life style,
176; and differences in school
facilities, 185–188; differences
in teacher quality, 190; and
differences in per-capita ex-

penditure, 195; and verbal achievement test averages, 199; and achievement, 214–215, 224; and effects of race on class, 532

Regression methods, 154n; reanalysis of, 34–43; defined, 34–35; findings, 36–41; conclusions, 41–43; "causal," 47; and school effects, 153–163; importance of variables in, 242–247

Reiter, Stanley, 536

Religion, 5, 7, 146

Remedial reading, 51, 82, 172, 426; teachers of, 98

Repeaters, of failed courses, 10. *See also* Promotion, of slow learners

Report on Equality of Educational Opportunity, *see Coleman Report*

Research, educational, 53, 139, 315–316, 384–418; descriptive studies, 384–392; expense factor, 388, 418; analytic studies, 393–406; experimental studies, 406–418; and models of educational process, 528

Residential patterns, 62, 312–313; and school quality, 125; and nonenrollment, 134

Resources, 15–16, 71, 73, 85–86, 298, 302, 313–316; allocation of, 37; and declining enrollments, 46; bias in Northern allocation of, 70; and student motivation, 84; measurement of, 117–119; discrepancy between disbursement and reception of, 150–153; distribution of public, 150, 152, 298, 302; and achievement, 241, 247–254, 257, 282–283, 297; fallacy in Report concerning, 249; principal's exaggeration of, 446–447; and family background, 483–484. *See also* Facilities

Resourcefulness, 57

Response rate, 250. *See also Coleman Report*, Nonresponse

Retardation, mental, 172

Retention rates, 6

Richmond, California, 351

Riesman, David, 545

Riley, Robert T., 25, 36, 40, 41, 43, 50, 475–476

Riots: Harlem (1964), 30; Watts (1965), 30

Role-playing, 534

Rosenthal, Jack, 62–63

Ross Pediatric Conference, 379

Rossi, Peter, 15

Rural areas, 374, 385

Russell, Bertrand, 15

Russia, *see* Soviet Union

St. John, Nancy, 50, 363, 365, 366

St. Louis, 89

Salary, teacher, 9, 28, 90–91, 99, 125, 150, 514; inner city, 151; and per-capita school expenditures, 180, 193, 195, 212, 218

San Francisco, 72, 89, 483, 484

San Juan, Puerto Rico, 402

Sanford, Nevitt, 545

SCAT series (vocabulary test), 154n

Scholastic Aptitude Test (SAT), and college grades, 476–477

School factors (characteristics), 130–131, 153–163, 166, 168–228, 407; and peer effects, 132–133; measurement of, 169; and family-background effects, 196–209; and achievement,

School factors (characteristics)
(*continued*)
209–221, 247–254, 464–470,
479–480, 484; assessment of
strength of, 241–242; and EEOS
students' test scores, 475–476;
in model of educational process,
531, 534. *See also* Inputs, school

School year, length of, 240, 514

Schools: Southern, 10, 153, 168; new
types, 56; and *de facto* segregation, 170; effectiveness in imparting knowledge, 172, 239;
black and white compared,
183–196, 206; base-line effect,
225; strong independent effect
lacking in, 239; size of, 281,
291, 325, 407; location, 281,
291, 325, 408, 448, 514; community relationship, 411; lowest grade, in principal's
questionnaire, 447; and response
to EEOS questionnaire, 482–502
passim; objectives, 529

Science, 29

Science laboratories, 13, 14, 94, 131,
281, 292, 324, 387; quality of,
282; utilization of, 314

Sears, P. S., 418

Secondary schools, 9, 40–41, 248–
249; enrollments (1970–1974),
46; in OE *Survey*, 119; relationship of home background and
achievement in, 262–265

Segregation, 7, 147, 170; in North,
30–31, 483. *See also* Desegregation; Integration

Selection practices, student's, 40,
232, 249, 255, 262, 263, 274–
277, 300–302, 314; and relation
between facilities and achieve-

ment, 283, 286, 297; and curriculum characteristics, 292; and
effect of racial composition,
350–354

Self-attitudes, 529, 533–535; -esteem,
6, 50, 171, 398, 517; -image, 6,
51, 398, 517; -expression, 432;
-management, 433; -acceptance,
522; -understanding, 522. *See
also* Environment, sense of control of

Self-selection, *see* Selection practices

"Separate but equal" education, 69–
70, 426, 514

SES level, *see* Socio-Economic Status
index

Sesame Street (television program),
57

Sewall, William H., 478

Sexton, P. C., 399

Shah, Vimal T., 478

Shaycroft, Marion, 461, 462, 471

Siblings, 254, 266, 268, 322; test
score correlation between, 462

Silberman, Charles E., his "A Devastating Report on U.S. Education," 30

Sills, David, 382

"Sink" parameters, 532–533, 540

Sioux Falls, 485

Size, school, 281, 291, 325, 407; in
principal's questionnaire, 448–
449. *See also* Class size

Skinner, B. F., 380

Slums, urban, 24, 25, 31; school principals in, 401. *See also* Ghettos

Smith, Frank L., 11n

Smith, G. M., 402

Smith, Marshall S., 21, 34, 39, 40,
43, 50, 86, 264, 319, 363, 365,
366, 437n

Social class, *see* Class, social

"Social distance," 403

Social environment (composition), 20–21, 25, 48; and achievement, 41, 43, 70, 82–84, 86–88, 157, 231; and child's academic orientation, 172–174; levels of, 172–173; family, 172–173; neighborhood (community), 173; peers, 173

Social mobility, 137

Social Science Research Council, 42

Socialization, 51, 413

Socioeconomic status, 17, 21, 29, 46, 73, 88, 118, 437; and achievement, 22–24, 37, 39, 70–71, 87–88, 105, 226, 399–400; upgrading of black family's, 43; and allocation of resources, North, 70; and schools' mean achievement, 71; and nonenrollment, 134; in child's social environment (life style), 172–173; black-white differences, 389; in principal's questionnaire, 450–451

Socio-Economic Status (ses) index, 22, 39; teacher, 304, 307, 308, 326

South, U.S., 9, 38, 161; school facilities in, 10, 153; inequalities in achievement, 15; response to eeor, 30; school desegregation, 60–61

South Carolina, 60

Southern Education Report, 8

Soviet Union, 57

Special Commission on the Social Sciences, National Sciences Board, 42

Special education, 431

Specialists, teacher, 411

Speech therapists, 98–99

Split session, 82, 93

Staff, *see* Personnel

"Standard deviation," described, 14n–15n; and variance, 16–19

Standard Metropolitan Statistical Area (smsa), 178, 439

Standards, educational, 517

Stanford achievement tests, 264

Stanford University, 416

Stanley, J. C., 411

Statistical models, 124–126, 128, 233, 235; absence of measure of initial endowments, 129–130; failures in Report, 137

Statistics, 374; crude, 12–14; bias, 13; and group policy, 14; and standard deviation, 14n–15n; and variance, 16–19

Stern, G. B., 401

Steubenville, 485

Stickler, W. Hugh, 546

Stodolsky, Susan S., 392, 393, 405, 428, 430–431

Student, individual: performance, 389, 390; questionnaire responses, 457–470, 495, 499–502; and background response reliability, 458–461; and assessment of family background variation, 462–470; tests, 470–479; development, 513

Student body (characteristic), 131, 132–133, 233, 237–238, 241, 322–323; and achievement, 154, 156–158, 160–162, 269–281, 300–302, 407–408; "growth rates" input, 166; and child's academic orientation, 173; quality, 271; and differential sensi-

Student body (characteristic)
(*continued*)
tivity hypothesis, 273–274; and
selection hypothesis, 274–277;
teacher's perception of quality
of, 277, 279, 280, 323, 400–
402, 408; relation to facilities
and curriculum factor, 286,
297; teacher's preference for,
307–310, 326
Substitute teachers, 102–103, 387
Suburbs, 8, 72, 152, 276
Student-change model, 520–526
Student-teacher ratio, 11n, 15–16,
46, 139, 239, 531; and achieve-
ment, 91, 94, 97, 154, 282, 283;
in New York ME Schools, 411.
See also Class size
Summary Report, EEOR, 8–9, 10, 29
Summer institutes, 412
Summer-loss effect, 48, 53
Summer programs, recreational and
educational, 140
Sumner, Charles, 514
Super, Donald E., 478
Superintendents, 93, 323; in OE *Sur-
vey*, 120, 490
Suppes, Patrick, 416
Supreme Court, U.S., 6, 30, 60, 62,
69–70, 170, 344, 426
Surrounding conditions, in student-
change model, 520, 522
Survey on Equality of Educational
Opportunity, *see Coleman Re-
port*, Survey
Surveys: sample, 374; descriptive,
385–392; analytical, 393–406;
experimental, 406–418
Syracuse, 485
Systems analysis, 393–395

Taba, H., 404, 412
Tables, mechanical errors in creation
of, 231
Talent needs, 391–392
Taubman, Paul, 57
Teacher aides, 387
Teacher selection, 72, 79, 99–100
Teacher training, 6, 29, 38, 72, 83–
84, 100–102, 304–305, 307–309,
326, 399; of black teachers,
100–101, 190, 193; in liberal
arts colleges, 101; and teacher's
transmission of knowledge, 172
Teachers, 19, 38, 40, 72, 128, 237,
238, 241, 325–326; of Negroes,
9–10, 62, 305; cultural background of, 20; and verbal ability, 38–39, 101, 157, 179, 188,
190–193, 195, 209, 222, 223,
274, 298–311, 325–326; potential supply (1974), 46; selection
devices, 72, 79, 99–100; background and training, 72, 80,
100–102, 179, 188–190, 195,
212, 218, 387, 514; professional
standing, 72, 81, 102–103; morale, 72, 81, 103–104, 147;
male, 100; preparation time,
103–104; in OE *Survey*, 119–
120; improvement in quality,
150; and external diseconomies,
152; attitudes, 153, 179–180,
400–402; and achievement, 154,
157–158, 160, 162, 165, 231,
234, 298–311, 412; black, for
black students, 157–158, 190;
and relationship between quality and imparting of knowledge,
172, 239; and community life
style, 176; quality measurement, 179–180; quality in black

and white schools, compared, 188–193, 212; and student-body factors, 271–273, 286; perception of student-body quality, 277, 279, 280, 323, 400–402, 408; localism of, 299, 304, 308–309, 314, 326; and cumulative effects, 303; and differential sensitivity hypothesis, 303–304, 307–308; SES level, 304, 307, 308, 326; student's perception of, 398–399, 405; parents' assessment of competence of, 399, 400; perception of their principals, 401; of the disadvantaged, 412–413; response to EEOS questionnaire, 455–457; response concerning school problems, 457; and classroom racial composition, 457; and missing questionnaire items, 495, 497–499; authoritarian, 531, 534; and new educational objectives, 534–535

Teachers' associations (unions), 102, 103

Teaching Disadvantaged Children in Preschool (Bereiter and Engelmann), 413

Teaching experience, 9, 38, 72, 82–83, 304, 326, 399; and verbal growth of students, 82, 85–86, 307, 309, 314

Team teaching, 411; at College of Basic Studies, Boston University, 542–543, 545

Television, 56–57, 392, 534

Tennessee, 60, 458

Tenure, teacher, 9, 99, 102; in principal's questionnaire, 451; in teachers' questionnaire, 457

Terman, Lewis M., 406

Teska, J. A., 413

Testing, 10, 87, 154n, 170, 387; verbal ability, 10, 22, 36, 134; regional differences in score, 188; nonverbal, 466; EEOS, of students, 470–479; and subsequent attainment, 476–478; and adult success, 478–479. *See also* Achievement tests

Texas, 60

Textbooks, 9, 95, 121, 151, 172, 387; in principal's questionnaire, 454

Theobald, Robert, 432

Thorndike-McCall Reading scores, 477

Time budgets, 54, 63

Title I programs, 51, 52

Toward a social report (H.E.W.), 146

Tracking, 54, 233, 262, 265, 281, 324–325; and school-input heterogeneity, 132; college-oriented, 271, 274, 276, 278–280; and curriculum characteristics, 292–293, 295–296; and classroom racial composition, 352–359; in principal's questionnaire, 452–453; in teachers' questionnaire, 457

Transfers, student, 133, 270, 279, 315, 323, 347, 408; at college level, 542, 543

Truant officers, 98

Tuddenham, Read D., 477

Tukey, J. W., 35

Tumin, Melvin, 427, 430

Turnover: pupil, 90; teacher, 103, 454–455

Twins, 462

Tyler, Ralph W., 428–430

Underachievers, 501

University of Michigan, Research Center for Group Dynamics, 375n

Urbanism, of pupil and parents, 254, 262, 266, 268, 321, 346

Urbanization, 14–15, 17, 21

Useem, Michael, 168n

Validity hypothesis, 438; areas covered, 438–439

"Value-added" concept, 393

Variance: described, 16–19; in Report, 114–126; of input factors, 127–130; between-school, 134, 164–165, 230; intergrade comparisons, 134; analysis of, and public policy, 135–140; and verbal achievement, 160, 164

Verbal ability (achievement), 38–40, 46, 73, 69–105 *passim*, 182, 233, 274, 381, 407; tests of, 10, 22, 36, 134; of teachers, 38–39, 101, 157, 179, 188, 190–193, 195, 209, 222–223, 298–304; and peer influence, 40, 271–281; and racial composition, 41, 157; early disadvantage for minority/black child, 49, 202–203, 211, 223, 225; and EEOR findings, 50; and school social composition, 70; and teacher experience, 82, 85–86, 179, 188–190, 195, 212, 218; within-school difference, 86–88; regional and community factors, 88–90; and effect of school resources, 153–154; and variance, 160; and Coleman's definition of school output, 170; black-white differences, 211–212, 222–225; and differential sensitivity hypothesis, 273–274; and selection hypothesis, 274–277; and school facilities and student achievement, 281–297; and self-concept, 398; Coleman's concentration on, 516–517

Veroff, J., 363, 364, 365, 366

Violence, 30

Virginia, 60

Vocational training, 292; and the Negro, 425

Wales, Terence J., 57

War on Poverty, 11n, 26

Washington, Booker T., 425

Washington, D.C., 62, 89

Watts, 30

Watts, Harold W., 147n

Weaver, Warren, 7

Weinfeld, Frederic D., 5

Weiss, Randall, 437n

West, U.S., 9, 62, 72, 88

White, Sheldon H., 49, 516

White majority, 59; and academic achievement, 14, 22; and social class, 22–24; and OE *Survey*, 119

Whitla, Dean K., 476

Wilder, David E., 11n

Wilkerson, Doxey A., 432

Wilson, Alan, 351

Wilson, Logan, 546

Wisconsin, 478

Woodring, Paul, 542, 546

Yeats, W. B., 15

York, Robert L., 5

DAVID J. ARMOR is Associate Professor of Sociology at Harvard University. He has written on computer methods in the social sciences, and on the school counseling profession.

JAMES M. BESHERS is Professor of Sociology at Queens College and the Graduate Center of the City University of New York. His writings have concentrated on demographic questions, urban social structure, and computer methodology.

DAVID K. COHEN is Associate Professor of Education and Director of the Center for Educational Policy Research at Harvard University. He has written on the subjects of social program evaluation, politics, and school integration.

JAMES S. COLEMAN is Professor of Social Relations at Johns Hopkins University. His writings include works on educational sociology, mathematical techniques in social science, and collective decision-making.

HENRY S. DYER is Vice President of the Educational Testing Service. He has written on the assessment of educational systems, problems in educational management, and the concept of professional accountability.

JOHN P. GILBERT is Staff Statistician at the Harvard University Computing Center, and also directs the Research Computing Group at the Massachusetts General Hospital. He has written in mathematical statistics, the application of computer models to kinship in anthropology, and on the safety of anesthetics.

EDMUND W. GORDON is Chairman of the Department of Guidance, Teachers College, Columbia University. His work includes studies of compensatory education, early childhood education, and the politics of education.

ERIC A. HANUSHEK is Assistant Professor of Economics at the United States Air Force Academy. His writing has concentrated on the economics of education.

CHRISTOPHER S. JENCKS is Associate Professor of Education at Harvard University, and codirector of The Cambridge Institute. He has written on questions of social mobility, educational reform, and American politics.

JOHN F. KAIN is Professor of Economics at Harvard University. He has written on housing and segregation, urban transportation, econometric analysis of housing markets, migration, ghetto labor markets, regional growth and development, and determinants of industrial location.

FREDERICK MOSTELLER is Professor of Mathematical Statistics at Harvard University, teaching in the Departments of Statistics and Social Relations, and in the Committee on Public Policy. He has written in theoretical and applied statistics, including industrial, medical, and social science applications.

DANIEL P. MOYNIHAN is Professor of Education and Urban Politics at Harvard University. His writings include studies of ethnicity, and of the role of social science in the formulation of public policy.

THOMAS F. PETTIGREW is Professor of Social Psychology at Harvard University. His work includes studies of racial conflict, racial segregation, and cognitive processes.

ROBERT T. RILEY is Associate in Education and Research Fellow at the Harvard Graduate School of Education. He has written on contextual models of school desegregation and on political attitudes in working-class populations.

GENE M. SMITH is an Associate Professor of Psychology in Anesthesia at the Harvard Medical School, a member of the Department of Anesthesia and Psychiatry at Massachusetts General Hospital, and Research Associate at the College of Basic Studies, Boston University. In addition to studies of personality based on peer-rating and self-report measures, he has studied pain and its response to analgesics, as well as psychological and physical performance in response to narcotics, stimulants, and sedatives.

MARSHALL S. SMITH is Assistant Professor of Education at Harvard University. His writings include studies of computer content analysis, program evaluation, and problems of racial integration.

V-365 ALPEROVITZ, GAR *Atomic Diplomacy*

V-604 BAILYN, BERNARD *The Origins of American Politics*

V-334 BALTZELL, E. DIGBY *The Protestant Establishment*

V-198 BARDOLPH, RICHARD *The Negro Vanguard*

V-60 BECKER, CARL L. *The Declaration of Independence*

V-494 BERNSTEIN, BARTON J. (ed.) *Towards a New Past: Dissenting Essays in American History*

V-199 BERMAN, HAROLD J. (ed.) *Talks on American Law*

V-211 BINKLEY, WILFRED E. *President and Congress*

V-512 BLOCH, MARC *The Historian's Craft*

V-513 BOORSTIN, DANIEL J. *The Americans: The Colonial Experience*

V-358 BOORSTIN, DANIEL J. *The Americans: The National Experience*

V-621 BOORSTIN, DANIEL J. *The Decline Of Radicalism: Reflections on America Today*

V-44 BRINTON, CRANE *The Anatomy of Revolution*

V-98 CASH, W. J. *The Mind of the South*

V-311 CREMIN, LAWRENCE A. *The Genius of American Education*

V-190 DONALD, DAVID *Lincoln Reconsidered*

V-379 EMERSON, THOMAS I. *Toward a General Theory of the First Amendment*

V-424 FOREIGN POLICY ASSOCIATION, EDITORS OF *A Cartoon History of United States Foreign Policy Since World War I*

V-498 FRANKLIN, JOHN HOPE *From Slavery to Freedom: History of Negro Americans*

V-368 FRIEDENBERG, EDGAR Z. *Coming of Age in America*

V-264 FULBRIGHT, J. WILLIAM *Old Myths and New Realities*

V-463 GAY, PETER *A Loss of Mastery: Puritan Historians in Colonial America*

V-400 GENOVESE, EUGENE D. *The Political Economy of Slavery*

V-676 GENOVESE, EUGENE D. *The World the Slaveholders Made*

V-31 GOLDMAN, ERIC F. *Rendezvous with Destiny*

V-183 GOLDMAN, ERIC F. *The Crucial Decade—and After: America, 1945-1960*

V-95 HOFSTADTER, RICHARD *The Age of Reform: From Bryan to F.D.R.*

V-9 HOFSTADTER, RICHARD *The American Political Tradition*

V-317 HOFSTADTER, RICHARD *Anti-Intellectualism in American Life*

V-385 HOFSTADTER, RICHARD *The Paranoid Style in American Politics and Other Essays*

V-540 HOFSTADTER, RICHARD and CLARENCE L. VER STEEG (eds.) *Great Issues in American History, From Settlement to Revolution, 1584-1776*

V-541 HOFSTADTER, RICHARD (ed.) *Great Issues in American History, From the Revolution to the Civil War, 1765-1865*

V-542 HOFSTADTER, RICHARD (ed.) *Great Issues in American History, From Reconstruction to the Present Day, 1864-1969*

V-591 HOFSTADTER, RICHARD *Progressive Historians*

V-630 HOROWITZ, DAVID *Empire and Revolution: A Radical Interpretation of Contemporary History*

V-514 HUNTINGTON, SAMUEL P. *The Soldier and the State*

V-242 JAMES, C. L. R. *The Black Jacobins*

V-527 JENSEN, MERRILL *The New Nation*

V-623   KRADITOR, AILEEN S.   *Means and Ends in American Abolitionism*

V-367   LASCH, CHRISTOPHER   *The New Radicalism in America*
V-560   LASCH, CHRISTOPHER   *The Agony of the American Left*
V-488   LYND, STAUGHTON   *Intellectual Origins of American Radicalism*

V-502   MATTHEWS, DONALD R.   *U. S. Senators and Their World*
V-552   MAYER, ARNO J.   *Politics and Diplomacy of Peacemaking*
V-386   MCPHERSON, JAMES   *The Negro's Civil War*
V-318   MERK, FREDERICK   *Manifest Destiny and Mission in American History*

V-84   PARKES, HENRY B.   *The American Experience*
V-371   ROSE, WILLIE LEE   *Rehearsal for Reconstruction*
V-212   ROSSITER, CLINTON   *Conservatism in America*
V-285   RUDOLPH, FREDERICK   *The American College and University: A History*

V-394   SEABURY, PAUL   *Power, Freedom and Diplomacy*
V-279   SILBERMAN, CHARLES E.   *Crisis in Black and White*
V-52   SMITH, HENRY NASH   *Virgin Land*
V-345   SMITH, PAGE   *The Historian and History*
V-432   SPARROW, JOHN   *After the Assassination: A Positive Appraisal of the Warren Report*
V-388   STAMPP, KENNETH M.   *The Era of Reconstruction 1865-1877*
V-253   STAMPP, KENNETH M.   *The Peculiar Institution*
V-110   TOCQUEVILLE, ALEXIS DE   *Democracy in America*, Vol. I
V-111   TOCQUEVILLE, ALEXIS DE   *Democracy in America*, Vol. II
V-103   TROLLOPE, MRS. FRANCES   *Domestic Manners of the Americans*

V-516   ULAM, ADAM B.   *The Unfinished Revolution*
V-540   VER STEEG, CLARENCE L. and RICHARD HOFSTADTER (eds.) *Great Issues in American History, 1584-1776*
V-265   WARREN, ROBERT PENN   *The Legacy of the Civil War*
V-605   WILLIAMS, JOHN A. and CHARLES F. HARRIS (eds.)   *Amistad 1*
V-660   WILLIAMS, JOHN A. and CHARLES F. HARRIS (eds.)   *Amistad 2*
V-362   WILLIAMS, T. HARRY   *Lincoln and His Generals*
V-208   WOODWARD, C. VANN   *Burden of Southern History*

VINTAGE CRITICISM,
LITERATURE, MUSIC, AND ART

V-418 AUDEN, W. H. *The Dyer's Hand*
V-398 AUDEN, W. H. *The Enchàfed Flood*
V-269 BLOTNER, JOSEPH and FREDERICK GWYNN (eds.) *Faulkner at the University*
V-259 BUCKLEY, JEROME H. *The Victorian Temper*
V-51 BURKE, KENNETH *The Philosophy of Literary Form*
V-643 CARLISLE, OLGA *Poets on Streetcorners: Portraits of Fifteen Russian Poets*
V-569 CARTEY, WILFRED *Whispers from a Continent: The Literature of Contemporary Black Africa*
V-75 CAMUS, ALBERT *The Myth of Sisyphus and other Essays*
V-626 CAMUS, ALBERT *Lyrical and Critical Essays*
V-535 EISEN, JONATHAN *The Age of Rock: Sounds of the American Cultural Revolution*
V-655 EISEN, JONATHAN *The Age of Rock 2*
V-4 EINSTEIN, ALFRED *A Short History of Music*
V-632 ELLMAN, RICHARD (ed.) *The Artist as Critic: Critical Writings of Oscar Wilde*
V-13 GILBERT, STUART *James Joyce's Ulysses*
V-646 GILMAN, RICHARD *The Confusion of Realms*
V-363 GOLDWATER, ROBERT *Primitivism in Modern Art*, Revised Edition
V-114 HAUSER, ARNOLD *Social History of Art*, Vol. I
V-115 HAUSER, ARNOLD *Social History of Art*, Vol. II
V-116 HAUSER, ARNOLD *Social History of Art*, Vol. III
V-117 HAUSER, ARNOLD *Social History of Art*, Vol. IV
V-438 HELLER, ERICH *The Artist's Journey into the Interior and Other Essays*
V-213 HOWE, IRVING *William Faulkner: A Critical Study*
V-20 HYMAN, S. E. *The Armed Vision*
V-12 JARRELL, RANDALL *Poetry and the Age*
V-88 KERMAN, JOSEPH *Opera as Drama*
V-260 KERMODE, FRANK *The Romantic Image*
V-581 KRAMER, JANE *Allen Ginsberg in America*
V-452 KESSLE, GUN, photographs by, and JAN MYRDAL *Angkor*
V-83 KRONENBERGER, LOUIS *Kings and Desperate Men*
V-677 LESTER, JULIUS *The Seventh Son*, Vol. I
V-678 LESTER, JULIUS *The Seventh Son*, Vol. II
V-90 LEVIN, HARRY *The Power of Blackness: Hawthorne, Poe, Melville*
V-296 MACDONALD, DWIGHT *Against the American Grain*
V-55 MANN, THOMAS *Essays*
V-720 MIRSKY, D. S. *A History of Russian Literature*
V-344 MUCHNIC, HELEN *From Gorky to Pasternak*
V-452 MYRDAL, JAN and photographs by GUN KESSLE *Angkor*
V-118 NEWMAN, ERNEST *Great Operas*, Vol. I
V-119 NEWMAN, ERNEST *Great Operas*, Vol. II
V-24 RANSOM, JOHN CROWE *Poems and Essays*
V-108 SHAHN, BEN *The Shape of Content*
V-415 SHATTUCK, ROGER *The Banquet Years*, Revised
V-186 STEINER, GEORGE *Tolstoy or Dostoevsky*
V-278 STEVENS, WALLACE *The Necessary Angel*
V-39 STRAVINSKY, IGOR *The Poetics of Music*

V-100   SULLIVAN, J. W. N.   *Beethoven: His Spiritual Development*
V-243   SYPHER, WYLIE (ed.)   *Art History: An Anthology of Modern Criticism*
V-266   SYPHER, WYLIE   *Loss of the Self*
V-229   SYPHER, WYLIE   *Rococo to Cubism*
V-458   SYPHER, WYLIE   *Literature and Technology*
V-166   SZE, MAI-MAI   *The Way of Chinese Painting*
V-162   TILLYARD, E. M. W.   *The Elizabethan World Picture*
V-35   TINDALL, WILLIAM YORK   *Forces in Modern British Literature*
V-194   VALERY, PAUL   *The Art of Poetry*
V-347   WARREN, ROBERT PENN   *Selected Essays*
V-218   WILSON, EDMUND   *Classics & Commercials*
V-360   WIMSATT, W. and C. BROOKS   *Literary Criticism*
V-500   WIND, EDGAR   *Art and Anarchy*
V-546   YATES, FRANCES A.   *Giordano Bruno and the Hermetic Tradition*

VINTAGE POLITICAL SCIENCE
AND SOCIAL CRITICISM

V-428   ABDEL-MALEK, ANOUAR   *Egypt: Military Society*
V-625   ACKLAND, LEN AND SAM BROWN   *Why Are We Still in Vietnam?*
V-340   ADAMS, RUTH (ed.)   *Contemporary China*
V-196   ADAMS, RICHARD N.   *Social Change in Latin America Today*
V-568   ALINSKY, SAUL D.   *Reveille for Radicals*
V-365   ALPEROVITZ, GAR   *Atomic Diplomacy*
V-503   ALTHUSSER, LOUIS   *For Marx*
V-286   ARIES, PHILIPPE   *Centuries of Childhood*
V-511   BAILEY, STEPHEN K.   *Congress Makes a Law*
V-604   BAILYN, BERNARD   *Origins of American Politics*
V-334   BALTZELL, E. DIGBY   *The Protestant Establishment*
V-335   BANFIELD, E. G. AND J. Q. WILSON   *City Politics*
V-674   BARBIANA, SCHOOL OF   *Letter to a Teacher*
V-198   BARDOLPH, RICHARD   *The Negro Vanguard*
V-185   BARNETT, A. DOAK   *Communist China and Asia*
V-270   BAZELON, DAVID   *The Paper Economy*
V-60   BECKER, CARL L.   *The Declaration of Independence*
V-563   BEER, SAMUEL H.   *British Politics in the Collectivist Age*
V-199   BERMAN, H. J. (ed.)   *Talks on American Law*
V-211   BINKLEY, WILFRED E.   *President and Congress*
V-81   BLAUSTEIN, ARTHUR I. AND ROGER R. WOOCK (eds.)   *Man Against Poverty*
V-508   BODE, BOYD H.   *Modern Educational Theories*
V-513   BOORSTIN, DANIEL J.   *The Americans: The Colonial Experience*
V-358   BOORSTIN, DANIEL J.   *The Americans: The National Experience*
V-621   BOORSTIN, DANIEL J.   *The Decline of Radicalism: Reflections on America Today*
V414   BOTTOMORE, T. B.   *Classes in Modern Society*
V-44   BRINTON, CRANE   *The Anatomy of Revolution*
V-625   BROWN, SAM AND LEN ACKLAND   *Why Are We Still in Vietnam*
V-234   BRUNER, JEROME   *The Process of Education*
V-590   BULLETIN OF ATOMIC SCIENTISTS   *China after the Cultural Revolution*
V-578   BUNZEL, JOHN H.   *Anti-Politics in America*
V-549   BURNIER, MICHEL-ANTOINE   *Choice of Action*
V-684   CALVERT, GREG AND CAROL   *The New Left and the New Capitalism*
V-30   CAMUS, ALBERT   *The Rebel*
V-33   CARMICHAEL, STOKELY AND CHARLES HAMILTON   *Black Power*
V-664   CARMICHAEL, STOKELY   *Stokely Speaks*
V-98   CASH, W. J.   *The Mind of the South*
V-556   CASTRO, JOSUE DE   *Death in the Northeast*
V-272   CATER, DOUGLASS   *The Fourth Branch of Government*
V-290   CATER, DOUGLASS   *Power in Washington*
V-551   CHEVIGNY, PAUL   *Police Power*
V-555   CHOMSKY, NOAM   *American Power and the New Mandarins*
V-640   CHOMSKY, NOAM   *At War With Asia*
V-554   CONNERY, ROBERT H. (ed.)   *Urban Riots: Violence and Social Change*

V-420   CORNUELLE, RICHARD C.   *Reclaiming the American Dream*

V-538   COX COMMISSION   *Crisis at Columbia*

V-311   CREMIN, LAWRENCE A.   *The Genius of American Education*

V-519   CREMIN, LAWRENCE A.   *The Transformation of the School*

V-734   DANIELS, R. V.   *A Documentary History of Communism*

V-237   DANIELS, R. V.   *The Nature of Communism*

V-638   DENNISON, GEORGE   *The Lives of Children*

V-746   DEUTSCHER, ISAAC   *The Prophet Armed*

V-747   DEUTSCHER, ISAAC   *The Prophet Unarmed*

V-748   DEUTSCHER, ISAAC   *The Prophet Outcast*

V-617   DEVLIN, BERNADETTE   *The Price of My Soul*

V-671   DOMHOFF, G. WILLIAM   *The Higher Circles*

V-603   DOUGLAS, WILLIAM O.   *Points of Rebellion*

V-645   DOUGLAS, WILLIAM O.   *International Dissent*

V-585   EAKINS, DAVID AND JAMES WEINSTEIN (eds.)   *For a New America*

V-390   ELLUL, JACQUES   *The Technological Society*

V-379   EMERSON, T. I.   *Toward a General Theory of the First Amendment*

V-47   EPSTEIN, B. R. AND A. FORSTER   *The Radical Right: Report on the John Birch Society and Its Allies*

V-692   EPSTEIN, JASON   *The Great Conspiracy Trial*

V-661   FALK, RICHARD A., GABRIEL KOLKO, AND ROBERT JAY LIFTON   *Crimes of War: After Songmy*

V-442   FALL, BERNARD B.   *Hell in a Very Small Place: The Siege of Dien Bien Phu*

V-423   FINN, JAMES   *Protest: Pacifism and Politics*

V-667   FINN, JAMES   *Conscience and Command*

V-225   FISCHER, LOUIS (ed.)   *The Essential Gandhi*

V-424   FOREIGN POLICY ASSOCIATION, EDITORS OF   *A Cartoon History of United States Foreign Policy Since World War I*

V-413   FRANK, JEROME D.   *Sanity and Survival*

V-382   FRANKLIN, JOHN HOPE AND ISIDORE STARR (eds.)   *The Negro in 20th Century America*

V-224   FREYRE, GILBERTO   *New World in the Tropics*

V-368   FRIEDENBERG, EDGAR Z.   *Coming of Age in America*

V-662   FREIDMAN, EDWARD AND MARK SELDEN (eds.)   *America's Asia: Dissenting Essays in Asian Studies*

V-378   FULBRIGHT, J. WILLIAM   *The Arrogance of Power*

V-264   FULBRIGHT, J. WILLIAM   *Old Myths and New Realties and other Commentaries*

V-354   FULBRIGHT, J. WILLIAM (intro.)   *The Vietnam Hearings*

V-688   FULBRIGHT, J. WILLIAM   *The Pentagon Propaganda Machine*

V-461   GARAUDY, ROGER   *From Anathema to Dialogue*

V-561   GALIN, SAUL AND PETER SPIELBERG (eds.)   *Reference Books: How to Select and Use Them*

V-475   GAY, PETER   *The Enlightenment:The Rise of Modern Paganism*

V-277   GAY, PETER   *Voltaire's Politics*

V-668   GERASSI, JOHN   *Revolutionary Priest: The Complete Writings and Messages of Camillo Torres*

V-657   GETTLEMAN, MARVIN E. AND DAVID MERMELSTEIN (eds.)   *The Failure of American Liberalism*

V-451   GETTLEMAN, MARVIN E. AND SUSAN, AND LAWRENCE AND CAROL KAPLAN   *Conflict in Indochina: A Reader on the Widening War in Laos and Cambodia*

V-174   GOODMAN, PAUL AND PERCIVAL   *Communitas*

V-325 GOODMAN, PAUL *Compulsory Mis-education and The Community of Scholars*

V-32 GOODMAN, PAUL *Growing Up Absurd*

V-417 GOODMAN, PAUL *People or Personnel* and *Like a Conquered Province*

V-247 GOODMAN, PAUL *Utopian Essays and Practical Proposals*

V-606 GORO, HERB *The Block*

V-633 GREEN, PHILIP AND SANFORD LEVINSON (eds.) *Power and Community: Dissenting Essays in Political Science*

V-457 GREENE, FELIX *The Enemy: Some Notes on the Nature of Contemporary Imperialism*

V-618 GREENSTONE, J. DAVID *Labor in American Politics*

V-430 GUEVERA, CHE *Guerrilla Warfare*

V-685 HAMSIK, DUSAN *Writers Against Rulers*

V-605 HARRIS, CHARLES F. AND JOHN A. WILLIAMS (eds.) *Amistad 1*

V-660 HARRIS, CHARLES F. AND JOHN A. WILLIAMS (eds.) *Amistad 2*

V-427 HAYDEN, TOM *Rebellion in Newark*

V-453 HEALTH PAC *The American Health Empire*

V-635 HEILBRONER, ROBERT L. *Between Capitalism and Socialism*

V-404 HELLER, WALTER (ed.) *Perspectives on Economic Growth*

V-450 HERSH, SEYMOUR M. *My Lai 4*

V-283 HENRY, JULES *Culture Against Man*

V-644 HESS, KARL AND THOMAS REEVES *The End of the Draft*

V-465 HINTON, WILLIAM *Fanshen: A Documentary of Revolution in a Chinese Village*

V-576 HOFFMAN, ABBIE *Woodstock Nation*

V-95 HOFSTADTER, RICHARD *The Age of Reform: From Bryan to F.D.R.*

V-9 HOFSTADTER, RICHARD *The American Political Tradition*

V-317 HOFSTADTER, RICHARD *Anti-Intellectualism in American Life*

V-385 HOFSTADTER, RICHARD *Paranoid Style in American Politics and other Essays*

V-686 HOFSTADTER, RICHARD AND MICHAEL WALLACE (eds.) *American Violence, A Documentary History*

V-429 HOROWITZ, DE CASTRO, AND GERASSI (eds.) *Latin American Radicalism*

V-666 HOWE, LOUISE KAPP (ed.) *The White Majority: Between Poverty and Affluence*

V-630 HOROWITZ, DAVID *Empire and Revolution*

V-201 HUGHES, H. STUART *Consciousness and Society*

V-514 HUNTINGTON, SAMUEL F. *The Soldier and the State*

V-241 JACOBS, JANE *Death & Life of Great American Cities*

V-584 JACOBS, JANE *The Economy of Cities*

V-433 JACOBS, PAUL *Prelude to Riot*

V-332 JACOBS, PAUL AND SAUL LANDAU (eds.) *The New Radicals*

V-459 JACOBS, PAUL AND SAUL LANDAU, WITH EVE PELL *To Serve the Devil: Natives and Slaves*, Vol. I

V-460 JACOBS, PAUL AND SAUL LANDAU, WITH EVE PELL *To Serve the Devil: Colonials & Sojourners*, Vol. II

V-456 JONES, ITA *The Grubbag*

V-451 KAPLAN, LAWRENCE AND CAROL, MARVIN E. AND SUSAN GETTLEMAN *Conflict in Indochina: A Reader on the Widening War in Laos and Cambodia*

V-369 KAUFMANN, WALTER (trans.) *The Birth of Tragedy* and *The Case of Wagner*

V-401 KAUFMANN, WALTER (trans.) *On the Genealogy of Morals and Ecce Homo*

V-337 KAUFMANN, WALTER (trans.) *Beyond Good and Evil*

V-482 KELSO, LOUIS O. AND PATRICIA HETTER *Two-Factor Theory: The Economics of Reality*

V-470 KEY, V. O. JR. *The Responsible Electorate*

V-510 KEY, V. O. *Southern Politics*

V-341 KIMBALL & McCLELLAN *Education and the New America*

V-582 KIRSHBAUM, LAURENCE AND ROGER RAPOPORT *Is the Library Burning?*

V-631 KOLKO, GABRIEL *Politics of War*

V-661 KOLKO, GABRIEL, RICHARD A. FALK AND ROBERT JAY LIFTON (eds.) *Crimes of War: After Songmy*

V-361 KOMAROVSKY, MIRRA *Blue-Collar Marriage*

V-675 KOVEL, JOVEL *White Racism*

V-215 LACOUTURE, JEAN *Ho Chi Minh*

V-459 LANDAU, SAUL, PAUL JACOBS, WITH EVE PELL *To Serve the Devil: Natives and Slaves, Vol. I*

V-460 LANDAU, SAUL, PAUL JACOBS, WITH EVE PELL *To Serve the Devil: Colonials & Sojourners, Vol. II*

V-367 LASCH, CHRISTOPHER *The New Radicalism in America*

V-560 LASCH, CHRISTOPHER *The Agony of the American Left*

V-399 LASKI, HAROLD J. (ed.) *Harold J. Laski on the Communist Manifesto*

V-426 LEKACHMAN, ROBERT *The Age of Keynes*

V-638 LEVINSON, SANFORD AND PHILIP GREEN (eds.) *Power and Community: Dissenting Essays in Political Science*

V-280 LEWIS, OSCAR *The Children of Sánchez*

V-421 LEWIS, OSCAR *La Vida*

V-370 LEWIS, OSCAR *Pedro Martínez*

V-284 LEWIS, OSCAR *Village Life in Northern India*

V-634 LEWIS, OSCAR *A Death in the Sánchez Family*

V-637 LIBARLE, MARC AND TOM SELIGSON (eds.) *The High School Revolutionaries*

V-392 LICHTHEIM, GEORGE *The Concept of Ideology and Other Essays*

V-474 LIFTON, ROBERT JAY *Revolutionary Immortality*

V-661 LIFTON, ROBERT JAY, RICHARD A. FALK AND GABRIEL KOLKO (eds.) *Crimes of War: After Songmy*

V-690 LIFTON, ROBERT JAY *History and Human Survival*

V-384 LINDESMITH, ALFRED *The Addict and The Law*

V-533 LOCKWOOD, LEE *Castro's Cuba, Cuba's Fidel*

V-469 LOWE, JEANNE R. *Cities in a Race with Time*

V-659 LURIE, ELLEN *How to Change the Schools*

V-193 MALRAUX, ANDRE *Temptation of the West*

V-480 MARCUSE, HERBERT *Soviet Marxism*

V-502 MATTHEWS, DONALD R. *U. S. Senators and Their World*

V-552 MAYER, ARNO J. *Politics and Diplomacy of Peacemaking*

V-577 MAYER, ARNO J. *Political Origins of the New Diplomacy, 1917-1918*

V-575 McCARTHY, RICHARD D. *The Ultimate Folly*

V-619 McCONNELL, GRANT *Private Power and American Democracy*

V-386 McPHERSON, JAMES *The Negro's Civil War*

V-657 MERMELSTEIN, DAVID AND MARVIN E. GETTLEMAN (eds.) *The Failure of American Liberalism*

V-273 MICHAEL, DONALD N. *The Next Generation*

V-19 MILOSZ, CZESLAW *The Captive Mind*
V-669 MINTZ, ALAN L. AND JAMES A. SLEEPER *The New Jews*
V-615 MITFORD, JESSICA *The Trial of Dr. Spock*
V-316 MOORE, WILBERT E. *The Conduct of the Corporation*
V-539 MORGAN, ROBIN (ed.) *Sisterhood is Powerful*
V-251 MORGENTHAU, HANS J. *The Purpose of American Politics*
V-57 MURCHLAND, BERNARD (ed.) *The Meaning of the Death of God*
V-274 MYRDAL, GUNNAR *Challenge to Affluence*
V-573 MYRDAL, GUNNAR *An Approach to the Asian Drama*
V-687 NEVILLE, RICHARD *Play Power*
V-377 NIETZSCHE, FRIEDRICH *Beyond Good and Evil*
V-369 NIETZSCHE, FRIEDRICH *The Birth of Tragedy and The Case of Wagner*
V-401 NIETZSCHE, FRIEDRICH *On the Genealogy of Morals and Ecce Homo*
V-689 OBSERVER, AN *Message from Moscow*
V-642 O'GORMAN, NED *Prophetic Voices*
V-583 ORTIZ, FERNANDO *Cuban Counterpoint: Tobacco and Sugar*
V-285 PARKES, HENRY B. *Gods and Men*
V-624 PARKINSON, G. H. R. *Georg Lukacs: The Man, His Work, and His Ideas*
V-128 PLATO *The Republic*
V-648 RADOSH, RONALD *American Labor and U. S. Foreign Policy*
V-582 RAPOPORT, ROGER AND LAURENCE KIRSHBAUM *Is the Library Burning?*
V-309 RASKIN, MARCUS and BERNARD FALL (eds.) *The Viet-Nam Reader*
V-719 REED, JOHN *Ten Days That Shook the World*
V-644 REEVES, THOMAS and KARL HESS *The End of the Draft*
V-192 REISCHAUER, EDWIN O. *Beyond Vietnam: The United States and Asia*
V-548 RESTON, JAMES *Sketches in the Sand*
V-622 ROAZEN, PAUL *Freud: Political and Social Thought*
V-534 ROGERS, DAVID *110 Livingston Street*
V-559 ROSE, TOM (ed.) *Violence in America*
V-212 ROSSITER, CLINTON *Conservatism in America*
V-472 ROSZAK, THEODORE (ed.) *The Dissenting Academy*
V-288 RUDOLPH, FREDERICK *The American College and University*
V-408 SAMPSON, RONALD V. *The Psychology of Power*
V-431 SCHELL, JONATHAN *The Village of Ben Suc*
V-403 SCHRIEBER, DANIEL (ed.) *Profile of the School Dropout*
V-375 SCHURMANN, F. and O. SCHELL (eds) *The China Reader: Imperial China, I*
V-376 SCHURMANN, F. and O. SCHELL (eds.) *The China Reader: Republican China, II*
V-377 SCHURMANN, F. and O. SCHELL (eds.) *The China Reader: Communist China, III*
V-394 SEABURY, PAUL *Power, Freedom and Diplomacy*
V-649 SEALE, BOBBY *Seize the Time*
V-662 SELDEN, MARK AND EDWARD FRIEDMAN (eds.) *America's Asia: Dissenting Essays in Asian Studies*
V-637 SELIGSON, TOM AND MARC LIBARLE (eds.) *The High School Revolutionaries*
V-279 SILBERMAN, CHARLES E. *Crisis in Black and White*
V-681 SNOW, EDGAR *Red China Today*

V-432   SPARROW, JOHN   *After the Assassination: A Positive Appraisal of the Warren Report*

V-222   SPENDER, STEPHEN   *The Year of the Young Rebels*

V-388   STAMPP, KENNETH   *The Era of Reconstruction 1865-1877*

V-253   STAMPP, KENNETH   *The Peculiar Institution*

V-454   STARR, PAUL AND IMMANUEL WALLERSTEIN (eds.)   *The University Crisis Reader: The Liberal University Under Attack*, Vol. I

V-455   STARR, PAUL AND IMMANUEL WALLERSTEIN (eds.)   *The University Crisis Reader: Confrontation and Counterattack*, Vol. II

V-613   STERNGLASS, ERNEST J.   *The Stillborn Future*

V-374   STILLMAN, E. AND W. PFAFF   *Power and Impotence*

V-439   STONE, I. F.   *In a Time of Torment*

V-547   STONE, I. F.   *The Haunted Fifties*

V-231   TANNENBAUM, FRANK   *Slave & Citizen: The Negro in the Americas*

V-312   TANNENBAUM, FRANK   *Ten Keys to Latin America*

V-322   THOMPSON, E. P.   *The Making of the English Working Class*

V-686   WALLACE, MICHAEL AND RICHARD HOFSTADTER (eds.)   *American Violence: A Documentary History*

V-206   WALLERSTEIN, IMMANUEL   *Africa: The Politics of Independence*

V-543   WALLERSTEIN, IMMANUEL   *Africa: The Politics of Unity*

V-454   WALLERSTEIN, IMMANUEL AND PAUL STARR (eds.)   *The University Crisis Reader: The Liberal University Under Attack*, Vol. I

V-455   WALLERSTEIN, IMMANUEL AND PAUL STARR (eds.)   *The University Crisis Reader: Confrontation and Counterattack*, Vol. II

V-145   WARREN, ROBERT PENN   *Segregation*

V-323   WARREN, ROBERT PENN   *Who Speaks for the Negro?*

V-405   WASSERMAN AND SWITZER   *The Random House Guide to Graduate Study in the Arts and Sciences*

V-249   WIEDNER, DONALD L.   *A History of Africa: South of the Sahara*

V-557   WEINSTEIN, JAMES   *Decline of Socialism in America 1912-1925*

V-585   WEINSTEIN, JAMES AND DAVID EAKINS (eds.)   *For a New America*

V-605   WILLIAMS, JOHN A. AND CHARLES HARRIS (eds.)   *Amistad 1*

V-660   WILLIAMS, JOHN A. AND CHARLES HARRIS (eds.)   *Amistad 2*

V-651   WILLIAMS, WILLIAM APPLEMAN   *The Roots of the Modern American Empire*

V-313   WILSON, EDMUND   *Apologies to the Iroquois*

V-208   WOODWARD, C. VANN   *Burden of Southern History*

V-545   WOOLF, S. J. (ed.)   *The Nature of Fascism*

V-495   YGLESIAS, JOSE   *In the Fist of the Revolution*

V-483   ZINN, HOWARD   *Disobedience and Democracy*

VINTAGE POLITICAL SCIENCE
AND SOCIAL CRITICISM

V-428   ABDEL-MALEK, ANOUAR   *Egypt: Military Society*
V-625   ACKLAND, LEN AND SAM BROWN   *Why Are We Still in Vietnam?*
V-196   ADAMS, RICHARD N.   *Social Change in Latin America Today*
V-568   ALINSKY, SAUL D.   *Reveille for Radicals*
V-286   ARIES, PHILIPPE   *Centuries of Childhood*
V-604   BAILYN, BERNARD   *Origins of American Politics*
V-334   BALTZELL, E. DIGBY   *The Protestant Establishment*
V-335   BANFIELD, E. G. AND J. Q. WILSON   *City Politics*
V-674   BARBIANA, SCHOOL OF   *Letter to a Teacher*
V-198   BARDOLPH, RICHARD   *The Negro Vanguard*
V-60   BECKER, CARL L.   *The Declaration of Independence*
V-199   BERMAN, H. J. (ed.)   *Talks on American Law*
V-81   BLAUSTEIN, ARTHUR I. AND ROGER R. WOOCK (eds.)   *Man Against Poverty*
V-513   BOORSTIN, DANIEL J.   *The Americans: The Colonial Experience*
V-358   BOORSTIN, DANIEL J.   *The Americans: The National Experience*
V-621   BOORSTIN, DANIEL J.   *The Decline of Radicalism: Reflections on America Today*
V-414   BOTTOMORE, T. B.   *Classes in Modern Society*
V-44   BRINTON, CRANE   *The Anatomy of Revolution*
V-234   BRUNER, JEROME   *The Process of Education*
V-590   BULLETIN OF ATOMIC SCIENTISTS   *China after the Cultural Revolution*
V-684   CALVERT, GREG AND CAROL   *The New Left and the New Capitalism*
V-30   CAMUS, ALBERT   *The Rebel*
V-33   CARMICHAEL, STOKELY AND CHARLES HAMILTON   *Black Power*
V-664   CARMICHAEL, STOKELY   *Stokely Speaks*
V-98   CASH, W. J.   *The Mind of the South*
V-272   CATER, DOUGLASS   *The Fourth Branch of Government*
V-290   CATER, DOUGLASS   *Power in Washington*
V-555   CHOMSKY, NOAM   *American Power and the New Mandarins*
V-640   CHOMSKY, NOAM   *At War With Asia*
V-538   COX COMMISSION   *Crisis at Columbia*
V-311   CREMIN, LAWRENCE A.   *The Genius of American Education*
V-638   DENNISON, GEORGE   *The Lives of Children*
V-746   DEUTSCHER, ISAAC   *The Prophet Armed*
V-747   DEUTSCHER, ISAAC   *The Prophet Unarmed*
V-748   DEUTSCHER, ISAAC   *The Prophet Outcast*
V-617   DEVLIN, BERNADETTE   *The Price of My Soul*
V-671   DOMHOFF, G. WILLIAM   *The Higher Circles*
V-603   DOUGLAS, WILLIAM O.   *Points of Rebellion*
V-645   DOUGLAS, WILLIAM O.   *International Dissent*
V-390   ELLUL, JACQUES   *The Technological Society*
V-692   EPSTEIN, JASON   *The Great Conspiracy Trial*
V-661   FALK, RICHARD A., GABRIEL KOLKO, AND ROBERT JAY LIFTON   *Crimes of War: After Songmy*
V-442   FALL, BERNARD B.   *Hell in a Very Small Place: The Siege of Dien Bien Phu*
V-667   FINN, JAMES   *Conscience and Command*

V-413   FRANK, JEROME D. *Sanity and Survival*

V-382   FRANKLIN, JOHN HOPE AND ISIDORE STARR (eds.) *The Negro in 20th Century America*

V-368   FRIEDENBERG, EDGAR Z. *Coming of Age in America*

V-662   FRIEDMAN, EDWARD AND MARK SELDEN (eds.) *America's Asia: Dissenting Essays in Asian Studies*

V-378   FULBRIGHT, J. WILLIAM *The Arrogance of Power*

V-688   FULBRIGHT, J. WILLIAM *The Pentagon Propaganda Machine*

V-475   GAY, PETER *The Enlightenment: The Rise of Modern Paganism*

V-668   GERASSI, JOHN *Revolutionary Priest: The Complete Writings and Messages of Camillo Torres*

V-657   GETTLEMAN, MARVIN E. AND DAVID MERMELSTEIN (eds.) *The Failure of American Liberalism*

V-451   GETTLEMAN, MARVIN E. AND SUSAN, AND LAWRENCE AND CAROL KAPLAN *Conflict in Indochina: A Reader on the Widening War in Laos and Cambodia*

V-174   GOODMAN, PAUL AND PERCIVAL *Communitas*

V-325   GOODMAN, PAUL *Compulsory Mis-education and The Community of Scholars*

V-32   GOODMAN, PAUL *Growing Up Absurd*

V-417   GOODMAN, PAUL *People or Personnel* and *Like a Conquered Province*

V-606   GORO, HERB *The Block*

V-633   GREEN, PHILIP AND SANFORD LEVINSON (eds.) *Power and Community: Dissenting Essays in Political Science*

V-457   GREENE, FELIX *The Enemy: Some Notes on the Nature of Contemporary Imperialism*

V-618   GREENSTONE, J. DAVID *Labor in American Politics*

V-430   GUEVARA, CHE *Guerrilla Warfare*

V-685   HAMSIK, DUSAN *Writers Against Rulers*

V-427   HAYDEN, TOM *Rebellion in Newark*

V-453   HEALTH PAC *The American Health Empire*

V-635   HEILBRONER, ROBERT L. *Between Capitalism and Socialism*

V-450   HERSH, SEYMOUR M. *My Lai 4*

V-283   HENRY, JULES *Culture Against Man*

V-644   HESS, KARL AND THOMAS REEVES *The End of the Draft*

V-465   HINTON, WILLIAM *Fanshen: A Documentary of Revolution in a Chinese Village*

V-576   HOFFMAN, ABBIE *Woodstock Nation*

V-95   HOFSTADTER, RICHARD *The Age of Reform: From Bryan to F.D.R.*

V-9   HOFSTADTER, RICHARD *The American Political Tradition*

V-317   HOFSTADTER, RICHARD *Anti-Intellectualism in American Life*

V-385   HOFSTADTER, RICHARD *Paranoid Style in American Politics and other Essays*

V-686   HOFSTADTER, RICHARD AND MICHAEL WALLACE (eds.) *American Violence, A Documentary History*

V-429   HOROWITZ, DE CASTRO, AND GERASSI (eds.) *Latin American Radicalism*

V-666   HOWE, LOUISE KAPP (ed.) *The White Majority: Between Poverty and Affluence*

V-630   HOROWITZ, DAVID *Empire and Revolution*

V-201   HUGHES, H. STUART *Consciousness and Society*

V-241   JACOBS, JANE *Death & Life of Great American Cities*

V-584   JACOBS, JANE *The Economy of Cities*

V-433   JACOBS, PAUL *Prelude to Riot*

V-332   JACOBS, PAUL AND SAUL LANDAU (eds.)   *The New Radicals*

V-459   JACOBS, PAUL AND SAUL LANDAU, WITH EVE PELL   *To Serve the Devil: Natives & Slaves*, Vol. I

V-460   JACOBS, PAUL AND SAUL LANDAU, WITH EVE PELL   *To Serve the Devil: Colonials & Sojourners*, Volume II

V-456   JONES, ITA   *The Grubbag*

V-369   KAUFMANN, WALTER (trans.)   *The Birth of Tragedy* and *The Case of Wagner*

V-401   KAUFMANN, WALTER (trans.)   *On the Genealogy of Morals* and *Ecce Homo*

V-337   KAUFMANN, WALTER (trans.)   *Beyond Good and Evil*

V-582   KIRSHBAUM, LAURENCE AND ROGER RAPOPORT   *Is the Library Burning?*

V-631   KOLKO, GABRIEL   *Politics of War*

V-361   KOMAROVSKY, MIRRA   *Blue-Collar Marriage*

V-675   KOVEL, JOEL   *White Racism*

V-215   LACOUTURE, JEAN   *Ho Chi Minh*

V-367   LASCH, CHRISTOPHER   *The New Radicalism in America*

V-560   LASCH, CHRISTOPHER   *The Agony of the American Left*

V-280   LEWIS, OSCAR   *The Children of Sánchez*

V-421   LEWIS, OSCAR   *La Vida*

V-634   LEWIS, OSCAR   *A Death in the Sánchez Family*

V-637   LIBARLE, MARC AND TOM SELIGSON (eds.)   *The High School Revolutionaries*

V-474   LIFTON, ROBERT JAY   *Revolutionary Immortality*

V-384   LINDESMITH, ALFRED   *The Addict and The Law*

V-533   LOCKWOOD, LEE   *Castro's Cuba, Cuba's Fidel*

V-469   LOWE, JEANNE R.   *Cities in a Race with Time*

V-659   LURIE, ELLEN   *How to Change the Schools*

V-193   MALRAUX, ANDRE   *Temptation of the West*

V-480   MARCUSE, HERBERT   *Soviet Marxism*

V-502   MATTHEWS, DONALD R.   *U. S. Senators and Their World*

V-577   MAYER, ARNO J.   *Political Origins of the New Diplomacy, 1917-1918*

V-575   MCCARTHY, RICHARD D.   *The Ultimate Folly*

V-619   MCCONNELL, GRANT   *Private Power and American Democracy*

V-386   MCPHERSON, JAMES   *The Negro's Civil War*

V-615   MITFORD, JESSICA   *The Trial of Dr. Spock*

V-539   MORGAN, ROBIN (ed.)   *Sisterhood Is Powerful*

V-274   MYRDAL, GUNNAR   *Challenge to Affluence*

V-573   MYRDAL, GUNNAR   *An Approach to the Asian Drama*

V-687   NEVILE, RICHARD   *Play Power*

V-377   NIETZSCHE, FRIEDRICH   *Beyond Good and Evil*

V-369   NIETZSCHE, FRIEDRICH   *The Birth of Tragedy* and *The Case of Wagner*

V-401   NIETZSCHE, FRIEDRICH   *On the Genealogy of Morals* and *Ecce Homo*

V-642   O'GORMAN, NED   *Prophetic Voices*

V-583   ORTIZ, FERNANDO   *Cuban Counterpoint: Tobacco and Sugar*

V-128   PLATO   *The Republic*

V-648   RADOSH, RONALD   *American Labor and U.S. Foreign Policy*

V-309   RASKIN, MARCUS AND BERNARD FALL (eds.)   *The Viet-nam Reader*

V-719   REED, JOHN   *Ten Days That Shook the World*

V-644   REEVES, THOMAS AND KARL HESS   *The End of the Draft*

V-192   REISCHAUER, EDWIN O. *Beyond Vietnam: The United States and Asia*

V-548   RESTON, JAMES *Sketches in the Sand*

V-622   ROAZEN, PAUL *Freud: Political and Social Thought*

V-534   ROGERS, DAVID *110 Livingston Street*

V-559   ROSE, TOM (ed.) *Violence in America*

V-212   ROSSITER, CLINTON *Conservatism in America*

V-472   ROSZAK, THEODORE (ed.) *The Dissenting Academy*

V-431   SCHELL, JONATHAN *The Village of Ben Suc*

V-375   SCHURMANN, F. AND O. SCHELL (eds.) *The China Reader: Imperial China, I*

V-376   SCHURMANN, F. AND O. SCHELL (eds.) *The China Reader: Republican China, II*

V-377   SCHURMANN, F. AND O. SCHELL (eds.) *The China Reader: Communist China, III*

V-649   SEALE, BOBBY *Seize the Time*

V-279   SILBERMAN, CHARLES E. *Crisis in Black and White*

V-681   SNOW, EDGAR *Red China Today*

V-222   SPENDER, STEPHEN *The Year of the Young Rebels*

V-388   STAMPP, KENNETH *The Era of Reconstruction 1865-1877*

V-253   STAMPP, KENNETH *The Peculiar Institution*

V-613   STERNGLASS, ERNEST J. *The Stillborn Future*

V-439   STONE, I. F. *In a Time of Torment*

V-231   TANNENBAUM, FRANK *Slave & Citizen: The Negro in the Americas*

V-312   TANNENBAUM, FRANK *Ten Keys to Latin America*

V-686   WALLACE, MICHAEL AND RICHARD HOFSTADTER (eds.) *American Violence: A Documentary History*

V-206   WALLERSTEIN, IMMANUEL *Africa: The Politics of Independence*

V-543   WALLERSTEIN, IMMANUEL *Africa: The Politics of Unity*

V-454   WALLERSTEIN, IMMANUEL AND PAUL STARR (eds.) *The University Crisis Reader: The Liberal University Under Attack*, Vol. I

V-455   WALLERSTEIN, IMMANUAL AND PAUL STARR (eds.) *The University Crisis Reader: Confrontation and Counterattack*, Vol. II

V-323   WARREN, ROBERT PENN *Who Speaks for the Negro?*

V-405   WASSERMAN AND SWITZER *The Random House Guide to Graduate Study in the Arts and Sciences*

V-249   WIEDNER, DONALD L. *A History of Africa: South of the Sahara*

V-557   WEINSTEIN, JAMES *Decline of Socialism in America 1912-1925*

V-585   WEINSTEIN, JAMES AND DAVID EAKINS (eds.) *For a New America*

V-605   WILLIAMS, JOHN A. AND CHARLES HARRIS (eds.) *Amistad 1*

V-660   WILLIAMS, JOHN A. AND CHARLES HARRIS (eds.) *Amistad 2*

V-651   WILLIAMS, WILLIAM APPLEMAN *The Roots of the Modern American Empire*

V-545   WOOLF., S. J. (ed.) *The Nature of Fascism*

V-495   YGLESIAS, JOSE *In the Fist of the Revolution*

V-483   ZINN, HOWARD *Disobedience and Democracy*